ROBERT BRIFFAULT

The Mothers

Abridged, with an Introduction

by

GORDON RATTRAY TAYLOR

ATHENEUM

NEW YORK

1977

ACKNOWLEDGEMENTS

I am indebted to Mr. R. G. Phillips, who introduced me to Robert Briffault, and to Mrs. Briffault-Hackelberg, Mrs. Herma Briffault, and several old friends of Robert Briffault, particularly Mme. Bradley and Mme. Stalio, all of whom helped me with biographical information.

I should also like to pay a tribute to my two secretaries, Mrs. Delgado and Mrs. Sawyer, who determinedly tackled the exceptionally demanding task of transcribing and typing several hundred thousand words of technical matter and obscure names, as the abridgement passed through progressive drafts.

G. R. T.

The Mothers, A Study of the Origins of Sentiment and Institutions
Three volumes, First published in 1927
The Mothers, Abridged, with an Introduction, By Gordon Rattray Taylor
Copyright © 1959 by George Allen & Unwin Ltd., London
All rights reserved
Reprinted by arrangement with Humanities Press Inc., New Jersey
Library of Congress catalog card number: 76-28642
ISBN 0-689-70541-7
Published simultaneously in Canada by McClelland and Stewart Ltd.
Manufactured by The Murray Printing Company
Forge Village, Massachusetts
First Atheneum Edition

CONTENTS

CONTENTS

INTRODUCTION

It is just over thirty years since Robert Briffault's prodigious work *The Mothers* was first published. Its enormous length—about $1\frac{1}{2}$ million words when the extensive footnotes and the vast bibliography are reckoned in—and its consequent relatively high price have prevented more than a very few people from studying it, for few libraries hold it in stock.

Furthermore, at the time of its first publication anthropologists were turning away from the larger questions of cultural evolution, which they felt to be insoluble, and Briffault's work tended to be seen as the last shot in a controversy which had already ceased to be interesting.

But today anthropologists are beginning to turn once more to these larger questions. For some forty years they have concentrated upon the detailed study of specific societies or 'cultural configurations'—a task made the more urgent by the rapidity with which modern technical progress and commercial expansion are destroying the social patterns of non-literate and technologically backward societies. During all this time, the attempt to erect large theories of cultural evolution has been in disrepute. While many of the criticisms brought against the theories of the older school of anthropologists—Tylor, McLennan and others—were just, it is nevertheless becoming recognized that the pendulum has swung from one extreme to the other, and groups like that headed by Steward at the University of Illinois are beginning to develop studies of a more synoptic character. The moment is therefore well chosen for a reissue of *The Mothers*, and the time is ripe for a reassessment of Briffault's remarkable work. That Briffault's ideas might be considered on their own merits, I suggested to the original publishers that the work be published in an abridged form, with an introduction to put the whole topic in perspective. They accepted this proposal, as did the owner of the copyright, Mrs Joan Briffault Hackelberg. The present volume therefore presents the original text reduced to about one-fifth of its original length and omitting almost all the footnotes.

I have attempted to preserve the order, proportions, and literary style of the original work, chiefly by omitting much of the overwhelming mass of illustrative material and by condensing some of the more discursive comments. As Briffault gives the reader few clues as to where he is going, preferring to let conviction grow out of the mass of the material, I have added a few verbal signposts to assist the reader in keeping track of the argument. Where passages are given in quotation marks they are in quotation marks in the original, and the source can be found by referring to the corresponding passage in the unabridged version.

It should perhaps be added that Briffault prepared for the Macmillan Company in New York a one-volume work which was published in 1931 under the title of *The Mothers*; it was a complete restatement of the material and in no way an abridgement of the original English three-volume work published under that title.

Briffault's Thesis

The form in which Briffault couched his ideas and the relative lack of interest with which they were greeted can only be understood in relation to the controversy of which they formed part.

This controversy was launched in 1851, when the famous jurist, Sir A. Maine, published his *Primitive Law*, in which he asserted that the patriarchal family was the original unit of society, and that larger social units had been built up by the aggregation of these family units into clan and tribe. In support of this view, he cited chiefly Biblical examples. In the same year, the Swiss jurist Bachofen was preparing his *Das Mutterrecht*, asserting that the original state of man had been one of sexual promiscuity, from which had emerged matriarchies, which had only later been replaced by or converted into patriarchies.

This set off a series of attempts to draw up schemes designed to account for the whole development of human society, and represented the application of the idea of evolution, which had proved so fertile in the biological field, to society as a whole. J. F. McLennan made the most important restatement of the matriarchal view in 1886, citing a great mass of new anthropological evidence. Early in the nineteenth century, Westermarck—a man without anthropological qualifications—published his *History of Human Marriage*, in which he attempted to re-establish Maine's position. He was not so much concerned to draw a picture of the whole development of human society as to assert that lifelong monogamy was the normal pattern of marriage throughout human society, polygamy representing a degeneration from the original monogamic pattern. This thesis was naturally much to the taste of Christian apologists and traditional moralists generally. Westermarck's works enjoyed wide acclaim, and he wrote a long series of works embroidering this theme, most of which are still to be found in the majority of public libraries. Largely as a result, this view of marriage is still held by very many laymen, in so far as they concern themselves with the topic at all, and is often given fresh currency by American anthropologists. It is asserted in the new Chambers's *Encyclopaedia*.

This view is, in point of fact, wholly untenable, and there can be little doubt that Briffault felt incensed by Westermarck's scientifically unjustified success, and that his main object in writing *The Mothers* was to explode this fallacy. This he undoubtedly achieves, adducing such a wealth of material to the contrary, and so decisively convicting Westermarck of manipulating his references and betraying other signs of bias, that one might have supposed that belief in the universality of monogamic marriage would have been abandoned for ever in a gale of laughter. In fact, as we know, his statement was ignored; and if this new version of his work does something to restore a more detached and speculative approach to the topic, it will have been worth while for this reason alone.

But Briffault was not content simply to destroy—he sought to establish an alternative theory. In contradiction to Maine, he asserted the former existence of a primitive matriarchy universally preceding patriarchy, but, unlike Bachofen, he did not define matriarchy in terms of actual mother-rule or inheritance through the maternal line, but in more general terms as a period in which women were socially predominant. As the crucial factor, he selects, for reasons which he adduces at length, the question whether, after marriage, the wife resides at her husband's abode or the husband at the wife's—i.e. what anthropologists term patrilocy or matrilocy. (The distinction is important, and several subsequent investigations designed to prove or disprove the matriarchal theory have gone astray through ignoring it.[1])

Furthermore, his inquiries lead him to the view that marriage was originally a contract between groups, in which it was agreed that a man of one group might have sexual access to all the women of another group while being denied access to his own. This primitive restriction on sexual behaviour was then elaborated into such forms as restriction to all the women of a particular family—that is, in our terms, if a man marries a woman he is thereby married to all her sisters. Briffault persuasively argues that 'sororal polygyny' and its complement 'fraternal polyandry' are not perversions of the basic idea of a monogamous marriage. Quite to the contrary, they are restrictions of an original group contract so different from marriage as we know it that we shrink from applying the word marriage to it. Indeed, where such group contracts are found they are usually termed by the scandalised Western observer 'sexual communism' or 'promiscuity'.

To establish these two main points, Briffault seeks to show that the alleged change from matriarchy to patriarchy was associated with the change from hunting to agricultural production and the essential emergence of property.

Into this landscape he also attempts to fit such well-known anthropo-

[1] E.g. R. Karsten: *Origins of Religion* (1935).

logical puzzles as initiation ceremonies and the prevalence of lunar symbolism.

Briffault develops his work in four main sections. In Chapters 1 to 5 he considers the domestic arrangements of animals, from which human arrangements presumably developed, and seeks to show that they were matrilocal in character. More precariously, he argues that the male instinct created the group or herd, while the female instinct created the family. Since he is going on, later in the book, to argue that the family is a feature of patriarchies, the relevance of this section is obscure, to say the least.

In Chapters 6 to 16 he considers the whole question of the emergence of marriage, arguing the universal existence of a primitive matriarchy in the prehistory of all peoples, and seeking to show in various ways that marriage was originally matrilocal.

In Chapters 17 to 24 he considers various indirect forms of evidence. In particular, he argues that lunar deities are indications of a primitive matriarchy, and that such cults were originally served only by women, who were the first hierophants. He seeks also to fit the concepts of totemism and taboo into his system, and here he is least successful, though he makes a number of interesting points.

Finally, in Chapters 25 to 30 he attempts to trace the growth of the modern Western conception of marriage as a sacrament, as a cultural remnant of the idea of a holy marriage between a deity and a woman. Ideas of this sort are indeed present in our thinking to a much greater extent than most of us realize, and Briffault's demonstration is fascinating; but on the sources of this need to preserve a sense of sacredness—so notably absent in many other fields—he has nothing to say. In conjunction with this, he traces the origins of the notion of romantic love.

Criticism of Briffault's Views

For some time before Briffault reached the point of publication of these views, anthropologists had been becoming increasingly critical of such attempts to provide a general schematic account of the development of society, on two general grounds.

Firstly, as anthropological studies developed it became even clearer that one could only hope to understand the meaning of a culture item by considering it in relation to the whole culture. A given social action may carry quite a different connotation in one culture from that which it has when part of another. Consequently, to pick out a given pattern— let us say, mother-in-law avoidance—from a number of different cultures and compare them was an unacceptable technique. (Like many before him, Briffault relies heavily on this 'comparative method.') Anthropologists therefore rejected the whole method, and turned to studying individual cultures in detail, seeking to profit from this new insight into their structure.

This argument was reinforced by another: we cannot assume that societies which are technologically primitive resemble equally primitive societies as they existed thousands of years ago. A long sequence of social changes may have occurred—the marriage customs of the technologically primitive Australian aboriginals are so complex that it seems certain they represent the outcome of a long process of elaboration. Hence (they felt) we have no information about primitive society, except what archaeology may uncover, and speculations about the past state of man are vain.

No doubt there is much truth in both these views. The horse has changed greatly from the Eohippos from which it is descended. But it is unnecessarily defeatist to say that nothing can be learned from such studies. If we had no skeletons of the Eohippos to go upon, we might not appreciate that the horse was so much larger, and we could only guess that the Eohippos had not developed the horse's specialized hoof; but we should at least be sure that the Eohippos did not swim or walk upright.

The passage of time may modify or complicate a given social pattern; it is not proved that it can bring about a change in kind. Indeed, it seems to me that it may be the case that technological advance is only possible when certain underlying changes of attitude or psychological make-up occur; such changes would also effect changes in social patterns generally, so that some aspects of social pattern may be correlated with the level of technical development, after all.

Though anthropologists tended to reject these synoptic attempts on *a priori* grounds, subsequently the advance of archaeology went far towards confirming their scepticism. It was observed that agricultural peoples, driven by population pressures out of Asia Minor into the steppe country, became pastoral—which is just the contrary of what Briffault asserts to be the normal process. Gordon Childe subsequently showed that various primitive peoples have passed through matriarchal and patriarchal stages in varying orders, and have adopted various methods of subsistence in quite a haphazard way.[1] Meanwhile anthropologists have noted tribes which, at the present time, are passing from patriarchal to matriarchal patterns of society; for instance, the neighbours of the Tsimshian in North-west America.[2]

It is now past all reasonable doubt that society does not evolve according to one single standard line of development. Of course, it might still be true that there was a normal line of development from

[1] V. Gordon Childe: *Social Evolution* (1951).
[2] J. R. Swanton: *Social Organisation of American Tribes* (1905).

which societies would occasionally depart in exceptional circumstances. The foregoing evidence does not justify the conclusion that all attempts to find any system in such data is vain. But once we admit that matriarchy can follow patriarchy, much of Briffault's material becomes ambiguous. When he draws attention to signs of an earlier matriarchy in a society which is now patriarchal, he may in reality be observing the signs of a future matriarchy which is only just developing.

A New Assessment

Briffault did himself much disservice by claiming too much: it was in the nature of the man to prefer the sweeping generalization, and he loved to shock the unimaginative out of their preconceptions. His data do not justify him in making the assertion that matriarchy always and everywhere preceded patriarchy, even if we neglect the facts just adduced. Even if in existing patriarchies signs of earlier matriarchy can be detected, this does not prove that a still earlier patriarchy may not have preceded the matriarchal phase. The periods of time in question are but a few hundred years—the pre-history of man runs to tens of thousands.

Briffault would have made a more convincing contribution if he had confined himself to asserting that in every patriarchy the existence of a previous matriarchal state can be shown or inferred, leaving unbroached the question of what had preceded that state during the thousands of years of pre-history. For the realization that these social patterns are labile is a novel and important one, to which we are only now coming. It never occurred to Maine that the Jewish patriarchy which he so much admired, and thought was fundamental and God-given, had actually developed out of an earlier mother-centred system, as Briffault shows. Even today, few people are any better informed than Maine. The belief that patriarchies were always patriarchal is almost universal. Briffault might justifiably have written his book to prove this one fact.

Again, Briffault invited ridicule or neglect by grossly over-generalizing his theory of marriage. It is certainly true that monogamy is not the universally preferred pattern; but it is going much too far to assert group marriage as universal. The likelihood is that humanity found a number of different solutions to the problem of regulating the relations between the sexes; group marriage may well have been one, perhaps even the most widespread one. The hypothesis certainly enables Briffault to reduce a great deal of otherwise baffling material to coherence, even if it does not explain quite as much as he claims. It is therefore well worth much closer examination than it has so far received.

His larger theory, in which the change from matriarchy to patriarchy is linked with changes in the method of subsistence, from pastoral to corn-growing and so forth, again attempts too much in asserting a single sequence of development. The more modest task of exploring whether certain social structures are always associated with certain modes of subsistence would have been more rewarding.

The Psychoanalytic Clue

Briffault's greatest mistake, one cannot help feeling, was to dismiss as valueless the entire contribution of Freud, for it is precisely Freud who could have helped him to solve the points on which he stumbles most hopelessly. First and foremost, Freud provides a comprehensive and consistent theory of the origin of incest fears. Since, as Briffault accurately notes, the whole system of exogamy rules is simply a system of incest-regulations, it is strongly supportive of his views that Freud attributes this preoccupation with incest to a preoccupation with the mother. That is, Briffault's contention that exogamy rules arose in societies in which mothers were dominant is completely in harmony with Freudian theory. Conversely, the jealousy which Westermarck thought a universal human instinct is revealed by Freudian theory to spring from a preoccupation with the father, and thus to be characteristic of patriarchal but not of matriarchal societies. Briffault, who justly rejects Westermarck's view on this point, could have proceeded to explain just why it is found in patriarchal societies, and indeed why Westermarck should have held such a view, had he not been so cavalier towards psychoanalysis. Unfortunately, Briffault derived his psychology from the teachings of Shand, now almost forgotten.

Again, Freud provided, in his description of the mechanism of *projection*, a theory which explains perfectly why those who are preoccupied with the mother-figure tend to envisage their deity as a mother, while those preoccupied with the father tend to postulate father deities. Briffault, who traces the tendency for the moon to be seen sometimes as a male and sometimes as a female deity (and occasionally as both conjointly) could—had he realized this—have related this dynamically to the corresponding social changes from matriarchy to patriarchy. Similarly, Freud's account of *decomposition*—the process by which people sometimes classify people into good and bad figures, and have difficulty in seeing that good and bad aspects can be combined in a single person —is accurately reflected in the way in which some peoples divide their deities into good and bad, God and Devil, while others feel that a deity may have good and bad features simultaneously. Briffault notes the anthropological fact quite correctly, but makes heavy weather of fitting it into his system because he does not understand (what Freud could have explained to him) the origins of these alternative attitudes.

Briffault was correct in his insight that the description of the deity could be used as a clue to the social structure of the people making the description, but tries to link the two in a mechanical way, instead of regarding both as reflecting an unconscious attitude. (In matriarchies, women have the priestly role, and the moon is their patron because it seems to control their menstrual periods, his argument runs.)

Freud's attempt to account for totemism and to explain taboos seems to me only partly successful.[1] On the other hand, Bettelheim's analysis of Australian initiation ceremonies, and the comparisons he makes with the disturbed children he has studied in the USA, seem to me the only writings which make any sense on this subject and, indeed, to be stimulating in the extreme. To say, as the anthropologist generally does, that initiation ceremonies mark the transition from youth to manhood may be true—if we assume that this transition takes place at puberty— but it certainly does not account for the frenzied violence which often accompanies them. It certainly offers no clue as to why the Australian aborigines should make a long and deep gash on the underside of the penes of these boys, and dress them in women's clothes—hardly a gesture designed to bring out their manhood. On the contrary, as Bettelheim points out, it is clearly a ceremony designed to turn them into substitute women, and it is the women who insist on this ceremony.[2] The anthropologist who is unwilling to accept a psychoanalytic interpretation of such odd actions would be more honest if he were simply to admit that he has no explanation to offer, instead of talking earnestly about *rites de passage*.

Briffault, though he takes a different view, is no more *à propos*. He argues that these ceremonies are designed primarily to demonstrate the young man's fitness to support a wife. This explanation at least recognizes the vital fact that it is the women who insist on these ceremonies. But tortures which maim, render impotent or even kill the victim do not really have this effect, and are clearly in a different category from demanding (as may also happen) that the young man demonstrate his prowess at hunting or fighting. At best, the aspect which Briffault stresses is but a single one; the other features—all the stranger because they seem to have no utilitarian value or even to be harmful—demand explanation.

Briffault is in even deeper water when he tries to explain the changes in the status of women. It is when men come to possess so much wealth that they can keep women in idleness that they become sexual playthings and lose status, he declares. He realizes that this view is quite inconsistent with the depressed status of women among the Australian aborigines, and suggests that this is because the aborigine has used his

---

[1] S. Freud: *Totem and Taboo* (1919).
[2] B. Bettelheim: *Symbolic Wounds* (1955).

superior strength to dominate his women. But elsewhere Briffault has argued that women are not only stronger but also fiercer and more cunning than men. And even if this were not so, it would still leave him under the obligation of explaining why, in matriarchal agricultural societies, men do not equally exert their strength. The Celts, too, whom he sees as matriarchal and deferring to women, had notable heroes; why did they tolerate their women's arrogance and sexual freedom? Finally, in our own day, in the West, man is more than ever able to earn sufficient to support his woman in idleness; but the American woman, for one, is hardly dominated by her male.

But here psychoanalytic theory provides a scheme which, though derived from quite other data, fits the anthropological facts as if it had been made for the purpose. The Oedipal situation, as described by Freud, accounts for men's fear that women will betray them sexually, and their sense that they are a threat to be kept under control. But the Oedipus situation can only exist where a strong father-figure is present, and is intensified if he is severe or thought to be so. Hence we should expect to find this attitude to women strongly marked in families of the patriarchal type, and absent in those families where the children are brought up by the mother alone (usually with the help of her brother), and where the biological father performs no parental role. It is many years now since Malinowski reported just this absence of sexual guilt and concomitant freedom of women from the Trobriand Islands, where the family structure is of the type just mentioned.

(Note how, in the West, the status of women has risen and sexual freedom has increased in proportion as the patriarchal nature of the family has declined.)

In making this estimate of Briffault's work, I am naturally influenced by my own speculations on these matters put forward initially in 1949, and developed in 1953 and 1958;[1] in them society is postulated as oscillating irregularly between phases in which the mother-figure is dominant and others in which the father is dominant, with the possibility of a balance between the two. Institutions, such as marriage or the inheritance laws, change so slowly, that institutions appropriate to a father-centred phase may persist into a mother-centred one, and no doubt the reverse also occurs. Hence we cannot safely classify a society by the little we know of its institutions, such as, whether marriage is patrilocal or descent patrilineal. Thus, as Margaret Mead has shown, the Tchambuli have all the social features—such as patrilineal descent—associated with a patriarchy, but in fact the women dominate the men.[2]

[1] G. Rattray Taylor: *Conditions of Happiness* (1949); *Sex in History* (1953); *The Angel Makers* (1958).
[2] M. Mead: *Sex and Temperament in Three Primitive Societies* (1935).

For the same reason, when Briffault succeeds in showing signs of the existence of a preceding matriarchal phase in a patriarchal society, this does not seem conclusive proof of a primitive matriarchy, since an even more primitive patriarchy may have preceded it.

Does this mean, then, that we should reject Briffault's contribution as worthless ? That is the conclusion which some contemporary critics reached; but in my view this is to throw out the baby with the bath-water.

The Problem Restated

The task which has fascinated so many anthropologists in the last hundred years—the attempt to devise a comprehensive account of the sequences of social development—turns out to be insoluble and perhaps meaningless. But this does not mean that this whole area of inquiry must now be abandoned; it means only that the task must be reformulated. The many extraordinary social phenomena which Briffault chronicles remain for the most part without any satisfactory explanation. Is it a matter of pure chance whether a given tribe adopts polygamy or monogamy, exogamy or endogamy ? Or are such practices related in some way to its mode of life, or to its religion ? Is it a matter of pure chance whether it adopts a father-religion, a mother-religion or a religion of some other type ? What is the explanation of the savagery which so often attends initiation ceremonies ? The remarkable range of human behaviour which Briffault records in such profusion still calls aloud for clarification, and if we object to Briffault's synthesis then we admit the need to find some alternative.

More than this: is it not possible that the explanations of many such cultural features are tied together ? To put it differently, is it not possible that there is only a limited number of basic sociocultural patterns, that the almost infinite variety of those we know consists only in variations on a few simple themes ?

If such patterns could be found, the task of analysing the history of cultural evolution would be greatly simplified. And if the conditions determining which pattern would be adopted could be established, it might be possible to make more reliable inferences about the social patterns of human communities in prehistoric times. Only by exploring the subject in this kind of way do we seem to have any hope of forming ideas about the manner in which social and sexual institutions have emerged in the long evolutionary scale of man's slow assumption of humanity.

If the psychoanalytic approach is adopted, we require, in order to account for the social changes which we observe on the historical scale, only to account for the changes in family structure. Perhaps it could be shown that economic factors make it inevitable that a pastoral society should be patriarchal. Perhaps, however, it may be the case that a patriarchally-minded individual prefers to occupy himself with flocks rather than with agriculture. We are most likely to find the answer to such choices when we can locate cases in which a change is actually occurring or is known to have occurred. Why are the neighbours of the Tshimshian, for instance, moving from matriarchy to patriarchy?

For the past half century, anthropology has taken a static rather than a dynamic approach: it has explored the structure of given societies in great detail. It has given little attention to the interaction between societies and to the change of societies with time. This is natural enough, and probably the harder task could only be fruitfully attempted when the easier had been performed. Naturally, too, the psychoanalytic tool has first been employed in order to explore the structure of given societies in more detail (e.g. by Kardiner, Linton, du Bois and others). But the time has come when it could be turned on these larger problems of historical change.

It is reasonable to believe that a new epoch in anthropology is now opening up. When we really understand the dynamic connections between social institutions, such as marriage, and economic conditions, and the connection of both with personality structure, we may reach a position from which we can attempt the task prematurely undertaken by Maine, McLennan, Briffault and others, of inferring how first social institutions were developed by the human race, and what form they may conceivably have taken.

Conclusion

Briffault opens the way for some development on these lines both by the devastating way in which he clears the ground of the forest of misconceptions which have grown up and enables us to view the data with less ethnocentrically-prejudiced eyes; and also by the many odd features of the terrain which he then points out, and the stimulating suggestions he offers to account for them.

It must be conceded that he is open to criticism in matters of detail. He not infrequently contradicts himself, and sometimes uses a fact to prove one thing at one stage and to support an equally plausible but quite different view at a later point. He is sometimes guilty of selecting his references to prove his point and glossing over those which are incompatible with it. The captious critic could make him look small, and it is easy to be persuaded that the writer who is inaccurate in detail is, *ipso facto*, wrong as regards his thesis. In point of fact, the kind of mind which is capable of conceiving a large theory is apt to be impatient of details; the mind that concentrates on details generally fails to see the wood for the trees.

We do not read Briffault for a text-book statement of incontrovertible fact, but for a challenging argument supported by a mass of fascinating detail. We can hardly expect that, having written a million and a half words, having impoverished himself and damaged his health in the process, he should then sit down and spend the next ten years trying to disprove his own theory. It is for others to raise the objections, and to see whether they can be met by minor modification of the main hypothesis or not.

Nor do we read Briffault exclusively for his main thesis; his inquisitive and radical mind explores many byways of anthropology, always throwing light, challenging preconceptions, and offering new insights. He is as instructive when he is discussing the origin of human clothing as he is when evaluating the role of the troubadours. Not the least fascinating feature of *The Mothers* is the way in which he weaves material from Biblical Jewish history or from Classical Roman and Greek sources into the general anthropological picture. It is intensely stimulating to see societies which we have come to know and take for granted in our schooldays, and which have thus acquired a special status in our minds, compared with societies which we regard as strange or primitive objects of anthropological study, and to see how they, too, are just as strange, their development just as complex. Just as our reading of the Bible, coloured as it is by religious presuppositions of a later date, seldom reveals to us the moon and mother-worshipping origins of Jewry, so our reading of the Classics is focused on a late phase of the society, and its curious matriarchal origins escape our eye.

BIOGRAPHICAL NOTE

ROBERT STEPHEN BRIFFAULT'S life starts with a mystery. He seems to have been born in Nice in 1873, although he later claimed to have been born in London in 1876. Briffault's mother—we should start by considering his mother, surely—was a Scotswoman of strong religious views; the daughter of a sea-captain. Nothing else is known of her life before she married—astonishingly—an elderly French diplomat, already retired, Charles Frederic Briffault. It was his second marriage, and of his first nothing is known either. Charles F. Briffault had been Chef du Secretariat du President de la Republique Napoleon in 1849, but left the service of Louis Napoleon on his unconstitutional seizure of power, and became naturalized British. He travelled a great deal on the Continent, where he had many friends. For many years he made his home in Florence, and it was there that Robert Briffault attended a private school for English boys until his 'teens, though he completed his education in England.

At the age of 19, his father being dead, Briffault went out with his mother to New Zealand, where, at 24, he married one Anna Clarke; by this marriage he had one son and two daughters. After much indecision as to a career, he decided to study medicine, and in 1901 he received an MB at Dunedin University, and a CH.B at Christchurch in 1905. He then set up in practice. After a visit to Europe, he returned to New Zealand, and was president for a time of the Auckland branch of the New Zealand Institute.

On the outbreak of the First World War, he returned to England to enlist, and served at Gallipoli, and later in Flanders and France, where he was rather badly gassed.

He had written a good deal in his spare time, without publishing anything, and while in the trenches he worked on a survey of human evolution which was published in 1919 as *The Making of Humanity*; *Psyche's Lamp*, an outline of psychology, followed in 1920. His wife having died at the end of the war, he established himself in London, where he alternated between frenzied spells of work on *The Mothers*, and working as locum tenens at one of the London hospitals. The death of his mother in 1924, followed by the death of one of his daughters, with other mental stresses, affected him so that at times he would slide to the floor in a trance lasting ten or twenty minutes. After sustained efforts, in which he gave up all medical work and depended largely on his daughter, *The Mothers* was finished and revised, appearing in 1927, when he was 54. With this he gained some reputation. Other books followed.

In 1930 he married Herma Hoyt, an American some twenty-five years his junior.

In 1931 he went to the U.S., but by the end of 1932 was living in Paris, where he remained until the end of the Second World War. While in New York, friends suggested that he should write a novel; the result was *Europa*, which, to his surprise, became a best-seller in several languages. A sequel, *Europa in Limbo*, followed, with other novels, and a number of essays.

In Paris, during the Occupation, Briffault was twice imprisoned for short periods. His principal difficulty was that he was cut off from the English language market, and presumably from the receipt of royalties also, and had to support himself with translations and hackwork. He also wrote, in French, *Les Troubadours et le Sentiment Romanesque*, which may be regarded as an expansion of Chapters 28 and 29 of *The Mothers*. After the war, he returned to England, in broken health, although he travelled restlessly several times to France and Italy. His wife, herself ill, returned to New York, believing that the State Department would then grant her husband an entry permit—this having been refused on earlier applications; but it remained obdurate. In December 1948 Briffault died of pulmonary tuberculosis at St Helen's Hospital, Hastings, aged 75.

Briffault's tastes were those of the Romantic. His favourite composer was Wagner; his favourite painter Hieronymos Bosch; his favourite play Goethe's *Faust*. Poetry he loved. His intelligence was encyclo-paedic. He spoke more than seven languages—French, German, Italian and English fluently. In addition he knew Latin, Greek, Dutch and Provençal French. He started learning Russian at 70.

As a general practitioner, he was much loved and even adored by his patients, particularly women, and by the nurses with whom he came in contact. The medical profession looked at him somewhat askance, it is said, because of his radical ideas and sometimes unorthodox methods of treatment. He seems to have been reasonably popular with fellow officers and men during the war.

Of Briffault's childhood and the forces which may have influenced him into undertaking the series of broad studies which culminated in *The Mothers*, we have no direct knowledge. *Europa* tells the story of Julian, the son of a retired diplomat living in Rome and his puritanical Irish wife—and from it we may gather some clues. The incident in *Europa* in which Nietzsche puts his hand on the head of Julian saying 'Thou mightest be He' is drawn from Briffault's own youth.

Julian is, as a boy, vaguely uneasy in the cultured setting of his father's many distinguished, wealthy friends. He is sensitive to the contrast between the ease of his own surroundings and the poverty of the peasants. He is much struck by Darwin's theories, and feels that knowledge is the key to the mystery of life; he must know everything. He asks a sympathetic teacher if it would be any good his reading the *Encyclopaedia Britannica* from cover to cover. His teacher tells him that nine-tenths of what is taught is untrue, and he must find out for himself what is true and what is not. A Catholic priest, attending his parents, finds him reading *The Origin of Species* and snatches it from him in a fury. A cardinal is brought in to dissuade him from accepting such ideas in a more subtle and intelligent manner, and he is shortly sent off to school in England. Here the science master lets him see the glories of the stars through his telescope; he is awed by the insignificance of the earth and the individual. This master warns him that the school does not teach what are now known to be historical facts, such as that Aeneas, Homer and King Arthur are not historical figures, for if the authority of tradition were flouted, all authority might be upset, even belief in the historicity of the Bible.

We can see here the gradual unfolding of doubt, and the desire to establish a scientifically tenable world view, which evidently animated Briffault's first books, although the Julian of the novel does not proceed to write works of this kind. If we ask where this curiosity came from, we may find the answer in the account *Europa* gives of Julian's awareness of sexuality. As a child he is represented as suffering considerable shock when a peasant woman, seeing him relieving himself against a wall, jokingly asks him if he knows 'what that is for', with other crude innuendoes. Sexuality ..... in the warm Italian air, and the adolescent Julian's sexual educ.... ludes a visit to a private collection of phallic emblems. While a psychoanalyst would certainly look for some earlier experience as the real starting-point of sexual shock—doubtless something concerned with the relationship between his parents—we can, in any case, see here the association between sexual curiosity and scientific curiosity which is asserted by Freudian doctrine. This, then, explains the possibly excessive interest in sexual matters which runs through *The Mothers*, and the violence of his attack on sexual ignorance in *Sin and Sex* and other writings. We can see, too, why the Church, and especially the Catholic Church, seemed to him to be the obscurantist force which opposed both scientific knowledge and sexual understanding.

Europa also depicts the disgust which Julian experienced when he was transferred from the cultured, adult world of Rome to the narrow and barbarous surroundings of an English school where, though not unpopular, he was an oddity who knew more Latin than the master teaching it, but nothing of cricket and who had never heard of *King Solomon's Mines*. This experience may well have reinforced the resentment which Briffault was developing for all established authority and morality, and against Britain, the country to which he nominally belonged.

This resentment was voiced in his book *The Decline and Fall of the British Empire* (though it must be noted that the title was devised by his American publisher, over his protests). A close friend has told me that his attitude to Britain was in reality highly ambivalent; at bottom he loved Britain, and he returned to his country to die. It was because he felt that Britain had rejected him that he hated it; such feeling must have been intensified by the grudging recognition accorded to *The Mothers*.

A psychoanalyst would surely see in this the reflection of an attitude towards parental figures, since native countries are either 'mother countries' or 'fatherlands'. And it is not unreasonable, when a man has devoted seven years of strenuous work to arguing the importance of mothers as against fathers, to ask whether he betrayed any marked attitudes towards his own parents.

Mrs Herma Briffault, however, informs me that he had little apparent attachment to his mother, but often spoke of his father. (He seems, nevertheless, to have had a picture of his mother in his room in the last decade of his life.) His mother was evidently a reserved, 'canny' Scotswoman, of strict views, whose capacity for personal warmth seems to have been limited, and perhaps he felt, as an infant, denied the acceptance he desired. He certainly rejected violently his mother's strong religious beliefs and teaching. Clearly there was strong ambivalence here, and the attacks—which suggest narcoleptic stupors—which assailed him at the time of his mother's last illness seem consistent with the idea of a powerful love-hate relationship. His attitude to his mother country was, as I have related, very similar, and the fact that he was brought up in isolation from that country, and regarded as an oddity when he visited it, may have completed the parallel.

His father seems to have been a broad-minded and cultured man; he wrote (probably at Louis Napoleon's request) a novel, *The Prisoner of Ham* (1846), in which may be found ideas and principles which reappear in the work of his son—such as faith in the power of truth, and dislike of those who proceed in everything merely from day to day, unable to conceive any grand idea or to create anything grand or useful, and convinced that poverty is unavoidable and evil necessary.

Briffault was generally regarded as having Communist views, and this is no doubt why he was refused entry to the u.s. He was certainly extremely interested in 'the Communist experiment', and learned Russian in order to study it; but there is no evidence that he ever took part in any Communist activities. Asked by his daughter, about 1922–3, to what political party he belonged, he replied, 'To none.' He did not agree sufficiently with any. He felt strongly that social reform could not be achieved by reforming the individual, but only by reforming the system. His conception of history was materialist: he accepted the desire for economic gain as the mainspring of human action.

It is not difficult to see how natural such attitudes were to one whose outlook had been conditioned by the experiences just described. I have observed elsewhere that, when a child has one parent who is easy-going and affectionate and another who is severe and apparently unloving, it identifies itself with the former and is preoccupied throughout life with its relationship with the latter. When it is the father who is severe, this seems to lead, in the case of a male child, to a homosexual tendency; when it is the mother who is unloving, this leads the male child to a preoccupation with women and with incest. This was certainly the case in Briffault's great contemporary, Havelock Ellis, for instance. It seems to have been equally true of Briffault.

GORDON RATTRAY TAYLOR

Richmond, 1958

CHAPTER 1

The Origins of Human Society

OUR object in this book will be to trace the origin of human society. What was the character of the first social groupings which arose as humanity evolved from the level of the animal? To ask this question raises the problem of what was the original nature of the family and of marriage.

Many writers have assumed that the family as we know it—the patriarchal family—was the first form of human grouping; that societies were created by the coming together of such families. Professor Maine, nearly a century ago, put this view forward, and early in the present century Professor Westermarck restated the idea with a much broader apparatus of anthropological information. Westermarck went further and claimed that the family had always been monogamous, polygamy being a late and decadent manifestation.

But this is by no means the only view of the origin of society which has been taken. In the year that Maine produced his *Primitive Law*, the Swiss jurist Dr Bachofen was writing his *Das Mutterrecht*, in which he maintained that the primitive state of man was one of sexual promiscuity and that the first social groups consisted simply of mothers and their children without the presence of any father. This view was further developed by others, notably McLennan, who introduced a novel conception when he claimed that the earliest human groups consisted of groups of kinsmen having an animal or plant for their badge, a state of affairs which he called totemism.

Founders of modern social anthropology—notably Morgan, Tylor and Robertson-Smith—also established the fact that in primitive society the role of women and their influence was much greater than has been the case during historical times in civilized societies. This conclusion is generally called 'The Theory of Matriarchy'—a name given to it by McLennan in opposition to the theory which traced social origins to a patriarchal age such as is presented in the Bible. The term has been loosely employed to denote a status of women ranging within wide limits, from the mere reckoning of descent in the female line instead of in the male line, to the exercise of supreme authority by women, or gynaecocracy. It may, I think, be used legitimately in a relative sense, in opposition to the term 'patriarchal', when referring to a society in which the interests and sentiments connected with women play a more important part than is the rule in the civilized societies with which we are most familiar.

Professor Westermarck's long series of books appeared after those of McLennan, and at the time of writing the view that society was primitively patriarchal is still widely accepted. In this work we shall attempt to re-examine the evidence, making use of anthropological material not available to McLennan.

In our inquiry we shall start from the fact that primitive societies approximate more closely to animal groups in structure than advanced ones, and their character is a consequence of this. In animals there is nothing corresponding to a patriarchal social group—the male has little or no share in the formation or maintenance of the animal family, and is often entirely absent from it. If human society developed out of such groups, it must have had its origin in an association which represented female instincts only, and human culture must have been moulded in the first instance not by the fierce passions of hunters battling for food and women but by the instincts of the mother.

The difficulties of such an inquiry are formidable. The remnants of uncivilized races at present existing are not truly primitive, inasmuch as they have survived the tribulations of hundreds of thousands of years. Even in conditions of isolation and stagnation, time must have deposited a detritus of culture. Fortunately culture—and I use the term in the contemporary sense of the inheritance of institutions and patterns of behaviour, of ideas and beliefs—has its own rules.[1]

Firstly, no human sentiment, no idea, no institution, has ever appeared completely *de novo*. Secondly, no phase of human ideas, sentiments or institutions ever fails to leave its imprint upon subsequent phases. However grotesque some institution, custom or idea, found in some uncultured tribe, may appear to us, nevertheless its equivalent is invariably to be found in our own customs, institutions and ideas. The quaintest cultural peculiarity from the Cannibal Islands or Central Africa can be matched in modern London.

But despite this undying persistence of primitive forms, it is a strange fact that primitive behaviour appears to us a fantastic and incoherent

---

[1] Briffault, in fact, does not use the word 'culture', which has been popularized since he wrote, but speaks of 'traditional heredity'. As the concept of culture is now much more widely understood, I have substituted the modern term, and have abbreviated his remarks on it very considerably, but it is only right to restore the balance a little by stressing that he was one of the very first to perceive the importance of cultural forces in moulding both behaviour and personality, and much of what he had to say was, at the time when he wrote it, of great interest and novelty.—G. R. T.

product of a mentality utterly different from our own. And despite our belief that human nature never changes or that it is the same the world over, many beliefs and customs and institutions which are found to be common to primitive humanity from the Poles to the Equator, from Polynesia to the American prairies, nevertheless appear to European man to be uncouth and strange. To interpret their significance and origin has been the standing puzzle of anthropology. Many interpretations have been put forward, but it must be confessed that these ideas and sentiments still remain to a large extent a riddle.

In attacking this problem, we depend upon two sets of facts. In the first place man displays a number of instincts which he appears to inherit and which must represent the result of evolution from animal instincts. At the same time, he learns from his society much which soon becomes 'second nature'; it is clearly important for our purpose to distinguish very carefully between what is inherited and therefore unmodifiable, and what is acquired from the culture and thus is peculiar to a given society. In point of fact, many attributes which are widely believed even today to be entirely inherited turn out upon examination to be largely or wholly cultural. In general, the instincts of man appear to be much less determinate in character than those of animals. With few exceptions, such as the infant's instinct to suck, they are quite general in nature, and their form of expression is largely determined by the culture.[1]

It is often thought that civilized man inherits a higher intellectual development than the savage, and a greater aptitude for education, which enables him to acquire more easily than backward races the cultural inheritance of his society. The facts are, however, that the children of savage peoples learn just as rapidly as those of Europeans, or even more so. Thus of the negro children of the coast of Guinea Captain Binger says: 'They have an extraordinary memory and capacity to learn anything that one may teach them. They are quite as highly gifted as our European children of the same age.' And a missionary in East Central Africa writes: 'It has been the general experience in other parts of Africa that negro children have no greater difficulty in learning to read and write than European children, but quite the reverse; and that experience is confirmed in our own schools.' When schools were first established in Hawaii, teachers were often embarrassed by being unable to keep up with their pupils; while in Samoa the natives developed such a craze for arithmetical calculation that the Hon. Frederick Walpole declared that his visit to that island was positively embittered

---

[1] For instance, a tailor bird can only make a particular type of nest. If man has an instinct to house himself, it is certainly not an instinct to make only one particular kind of house.—G. R. T.

by ceaseless multiplication and division. Scientific tests have shown on a number of occasions that although individuals differ there is no appreciable difference in the natural mental capacity between savage races and modern Europeans. It seems, however, to be true that this aptitude reaches an early ceiling, whereas the European out-distances the savage in the long run.

It is often supposed that artistic talents are inherited, and attempts have been made to demonstrate a specific aptitude for music. In particular, it has been thought that the ability to recognise the pitch of a musical note when sounded is a rare inborn capacity. However, it has been shown that almost every child is capable of acquiring it quite easily; it is only that the majority of children lose their natural musical ability through lack of training during the most susceptible period.

To many it seems evident that the progress of the human race is correlated with the development of moral qualities. But Professor Boas says: 'As the civilization is higher we assume that the aptitude for civilization is also higher; and as the aptitude for civilization presumably depends upon the perfection of the mechanism of body and mind, the inference is drawn that the white race represents the highest type of perfection. . . . There is no satisfactory evidence that the effects of civilization are inherited.' And as Mr Burt says: 'In inborn mental constitution the civilized inhabitant of Paris or London today is, if any-thing, inferior rather than superior to the Athenian at the time of Pericles or the Englishman at the time of Shakespeare; and indeed, if anything, inferior rather than superior to his prehistoric ancestors. . . . The superiority of the modern, civilized man is due, not to the heredi-tary powers and capacities but to mental contents and achievements accumulated not by inheritance but by tradition.'

Social co-operation and other moral factors are often thought to be inborn, yet many observers have noted how well-conducted young men can become lazy, disrespectful and dishonest as a result of mental injuries or even exposure to a different social environment. What are supposed to be racial characteristics also seem to be derived from culture rather than inheritance. As Professor Boas says: 'Much has been said of the hereditary characters of the Jews, or the Gypsies, or the French and Irish, but I do not see that the social causes which have moulded the character of members of these peoples have ever been eliminated satis-factorily.' The French feeling for 'logic' and the English tendency to blunder through by 'horse-sense' can be deduced from their respective social histories. The French language itself developed its lucidity and logical qualities in the French salons and had previously been as un-couth as English. It is a current view that the acquirements or contents of the mind are of secondary importance to 'good stock', and if a Briton behaves well in difficult circumstances it is often attributed to his hereditary background or breeding. In much the same way the Gothic barbarians despised the culture of ancient Europe and refused to have their children educated because they said 'education enfeebles the mind'.[1]

Sir Thomas Browne affirmed the inborn character of all the virtues. 'Rejoice that thou wert born of honest parents, that honesty, modesty and veracity lay in the same egg and came into the world with thee.' Such beliefs die hard. The absolute validity of moral ideas is thought to demand that they should be rooted in the very structure of human nature. Even social institutions such as private property, monogamic marriage or male dominance tend to be viewed as embedded in human nature. Able writers have sought to show that regard for chastity and the sentiment of modesty are also implanted in the human mind.

The transmission of culture takes place by words, and since animals have no language there can be no true equivalent of human society in the animal world. Without language it is impossible to form concepts or to think in any but the most primitive manner. Thought is but un-uttered speech; the infant learns to think and to speak at the same time —it thinks aloud, and its thoughts take the form of a continuous babble. Though later the child learns 'to hold its tongue', the adult, when no one else is present, will often talk to himself.

While some germ of thought no doubt exists in the higher animals, nevertheless, as Professor Lloyd Morgan says, animals are without the perception of relations; their memory is desultory and 'the evidence now before us is not sufficient to justify the prophecies that any animals have reached that state of evolution in which they are even incipiently rational'.

Man is man by virtue of language alone.[2] The point is so important that it is worth a little development. Thus we may draw attention to the fact that in Latin as in Greek, the same word meant both dumb and stupid, while our own word dumb derives from the German 'dumm'— stupid. The name of a thing has widely been regarded as intimately connected with its very nature. Plato's famous doctrine that a word is not a mere label or representation but is the true reality, as an indepen-

---

[1] In many cases apparent racial differences are due to malnutrition or endemic disease. Where aristocratic classes are of a finer physical and mental type than the common people, this is probably the result of their privileged position, not the cause of it.

[2] Controversy sometimes arises as to whether thought is possible without language. The answer is that language is but a particular system of symbolism and thought is possible by means of any other symbolic system. Mathematicians can think in terms of mathematical symbols, and the blind deaf-mute Laura Bridgman was observed to move her hands in sign-language when dreaming.

dent existence, is merely a developed form of a theory found in many phases of primitive society. The Babylonians believed that the name was the essence of the person or thing to which it was attached and that that which had no name did not exist. The Egyptians also held that all things had their true name—the essence of their being. Thus it is that things can be created by uttering their names and that creators so create the world. 'There was a time', states an ancient Egyptian papyrus, 'when no one and nothing existed except the creator. A desire came over him to create the world, and he carried it into effect by making his mouth utter his own name as a word of power; and straightway the world and all therein came into being.' That creative utterance was known to the early Sumerian priests as mummu, and in later Babylonian theology as the God Nebo, called by the Greeks Hermes, who had been identified with the word as far back as the sixth century. Among the Persians and in the Vedanta the same conception is found. 'The world', says a Vedic hymn, 'originates from the word.' We find the same ideas among rudest humanity. For example, among the wild tribes of Brazil every creative thing has as they say 'its mother', every lake, every stream, every species of animal, vegetable has its determinal paradigm or 'mother'. Father D'Acosta, writing of the Caribbean natives, remarks 'that they approach somewhat near the proposition of Platoes Idees'. The same comment was suggested to Father Lafitau when he saw the American Indians.

The person's name is therefore regarded as his spirit or soul—the very word soul is from a root denoting wind, and the Greek $\Psi v \chi \acute{\eta}$ is derived from the word $\Psi \acute{v} \chi \omega$ —I blow.

In many languages the word for breath and spirit are identical. Hence if one utters one's own name one is liable to lose one's soul, and names are commonly kept secret so that magic cannot be worked with them. Sneezing, which is an expiration of the breath, is also liable to cause the soul to depart, and the Malays when they sneeze call back their soul in a loud voice.

It is by the same conception of the importance of the word that spells, curses and blessings and incantations operate. The Bechuana, when they go to war, have a priestly personage who marches with the troops and continually calls out 'the army is not seen', which effectually conceals the troops from the enemy. No sorcerer can harm a person if he is ignorant of his name, and an Irish poet quite failed to curse a certain King of Ulster whose name would not scan in any known metre. Accordingly, to work magic it is necessary to know the correct words and in Persia the magic art was called 'The science of names'. All that Eskimo require to command the spirits is a knowledge of their names. The power which such knowledge bestows is illimitable. Australian medicine-men can stop the sun, cause thunder, raise mountains, create lakes and rivers; in Brazil they can control the course of nature and human life.

By the same argument, poets are creators and even sorcerers. 'None merits the name of creator save God only and the poet', said Tasso. The word magic is derived from the word for 'making' and *vates* means both prophet and poet. The word *runa* meant first of all the poet's magic word and then poetry in general. The classical invocation 'Sing, heavenly muse!' was originally the formula by which the poet invoked the god who possessed him. The Hindus and Arabs have a simple means of depriving a sorceress of the power to do harm: they extract her front teeth, so that she is unable to sing or articulate distinctly; and it was for analogous reasons that Odysseus had the power to tame animals, heal sickness and compel the affection of women. Vergil assures us that poetry can draw down the moon from heaven; while the ancient Irish were convinced that a satire inevitably caused blisters to appear on the face of the victim.

It follows that to doubt that language is innate in every human being when born is tantamount to denying the existence of the soul. Eunomius charged St Basil with atheism for maintaining that babies learn to talk. Many rulers have sought to put the matter to the test: James IV of Scotland put two bairns in charge of a dumb woman on the Island of Inchkeith and we are assured that when they came to the age of speech 'they spak guid Hebrew'—for Hebrew was, of course, the primitive language of the world. The view that language was given to man and not invented by him was maintained even as late as the nineteenth century by the famous Catholic philosopher Vicomte de Bonald.

But in fact the numerous discoveries of children who have been brought up wild by animals shows that in no case could they speak, nor could they even think. Madamoiselle Leblanc, the wild girl found near Chalons in 1731, said that in her pre-linguistic days she had no thought at all and had now only very dim memories of the period. Kaspar Hauser, the youth found in 1828 near Nuremberg, had the mind of a child and mistook inanimate objects for living things. It would appear that the same is true even of animals—a cow which is born deaf will not low, and sparrows brought up with canaries have acquired the trills and call-notes of the latter. The paradox is that human culture must be acquired in order to be inherited—a paradox which Goethe expressed by saying, 'That which from thy fathers hast inherited, acquire it!—that it may be thine.' Nevertheless, the belief in inborn character dies hard.

We may see in the most ordinary child evidence of the primitive character of the human animal before it has become influenced by culture. The child is amoral; it is callous, if not cruel; it is attracted by dirt and those things which we regard as obscene; it is selfish, passionate, gives way to anger and resents deprivation bitterly. In an adult such behaviour would be regarded as insane, and it is hardly too much to say that we derive our sanity from the culture. It is this socially and traditionally acquired mind which thrusts our physiologically inherited attributes into the obscurity of unconsciousness, and which may be equated with Freud's super ego and id.

In short, all those mental characters which are specifically human are derived from the culture. They include not only the conceptual forms of consciousness—thought and ideation, but also those feelings, sentiments and effective values by which the behaviour of the social individual is for the most part determined. The human mind, in all that distinguishes it from the mind of animals, is thus a social product, and it is for this reason that I have already said that there is nothing properly corresponding to a human society in the animal world. Thus it is in the social history of the human race itself that the origin and development of the human mind—in so far as it is human at all—are to be sought. The true field of investigation into the psychology of mind is that of social anthropology and social history.

CHAPTER 2

Motherhood

THE nearest thing to an emotional relationship among animals, and the presumable point of origin of all social relationships and structures, is that which subsists between some primate animals—mother animals and their offspring. If, as I hope to show, it is from this germ that human society sprang, we must start by asking how the maternal instinct originated.

As we ascend the evolutionary scale, the role of mother becomes increasingly important, but let us take the argument back a stage further and ask how it is that mothers come to exist at all. In the simplest forms of life reproduction can take place asexually. In many higher forms reproduction is effected by the female alone parthenogenetically.[1]

Sexual differentiation is not rooted in the constitution of life, but is a biological accident, a special device designed to meet certain conditions. This differentiation becomes marked in the higher organisms. Whether males or females are produced of such unions depends essentially upon nutrition—good food giving rise to an excess of females.

While the function of the primitive female is fulfilled when she has produced an ovum, as we advance up the evolutionary scale another duty becomes thrust upon her—that of care for the offspring. In the simplest stages this care is perhaps involuntary. The young of some animals attach themselves parasitically to their mother and suck the fluids of her body. In the case of some gall-flies the young actually eat their mother, and creep out of her empty skin only after the matricidal feast is over.

As we ascend the evolutionary scale we find that the period allowed

[1] This is the ordinary mode of reproduction among wheel-animalcules and is common among many species of crustaceans. It has been observed among thrips and nematode worms, and is the rule among saw-flies and caddis-flies. 'Among gall-flies the male is useless; the continuation of the species being effected by virgin females, although males exist.' It commonly takes place among several species of moths and butterflies. Reproduction of males without the female is, however, unheard of. In some species which habitually reproduce parthenogenetically males may be entirely absent, as for example in *Cypris ovum* and other ostracod crustaceans and in fresh-water rotifers. In the Solenobia butterfly, males appear only occasionally, sometimes at intervals of years. In some species of rotifers the males are not sexually functional.

for gestation steadily increases in length. It is true that an elephant carries its young for two years but, proportionately to weight, human beings carry their young longer than any other animal. This increased period of gestation allows for an increasingly complex development in the organism, and is generally associated with the reduction in the number of young produced. Furthermore, the young require increasing amount of care after birth in the highest stages of development. Rats, for instance, shift for themselves when thirty-nine days old and reach maturity in six months; a hartebeeste antelope, one week old, can outrun the fastest man. A young elephant is capable of following its mother when two days old. Carnivorous animals, on the other hand, are born helpless; they are unable to stand for several days, and are entirely dependent upon their mother for many months. Young lions are unable to stalk for themselves until they are about a year and a half old. In the case of monkeys the period of care is even longer; a baby gibbon remains clinging to the body of its mother for seven months; the orang-outang at the end of one month is as advanced as the human baby when a year old; a lamb a day old has proceeded farther in its development than either. This period of immaturity is not required for bodily growth but for completion of the brain and neural system.

Similar differences in rapidity of growth and maturation can be seen between the lower and more civilized races of men; savage children develop more quickly than Europeans but, their development being completed earlier, are less capable of further progress. For example, children among the Baholoholo of the Congo know how to paddle a canoe and catch a fox at an age when civilized children are still in the arms of their nurses. Among the Kirghis a child of three can already ride a horse and at six takes charge of a herd of camels. Among the Habbe of Nigeria children of six or eight leave their home, build a hut and provide for themselves. Among the Aleuts, children of ten have already become hunters and not infrequently keep a wife. Chiriguano children of seven or ten go on war and hunting expeditions with their fathers. Unfortunately mental development ceases about the time that sexual maturity is reached. Captain Binger remarks: 'Not only does the intellect of the child cease to develop, but it might be said that it retrogresses; the memory becomes impaired. He becomes stupid, mistrustful, vain and deceitful as he was formerly intelligent.'

Thus it would appear that the congenital superiority of what are regarded as the higher races of man consists essentially in a slower rate of development, and this slower development is rendered possible, and perhaps caused, by the prolonged relief from the necessity of providing for subsistence and protection—in a word, by mother-care.

But the mother animal's instinct to look after her children is, in animals, of a purely physiological kind. It is not something which is always with her, but comes into being only at the time of pregnancy or just before birth. Unimpregnated female mice take no notice whatever of young mice, and it is not until the later phases of pregnancy that they will lick them and endeavour to carry them away. Manifestations of this instinct cease about six weeks after birth; moreover, it is often satisfied by substitutes—a pregnant bitch, noted Loisel, searched restlessly until she was presented with a litter of young rabbits, when she was entirely satisfied and licked and fondled them. A female crab bristles with anger if the maturing larvae on its appendages are touched—behaviour which would provide a text for maternal devotion—but the crab behaves in just the same manner when the brood-stalks have been appropriated by noxious parasites.

Maternal reactions generally take place in response to gross physical stimuli. Suckling is sought by the female to relieve the tension in the mammary glands, and brooding in birds is caused by exhaustion and irritative congestion of the abdominal wall. In birds that are not good sitters, the defect may be remedied by rubbing their abdominal skin with nettles. Consequently when we speak of maternal 'care' and 'devotion' in the lower animals, we are really projecting human sentiments into behaviour which is in fact purely physiological.

That the maternal instinct is a product of evolution and not of primary impulse is indicated by the fact that it requires an appreciable time to develop fully. The same females that will offer their life for their young will commonly eat them when they are new-born. Carnivores are prone to eat their young whenever they are frightened, as are sows, and even dogs and cats, while the reindeer is said invariably to kill its second fawn. Even in humans mothers not uncommonly take a day or two until they become attached to their children, and at the moment immediately following birth infanticide is common among both savage and civilized mothers, whereas a little later it would be difficult or impossible.

Maternal instinct is also frequently limited in duration. Few animals pay regard to earlier offspring after the birth of fresh young ones, and many animals throw out the young after lactation has finished. Birds, for instance, change from 'unceasing solicitude to open hostility' and drive forth their young from the neighbourhood. Swallows and house-martins when migrating frequently abandon their nestlings. While carnivores frequently defend their brood, the practice varies—for example, the offspring of a seal can be killed before its mother's eyes without causing her the slightest concern, whereas the walrus mother will fight to the death in defence of her young. Nevertheless, on maturity the maternal instinct ceases.

Among monkeys and apes, however, the maternal instinct is so intense and uniform as to contrast with all other mammals. The tense and watchful anxiety of the monkey mother has often been noted. Baboons will wash their young in a stream, and the Cebus has been seen to drive away the flies which plagued its infant. Some monkey mothers will die from grief when deprived of their young, and there are several cases on record of a monkey placing its body between its child and the hunters' gun and so sacrificing its life for its offspring. In contrast, carnivores, although they may fiercely defend their young, will occasionally abandon them. Starving tigresses have been known to kill and eat their young—behaviour which has never been reported of monkeys.

The new relations which are established by protracted mother-care transform the very springs of action and behaviour, for they cause the individual mind to be linked up with others to form a new organism—the group bound by social ties. Let us consider next what we can infer from animal societies about the origins of social feeling and gregariousness and the character of the primordial family.

CHAPTER 3

The Origin of Social Feeling

I T has been generally assumed that feelings of tenderness and affection are part and parcel of the attraction between the sexes, an attraction commonly spoken of as love. Love is generally identified with the sexual impulse, and is assumed to be one of the mainsprings of the universe. Life, says Schiller, is ruled by Hunger and Love.

But love, far from being a basic force in the universe, has arisen late in human evolution. Primitively, sexual feelings are associated not with tenderness but with delight in the infliction of pain. Animals are preying beings and the sight of a mangled or a weak and helpless creature means to them food. All carnivores are cannibalistic; lions frequently eat their mates or their cubs. A jaguar in the New York Zoo showed every sign of fondness for a female kept in an adjacent cage. He purred, licked the female's paws, and behaved like the most love-sick admirer, but when the partition between them was removed, his first act was to kill her. Sexual hunger, as it is aptly called, is a form of voracity. The object of the male cell in seeking conjunction with the female cell is primarily to improve its own nutrition. The female requires the male also to assure her nutrition, and in some forms of life the female devours and assimilates the male.

With both sexes, sexual attraction is pre-eminently sadistic, and is gratified by pain. Rutting animals maul each other, and emerge from the sexual combat bleeding and mangled. Crustaceans usually lose a limb or two in the encounter. All mammals, without exception, use their teeth on these occasions. So fundamental is the association between sex and cruelty that it is probably never wholly absent even in humanity. According to M. d'Enjoy, the kiss has developed out of the love-bite. Among the ancient Egyptians the word translated by 'to kiss' meant 'to eat'.

Sentiments of tenderness between the sexes are originally connected not with the sexual impulse but with the mating instinct—something very different. Mating, meaning association between the sexes, is an adaptation to the reproductive functions of the female. With the extension of maternal care, the female needs protection and help in procuring food, and so requires the co-operation of the male. For birds, where the female sits on eggs, such help is almost indispensable; hence it is among nidicolous birds that the mating instinct has achieved its most striking development, but even here it is confined to those species which hatch their eggs by prolonged brooding.

Many mammals, far from associating after the sexual act, appear to be actually repelled from one another. In general, mammals do not mate, but the sexes roam in separate herds. This is true of all herbivores. Elephant cows, after being impregnated, form bands, from which males are driven off, as do seals and walruses, bears and leopards. Among carnivores, the female generally conceals herself and her brood from the male lest he eat the cubs. Even where an association exists between the parents, it is the female which attends to the feeding of the young. The male lion is frequently represented as bringing his kill to the female while she remains with her cubs, but in fact he drags his kill to his lair, whether there are cubs or not. Not only is it the female alone who protects the offspring, but in some cases she protects the male also, as among deer and antelope, and also elephants.

Among primitive human races the mating instinct is almost equally unimportant. As will later be shown, cohabitation is very transient in the lower phases of human culture. Conjugal affection is almost unknown. 'If you wish to excite laughter,' says Father Petitot, 'speak to the Déné of conjugal affection.' Similar reports come from many parts of the world—from Africa, New Zealand, Papua and elsewhere. The point has been the subject of controversy, but the data which will be brought forward later in this book will show that in primitive peoples, sexual love, as we conceive it, is at best rudimentary.

On the other hand, there is no doubt that among savages the love of mothers for their offspring is unambiguous. In the very peoples who are described as being devoid of love between man and woman, the strength of maternal affection is constantly noted. For example, among the Eskimo the coldness of the sexual relation is conspicuous, but maternal love is said to be 'lively and tender', more so, as Father Petitot remarks, than among ourselves. Among the Déné 'maternal love is developed to the point of obliterating every suggestion of prudence, and even every reasoned act of intelligence.' The Patagonians display a love for their children 'which is quite extravagant; they show such extreme compliance with regard to them that whole tribes have been known to leave a district or to remain there longer than was advisable simply to gratify the whim of a child. Primitive women will court danger or pain for their children. During a tribal war in Samoa 'a woman allowed herself to be hacked from head to foot, bending over her son to save his life'. Women will not eat until their children have been satisfied; they offer themselves to redeem children who have been taken as slaves. This intensity of maternal affection is equally noted in the lowest races, such as the Fuegians, the Seri Indians, the Veddahs, the Ainu and others.

It might seem that the widespread practice of infanticide was irreconcilable with the existence of maternal love, but it must be recalled that in primitive society murder is often not a crime, and it is believed that the dead are still with us. Thus in the Cameroons, during the German invasion, the natives, who are devoted parents, killed most of the new-born, 'in pity for their sufferings and in the firm belief that their spirits would return to earth as soon as all was peaceful once more'. In primitive society corporal punishment of children is unheard of. Father Le Jeune complained that 'all the savage tribes of these parts, and those of Brazil, as we are assured, cannot chastise a child or bear to see one chastised. What trouble this will cause us in carrying out our intention of instructing their young!' In fact, many missionaries have stirred up trouble by their chastisements.

In other respects, the primitive mother is far from gentle. Her feeling for her mate is primarily that of loyalty. She is content to leave the choice of mate to her parents, and her estimate of the husband's value is a hundred per cent utilitarian. His appeal therefore grows with the closeness and stability of his relationship with her. Among the lower races, where sexual selection exists, it is predominantly exercised by the women, as we shall see in detail later. In those races where the men are indifferent or brutal to the women, strong and genuine attachment to them is nevertheless displayed, and their widows are inconsolable when their brutal husbands die. Fijian women, who are among the most brutally treated, insist upon being killed on the graves of their husbands. It is probable that the custom of 'suttee' was originally voluntary. The numerous wives of an African chief, whom he uses as pillows and footstools, vie for the honour of being so employed.

The female's affection provides a powerful inducement for the male to modify his sexual instincts to suit her mating needs, for her affection is the equivalent of the maternal tenderness which he knew in infancy. Biologically, however, his sole function is the impregnation of the ova, and his instincts are limited to that. These instincts are indeed in antagonism with the mating instincts. The sadistic hunger of the masculine impulse can never become entirely blended with mating attraction. 'Il n'y a rien de si loin de la volupté que l'attendrissement,' observes Lamartine. Indeed, the two forms of sexual attraction are essentially incompatible. Love—tender feeling—is a common cause of 'psychical impotence'. The two instincts, sexual and the mating, may exist in the male quite independently, and this, as we shall see, is common in primitive humanity. The sexual impulse may have no trace of affection, while genuine attachment may be unattended by sexual jealousy. Throughout primitive societies the distinction between the two functions is much more consciously recognized than in our own, where sentiments and institutions have tended to obliterate the distinction.

The moral qualities, such as courage and character, which are supreme in the woman's sexual choice have no place in the man's in so far that the choice is purely sexual; he discriminates chiefly with regard to sexual values; that is, the physical qualities of youth and beauty, which are ultimately expressions of the suitability of the female for rearing the best offspring. Hence the feminine taunt that a man may be attracted by a woman whom he neither esteems nor respects.

Since the female instinct is more directly founded on biological need, and is developmentally older than the male, it tends to retain its primitive character, even in advanced stages of culture. This is why.it is less subject to cultural transformations in women than in men. Even a cursory study shows what a wide range of fashions in love have existed, and it has frequently been remarked that romantic love is profoundly influenced by literature and traditions, and that no one would be subject to it in the same form had he never read a novel nor seen a play.

Yet people constantly treat animal and primitive sex impulses as identical with the love of cultured humanity. Sexual love is spoken of as if it were a simple basic emotion or impulse, when it is really the most complex of sentiments. It is compounded of self-esteem—'amor a nullo amato amar perdona', of aesthetic elements—few men would be attracted by a woman who was a habitual frump or slut—and, by participation in common tastes, mostly imaginary. As Spencer says, love 'fuses into one immense aggregate most of the elementary excitations of which we are capable'.

Just as the transferred affection of the female for the male is a derivative of maternal love, so all feelings of a tender, altruistic character are extensions and transformations of the maternal instinct. Altruism is almost unknown in animals, and is in contrast to basic biological demands. These sentiments, being of female origin, develop more strongly in the female. The sympathetic, protective, affectionate attitude, transferred by the female from the offspring to its father, is gradually extended towards all males, towards females who are not possible rivals, towards animals and all living things, and even towards plants, flowers and inanimate objects. These are handled tenderly, whereas the male is disposed to be rough and to destroy. For the male the extension of sentiments in this way is much more difficult, more unnatural. The male child is born cruel. It is his natural propensity to inflict suffering and to destroy. Only social education can develop a tender disposition in him to any degree.

Long before such a transformation occurs maternal instincts produce an even stronger bond of attachment in their direct object, the offspring. The strong feeling of the child for his mother, founded upon infantile experience, is highly developed in primitive societies, but is weakened in advanced societies where sentiments of manliness and independence are stressed.[1] Savages remain children.

The primitive's continued dependence upon the mother's affection is a feature of primitive psychology. The Indians of California 'scarcely acknowledge their father but they preserve a longer attachment for their mother who has brought them up with extreme tenderness'. Among the Iroquois 'the crime which is regarded as most horrible and which is without example is that a son should be rebellious towards his mother'. In Melanesia, when engaging a boat's crew, one comes upon men of forty who say that they must first obtain their mother's consent. The Dayaks of northern Borneo are devoted to their mothers and honour them all their lives, but 'their father they may like or they may not; they recognize no duty towards him; but their mother is something holy to them, whatever she is like, and no one is ever allowed to breathe a word against her'. Similar examples are found in almost every part of the world. The strongest of all natural ties, says Wilson of the West African negroes, 'are those between the mother and her children. Whatever other estimate we may form of the African, we may not doubt his love for his mother. Her name, whether dead or alive, is always on his lips and in his heart.'

Daughters, too, are more closely bound to their mother than to their husband. In Togoland, 'the bond between mother and daughter is so strong that both remain bound to one another until one dies. Never can love towards the husband displace in the heart of a daughter the love towards her mother'.

The attachment of the young towards the mother consists, not so much in the sentiment of tenderness, as in the sense of dependence and fear when protection is withdrawn. The child is therefore ready to accept a substitute protector. All young animals will attach themselves to the first creature, animal or human, that will look after them. Mr Selous mentions that, having shot a female rhinoceros which had just dropped a calf, the latter at once trotted behind its mother's slayer, and quietly followed him to his camp. (Such instances show how animals were first domesticated.) The reliance upon the mother extends to all companions who are recognized as not being hostile or dangerous, and results in the general disposition to friendliness.

Brothers and sisters are naturally the first substitutes adopted to

[1] In some tribes boys are taught to use violence towards their mothers in order that they should grow up manly.

satisfy this desire for dependence and to appease the fear of solitude. Such feelings are even more prone to assume the character of affection when directed towards companions of the same age than when directed to the mother. An instinct of clannishness becomes a marked feature of such a group.

It is often held that gregariousness is a fundamental instinct. In fact, it is evolved from family feeling. The majority of animals are not gregarious; in those that do form herds, the herds are constituted of family groups. Far from there being any natural tendency to congregate, most living organisms tend to disperse, for there are biological advantages in wandering to fresh fields and pastures new, and concentration tends to exhaust the food supply. Primitives, far from displaying signs of any general social instinct, exhibit profound distrust and hostility towards those who are not members of the group. 'In primitive culture', observes Dr Brinton, 'there is a dual system of morals; the one of kindness, love, help and peace, applicable to the members of our own clan . . . the other of robbery, hatred, enmity and murder, to be practised against all the rest of the world.' It is for this reason that small groups are so unwilling to merge, and that tribes in the same territory are deeply suspicious, and their languages diverge so far that they cannot converse with one another.

Wherever groups exist, it is as the result of specific needs and instincts, not the result of any generalized mutual attraction. In the higher forms of animal life the so-called social instinct is the direct outcome of the relation between mother and offspring, and of the reflection of maternal instincts between members of the same brood or brotherhood, as Darwin perceived. The material out of which all human society has been constructed is the bond of those sentiments. The origin of all social bonds, the only one which exists among the higher animals and in the most primitive human groups, is that created by mother-love.

CHAPTER 4

The Herd and the Family
amongst Animals

LET us now consider animal societies and herds.

Supposed Animal Societies

Every association of individuals in the animal kingdom is, without exception, a reproductive organization, even though such groups often serve other purposes, such as mutual protection or the securing of food.[1] True, in insect communities the correlation which takes place between the male and the female is elaborated so that a large number of differentiated individuals co-operate to achieve the reproductive end, but the principle is the same. Insects are, however, an offshoot from the main stem of evolution, and lie outside the direct line of human ancestry.

Many visible assemblages of animals are not true associations. Fishes collect in shoals simply because they seek the most favourable conditions; just as sea-birds congregate on rocks. Flocks formed for migration are of analogous origin, and revert to separate groupings as soon as the migration is accomplished. The same is true of deer and antelope. Sometimes the presence of a large number of species, such as African reed-bucks, in one place, gives rise to the impression that they are gregarious.

The association of lions in groups of as many as forty is, as Selous remarks, only of a very temporary nature. Hyenas, too, are solitary animals, even though they are often seen in packs, since they scent the blood of a dead animal from afar and collect for the feast. Wolf packs are the nearest approach to an organized association, but they are not permanent associations, and the South American wolf never forms packs. The 'pack law' of the Indian wolf, so eloquently described by the author of *The Jungle Book*, exists only in imagination; it is scarcely ever known

[1] The tendency to interpret biological phenomena in terms of human traditions and assumptions is illustrated by the conceptions put forward at different times about bees. The ancients regarded the egg-laying female as a patriarchal male, and called it 'the king'. The hive was divided into patricians and plebians. When the true sexes of the insects became known, the female was called 'the queen', and the hive was regarded as a more democratic organization, and compared to an industrial community under the term, 'hive of industry.'

to gather in larger numbers than three. Another animal frequently spoken of as organized into communities is the beaver, and beaver colonies have been described as working under a leader. Actually beavers live in families and have no leader. The largest communities ever seen by Agassiz consisted of five families. 'It is evident', he says, 'that beavers are not really gregarious in their habits, and that the dams and canals are the work of a comparatively small number of animals.' A dam has been known to be constructed by a solitary beaver. Equally romantic descriptions have been given of the 'societies' of 'prairie dogs'. According to Captain Marryat, their burrows are laid out in regular streets, forming prairie-dog cities. They are in the habit of paying afternoon calls on one another. It is scarcely necessary to say that this is pure fable.

Polygamy and Monogamy amongst Animals

Are any animals 'monogamous'? Woods Hutchinson has made the extraordinary claim that among animals 'monogamous marriage lasting for life' has 'become adopted by every dominant race on account of its resulting in the largest number of most efficient offspring'. Several writers have been anxious to discover such a relationship, and to suggest that ideas of sexual morality which developed at a late stage in human history have some sort of validity among the lower animals. The facts show, however, that whether such relations are polygamous or mono-gamous has no bearing on reproductivity. Actually the terms, 'mono-gamy' and 'polygamy', applied to animals, do not have the same mean-ing as when applied to human marriage, for they refer only to the associations which take place during one breeding season. The so-called 'true marriage' of birds merely means pairing during a single season. Thus the mallard, while essentially monogamous during the pairing period, as soon as the duties of incubation have begun, savagely pursues every other female that ventures in his neighbourhood. Simi-larly, the bull moose, which is spoken of as monogamous because it is rarely found with more than one cow at a time, does not remain with her for more than a week, and, since the rutting season lasts about two months, he mates with a considerable number. The same is probably true of the majority of animals which, though not forming polygamous herds, do not remain with the female after sexual union. The lion is no more monogamous than the domestic cat. Among mammals 'a union in pairs lasting beyond one season', say Brehm's editors, 'has been ob-served only in the case of the dwarf antelope . . .', in which species pairing depends upon the circumstance that two young, a male and a female, are generally born together, and these subsequently pair, the species being perpetuated incestuously.

While monogamous associations are found among the lower mammals, such as the rodents, polygamy is universal amongst the highest mammals, the monkeys and the anthropoids. A report, often quoted, that some species of monkeys are monogamous seems wholly unsubstantiated. Dr Westermarck quotes the assertion of Dr Hartmann that 'the gorilla is monogamous' as a foundation for his theory of human marriage. It is quite incorrect. Gorillas live in groups polygamously, as numerous observers have reported. Hartmann bases his assertion on an article in a popular magazine, and this, when inspected, proves not in fact to make such a statement.

Jealousy among Animals

If the patriarchal group derives from animal society, we should expect animals to display sexual jealousy. Among carnivores, competition among males for the possession of females is much rarer than in the herbivores, and it is the latter which are equipped with weapons of sexual combat. Lions never fight; bats queue quietly for their turn, while other males pair with the female. Though deer fight, they do so only during rut, and this combativeness does not denote anything corresponding to jealousy, which, as we use the term, implies the choice of a particular female, the appreciation of differences. The displays of male decoration serve to attract attention, as do call-notes, but not to influence individual choice. Some animals, such as salmon, fight in order to protect their eggs, as does the stickleback, whose combats are so furious that they have often been described in terms of human sentiments, but the stickleback is by no means monogamous, as was once believed, but endeavours to induce a number of females to deposit eggs in the nest he has built.

The struggles of male animals are not for the possession of particular females, but for access to females in general, and commonly take place when no females are actually present. Male animals fight for the opportunity of reproduction, as they fight for food. Brehm placed two pairs of bears, which appeared to be affectionate couples, in the same pit. The males immediately fought for the possession of both the females at the same time, and the winner immediately paired with the she-bear of the loser. The carnivora are jealous of all rivals, and imprisoned lions are even jealous of the keeper who approaches the cage. Stags often herd their does and force hinds to stay in the herd, but they have often been seen to leave the whole herd and take possession of a new one; sometimes to exchange herds. Often several stags keep possession of a herd together, and fights are by no means as frequent as some people believe. Though seals fight, the bull does not appear to know his own females individually. Once one has strayed outside his marked-out territory, he

pays no further attention to her. 'It is the cows and not the bulls', says
Major Hamilton, 'which have the real control of the harem system.'
Some young bulls were even observed to mate with females under the
eyes of the old bull without his paying any attention. The male becomes
spent after a short period of rut and loses interest.

The Female in the Animal Group

Though it is the male which keeps the females in a polygamous herd
together, his control is purely in sexual matters. An animal group is not
usually led by a patriarch—an old male—but by a female, who guides it
and keeps watch against possible dangers. Whereas stags will often walk
blindly into danger, the females seem more alert; the same is true of
buffaloes, of African antelopes, of gazelles, chamois, zebras and so on.
'Sometimes', says Dr Hornaday, 'a herd of elk is completely tyrannized
by an old doe, who makes the young bucks fly from her in terror, when
one prod of their sharp antlers would quickly send her to the rear.'
When a male and female tiger are found in company 'the tigress is
generally in advance of the male'; and the same is true of the lioness.

The migrations of mammals are led by the females, and appear to be
determined mainly by the females' search for favourable grounds to
bring up their offspring. In short, even in the typically polygamous herd,
the dominance of the male is qualified, and the protective social functions
are discharged chiefly by the female. It is in the field of sexual relations,
in the narrowest sense, that the herd is dominated by the male, and then
only during the period of rut. Thus, the real animal group depends on
the bond between mother and offspring, and not upon the association
between the sexes. Indeed, the male sexual instincts tend to break up
the herd. In the typical herbivorous species—for instance, the red deer
—the female withdraws from the herd after impregnation, and leads a
solitary life with her calf until the autumn. If the hind then joins a herd,
her male offspring is driven off by the stag, and is thus weaned, although
a female calf is allowed to remain.

In short, there is opposition between the maternal and the sexual
instinct. The tendency of the female is to segregate herself with her
offspring, and the more prolonged the maturity of the offspring the
more complete will that segregation be. Since the herbivorous mother
neither feeds nor trains her young, maternal instincts must be regarded
as more highly developed in the carnivores than in the herbivores. Thus
we have the paradox, as it seems to us, that those animals termed
gregarious are devoid of any binding social sentiment, and it is among
the supposedly non-gregarious creatures that the germs of the social
instinct have developed. It is in the maternal not the sexual association
that the growth of the so-called 'social instinct' takes place.

The mother is the centre and bond of the animal family. When the male attaches himself to it, his association with it is loose and precarious, and in no animal species does it appear to survive the exercise of the sexual function. Nor is any tendency towards a closer association of the male with the family discernible as we ascend the scale of evolution.

It is usual to apply the term 'family' to animal groups, but there is, in fact, no analogy between the animal family and the patriarchal human family. The former is entirely the product of the female's instincts, and she, not the male, is the head. The male may be more powerful, though this is not invariably so. But, in any case, this has nothing to do with his relation to the female. Nowhere do we know of the male using compulsion towards the female. Nor is the position of the male in the animal group affected by mental superiority, for in animals, whatever may be the case with humans, it is clear that the female is superior. Masculine intellectual superiority, if we assume it, is the product of advanced social evolution, and has no application in primitive conditions. The female animal is the more cautious, ingenious and sagacious, the male is reckless and often stupid. With most animals males are much more often caught or shot than females. It has been said that monkeys, however, are led by old males. If this is true, it may be due to the females being burdened with their young, which they carry in their arms. In a troop of chimpanzees observed in a reserve in Teneriffe the group was led by a male, but the rearguard was brought up by an old female, to whom the group ran in time of danger, and who seemed to carry the group with her when she changed her place.

The female, not the male, determines the condition of the animal family, and when she can derive no benefit from association with the male, no association takes place. It is the female which does the house-hunting; which, in the case of beavers, builds the dams or makes the burrows. It is the female bird which builds the nest.

While the female instinct produces the family, the masculine instinct produces the herd, for the masculine instinct compels the male to impregnate as many females as possible. The stability of the herd is, therefore, limited by the operation of the sexual instinct. It is not an assemblage differing merely in size from the family, but is opposite in kind, and, when true herd association takes place, means the dissolution of the maternal group or family. Thus the herd results from atrophy of the maternal instinct. As Mr Pycraft observes of animals, this 'polygamy' arises not because the males capture the females but because the females seek the males in their desire to satisfy their natural craving. This extinguishes any feelings of jealousy.

From these facts, it can be understood that the masculine herd is patrilocal; that is, the female follows the male's place of residence, whereas the animal family is matrilocal; that is, the males goes to the female's lair. Wherever circumstances bring together a large number of animals, there is a tendency for the family to lapse into the herd. Rodents, such as rats or rabbits, which gather in large numbers, become promiscuous. It is, on the other hand, well-nigh impossible for the herd to become transformed into a group of families except by breaking up completely.

CHAPTER 5

The Primitive Human Group

WHAT was the form of the most primitive human groups? This is a question of the first importance, for upon the answer all subsequent human development, social and mental, has depended. Presumably the earliest human societies developed out of some form of animal assemblage. They were, therefore, like all animal groups, primarily reproductive in function, and not, like existing human societies, co-operative organisations.

Certainly the human group did not develop out of the animal *herd* for, as we have seen, the herd is incompatible with prolonged maternal function. It must therefore have been derived from the animal *family* based on the maternal instincts of the female.

At the same time it is impossible to suppose that nascent human society consisted of small isolated groups corresponding in size to what we understand by families. Such limited groups could offer no scope for the development of those distinctively human social relations and feelings which are essential for the mental evolution which took place.

Some races on the lowest level of culture are, it is true, found in small scattered groups which include sexual societies and may be called families—for instance, the savages of Tierra del Fuego, the Eskimo and some of the most wretched tribes in the forests of the upper Amazon and Parana. The forest Veddahs of Ceylon are also found in small groups, consisting for the most part of sexual partners, or single families.

Such populations are not simply 'primitive' in the sense of having remained wretchedly backward; they are also unsuccessful races which have been driven towards the least habitable parts of the earth. The Fuegians, who belong to the same stock as the other races of South America, have been 'pushed off the edge of the world', and 'forced to break up into small clan or family groups'. The forest tribes of Brazil have been driven to their present habitat by Caribbean invaders. In these unfavourable conditions 'it is safe to assume that they never could have emerged from their savage state'. Likewise there are clear traces among the Eskimo of a former organization into clans, now fallen, owing to physical circumstances, into almost complete decay.

The Veddahs of Ceylon are the descendants of the aboriginal royal race who were driven into the jungle by invaders.

In short, such societies represent, not the primitive condition of human society, but the effects of its dissolution under the pressure of unfavourable conditions; we cannot infer from them the condition of incipient humanity. They are defeated unsuccessful races; the animal race which developed into humanity must have been a favoured race living in exceptionally propitious conditions.

All that is involved in human evolution postulates a much larger group than the family—and, in fact, we find all human communities above the most miserable and degenerate in much larger groups; and the larger those groups, the greater, as a rule, is their cultural and social development.

How came those larger groups to be formed? The question may surprise the reader. The formation of a larger group from the original family group appears to be a quite obvious process. It might take place in two ways: either a number of neighbouring families might come together; or the mature offspring of the original family, instead of separating from their parents, might remain with them and found secondary families.

Such a simple view of the origin of human society has been taken for granted from ancient times until the present.[1] However, it begs the question, for it assumes that such family groups will continue distinct within the larger group, and will retain their character and constitution; that is to say, it is postulated that those characters are already consolidated in such a manner that they will be preserved unaltered, notwithstanding the conditions presented by a different type of association. There is nothing to justify such an assumption. On the contrary, it follows from all that we know of animal groupings that the association of a number of separate families must put an end to a form of organization which demands isolation as the first condition of its existence.

Whenever, among animals, such an assemblage of a large number of families takes place even temporarily, the family grouping tends to be broken up, and the constitution of this larger group lapses into that of the promiscuous herd. This takes place even among the most typically pairing and family-forming animals, viz. among birds; it does so in the short period in which they gather in large numbers during the breeding season. The larger grouping no longer depends on the manifestation of maternal instincts, but on the male instincts. From a maternal group it is changed into a masculine group, from a family into a herd.

Among the apes we find large assemblages, it is true, and the maternal instincts are more highly developed than among other animals. But

[1] Cf. Westermarck, E.: *The History of Human Marriage* (1901), p. 49.

these assemblages are not under the dominance of the males. In human groups the conditions are quite different. There is no division of labour amongst the apes; in the human group, the male is differentiated as a hunter and a warrior. In a promiscuous human herd a struggle would inevitably take place for the possession of the females, and would at once result in the dominance of the most powerful males. The group would, in fact, be a patriarchal herd, in which a few of the stronger males would hold the weaker males and all the females in subjection.

In short, unless some principle can be shown to operate which will maintain the arrangement—unprecedented in biological history—of an associated group of separate families, the result of simple aggregation will not be a group of families but a promiscuous herd. We explain nothing by supposing that a number of families are brought together.

If, on the other hand, the compound group is supposed to be formed by the offspring of a single family continuing with their parents and giving rise to new families, the difficulties are even more marked. If the sons, after they grow up, continue with their parents, they must either marry their sisters or else import women from another group. The effect on an incipient human society would be equivalent to the haphazard fusion of family groups into a herd family. The capture of females from another group and their introduction into the parental group would result in a complete transformation of the group's constitution. If the compound family grouping is to grow out of the original animal family and to retain its distinctive advantages, the feminine constitution of the family must be maintained; it cannot be maintained if the sons remain and import their wives, while the daughters are taken away by strangers. The structure of the group would then be transformed. The female line of influence would be destroyed, and a grouping, based on male initiative, would be formed. Such a transformation has occurred in later stages of social evolution; and, where racial development is already fairly advanced, it is not attended with untoward effects; but in the initial stages of that development, it would abolish those conditions upon which the emergence of the social group has depended. The group would cease to be a maternal animal family; it would become a masculine herd.

There is, in fact, one way, and one only, whereby the feminine constitution of the family could have been maintained while it expanded at the same time into a larger assemblage—namely, by the sons leaving the group, and the daughters remaining and pairing with the males from some other group.

This peculiar arrangement is, in point of fact, the one which was adopted by nascent humanity. Everyone who has even a passing acquaintance with anthropology knows that the most general rule governing the organization of primitive social groups is that of 'exogamy'—the rule that marriages shall not take place within the group but always with members of another group. The manner in which that rule is carried out in a large number of primitive societies is by the males either leaving the parental group and being adopted into the group to which their wives belong and living with them, or simply visiting them while they continue to live in their own group. In either case, the daughters do not leave the family group in which they were born.

The great majority of primitive societies regard the exogamic system as the most inviolable principle of their social organization. In many communities it has assumed complicated forms.

The group is subdivided into two, four or even eight sub-groups, and frequently the members of one group may intermarry with members of only one other group. With those complexities we need not concern ourselves here. They are necessary effects of the development of the exogamic group which in time must needs subdivide. Fundamentally this principle is identical with the prohibition of incest, for in the primitive family group there is no alternative to the marrying out of the males except union with their own sisters; thus our own horror of incest represents the very principle which appears to us so strange in the exogamic regulations of primitive man.

It is significant that nothing approaching to a satisfying explanation has been offered of this principle. That failure seems to point to some radical fault in our method or in our assumptions.

J. F. McLennan, the first expounder of the principle of exogamy, had no better hypothesis to offer than that exogamy arose from the scarcity of women resulting from the prevalence of female infanticide among savages. Both his arguments and his facts have been fully refuted. Lord Avebury ascribed the law to the practice of capturing wives, but this would produce results exactly opposite to those that are known to accompany exogamic organization, and there are, as we shall see, definite grounds for regarding wife-capture as a much later development than exogamy. To appeal to the 'natural horror of incest' is to beg the question at issue.

Alleged Injurious Effects of Inbreeding among Animals

It has been thought that the rule of exogamy is connected with the supposed injurious effects of inbreeding. Though belief in such ill-effects has been practically universal from time immemorial, attempts to substantiate it scientifically have failed completely.

Since some writers continue to assume it as a basis for explaining the constitution of human society, the following points may briefly be made:

(i) All animal species propagate without regard to inbreeding, and some propagate exclusively by what we should term incest. Thus the African reed-buck usually brings forth two young at a birth, a male and a female; these, when mature, pair with one another. The same appears to be true of most of the smaller species of antelopes and all red-deer, tigers, buffaloes, etc.

(ii) Whole countries have been rapidly overrun by the offspring of single pairs or of a very small number of individuals. Rabbits have become a plague in Australia; they are the progeny of a few individuals brought there in 1863. In New Zealand a hardy race of wild pigs, much sturdier than any of our domesticated breeds, is the offspring of a couples of sows and a boar left there by Captain Cook on his second voyage, and of a few animals similarly turned loose in subsequent years.

(iii) Numerous experiments have been carried out on rats, mice, guinea-pigs and rabbits, by causing them to inbreed closely for many generations. They have in most instances shown no perceptible evil effects as regards the quality and size of the animals, but a diminution in fertility has been observed. It is, however, well known that all animals, especially rodents, suffer a diminution of fertility when kept in close confinement. In recent large-scale experiments by Dr H. D. King on white rats, it was found that: 'These laboratory rats, which have been inbred as closely as possible for twenty-two generations, are in every respect superior to the stock rats from which they took their start six years ago, and which have since been bred in the usual indiscriminate manner.' The largest albino rat ever recorded was produced. The inbred rats 'live fully as long as do the stock rats, and they appear equally resistant to disease'. The fertility of the inbred rats was nearly 8 per cent greater than that of the stock rats.

(iv) The experience of breeders of domesticated animals has been supposed to afford evidence that inbreeding results in degenerative changes and impaired vitality and fertility. The English racehorse is one of the most closely inbred of existing animals. Several elaborate investigations have been made of the stud records of famous English racehorses, and it has invariably been found that noted winners excelled in almost exact proportion to the close inbreeding shown by their pedigrees. The Percheron horses are also a closely inbred race, most of the individuals being traceable to two original sires. Numerous similar illustrations of exceptionally fine breeds of domestic animals, the products of prolonged inbreeding, are mentioned by Darwin in his book on *The Variation of Animals and plants under Domestication*—a work in which he seeks to uphold the evils of inbreeding while showing the benefits sometimes observed in domesticated animals from occasionally crossing them with another breed.

Inbreeding may indeed, produce injurious results where the animals are bred for the improvement of a *single characteristic:* thus pigs bred for fat sometimes become less fertile and the sows are unable to nourish their young. The surprising circumstance is that such evil effects are not more common and more conspicuous. It is only where the stock has been thus inbred that the 'occasional cross' is beneficial. In Central Europe and the Baltic countries the art of stock-breeding was for long a complete failure; until recently nobody ever heard of a reputable breed of German or Scandinavian horses or cattle, and breeds of domesticated animals had constantly to be improved by importations from England, France and Spain. The chief reason for this was the great authority attached in those countries to the works of Professor Settegast, who fiercely denounced inbreeding in any form, until Count Lehndorff and de Chapeaurouge exposed the baselessness of his dogmas.

If the results of the breeding of domesticated animals prove anything, it is the absolute innocuousness, if not the actually beneficial effects, of inbreeding. Thus in many British parks, such as Cadzow Castle, Chartley, Lyme Park, Somerford, herds of cattle have been left to inbreed from time immemorial. The Arabs inbreed their famous horses as closely as possible without any scientific refinements. In the records of breeding from domesticated animals there is not a single fact, alleged or verified, which indicates, much less evidences, that inbreeding, even the closest, is in itself productive of evil effects.

Results of Inbreeding in Human Communities

In the human race the evidence is, if anything, even more definite. Close inbreeding takes place habitually among many peoples; for, even where the principle of exogamy is strictly observed, if marriage outside the group takes place for generation after generation in one particular other group, the intermarrying members stand to one another in the relation of cousins. It is a very widespread custom for a man to marry his first cousin; such marriages are regarded in many parts of the world as obligatory. Yet nowhere have any evil effects been observed, and the races which practise those marriages include some of the finest physical types of mankind. Thus the Bataks of Sumatra are described as being physically the best-developed race in the Indian Archipelago; the men, Junghuhn remarks, might have stood as models for the sculptors of Greece. An elaborate census of the population of Fiji, among whom marriage between first cousins was regarded as a sacred duty, showed that such marriages were associated with a higher birth-rate and a markedly greater vitality in the offspring than unions between non-relatives. So much so that the former are maintaining their numbers while the latter are rapidly dying out.

From the large number of peoples who favour cousin-marriages no instance has been brought forward which might be set against the testimony of such instances.[1] In almost every part of the world small, isolated communities exist where, for centuries, marriages have of necessity taken place between closely related individuals. They are almost invariably distinguished by conspicuously fine bodily development and robust health. For example, in the Tengger Hills of Java the Surabaya community, numbering some 1,200 people, has intermarried for ages. 'They differ from the people of the plain, being taller and more robust'. The same is true of a small segregated community, the Baduwis, in West Java, who number no more than about forty familes all told. In Europe such intermarrying communities are common enough in hill districts and among fisherfolk. That of Batz, near Croisic, which numbers about 3,300 people, was made the subject of a very thorough investigation by Dr Voisin. He did not find an instance of malformation, mental disease or any of the evils ascribed to inbreeding; marriages between first cousins in that community were found to produce an average of 4·6 offspring, whereas the general average for France at that time was only 3·3. The island of St Kilda contains [I.e. in 1927] twenty seven families, and supplies, as Dr Kerr Love remarks, the proper conditions for the production of all the evils ascribed to intermarriage. The inhabitants are poor and badly housed. Dr C. R. Macdonald, the Chief Medical Officer of Health for Ayrshire, has assured the writer 'that there is no history of any case of deaf-mutism in this remote islet, nor, moreover, of other signs usually attributed to the results of intermarrying.' In an article (1888) he says: 'There are no cases of deaf-mutism; insanity and idiocy are unknown, and cases of imbecility are extremely rare.' This is after centuries of intermarrying.

Many similar examples are forthcoming. The Pitcairn islanders are descended from nine of the mutineers of the *Bounty* who in 1790 were deposited on the island, together with six men and twelve women from Tahiti, and in 1800 consisted of twenty-five people. They are described by all observers as remarkably strong, healthy and well-built; the men averaging six feet in height, both sexes being well formed and handsome; the women being as muscular as the men, and taller than the generality of women, and the children uniformly healthy.

While the manifestations of racial degeneration in royal families, such as the Hapsburgs and the Spanish Bourbons, are often popularly referred to—it is hard to see on what grounds—as illustrating the evils of inbreeding, those royal families which have systematically practised

[1] Dr Westermarck has ransacked ethnological literature for examples, yet he feels compelled to apologize for the results and for 'their vagueness and more or less hypothetical character'.

dynastic incest furnish no evidence of those supposed evils. None is afforded by the Ptolemies; the practice which they adopted when they took over the throne of Egypt had been regularly observed in that country for at least 3,000 years. In the golden age of the Egyptian monarchy, during the XIXth and XXth Dynasties, every king of the former married his sister as the lawful mother of the heir to the throne. Yet the race that produced Seti and Rameses affords no evidence of degeneration, nor does there exist in the age-long records of by far the longest line of kings in the world's history, among whom, not mere inbreeding but actual incest was a fundamental principle, any fact lending support to the doctrine of the evil results of inbreeding.

No attempt to demonstrate this theory by statistical investigation has met with any success. The most thorough general investigation of the kind is still that undertaken by Sir George H. Darwin, who was, like his father, strongly disposed to believe that inbreeding is attended with injurious effects. As regards fertility, he found that balance was slightly in favour of cousin-marriages. He found no differences as regards insanity or deaf-mutism.

When the belief that consanguineous marriages produce deaf-mutism and other physical conditions, such as mental deficiency and sterility, are scientifically examined, they turn out to be equally unjustifiable. Thus a Mr Huth, at the end of an exhaustive discussion, declares that 'statistics on which so much reliance has been placed as a proof of the harmfulness of consanguineous marriages are, when not absolutely false, miserably misleading and defective'.

The belief that the offspring of parents consanguineously related will be stricken with deformities or diseases is much older than any attempt at scientific inquiry, and in more recent times is often derived from the fact that such marriages are condemned by the Roman Catholic Church. But this belief is firmly held not only in Europe but among almost all savages. The mountaineers of Albania believe that incest results in deaf-mutism; the Aleuts that it produces malformations and that the offspring of such unions will have tusks like a walrus. The Kaffirs believe that it causes idiocy, and the Basoga of Uganda are even scandalized at the thought of incest being committed by their cattle and punish the criminals. The consequences are not limited to the children, but may extend to the parents and even to the more distant relatives or sometimes to the whole tribe. In the Celebes such unions are regarded as causing earthquakes and floods and volcanic eruptions. (These are, of course, the usual effects of infringing a tabu.)

But the definition of what constitutes a consanguineous marriage varies widely. Thus the Murung of Borneo permit marriage between brothers and sisters, and believe that their offspring will be remarkably healthy, yet regard with horror marriages between cousins and certain other relationships. The Bhotias prohibit cousin-marriages on the father's side only; while the Herero consider that, while the children of a brother and a sister may marry, the children of two brothers or two sisters may not. Some people regard all marriages between close relatives as particularly lucky. The Kalangs of Java believe that incestuous unions between mother and son are blessed with prosperity, while the tribes of British Central Africa believe that incest makes one bulletproof. Current ideas of the evils of inbreeding are, in fact, a survival of an ancient superstition.

Theories of the Origin of Exogamy

Sir Henry Maine and Lewis Morgan accounted for incest prohibitions and exogamous practices by supposing that men noticed the evil results of inbreeding and forbade it. Many savages give a similar account. Yet it may be noted that they give no similar account of marriage between extremely young persons which invariably produces undersized offspring of poor vitality. The physical decay of many primitive peoples is due to this practice, but it has scarcely anywhere led to a prejudice, still less a rule against it. Although the belief that inbreeding is damaging has now been generally abandoned, Dr Westermarck, while professing his inability to find conclusive proof, nevertheless decides that 'inbreeding generally is in some way or other more or less detrimental', and suggests that the peoples who failed to preserve such principles were exterminated by these injurious effects. The practice of exogamy itself he ascribes to the lesser sexual attraction of habitual companions.

M. Durkheim starts from the proposition that defloration of a female of one's own group must be regarded with horror. Unfortunately defloration in primitive society does not happen in marriage, but is usually performed by the very members of the group whose relations with the females would normally be considered incestuous.[1]

Darwin believed that the emigration of young males was due to the jealousy of the old males, but such a procedure—even if it exists—could not account for the abhorrence of incest; and the tyranny of the older males would surely operate as strongly against strange males as against their own male offspring, so that young males would thus never obtain wives in a strange group, except by fighting old males.

Havelock Ellis is one of those who feel that the explanation is 'really exceedingly simple'—boys and girls brought up together from infancy fail to evoke the pairing impulse because familiarity has dulled the sexual stimulus. But, as is widely known, men frequently marry the companions of their childhood, and relationships which have for a long

[1] See p. 397.

time been platonic end in marriage. Dr Ellis confounds the sexual impulse with the mating impulse. The latter is based on companionship and affection and not on sexual desire; indeed, it involves subordination of the male sexual impulse.

In primitive societies in every part of the world children are commonly betrothed to one another and grow up like brothers and sisters. Such marriages are attended with the greatest success. Thus we are told of the tribes of the Upper Congo that it is rare for children brought up together to fail to marry and to dislike one another. Drs Hose and McDougall, speaking of the intercourse of a youth and his sister by adoption in Borneo, point out the difficulty of reconciling these facts with Westermarck's theory. The occurrence of brother-sister incest and the strong objection of the Sea Dayaks to newphew-aunt incest—these often being members of distant communities—seem fatal, they add, to Westermarck's theory.

The fact, adduced by Mr Walter Heape, that animals will neglect their accustomed harem to attend a newcomer does not illustrate the greater attraction of the stranger but the male's instinct to impregnate as many females as possible. And he does not explain why the buck rabbit, which is so susceptible to the fascination of the strange female, is yet incorrigibly endogamous.

Derivation of the Rule of Exogamy from the Constitution of the Maternal Group

All these theories have one feature in common—they refer exclusively to the operation of the male sexual instincts and assume a patriarchal social state in which those instincts are dominant. As soon as we postulate that primitive human groups were not patriarchal but matriarchal, we see that observance of the rule of exogamy is essential to the preservation of the maternal character of the group. If the women left their family to join their husbands, that family would cease to be a maternal group. If the men were the sexual mates as well as the brothers of the women, patriarchal succession would be established, and their authority and rivalry would bring about patriarchal dominance. The mothers are the basis and bond of the primitive group, and the only relation originally taken into account is the maternal relation. Kinship and descent are reckoned exclusively through the women; the relationship through the father is ignored. To permit women to follow strange men, to sever their connection with the group, would be to break up the social unit, and would be opposed to its most basic sentiments.

Such principles do not, of themselves, impose upon the men the need to mate outside the group, but the distinction between the permanence of the women and the freedom of the men being established, there are many factors to lead men to make use of their freedom. Thus while men are naturally of a roving disposition, the women are home-loving. The man instinctively seeks for food, the woman to settle down. But while such facts make for the association of males with females from another group, they do not imply an actual prohibition of sexual intercourse between members of the same group. However, a habit which has hardened into an established rule that one should seek one's partner elsewhere inevitably gives rise to a corresponding prohibition, not to seek them in one's own group. This prohibition is reinforced by the sense of ownership implicit in maternal instinct. In the human family the maternal instinct does not, as in animals, cease to operate when the males reach sexual maturity. It is not the mother, therefore, who drives off her male offspring, but the son who at sexual maturity tends to transfer his allegiance to another female. The animal is wholly unreasonable and responds at once to impulse; the semi-human mother was not the gentle creature of our conceptions, but a wild animal to whom the idea that one of her sons should transfer his allegiance from herself to one of his sisters was a horrible thought, because a blow to her jealous love. Darwin describes how female baboons protect their young from being teased by one another; since any attempt by a male to perform intercourse with another member of the brood would be regarded by the female as violence, this would infallibly bring the mother to her assistance.

Though it is not a trait likely to be noticed much by observers, there are several references to the jealousy of primitive mothers. In New Britain 'sometimes fond old mothers are desirous of keeping their sons with them as long as possible'. One very intelligent Dutch peasant said that mothers are more jealous with regard to their favourite son than wives as regards their husbands . . . 'if mothers had their own way their sons would never marry—at least not for a long time'.

The incest prohibition applies primarily to relations between brothers and sisters. In the simplest forms of exogamy, as found in South-eastern Australia, where there are two intermarrying classes, the system prevents marriage between brothers and sisters but not between parents and children. In the Island of Kiwai, a father may take his daughter to wife, although brother-and-sister unions are regarded with abhorrence. Similarly in some of the Solomon Islands. It is easy to see why this should be extended from the sister to the mother, for the awe and dread attaching to the head of the family would make it even less likely that she would be the object of incestuous advances.

These rules are, of course, generalizations. It is most unlikely that in every primitive human group the males sought their partners elsewhere, and instances in which incestuous relations habitually take place have already been noted. And if this prohibition is the most primitive of all the regulations imposed upon sexual relations, every subsequent regulation must have tended to consolidate it.

The Mother-in-law

Connected with the rule of exogamy is the fact that in savage society it is a constant rule that a man may not speak to his mother-in-law and generally may not even look at her; the breach of this rule is regarded with as much horror as incest. In Australia a man is warned of the approach of his mother-in-law by the sound of a bull-roarer; it was formerly death for a man to speak to her—later banishment. In Tasmania a native, concerned about the attentions a younger man was paying to his wife, betrothed his new-born daughter to the suspected rival—thus making it quite impossible for the latter even to look at his future mother-in-law. In New Britain a man must not only not look at his mother-in-law, but must avoid meeting her and must hide if he sees her coming. Suicide of one or both would be the only course if he inadvertently spoke to her. In the Banks Islands a man would not follow his mother-in-law along the beach until the tide had washed out her footsteps. The rule is as rigorous in Africa as in Australia and Melanesia. Among the Baholoholo the ceremonial avoidance is observed even after the death of the wife. The Yukatans believed that if a man even met his mother-in-law he could never beget children. The Baganda regard the prohibition of meeting the mother-in-law as more sacred than the prohibition against incest, and the remark would appear to be generally applicable. The well-worn jokes of the British music-hall are probably therefore an echo of a very primitive sentiment for which no satisfactory interpretation has ever been offered.

Lord Avebury's hypothesis that the rules of mother-in-law avoidance are connected with wife-capture is ruled out by the fact that those usages are commonest where wife-capture does not obtain, and are rare where it does. Moreover, they would not account for singling out the wife's mother for avoidance, but would require rather avoiding the menfolk of the wife's tribe, and especially brothers and uncles on whom the duties of revenge would fall. The rule of avoidance does in several instances extend to other relatives, and even in Australia to the whole clan, but in most cases it applies to the mother-in-law alone and where others are included to her chiefly. Father-in-law avoidance by women is found for the most part in advanced Oriental nations, such as the Hindus and Chinese, where patriarchal domination is established. Significantly, avoidance rules also sometimes apply to the grandmother. The suggestion frequently made that these rules are intended to prevent improper intercourse between the mother-in-law and the sons seems to be excluded by certain curious derivative practices found in several tribes. Thus among the Navaho, although mother-in-law taboos are exceptionally strict and extensive, yet a Navaho can sometimes avoid them by the simple expedient of marrying his mother-in-law *pro forma* before he marries the daughter. The Cherokees and the Caribs have hit on the same plan, while with the Wagogo and the Wahele of East Africa a man must cohabit with his future mother-in-law before he is allowed to marry the daughter. It seems clear that tabus which can be evaded by marrying one's mother-in-law are not intended to guard against incestuous relations with her.

On the view that the feeling against incest and the rule of exogamy are consequences of the matriarchal character of primitive groups, these avoidance customs present no problem. It is because he *fears* the mother-in-law that primitive man originally avoided her so sedulously. It is a memory of the awe which was originally inspired by the mother that, even where the supremacy of the mother has passed away, it still survives in these rules whose widespread distribution betrays their original importance.

Moreover, mother-in-law restrictions can be commuted by presents. Among the Arapahos, all restrictions are removed if a man presents his mother-in-law with a horse. That the supposed danger which these rules were designed to obviate comes from the mother-in-law and not from the son is further shown by the fact that among some peoples (e.g. the Warramunga of Central Australia), though a man may not go to a camp where his mother-in-law resides, *she* is quite free to visit him in his own camp. The idea underlying these observances is also betrayed in other instances. Among the Banyoro of East Africa, for example, a man is not obliged to avoid meeting his mother-in-law, but it is absolutely essential that he kneel down and remain in a reverential position whenever he meets her. In these and other customs the mother-in-law does not appear as a possible object of unlawful desire, but as an offended personage who it is needful to conciliate.

If my conclusions concerning the origin of the rule of exogamy are correct, such customs present no real enigma, but confirm these conclusions and serve to exhibit the natural authority of which the primitive group was the expression.

CHAPTER 6

The Motherhood

MONTESQUIEU was considerably amused when he read in a missionary's account that in Formosa the groom remains in the house of the bride's parents, but in fact this custom, which is known as matrilocal marriage, is widespread, and is of especial interest since it suggests the existence of former female supremacy.

It is found among many varieties of Eskimo; it was formerly the general rule among all North American Indians. The Senecas, the most important of the members of the Iroquois confederation, formerly dwelt in 'long houses' under the authority of a matron. The female portion ruled the house, and any man who disobeyed orders might be forced to retreat to his own clan or to leave and start a new matrimonial alliance elsewhere. Among the Crees, when a man marries he resides with his wife's parents, who treat him as a stranger till the birth of his first child.

Matrilocy is also a feature of the Pueblo Indians of New Mexico. It has been suggested that, as these are the most advanced in culture of North American Indians, matriarchal society is not primitive but a product of advanced development. However, the matriarchal organization is also found in an even more absolute form in the rudest and most uncultured tribe in the whole North American race, namely the Seri of the Californian gulf. To say that they are in the Stone Age is scarcely accurate, for they do not even fashion stones but merely pick up a cobble for crushing bones or severing sinews. When provided with knives, they do not know how to use them. No other human tribe is so devoid of material devices. They have no form of agriculture, they do not cook their food, and, in eating a heavy joint, so rotten that the flesh could easily be scraped off with a knife, they lift the whole thing to the mouth and gnaw it. So fierce is their hostility that it has not been possible to observe them as fully as is desirable; they have murdered many would-be observers.

The most noticeable feature of their organization is the prominence of the females. The social unit is the maternal clan, determined by descent from a common line of mothers. The clan is headed by a clan-mother and comprises a hierarchy of daughters and granddaughters.

The indigenous name of the tribe is 'kunkak', which means Womanhood or Motherhood. Their rude dwellings are erected by the women without help from the men, and belong exclusively to the matrons. It was often difficult to identify the husband, partly because he was often incongruously younger than the mistress, and partly because of his lack of authority. The females have no term for father, and there is some question as to whether the Seri recognize paternity. The women are the only real workers; the men tacitly accept the decisions of the mother. Though male chiefs are elected, mainly for leadership in war, all magical powers are considered to reside in the women, and the election of a chief depends largely on the magical powers of his wife. A man generally marries all the sisters of one family and there are indications that formerly, when the men were numerous, all the brothers of a family were conjugally bound to all the sisters of another. The prospective bridegroom is subjected to a series of elaborate tests before acceptance by the mothers.

Matrilocal marriage is also widespread among the Caribbean races, and was practised in Mexico by the tribes of Yucatan, as also in Peru under the Inca monarchy. Old missionaries noted it with astonishment among the Mozcos of New Granada and among various tribes of the Orinoco. It is reported of the Gran Chaco tribes, of several tribes of Southern Argentina and those of Tierra del Fuego.

In Africa, the matrilocal rule is strictly observed both among such primitive tribes as the now almost extinct Bushmen, the Basuto, the Barolong and all other Bechuana tribes. The practice is very general in East Africa, chiefly among the Marotse, the Yahos, the Anyanga, the Tumbuka, the Wakamba, the Mosuto, as well as among the primitive pygmies of the Congo forest.

The social constitution appears to have been characteristically matriarchal throughout the vast region which extends south of the Sahara, from the Atlantic to the Nile, property being transmitted by a man to the children of his sister, and matrilocal marriage being general; thus among the Kona, the Fulani, the Kilba, the Kulangas, the Madi, the Buduma and Baele of Lake Chad, the Nuer of the Upper Nile, the Barabra of Nubia and many others. Special interest attaches to the white races of Northern Africa who now inhabit the Sahara region, for, according to a common view, these populations are direct representatives of the race which laid the foundations of Western civilisation on the islands and shores of the Mediterranean. These people are now matriarchal and there are strong grounds for thinking that these early invaders were also pronouncedly matriarchal in character. All the peoples of Northern Africa west of Egypt belong to the Berber race (which the Greeks called Libyans), a white race scarcely different from the inhabitants of

Southern Europe, some being so fair they might pass for Irishmen or Scotsmen. The Berbers of Algeria and Tunisia are now largely Muslim and thoroughly patriarchal, but those which withdrew to the interior rather than yield to a foreign invasion—the Tuareg—have preserved both their ancient language and their matriarchal constitution. Descent among them is reckoned in the female line, and property descends from a man to his sister's children. Though there is an Eve in their myth there is no Adam. Their ancestors in Roman times, the Numidians, had the same customs, and were named after their mothers. Ibn Batuta was the first modern traveller to describe them. He says: 'The women . . . are not timid in the presence of men, nor do they cover their faces with the veil. . . . The women do not follow their husbands, and should any of them wish to do so, her relatives would prevent it.'

Every traveller has commented on the independence of the women among the Berber races of the Sahara, such as the Tibbu. 'In all matters their word is law.' The culture of the Tuareg is almost exclusively confined to the women (the men are entirely illiterate); and it is they alone who preserved knowledge of the ancient Libyan tongue and script, which appears to resemble that of Minoan Crete.

The Malay race which has spread over the whole Indonesian region, sending off-shoots as far as Madagascar and China, has for centuries been under the influence of Hindu and Islamic religions, but they always distinguish between the customs of their adopted religion and their traditional law known as *adat*, and cling persistently to the latter. Many Malays prefer the older form of matrilocal marriage to the new patrilocal form introduced by Islam. Chinese travellers of the time of the Ming Dynasty (1368–1643) noted the Malays of Sumatra were matrilocal. Pistorius describes how the Malays of Negri Sembilan live in barrack-like rows of dwellings, forming a Sa-mandei or Motherhood, consisting of a house-mother and her descendants in the female line. He was much amused to see the husbands walking across at dusk from their own homes to join the wives; if a man has several wives, he visits each in turn. (This practice is also true of many other matrilocal tribes where polygamy is practised.) The husband has no obligation to maintain his wife; this falls on the maternal family, and the head of the family is usually the brother of the mother. The property of a Malay passes on his death, not to his wife and her children, but to his brothers and sisters and to his sisters' children; that is, to his maternal family.

An unmodified matriarchal organization is found in Northern Sumatra, among the Orang Mamaq, who are divided into strictly exogamous clans: husband and wife seldom live together, but if they do the husband comes to his wife's clan. The Sakai tribal organization is strictly matriarchal, and it is the rule among the primitive races of Timor, of the neighbouring islands of the Southern Malaccas and in the Celebes. In the Northern Malaccas, as in Java, Islamic marriage customs have now become universal, but in many of the islands between the Celebes and the Philippines matrilocy remains the practice. It is also the rule in Borneo among both land and sea Dayaks, and was formerly the general native custom in the Philippines. The Spanish conquerors noted that the Pintados took sides with their wives' relations, even against their own fathers and mothers, and thought that this indicated that they loved their wives very dearly.

The natives of the Micronesian region—the Carolines (with the exception of Yap), the Marshall, Mortlock, Pelew and Gilbert Islands— are matriarchal in their social organization. Similarly in the western islands of the Torres Straits, where matrilocal marriage is the rule. It also appears to be the typical usage in most parts of New Guinea, though there are many gaps in our information about that vast island. Several regions appear to be in a state of transition from matrilocal to patrilocal usages. Thus in some parts of Dutch New Guinea, a man may take his wife to his home for a year, after which she returns to hers and he visits her. The fundamental matrilocal character of their customs is indicated by the fact that no boy can go through puberty ceremonies until he has resided for a while with his mother's family.

Evidence is also adduced from New Zealand, from the Marquesas, the Nicobar Islands, the Ainu of Japan, the Kurile Islands, etc. In Northern and Central Asia, the custom that the bridegroom resides for a more or less prolonged period with his wife's family or that the bride, after a short residence with her husband, returns home for a prolonged period, is widespread. These customs, so similar to the practices in New Guinea and Africa, where we know that the culture is in a state of transition from matrilocal to patrilocal usages, suggest that this is the case in Asia also; an inference which is confirmed when we find, in several cases, that this is indeed occurring. Thus among the Buryat, a Mongolic tribe of Southern Siberia, the bride returns home after marriage for six months or more, and this visit is several times repeated. Buryat tradition states definitely that it was formerly the usage for the husband to take up his abode permanently in the home of his wife.

Matriarchal societies are found in several parts of China, among aboriginal populations of non-Chinese race. Thus the Nue'kun is said to be permanently ruled by a woman, and the tribes in the mountains of Kwei-Chow are matrilocal. Matrilocal marriage is characteristic among the peoples of Siam, Burma, Indo-China and Tonkin.

In India, in the hills of Assam, there are various tribes so little disturbed by change that they still erect large standing stones like the

menhirs of Brittany over their dead. The social unit of the Khasi tribe
is called Mahari, that is 'Motherhood', and Sir Charles Lyall says it
'presents one of the most perfect examples still surviving of matriarchal
institutions, carried out in a logical and thorough manner which, to those
accustomed to regard the status and authority of the father as the foundation of society, are exceedingly remarkable'. The mother is the only
owner of real property. Among the Synteg, the husbands only visit
their wives at night and are known as 'the Begetters'. A similar organization is found among other tribes of the region, such as the Garos.

Among other of the aboriginal races of India, where Hindu customs
have not influenced the original institutions, matrilocal marriage is
found, as among the Kehal, a tribe of boatmen on the Indus, who are
now Mohammedans, among the Gonds, the Santals and the Mundas.

The term 'the Motherhood' is also applied to the family group
among the famous Nayars of Southern India, where the household is
constituted by the mother and her children, and a Nayar husband may
not even partake of food in his wife's home, but must visit after supper.
At the present day much of the social organization of these Motherhoods
has disintegrated, but the matrilocal element still remains strong.

In several of the above instances, marriage is not permanently
matrilocal, but the woman resides in her own home for a limited period
after marriage. Sometimes this becomes a mere ceremonial, a period
of a few days or even simply the wedding night. Perhaps the most
attentuated form is found among some tribes of Southern India, such
as the Mappellas, where the bride and bridegroom are locked up for a
few moments in a room in the bride's home after the wedding ceremony. The marriage is supposed to be consummated during these
moments, though, in fact, the custom is purely ritual. In our own society,
the practice survives in the practice of taking the wedding-lunch at the
bride's house.

In many parts of Africa and among uncultured societies elsewhere,
even where the wife is brought to her husband's home, connection with
her own family remains much closer than is the rule in advanced
patriarchal societies. Missionaries complain of the way the women tend
to go back to their mother on the least occasion.

Such limited matrilocy is sometimes difficult to distinguish from a
marriage by service in which the bridegroom gives his services for a
stipulated period, and it is sometimes thought that these practices
merely represent a commutation of a payment. We shall consider the
matter more fully later, and it will become clear that, on the contrary,
making a payment is a commutation of service rather than the reverse.
Marriage by service is found nowhere except where permanent matrilocal marriage is also customary or is known to have been formerly

general. Thus among the tribes of Assam, where complete matriarchal organization obtains, we are told that among the Bodo and Dhimal, who now pay a 'bride-price' on marriage, 'a youth who has no means of discharging this sum, must go to the home of his father-in-law-elect and literally earn his wife by the sweat of his brow, labouring "more judaico", for up to seven years.' Indeed, in some instances, instead of the service being regarded as a form of payment, the husband himself is paid by the wife's parents in order that he should forgo any claim to remove her and her children from their home.

Missionaries, with the Biblical precedent of Jacob's marriage in their mind, have frequently misreported matrilocal marriage as 'serving for a bride'. But in many of their accounts it is clear that this is a misunderstanding based on the fact that, after the end of the service period, frequently on the birth of a child, the relationship is terminated, not confirmed. In some cases, the fact that the husband erects his own wigwam, because of the limited accommodation in the wigwam of the wife's parents, has been taken to be the termination of his residence with the family, but it is clear that this is not a taking-back of the woman to the husband's clan. Indeed, the marriage of Jacob which causes this misunderstanding is itself not an example of the commutation of services by a payment, for the Bible expressly tells us that Jacob's father-in-law denied that he had any right to remove his wife even after twenty years (Genesis xxxi. 26, 43).

As we have seen, the fact that the female, not the male, determines the dwelling-place arises from the biological fact that it is the female of the species who chooses a suitable lair. (All animals may be said, in so far as they form sexual associations, to be matrilocal in habit, and it is natural to infer that habits of primitive humanity were similar.) The validity of this inference is proved by a social fact to which there are no exceptions. Whenever the man removes the wife from her home and brings her to his own, the procedure *invariably* involves a transaction whereby the woman's family sanctions this removal. In all but the highest cultures this sanction involves the payment of a compensation.[1] Among the Alfurs of Ceram, a man has the option of marrying his wife without payment and taking up residence in her village, or of paying a bride-price and removing her; but if he marries a woman of the same village, there is no question of payment. The same is true among the Alfurs of Buru and in the Kei Islands. Hence there is no alternative but to conclude that the practice of matrilocal marriage was the original form of marriage union and is coeval with the origin of humanity.

[1] A woman might, it is true, be removed from home by abduction, but, as we shall see, it is impossible that this was ever the usual and general mode of obtaining a wife.

This conclusion is confirmed by ethnological documents, for though there are numerous societies where matrilocy clearly prevailed at a former date, there is no single case where it appears that patrilocy preceded matrilocy.

The usage most frequently associated with matrilocy is matriliny, or the reckoning of descent from the mother and not from the father. When Herodotus noted it among the Lykians in Asia Minor, he thought it singular, but we now know it to be the rule with about half the people of the world below the most highly developed stages of culture. With most of those who reckon descent in the paternal line, clear evidence exists that the opposite was formerly the case.

It is sometimes thought that matriliny is the most distinctive feature of matriarchal society, but, in point of fact, matriliny is compatible with a very depressed status for women, as for example, among the majority of Australian tribes. On the other hand, matrilocy inevitably gives a woman a high status, for she remains among her blood relations while the husband is more or less a stranger. As Dr Kroeber says of the Zuñi: 'Upon her permanent occupancy of her house rests the matrilinear custom of the tribe.' The husband is economically destitute, for all the property is owned by the wife. Matrilocy necessarily implies a matriarchal form of society.

The Status of Women in Uncultured Societies

It used to be asserted that the more civilized a society the higher the status of the women in it. It was held that in uncivilized societies their position was one of outrageous oppression. If this were true, the Redskins and the Papuan cannibals would have to be accounted more civilized than the Chinese and the ancient Greeks. In point of fact, the exact reverse is the case. In the great majority of uncultured societies, women enjoy a position of independence and of equality with the men, and exercise an influence which would appear startling even in the most feministic of modern societies.

It is true that there are a few primitive societies where women are subjected to the despotism of brute force. Thus among the Australian aborigines the condition of the women is utterly degraded, and they are treated with 'about the same consideration as the dogs'. A girl of seven to ten is handed over to a man old enough to be her grandfather. For the slightest offence she is beaten with a yam-stick and not infrequently speared. Government records in Adelaide furnish numerous cases of Blacks murdering their Lubras. In times of scarcity, she is the last to be fed. 'Few women', says Eyre, 'will be found upon examination to be free from frightful scars upon the head or the marks of spear wounds about the body.' 'It is not uncommon', says Mr Hodgson, 'to meet a woman with scarcely a single hair to be seen, from the frequent strokes which have descended upon her unfortunate pericranium.' Any female, whether old or young, if found unprotected, is invariably ravished and, in most instances, killed afterwards. Queensland natives chastise their wives by rubbing hot coals over their stomach.

A similar state of things is found in most Melanesian islands. 'The New Caledonians take no more account of a woman than of a pig.' A New Caledonian chief, having acquired an old flintlock, practised shooting, using women set up in rows as targets. Another native, who was converted by a missionary, asked to be received into the Church, but was told that he could not be admitted as he had two wives. He returned next morning saying that all was in order, as he had now eaten the superfluous wife.

In some parts of Africa things are as bad. The Bangala of the Congo quite commonly eat their wives. In 1887, a Bangala chief informed a missionary that he had eaten seven of his wives, and had invited their relatives to the feast, in order that there should be no family unpleasantness. Among the Somalis, as among the Sifan of Tibet, the bride begins married life by receiving a sound flogging from her husband.

In low phases of culture where man is dominant such a state of affairs tends to come about. No innate scruples and no external compelling force restrain primitive man from using his power ruthlessly towards the women whom he regards as his property.

Yet there are numerous exceptions universally distributed; a few have already been noted. Among the Eskimo, 'the women appear to stand upon a footing of perfect equality with the men'. Among the North American tribes, the position of the women is one of complete independence. As the missionary Lafitau said: 'Nothing is more real than the superiority of the women.' The importance of the counsels of the women among the Iroquois confederation is shown by the fact that the deeds of land-transfer of the colonial government nearly all bear the signatures of women. The compensation due for the murder of a woman was double that for the murder of a man. Similar data may be adduced for Pre-Columbian Central America, Western Peru, New Britain and many parts of Melanesia. In Dutch New Guinea, a traveller saw a man subjected to a sound drubbing from his wife because he had brought some trinket to the boats for barter. Throughout the Malay archipelago women are treated with uniform consideration, and in all parts of Micronesia the position of women is notably exalted. As one missionary reported: 'The women in this country have arrogated to themselves those rights which everywhere else are claimed by the husband. The wife absolutely rules the house: she is the master and the husband is unable to dispose of anything without her consent.' If he displeases her, she maltreats him or quits him altogether. Throughout Polynesia, the position of women, though theoretically subordinate, is invariably one of great independence and influence. Similar data can be adduced from many African tribes, including the Bagisu, the Ekoi, the Bega, the Bantus and many others. It has already been noted that similar conditions obtain among the Tuareg.

In Asia, while among the most highly civilized races, such as the Hindus and the Chinese, women occupy a position of great subordination, among the most primitive and secluded races their status is high. In Kamchatka, for instance, 'husbands are under the iron rule of their wives'. Among the primitive Ainu, 'the wives dictate to their husbands and make them fetch and carry'. Of the Giak of Sakhalin, a Japanese traveller writes: 'In this country it is the custom that the women should rule over the men; they treat these like servants and make them do all the work.' Among the Moi, the most primitive race of Indo-China, 'nowhere does woman enjoy more consideration and esteem.'

One writer asks how women could possibly have gained such ascendancy over the men. In fact, there is no conceivable process whereby this could have happened. Not only is the savage strong, but woman is immeasurably orthodox; revolt is alien to her nature.

In judging these matters, many writers have been misled by the hard work done by women to suppose that their status was one of slavery and oppression. But, in fact, the toil with which they were burdened was freely and eagerly accepted by them. Generally speaking, it is in those societies where they toil most that their status is most independent. Where they are idle, they are as a rule little more than sexual slaves. As Roscoe says of the Baganda, no woman would remain with a man who did not give her a garden and a hoe to dig with; she would return to her relations to complain of her treatment. Seri women do all the labour of the community. The toil which woman performs is regarded by her as a functional division of labour. Indeed, the Australian women are much attached to the husbands who beat them so brutally, and even the custom of suttee is nowise resented by women, who often compete among themselves for the honour of being burned on the funeral pyre. Herodotus tells us that the same competitive eagerness for the honour of being immolated was the rule among Scythian women, and similar data can be found among the Maori of New Zealand, the Natchez of North America and elsewhere.

How then did the revolution take place? Bachofen, the first to draw attention to some of the evidence for former female dominance, suggested that the women rebelled in disgust at the promiscuity imposed by the males. Nothing could be more fantastically impossible. There is no tendency in women to object to the sexual standards which rule in

her environment, and it is a delusion that she in any way resents polygamy, as many missionaries have noted with surprise. One writes: 'A
woman would infinitely prefer to be one of a dozen wives of a respectable man than to be the sole representative of a man who had not the
force of character to raise himself above the one-woman level.' And
Miss Kingsley says she knows men, who would rather have had one wife,
driven to polygamy by the women.[1]

Similarly women accept promiscuity and sexual freedom where that
is the rule. As the daughters of an African chief said to an explorer:
'Why do you disdain us ? Are the women of your country prettier . . . ?
We are the daughters of a chief and will not submit to being insulted.'
Similar indignation, when a guest has refused a like offer, is expressed
by Eskimo, Chinook and other women.

The Establishment of Male Domination

Some writers have supposed that the high status of women in certain
communities is the outcome of special economic conditions, such as
their having acquired land or property, and thus that this is a late
development; but the fact that matriarchal organizations exist in
societies which have the barest minimum of economic development,
such as those of the Seri Indians, disposes of this explanation.

Furthermore, there is no evidence of a transition from patriarchal to
matriarchal customs anywhere. On the other hand, in every society,
uncultured or not, where patriarchal usages obtain at the present day,
indications are to be found of a previous higher status of women or of
an actual matriarchal organization.[2]

Among matriarchal primitive races, the change to patriarchy is everywhere taking place before our eyes, under the influence of European
contacts. The North American Indians who have adopted paternal
descent, have probably done so within the period of European occupation. In the islands of Torres Straits the social organization is now
patriarchal, but the guardian of the children at their initiation is not
their father but their maternal uncle. In Nigeria, as among the Malays,
two forms of marriage are found. In one, the children belong to their
father's clan; in the other, to the mother's. It is curious that in the island
of Yap, which alone among the Caroline and Marshall groups transmits
property in the male line, matrilocal marriage nevertheless persists, due
to local conditions which do not permit the clans to be sufficiently
segregated.

[1] For further examples, see pp. 210–11.
[2] Certain Kwakiutl Indians reckon descent in the male line, but are in the
habit of adopting the crest or totem of their mother's father. This may be due
to the influence of neighbour clans who reckon descent in the female line.

Sir Edward Tylor compared the two forms of marriage residence with the custom of mother-in-law avoidance. He found a greater correlation between matrilocy and avoidance than would develop by chance. Certain tribes, however, display the curious anomaly that, though the husband takes the wife home to his own tribe, yet mother-in-law avoidance is carried to a ridiculous extreme, and Tylor concludes that matrilocal residence must have formerly been customary, adding in support that, when a native kills game certain parts of the meat are allotted to the wife's parents—the duty of supplying game to the wife's household is, of course, a well-marked feature of matriarchal law. I therefore wrote to Mr Howitt, the leading authority on Australian anthropology, suggesting that inquiry would probably disclose further evidence of a maternal stage in Australian society. Mr Howitt, after investigating, replied that this surmise was correct—for instance, in the event of a war expedition, a daughter's husband fights on behalf of his wife's family and even against his own blood relations. In fact, there can be no doubt that the patriarchal character of Australian society and the low status of women are features of comparatively late origin.[1]

After Australia, Melanesia is perhaps the area in which the low status of women is most pronounced. Yet here, too, social organization presents countless typical matriarchal features, such as the system of maternal clans, the strict observance of mother-in-law tabus and the special position of the maternal uncle. Thus, among the natives of the Gazelle Peninsula of New Britain, though women are dominated by the men and excluded from religious functions, yet the society is organized throughout on purely matriarchal principles, descent being matrilinear. From similar arguments, it would seem that the people of Tierra del Fuego were also formerly matriarchal. One of their chief traditions is that 'formerly the women exercised supreme domination over the men', maintaining this by a system of terrifying apparitions of supposed ghosts, and the tradition adds that this was terminated by a sort of revolution in which many of the women were killed. Hence it seems that the change from matriarchy to patriarchy, which so often does not occur until a late phase of culture, may also take place at the rudest levels. The low status of women is such tribes is probably connected with their cultural isolation, for among less-isolated uncultured races the status of women is generally high.

[1] Spencer and Gillen, though they found no instance of matrilocy, also noted the practice of giving game to the wife's relations, and concluded that it indicated a former state in which a man owed allegiance to his wife's group; in Western Australia, where the condition of women is particularly degraded, it is nevertheless traditional that certain elderly females are invested with the status of moyram, or grandmother, after which they can no longer be carried off for a drudge or made the victim of revenge, and they become influential.

On the other hand, those peoples of whom we speak as civilized, such as the inhabitants of Europe, the so-called Aryan races of India, the Chinese, the Semitic races of Arabia and their descendants, together with those who have been converted to their religious systems, are normally patriarchal, and this association suggests that this is not a racial peculiarity of certain peoples but the outcome of conditions connected with their state of civilization. It is reasonable to suppose that, in an earlier stage, these societies too were matriarchal in organization, or at least less pronouncedly patriarchal than they have been during historical times, and, when their records are examined, strong evidence of this is invariably found, as the next chapter will show.

CHAPTER 7

The Matriarchal Phase in Civilized Societies

The Indian Aryans

AMONG the Hindus the subordinate position of woman was even more pronounced than in patriarchal Rome. The laws of Manu assert that 'in her childhood a girl should be under the will of her father; in her youth under that of her husband; her husband being dead, under the will of her sons. A woman should never enjoy her own will. . . ." Her husband must be worshipped 'like a god'.

But the oldest Indian records reveal a very different position. 'Let a wife', a Vedic hymn declares, 'be absolute mistress over her fathers-in-law, absolute mistress over her mother-in-law; let her be mistress over her husband's sisters, let her be mistress over her husband's brothers.' Writers of the epic period were aware of the change. Thus, Pandy in the Mahâbhârata says: 'Women were not formerly immured in houses and dependent upon husbands and relatives. They used to go about freely, enjoying themselves as best they pleased. . . . They did not then adhere to their husbands faithfully; and yet, O beauteous one, they were not regarded as sinful, for that was the sanctioned usage of the times. . . . The present practice of women being confined to one husband for life hath been established but lately.'

Most significantly, while in the historic and epic periods women were excluded from religious functions, in the Vedas, on the other hand, they were present and were even 'the orderers of the sacrifice'. In the most solemn function of Vedic religion, the Sacrifice of the Horse, the part they played was even more essential.[1] At least one of the Vedic hymns was composed by a woman. The erudite Princess Gargi Vakaknavi was renowned for disputations with the sage Yajnavalkya.

The society depicted in the Vedas is clearly not in a primitive condition: it appears to be essentially patriarchal, as might be expected of a pastoral society; it is marked by private ownership of cattle and horses, by well-defined aristocratic classes of warriors and priests, and a highly-developed religious cult and literature. It is fantastic to speak, as some

[1] See p. 379.

writers used to do, of the Vedas as 'the most ancient literature of which we possess written records'. The Vedas do not, in all probability, go back much farther than the first millenium B.C., if indeed as far. The 'Aryan' tribes of Hindustan also retained a matriarchal type of social organization, as is clear from Chinese accounts.[1] Of the people between the Oxus and the Jaxartes we learn: 'They hold their women in high honour, for whatever a woman says her husband invariably agrees to it" Of the Hu tribe of the Great Get-ti, the historian Hu-Han-Shu writes: 'They also take their personal name after their father, but they take their family name after their mother.' Thus it would appear that some of those Aryan tribes had retained a considerable degree of matriarchal organization. In ancient Indian society itself there are several indications of the previous existence of matriarchy. Thus, in the Mahabharata we are told that a man should avoid marrying a girl of the same family as his mother, a prohibition still emphasized in Hindu law. The Pandava dynasty traced its descent from a divine foundress, Pandaia. In Vedic India the guardian of a woman is her brother. The Rajputs, the purest representatives of the ancient Aryan conquerors of India, retain many of the archaic rules which have disappeared among the Hindus. Thus a woman may only marry into a clan equal to or more noble than her own, while the first step in any proposal of marriage must come from the woman or from her family, a characteristic matriarchal usage. Reverence for women, and especially for a man's mother, is a trait of Rajput manners. In Hindu custom, a bride is not at once permanently transferred to her husband's family, but at the end of a month her parents come and take her home, and for five years or until she has children she lives alternatively in her parents' or her husband's home.

China and Japan

China is the country where patriarchal principles are more strongly emphasized and women more completely subjugated than anywhere, and it is generally considered that indications of a former matriarchal

---

[1] Whether or not there was ever, strictly speaking, an Aryan race is a speculative matter. We know, however, that the Medes, the original inhabitants of Persia, and a neighbouring Scythic tribe in what is now Turkestan, called themselves thus. The Medes called themselves Ariyas, and the eastern portion of Persia was called Ariana—Iran is probably a variant of it. The peoples included under the denomination Scyths were an Iranian race, and spoke Iranian languages and had similar religious conceptions. In India the term 'Arya' was used with reference to the three upper castes rather than as an ethnic designation. With one important exception, no Hindus called themselves Aryas. The tribes which the Romans called the Great Getae inhabited the deserts of Scythia, and seem to have been the same as the tribes in India called Jats.

state are completely lacking. The early social history of China is obscure, but nevertheless there are indications that China is actually no exception. Thus, while emphatically patriarchal, the Chinese are exogamic. A man is strictly forbidden to marry a woman bearing the same clan-name as himself. The names of these clans are made up of the signs meaning 'woman' and 'birth', and their combination thus means 'born of the same woman' or 'one woman's brood'. Chinese marriage customs are essentially identical with those of the Mongol and nomadic Tartar populations of Central Asia, except for the more emphatic consolidation of marital power. The continuity of evolution between the ruder tribes and the Chinese can be clearly traced. Thus, among the Mongols and Tartars, as in China, the bride is purchased. Nevertheless, the bride is obliged to supply the house itself, which, as Robertson Smith pointed out, is a survival of the time when it was in the wife's house that the husband took up his abode. The relationship between this rule and the matriarchal order of society has been noted by the Chinese. As one writer says: 'The girl's dwelling and trousseau all come from her own family; hence the custom of counting genealogies from the female side.'

It follows that such usages must have been preceded by a stage in which marriage was matrilocal, a conclusion supported by the fact that, at the present day, it is only after living several days in the house of his parents-in-law that the bridegroom takes his bride to his own home. Throughout China it was once customary with the aristocratic classes that the wife, after a short residence in her husband's home, should return to her own house for several months. Moreover, complete matrilocal marriage is still sometimes practised at the present day, and Chinese law provides for the case of a husband who takes up residence in the home of his wife. Such a husband generally assumes the wife's family name instead of her taking his. It appears from the language of Li Ki that such marriages are a very ancient practice which has only recently become rare. In many districts there are anti-marrying leagues among the girls, who refuse to accept the complete effacement which is the lot of a Chinese wife. In Lung Kong they refuse to marry except on the condition that the husband go to the wife's home to live. In Yunnan the women appear to retain a degree of independence, and as a preliminary to marriage the bridegroom comes to the girl's house and knocks. His intended then asks who is there and, on hearing his name, asks if he wishes to come to her house and stop with her. The children take the wife's family name.

Such facts cannot be interpreted as indicating an evolution from patrilocal towards matrilocal usages. According to a Chinese tradition, the present form of marriage was instituted by Fu Hi, the legendary founder of Chinese civilization, previous to which children did not know their fathers and sexual relations were promiscuous, which is the usual expression used by patriarchal peoples when referring to matriarchal marriage. Fu Hi himself had no father, and the same is true of all the legendary and of many later Chinese emperors. Early Chinese history offers many examples of powerful and masterful empresses who either ruled as regent or forcibly seized the reins of government. Famous among them are Lu-Kao-Heu (187 BC), Sing-Zche (AD 1) and Hou-Zche (AD 15). The position of the women of the royal family, where archaic usages survived, constitute an exception to the rule concerning the position of women in China. When a minor was emperor, the dowager empress ruled for him. She selected the empress—his chief wife—his eight queens, and also his ministers, generally appointing her own brothers. Though, in later times, only the Son of Heaven could perform the sacrifice to Sanf-Tien, and scandal was caused when the adventuress, Hou, arrogated to herself this privilege, yet one of the earliest references to that sacrifice reads: 'The Empress Kiang-Yun, together with the Emperor, offered a sacrifice to Shang-Ti.' It is clear, therefore, that the status of women in religious matters must have undergone a transformation. As late as the third century of our era, women could hold office and exercise administrative functions, a right which did not completely disappear until the eighth century.

Turning to Japan, it might seem, at first sight, that the position was identical with that in China. Until recently the position of the Japanese upper-class wife was quite as servile as that of the Chinese wife. Yet, it is clear even from existing customs that such usages were mere imitations of the Chinese conception. For instance, instead of marriage being regarded as a solemn contract which even death cannot dissolve, there is complete liberty of divorce for both parties: 33 per cent of Japanese marriages are said to end in divorce, and both parties usually marry again without delay. When a daughter is the sole heiress, she continues to live in her parent's house, instead of going to her husband's, and her husband assumes her name and becomes an adopted son of her parents.

The features of marital relations which resemble those of China are much more pronounced among the upper-class than among the common people. Among the latter the wife is treated with deference, and exercises her right to dismiss the husband on the slenderest grounds. This, together with the matrilocal custom, suggests that the Chinese usages are recent adoptions. Patrilocal marriage did not, in fact, come into use in Japan until the fourteenth century. Previously, the husband merely paid occasional visits to his wife, who remained in her parental home. The Japanese family was entirely uterine, the children taking the name of the mother. A ceremonial survival still exists in the obligation of a newly-married couple to spend a night or two in the bride's home. Still older records represent an even more pronounced degree of the same condition of things. There was, properly speaking, no marriage—that is to say, no contract. Sexual cohabitation constituted marriage, and in older Japanese literature it is not possible to distinguish the relations of a wife from that of a mistress or concubine. Powerful chiefs are described as having a wife in every island and on every headland.

The Semites

The patriarchal clans of the Hebrews have always stood for the very type of patriarchal organization, yet it was from a study of their customs that Robertson-Smith illustrated the transition from matriarchal to patriarchal institutions. Semitic kinship terms refer, as among most peoples, to maternal rather than to paternal descent, and the clan or tribe to which a man belongs is frequently spoken of as his 'mother'. The Arab genealogists of the time of the rise of Islam, when patriarchy was strongly established, were at pains to exhibit Semitic descent as patriarchal, but they were often compelled to recognize that the older clans were metronymic. Among the Hebrews who had left the peninsula many centuries before the Arabs, the same situation had arisen long before, and they endeavoured also to interpret their genealogies in terms of a male descent. Yet the Jewish rabbis themselves, at a comparatively late date, acknowledged that the 'four Matriarchs', Sarah, Rebecca, Rachel and Leah, had occupied a more important position than the 'three Patriarchs', Abraham, Isaac and Jacob. According to Robertson-Smith, the tribe of Levi was originally metronymous, being the tribe of Leah for whom the husband Levi had to be invented. Israel itself, the tribe which gave its name to the whole nation, was originally the tribe of Sarah, Israel being her son. Even in patriarchal times, women built cities, i.e. founded families. Sherah 'built Beth-Horon the nether, and the upper, and Uzzen-Sherah.' (1 Chronicles vii. 24)[1]. With the early Hebrews the regular practice was for the man to 'leave his father and mother and cleave to his wife'; that is, to take up his abode with his wife's clan. Isaac takes it for granted that Jacob, when he marries, will dwell with his wife's people. In fact, Jacob lives twenty years in the home of his wives and, when he departs by stealth, Laban pursues him and tells him that he has no right to take them, or even his own children, away, and claims them as belonging to their mother's father. Samson's wife remains with her own people. Joseph's

---

[1] The Jewish practice of marrying a father's daughter or his sister (Genesis xi. 29; Exodus vi. 20; Ezekiel xxiii. 11) also points to former matrilocal usages.

children by his Egyptian wife have to be adopted before they can be regarded as belonging to his tribe.

Matrilocal marriage passed away when the Jews settled in Canaan, but survives to this day among the Bedawi of Arabia. To the true Bedawi, marriage is almost always matrilocal. 'The wild men', says Burton, 'do not refuse their daughters to a stranger, but the son-in-law would be forced to settle amongst them.' Even after the introduction of patrilocal marriage, contracts were sometimes drawn up stipulating that the wife should remain with her own people.

Ammianus Marcellinus noted that in his day the common marriage ceremony among the Arabs consisted in the woman's presenting to the man a spear and a tent. The tent has always been regarded by the Arabs as the property of the woman and, indeed, as a synonym for the woman. An Arab author mentions that the women of Jahiliya could dismiss their husbands by merely turning their tent round, a custom which still persists. Among the Bedawi of Mesopotamia a special tent called 'hofah' is erected for the newly married couple. The ordinary expression for 'to get married' in Jewry was to 'go into the "huppah" ', i.e. the tent. The marriage was not concluded until this had been done. When the practice of the husband visiting his wife in her tent gave place to patrilocal marriage, he did not bring his bride immediately into his own house, but a special tent, presented by the bride's family, was erected to represent the woman's home. 'Huppah' is still the ordinary term for the marriage ceremony among the Jews and, until quite lately, was represented in every Jewish marriage by a canopy under which the bride proceeded to the synagogue.

As we should expect from the former existence of matrilocy, there are indications that formerly the position of women, both among the Jews and in Arabia, was high. The oldest existing fragment of Hebrew literature represents the Hebrew tribes as led by a woman (Judges iv–v). Among the Arabs likewise many of the judges were chieftainesses. Queens, from the Queen of Sheba to Zenobia, occupy a prominent place in Arab history. In every one of the references to Arabian kingdoms in the historical inscriptions of Assyria, it is with a queen that we have to do. The position of those queens appears to have been exalted. Their husbands were merely their consorts. 'The female sex rules among the Sabians,' says Claudian, 'and a large proportion of the barbarians is under the armed domination of queens.' Women in ancient Arabia were commonly the owners of wealth, possessing large flocks and herds; their husband commonly acted as herdsman. Mohammed himself was able to carry out his mission thanks only to the wealth which he acquired from his first wife. In early and pre-Islamic literature we come upon women like Mawia bint Afzar, who changed her husband whenever she pleased; but, though courted by the most famous warriors and poets of the age, her choice was never frivolously determined. There is nowhere to be found a nobler type of dignified yet unfettered, free yet self-respecting, womanhood than the women of ancient Arabia up to the time of ancient Saracenic civilization. The women were always close behind the warriors in battle, and more than once rallied them to victory. Many an Arab woman personally led the men to battle. As late as the time of Rashid, Arab maidens fought on horseback and commanded troops, and royal princesses clad in mail fought under Mansur against the Byzantines. Yet those proud Amazons were not barbaric viragoes, but cultivated beauty, grace and elegance and all the accomplishments of their age. The record of their sentiments is contained in their own impassioned poems, which form a considerable proportion of pre-Islamic poetry. The tent of many an Arab woman was the scene of tournaments of song. Like archaic Greece, ancient Arabia had its seven sages, but they were women.

Ancient Egypt

The conservative society of Egypt never lost its essential matriarchal character, though continuous progress towards patriarchal institutions is clearly traceable through the various phases of Egypt's four-thousand-year career. We shall have to consider elsewhere the rules of succession to the throne of the Pharaohs, and we shall see that the functions of royalty were transmitted in the female line. While every Egyptian princess was born a queen and bore the titles of the office from the day of her birth, a man only acquired them at his coronation, and could do so only by becoming the consort of a royal princess. It was in the queen that mystic or divine virtue resided.

Such features are substantially identical with those obtaining in all other African kingdoms. Royal families naturally tend to preserve a more archaic constitution than the families of ordinary people, and these matriarchal features would not in themselves be sufficient ground for inferring the matriarchal character of Egyptian society as a whole. Nevertheless, scanty as our information is we have enough to see that Egyptian social life generally was in the highest degree matriarchal. Dr H. R. Hall says that the constitution of Egyptian society was characterized by 'a distinct preservation of matriarchy, the prominent position of women and a comparative promiscuity in sexual relations'. Professor Mitteis confirms that Egypt was immemorially a land of matrilinear descent, a usage which continued in Christian times until the seventh century. 'The maternal uncle is often named as important. The father of the mother was more important than the man's own father.' In consequence, there were no illegitimate children in Egypt, a child born out of wedlock enjoying the same rights as one born in marriage. All children belonged to the mother. The Nomes, or primitive totemic clans, of which the nation was formed, were maternal clans or motherhoods, and their headship was transmitted through women.

Flinders Petrie observes: 'The family in Egypt was based on a matriarchal system. . . . The house and property went with the women and daughters.' Sir Gaston Maspero says: 'The Egyptian woman of the lower and middle class was more respected, more independent, than any other woman in the world.' The husband had no power as head of the household, and the word 'husband' is only found in marriage contracts after the reign of Philopator. Marriage was matrilocal, and where there were two wives each remained in her own house, the husband visiting them in turn. 'As late as the XIXth Dynasty, there was still surviving the idea that a man was only a boarder in a woman's home.' All landed and house property was in the hands of the women, and if a man built a house it passed immediately to his wife.

Marriage does not appear to have been associated with any religious ceremony, but was essentially an economic transaction and was made the subject of a written contract. We possess hundreds of these contracts dating from the Ptolemaic period. In them the woman imposes her conditions on the man. Thus: 'If I leave thee as husband because I have come to hate thee, or because I love another man, I shall give thee two and a half measures of silver, and return to thee . . . the bride-gift.' In a love poem of the period of Rameses II, addressed by the lady to her beloved, she opens her heart thus: 'O my beautiful friend! My desire is to become as thy wife, the mistress of all thy possessions!' The eagerness which Egyptian husbands seem to have shown in making over their property to their wives was probably due in part to the fact that, according to matriarchal usage, it would otherwise have passed not to their own but to their sisters' children. Thus, by a curious paradox, the anxiety to secure patriarchal succession contributed to accentuate the economic power of women. To the same desire to combine inheritance in the male line with the matriarchal organization of the family was also doubtless due the practice of marrying sisters, which appears to have been more prevalent in Egypt than among any other people of which we know. The majority of marriages were between brothers and sisters as late as the second century AD in some districts.

Generations of Egyptologists have treated with contempt the statement of Diodorus Siculus that under the marriage agreement the husband appertains to the wife and must obey her, but this is now known to be strictly accurate, and obedience is urged on the husband as a duty in 'the oldest book in the world', the 'Maxims of Ptah-Hotep', dating from about 3200 BC. Indeed, the marriage contracts which we possess go even further than does Diodorus; the tone of servility which pervades them is almost incredible. 'I acknowledge thy rights as wife,' says one of them, 'from this day forward I shall never by any word oppose thy claims. I shall acknowledge thee before anyone as my wife, but I have no power to say to thee: "Thou art my wife." It is I who am the man who is thy husband. From the day that I become thy husband I cannot oppose thee, in whatsoever place thou mayest please to go. I cede the . . . [here follows a list of possessions], that are in thy dwelling. I have no power to interfere in any transaction made by thee, from this day. Every document made in my favour by any person is now placed among thy deeds, and is also at the disposal of thy father or of any relatives acting for thee. Thou shalt hold me bound to honour any such deed.'

Can we wonder at the gibes of the Greeks at the 'topsy-turvy world' of Egypt and its hen-pecked husbands? It is not surprising therefore that the position of women in society was equally prominent. Whether married or single, from the earliest age a girl had the fullest legal rights and could enter legally into any transaction. Guardians were entirely unknown in Egypt. 'No people, ancient or modern,' says Max Miller, 'has given women so high a legal status as did the inhabitants of the Nile valley.' Herodotus declares that, 'the women go in the market-place, transact affairs and occupy themselves with business, while the husbands stay at home and weave'. Even the role of priestess was open to a woman. We have full details of the career of a woman who, beginning as a clerk in her father's office, was promoted to various administrative posts, and became governess of the Fayum, and, what appears more remarkable, commander-in-chief of the western military district. To this was added later the governorship and the military command of Kynopolis and the eastern frontier, and she became one of the most important and wealthiest personages in the realm.

The continuous restriction of these privileges can be traced. During the first dynasties the number of women exercising the function of priestesses are numerous, but there is not a single example after the XIIth Dynasty. Thus it would appear that, as in many primitive tribes, the first step in the limitation of the status of women is to take over from them the monopoly of religious and magic functions. By Ptolemaic times, it is the husband not the wife who claims complete freedom of divorce, and husbands are found administering the estate of the wives.

The Ægean and Greece

The marvellous remains of Krete provide eloquent testimony to the matriarchal character of Kretan society. The enormous predominance of female over male figures is without parallel. Kretan divinities are almost exclusively feminine, as are the innumerable votive figures.

Women alone figure as priestesses in religious ceremonies. These characteristics are equally marked from ancient Neolithic times to the height of Minoan culture. 'It may be admitted without reserve', remarks Dr Mosso, 'that at this epoch, that is to say, about 1500 BC, Minoan religion had preserved its matriarchal character. The supremacy of women in religion was thus maintained until Mykenean times.' Secular art also speaks for the predominance of women. There are numerous representations of men in Minoan art, but they are all engaged in subordinate occupations: cup-bearers, pages, musicians, harvesters, soldiers and sailors. Not once does it depict a king, prince or hero, or show a man in a position of domination. The female figures, on the other hand, invariably exhibit an attitude of self-possessed independence. Minoan women are seen mixing freely with men at festivals, riding in chariots driven by female charioteers. 'It is certain', remarks Dr Hall, 'that they must have lived on a footing of greater equality with the men than in any other ancient civilization.' That the state was governed by women is suggested by Klidemos, who tells us that after the death of Deukalion the throne passed to Ariadne, who concluded a treaty of peace with Athens.

Marriage in Krete was matrilocal, as appears from Strabo, and from the laws inscribed on the walls of the temple of Gortyna, which contain many traces of older matriarchal usages. Thus the mother's brother occupies an important position and is responsible for the bringing up of the children. A woman, on marriage, retained full control of her property and, like the husband, had the right of divorce at pleasure. A man's property passed to his children, but in the absence of children his sister's children might be heirs.

Krete was the most brilliant focus of a culture which, at that time, was common to all the peoples of the Aegean. The various peoples of the Aegean were culturally, linguistically and doubtless ethnically one. Lykians, Karians and Lydians are all one race, and what we know of them confirms their matriarchal character. Thus Nicholas of Damascus tells us that 'amongst the Lykians the women are more honoured than the men', and that not only kinship but property was transmitted in the maternal line. Of the Lydians we are told: 'The men are subject to female domination. The throne went with the queen and not with the king.'

Probably the same race that peopled the Aegean also peopled the greater part of the Mediterranean coast. Every advance in our knowledge tends to confirm the view that the Neolithic race of the Mediterranean came from Africa at a time when land-bridges still spanned the inland sea. The Berbers and Tuareg would thus be the surviving African relatives of the race which gave birth to European culture, and the similarity of the scripts of Minoan Krete with the archaic script preserved by Tuareg women seems to confirm this.

Female figures are equally predominant in the Neolithic art of the whole Mediterranean region; there is not a single male idol to be found before the Bronze Age. Dr Rodenwalt says that the prominence of women is even more pronounced in continental Greece than in Krete, and points out that, whereas in Kretan frescoes women are assisted by men, in the Mykenan palaces of the Peloponnesus 'we see, everywhere, women and women only taking part in religious cult'. At the opposite end of the Mediterranean the evidence of matriarchy is even more emphatic. 'Among the Cantaberians', says Strabo, 'the men bring dowries to the women. With them the daughters alone inherit property. Brothers are given away in marriage by their sisters. In all their usages, their social condition is one of gynaecocracy.' Until quite recently the custom lingered in the Pyrenees that all property passed to the eldest child, son or daughter, and, if the latter, the husband took up his residence at the house of his wife, but acquired no rights over her property.

It has frequently been suggested that, while the aboriginal or Pelasgian populations of the Aegean were matriarchal in their social organization, the invaders, or Hellenes, brought with them 'as a precious possession, the patriarchal system'. It is extremely doubtful, however, whether there exists any fundamental ethnical difference between the authochthonous inhabitants and the invaders. The Dorians, whom alone Herodotus calls 'Hellenes', came from the north, but there is no evidence that their habitat was any farther than the southern shores of the Danube, a region where we find the Neolithic culture of Butmir identical with that of Krete.[1]

Be that as it may, the Spartans appear to many 'the embodiment of the specially Hellenic elements in Hellenism'. Their social organization was purely matriarchal. Their customs were so similar to those of Krete that it was believed at the time that they had been borrowed from the Kretans. Spartan women were entirely unrestricted in their social and sexual relations. Virginity was not demanded of a bride. Children born out of wedlock were called 'virgin born', and were regarded as equal to those born in wedlock. At the time of Argesilaos, the number of them exceeded those born in regular wedlock. The Spartans practised fraternal polyandry, and their marriage was matrilocal. In the Spartan version of the story of Penelope, when she follows Odysseus home, she is represented as breaking the custom. Plutarch says that the Spartan women

---

[1] The assumption that the Greeks, or 'Achæans', were a separate race from the Aegeans is based upon the Aryan theory, a speculation which has now crumbled to pieces. It is not without significance that Dorian invasion was invariably spoken of by the Greeks as 'the return of the Heraklides'.

were 'the only women in Greece who ruled over their men'. They were commonly consulted on political questions, and could inherit and bestow property, nearly all the property in Sparta being in their hands.

The Lokrian colony of Cape Zephiros was also regarded as having preserved more archaic usages than other Hellenic states. Of them we are told: 'All fame and honour attaching to descent is derived through the women, not through the men.' Ritual sexual licence, quite opposed to the sentiments of most Greek communities in historical times, survived among them until a late date. The view that the Greeks were originally matriarchal is confirmed by traditions of the historical period, when it was held that the status of women in the form of marriage had, in primitive times, been entirely different. It was said that in primitive Athens 'at one time, because of the general promiscuity, men did not know their own fathers'. Marriage was said to have been instituted by Kekrops, who was therefore named 'diphues'—'of a double nature'— for before him children had a mother but no father. Aeschylus in his *Eumenides* represents the change from the ancient law to that of the new gods as chiefly manifested in the way of viewing maternal and paternal kinship. The tradition of the contest between the old and the new gods to which the *Eumenides* referred, gives an account of the changes in the status of the women. The famous contest between Athene and Poseidon for the possession of the city was decided by the votes of the Athenian citizens. The women voted for Athene, the men for Poseidon. When the victory went to Athene, Poseidon vented his anger by flooding the land, and in order to pacify him, it was ruled that the women should be disfranchised, that no child should receive the name of its mother and that women should no longer be regarded as Athenian citizens.

While such traditions are of course mythical, no mythologist nowadays doubts that such myths indicate an actual conflict between native and foreign cults. It would be difficult to imagine why a strictly patriarchal people should devise a theory of their primitive matriarchy. A considerable body of evidence confirms these traditions. As we shall see elsewhere, in primitive Greece the religious functions connected with agriculture were exercised chiefly if not exclusively by the women. The chief civic function in this connection continued in historical Athens to be exercised, not by the male magistrate or 'archon', but by a special female functionary, the 'queen archon', assisted by a council of matrons. Gods and heroes are commonly referred to in Greek genealogies by the names of their mothers, as 'Apollo, the son of Leto', 'Dionysos, the son of Semele', and so on. Such gods and heroes were in fact, 'virgin-born'; that is, they were in the same case as the Athenians are reported to have been before Kekrops instituted marriage. Jason is expressly asserted to be 'virgin-born'. The Argonauts, or Minyans as they are commonly called, all trace their descent through women to a common ancestress, Minya, or to Klymenes, mother of Jason. Early Greek genealogies are, in fact, little else than catalogues of women. The relationship between Theseus and Herakles, to which so much importance was attached in archaic tradition, was traced through women. In primitive Greece the women gave their names, not only to their children but to their clans and tribes. Thus, the Athenians claimed to be descended from Atthis, the daughter of Kranaos; the Spartans from Sparta, the daughter of Eurotas, and so forth. The grammatical ending of Greek family and tribal names in '-ida', is a purely feminine form. Later traditions substituted obscure male eponyms for the original eponymae. Thus the Ionians were supposed to be called after a certain Ion, but their true eponym is revealed by the fact that the Ionian sea was understood to be named after Io. Similarly the Dorians were more probably derived from the lunar goddess Doris than from an obscure Doras, a son of Helen. Both Ionians and Dorians traced their descent from Helen, the daughter of the Moon, and there can be, I think, little doubt that she was the true ancestress of the Hellenes.

Greek thinkers in the classical age held that the mother had little or no share in the process of procreation, that the seed proceeded from the father, and the mother's womb was but a suitable receptacle to protect it. The mother, it was said, was little more than a nurse; the father was, strictly speaking, the sole progenitor. This view contrasts not only with older usages but with the very structure of Greek speech and legal customs. In Homer a sharp distinction was drawn between a uterine brother, ὁμογάστριος, and a brother on the father's side, ὄπατρος, and the former relationship is invariably emphasized as more important. Moreover, in contradiction to this ingenious patriarchal theory of procreation, the ordinary appellation for brother continued to be 'adelphos', which means 'from the womb', and is therefore a relic of the time when the relationship of a brother was reckoned on the mother's side only. The distinction persisted in the most concrete manner in historical times, for, according to Athenian law, a man was at liberty to marry his half-sister on his father's side, but was forbidden to form an incestuous union with his half-sister on the mother's side.

In princely houses, of which alone traditional records have reached us, it is the women who transmit both titles and property. They remain in the maternal homes, and the sons regularly depart to marry in some other town princesses whose titles they share. This is the form of marriage which Alkinoos proposes to Odysseus. 'I should wish', he says, 'that so goodly a man as thou . . . would take my daughter to wife and be called my son and abide with me.' Gilbert Murray thus briefly sums the social conditions in the heroic age of Greece: 'House property belonged to the woman, and descended from mother to daughter. The father did not count—at least not primarily—in the reckoning of relationship. He did count for something, since exogamy, not endogamy, was the rule. The sons went off to foreign villages to serve and marry women in possession of the land there. Their sisters, we have reason to believe, generally provided them with dowries.'

In Athens, in historical times, it was the custom that after an Athenian husband had removed his wife to his own home and spent the wedding night there, the couple should return on the following night to the bride's home and sleep there—a custom observed by many peoples who formerly practised matrilocal marriage; for instance, the Baila of Rhodesia. In fact, Athenian marriage never became thoroughly patrilocal. The Athenian wife, though she removed to her husband's home, never became legally regarded as a member of his family. Her father could, at any time, take her away and bring her home or marry her to another man. If she had no father, her next-of-kin or legal guardian could do the same. A wife had no claim on any of her husband's property except her dowry, and when he died the widow returned to her own people. It is, I suggest, impossible to conceive such laws as having developed in a state of society where the tradition was for the husband to transfer the wife to his household, and to become the founder of a patriarchal society.

In the islands of Greece, little touched by the passage of events, the traveller often comes upon scenes that answer in every detail descriptions in the *Iliad* and the *Odyssey*. In the island of Kythnos, at the present day, it is the invariable custom for a husband to take up his abode after marriage with the family of his wife.

The adaptation of the laws of matriarchal society to patriarchal ideas is no less clearly exhibited by the legislation concerning inheritance; Athenian law in this respect being very similar to the Kretan law. An heiress must marry her nearest male kinsman, except in the forbidden degrees, starting with her father's brother, if any. This is clearly a provision to ensure that property shall remain with the male members of the family without going so far as to make it transmissible in the male line only. Athenian law was very similar but even stricter, for if the woman was already married at the time she inherited, the male heir had a right to take her away from her husband, whose marriage became null, and to marry her. Professor Ridgeway feels that this points 'to a time when all property descended through women'.

No contrast could be more glaring than that presented by the position of women in the Homeric poems and that found in historical Greece, which, as will be noted later, was beyond all comparison degraded. Throughout the *Odyssey* it is the women who direct, counsel and protect the men. Wherever Odysseus goes, he comes upon a queen or queen-goddess ruling the land alone, or with a subordinate consort. The royal office is transmitted by dynastic incest. He recites catalogues of women, giving the female genealogies of the Minyan and Aiolian houses. So marked is this that Richard Bentley, the scholar, declared that the *Odyssey* had been specially composed for women, and Samuel Butler had the whimsical idea that it must have been written by a woman.[1] The *Odyssey* recalls a society in which women held a great place.[2] Klytemnestra, Alcestis, Kassandra, Medea, Polyxena, Hermione, Antigone differ completely from the sequestered Greek wife, artificially stunted in mind, who was not even permitted to witness the representations of her ancestresses on the stage.

The Teutons

Passing to the barbaric nations of Europe, everyone is familiar with the account given by Tacitus of the influence wielded by women among the Teutons. In the oldest Nordic and Germanic documents persons are often referred to by the names of their mother without mention of the father. The Lombard nation traced its descent from a woman, Gambara, the father not being mentioned. Tacitus notes that 'the sons of a sister have the same position as regards their uncle as with their father. Some even consider the former as the stronger tie'. Down to a late date the uterine relationship was regarded as more important than the paternal. In the time of Tacitus the organization of the Teutons was patriarchal, for a man transmitted his property to his own children. This was combined with purely matriarchal juridic usages. Thus, according to the laws of the Thuringians, if a man died without children his property

[1] Note that the lines in which Alkinoos and Arete are unambiguously stated to be brother and sister are immediately followed by a genealogy which represents them as uncle and niece—a concrete illustration of the adaptation of matriarchal to patriarchal ideas.

[2] It must be concluded that the *Iliad* and the *Odyssey*, in their present general form, were composed not earlier than the eighth century B.C., and probably in the seventh by the remodelling of much older material. Thus, they cannot be regarded as affording a contemporary picture of the world they depict. In many respects, they represented the world they depict about as accurately as Shakespeare's *Hamlet* represents fourth-century Denmark. Thus, among Homeric heroes iron is not only in general use, but its use is so familiar that it has passed into proverbial expressions; whereas Mykenean Greece belonged to the Bronze Age and iron was completely absent, except in the form of very rare finger-rings. Again, Homeric heroes are cremated. Mykenean Greece invariably buried its dead. And so on. Homer seems deliberately to have archaized his material; he carefully avoids, save in one ambiguous instance, mentioning writing, although writing had been in use in the Aegean from time immemorial. At the same time, he adapts myths such as that of Penelope to suit the moral notions of his time.

passed to his sister, or failing her, his mother. Similarly, in Burgundy a man's property, in the absence of children, went to his sister and, failing her, to his brother. Of the famous Salic laws, there are ten somewhat different redactions. In the four oldest a man's heirs, after his son, are his mother, his brother, his sister and his mother's sisters. In none is the father mentioned; in one only is the father's sister named, and she owes precedence to the mother's sister. The later redactions show Roman influence, and a gloss informs us that 'the laws which were observed in pagan times are no longer valid, for according to them many persons were deprived of their rights'. It was not until the end of the sixth century that the legal equality of the father's and of the mother's relations became fully established. Ample evidence confirms that property and titles, at least in royal houses, were transmitted through the women. Saxon aspirants to the throne did not consider that they had fully established their claim until they had married the queen.

Thus Hermigisil, King of the Varini, on his deathbed, begs his son Radger to be sure and marry his stepmother in accordance with their ancestral custom. Edbald, King of Kent, does likewise; as does Ethelbald, King of the West Saxons, who marries the widow of his father Ethelwulf. The West Saxon Queen Seaxburg, however, preferred to retain the kingdom for herself. Similarly, Canute the Dane, after having overthrown Ethelred, sends for the queen, an old woman who was then living in Normandy, and does not regard his usurpation as complete until he has married her. Hamlet's uncle, Feng, obtains the Danish crown in the same manner; and Wiglet killed Hamlet in order to obtain possession of Hamlet's wife and of the kingdom. Similarly among the Scandinavians the kingdom passed to the daughters and to their husbands as late as the eighth century; and it is usual in Nordic records for the kingdom to be inherited through a man's mother, or by marrying the queen or a royal princess.

We have no express information as to whether marriage was patrilocal or matrilocal among commoners, but we know from Procopius that the Gothic tribes were familiar with matrilocal marriage.

The Celts

Though we have no systematic account of the Celts as a whole, we know a great deal about the Irish Celts, and there appears to have been great uniformity in the usages of all Celtic peoples, whether they dwelt in Ireland or on the banks of the Po or the Tagus. Irish traditional narratives show that marriage was essentially matrilocal. Even Cuchulainn, mightiest of all the heroes, was constrained to go and live with the fairy queen, Fand, who had wooed him. Throughout, the mistress or wife retains superiority. 'She chooses whom she will and is no man's slave.

Herself she offers freely but she abandons not her liberty.' Irish and Welsh heroic groups are named after the mother and, especially in the older strata of tradition, heroes are commonly metronymous. Ireland and Scotland derive their names from eponymae, Erin and Scota, and the earliest settlers in Ireland are represented as having been women. The queens and princesses of Irish traditional history are pictured as viragoes, of whom their husbands generally stood in dread.

Among the Picts, property was transmitted exclusively matrilineally, a man's estate passing to his sister's children. 'It is in the right of mothers they succeed to sovereignty and all other successions'. Accounts of early Scottish history confirm what we should expect from this. Women did not leave home on marriage, a usage of which traces survive in the Highlands even today. 'It is a practice among the better sort in these days for the bride to remain with her parents for some weeks.' The accounts of the Book of Leinster and other documents state that matriarchal organization was imposed upon the Picts by the Irish Gaels after a victory. This, of course, is unlikely, but implies that the Irish themselves had the same social customs, for they would hardly impose upon other peoples usages foreign to themselves. Throughout the literature of the Irish and British Celts heroes are represented, as in the archaic Greek sagas, as leaving their homes to seek in some foreign tribe an heiress whom they will marry and with whom they will share dominion over her estates. The ancient laws of Ireland and of Wales lay down that when a daughter is married to a stranger her son shall inherit the estate, and the principal personage after the chieftain is invariably his sister's son, not his own. There can be no doubt that matriarchal succession was the immemorial rule with all Celtic-speaking peoples.

Ancient graves of the Bronze Age in Britain show that women were buried with at least as much pomp as the men, and Tacitus reports with surprise that Britons, brought before the Emperor Claudius to make their obeisance, went straight to the Empress Agrippina and did homage to her.

The little that we know of pre-Roman Gaul is also consistent with the matriarchal interpretation. Several accounts testify to the influence of women, who took part in a tribal council. Almost the only account of their marriage customs we have is one given by a Greek merchant who witnessed a wedding. He was surprised to be invited to a banquet to which a large number of marriageable young men had been invited. After it the bride entered and surveyed the assembly, then signified her choice by presenting a cup to the man she had selected as husband. Similar matriarchal usages are found in various parts of the world; matrilocal marriage is found nowadays in some secluded mountain districts of Savoy and is known as 'goat marriage', an allusion to the practice of bringing the he-goat to the female, while cows and ewes are taken to the male.

Rome

Rome stands for the very type of the patriarchal organization of society, and, in large measure, it is from her that our own patriarchal organization has been derived. Modern jurists and historians have analysed the Roman tradition as it is embodied in the interpretations of Roman jurists, and have derived from it the patriarchal theory of society, which has been worked out with great learning, notably by Sir Henry Maine. It assumes that the patriarchal family as we know it is not only the unit of human society but the primitive and original form of the human social group, and that all other groups, such as the clan or gens, the tribe and, finally, the city and state, have been formed by the aggregation of patriarchal families and 'organized as a collection of patriarchally governed families'. Apart from the biological and comparative ethnological reasons for rejecting such a conception, it leads to a tangle of difficulties and inconsistencies within the domain of Roman and Greek archaeology itself. Sir Henry Maine candidly admits that the origin of the patriarchal family itself is a complete mystery. One of the most distinguished of classical social students, M. Fustel de Coulanges, working purely from the classical point of view, felt obliged by his difficulties to break away from current theories, and to regard the original unit, not as a family, but as a gens or clan. I have already given some reasons for thinking that such a group could not have rested upon patriarchal principles.

In the light of present knowledge, the evidence that Roman society was preceded by a matriarchal constitution is no less conclusive than in regard to other people. The primitive Romans were divided into tribes, and those tribes into curiae, which, as Livy reveals, were named after each of the Sabine women: that is, they were named after the mothers and not the fathers of the clan. Thus, the primitive organization of the Romans consisted of motherhoods. The Latin people as a whole derived their name from a tribal ancestress, for the first king of the Latins was, according to tradition, Saturnus and his wife, Latia. Furthermore, the land upon which Rome itself was built was traditionally inherited from women. Acca Larentia, who is curiously described as 'a most noble prostitute' married a wealthy Etruscan 'whose home she ruled,' and left the land to the Roman people when she died. Moreover, succession was not in the male line. If a male of the royal family had a claim to the throne, it was through his mother, and he did not succeed his father, but his uncle. When Tarquin the Proud caused one of his nephews to be murdered in the hope of securing the succession for his own son, the other nephew feigned insanity; and it was upon him, in accordance with matriarchal law, that the duty of blood-revenge evolved, when his niece Lucretia was assaulted. As in all patriarchal society, the distinction between paternal and maternal uncles was clearly drawn, the former being called 'patruus', the latter 'avunculus', a diminutive of avus; that is, ancestor. Thus our word 'uncle', a corruption of avunculus, preserves a trace of the matriarchal order of succession.

The Etruscans, the most important of the Italian populations, and probably the actual founders of Rome, are known to have been definitely matriarchal. There is no instance of an Etruscan agnomen—that is, of a name derived from the father—and on funeral monumenta the deceased is usually designated by his metronymic.

In bilingual inscriptions, the father's name is inserted in the Latin version only, while the mother's name, always given in Etruscan, is sometimes omitted in the Latin. Etruscan girls were unrestricted before marriage and were said to earn their dowry by prostitution. Their freedom after marriage was scarcely less. 'It is a custom instituted by law among the Etruscans', says Theopompos, 'that wives should be in common.' In their frequent feasts the married women lay on couches with any man they chose and had freedom of intercourse with him. Paternity, we are told, was unknown. No word for father has yet been detected in the inscriptions. The words denoting husband and wife are also somewhat doubtful.

It is difficult to imagine how in primitive times two populations so closely intermingled as were the Etruscans and the local Italic tribes could have maintained a separate and totally different form of constitution, one matriarchal and the other patriarchal. In the bilingual sepulchral inscriptions special devices were adopted to render the matriarchal nomenclature in accordance with later Latin usage. The word 'agnomen', the correct term for a patronymic, derived from the paternal relatives, was only introduced in the fourth century. Theopompos uses the same language in speaking of the Roman plebs as he does of the Etruscans: they were said not to know their fathers. But originally the nobility were in the same case, as Virgil discloses. The most eminent of the Latin nobles, Drances, 'was proud of the nobility derived from his mother; as to his father he was uncertain'. This uncertainty was shared by the kings of Rome themselves—Romulus, Ancus Martius and Servius Tullius.

The patriarchal principle of transmission of property to the son was evidently an innovation of the patricians, the owners of property. We find, in other parts of the world, the propertied classes adopting identical measures to transmit it in the male line. Thus, the wealthy of the

Tlinkits of Alaska are patriarchal while the poorer classes are matrilinear. The same is true in Dahomey.

The contest between plebeians and patricians which occupies so great a place in early Roman history is not merely part of the conflict between the poor and the rich, but also a conflict between two forms of social organization. The transition from one to the other appears to have taken place almost within historical times. The elder Cato refers in pretty clear terms to the event. 'Our fathers have willed that women should be in the power of their fathers, of their brothers, of their husbands.' Plutarch represents Roman senators as scandalized at the notion of a woman raising her voice in the Senate, yet in the age of Romulus women commonly delivered orations in the Senate. Tacitus notes as a peculiarity of the Germans that they insisted upon female hostages, but Porsenna did exactly the same thing with regard to the archaic Romans. Much in Roman cult survives from an earlier time. In the temple of Ceres, for instance, the names of male relatives were never pronounced, and in the rites of Mater Matuta it was the custom for Roman women to pray first for their sisters' children; that is, for the children of the maternal clan. The Romans, observed one historian, 'had a most remarkable predilection for ascribing to women the most important events in their history.' Virgil describes the Italic tribes as being led against the invader by an unwedded queen, Camilla, high-priestess of Diana, who, though she has a brother living, reigns over the Volsci in her own right. He pictures the Latin queen, Amata, claiming the right to choose a husband for her daughter, that is, an heir to the throne, and inciting the Latin women to resist her husband's nominee, as their 'maternal right'.

It is owing to its original matriarchal character that, in spite of the 'patria potestas', women nevertheless retained in that society their dignity and privileges, which contrast with their position in Greece. As we shall see later, their status in Rome was marked by a strange combination of patriarchal institutions and matriarchal sentiment.

To conclude, we see that even in those countries which are now regarded as strongholds of patriarchy, the former status of women was higher and more independent than in later times. Possibly the only exceptions to this rule are the Australian aboriginals and the Melanesian savages.

CHAPTER 8

Division of Labour

THE difficulty which many experience in recognizing the matriarchal character of primitive societies arises, I believe, from a fundamental misconception. It is assumed that in a matriarchal society the women dominate the men in a way similar to that in which men dominate women in a patriarchal society, the difference merely being in the sex which exercises power. But in fact the relationship is quite different, for in advanced patriarchal societies men's power depends upon the fact that they are producers, whereas women are economically dependent. In primitive society, however, where private property scarcely exists, no such relationship is possible and the conception of authority is not understood.

It is the development of private property and the desire of the male to possess it which is the commonest cause of the change from matriarchy to patriarchy, the other frequent motive being the desire for a monopoly of certain magical powers. The term 'mother-right', which is so often employed in speaking of matriarchies, therefore contains a misleading implication, for it assumes the notion of established claims, which are in fact peculiar to patriarchal societies. The primitive ascendancy of women is founded not on economic power but on the constitution of the social group. The primitive human group is matriarchal for the same reasons that the animal group is matriarchal. The group subserves the maternal instincts and is governed by them, but this fact does not impose a female domination on the male.

Where the matriarchal order exists after the development of private property, and such wealth continues to remain in the hands of the women, the result is indeed a female economic domination, similar to that of men in patriarchies. This state of affairs may be called a gynaecocracy, as distinct from primitive matriarchy.

This does not mean that there are not distinctive economic relations in the primitive group. The sole form of wealth and power at such levels consists in power to produce, and the advantage in such power is in favour of the women, for in primitive society women are the chief producers. This power is associated with agriculture, which appertains to women, for the productiveness of the hunter can never go beyond hand-to-mouth subsistence.

Women's Labour

It is precisely because the women sustain the main burden of labour that they are in a position of independence, and it is a fallacy to suppose that the hard work which they do is an indication of inferiority. No labour in primitive society is other than voluntary. Numerous accounts exist of the slavery and oppression of North American squaws; they rest upon complete misunderstanding. 'The work is not only voluntarily but cheerfully performed', Father Theodat observes. 'It is perfectly voluntary labour. All labour with Indians is voluntary', says Schoolcraft. Furthermore, though the women work hard, the work of the men is generally far more strenuous and dangerous. The women themselves say that they have no hardship, for while their labour in the fields employs them, at most, for six weeks in the year, the men work the whole year. A single man may have to find food for as many as fifteen people. He may have to walk twenty-five or thirty miles over rough ground, fasting, in order to find game and may have to drag home an 150 lb. deer.

Some travellers have noted that, when savage people make a journey, the women bear the burdens while the men only carry weapons: but such an arrangement is essential both for safety and to free the men to take advantage of any game which may be encountered.

What is true of North American Indian society is true of almost all primitive societies. Even where women are roughly handled, as in Australia or Melanesia, this treatment is not used to compel them to do tasks against their will. The state of such women is by no means so oppressed as one might imagine. Thus a missionary writes of the Zulus: 'Whoever has observed the happy appearance of the women at their work, their gaiety and chatter, their laughter and song . . . let him compare them with the bearing of our own working women.' And as Shepstone says: 'The labour performed by the women bears no comparison to what is performed by the women of the lower classes in England. . . . As a rule, women only work during these eight weeks in the year.'

How did this division of labour between the sexes arise? Among mammals there is no economic division of labour except in so far as the mothers of the young carnivora assist them in procuring food. The same is true of the higher primates; in a band of gorillas each animal, male or female, forages for itself. No doubt, primitive humanity was also mainly frugivorous, and in those conditions very little division of labour could take place. As we shall presently see, in primitive society there is very incomplete division of labour. Women hunted equally with men and fishing was done more commonly by the women than the men. It was the development of hunting which finally established the primitive division of labour between the sexes.

This division of labour was not chiefly determined by the respective aptitudes of the sexes, nor by any physical inferiority in women, but by woman's need to care for her offspring, which prevented her from undertaking pursuits entailing prolonged absence. This handicap is much greater in mankind than in any animal species, because of the much longer duration of infancy. An Iroquois myth recognizes this, representing early men and women as hunting together in the forest, whereas when children were born there were so many things for the wife to do that she stayed at home.

Physical Difference between the Sexes

The disparities between men and women in physical power, enterprise and capacity for endurance, observed in civilized societies, are often regarded as due to organic differences, but they are much less marked among primitive men and women. Such differences are often assumed to be the cause of the division of labour, but seem to be largely a result of it.

Throughout most of the animal kingdom the females are larger and more powerful than the males. This is true, for instance, of all spiders, all teleosteous fishes, all snakes, most lizards and many birds, as well as invertebrates generally. But among mammals the male is almost invariably larger. It would appear that there is some correlation between the physiological development of motherhood, prolonged pregnancy, etc., and the reduced size of females among mammals. But, though the mammalian female is generally smaller, there is no sign of physical inferiority. On the contrary, female carnivores are more formidable than the males. 'A lioness', says Mr Rainsford, 'is, I think I am safe in saying, a hundred per cent more dangerous than a lion.'

While women are generally smaller than the men of the same race, even this is not invariably true. Thus among the Bushmen the women are, on an average, about four centimetres taller than the men, and among the Adombies of the Congo the women are reportedly stronger and better-developed than the men, as also among the Ashira, the Bashilanga, the Wateita and others. In Dahomey 'the women are generally tall, muscular and broad, and the men smooth, full-breasted, round-limbed and effeminate-looking'. A Kikuyu man is quite unequal to carrying a load that his women think nothing of. The same is true of the Manyema women of the Congo, the Krus, the Iyashi of Nigeria, the Lala tribes and others. Similar reports come from Patagonia, Tierra del Fuego, Tibet, the Khasi women of Assam, the Gond tribes of Central India, the Chinwan of Formosa, the Dayaks and others. In Butan, the women carry the men on their backs when travelling.

Speaking generally, the physical differences between the sexes are less pronounced in primitive races than among civilized peoples. In prehistoric skeletons, the determination of sex is often difficult, since the bones are as massive in the female as in the male, while the muscular attachments are nearly as pronounced. Among the Bushmen, it is often difficult to distinguish the sexes in life, even where the individuals are almost naked. (The breasts constitute no distinction. They are so developed in the males that these are sometimes able to suckle.) Similar difficulties are reported by Phillips of the Lower Congo races, and of the Eskimo and other peoples.

Women as Hunters and Fishers and as Warriors

That men took on the labour of hunting was not due to incapacity on the part of the women. In British Columbia the women used to hunt; the women of New Spain and of Nicaragua hunted regularly; the same is reported from Tierra del Fuego, Tibet, West Africa, Tasmania and elsewhere. Procopius mentions certain barbarians of Thule among whom men and women hunted together.

Fishing is often exclusively a women's occupation (as for instance among the Bambala, the Tasmanians, the Fuegians), and in some seasons the women provide the whole food supply of a tribe.

In short, the primitive division of labour has become established more by a spirit of professional exclusiveness than by a difference in aptitude.

Similarly the tendency of the man to take on the role of warrior and fighter is also due to economic necessity, rather than to any constitutional incapacity of women. In New Guinea, Malaya and many parts of the Pacific, including New Zealand and Hawaii, women were accustomed to fight alongside the men, and in the Ladrones they fought under female leaders. As late as 1900, when punitive expeditions were sent against an inland tribe in Papua, the police found that the houses were garrisoned by as many women as men. Women frequently accompanied the men to war among the North American Indians; the title of 'Beloved' was bestowed upon those who had distinguished themselves by warlike deeds. During their expedition on the Klamath in 1854, the US troops frequently saw women fighting or found them dead. 'One day the savages came suddenly upon them . . . filling the air with a perfect shower of arrows. But not a male barbarian was in sight. Before them, in serried line of battle, their women were moving to the charge, while the warriors slunk behind them, discharging their arrows between the women.' In the province of Cartagena the Spaniards found that 'the women fight as well as the men'. Columbus and his companions were attacked by female archers.

In many Arab countries the women fight with the men; the Sultan of Zanzibar had an army of six thousand female soldiers. These were certainly not ornamental. In the case of the famous corps of Amazons of Dahomey, to whom King Gueso owed his safety, the women alone stood their ground, in spite of appalling losses, while the rest of the army scattered. Their strenuous training involves taking fortified positions by assault, charging through obstacles formed by cactus and spikes and, as they march past after these sham fights, their bodies stream with blood and the skin hangs in shreds from their torn limbs.

The Tartar and Mongol women of Central Asia have long been noted for their war-like qualities; Matthew Paris, describing the Mongol hordes of Jinghis Khan, refers to the fierceness of their wives who 'fight like the men'. The kings of Siam used to keep an Amazonian guard, as did the Nizam of Hyderabad; the kings of Kandy kept a body-guard of female archers, as did the Persian kings. Of the ancient Scythians, Diodorus reports that 'the women fight like the men and are in no wise inferior to them in bravery'. There is therefore no reason to dismiss the Greek accounts of their battles with Asiatic Amazons.

Celtic women regularly followed their male relatives in war, and such military service was not abolished until 590. Irish literature abounds with references to war-like women. Tradition preserves the memory of chieftainesses such as Geraldine Desmond who 'was of a fierce and restless character', and led her clansmen constantly into frays, killing all who opposed her.

When the Romans had their first terrible encounter with the overflowing barbarian tide at Aquae Sextiae, 'the fight had been no less fierce with the women than with the men themselves'. When the barbarian onslaught broke, the women erected barricades and fought fiercely amidst the mountains of dead; when summoned to surrender, they killed their children, slaughtered one another and hanged themselves on trees. Among the slain Marcomanni and Quadi, the Romans found the bodies of women in full armour. Several of the Gothic warriors taken prisoner turned out to be women, and the same was observed by the Byzantines when they were attacked by the Varangians. Queen Boudicca boasted that British women were quite as good warriors as the men.

Of the endurance and courage of primitive women, an even more general test is constituted by their behaviour in childbirth. Though childbirth appears to be, as a rule, easier with primitive than with civilized women, nevertheless their endurance is remarkable, and in many tribes if a woman uttered a cry during labour she would be disgraced.

Primitive Industry

Thus it is clear that the differentiation of men as hunters was not due to the more limited powers of endurance of women. At the same time, the industrial occupations which give rise to material culture belong in the rudest societies almost exclusively to the women. All industries were at first home industries, and developed therefore in the hands of the women.

The preparation of skin as apparel was a function of women, and was carried to high levels of skill. The scrapers used by Eskimo women today for preparing skins are identical with those found in the drift gravels of the Ice Age, and in South Africa the country is strewn with scrapers, manufactured by the women of the Bush tribes, which are identical with those of Palæolithic Europe. The flint arrow-heads of the Seri Indians, which are identical in type with those of Palæolithic Europe, are said to be manufactured by the women.

The decorations on a fur robe and the combination of various furs may be so elaborate that it may take a whole year to complete a single garment. The sewing and ornamenting of robes even form the chief purpose of a kind of 'secret society' among North American Indians; a society from which men were excluded.

A similar development occurs in those areas where women concentrate on weaving or plaiting. Thus in New Zealand, where there are at least twelve different styles of mats differing in the fashion of plaiting, each is the speciality of the women of a particular tribe. Initiation into the art was conducted as a religious ceremony; a consecrated workshop was reserved for the purpose, and if a man entered the precincts all work was stopped and put aside. Similarly, among the Manipur tribes, cloth in ten different patterns is produced in certain villages only, this industry being carried on by the women alone.

Pottery

The art of pottery is likewise found in the hands of women among all primitive peoples. Only under the influence of advanced culture does it become a man's occupation. Thus, out of seventy-eight tribes investigated by the ethnologists attached to the Belgian Congo Museum, 'the men had no hand whatever in the making of pottery in sixty-seven'; the others 'are exceptions arising from special circumstances which in almost every instance it is easy to trace'. If we follow the course of the Nile we find a complete series, from Nubia where, at the present day, the pottery is made exclusively by the women, through Upper Egypt, where the head-potter is a man with women working under him, to Lower Egypt where the pottery is made by the men. And there is no reasonable doubt that prehistoric pottery was the work of women. Remains found in the lacustrine dwellings of Switzerland bear numerous imprints of thumbs and fingers; undoubtedly those of women.

In this field, too, the art becomes a mystery, the secrets being transmitted in the female line. Every Samoki woman must be proficient in the art, but she is forbidden to practise it if she marries in another district. The same thing is noted in Ceram and among the Massims of New Guinea. Pottery is unknown in most parts of Melanesia, but in those where it exists it is likewise a monopoly handed down from mother to daughter. In East Africa, among the Nandi, no man may go near the hut where women are engaged in making pottery, and if a man should take a woman's pot he would be sure to die. In Manipur if a man approaches while a woman is making pots they will crack in the firing; as also in Brazil among the Tupis.

The Greek tradition that the first 'patera' was moulded on the breast of Helen is illustrated by the practice of the Zuñi women who, as of old, make their pitchers in the shape of a female breast. The nipple is left open to the last and the sealing of it is performed with the solemnity of a religious rite. The vessel is thus assimilated to the woman herself, for unless this ritual were observed that woman might be barren. Such an assimilation is widespread. In the earliest Egyptian hieroglyphics the pot is the symbol of womanhood, and vases used among the archaic populations of the Ægean were frequently in the shape of a woman. In Greece the pot was an emblem of fecundity. In Cyprus, at Lithrodonto, a potter of today puts two little dabs of moist clay on the right and left side of the rounded surface, slightly above the middle, little knowing why he does so. But vases disinterred by archaeologists from tombs 2,500 years old display numerous specimens with the same finishing touch—the two dabs representing two breasts. 'The Mother Pot is really a fundamental conception in all religions,' observes Dr Elliott Smith, 'and is almost world-wide in its distribution.'

The sacred vessels used in religious cults often retain their archaic character. Thus the pots used by the Roman vestals were, even in the height of Roman splendour, made in the coarsest fashion without the use of a wheel, and were spoken of as 'Numa's crockery'. There can be little doubt that in early times the potters were the vestals themselves. In the same manner the vestals of Peru served their God in very coarse vessels of clay, until the Incas, shocked at this, had them replaced by vessels of gold. The Zuñi women, with an aesthetic sense that would have rejoiced Ruskin, scorn the wheel—a comparatively late development—as giving a machine-made appearance to the products, and trust entirely to the eye.[1]

Thus we may conclude that the art of pottery was a feminine invention.

---

[1] The patterns with which the clay is ornamented are commonly derived from the braiding of basket-work, and early pots were no doubt shaped in or upon baskets. Much contemporary pottery preserves these patterns, and the 'Greek fret' need be no more than a basketry version of a 'loop-coil' meander.

Building

We are not accustomed to think of architecture as a feminine occupation. Yet, just as the animal builds its nest or burrow, so also primitive woman was the actual home-builder. The huts of the Australian, of the Andaman islanders, of the Patagonians, of the Botocudos, the rough shelters of the Seri, the skin lodges and wigwams of the American Indian, the black camel-hair tent of the Bedouin, the 'yurts' of the nomads of Central Asia, are all the exclusive work of women. But even the most elaborate buildings of the uncultured world were fashioned by women. The earth-lodges of the Omahas were built entirely by them, as were the elaborate pueblos of New Mexico and Arizona, with their court-yards and piazzas. Among the Zuñi today the men assist with the heavier work of timbering; but among the Hopis the work is still done entirely by the women. When the first Spanish priests settled among the Pueblo Indians, no man had ever set his hand to the erection of a house. In the building of the larger and more substantial timber houses most of the heavy work is generally undertaken by the men, but the tradition of the primitive division of labour survives in the fact that the men are invariably assisted by the women. In Samoa, for instance, the women do the thatching, though the men erect the framework. In Egypt even in the present day the building is done by the women, and the assistants of the master builder are invariably girls.

It is a significant detail that, in most parts of the uncultured world, the maximum of care is bestowed on buildings in which food is stored, and which therefore belong to the province of women. Sir Charles Fellows was one of the first to remark that the food stores in Lykia and other parts of Asia Minor at the present day are the exact counterpart of the ancient tombs and temples.

The primitive temples of Greece were built of wood. The earliest temple of Delphi was a thatched hut. In Lydia, the dwelling-houses, as Herodotus mentions, were mostly built of reeds and mud. There can be little doubt that, like the African kraals which they resembled, they were built by the women. The most imposing monument in the country, the heroon of Alyattes, bore on one of its columns an inscription stating that, for the most part, it had been built by women.

Primitive Trade

Since all surplus production belongs to the women, both as cultivators of the soil and as keepers of the food store, it is theirs to dispose of. In all early culture, the barter and traffic is in the hands of the women. This is true throughout Africa, where trade is almost exclusively carried on by the women. Formerly the North American fur trade was in the hands of the women who prepared the skins. In Nicaragua 'a man may not enter the market or even see the proceedings, at the risk of a beating'. Throughout Central Asia trading is entirely in the hands of the women, as Marco Polo also reported. This is also true of Tibet, Burma and many parts of the Pacific.

Medicine and Surgery

The search of women for edible vegetables acquainted them with the properties of herbs and made them the first doctors. The word 'medicine', and the name Medea, the medical herbalist witch, come from the same root—a root meaning knowledge or wisdom.

Primitive medicine is of course for the most part a department of magic, and women, as we shall see, were the primitive practitioners of this art. In addition, in many areas the women are the surgeons and treat all injuries received in warfare. Thus, throughout the primitive populations of Indonesia, the treatment of the sick is almost exclusively in the hands of medicine-women. Among the Land Dayaks, while there are both male and female doctors, the service of women is regarded as more valuable and is more highly remunerated. Among many North American tribes, as also among the Eskimos, the profession is practised solely by the old women. The same is true in Patagonia, Chile, Mexico and elsewhere.

In early Arabia and down to the Middle Ages the treatment of wounds and the practice of medicine were recognized occupations of women, and even at the present day this tradition survives in the more secluded Muslim countries. Among the ancient Germans, Scandinavians and the inhabitants of Gaul, women were regarded as especially qualified in medicine.

In short, to a far greater extent than is generally realized, the sexual differences between men and women are products of social development. Primitive woman is anything but 'effeminate', and is as capable as the man of providing for herself, if she is not indeed his superior.

It is commonly supposed that the facts of primitive matriarchy favour the doctrine of feminism—that is, the view that women are fitted for all the pursuits which in our society are regarded as masculine. This view, whether correct or not, does not follow from the respective capacities of men and women in primitive society. The predominance of women in primitive society, which appears to some so paradoxical, would be largely restored in our own society if culture were limited to the range of activities of the primitive household.

In the spheres which are important at this cultural level, intellectual advantage is with the female. She is more wary and ingenious than the male, and it is little wonder that the savage habitually goes to his womenfolk for advice. In many societies it has been remarked that the women are mentally higher than the men, and they are far more self-possessed. For instance, according to Mr Landor, 'the Tibetan woman is far superior to the Tibetan man. She possesses a better heart, more pluck and a finer character than he does. Time after time, when the male, timid beyond description, ran away at our approach, the women remained in charge of the tents and, although by no means cool and collected, they very rarely failed to meet us without a show of dignity.' The same thing may be observed in the ruder strata of western society: the French peasant woman, for instance, is a more intelligent, alert and less awkward person than her man.

Position of Chiefs

It has sometimes been thought that the fact that in matriarchal societies the headman or chief is commonly a man is an argument against the view that primitive society was essentially matriarchal. This is due to a misunderstanding: the position of the headman in primitive societies entailed nothing of authority, for there is no such authority in truly primitive societies. Those whom the whites call headmen are usually little more than spokesmen, put forward to voice the views of the group and without any power to act on their own initiative. In Northern Melanesia, the transacting of any business with the natives is 'rendered very difficult by the fact that they have no chiefs', while in New Caledonia the chiefs have 'absolutely no political power'. Among the tribes of Assam, 'each village is a small republic and each man as good as his neighbour; indeed, it would be hard to find anywhere else more thoroughly democratic communities. Headmen do exist, but their authority is very small.'

Such tribes have often found the necessity of appointing a leader for hunting or war. Thus a missionary reports of the Indians of Brazil, that 'they know neither princes nor kings; each family regards itself as absolutely free; every Indian looks upon himself as independent. As the continual wars which they have to wage against their neighbours place that liberty in danger, they have learnt the necessity of forming a sort of society, and they choose a chief who is called "cacique". But in choosing him, their intention is not to give themselves a master but a protector and father under whose guidance they desire to place themselves.' Similarly, among the Iroquois, the chiefs are nothing more than the most respected among their equals in rank. Their principal duty is to conduct negotiations, and if they make a mistake they are reprimanded or dismissed.

Among the Arabs, the chief is merely 'influential', and is obliged at every turn to consult the tribal council. Even in Africa, the land of despots, the chiefs are not always what the European assumes. Often they are no more than war-leaders. Thus Dundas states, of a number of tribes of East Africa: 'After the most careful inquiry . . . I feel convinced that these tribes have no heads or leaders who could be dignified with the names of chiefs.'

Thus the existence of male chiefs in primitive social groups, far from constituting a difficulty as regards their matriarchal nature, appears, on the contrary, to prove the impossibility that such groups could ever have been formed in the first instance around the authority of a dominant male. Such domination is incompatible with the equalitarian character of primitive societies.

The desire to dominate takes different forms in men and women. Woman's ambition is not to exercise physical compulsion, but to bend the will of others to her desire, to overcome not physical but psychical resistances. Her object is to have her way. The man, however, delights in the display of power, is flattered by hostile envy and desires his power to be felt and known. Thus it is that, where tribes have conquered other peoples, the war-leader has acquired absolute authority over them.

The point is further emphasized by the fact that, in matriarchal communities, the authority of the male headman is even more insignificant than in other primitive communities. Thus among the Seri the chief appears to do little more than communicate the decisions of the matrons to the men; he is not chosen with regard to his own qualifications but to those of his wife. In Khyrim, the chieftainship is limited to the male relatives of the high-priestess. Among the Pelew Islanders the authority of male chiefs is exercised over the men only; women do not even salute them, and they can take no action without consulting the council of matrons.

But even when the theory of male rule has become fully developed, the authority of the woman is completely recognized within the home and the economy of the family. The primitive division of functions has sometimes left its trace in comparatively advanced communities. In Hawaii the administration of all internal affairs was under the control of the queen, the king being concerned with foreign politics only.

Position of the Woman's Brother

In his character of warrior, the man is defender of the home, and in him is vested the executive power of action in the relation between the home and a hostile environment. But the male to whom a woman looks for this protection is not her sexual mate but her brother. The word brother, in Sanskrit 'bhratr', comes from the root 'bhr', to support.

The position of the eldest brother of the woman is so well-known a feature of primitive society that it need not be described in detail. It has frequently survived the original constitution. Thus, in North America the relationship of uncles is, in several particulars, more important than any other. In every part of the African continent the mother's brother is responsible for his sister's children. For instance, on the Gold Coast a man may chastise or even sell his sister's children, but in no circumstances may he do so with his own, since they do not belong to his family but to the mother's. Among the Adiokru of the Ivory Coast province, legitimate children are under the care of their father, illegitimate children (who suffer no social disability) under the care of their mother's brother—the matriarchal and patriarchal customs thus existing side by side. Among the natives of Timorlaut, although the social organization is now essentially patriarchal, the mother's brother occupies a fundamental position and performs most of the parental functions.

We have already noticed this relationship among the ancient Germans, and we have found distinct traces of it in primitive Rome. Among the Christian Ossetes of the Caucasus, before a man can marry he must present a horse to the bride's maternal uncle. Today no social organization is more definitely patriarchal than theirs. In Krete, in the seventh century BC, when patriarchal usages had become well-established, a woman's illegitimate children were brought up by her brother.

The brother is also the partner in the economic association which constitutes the primitive group. Moreover, the main object of a woman's affection is her brother rather than her sexual mate. If we have grasped the fact that the extension of affection towards the male has the sole object of enlisting his co-operation, we shall have no difficulty in understanding why a woman's affection for her brother may be as lively as that for her husband—if not indeed more real, for sexual love always contains a hidden element of opposition. In primitive societies, the bonds between brother and sister are generally stronger than those between husband and wife, and the existence of the latter is often doubted. Thus among the Hovas of Madagascar, where love between husband and wife is said to be 'not even thought of', there is 'no lack of affection between brothers and sisters'. The closest relation existed between brother and sister among the North American Indians: if a young warrior captured a horse it was to his sister that he presented it; it was invariably his sister who advanced to meet him when he returned from battle. Even where traditional usages of avoidance place a barrier between brother and sister, as in New Caledonia, they remain extremely fond of each other. In Samoa, the relationship is regarded as 'semi-sacred'.

In Sophocles' *Antigone*, the heroine sacrifices herself not for her lover, who plays a subordinate part in the drama, but for her brother, and expresses emphatically her reasons for the preference. This passage horrified Goethe, but exactly the same sentiments are expressed in the oldest Teutonic literature. Herodotus also relates how the wife of Intaphernes, when Darius gave her the boon of asking for the life of one of her kinsmen, chose her brother, and this so pleased Darius that he gave her the life of her eldest son also.

A widely current Arab proverb reproduces this reasoning. 'A husband can be found, a son can be borne, but a brother cannot be replaced.'

The Marital Group Family

Prescientific theorists have generally regarded the family as the original unit of primitive society, for as an eighteenth-century writer elegantly puts it: 'The husband and the wife of his bosom, whom love unites by the silken ties of matrimony, form the first society; this union is first founded on the call of nature, in mutual assistance, and the sweet hopes of seeing themselves reproduced in numerous offspring.' The facts of ethnology do not accord with this dogma. Primitive social organization, on the contrary, is based on common blood and on derivation from the same womb—the so-called uterine family. Thus among the Fanti, each family includes members of the mother's side only; the mother and all her children, male and female belong to her family, as do her mother and maternal uncles and aunts, but her father and all his relatives are nothing to her nor are her husband nor any of his relatives.

In many primitive societies there is no word for the concept of family, though there may be a word which indicates marriage. Thus Mr Joelson says, speaking of the natives of East Africa generally: 'For want of a better word, I must needs refer to the Negro "family", but my readers will realise that the term in this connection is used to convey an idea essentially different from the construction put upon it in modern society.' Of the 'family' in West Africa, Clozel said: 'Although apparently it resembles that of European societies with father, mother and children, the father's authority scarcely exists and from the civil point of view he is not the parent of his children. The true family among the Alladian only takes account of the uterine parentage'. Among the Wyandots, says Mr Powell, 'the family household is not a unit, as two gentes are represented in each, the father must belong to one gens, the mother and her children to another'. 'The Indians consider their wives as strangers', says an old missionary. 'It is a common saying among them, "My wife is not my friend", that is "she is not related to me and I need not care for her".'

The husband was isolated; plans and secrets existed among the members of the gens rather than between husband and wife. The children do not regard their father as a relative by blood; if he requires assistance they consider that 'his people' should look after him. In disputes, the children and the father in primitive society fought on opposite sides. Among the Haidas 'it appears as if marriage were an alliance between opposite tribes, a man begetting offspring rather for his wife than for himself, and being inclined to see his real descendants rather in his sister's children than in his own. Husbands and wives did not hesitate to betray each other to death in the interests of their own families'. Among the Goajiros, we are told again in so many words, 'what we call the family does not exist'. Numerous other cases can be instanced.

Not only does the family not exist as a juridic or social unit, it frequently does not even comprise a physical association. It is common in primitive society for husband and wife to live apart. In New Caledonia 'domestic life does not exist'. Men and women are seldom seen talking or sitting together. The men generally associate with other men and live in their club-house. The Nayar husband is not even permitted to take food in his wife's house; indeed, it is a universal rule in India that men and women do not eat together. There is no common life between husband and wife in China; the house is divided into two and the sexes live in separate compartments. In Korea 'family life as we have it is quite unknown'. The same is true of the Eskimo. There was scarcely any intercourse between men and women in any of the North American tribes; a man did not take his meals with his wife, and rarely spoke to her in public. So fundamental was the custom that it was kept up by the completely Christianized and semi-Europeanized Indians living on the outskirts of Quebec. Similar customs can be found among the Pueblo Indians, the Caribbean tribes, the Carajas of Brazil and in many parts of Africa.

Even more extraordinary in our eyes is the fact that the husband is commonly a clandestine and surreptitious visitor to his wife. One of the Japanese words for marriage is 'yome-iri', which may be interpreted 'to slip by night into the house', and this is the common mode of connubial intercourse among many primitive peoples. Among the Khasis 'the husband came to his mother-in-law's home only after dark, and he did not eat, smoke, or even take betel-nut there'. Among the Tipperah, the Takut, the Samoyeds, the Kurils, the Tartars and other tribes, the husband slips surreptitiously to his wife's room after dark and leaves before dawn. If a Tartar is seen leaving, he receives a sound drubbing from his wife's relatives. In Khorassan, it was the rule for the mother of the bride to introduce the bridegroom secretly into the house by the back door, and he had to depart before dawn. Among the Cherkiss the husband gets in through the window; much the same is true throughout the Caucasus.

The same practice was found in the primitive community of Sparta. It is reported from Africa, and of the Algonkin and Iroquois in North

America, the Caribs of the West Indies and many tribes of New Guinea, as well as those of Fiji and elsewhere.

The idea that this behaviour was due to some innate sense of delicacy, though met with in apologetic literature, cannot be taken seriously, for those natives who would be filled with confusion if seen approaching the hut of their wife have at the same time no scruple against indulging in promiscuity, and even incest, *coram populo*. There is good reason to suppose that the relations between husband and wife were attended with real danger. The beating which the Tartar husband incurs, if detected, is more than a ritual; and similarly in Kamchatka it is 'beyond a joke'. A Russian story describes how a suitor, when he finally obtained his bride, was unfortunately rendered impotent by the barbarous treatment he received. Among the Mongols not only the bridegroom but all his male friends were thrashed by the dowagers of the bride's family. The same sort of thing, it would appear, happened in ancient Arabia. Among certain Germanic tribes patrilocal wedding appears to have been somewhat risky; the ancient laws of Frisia provided for the bridegroom being murdered during the ceremony—the bride was instructed to follow his corpse home if she wished to claim her share of the inheritance. Many of the customs which have been described as survivals of 'marriage by capture' are in reality manifestations of this general hostility between the wives' and husbands' group, especially when it is required that the woman should leave her group and join her husband's tribe. Swanton goes so far as to say that among the Haidas the members of the two clans regarded each other as downright enemies.

Accordingly it is difficult to believe that the family as we know it was the germ of social organization, and that society was formed by the aggregation of family groups. Indeed, it is clear that the patriarchal family group is actually in direct conflict with the instincts which have determined human association. The basic group which the patriarchal group has superseded is the Motherhood—that is, the mother and her offspring. It follows that the primitive social instincts of society are not the sexual instincts but the maternal instincts and the ties of kinship that derive from them. To these forces sexual instincts are secondary. 'Love of the clan', says an old Arab poet, 'is greater than the love between husband and wife.'

CHAPTER 9

The Institution of Marriage

WHAT is the origin of marriage? It is sometimes said that the purpose of marriage is the procreation of children, but evidently marriage is not essential to procreation. Among animals, mating is far rarer than is supposed. There is no evidence of it among the anthropoid apes, and among those mammals which do mate it usually takes the form of an association which nearly all human races would regard as incestuous. Although certain birds and mammals gain economic advantages by associating, this is not so in maternal clans, where these advantages are already secured by the female's association with brothers or with other males of the group who are not sexual partners.

In some communities only a small minority of the people enter into marriage, even though the marriage institutions are themselves fairly elaborate. For example, among the Line Islanders marriage is a method for conveying landed property, and only the property-owning class marries. In the Society Islands marriage seems to have been confined to the higher class of chiefs; while in the Pageh Islands marriage is sometimes contracted by elderly men who wish to provide a home for their old age.

Even those who seriously believe that husband and wife constitute the primary social unit recognize that marriage is a social institution and not an instinctive necessity. Most peoples in all stages of culture have held this view. The Roman jurists were quite clear on the point. They made a basic distinction between natural and social or juridic facts. Natural law, they said, is what nature has taught all animals; it is not a law peculiar to the human race. The maternal relation, they considered, was a natural fact, but the paternal relationship belonged to the sphere of juridic institutions. Again, matrimony is the name of a natural fact, for it derives from the relation of motherhood; marriage, however, is the name of a civil institution.

In many traditions, marriage is stated to be a relatively late institution. The Greeks believed that marriage had been instituted by Kekrops, and that previously promiscuous cohabitation had been the custom. The Chinese thought similarly, substituting Fu-Hi for Kekrops, while the Peruvians attributed the establishment of marriage to Manco-Capac.

Even such uncultured people as the Lapps, the Wogul and the Australian savages attribute the invention of marriage to some traditional legislator.

If there were really any 'mating instinct' which determined marriage, such an instinct should, in primitive society at least, take precedence over all other considerations. The personal desire of a man and woman to enter into a fundamental association should be the basis of the social order; but in point of fact the exact reverse is the case. It is regarded almost everywhere as irregular that a man and a woman should spontaneously form such an association on their own initiative. Such a thing would have shocked our own grandmothers; and the Australian Blackfellows, like most other savages, would have shared their feelings. Marriage, on the contrary, is a matter arranged by the families: among the Hidatsa Indians a marriage not so arranged is scarcely looked upon as deserving the name of marriage; indeed, they do not call it a marriage, but have a special term for so disreputable a relationship. The same is true among the Haidas; a West African negro explained in court that a certain person would hardly be regarded as better than a bastard since 'his parents married for love'. Among the Malays of the Patini States, a runaway match is not regarded as legal. This is, in fact, almost universally true in primitive society. Even in England, where personal freedom in such matters has always been greater than in most other countries, up to the eighteenth century a marriage without parental consent was null and void when one of the parties was under the age of twenty-one, and the position is similar in most other European countries today.

In Russia, 'among the upper classes the bride and bridegroom never saw each other before the wedding; among the people they saw each other but never dared to speak about marriage, that being a thing which did not depend upon themselves'. Among the Romans marriage was purely a family contract, and in ancient Athens, 'we have not a single instance of a man having loved a free-born woman and marrying her from affection'. The Spartans, who represent a more primitive state of Greek society, 'considered marriage not as a private relation . . . but as a public institution'. The same views obtained among the barbarians of Northern Europe. The laws of the Aryas expressly condemn as immoral 'the voluntary union of a maid and her lover'. Such unions are 'blameable marriages'.

In China the most fundamental principle of the elaborate marriage institution is that marriage is an alliance between two families, and that the bride and bridegroom have no concern in it—so much so that it is not uncommon for two families to be united by matrimonial alliance, even though one, or both, of the parties concerned is dead. Furthermore, the negotiations must be conducted by a professional go-between, and the young people first make each other's acquaintance when the transaction is completed. Any infringement of this rule is looked upon as profoundly immoral. 'When children do not await the decision of their fathers and mothers and the words of the go-betweens, but bore holes in walls in order to see each other, leap over walls in order to meet, their fathers and mothers and all the people of the realm despise and condemn them.'

Marriages negotiated by Go-betweens

Go-betweens are, indeed, used widely; in Australia, for example; in Borneo, among the Dayaks; in the Ladrones, the Banks and Loyalty Islands; in Africa among the Basutos and Bambara, as well as a number of other African peoples. They are an indispensable institution among the Arabs, as well as among many South American tribes. Among the North American Indians, 'courtship is always begun by proxy'. Go-betweens are found in much the same forms in Tibet, upper Burma and among the Tamil populations of Ceylon, as in Cambodia, Cochin-China, Siam, Java, Formosa and the Philippines. In Europe the same is true among the Poles, the various Slav races and the Finns.

In many societies the marriage is arranged when the parties concerned are still infants, a practice by no means confined to sophisticated aristocracies. The allotting of girls at birth, or before, is the universal rule among the Australian aborigines.[1] The usage is prevalent, though not universal, throughout Melanesia, and was common in the case of men of distinction among the Polynesians.[2] It is general in New Guinea, and the children are commonly married and cohabit when hardly able to toddle.[3] It is found in every part of Micronesia and the Philippines, although there it is an occasional means of cementing an alliance between families and not a general practice. It is common in Indonesia, it is very prevalent among all the peoples of Northern Asia, and appears to be almost universal among the Turkic populations. As is well-known, it is an obligatory practice among the Hindus, and appears to be an original usage with the Tamil populations. It is the rule among the primitive forest tribes of Malaya; and in Africa, where marriage by purchase has reached its highest development, that purchasing power is extensively used to secure girls in infancy. Though prevalent among the Eskimo and Alaskan tribes, it is comparatively rare among the North American races of the eastern regions and the plains. Infant betrothal is also general in South America.

---

[1] A bibliography of forty-two titles is appended in support of these and the following assertions in the unabridged edition.
[2] A bibliography of forty-three titles is appended.
[3] A bibliography of fifteen titles is appended.

Where patriarchy is the rule, it is almost invariably the father who has the right to dispose of his daughters, as for example among the Kaffirs of South Africa. Among the Papuans of Geelvink Bay, the father obtains a wife for his son while the latter is still an infant. Sometimes the selection of a wife is left to a chief or king, as among the Bantu. In matriarchal societies and those which have preserved matriarchal traditions, the duty often devolves upon the maternal uncle, and it is his consent which is essential among the North American Indians. This idea is so inherent in Indian thought that a current proverb asks: 'If a girl is not given in marriage by her mother's brother, then who will give her?' We have already noticed the same fact in many parts of Africa. Elsewhere, however, it is the mothers of the respective families who arrange the marriages, as among the Western Eskimo. Among the North American Indians, 'the first proceedings must be initiated by the matrons'. (Though it is the father who gives his consent.)

Personal Inclinations

Some writers think this custom tyrannous; others note that the personal wishes of the parties are often deferred to. These opposed points of view rest upon a misconception—upon the fallacy of attributing to primitive humanity sentiments which are really peculiar to advanced cultures. The majority of those concerned have no personal preferences in the selection of partners and, in general, there is no objection to the selection made by the authorities. Where objection is made it is often deferred to, and frequently the objection is only to the partner being too old, not an objection to his particular personality. The selection of a wife is often undertaken by the authorities at the young man's request; it is a wife he wants, not a particular young woman. Thus among the Basutos, when a young man wishes to marry, all he does is to drive the cows out of the kraal and let the calves be suckled by their mothers. This conventional sign is understood, and the young man's parents immediately set about procuring a wife for him. A Catholic missionary among the Déné relates how the Indians often consulted him about a proposed match, and he at first endeavoured to give them his best advice as to the pros and cons of the alliance. He soon discovered that what they wanted was not advice but a peremptory order to marry. Often, too, he would be told by those whose marriage had turned out unhappy that they were perfectly aware when they married that they could not agree, but they were told to marry and therefore had no option. Similarly, among the Bataks of Sumatra girls readily refuse suitors possessing every attraction in order to marry the young man to whom they are assigned by custom. If questioned, they say: 'It is the custom. What else is one to do?'

So universal a practice could not have arisen or have been maintained in equalitarian primitive societies had there been any real antagonism between such actions and the individual desires of each member. It is easy to show that in such contracts the wishes of individuals are very seldom set aside. In West Africa, for example, should a girl refuse to fulfil the contract, 'the tendency is not to bring compulsion to bear on the woman but to enforce restitution of the dowry paid to the girl's father'. Indeed, the deference paid to the personal objections of the young man or woman is much more marked in primitive societies than in most civilized communities where prearranged marriages are the rule. The individualistic interests aroused by the profitable disposal of marriageable daughters may, on the other hand, lead to the use of coercion, and an incompatibility which did not originally exist between the wishes of the individual and the authority of the group thus develops. The objections then raised are a sign of the decay of old customs. In the state of society in which such customs originated, there was no conflict between the individual and the tribal will.

Marriages Celebrated among all Members of Two Groups

The authority in such matters derives not from the father but from the group, and defiance of the group's authority is the most heinous of crimes; it is usually punishable by death. But in its original form the group's control refers not to unions between individuals but between *groups* of individuals. A person is bound to marry within a certain group, but within the group freedom of choice is, as a rule, not interfered with. For primitive legislation takes little account of private affairs, and concerns itself exclusively with matters which affect the whole group. Thus, among the Arawak a man is bound to marry—and is, in fact, allotted at birth to—a certain group of females. To marry outside that group would be inconceivably impious, but within it he is free to choose as he pleases. Thus it is that stringent determinism may be combined with the greatest freedom of personal inclination. Countless primitive peoples are in the same situation. Thus among the Gonds, if a brother and a sister have respectively a son and a daughter, it is compulsory for these to marry, but if a girl has several cousins she has the right to choose among them.

In those societies where the father, maternal uncle or mother dispose of the young person, they do so not in their personal capacity but as representatives of the family; it is true that, especially in patriarchal society, this may develop into a personal despotism, but this is a later abuse. The will of the head of the group is rarely exercised without consultation with all its members. Thus when the Malaiali father sets out to find a bride for his son he is accompanied by his relatives, and the first person he approaches is neither the intended bride or her parents but the headman of a neighbouring village. A Kadir young man must work in some village for a year, and then generally has an opportunity of selecting a bride—but before he can enter into any negotiations, he must return home and inform the villagers of his intention and obtain their sanction. The practice of referring a marriage to a tribal council or a whole group is widespread. In New Zealand when a young man married a girl of different tribe, failure to obtain the permission of both might lead to war. Among the Hurons of North America 'proposals made to the girl's mother were submitted by her to the women's council, whose decision was final'; while among the Pawnees a marriage was discussed in a solemn assembly by all the relatives of both parties. In Western Australia the consent of the whole tribe is necessary to the conclusion of a marriage, while in the Gilbert Islands all the males of the clan must signify their consent, as also with the natives of San Cristobal in the Solomons.

The presents which it is customary to exchange on the occasion of a marriage, or the bride-price which is paid, are in many of the most primitive groups supplied by all the relatives of the one group, and distributed among all the members of the other group. Thus among the North American Indians such presents are collected from the husband's kindred and are equally distributed among the members of the wife's family. Among the Araucanians all the relatives share the bride-price. Among the Yakut there are two distinct bride-prices, one payable to the bride's parents and the other to the whole of her clan. In Samoa, the immediate relatives of the bridegroom 'had to go on begging expeditions to all who were connected with them, and collect from them large quantities of property', and the family of the bride did the same. Similar procedures are widespread in every part of Africa. The whole tribe contributes towards the payment among the natives of Central Ceram and the Toradjas of the Central Celebes.

Furthermore, a marriage is commonly celebrated not by the happy couple but by the two families; indeed, the bride and bridegroom are sometimes absent from the ceremony. They do not appear at the wedding celebration among the Kirghis, the Yurok or the Buryat; while among the Pathans the one person who is conspicuous by his absence in the wedding procession is the bridegroom. The wedding banquet might, at first sight, appear to be an institution calling for no explanation beyond the natural one that it serves as an occasion for conviviality. But closer examination suggests that there is more to it. Among many peoples the eating of food together by the bride and bridegroom is the essence of the marriage ceremony, and often it is the only occasion on which they take a meal together. It seems possible that it is this rite which actually joins together the peoples in matrimony,[1] and this conjecture is strengthened by the forms which the banquets sometimes assumed. Thus among the Yakut the bride and bridegroom do not take part in the banquet, but sit with their faces towards the wall. The relatives exchange pieces of meat, symbolizing the union of the families which henceforth are to be 'flesh of one flesh, and bone of one bone'. Among various tribes of British Central Africa, unless the parents of both parties eat the food cooked by the bride's parents, the marriage is neither legal nor binding. Similarly among the Rajbansis of Purnea, in Bengal, a man who is too poor to afford such a meal may marry a woman with elaborate religious ceremonies, but until he has saved up enough money to provide a wedding meal he is regarded as living in a state of concubinage. The Chuhra of the Punjab do not admit the other party to family privileges until after the ceremonial meal. The wedding cake is, of course, an essential constituent of such banquets. Among the Kolarian tribes portions of the cake are presented to the totems of the respective parties. Certain clans which have trees for their totems offer wedding cake to the sacred trees; others of the cobra-totem deposit pieces of wedding cake in cobra holes, and so on. Certain Basors, who express their religious emotion by violent dancing, partake of the wedding cake while performing somersaults. It is of course obligatory for all guests to eat some of the wedding cake, but among the Kols it would be highly improper for any persons who are forbidden by law to intermarry to do so, for they would thus be married and hence become guilty of incest.

Elsewhere it is necessary to eat the wedding banquet hastily. Among the Karubas of Southern India, should anyone choke during the proceedings or afterwards be seized with flatulence or indigestion, this is a bad omen. Among the Yurok, a Samoyed tribe of Siberia, the wedding guests must not only eat as hastily as possible but must depart immediately the last mouthful has been swallowed. It would therefore seem that the banquet does not really have the character of a convivial gathering, as we so generally assume, but rather echoes other ritual meals of which we know, which are a means of effecting a communion of flesh between the participants. In short, it would seem that such banquets are intended to unite, not only the bride and bridegroom but their respective families.

Another common marriage rite is the marking of the bride and bridegroom with blood, the contract being assimilated to the blood-bond by which a person becomes adopted into the tribe. Now, in some instances, not only are the bride and bridegroom thus marked but all their relatives also, as in Cambodia and among the Papuan savages of

[1] See also p. 262.

the western coast of New Guinea. In some parts of Polynesia, it is not
the parties concerned who mingle their blood but their respective
mothers.

Reasons for Marriage between Groups

Marriage, then, is almost universally regarded as a contract not between
a man and a woman but between the groups to which they belong. No
feature is more marked and more general, and it is even more pronounced
in the most primitive phases of society. The Blackfellows of Australia,
the wild Seri of Tiburon, are one with the Chinese and the French
nobility in viewing marriage as a matter primarily concerning two contracting groups. Evidently, a contract between two groups must, in the
conditions of primitive society, have been a matter of far greater importance than any possible individual relationship. These elaborate
negotiations can be better understood if we remember that, under the
rules against incest, a man must, if he marries, marry someone from
another group; but in primitive societies there is very little intercourse
between groups, and this may be a very difficult task. The members of
one's own group are, in primitive society, 'our people', all others are
enemies. Mr Mathew remarks: 'When a Blackfellow crosses the boundary lines of his own territories, he takes his life in his hands.' Furthermore, clandestine visiting is even more difficult than open intercourse,
for almost all savages are restrained by superstitious fears from going
out of their camp after sunset. Unless there exists some friendly
understanding between the two groups, it is impossible to do so during
the daytime. For example, among the Bakyiga, a tribe inhabiting the
shores of Lake Edward, a man must, by the laws of exogamy, procure
a wife from one of the neighbouring clans, but, since all the clans are
in a perpetual state of deadly war, it is quite impossible for him to visit
another clan without a virtual certainty of being murdered. Negotiations for marriages are accordingly conducted by women only, and when
the bride comes to join her husband, she is brought by female relatives
only. There is, in fact, but one way in which such difficulties can be
overcome while observing the prohibition of incest; that is, by some
pact between the two groups, such as that which the sons of Hamor
proposed to the sons of Jacob: 'Then will we give our daughters unto
you, and we will take your daughters unto us.'

This is what in fact takes place in primitive societies. The elaborate
tribal conferences and conciliatory exchanges of presents which have
been noted in Australia and Melanesia or Polynesia, do not, of course,
take place on the occasion of every marriage, but only when a marriage
takes place between members of two different tribes between whom no
such practice has become established. The negotiations which take

place refer only incidentally to the individuals. Primarily they concern the relationship between the two groups.

Thus it is that the original character and purpose of the juridic transaction of marriage is not to legalize the sexual relations of individuals nor to safeguard the claims of individual possession; it is a contract about the relationship of groups, rendered necessary by the rules against incest.

The Marriage of Cross-cousins

Such an agreement between the two groups implies that every member of each group shall marry into the other group. This relationship, if continued long enough, results in an institution known as cross-cousin marriage. Let us suppose, for the sake of example, that in each of two primitive groups which we will call 'Bears' and 'Wolves', consisting of two generations only, all the Bear men will be married to Wolf women, and all the Bear women married to Wolf men. Then, if children are regarded as belonging to their *mother's* clan, since the eldest male Wolf will be married to a Bear woman, the father of every Bear will be a Wolf, and similarly the father of every Wolf will be a Bear. The wives of the younger Bear men will be Wolf women—that is, they will be the daughters of their father's sister, and they will also be the daughters of their mother's brother. In short, every Bear man and every Wolf man will marry a daughter of his mother's brother, and every Bear woman and Wolf woman will marry a son of her mother's brother. In other words, all unions in the two groups will be between cross-cousins. (In our own language we make no distinction between a father's brother's child or a mother's sister's child, calling both first-cousins, but among the vast majority of peoples a distinction is drawn between the two, the first kind being known as cross-cousins, the latter as ortho-cousins.)

Furthermore, among many peoples, while marriage between cross-cousins is allowed, marriage between ortho-cousins is prohibited as incestuous, those relatives being regarded as brothers and sisters. The reason for this distinction is manifest: daughters of a father's brother or of a mother's sister were members of the same group, or clan-sisters. Nor is this all. Not only are marriages between cross-cousins encouraged, but what is regarded as being a peculiarly desirable union is to marry a girl who is at the same time the daughter of one's mother's brother and of one's father's sister.

In Melanesia this system is the foundation of social organization. Thus in New Britain a man is expected to marry the daughter of his mother's brother, but may on no account marry the daughter of his mother's sister. Among the majority of the more primitive populations of the Malay Archipelago, to marry a cross-cousin is regarded as a moral obligation, and failure to do so is visited with a heavy fine. The fine is similar to that imposed on anyone who has incestuous relations (as they are considered) with his father's brother's or his mother's sister's daughter. The same customs obtain in the various islands of the Southern Moluccas and also in Ceram.

Cross-cousin marriage is a fundamental social law with a large proportion of the aboriginal races of India. It appears to be widespread among the primitive populations of Northern and Central Asia, although owing to the ambiguity of our terms of kinship, the reports of explorers do not always make it clear whether cross-cousins are meant. The Aleuts, according to Father Veniaminoff, 'marry by preference the daughter of their uncle'. A similar preference is shown by the Ainu, the Kamchadals, the Chukchi, the Koryaks and others. This view obtains in several parts of Africa, for example among the Bakongo, the Herero and others, while among the Bechuana the practice is so common that it must almost be considered the general practice of the tribe. These rules appear to have been common to all the Caribbean races of Central America. 'Marriage among the totem-societies of Australia, America and India is both exogamous and endogamous; a man is forbidden to marry either within his own clan or outside a certain kinship group.'

As Dr Codrington very lucidly explains when speaking of the Melanesians: 'In the native view of mankind . . . nothing seems more fundamental than the division of the people into two or more classes which are exogamous, and in which descent is counted through the mother. This seems to stand foremost as the native looks out upon his fellow men; the knowledge of it forms probably the first social conception which shapes itself in the mind of the young Melanesian of either sex, and it is not too much to say that this division is the foundation on which the fabric of native society is built up.' Sometimes a clan is divided into two groups, the members of any one group being prohibited under pain of death from intermarrying and being obliged to draw their sexual partners from the other group. Or instead of two exogamous groups, there may be four or even eight. Totemic considerations may also apply, so that the restrictions become very complicated. Since marriage between members of the same village is regarded as incest, it often happens that, as among the Zayeins, the unmarried males and females dwell separately in two large houses at the opposite ends of the village, and so afraid are they of incurring suspicion that any amatory relations exist that they are careful to lower their eyes discreetly should they happen to meet. If such a crime comes to light the culprits are made to dig their own graves, then they are pushed in and buried alive.

It can cause no surprise to learn that the Zayeins are steadily diminishing in numbers.

The custom of cross-cousin marriage is now well enough understood for it to be unnecessary to adduce further evidence here. As Dr Rivers remarks: 'It would seem impossible to find any direct psychological explanation in motive of any kind, whether religious, ethical or magical. They [the customs] seem to be meaningless except as a vestige of an old social order, while when considered from that point of view they become at once intelligible and natural.' It has been suggested that cross-cousin marriage may be explained by the economic advantage of keeping family property undivided. This cannot apply to the savages of Australia, Melanesia or the Caribbeans, who transmit no family property. Moreover, it is patriarchal societies which care most about property, and yet few such societies practice ortho-cousin marriage; it is virtually confined to the Arabs and some other Muhammadan peoples of Egypt, the Sudan, Morocco and India, and in each of these cases it is said to be adopted precisely with the object of keeping property in the family. The ancient Greek 'laws of Gortyna' make the matter very clear: 'An heiress shall be married to the brother of her father, to the eldest of such brothers as there may be. If there be several heiresses and several brothers let each of the younger ones be married to one of the brothers in the order of their ages. If there be no brothers of her father . . . then let the heiress marry the son of the eldest brother.' Inheritance through the daughters is here adapted to patriarchal aims, not by cross-cousin marriage but by ortho-cousin marriage. It is, in fact, unlikely that a custom devised to keep the property of a matriarchal family undivided should be preserved under a patriarchal system—the chief purpose of which is to abolish such a mode of succession.

Bakongo society offers a striking illustration of the essentially matriarchal character of clan organization and the patriarchal character of the family group. The exogamous clans are reckoned to have sprung from the offspring of a common ancestress, and descent is reckoned in the uterine line, yet the father is the absolute head of the family and the property is transmitted in the male line. Nevertheless, the Bakongo strictly observe cross-cousin marriage. A similar paradox is found among the Rabhas of Assam. Often economic advantage is set aside, as among the Bataks of Sumatra, a severely patriarchal people who nevertheless set advantageous alliances aside in order to make cross-cousin marriages.

Westermarck makes it a principle that customs should be explained by existing conditions and not as survivals of hypothetical past conditions. Quite to the contrary, a sounder rule would be: whenever a usage of world-wide distribution is found to be observed by races of widely different cultural levels, the explanation of its origin is to be found in interpretations which apply to the least-advanced of these peoples. Westermarck's principle leads to error since plausible current reasons can always be found—for instance, the explanation of the rule of exogamy as a provision against the injurious effects of inbreeding. On this principle, we should have to interpret the observance of sabbath days as due to the advisability of regular rest intervals, whereas we know the explanation to be quite different.[1] Similarly, we might think mourning customs prompted by respect for the dead when in fact they are prompted by dread of the spirit of the departed. In modern society no one supposes that such customs as raising one's hat to a magpie are to be explained by reference to existing conditions.

The Change from Clan-kinship to Family kinship

Once the primitive maternal clan organization has broken down and kinship comes to be viewed in relation with another form of group, i.e. the family, both ortho- and cross-cousins are regarded as equally close relatives, and marriage of either may be seen as incestuous. Thus many societies condemn marriage of first cousins of either sort and even of second, third, fourth and more remote ones, so that the very relationship which is prescribed under one system is condemned under the other. The transition is clearly seen in India where among some tribes and castes the one form of marriage is an obligation, in other commendable, in others permissible, while yet others condemn it. Sir Denzil Ibbetson writes of the Punjab: 'The people are beginning to add the mother's mother's clan to those in which a man is forbidden to marry or even to substitute it for the father's mother's clan, and this is apparently the last stage in the change from relationship through women to relationship through men.'

The clan-group organization tends to break down in time into family-group organization. Since exogamous clans or classes are general throughout Australia, Melanesia and primitive Indonesia, there can be little doubt that they were once general in Polynesia, but they have vanished. Again, the Yakut were once so strictly exogamous that blindness was thought to be visited upon the trespasser, but today a man marries any woman outside his own family. Similarly with the Iroquois. Moreover, even where, as in Fiji, the clan organization has fallen into complete decay, cross-cousin marriage may persist.

Primitive Kinship and Group-motherhood

We must dismiss the idea that while the family is a group depending upon reproductive and economic relations, the clan is a group resting

[1] See below, p. 250 ff.

upon some other principle of a social or political character. Primitive humanity is innocent of political organization, and organization through the authority of a chief is a late phenomenon. 'Cohesion in a community', remarks Mr Mathew, in speaking of the Australians, 'depends entirely upon consanguinity, and derives no strength at all from governmental authority.' Primitive kinship terms support this idea; all male members of the clan of about the same age, including those we should call cousins, are reckoned as brothers, and all females as sisters; the older male members are called by a term which includes both 'father' and 'uncle'; the older female members by a term including both 'mother' and 'aunt'. The younger members of the corresponding marriage class are called 'wives' and 'husbands', i.e. a wife's sisters or a husband's brothers. This is the so-called *classificatory* system, as against the system which obtains in our own society which is known as the *descriptive* system. This label assumes that our own system is somehow natural. We tend to think that when the term 'mother' is applied to all women of the same generation as the actual mother that this is a convention but, as Mr Thomas explains, when we find that the term which is translated 'son' is applied not only by the biological mother but by all the other women of the group to a particular boy, we 'may discard the hypothesis that "wife" means wife, "husband" husband, and conclude that if there was a period of group marriage there was also a period of group motherhood. This interesting fact may be commended to the attention of zoologists.'

But zoologists would tell him that there is an absence of any relationship between the operation of the maternal instinct and actual consanguinity among animals—as we know from the case of the cuckoo and many others. Thus filial and fraternal instincts operate in accordance with the classificatory and not with the descriptive system of relationship, and it is the former which is, in the biological sense, natural. The idea that a system of relationship must rest upon the biological fact of generation arises from the fallacy of ascribing to primitive ideas an intellectual character which is foreign to them. This fallacy is embodied in the very word 'system'—it is assumed that the reckoning of kinship is based on a deliberately devised and intellectually sound scheme. That this is equally true of humans is shown, for instance, by the reply of an Iroquois to Father Lejeune when he asked him how he could be so fond of children of whose parentage he could not be sure. The Indian looked at him contemptuously and replied: 'You Frenchmen love only your own children, we love all the children of the tribe.' Wives who attend to their own children and to those of other women without distinction are widely found among primitive races, and it is an 'almost universal custom that a child should be suckled not only by its mother but also by its grandmother, and by other near female relatives'. In many cases foster-relationship systems are maintained and children are interchanged. In the Hindu Kush these foster relationships are regarded as so close that marriage between foster relations would be looked upon as incestuous. If a man is suspected of adultery, any further misconduct is insured against by obliging him to put his lips against the woman's breast—she is henceforth regarded as his foster-mother, and no other relationship but that of mother and son can exist between them. These fostering usages are common in India, are prevalent in primitive Indonesia, especially among the Dayaks, and are found in Polynesia and Melanesia. In the Gilbert Islands the persons who pass for a man's or woman's parents are never the real parents, for every child is adopted at birth by foster-parents, as soon as suckling is terminated. The children are so completely assimilated as to be unconscious of their relationship to their real family. Similar customs are found in West Africa, as well as among such tribes as the Aleuts and the Cheyennes.

Yet Dr Westermarck exclaims: 'Where in the world has a society been found in which it is the custom for infants to be taken away from their mothers when weaned, or for mothers to desert their infants?' His inquiry is all the more remarkable inasmuch as the usage is found among some of the peoples of Morocco, a country about which he claims a special knowledge.

To summarize, the aspect of the clan which is foremost in the primitive mind is the sexual aspect; all primitive marriage regulations are dominated by the desire to avoid incest. To the Australian, the Melanesian and the North American Indian the primary purpose of clan divisions is to indicate who may marry whom.

Primitive Marriage Relationship

These inter-marriage rules refer exclusively to the relations between groups, and are not designed to safeguard claims to individual sexual possession—which *we* regard as the main purpose of marriage laws and morality. The relationship of individual marriage is denoted by no specific term in primitive nomenclature. A wife's sisters and a husband's brothers are not merely called wives and husbands, but act and are treated as such, as we shall see in the following chapters. In most cases such usages are associated with some form of individual marriage, i.e. the continuous cohabitation of one man with one or more women. But this association does not necessarily exclude collective sex-relations. The sexual and economic aspects of association are, in fact, quite independent. Individual marriage rests upon the economic relation, for a man may contribute the products of his hunting or his services as a warrior to the whole group, but the economic value of a woman lies in her personal service. To obtain this service is the chief motive of individual marriage in most primitive communities. Jealousy among most primitive races refers not to exclusive sexual possession but to economic loss, and claims to exclusive sexual possession have developed out of this.

In the societies which have preserved their primitive organization, freedom of access between any male of the one group and any female of the other is the rule rather than the exception. Where individual sexual rights exist, penalties for infringing them, i.e. for adultery, are usually much less severe when the infringer belongs to the same group as the husband than when he does not. Indeed, in the former case there may be no penalty: a temporary loan or exchange of wives between members of the same marriage group is quite common.

Nevertheless, complete promiscuity is nowhere found as an accepted social pattern. Though sexual relations are, in primitive societies, often loose and casual they are by no means unregulated, for the incest prohibitions both exclude certain relationships within the group and necessitate an agreement with some other group. To assess this early form of the marriage institution by current standards of sexual morals and to regard it as approaching promiscuity—as many missionaries have done—is unscientific and inaccurate. People always feel that systems different from their own are barbarous. Thus the polygamous Singhalese spoke of the wild Veddahs, who had only one wife, as being 'like monkeys', while in South Africa coastal natives who have given up such practices speak of the inland tribes as 'no better than dogs', in this respect. The Jews looked upon the marriages of Christians as wholly invalid.

Far from being unregulated, Australian and Melanesian sexual relations are subject to much more elaborate regulations than our own, and these may make the choice of a wife much more restricted than in modern society, or may even make it impossible. These rules may become, as among the Zayeins of Burma, an intolerable tyranny. As a matter of fact, if we seek for the nearest approach to promiscuity we find it in societies which are formally 'monogamous', such as some forest tribes of Brazil and Malaya.

To recapitulate: marriage originated in a contract between two kinship groups, and only later became a contract between individuals, when clan kinship broke down into family kinship. In the next two chapters let us pursue this novel idea further, examining every quarter of the world for evidence of group marriage.

CHAPTER 10

Group Marriage (1)

Sororal Polygyny

IT is a widespread principle in uncultured societies that when a man marries a woman he thereby acquires marital rights over all her sisters. Thus, among the Kurnai of South-east Australia, when a man elopes with a woman from another tribe, her parents, after their anger has blown over and the matter has been amicably settled, hand over her sister also. Among the tribes of Gippsland the men cannot be made to understand the distinction between a wife and a sister-in-law; the latter, they insist, are just as much their wives as the former. So also in the western islands of the Torres Straits before conversion of the natives to Christianity, a man's wives were all sisters or cousins, and even today there is little doubt that husbands normally have marital relations with the wives' sisters. This principle, like the rule of cross-cousin marriage, is a translation into terms of family relationships of the sexual claim of a man to all the women in the group with which his own group has entered into a marriage agreement.

This arrangement, which is called sororal polygyny, was almost universal among the North American tribes, and appears to have been equally general in Central and South America, where it is found from the Canebo of the Upper Amazon to the inhabitants of Tierra del Fuego. It is very common in Africa (e.g. among the Zulus and Kaffirs), especially among the primitive races, being a matter of course among the Upper Congo tribes.

It is also usual among the primitive races of Siberia, and is old-established among the Mongols and Chinese. Jinghis Khan married two sisters, and the practice was taken for granted among his warriors and khans. We read of the Emperor Yao bestowing both his daughters on the Chinese prince Sheunn. Among the ancient Japanese, 'to wed two or more sisters at the same time was a recognized practice'. We also find it in Tibet, Cambodia, Siam, among the Malays of the Patani States, and among the tribes of Upper Burma and Manipur. It was in vogue among the ancient Indo-Aryans, and is common in the Punjab, as well as among various native tribes of Central India, and is prevalent in Mysore and Southern India. We know from the account of the marriage of Jacob that it was a recognized usage among the ancient Jews.

In the Pacific area, similar evidence comes from the Philippine Islands, the Marshalls, the Gilberts, the Mortlocks and elsewhere.

In practice, sororal polygyny is limited by the factor which limits every kind of polygamy—the financial strain of marrying a whole family. This difficulty is often relieved by the fact that, since in primitive society girls usually marry at puberty, the younger sisters are not yet marriageable when their elder sister marries. By the time they are eligible the man's circumstances may have improved, enabling him to maintain a larger family. Hence the rule, observed in most parts of the world, that the younger sister shall not marry before her older sister—a rule on which Laban insisted when he gave his daughter to Jacob, and one which has left traces even in England and Scotland.

If a husband does not wish to exercise his claim on his wife's sisters, he may allow them to marry other men and, in some cases, may receive the bride-price instead of the girl's relatives. An additional sister is given as a matter of course if the first sister proves barren. Among the Tartars, if the wife dies before the payment of the bride-price is completed, the sum already paid goes towards the acquisition of her sister, but if there is no sister to take her place, the deposit is lost. In other instances, the bridegroom may demand a refund of the bride-price.

Among the Flatheads and other Oregon tribes, when a man's wife dies, if her sister is already married to another man she is obliged to leave him and marry the widower. Among the Wabemba of the Congo in a similar situation, the husband of one of the deceased wife's sisters must allow his wife to cohabit for one or two nights with the widower. Unless this is done, the latter cannot remarry. If the sister is still an infant, she is nevertheless handed over to the widower, but a slave-girl is sent with her to act as a substitute until she is of marriageable age. Similarly among the Baholoholo, who observe the same rule, if the surviving sister is a mere infant the widower goes through the form of imitating the sexual act with her. (We shall see that similar ritual survivals are associated with the corresponding custom of fraternal succession.)

Marriage with the deceased wife's sister is sometimes regarded as a moral obligation rather than as a claim or privilege. Among the Shuswap of British Columbia, the widower was actually kept prisoner by his deceased wife's family, and was released only on condition that he married the sister. The notion that it is reprehensible to marry one's deceased wife's sister is an anthropological curiosity which appears to be found only among the natives of New Britain, some Chinese tribes and some natives of Ashanti. Nevertheless, the people who observe this rule but who have given up sororal polygyny do not admit that they practise the former custom because they once practised the latter, but give some specious explanation. In the same way, certain anthropological writers to whom the application of the theory of evolution to the human race is repugnant have no hesitation in declaring that they cannot 'find any reason for the assumption that the custom of marrying a deceased wife's sister is derived from the custom of marrying her other sisters in her lifetime'.[1]

The favourite explanation given by travellers and missionaries who last observed the custom is that it is desirable in a polygynous family that the wives should be sisters because sisters are more likely to live together in harmony. In fact, where polygyny obtains, the women are the most persistent advocates of the practice, and there is nothing to indicate that the wives in polygynous families are more prone to quarrel among themselves than other persons who live together. Indeed, according to La Potherie, among the North American Indians sisters are particularly quarrelsome and sometimes attack one another with knives; while the Ostyak, who have immemorially practised sororal polygyny, state that the arrangement is unsatisfactory since sisters are particularly liable to disagree in such marriages.

Actually it may be doubted whether Melanesian savages are much concerned about the amicable nature of the relationships between their wives, about respect for their deceased wives, or the proper qualifications in the nurses of their children—to name some supposed reasons for the practice. In any case, none of these alleged benefits account for a man having to marry his wife's sisters against his will, or for his collecting the bride-price when they marry other men, or for his having to wait with a slave-girl as a substitute when those sisters are still infants-in-arms.

Like cross-cousin marriage, sororal polygyny is a translation in terms of family relationship of the wider conceptions of clan relationship. From the point of view of the clan-group, the term 'wife' includes all women of the corresponding marriage-group, and all those women are sisters. Dr Codrington, speaking of the Melanesians, declares that, 'to a Melanesian man, all women, of his own generation at least, are either sisters or wives' [actual or potential], and that 'all women who may become wives by marriage and are not yet appropriated, are to a certain extent looked upon by those who may be their husbands as open to more or less legitimate intercourse. In fact, appropriation of particular women to their husbands, though established by every sanction of native custom, has by no means so strong a hold in native society, nor in all probability so deep a foundation in the history of the people, as the severance of either sex by divisions which most strictly limit the intercourse of men and women to those of the section or sections to which they do not themselves belong.'

[1] Westermarck: *History of Human Marriage*, III, 263.

The complement of the rule of sororal polygyny is that of fraternal polyandry; i.e. that when a woman contracts a marriage with a member of another family she marries all the marriageable males of that family. The simultaneous observance of both these rules constitutes a marriage between the two groups, irrespective of the relations between the members composing them. However, the one-sided observance of sororal polygyny, and perhaps also of fraternal polyandry, are much more common today than the combination of the two practices as complete group-marriage. The reason for this is plain. The combination of the two practices is an unstable arrangement, and can only operate in a modified form where sexual relations do not entail permanent co-habitation. As soon as marriage involves economic interdependence the arrangement becomes impracticable, for economic association can only take place when the labour of the woman or women is in some degree specially allotted to the husband, and it necessarily breaks up into one or another of its aspects—that is, into sororal polygyny or fraternal polyandry. But since the development of individualism and individual property has taken place in the hands of the men, it is natural that when it breaks up it does so in the form of sororal polygyny. In point of fact, fraternal polyandry, though geographically widespread, is considerably less common than sororal polygyny, being rarer than is generally supposed. Many of the customs usually described as fraternal polyandry turn out, on inquiry, to be associated with sororal polygyny and thus to represent, in reality, group-marriage. We shall now survey the two subjects together.

Northern Asia

The confusion to be found in many early anthropological reports is well illustrated by the Gilyak. As the careful investigation by Dr Sternberg has shown, they are strictly organized into exogamic classes, and every member of each marries into his allotted class on the basis of cross-cousin marriage. Individual 'marriage' takes place in the sense that a woman becomes the particular economic associate of a man but her economic husband possesses no sexual rights over her.[1] Earlier reports misunderstood the position. An old Japanese traveller says that Gilyak women had several husbands, while another traveller reports that their sexual relations are indiscriminate.

Of the Chukchi of extreme North-east Asia a Russian traveller mentions that 'among other customs they have the usage of contracting so-called "exchange-marriages". Two or more men enter into an agree-

---

[1] Among the Western Gilyak all tribal brothers have marital rights over the wives of each other indifferently, but among the Eastern Gilyak the older brothers have no right to the wives of the younger brothers.

ment whereby they have mutual rights to each other's wives. This right is exercised whenever the contracting parties come together, as for instance on the occasion of a visit.' However, the elaborate monograph of Mr Bogoras makes clear that the Chukchi are commonly betrothed in their infancy to their first-cousins, and that they observe sororal poly-gyny. In this instance we have clear testimony that licentiousness has nothing to do with the institution. The Chukchi are indeed described as a sensual race, but their group-marriage organization is not exploited for licentious purposes. They are careful not to form such an alliance with persons dwelling in the same village, and in general avoid exercis-ing the rights it confers on them. Sometimes cousins exchange wives for several months, for years or permanently. So seriously is the arrangement regarded that children in the same marriage-group are regarded as brothers and sisters, and are not allowed to marry among themselves. It appears that, although the group-marriage of the Chukchis is to a certain extent artificial, since it depends upon an individual compact, it nevertheless is a derivative of established marriage-rights between two marrying classes or groups, modified by the necessities imposed by their isolated and scattered way of life.

This view is confirmed by the position among the Aleuts, where thorough investigation has been made by Mr Jochelson, who says: 'To participate in group-marriage is the duty of cousins.' Here, again, earlier reports described the system as consisting of loose polyandrous unions.

Sexual Hospitality

Let us pause for a moment to consider how it is that participation in group-marriage, which we tend to regard as a form of licence, should be regarded not only as a right and a privilege but as a moral obligation. Community of wives was originally regarded as essential to the relation-ship of tribal brotherhood. To primitive man all men are either tribal brothers or strangers, and the latter term is equivalent to 'enemy'. If a man, not being by birth a tribal brother, is admitted into a community and is regarded with good-will—in short, if he is not an enemy—he must needs be a tribal brother. Hence the sacredness of hospitality in all primitive sentiment. If a man has touched the tent-rope of an Arab's tent, his life must be defended against all enemies. The hospitality of savages knows no bounds. If they are on the verge of starvation, they will give what little they have to the stranger who has been admitted to their midst. The first thought of the savage, when the stranger to whom he feels himself attracted is in his company, is to take the necessary steps to make him a tribal brother. In Australia, if the member of a strange tribe refuses to drink the blood of his hosts, it is forcibly poured down his throat. Among the Koryak the guest is obliged to undergo a somewhat strange rite of brotherhood with his host's wife before he can avail himself of her hospitality. 'Elle lache son urine en presence de l'étranger et lui en offre une jatte pour s'en rincer la bouche.' It follows that the host's lending his guest his wife is not misguided benevolence but a necessary pledge of friendship. For the guest to refuse this so-called 'hospitality prostitution' is the equivalent to repudiating the assumed brotherhood and is thus tantamount to a declaration of war. The sedentary Koryak 'look upon it as the truest mark of friendship when they entertain a friend to put him to bed with their wife or daughter; and a refusal of this civility they consider as the greatest affront, and are capable of even murdering a man for such contempt. That happened to several Cossacks before they were acquainted with the customs of the people.' The same is reported of the Chukchi. In Madagascar a missionary closely escaped being murdered because he refused the proffered hospitality. The custom is very general in all primitive societies.[1]

Thus it is that the existence of clan-brotherhood is, or was, formerly considered to imply sexual communism. Naturally the practice of sexual hospitality has tended to become modified in the same way that sexual communism has become modified by the development of individual marriage. All manner of transitional forms are found. Thus, the Missouri Indians were so averse from intercourse with members of another tribe that they never offered their wives or daughters to strangers. Nevertheless, they regarded themselves as under the obligation of offering sexual hospitality to a guest, and accordingly provided him with a captive from another tribe. It may safely be concluded that this was a compromise between their endogamic tribal principles and their equally strong conviction that a clan-brother was entitled to access to his host's women. Again, among the Krumir Berbers a stranger visiting the tribe is lodged by one of the tribesmen, and is invited to spend the night in the company of his host's wife. The host mounts guard outside the tent, and should he hear any suspicious movement would have no hesitation in instantly shooting his guest. So-called 'hospitality prostitution' has here dwindled to an empty ceremonial. Similarly, since the Arabs attach great importance to hospitality and clan-brotherhood, we may infer that at some previous period sexual communism among clanbrothers was customary. And in fact the learned Arab jurist, Ata ibn-Abi Rabah, states that the custom of offering one's wife to a guest was of old a universally-sanctioned custom of the Arabs. In some Arab tribes this has survived down to the present, or quite recent, times. Thus the clan organization of a people whose notions of individual

[1] A bibliography of 116 titles is appended.

marriage are today even severer than our own nevertheless entailed the same conceptions as among the most primitive savages.

Collective Sexual Relations in America

There can be little doubt that the practice of exchanging wives temporarily, universal with all sections of the Eskimo race, is a survival of tribal sexual communism, which has become disintegrated by the dispersion of these small communities. In Repulse Bay, 'it is the usual thing among friends to exchange wives for a week or two about every two months'; and Dr Murdoch was informed that 'at certain times there is a general exchange of wives throughout the village, each woman passing from man to man until she has been through the hands of all'. In Northern Greenland, as Dr Bessels delicately puts it, 'somewhat communistic tendencies seriously interfere with the sanctity of marriage'. The most important race of the extreme north-western region of America are the Tlinkit. They are divided into a number of totemic clans grouped into two large exogamic marriage classes. Polygamy is very general, a man of distinction having as many as forty wives; the Tlinkit are also polyandrous. Here again we see the deceptive manner in which such an organization is apt to be reported. Some writers report that their customs allow 'great looseness in sexual relations'. Count Langsdorf, on the contrary, says that their decent and orderly behaviour and the modesty of their women stand in striking contrast with the manners of neighbouring races. Adultery is severely punished, but it is only a serious offence if the seducer belongs to a clan other than the husband's. The rules governing their sexual organization seem fairly clear, but the Russian bishop, Father Veniaminoff, feels it necessary to go to Sicily for a parallel; many ethnological writers have taken the hint and term these arrangements 'cicisbeism'. It does not appear that the customs of the Tlinkit bear any resemblance to the practices of eighteenth-century Italian society, of which the relations between Nelson and Sir William and Lady Hamilton are a famous instance; they resemble far more closely group-marriage. It should be noted that their marriages were matrilocal.

Making due allowance for the difficulty of observation, it would appear that, from Manchuria on the Asiatic side to British Columbia on the American, the principles governing sexual relations are substantially identical among all tribes, and with the large majority, reciprocal sexual rights between all the males and all the females, through intermarrying groups, are recognized, or were so until quite recently. The general prevalence of those customs among the peoples of the ruder north and west suggest that they may also have obtained among the North American Indians, a presumption confirmed by several characteristics, such as the existence of the classificatory system of clan relationship, and the practice of sororal polygyny which, as we have seen, is universal among the North American Indians.   In conjunction with it, levirate marriage is a rite and an obligation.[1] Father Charlevoix adds that, among the Senecas, who practise sororal polygyny, there is 'a far greater disorder, namely a plurality of husbands'. Thus there is ample evidence to confirm the presumption that the marriage customs of North American Indians were the result of decay of clan organization under the influence of individual economic marriage.

Similar principles appear to have been widely current in South America, and are reported of the natives of New Granada, the tribes of Brazil, the Zaparos of Ecuador and many others. In Guiana, at the present day, polyandry is common, and when a missionary endeavoured to persuade an Indian to give up polygyny by asking him what he would think of a woman having several husbands, he replied that both customs were equally honoured in his tribe.

Collective Marriage in Tibet

Although Tibetan polyandry is constantly referred to and was used by McLellan as the type of fraternal polyandry, the polygyny which goes with Tibetan polyandry is overlooked by most writers. However, Mr Savage Landor, who had exceptional opportunities of obtaining first-hand information, gives us the most definite account. 'A Tibetan girl on marrying does not enter into a nuptial tie with an individual, but with all his family. . . . If an eldest son marries an eldest sister all the sisters of the bride become his wives. . . . At the same time, when the bridegroom has brothers they are all regarded as their brother's wife's husbands, and they one and all cohabit with her as well as with her sisters if she has any.' Tibetan marriage is, therefore, not simple polyandry but a complete group-marriage.

On the current assumption that polygyny and polyandry are different and opposite forms of marriage, the mistake has occurred of describing Tibetan group-marriage sometimes as polyandry and sometimes as polygyny. But all reports agree to the existence of both these customs in Tibetan-speaking countries.[2] Mr Landor was surprised by the rule of seniority, by which, if an elder son marries the second sister, then

[1] See pp. 153–6, for an account of the 'levirate'.

[2] For reasons presently to be noted, limitation of the number of wives appears on the whole to be more common in the higher uplands, while plurality of wives is more prevalent in the lower valleys; and in one and the same valley polyandry is stated to obtain in the upper portion and polygyny in the lower. It seems clear, however, that the polygyny of the lower valley is, in reality, part of the same organization as the polyandry of the upper.

only the sisters from the second down become his property; but this is, in fact, a characteristic feature of group marriage. It is understandable when we realize that when an elder brother marries he does so as the representative of a whole group of brothers. The younger brothers can make no valid contract except through the medium of their elder. The elder brother inherits the father's property, and is under the obligation of supporting his brothers. Since, on the marriage of an elder brother his younger brothers have rights over his wives, it follows that any marriage contracted by a younger brother independently would be supererogatory. It would, in the Tibetan view, be bigamous.

Similarly among the Brahmans of Travancore and Malabar, when an elder brother marries all the younger brothers are debarred from contracting any regular marriage within their own caste. The same principle is observed in that residue of fraternal polyandry known as the levirate, the right to marry a deceased brother's wife. But while a younger brother has this right as regards the widow of his elder brother, there is no converse right of an elder brother to the widow of his younger brother. The same is true of other tribes such as the Zulus and the Thonga of Mozambique. On the same principle it is considered wrong for a younger brother to marry before his elder brother. In China any infraction of this rule is atoned for by carrying in the bridal procession a pair of trousers, representing the elder brother, and laying them on the chair of the bride.

Since there is every reason to believe that group-marriage derives from an organization in which the marrying groups were originally clans, or in later stages marrying classes, it is interesting that traces of these classes have not completely disappeared in Tibet. Father Desideri, a Jesuit, who visited the country at the beginning of the eighteenth century, reports that there are two different kinds of kinship in Tibet, kinsmen 'of the same bone', and kinsmen 'of the same flesh'. The first kind comprising all individuals issued from the same stem, whether begotten in the direct line or belonging to side branches however remote. Those, on the other hand, designated as kindred of the same flesh are matrimonial allies. The first type of kinship is regarded as absolutely inviolable. This implies that the proper wife of a young Tibetan is his cousin, which is confirmed by the fact that no marriage can be concluded without the authority of the bride's maternal uncle— who would normally be the father of the bridegroom. Thus Tibetan society, although essentially patriarchal at present, is not far removed from a matriarchal phase. Formerly it was under a complete system of gynaecocracy. The high position occupied by Tibetan women, in marked contrast to the women in India or China, has already been noted. By a strange paradox, despite the importance of the patriarchal household today, the patriarchal family has no name, and children are named after their mother, not their father, whose name indeed must not even be mentioned. In some districts polyandrous Tibetan marriages are also matrilocal. Marriage is not regarded by the Tibetans as a sexual but as a social and economic relation, the two aspects being kept distinct. Marriage is regarded rather as a sacrifice in the interests of the family group. Perhaps this is what Captain Turner meant when he wrote that 'marriage amongst them seems to be considered rather as an odium and a heavy burden, the weight and obloquy of which a whole family are disposed to lessen by sharing it among them.' (The question about which Warren Hastings was curious to obtain information—namely, to which of the fathers the children were supposed to belong—is entirely irrelevant.) It has several times been stated by older writers that polyandry is peculiar to the poorer classes and is not practised among the well-to-do. This is quite untrue.[1]

The polyandrous organization of Tibetan marriage is not imposed upon the women, who are staunch supporters of the system.

It is worth noting that the degree of sexual promiscuity is small, except where group-marriage organization has been undermined by individual marriage. Frequently, the several husbands are absent from home for long periods, and in practice a woman seldom cohabits with more than one man at a time. Group-marriage is indissoluble, and the easy dissolution of marriage owes its introduction to the infiltration of marriage customs of the plains. Dr Westermarck takes occasion to remark that—'in decay, polyandry is modified in directions tending towards monogamy'. But, in point of fact, it is not towards monogamy but towards the highest degree of polygamy that group-marriages actually lead. The Marquis Cortanze, impressed by the high moral character of the Tibetans, remarked: 'There does not exist in the whole province of Ladakh . . . a single Tibetan woman who is a prostitute;' whereas the lowlands, where Tibetan customs have decayed, swarm with them.

In Tibet there is no tradition of any origin of group-marriage, which is regarded as 'indefinitely old', and these institutions have no connection with the Lamaistic Buddhism which was introduced at a comparatively late date. Mr Wilson reports that polyandry is almost universal all through Chinese Tibet and in almost all Tibetan-speaking

[1] No importance can be attached to the various theories put forward 'to explain the origin' of so-called Tibetan polyandry. For instance, it has been said that it is due to the disproportion between the sexes, though there is no evidence of such disproportion. Mr Rockhill and other writers are of the opinion that 'the numbers of women and men are probably equal', while in Lahul, where polyandry is extensive, the censuses of 1881 and 1891 show that women actually outnumber the men.

provinces. It is probably the common marriage custom of at least thirty million people in this area.

Polyandry is found throughout the Himalayan region in various stages of decay and obsolescence. It is general in Saraj, the Simla hills and the valleys of the western Himalayas. The gradual decay of polyandrous institutions in the lower Himalayan valleys appears to be due, not to changes in ethical conceptions but to the disintegration of the old social organization. It is bound up with the communal undivided economic household, in that all brothers remain in one family and share alike. With the rise of individual economic interests, the polyandrous marriage is necessarily broken up also. The highland regions of the Himalayas are but a cultural island preserving social customs which once were far more extensively distributed. Biddulph considers that polyandrous marriage was once general in Hindu-Kush and Chitral, a view substantiated by the eleventh-century Arab traveller, Al-Biruni. In Turkestan, according to a thirteenth-century Chinese geographer, polyandry was obligatory. It is curious that in the exogamic clans of China the same terms are used as in Tibet to indicate distinction between kinsmen of the same flesh and of the same bone; and sororal polygyny was once as customary in China as with the ruder Mongol tribes of Central Asia. Today, to marry the widow of one's brother is so criminal an act that the guilty man is condemned to be strangled. Nevertheless, it was at one time an established usage among the Chinese.

Polyandry in North India

Polyandrous institutions were common in many parts of India, and attracted the attention of the English when they colonized the mouth of the Ganges. These people 'stretch the Levitical law so that a brother not only raises up seed to another after his decease, but even during his absence on service, so that no married woman lies fallow.' The writer was probably referring to the Khonds—the most important of the non-Aryan tribes in India. Similarly amongst the Santals, also representatives of the aboriginal race, man has right of access to all the younger sisters of his wife, and so have his younger brothers. In other words, there is complete group-marriage. In addition, a Santal uncle 'is permitted a good deal of freedom of intercourse with his wife's nieces', a feature which derives from the age-grade organization.

Attempts have been made to 'explain' polyandry by suggesting that it is caused by mental abnormality. Thus Mr Wilson says that Tibetans are peculiarly cold-blooded. On the other hand, Father Desideri says they are of lively temperament. Many travellers assert an absence of jealousy to explain it, among them Westermarck. 'Jealousy', he tells us, 'is a passion of very great intensity . . . belonging to the nature of man.'

So that 'promiscuity is to be explained by the absence of that part of human nature'. Westermarck has not thought it worth including in the instances he cites the Santals who, far from possessing 'an abnormally feeble disposition to jealousy' are 'usually frantically jealous'. Their jealousy, however, assumes a peculiar form; they 'often complain that their husband's younger brothers are carrying on intrigues with other girls when they can get all they want at home'.

Polyandry among the 'Aryan' Hindus

It would be a mistake to suppose that the disappearance of polyandry among the Dravidian and Mongoloid races of India was due to the influence of the conquering 'Indo-Aryan' race, for the latter had the same polyandrous institutions as the races they conquered. The 'Aryans' established themselves first in the Punjab, and it is there, if anywhere, that their existing representatives are to be found—the Rajputs and the Jats. Among them fraternal polyandry persists to the present day, particularly in the district of Dehra Dhun, one of the chief cradles of Hindu civilization, where the fair-skinned Rajputs and Jats predominate. Polyandry was reported as on the decline there in 1827, but in 1874 it was still described as 'unquestionably common to this very day'; the writer adding that, if a woman dies leaving an infant son, her daughter-in-law is bound to rear the boy and marry him herself. Rajput polyandry is strictly fraternal, only sons of the same mother by the same set of fathers being permitted to enter into collective marriage relations; and it is associated with polygyny, although elsewhere other kin, including first cousins, are admitted. The women enjoy the highest status and freedom, being at liberty to leave their husbands and remarry provided that the new husbands refund the wedding expenses of the old.

Among the Jats, of whom the Rajputs are the aristocratic class, the custom appears to be universally recognized, though not always openly acknowledged owing to Brahmanical influence. Thus of the Kanaur district Sir Denzil Ibbetson says: 'Polyandry is practised without disgrace by both Kanets and Jats; it is the rule, not the exception, for the wife to cohabit with all the brothers.' Among the eastern Jats it is 'a common thing, when women quarrel, for one to say to the other: 'You are so careless of your duties as not to admit your husband's brothers to your embraces.' Much other evidence can be adduced; for instance, in the Sikh regiments of the Indian Army in the middle of the last century it was the recognized plea for leave of absence for Rajputs and Jats that their brothers were away from home and their wife left alone. Mohammedan historians record that before embracing Islam many infidels of the Punjab observed polyandry.

It has also been suggested that the Indo-Aryans adopted polyandry from the aboriginal inhabitants or from neighbouring peoples; this is intrinsically improbable, since individualistic marriage usages rarely give way to communal ones, and still more because polyandry among the Indo-Aryans of the Punjab is associated with survivals of an archaic order of society culturally identical with that of the polyandrous peoples of the Hindu-Kush, whence the invaders came.

As we have seen, polyandry was obligatory among the peoples of Turkestan—that is, the ancient Baktria and Sogdiana—the main habitat of the Indo-Aryans. Chinese annals of both the earlier and the later Han dynasties refer repeatedly to the same customs among the Great Get-ti, or Ye-tha. These are the same customs to which Herodotus refers in speaking of the Massa-Getae: 'Each man marries a woman, but all wives are in common; for this is the custom of the Massagetae, and not, as the Greeks think, of the Scythians. And when a Massagetae desires to have company with a woman, he hangs up his quiver in front of the chariot and has intercourse with her openly.'

The ancient literature of the Indo-Aryans refers everywhere to their polyandrous institutions. In the sacred laws of the Aryans it is laid down that 'a bride is given to the family of the husband and not to the husband alone', although 'a husband shall not make over his wife, who occupies the position of a clanswoman, to other than to his own clansmen in order to cause a child to be begot for himself.'

The two great national epics of the invading race, the 'Râmâyana' and the 'Mahâbhârata' depict the marriage of the heroes as a group-marriage. These two epics derive from sagas of the two main groups into which the Aryan invaders appear to have been divided. Thus in the marriage of the five sons (or brothers) of Pandu, which forms the theme of the first book of the Mahâbhârata, the princes declare 'Thy daughter, O King, shall be the common wife of us all', and the daughter dwells with each of them for two days at a time. The sage Ydhishthira, in commending this marriage, says: 'Let us follow in the way that has been traced by the illustrious of former ages; this practice hath been established, it is to be regarded as old and eternal.' Similarly in the 'Râmâyana'. The full force of the evidence cannot be appreciated without a survey of the entire literature.[1]

The sage's assertion that the practice is an ancient one is amply borne out by the Vedic hymns, which refer repeatedly to plurality of husbands. The Vedic family was constituted in the same manner as other polyandrous families; that is, the brothers continued to live together even after the death of their fathers, and the eldest brother acted in all things for the others, an arrangement almost invariably associated with polyandry.

[1] The Mahâbhârata contains some passages expressing disapproval of group marriage which appear to be late Brahmanical interpolations.

The converse rule that a man would have right of access to his wife's sisters is also explicitly referred to.[1]

Finally it must be noted that nowhere in the Vedas or in the Sutras is there a word of condemnation of the practice, although they are meticulous indeed in their moralizing. This fact negatives the argument that polyandry was a later adoption.

It was Brahmanism which lead to the gradual suppression of primitive marriage customs among the Hindus. The Brahmanical system was individualistic; it was not an organization comparable with the Church of Rome, but a collection of sacred individuals acknowledging no authority. Hence it caused a change from a clan system to a caste system, and the clan to which the individualistic priest belonged was of no significance to him. The caste organization, based on the exclusive priestly caste, broke up the clan organization based on group kinship. To treat, as is often done, Brahmanical ideas as being 'primitive Aryan' usages is to ignore the whole course of Indian history. Indeed in southern India, remote from the contest with the aristocratic clans, the Brahmans themselves retained the constitution of the undivided family—the elder brother alone being permitted to marry and his children being accounted the offspring of the entire family. As a seventeenth-century traveller noted: 'It is a law with the Brahmans that one son only takes a wife, who is common to all the brothers but to no one else.' The learned Hindu judge Sir T. Muttusami Aiyar comments that 'the personal law of these Nambudiri Brahmans' was not the modern Hindu law but 'the ancient Hindu law as it is probably understood and followed about the commencement of the Christian era'.

Polyandrous Marriage amongst other 'Aryan' Peoples

One way of dissociating ourselves from customs different from our own is to suppose that the latter are a peculiarity of an imaginary 'Aryan' or Indo-German race. (Actually the term 'Aryan'—as Mueller, who popularized it, stressed—applies solely to language.) It has been a point of honour, especially with German scholars, to depict in the most exalted terms the moral standards and social institutions of the supposed first-cousins of the progenitors of their race; and in their zeal for the principles of the Hindus of three milleniums ago they have often appeared

---

[1] European commentators have attempted to explain such references away. Thus Professor Hillebrandt claims that the sister dwelling with her father must mean with her forefathers, i.e. dead. Some have even asserted flatly that 'polyandry is not Vedic'. Dr Keith finds this too much, and rejects the suggestion that the reason that the word for 'wife' usually occurs in the plural is that it may refer to 'hetairai', as unlikely, since the Rig-Veda uses the phrase meaning 'wifehood to a husband', besides containing passages clearly referring to marriage.

to lose all concern for intellectual honesty. In point of fact, the sexual standards of inhabitants of the Hindu-Kush and the Punjab are remoter from modern conceptions than those of any comparable people. The only Aryans known to history, as we have seen, were the Medes, and the Central Asiatic offshoots of the same race, to which the early invaders of India belonged. These Aryans were polyandrous, as Strabo tells us. To have fewer than five wives or five husbands was accounted a misfortune.

There is no reason to suppose that the conceptions of peoples speaking languages related to Sanskrit have passed through phases different from those passed through by other ethnic groups. The differences between advanced and primitive peoples in this respect are due not to racial characteristics but to the extent of their social evolution. Everything goes to show that Western races have passed through the same phases as primitive people of other races.

Evidence of sexual communism and polyandry are by no means unknown among the peoples from whom European civilization has derived, whether or not culturally or racially related to the Aryans. Thus in Sparta, the community which preserved most faithfully the primitive organization of the Hellenes, fraternal polyandry was legal. 'In Sparta', says Polybius, 'several brothers had often one wife between them and the children were brought up in common.' It was the custom to exchange wives and to offer them to strangers, and, during the absence of their spouses, Spartan women might take 'secondary husbands'. Circumstances, such as the rituals of sexual promiscuity practised in some Greek communities, confirm the inference that the Spartan institution was a survival from a phase through which the Greek race as a whole had passed.[1]

The Etruscans, according to Theopompos, held their wives in common. We have already indicated that the institutions of Rome were once very different. Those primitive Latin princes who did not know their fathers can scarcely have been monandrous. From the most brilliant epoch of the Roman Republic, Plutarch reports an incident which divorced from this background, would appear utterly inexplicable. Quintus Hortensius, a man of exalted character and a friend and admirer of the second Cato, expressed a desire 'to be more than a mere associate and companion of Cato and in some manner to bring his whole family and blood into community of kinship with him'. To this end he proposed that Cato's daughter, already married to Bibulus, should be lent to him 'as noble soil for the production of children'. Lest Bibulus be averse from the proposition, he promised to give him back his wife as soon as

---

[1] Sexual promiscuity, of course, does not constitute collective sexual organization; nevertheless, it rarely survives in a society where individual sexual claims are fully established.

she had borne a child. Cato was far from being offended, but refused the request on the grounds that Bibulus would be unwilling. Hortensius then suggested that Cato should lend him his own wife. To this Cato could see no objection, but thought it only fair to talk the matter over with his wife's father. The latter entirely concurred, and Cato accordingly lent his wife to Hortensius. Plutarch reports this with obvious embarrassment, but Strabo saw the incident in its proper perspective. He refers to it after mentioning the polyandrous customs of the Medes, adding: 'In the same manner in our own day Cato lent his wife to Hortensius, upon the latter's request, following in this an ancient custom of the Romans.'

Among the barbarians of Northern Europe, it was not unusual for men to exchange wives. In Germany, until quite late in the Middle Ages, it was legal for the husband, if his marriage proved without issue, to introduce a friend to his wife, a usage which is said to have lingered almost to our own time in some of the remoter districts. In Nordic mythology the goddess Frigga, when her husband Odin goes on a journey, cohabits with his brothers, like a Tlinkit lady.

Cæsar states that the ancient Britons practised community of wives—groups of ten or twelve, especially brothers, having their wives in common. Dio Cassius makes Queen Boudicca say: 'It is over Britons that I rule, men . . . who have even their wives and their children in common.' Similar usages are reported of the Caledonians and border tribes: 'They live in tents, naked and barefooted, having wives in common and rearing the whole progeny.' Strabo was told that the Irish had free access to one another's wives and did not even bar incest. St Jerome, with theological exaggeration, says of the northern Britons: 'The nation of the Scots have no individual wives, and, as if they had been reading Plato's *Republic* or wished to imitate the example of Cato, a man amongst them has no wife of his own . . .'

There appears to be no reason to question, as has been done, the accuracy of these statements. That they do not appear in Celtic literature is to be expected, since all this literature has been set down in Christian times by Christian priests. Nevertheless, the 'Ulster Saga' mentions that the princess Clothru married three brothers and that her son had thus three fathers. Multiple fatherhood is also referred to in mythological texts. In the Celtic family property was indivisible, and, unless a son went to seek his fortune, brothers continued together, forming one common household. The name of that household was not the house but, significantly enough, 'the bed', and the Celtic family was called 'the common bed'. In short, there is no indication of a monogamic tradition or disposition among the peoples who have been called 'Aryan', whether in Europe or in Asia.

Collective Marriage in Southern India

In southern Hindustan the survivals of collective sexual organization are so general as to leave little doubt that this once constituted the usual form of marriage. Group-marriage is in full force at the present day among the tribes of the Nilgiri Hills, especially among the Todas. It has been described as simple polyandry, but, as Gait's account makes clear, it is actually sororal-fraternal group-marriage. Not only are the brothers of one family co-partners in the group-marriage of that family with another, but tribal brothers are also admitted to the connubial group. 'Notwithstanding these singular family arrangements', says Major Ross King, 'the greatest harmony appears to prevail among all parties—husbands, wives and lovers. The children live happily with their putative parents, equally well treated on every side.'

According to Dr Rivers, there is reason to believe that the Todas migrated to their present habitat from the coasts of Malabar at the time of the Aryan invasion. Hence they must be regarded as representing the original form of organization of all the native races of Malabar and Travancore—a conclusion supported by the reports of the older travellers and by what we know of the usages of the populations of that country at the present day. Thus fraternal polyandry is reported of the Krisnavakkakars of Travancore. The Kanisans admit that fraternal polyandry was formerly common among them. Today in Malabar polyandry is most prevalent among the poorer classes. In former days it existed among the noblest and wealthiest aboriginal caste of the land. Concerning the marriage system of the Nayars, we have a considerable number of accounts dating from the time of the first landing of the Portuguese in India to the present day. Apart from a few misconceptions, the numerous accounts are remarkably consistent and, in the light of present knowledge, accurate.

As already noted, the social organization of the Nayars is one of the purest examples of unmodified matriarchal organization, the motherhood, or 'tarwad', being composed of all the descendants of a common ancestress in the female line and constituting the only unit of Nayar society. These tarwads, of which there are a hundred, are classified in order of nobility, and the strictest rule is that no Nayar woman may associate with a man in a caste lower than her own. Apart from this limitation, either sex is free to make whatever associations it wishes; there is no permanent cohabitation or economic association between men and women and no initiatory ceremony. As one Nayar says: 'Marriage among the Nayars is indeed pure and simple and unmixed with considerations of civil rights of property—a marriage for the sake of marriage alone. It is not an institution intended, as in more advanced

Hindu societies, for the perpetuation of the family, but a social arrangement intended for the peaceful satisfaction of the "blindest appetite" of man.' The association can be dissolved with the will of either party without further ceremony. Mr Gopal Panikkar says: 'There are two sides to a marriage, a legal and a religious. Now, in the case of our marriage both elements are wanting. . . . There is, in fact, no fixed rule or custom as to marriages in Malabar. They are terminable at the will of either party and the law takes no notice of them.'

While Nayar associations are limited by the law prohibiting the woman to associate with an inferior caste, caste organization is not an aboriginal institution and this must have been borrowed from the Aryans. Probably relations were originally confined by tribal law to certain intermarrying tarwads, a suggestion confirmed by the fact that today a Nayar is supposed to marry his cross-cousin; that is to say, in the same tarwad as the other members of his own tarwad.

McLennan regarded Nayar polyandry as the type of non-fraternal polyandry, in contrast with the Tibetan form, and the impression that it was non-fraternal has continued among ethnological writers to the present day. But there is every reason for thinking that this is an error. Non-fraternal polyandry, as a traditionally established institution, is extremely rare, if it exists at all. Instances, such as the collective marriages of the Chukchi, or the polyandry still surviving in the Darjeeling district, which are described as non-fraternal polyandry, are seen on examination to be but degenerate forms of collective relations, in which the husbands were originally brothers, own or tribal. The organization of Nayar marriage has been obscured by the fact that Nambutiri Brahmans were admitted to 'marriage' with Nayar women; and in the lower castes, and wherever polyandry still survives among Nayar castes at the present day, it is confined to the fraternal form.

Gemelli-Careri expressly states that the husbands in Nayar marriage were brothers; 'when one brother marries a woman,' he states, 'she is common to all the others'. Other travellers, misled by the part played by Brahmans in such unions, and also by the fact that in the Nayar social system there were no 'actual' but only 'tribal' brothers (that is, members of the same 'tarwad') have described Nayar polyandry as non-fraternal. Since there was no 'family', there were no brothers in the family sense, but only in the clan sense. That Nayar polyandry was fraternal follows from the obligation to marry in certain 'tarwads' only, and seemingly in that into which a man's mother's brothers have married. At the present day, cultured Nayars, who are extremely reluctant to admit any survival of the polyandrous customs of their ancestors, acknowledge that a trace of it is retained in the relations between brothers. 'The wife of a brother', says Mr K. M. Panikkar, 'is looked upon as a person to whom one could openly, though not legitimately, pay court, and any favour short of sexual relationship which she confers upon them is allowed by public opinion. . . . All brothers treat her half as a sister and half as a wife.'

Nayar marriage was, in fact, identical with all the other institutions of fraternal sororal polygamy, and differed only from the modern Tibetan form in being of a more primitive type, the marrying groups being unmodified matriarchal clans and not, as in Tibet, semi-patriarchal families. It is significant that no instance of non-fraternal polyandry, as a general custom of spontaneous and independent origin, is definitely known; and that, where such a practice is found, it appears invariably to be derived from fraternal group-marriage. For if, as some have supposed, polyandry were simply the outcome of various local and accidental conditions, such, for instance as scarcity of women, there would be no apparent reason why it should not commonly take the form of a deliberate partnership between persons not necessarily related. But no instance is known of polyandry having become customary except as a modification of already existing fraternal group-marriage.

The connubial relations of Nayar women were preceded by a ceremony, the tying of the 'tali', which was performed on Nayar girls before the age of eleven. The 'tali' is a small gold leaf through which a hole is bored with the finger, and which is tied round the neck of the girl. (This rite is general among Dravidian races.) It is often performed on batches of girls, including infants. In one form of the usage there were as many ritual bridegrooms as marriagcable girls, and it is thus possible that the ceremonial marriage constituted in those instances the actual marriage of a group of girls to a group of bridegrooms.[1]

The marriage customs of the Nayars have now become almost, though not entirely, obliterated, but polyandry is, according to Mr Gopal Panikkar, observed at the present day by the barber caste of Nayars. Strange as it may seem, the group-marriage of the Nayars has been strenuously denied *in toto*. Such repudiations are inevitable wherever new moral values have been adopted and old usages abandoned. The Parsee scholars attempt to repudiate the existence of the well-known law of next-of-kin marriage, or 'xvaetvadatha', of Mazdanean religion, an institution laid down in their Sacred Books, the practice of which for centuries is a matter of history. The Todas indignantly repudiate the practice of female infanticide, although it is well known that they

[1] Nayars, to defend themselves against the sort of ethnical persecution to which they have been subjected, have sometimes adduced the 'talikettu' ceremony, but Sir T. Muttusami Ayer, the chairman of the Malabar Marriage Commission, concludes in his report that 'in relation to marriage it has no significance save that no girl is at liberty to contract it before she goes through the "tali-kettu" ceremony'.

practise it at the present day. In Africa, tribes mutually accuse one another of cannibalism, while each denies the impeachment.

In conclusion it may be added that the institutions which were general among the aboriginal races of India were, as might be expected, common to the peoples of the same race in Ceylon. Among the Singhalese, fraternal polyandry was an established institution and was recognized by law until the year 1859; it continued to be practised much later in the interior.

Evidence of Polyandry among the Ancient Semites

Polyandrous marriage was a familiar institution among the ancient Semites. As we know from the Arab philosopher Al-Biruni and others, 'all the kindred have their property in common, the eldest being lord; all have one wife, and the first that comes has access to her'. This account is confirmed from the inscriptions of southern Arabia, which commonly refer to a man's 'fathers'. These have sometimes been interpreted as referring to the person's father, grandfather and great-grandfather, but this interpretation is excluded by some inscriptions in which the fathers are described as brothers. In one, a whole genealogy is given in which brothers twice appear as the common fathers of their descendants.

Early Babylonian records refer also to polyandrous marriage; the important part played by the institution of levirate marriage which, in Mosaic legislation, is expressly connected with the custom of brothers living together in an undivided household, indicates the former prevalence of similar usages amongst the Hebrews.[1]

[1] Levirate marriage is described on pp. 153–6.

CHAPTER 11

Group Marriage (11)

IN Africa, owing to the extensive development of private property and consequently of individualism, marriage has tended to assume the form of personal economic, and even purely commercial, transactions. Nevertheless, the continent presents examples of collective sexual relations. Thus, among the Banyoro of Uganda it was legitimate for a man to have relations with the wives of the men he called brothers, i.e. his clan fellows. A man might use his influence with his wife to make her refrain from such action, but he could not accuse her of unfaithfulness for so doing. A woman, however, was restricted to men of her husband's clan. Similarly among the Banyankole or Bahima—except that the restriction to clan-brothers is not insisted on for either sex. Much the same is true of the Akamba, a Bantu tribe, but here limited to members of the same clan or occasionally to intimate friends of another clan. Half-brothers have a recognized right of habitual access to the wives of their half-brothers of a corresponding age.

Among the Masai and other kindred tribes there is right of access among members of the same marriage class, such classes being based on age-groups of the men who passed through puberty ceremonies at the same time. Individual marriage does not take place until comparatively late in life, prior to which the young men live in separate kraals and the unmarried girls of corresponding age with them. But when individual marriage takes place, the members of the age-grade claim priority of intercourse with the bride. After marriage, temporary exchange of wives is usual between members of the same age-grade. So also among the Nandi and elsewhere.

The Herero, the great western branch of the southern Bantu, have an elaborate institution of sexual communism which presents interesting features. Owing to their isolation, they have preserved customs of more primitive character than have the majority of Bantu. They are divided into totemic clans, some strictly matriarchal, others patriarchal, and appear to be in a state of transition from matriarchy to patriarchy. Cross-cousin marriage is strictly observed. Sororal polygyny and the levirate are customary. Speaking of the Ovaherero in particular, Dr Hahn says that every man and every woman stands towards certain other men and women in a particular relation called 'upanga', a word originally meaning 'companion'. Every man can claim access to tne wives of his 'upanga' at any time, and conversely for women. These customs are observed in all the neighbouring tribes. According to Dr Dannert, actual brothers and all persons closely related by blood are prohibited from entering into the relationship of 'upanga', though this does not apply to the women. Though other writers contradict this, if Dr Dannert is correct the sexual communism of the Herero presents a remarkable anomaly. But this might have come about easily enough in relation to the development of private property. The Herero are great pastoralists: and communism tends to be abolished wherever property becomes of great value. It is noticeable that the prohibition regarding relatives applies only to the men. Among the Bantu the women are never owners of cattle; it therefore appears to refer to the economic consequences of the relationship rather than the relationship itself.

In every part of Madagascar relations are permitted between a man and the sisters and female cousins of his wife, and with the wives of his brothers and cousins; conversely for women, The only forbidden relations are those between a married woman and a slave, or a stranger who is not the guest of her husband.

Sexual Communism in New Guinea and Oceania

Sexual communism is found in northern Papua, among the Kai, and among the southern Massims of British New Guinea. Similar institutions flourish in Polynesia. Thus in Tahiti and in the Friendly Islands the aristocratic classes were united in a brotherhood known as 'areoi'. A wife might sleep with fellow-members of her husband's 'areoi', but relations with non-members were accounted adulterous. Sexual promiscuity was practised at periodic feasts.

The Marquesan group long escaped civilizing influences, and Dr Tautain, the French administrator there, found fraternal sororal polygamy derived from an originally wider form of tribal sexual communism, as shown by the fact that it was obligatory for the bride to be placed at the disposal of all the tribal brothers of the husband before marriage. Similar customs are found at the other extremity of the area inhabited by the Polynesian race, in Hawaii, which was probably the first Polynesian settlement in the Pacific. Although they are not definitely reported from the intermediate parts, there are indications that they were not local peculiarities of Hawaii and the Marquesas. For example, the word 'punalua', now translated as 'intimate companion', is in general use throughout Polynesia and its exact meaning is 'a multiplicity of spouses'. Very much the same customs obtained throughout Micronesia, polyandry being reported as common among the upper classes in the Gilbert Islands, the Marshalls and elsewhere.

Collective Marriage in Australia

As we have seen, the collective sexual organization varies; the group of husbands may consist of actual or half-brothers or may include other near relatives; sometimes the eldest brother is paramount; sometimes the group consists of a limited number of clan members, or of all clan members, or of all members of a given marriage class or age-group. And we have seen that in organizations of the fraternal type there are signs that they were formally associated with an organization into clans or marriage-classes. If, as we concluded, the earliest pattern was an understanding between two primitive groups or clans and had no reference to individual marriage, then the most primitive form of marriage would consist of sexual communism between clan brothers—that is, the right of access of all members of one group to all those of opposite sex in the corresponding group.

Special interest therefore attaches to Australian clan organization since there the primitive pattern has remained substantially unchanged. Their material culture has, of course, undergone important changes, and, as we have seen, male domination has attained its most despotic form. Australian society exhibits several different principles of organization which have become combined and have modified one another. There are three basic principles of organization—totem groups, territorial classifications (members of the same camping-ground) and marriage classes. Each varies from one tribe to another: thus in one case the totem is transmitted through the mother, in another through the father and in a third the community decides to which totem a particular child shall belong. Sometimes change of residence transfers an individual from one territorial group to another.

This complexity of organization means a corresponding complexity in the rules governing sexual relations, and indeed this is the sole purpose of all this organization. It is therefore inappropriate to speak of promiscuity, and these rules may properly be described as concerned with morality, although so different from the moral rules of civilized communities. The Australian rules are not concerned with safeguarding the claims of individual marriage but with the prevention of incest. To marry within the prohibited degrees would have dire consequences for the whole tribe. Among the Dieri, the elders in their leisure lecture the young people on the heinousness of incest, the penalty for which is usually death. Even in cases of rape, the victim is first asked by her assailant to what class she belongs. The totemic system is regarded as having been instituted solely in order to distinguish between those who may and may not have sexual relations.

Individual marriage for economic purposes is widely found in the present day, but is regarded simply as due to economic necessity. But while it establishes the rights of the husband to the company, obedience and labour of the woman, it does not regulate sexual relations. Group marriage between members of corresponding marriage classes has long been widespread, and was accurately described for the first time in 1832 by Scott Nind, who noted that men did not marry until after thirty, as a rule, but that they often courted a wife while her husband was still living. Exchange of wives among tribal brothers is 'extremely frequent' in Western Australia, and, as one cleric observes, 'it may be said that they have their wives in common'. Among the Dieri, when two brothers are married to two sisters they probably live together in a group marriage of four. In the Kunandaburi tribe intercourse constantly takes place between 'a group of men who are own or tribal brothers and a group of women who are own or tribal sisters'. Among the northern tribes fraternal polyandry is so much a matter of course that it is usually not the husband but one of his brothers who chastises a woman guilty of adultery.

However, Australian sexual organization differs in some respects from the examples of fraternal polyandry earlier considered, and represents a more primitive form. Thus it is not an organized marriage of the whole fraternal family group, as is the marriage of the Tibetans or the Todas. Indeed there is no such thing as a juridically-recognized family group in Australian social organization.

Missionaries have often been misled by these institutions to suppose them licentious aberrations. Any promiscuity which exists is a rigidly defined group promiscuity. Thus among the four clans of the Aldolinga tribe, a Beltare man can cohabit with any Kumare woman and a Burule with any of the Bunanke women.

Spencer and Gillen have described some aspects of sexual relations among the Dieri and the Urabunna tribes of Central Australia; among the Dieri, at the great tribal gatherings in connection with puberty, a special ceremony known as 'Kandri' is performed at which the names of various couples are solemnly read out by the head of the totem group. The various persons thus allotted to one another are not consulted, and they are expected to cohabit immediately. These pairs are known as 'pirrauru', a term which appears to mean 'moon spouses'. (In the Warramunga tribe, it is the moon god which is supposed to have established the marriage classes and sexual rules.) All the marriageable and married people, even those who are already 'pirraurus', are allotted in batches, and once a 'pirrauru' always a 'pirrauru'. These relationships are independent of the individual economic marriage known as 'tippamalku', and are attended with special solemnities. Every man, married or unmarried, has one or more 'pirrauru' wives, and each woman may have a number of 'pirrauru' husbands in addition to her 'tippa-malku' partner. A man exercises marital rights over his 'pirrauru' with the formal assent of the 'tippa-malku' husband if the latter is present, and as a matter of course if he is not. Similarly among the Urabunna tribe the normal marital pairs are called 'nupa', but in addition each man has certain 'nupa' women with whom he stands in the relation of 'piraungaru'. Conversely a woman is the 'piraungaru' of certain other men while being the 'nupa' of one particular man. In this tribe individual marriage does not exist even in name, as far as sexual rights are concerned.

The marriage organization of the Australian aborigines suggested to Fison and Howitt the view that collective group relations must have preceded any form of individual marriage, a view which has been endorsed by most eminent authorities, though not by Dr Westermarck, who is severely criticized by Spencer and Gillen for his scepticism.

The existence of group-marriage is not at issue; the questions which are in dispute are: (1) whether the individual association was anterior or posterior to the sexual communism, and (2) whether sexual communism does or did extend to the whole of the inter-marriage classes. Dr Westermarck founds his hypothesis that individual marriage came first on nothing more than the supposition that such ideas are innate in human nature; but, as we shall show in more detail later this rests upon a misconception. What is spoken of as jealousy in primitive societies does not refer to sexual possession. The Rev. J. Mathew bases his objection on the ground that this would 'reduce mankind to a state of degradation lower than the brutes'; adding 'if gorillas have the decency to pair off, why may not primitive man have done the same?' He doubtless derives the notion that gorillas pair from Dr Westermarck, who gave considerable currency to that piece of misinformation at one time.

To suppose that individual marriage was replaced by sexual communism is difficult, for such a trend is of course unknown in any sphere of social development. The whole of history proves the difficulties of checking individualistic tendencies once they have developed. Westermarck remarks that polygyny and polyandry are prone to be modified towards monogamy, but elsewhere claims that the Urabunna custom may have developed from ordinary individual marriage. It is hardly possible for both views to be correct.

The existence of sexual communism has usually been assigned to the difficulty of obtaining wives when there is a scarcity of women, and to the benevolence of the older married men in remedying the distress of the younger members by allowing them access to their own wives. Unfortunately almost every account tells us that the scarcity is caused chiefly by the older men monopolizing the women, and that, far from attempting to remedy the situation, they go out of their way to make matters more difficult.

The bulk of the criticisms have been directed against Dr Howitt's account of the customs of the Dieri, but it seems to me that the 'pirrauru' institution constitutes but a small part of the evidence pointing to the fundamentally collective character of aboriginal social organization. Certain inconsistencies due to misinformation or misunderstanding have been made much of, and it is easy to draw up a list of points concerning the institutions of this tribe which still remain obscure, but there are many points which are clear. For example, while a man may have several 'tippa-malkus', a woman can have but one; and, in general, the system is more beneficial for the male, as one would expect in a state characterized by male supremacy. Mr Thomas argues that, since the 'pirrauru' relationship comes after a 'tippa-malku' marriage in the case of the woman, it must be evolutionarily later; but since both forms of marriage are preceded by free love, he should therefore infer that this was the earliest state of humanity. He claims that the 'pirrauru' relation cannot be a survival of unregulated relations, since it is regulated; but, in fact, throughout the world many forms of promiscuity are subject to a certain regulation, from the Nanga gatherings of Fiji to the Babylonian rites of Mylitta.

It is recognized that ritual licence, which often has a semi-religious or magical character, cannot be adduced as evidence of normal social relations, but in practice it is often difficult to draw a hard-and-fast line between the two phenomena. In Australian tribes, which are fragmented into small camps which only meet at periodic gatherings, promiscuity can never be other than ceremonial. The fact that the husband's consent must be requested, if he is present, before a 'pirrauru' relationship is consummated has been thought to indicate the vested right of the husband to dispose of the woman at his pleasure, and thus to make the whole thing merely an instance of husbandly authority. But it is clear that the husband never refuses his consent, and the object of asking it is to assure him that his wife will not be permanently taken from him. Again, the fact that a man who has access to a man's wife offers the latter some present has been taken as indicating that the transaction has the character of a prostitution. Actually, so little mercenary is the custom that the presents are commonly given away again by the husband.

Turning to the second controversial aspect: though it is true that own brothers frequently have connubial rights, nothing in Australian institutions resembles the fundamentally fraternal polyandrous organizations of the Tibetans or of the Todas. The circumstance that own brothers are preferential co-partners is a consequence and not the foundation of

Australian sexual collectivism. There is no sign of any evolution from fraternal to some wider group; on the contrary, the fraternal group and the family itself remain an unrecognized, and indeed nameless, accretion within the collective marriage-class organization.

The relations between members of corresponding marriage-classes are entirely different from those between other men and women. They are called 'spouses' (husband or wife)—the word 'noa' means spouse or partner—but the term 'noa,' and corresponding terms such as 'nupa' among the Urabunna, apply equally to all members of the opposite sex in corresponding marriage-classes. They are therefore frequently interpreted in English by the term 'potential wife' or 'potential husband'. Many of the controversies on this topic have arisen from the misconception created by this misleading expression. Thus in England almost all unmarried women, except the few within the prohibited degrees, are potential wives of any unmarried man, yet for an Englishman to ravish an unmarried girl is a serious offence. In Australia the relationship of 'noa' gives him the right to do this with impunity. Furthermore, a European woman ceases to be a potential wife when she marries, but in Australia she does not. In Australia, this relationship gives a native a claim to sexual access to a woman, whether he contemplates marrying her or not and whether she is married or not. A better term would be 'facultative' wife. When the Rev. J. Bulmer pointed out to a native of unusual independence of mind what he called 'the absurdity of the native classificatory system', the native replied that it was the European system which was absurd. 'Why should I be so foolish', he said, 'as to call my wife's sister 'sister'? She is *not* my sister and she *is* my wife.'

To sum up: of actual group-marriage relations, in the sense of regular, recognized and habitual sexual cohabitation, we have evidence only in the 'pirrauru' and similar institutions and in the collective sexual communism prevalent among Australian tribes in every part of the continent. But Australian social organizations are not founded on any system of fraternal-sororal polygamy, and their especial significance lies in the fact that they cannot have developed out of a system of individual marriage, but must, from the first, have been collective and polyandrous. Hence there is no alternative but to conclude that the collective marriage groups were originally co-extensive with the present intermarriage classes, for there is a total absence of groups or relationships of any other kind, apart from individual marriage. Dr Westermarck argues that, even if group marriage was once common in Australia, this would not prove that it was once common among mankind at large; and he adds that the existence of kangaroos in Australia does not prove that there were once kangaroos in England. But, in point of fact, no less than twenty-three different species of marsupial mammals have been found in the Oligocene desposits of the south of England and northern France. To the truly scientific mind the discovery of marsupials in Australia would certainly suggest that mammals of the present day might not be unrelated. Similarly if we turn to the first account ever published of the married usages of the British, we find Caesar remarking: 'In their domestic life they practise a form of community of wives, ten or twelve men combining in groups, especially brothers with brothers and fathers with sons.'

This lengthy survey shows that, however rare collective sexual organizations may be today, they are not as rare as supposed, and that there is scarcely anywhere in the world where evidence of their recent existence or actual existence is not to be found. The remarkable fact is not that they are rare, but that they have survived at all down to the present time. The only favouring factor common to these cases is the comparative isolation of the peoples among whom they survive. They are chiefly found among mountain populations, and it is not among such populations we should look for aberrations, innovations or eccentricities. Taken with the fact that the stranger who is made a tribal brother is commonly regarded as entitled to sexual hospitality, these facts all confirm the conclusion already reached on other grounds that the regulation of collective sexual relations has everywhere preceded the regulation of such relations between individuals.

The Levirate

The custom that a man should marry his deceased brother's widow, known as the 'levirate', is well-nigh universal in distribution, and it is invariably continuous with fraternal polyandry.[1] If it is, in fact, a survival of it, additional evidence is provided of the universality of the principles which we have been discussing.

The levirate is observed with particular rigour among just those people among whom fraternal or clan polyandry also obtains, such as the Australian aborigines, the Tibetans, the Eskimo, the Tlinkit and others. Moreover, just as when a man marries his wife's sister no new ceremony is necessary, so also when the deceased man's brother takes his wife no ceremony is necessary. In Ladakh, however, the woman can be relieved from the obligation of marrying her deceased husband's brother if she goes through a ceremony of divorce with her deceased husband's corpse.

Again, the rule that younger brothers have sexual rights over the wives of their elder brothers, but that the latter have no rights over the wives of younger brothers, is also true of the levirate. On the other hand,

[1] A bibliography of 240 titles is provided in support of this point.

in a purely tribal society the widow may go indifferently to an older or a younger brother. Among the Shuswap the widow is kept a prisoner until she marries her husband's brother, in the same way that a man is kept under lock and key until he marries his deceased wife's sister. Frequently these two customs co-exist. In fact, among those who observe the levirate, it would be difficult to find many instances in which the custom is not associated either with actual sororal polygyny or with its residual form, the right or obligation to marry a deceased wife's sister.

Nevertheless, one fundamental difference between the two situations exists: in certain phases of society women tend to be regarded by the men as acquired possessions, and are in fact 'purchased'; whereas, with rare exceptions, men are not 'purchased' by women. The woman acquired by a family or clan is commonly regarded as permanently acquired. As an educated Yoruba explained: 'Women are never really married twice. . . . Once married, they are attached for ever to the house and family of the deceased husband; hence it is more usual for widows to choose another husband from the same family.' But the view that the woman is acquired property, in which the whole family has an interest, is so closely allied with the view which regards the brothers as having a claim on the woman even during the first husband's lifetime as to be indistinguishable. As Dr Lindblom said of the Akamba, fraternal succession is with them a sequel to the recognized rights of access during the husband's lifetime.

Juridic notions of property and of its transmission by inheritance are of comparatively late emergence. Unless, therefore, we suppose that the levirate did not come into use until such ideas had developed, we must look for some prior social cause. The practice is found among peoples, such as the Australians, who have no juridic idea of property. Even if the wife is assimilated to property, such property must be regarded as having been originally communal, like all other clan property. The North American Indians, among whom the levirate was general, not only have no conception of individual property but do not acquire wives either by exchange of goods or of another female. Moreover, even where the custom of the levirate appears to be interpreted as an inheritance of property, it is found that the laws governing it are different from those governing property. This is true even in Africa, where the assimilation of the wife to property has been carried farthest. Thus among the Koro of Northern Nigeria a man's property passes to his son, but his widow's goes to his younger brothers. It is a very general usage among the advanced African tribes for a man to inherit his father's wives, with the exception of his actual mother. Thus here the law of inheritance, instead of enforcing the levirate, has the effect of abolishing it. Again, we find rules regarding the disposal of widows which have no reference to juridic property. Thus among the Banyankole, if a man has as many wives as he can keep, he may decline to take on his deceased brother's widows, and permit them to marry whomever they choose; but he, nevertheless, retains his right of sexual access to them, and is, in fact, expected to visit them as husband now and again. Similarly among the Gwari, a widow is at liberty to return to her own people and to marry whom she likes, but is under the obligation of cohabiting, if only for three days, with the brother of her deceased husband, and any children resulting are his. A similar custom is found among the Baluba in the Congo and the natives of Theraka in East Africa.

Another interpretation put upon the levirate is that of the ancient Hebrews, who regarded it as an obligation to raise seed to the brother, or to build up his house, an interpretation also given by other people, both savage and cultured. Among the Ossetes, while a widow is obliged to remain unmarried if her deceased husband has left no father or brother, yet she is not prohibited from living with other men; however, any children which may result are considered the legitimate offspring of her first marriage. A boy born in this way will succeed to the property at the expense of daughters born in wedlock. The Ossetes display the unusual but not unique feature that the widow passes, as often as not, to the *father* of the deceased rather than to his brother. Thus the Ossete father not only raises seed unto his son after the latter's decease but during his lifetime also. A father sometimes purchases a wife for his son and cohabits with her until the son reaches the age of puberty. He may even purchase a wife for the son which he has by this girl and cohabit with her in turn.

The Ossetes are the same people whom the Romans called Alani, a tribe of the Massagetae, among whom the fraternal household is the foundation of the social order; thus, the levirate custom is traceable, both in the economic and the Hebraic interpretation, to its original source in fraternal sexual communism or polyandry.

Among the Dinkas the theory of raising seed is carried out even more thoroughly, for if the widow is past child-bearing age it is incumbent upon her to furnish a young girl to the brother or the nearest relative of the deceased, and if there is no such relative she must also provide a man to act as husband to the girl, the children still being accounted as the offspring of the deceased husband, who with luck may go on procreating a family in this way for more than fifty years after his death.

However, the view that the function of the levirate is to raise seed to the husband is manifestly an interpretation subsequently invented to explain an immemorial usage. And many who practise the levirate have no notion of such a theory. Furthermore, it is obviously not a need to raise seed which renders it obligatory among many peoples for the widow to wait, if her late husband's brother is still an infant, for the latter to grow up. Again, when a man inherits his father's wives, the sons which he has by them are not called his sons but his brothers. Similarly the sons of a man by his brother's widow do not call him father, but uncle.

In some parts of Africa, the levirate is viewed as a sort of purificatory rite, designed to avert the anger of the deceased's ghost. Interpretations of the levirate cannot be seen as anything but variations of the usage of succession to the wives of the fraternal group. This is the only explanation which is applicable in all cases. It is highly improbable that a usage so universal in distribution and so deeply rooted should owe its rise in the first instance to the adventitious operation of a multiplicity of diverse local causes.

CHAPTER 12

Promiscuity and Individual Marriage

WHEREAS the regulation of relations between intermarriage groups is sexual, individual marriage has its foundations in economics. In the vast majority of uncultured societies marriage is regarded in an almost exclusively economic light, and the changes which it has undergone had economic causes.

In modern Europe, the sexual and economic aspects of marriage are combined, and the former is conventionally regarded as the primary one. This convention has been maintained even where, as in marriages of convenience, the motive for the association is primarily economic and social.

The origin and development of marriage have hence been discussed by social historians almost exclusively in terms of the operation of the sexual instinct—the exercise of personal choice, of jealousy and of romantic love. Actually these are the products of the association rather than its causes. To be sure, individual economic association between sexual partners has inevitably tended to establish individual sexual claims. These claims have brought about new restrictions on sexual relations: the married woman tends to become prohibited to all but her individual associate. In comparatively advanced stages of development, infant betrothal has led, especially in the aristocratic classes, the restriction on women's sexual freedom to operate retrospectively, and so to the demand that a bride should be a virgin.

Such restrictions did not become fully established until quite late in the growth of advanced societies, and have contributed to the European identification of the economic with the sexual aspect of marriage. With us, marriage is, in theory and to a large extent in practice, the only licit sexual relation. But in primitive society it is nothing of the sort. Far from being a means of satisfying the sexual instincts, it is one of the chief restrictions imposed upon them. Without a single exception, unmarried females outside the prohibited degrees are accessible to all males.[1] If ever a case were found where chastity was obligatory on unmarried

[1] A bibliography of 422 titles is provided in support of this point.

females other than as a result of the influence of some more highly developed culture, the fact would be momentous, for it would be an example of the appearance in mankind of a sentiment entirely absent in animals. It would thus jeopardize the whole evolutionary conception of human development.

Until the theory of evolution was propounded, men and animals were regarded as having had separate origins. The accepted view was that the primitive state of mankind was one of primal virtue—that is to say, it accorded with the moral standards recognized in European societies, and these sexual codes were supposed to represent the innate endowments of primitive humanity; any variations were regarded as aberrations due to corruption. When travellers first began to report the customs of uncultured races, they were found interesting chiefly because it was believed that they would corroborate this theory. The science of comparative social anthropology owes its origin largely to the interest of the Jesuit Fathers. Father Lafitau's *Manners of the American Savages compared with those of the Earliest Times* was the first systematic book on the subject. It was intended to uphold the theory of a primitive moral revelation. The good Father scorns those authors who, like Athenaeus, believed that 'the men of the earliest times observed no solemnity in their marriages, mixing indifferently like animals, until the time of Kekrops, who laid down the laws of matrimony'. He attributes this to the error in which men were sunk in the last days of paganism. 'It appears to me evident, on the contrary, that marriage has always been regarded by all peoples as a thing sacred and solemn, the rights of which have been respected by even the most barbarous nations. . . . We have seen that virginity has been honoured from the most ancient times, consecrated in persons specially appointed to the cult of the gods and held in regard among barbarians. That virtue could not be extended to all persons for all the days of their life on account of the necessity of procreating the human species; but, mankind being in that necessity, conjugal faith has been respected, and marriage, shameful in its use, has been subject to laws of propriety, modesty, pudicity and continence, which are inspired by nature, upheld by reason and which the institution has preserved in the midst of barbarism.' And he adds: 'I admit, of course, that among some peoples, depravity and grossness of manners have at various times and in diverse places introduced abuses and even shameful customs in this respect.'

The doctrine of organic evolution completely changed the premises of social anthropology, and a galaxy of brilliant scholars soon placed the social history of the human race upon a scientific basis by showing that the organization and conceptions of primitive society differed profoundly from those of modern Europe. However, the views of Father

Lafitau have been recently revived by a Finnish writer, Edward Westermarck, who, taking little note of anthropological discoveries, 'boldly
challenged the conclusions of our most esteemed writers', and 'arrived
at different, and sometimes diametrically opposite, conclusions'.[1] Supported by unparalleled bibilographical industry, his views have exercised
enormous influence. If his views were substantiated, we should be
compelled to abandon scientific methods in studying the social development of humanity. For Dr Westermarck, though he has endeavoured to
trace the institution of marriage to the apes, has not offered any examples
of regard for chastity among monkeys. Hence, there would be no alternative but to account for such sentiments by supposing a special revelation. The hope that we may continue to employ the methods of science,
however, is strongly supported by many thousands of accounts and
statements referring to the sexual habits of uncultured races, derived
from all sorts and conditions of witnesses, many of them entirely devoid
of scientific notions, and many zealously anxious to represent the European conceptions of morality as universal.

As Dr Westermarck has most industriously collected such statements
as seem to support the moral theory of the last century, we cannot do
better than to examine the examples he cites.

Alleged Instances of Primitive Pre-marital Chastity

Some of Dr Westermarck's instances refer to highly patriarchal peoples;
others to tribes which have long been Christianized. With these we are
not here concerned.

In other cases, however, he asserts pre-nuptial chastity to have been
a general usage when in reality it was confined to the ruling classes and
to chiefs. Thus he asserts it to have been general among the Yoruba, the
Ewe and the peoples of the Gold Coast, and, still more unwarrantably,
among the Tongans, Samoans and other Polynesians. This is profoundly inaccurate. Similarly, he cites several Californian tribes in
which the wealthy class required a high bride-price for their daughters,
and therefore prevented access to them. The Californian Indians were,
however, 'a grossly licentious race'. Among some peoples, where boys
and girls are mated as soon as they attain the age of puberty, while there
cannot be said to exist either pre-nuptial chastity or unchastity, neither
can it be said that any account is taken of purity. Again, it is no evidence
of pre-nuptial chastity to report that the married women are chaste. For
example, Comanche girls made ample use of their pre-marital freedom,
but were strictly faithful as wives. There are numerous other examples.

Again, statements to the effect that unmarried girls are chaste and

---

[1] A. R. Wallace (who introduced Westermarck to the English public) in his
introductory note to Westermarck's *History of Human Marriage*, i, ix sq.

are strictly guarded often refer only to their attitude towards strangers, and Europeans in particular. Many North American tribes would not even permit their women to become the legitimate wives of Europeans, although intercourse was almost promiscuous with members of the tribe. This was also true of many Caribbean races of the Mosquito Coast. Although sexual relations were entirely unrestricted within the tribe, a girl who had intercourse with a white man was killed by being slowly whipped to death. In Benin, not even prostitutes were permitted to consort with Europeans. In other cases, while no girl is expected to observe chastity, neither is she expected to suffer violence, and she may be guarded for this reason, for the dangers of such violence are very real. In East Africa, among many tribes, a man will not pass a solitary unmarried girl without entering into sexual relations with her; if she refused, he would probably kill her. Among the Siouan tribes of North America, 'a man has as little control over his passions as any wild beast'. Among the Pima Indians, the young men actually used lassoes to catch any stray female they might find. Among the Plains tribes, unmarried girls, when they went out to dance, tied a rope around their thighs in such a way as to prevent any violence on the part of the men. Such precautions in no way prevented their liberty to have as many lovers as they pleased.

Dr Westermarck cites the Rev. Owen Dorsey as saying that extra-matrimonial intercourse is only practised among the Omaha by prostitutes, but at the time Dorsey described the Omahas they were Christian farmers sending their children to Sunday-school, and he warns us that their customs were formerly quite different.

A retiring attitude in the bearing of girls is commonly regarded as evidence of chastity by superficial observers, who imagine that women ignorant of European moral restrictions must necessarily behave like European prostitutes. In fact, the combination of modesty of manners and unchastity is common. Thus, Dr Finsch says that the girls of the Caroline Islands (who were entirely unrestrained in their sexual relations) were remarkably modest in their demeanour; and also in New Zealand and elsewhere.

Many of Westermarck's examples consist of statements to the effect that it is rare to come upon pre-nuptial children, or even that a girl is blamed or punished for having such a child. But it is an ethnological commonplace that, in many uncultured peoples, though sexual relations are unrestricted before marriage, pregnancy must be avoided or the resulting children killed at birth. This rule is stringently enforced among peoples with whom pre-nuptial intercourse is not merely permitted but is obligatory, such as the Masai. Similarly of the Banyoro, 'there was no idea of sexual union being wrong so long as there was no conception, and the only risk run by the girl lay in her being discovered to be with child.' The disposal of pre-nuptial children by infanticide or abortion, which was very general in uncultured societies, is apt to suggest to us that shame and dishonour attach to pre-nuptial motherhood; but infanticide is not regarded as a criminal act in the lower stages of culture, but simply as a measure of expediency. The Australian aborigines destroyed most of their offspring simply because the babies were 'too much trouble to look after'. In seasons of drought, the tribes near Adelaide killed all new-born children and ate them. Among the Queensland tribes a girl's first child was almost invariably killed. Among the Veddahs a man is not allowed to have more than three children; all above that number are killed, as also in the Marshall Islands. A young married man in the Island of Rook, being asked if he had any children, replied that he had killed them all; he was still too young, he modestly explained, to have a family. Failure to exercise such moderation is regarded as unpardonable improvidence. In Papua the custom was to despise the mother of a numerous family. Among the Tshi-speaking peoples of West Africa a woman cannot have more than nine children. When the tenth is born, it is buried alive and the husband and wife separate. Among the Lala of Nigeria it is customary for the father of the bridegroom to have the use of the bride until she has conceived three times, abortion being procured by means of a compression bandage around the lower part of the abdomen. Children born in wedlock are disposed of as commonly as those born out of it. Among many North Indian tribes a young woman's chances of marriage were augmented by her having had many lovers, but the unmarried women destroyed their offspring in order to prolong their period of sexual freedom. No evidence could therefore be more irrelevant as regards pre-nuptial chastity.

When all such invalid instances are eliminated, Westermarck's enumeration of statements concerning peoples said to enforce pre-nuptial chastity is reduced to very moderate dimensions. In several of these remaining instances there can be no doubt the facts are quite the reverse of what he suggests. In others, the authorities he cites do not say what he ascribes to them, and sometimes they say the exact opposite. Thus he cites from Petroff a statement, ascribed to Father Veniaminoff, in which it is asserted that, among the Aleutians, girls 'who gave birth to illegitimate children were to be killed for shame and hidden'. But what Father Veniaminoff actually says is just the reverse. After stressing that irregular relations were common, that guests shared the marital rights of the husband, and that prior to 1825 scarcely a virgin was to be found above the age of twelve, he adds, 'infanticide was indeed very rare. For down to the present day the belief is prevalent that if a girl, in order to hide her shame, should kill her child before or after birth,

countless misfortunes would be brought down upon the whole village.'
All other testimonies as to the morality of the Aleutians are in agree-
ment, and they do not differ from the other Eskimo races. Yet Dr
Westermarck cites the latter also in support of his case.

He gives a list of references concerning North American tribes,
asserting that in the passages indicated 'we read that the girls were chaste
and carefully guarded'. In the majority we read nothing of the sort, and
in some we read the exact opposite. Thus, Father Morice is accused by
Dr Westermarck of reporting this of the various Déné tribes. What
Father Morice actually said on the subject was that the Déné had no
word for a virgin—a deficiency which becomes intelligible when we
learn that the Déné regarded sexual intercourse before puberty with
strangers as absolutely imperative. They believe that menstruation cannot occur without it, and when missions were established amongst them
nothing astonished them more than the discovery that a virgin can
menstruate. Father Morice also refers to the account of McLean who
says that 'the lewdness of the women could not possibly be carried to a
greater excess; they are addicted to the most abominable practices,
abandoning themselves in early youth to the free indulgence of their
passions. They never marry until satiated with indulgence.'

Father Chrestien Le Clercq represented the Canadian Indians not
only as chaste but as ascetic. Men and girls resorted at night-time to one
another's couches without any impropriety, and even preserved their
chastity for a year after marriage. This was not the view taken by other
missionaries, who untiringly denounced the usage: when one of them
preached against the custom a young Indian accused the Fathers of
desiring to gain possession of their mistresses for themselves. Father
Theodat describes the usage thus: 'The young men have licence to
addict themselves to evil as soon as they are able, and the young girls
prostitute themselves as soon as they are capable of doing so. Even
fathers and mothers commonly act as pimps to their daughters. At
night the young women and girls run from one hut to another, and the
young men do the same, and take their pleasure where they like, without,
however, using any violence, for they rely entirely upon the will of the
woman. The husband does the same with regard to his nearest female
neighbour, and the wife with regard to her nearest male neighbour; nor
does any jealousy appear amongst them on that account, and they incur
no shame or dishonour.' Westermarck refers to Le Clercq's story on
the authority of Father Charlevoix, who in fact comments that 'it
appears quite improbable.' (He also refers to Heriot's account which is
merely a transcription from Charlevoix and Lafitau.)

The statements adduced by Dr Westermarck in reference to the
alleged regard for pre-nuptial chastity in Africa are, when not irrelevant

and misleading, as questionable as the foregoing. We are informed, for instance, that in the Madai or Moru tribe the girls are carefully looked after. But Emin Pasha, a most accurate observer, stated that the unmarried Madi girls slept in special huts for the express purpose of allowing the young men to have access to them. Major Stigand reported that a man is allowed to pass the night with an unmarried Madi girl if he gives her a present of five arrows. Dr Westermarck refers to the Dinka of the Upper Nile, concerning whom we have Captain O'Sullivan's detailed study. He tells us that 'simple seduction is not a grave offence among the Northern Dinka'. Among the ancient inhabitants of the Canary Islands, we are told that a woman who lost her virtue was ostracized for life. We are, however, only told this on the authority of the grossly inaccurate Father Abreu de Galindo, whose reports are uniformly contradicted by every contemporary testimony. It was, on the contrary, obligatory for every Guanche girl to lose her virtue before she could be married.

Dr Westermarck is no happier in India where, for example, he reports, on the authority of the Rev. Sydney Endle, that among the Kacharis, Rabhas and Hajongs 'sexual intercourse before marriage is rare . . .'. A different view is taken by the authors of the last Government Report on those tribes. Concerning the Sayeins, Westermarck reports that the young people of both sexes are domiciled in two long houses at opposite ends of the village, and when they may have occasion to pass each other, they avert their gaze so that they may not see each other's faces'. In fact, this tribe is rigorously exogamic, none being allowed to marry except his cousin in another village. The scrupulous avoidance rules are therefore not directed against unchastity, but against what, by their tribal law, is incest. When a meeting takes place between two intermarrying villages, as on the occasion of a wedding, orgies marked by unrestrained promiscuity take place.

Our knowledge of the wild tribes of the Malay forests is defective, and various edifying accounts have been circulated. Father Bourien denies them, saying: 'A long sojourn among erratic tribes has taught me that from among carnal sins they only exclude one, viz. rape.' A Russian traveller has described the sex-relations of the Jakun as a 'round of temporary cohabitations regulated by chance and inclination'. Mr R. J. Wilkinson says that the Sakai 'leave everything to sexual passion'. These tribes are included by Dr Westermarck in his list of peoples who show an innate regard for chastity.

Though he has not been able to discover any example of primitive chastity in Micronesia, he finds one in the Philippine Islands to which he appears to attach much importance, and makes it part of the main evidence for his thesis. While other accounts tell us that 'the women are extremely lewd, and even encourage their daughters to a life of un-chastity', Dr Westermarck cites from the German poet Chamisso, who spent nearly a week at Manila, the statement that 'some of the independent tribes of the Philippines held chastity in great honour . . .'.

The extreme licence notoriously prevalent in every part of Polynesia is alluded to by Dr Westermarck with the characteristic concession that 'there is said to be, or to have been, the greatest freedom before marriage'. However, he gives prominence to statements calculated to convey the impression that the ritual virginity required of the brides of chiefs in Tonga and Samoa represented general customs. In fact, these were exceptions. In Samoa, there was exactly one virgin per village.

In support of his assertion that 'among many uncivilized peoples both sexes enjoy perfect freedom previous to marriage . . . the same can certainly not be said of the Australian aborigines while in their native state', he adduces a statement from Pastor Strehlow; this invests the Aruntas with a fanatical asceticism which has escaped the notice of every other observer, including Sir W. B. Spencer and Mr Gillen, who spent some four years amongst them. Mr Collins, after referring to the habitual practice of rape, says: 'Even children make it a game or exercise, and I have often, on hearing the cries of the girls with whom they were playing, run out of my house thinking some murder was committed, but have found the whole party laughing at my mistake.'

Dr Westermarck has frequently lectured or admonished Australian scientists who have spent their lives in the study of the native races, and has passed unfavourable judgments upon their critical standards. Had any of them made inferences concerning the past upon such slight evidence as Dr Westermarck produces about the present, the reproofs which he has bestowed upon them would not be impertinent.

Effects of Contact with Europeans

The glaring discrepancy between moral theory and observed fact was accounted for by the Jesuit Fathers by assuming that the primal innocence of unsophisticated savages had been corrupted by contact with civilization. General Denys, the Governor of New France, was persuaded that the morality of the Canadian Indians was due to European contact; as an instance, he mentions that a girl found a husband more readily if she had already borne a child, because he was then assured that she was not barren—a preference which seems difficult to trace to the corrupting influence of European ideas! He adds that the men do not repudiate their wives as readily as formerly, and that polygamy is disappearing—changes which are to be regarded, apparently, as the effects of European corruption. Dr Currier, after a full review of the present condition of North American tribes, concludes that 'in nothing has the influence of education and Christianity been more positive and noteworthy than in the improvement which has taken place in some localities with regard to marriage and the sexual relations'.

This somewhat puerile theory has been revived by Dr Westermarck who assimilates the absence of extra-connubial restrictions in primitive societies to prostitution, and suggests that this absence is due to corrupting influence. European society has, among other things, introduced venality and prostitution for profit, which in fact does not exist in primitive societies in the form known to us. In Australia, wherever white men were settled near the aborigines, wholesale prostitution of the native women took place, but this cannot be ascribed solely or even chiefly to the whites. Natives who are favourably disposed towards any white man may place their women at his disposal; while many of the women were attracted by the knowledge that the white men would treat them with kindness.

In Polynesia, while girls freely offered themselves to the crews of the first European ships, far from this being for profit the natives overwhelmed their guests with presents as well.

In India, wherever premarital sexual freedom is recognized within a tribe, it is punished when exercised with members of another tribe, in almost every case. Among the tribes of the Chittagong Hills who practise it most uniformly, it is precisely the most inaccessible tribes which do so most generally, and it is becoming discouraged among those in contact with European civilization. Hence, as Mr Gait says, Dr Westermarck's theory (of the contaminating effect of civilization) 'is not in accordance with our experience of India'.

With regard to Africa, Mr Dudley Kidd uses stronger language, saying that those who believe that the Kaffir races guarded female purity and were subsequently corrupted by Europeans, must 'be either fools or knaves'.

Difficulty of Distinguishing between Marriage and Other Sexual Relations

The primary purpose of marriage could not have been the satisfaction of sexual impulses, since sexual relations (within the prescribed limits) were freer before marriage than after. So much so that of the Angami Nagas it is said that 'chastity begins with marriage', and among the tribes of Upper Burma 'it is claimed that unchastity after marriage does not exist owing to their freedom of experiment before marriage'.

It has been represented that such freedom may be a crude way of affording young people an opportunity of choosing permanent partners. However, among many primitive peoples there is no relation between the two. Among the Bhuiya 'intimacy between boys and girls of the same village does not commonly end in marriage, for which a partner should be sought from another village'. While, among the Kumbi, if young people have had intercourse with one another they are forbidden to marry.

As we shall see, primitives commonly undertake more permanent relations in mature age only, usually for economic reasons and quite irrespective of the sexual relations of their younger years. Among the Masai the risk that pre-nuptial freedom might lead to marriage alliances was strictly guarded against by tribal law.

Among other peoples indiscriminate unions may develop into more stable ones, and the husband may be chosen from among pre-nuptial lovers, as among the Trobriand Islanders. And sometimes, as among the Igorots, when a girl has become pregnant she commonly marries the father of the child. Among the Lolo of Upper Tonkin, an experimental marriage is contracted by a girl spending a night with a suitor at his house. She then returns home, and continues to live a life of sexual freedom as before. If, after a while, she goes back to her suitor pregnant, she is received as his wife, although he knows that he is unlikely to be the father of the child. If she does not, the engagement lapses. In Cambodia the parents absolutely refuse to entertain propositions from a suitor for the hand of their daughter unless he has first seduced her; should he suggest marriage before this, he is scorned as a fool. Similar freedom of experiment is common among many peoples without the fact of pregnancy constituting an obligation to marry; for instance, among the natives of the lower Congo. As Father Merolla said: 'These people were accustomed to commerce with their wives for some time before they married them, to try if they could like them; and after the same manner the wives were to experiment their husbands.' Among the Munshi of northern Nigeria 'a boy may live with a virgin as his wife if he gives her mother ten cloths and a pig, on the understanding that the girl's offspring belong to her family, and that, unless he can presently make an equivalent exchange, he must give her up'.

Many Central and South American races advocated child marriage, among them the ancient Peruvians. The agreement was binding for one year. Previous cohabitation was regarded as so essential a preliminary that a woman who had married without such preparation was not regarded as respectably wedded, and was liable to have the fact thrown in her face if the marriage turned out unsuccessfully. In spite of the efforts of the Church and severe decrees issued by the Spanish authorities, such customs are still regularly observed among the Catholic Indians of Bolivia; the Arawak races of Guiana also have the same usages. Among the ancient Egyptians a trial year was so ingrained a conception that it persisted into Christian times and even after the Arab conquest.

We thus find every degree of transition between general pre-sexual relations wholly unconnected with prospective marriage, the right of experiment or trial marriage, and recognized freedom of relations between prospective spouses. It is difficult to draw a line between such customs. Among many peoples such customs have become less free and open as a result of contact with higher cultures or the development of individual proprietory claims; they have often survived as a right to trial marriage. But it is equally difficult to draw a line between trial marriages and true marriages, for with many primitive peoples the latter are scarcely more stable.

In point of fact, it is impossible to frame a definition of marriage which will apply to all forms of the relation as found in uncultured societies, while excluding the most casual sexual congress—as we must do if marriage be regarded as essentially a sexual relation in accordance with the usual European sentiments. Dr Westermarck has proposed, as a definition, to regard marriage as 'a more or less durable connection between male and female, lasting beyond the mere act of propagation till after the birth of the offspring'. But where the whole distinction, as we conceive it, between sex relations which are, and those which are not, marital turns precisely upon their degree of permanency, the use of such a phrase as 'more or less' vitiates the definition—as we have seen with regard to the North American Indians whose associations were in widely varying degrees 'more or less durable'. Among all the tribes it was customary for a young man, when he went on a prolonged hunting expedition, to arrange for a young woman to accompany him, both as a sexual companion and to assist him with carrying, cooking, etc. The woman received a liberal share of the profits, and the transaction was on a business footing. Similarly, young men with no female relatives to look after them would engage some young woman to perform the duties of a wife, though both of them would remain free to visit their other mistresses or lovers from time to time. But the relationship spoken of as marriage among the Indians was not much more durable than these associations. 'The Delawares and Iroquois', says Loskiel, 'have seldom marriages of long continuance, especially if there are no children soon. . . . The family connections of Indians are commonly very extensive on account of their frequently changing wives.' The Cherokee Iroquois 'commonly change wives three or four times a year. . . . Marriage is accounted only a temporary convenience.' Separation takes place without any formality. 'Those savages are not even able to imagine that there could be any difficulty about the matter.' They 'laugh at Europeans for having only one wife, and that for life; as they consider that the Good Spirit formed them to be happy, and not to continue together unless their tempers and dispositions were congenial'. As will be seen, La Hontan was scarcely exaggerating when he said that 'what is spoken of as "marriage" amongst the North American Indians would, in Europe, be spoken of as a criminal connection'.

How can we distinguish irregular intercourse and marriage in such cases ? There was no ceremony or solemnization of any kind. The associations which turned out more permanent were not distinguished from the more transient ones by any special contract. No distinction can be drawn on economic grounds, for economic contributions from both parties took place whether the association lasted a hunting-trip or a lifetime. Lieutenant Timberlake says of the Iroquois: 'Courtship and all is concluded in half an hour without any other celebration, and it is as little binding as ceremonious.' In the union of the most permanently married and confirmed old couple, the man acquired no more rights over the children than the casual lover had. The children in either case were part of the mother's family. Father Le Jeune remarked: 'The bond so strong, which holds man and wife under one yoke, will be very hard to fasten upon these savages.'

The same difficulty in drawing a distinction between marriage and other sexual relations is found in many parts of the world. For instance, among the Dayaks of Borneo, in the Nicobar Islands and elsewhere. Among the aboriginal tribes of Malaya, 'it is nothing rare to meet individuals who have been married forty or fifty times'. Of the natives of the Maldive Islands, we learn that it very often happens that a man would marry and divorce the same woman three or four times in the course of his life. Among the Ainu, as formerly among the Japanese, there was no clear distinction in language or in usage between transient and more durable unions. Similar reports come from such northern tribes as the Samoyeds and Aleutians, throughout Central Asia and from many parts of India. Sir Henry Yule says of the Khasis, 'their unions can hardly be honoured with the name of marriage'. Almost identical words are used by African travellers about the Bushmen and many others. Turning to South America, we learn that the lives of the Guaycurus are 'a quick succession of marriages, separations and re-marriages, in the course of which everyone mates with everyone else, and the same couples come together several times'. Such examples might be greatly multiplied. As Dr Westermarck quaintly puts it: 'There are unions which, though legally recognized as marriages, do not endure long enough to deserve to be so-called in the natural history sense of the term.' Most writers in speaking of them are, on the contrary, reminded of the natural history of animals.

However, there is one thing which has a consolidating effect upon individual unions: the birth of offspring. Indeed, it is considered by most uncultured people as constituting the consummation and establishment of the marriage relation, and a sexual association is not regarded as a marriage until children are actually born. Among the Todas the expression for 'to be married' is 'to have a son'. Among the Baila of Rhodesia the marriage ceremony is not completed until after the birth of the first child; while in other cases the topic is not broached until this stage. A woman who has not borne a child is usually treated in primitive societies as an unmarried girl, and is called a virgin. Sometimes, and this is true even of advanced societies, a man does not contribute to the maintenance of his wife until she has borne a child, until when expenses are defrayed by the bride's father. Such usages pass imperceptibly into the almost universal rule that the barrenness of the wife is a legitimate ground for divorce, and for the refunding of the bride-price, if any. Thus among the Baele of the Sahara, after the bride-price is paid, the father builds a house by the side of his own for the couple; if, after a reasonable time, no child is born, the payment made is refunded and the husband departs.

Since the association is recognized by the woman's family only after the birth of offspring, it tends to acquire a more durable character after that event. But it would be incorrect to suppose that this is a general rule. Indeed, in some cases the birth of children, far from consolidating the association, causes its dissolution. Among the Iroquois, 'sometimes an Indian forsakes his wife because she has a child to suckle, and marries another whom he forsakes in her turn for the same reason'. Separation after the birth of children was, we saw, the rule among all North American Indians. In many parts of the world, married couples separate if they do not get on happily together, the woman usually taking the children with her, and sometimes she settles down with her progeny and a new husband on the very day on which she leaves the old.

The Juridic Conception of Marriage

Even though the native tends to distinguish marriage from other sexual associations by the fact of a child being born, nevertheless we cannot make the formation of a permanent association the grounds of the distinction, for little or no greater notion of permanency attaches to unions held to constitute marriage than to others. Moreover, in all societies which preserve their matriarchal character the birth of offspring does not necessitate the continued association of the parents, for the mother's family and not the child's father are responsible for the maintenance of the child. Nor does any new grouping, or family, result from the birth of children; the father may or may not live with the mother, and if separation takes place, he has no claim or liability in regard to the children. Only in more advanced social phases, as a result of somewhat elaborate transactions and indemnities, does he acquire the right to remove any of his children from the maternal group.

In short, individual marriage cannot be based upon the formation of a family group, since none is formed. What the birth of offspring does is to establish, not a new group but a relationship between the husband and the wife's family. Thus among the Cree Indians the young husband coming to live with his wife's parents is treated as a stranger until his first child is born, whereupon he takes its name and is attached thereby to his parents-in-law rather than to his own parents. Such usages are very widespread, especially among peoples who have preserved a matriarchal organization, but they still subsist among many who have long since adopted patriarchal usages—for instance, among the Arabs, where the custom is firmly established.

The relation thus established between a man and his wife's family remains unaffected when actual relations between the two are severed. However transitory the association, this cannot in any way alter the relation of the father to his child's maternal family once it has been established.

These circumstances have confused observers more concerned with stretching primitive conceptions on the Procrustes' bed of European ideas than with understanding them, and have led them to strange inconsistencies. Thus the writer who describes the utterly transient nature of marriage among the Guaycurus of Brazil, nevertheless states that, if a woman has a male child, she does not separate from her husband until death. Yet he mentions at the same time that a woman having a son by one husband is commonly married to another, while the father of the boy marries another woman. The writer who makes such contradictory statements obviously confuses the 'indissoluble' character of the relation established between the father and the mother's *clan*—the tribes are strictly exogamous—with the supposed indissolubility of the association between them. Perrot makes the same kind of statement concerning North American Indians. In Samoa young men belonging to a chief's family used to form temporary unions with young women of good family. The union was celebrated by exchanges of valuable presents, and they were regarded as the most honourable unions into which any Samoan girl could enter. After their termination the women were debarred from contracting other alliances, and devoted themselves to the entertainment of visitors, their function of public prostitutes in no way detracting from their enhanced respectability. In the island of Engano, so indissoluble is the connection established between the husband and the wife's family that if a man marries after his wife's death he must pay compensation to her family.

Of some peoples it is said that they draw no distinction between marriage and cohabitation, or that cohabitation constitutes marriage. But with the majority of even the most primitive peoples a distinction is indeed drawn, as with ourselves, between the two relations, and the distinctive character of marriage, with them, as with us, lies in the establishment of a social and juridical relationship, although the nature of that juridic foundation necessarily varies with social and cultural conditions. Thus among the Australian aborigines, who usually give a sister or some other female in exchange for a wife, a woman for whom no other female has thus been given is not regarded as being 'properly married'. Elsewhere a woman is not regarded as legally married if the bride-price has not been duly paid. In every instance, the sanction of her family or immediate guardian, and sometimes of all her relatives, is regarded as essential. In the later phases of civilization other sanctions of a religious or moral nature may be added to these, and the performance of the ceremony may come to be regarded as essential. For instance, where a feast is regarded as essential, the man who has been unable to afford such entertainment is regarded as not being married, even if he cohabits with the woman for many years and has a numerous family by her.

The distinction drawn between individual marriage and other sexual relations is thus essentially the same in primitive societies as in our own. In England, at the present day, a man and woman may cohabit in the most devoted manner for fifty years and rear a family, yet, unless the union has been legally registered, they are not married and their children are bastards; whereas the most transient association, or even one without any cohabitation, constitutes, if legally established, a true and valid marriage. The distinction does not rest upon the association or its permanency, or even upon the formation of a family group, but solely upon the juridic and legal transaction. In short, in its origin individual marriage is not rooted in any form of association between sexual partners, or in any group or family resulting from such association, but even in its most primitive and rudimentary forms it is distinguished as a juridic relation irrespective of its stability. There is, however, a difference between the primitive and the advanced view of the distinction, since in the latter all other relations between the sexes have come to be regarded as illegal, or illegitimate, and subject to censure. Far from this being the case among the North American Indians and others, the young women freely employed abortion and infanticide in order to avoid establishing a relationship which would have constituted a legal bond. Again among the Line islanders and the Hawaiians, juridic marriage served certain specialized economic purposes in the transmission of landed property, and was not entered into by the majority of the people, who had no interest in such transactions. But there is no ground for supposing that the one sort of union was more durable than the other. On the contrary, we are told that all were equally loose. The distinction lay purely in the juridic conditions attending the union.

A tendency must inevitably develop for a juridically-established rela-tion to cause a depreciation in the esteem in which relations not so established are held; the correlative of the sanctioned and legitimate union comes in time to be an unsanctioned and illegitimate one—though, as we shall see, several other factors have contributed to giving marriage the character of being the sole recognized form of sexual association.

CHAPTER 13

Primitive Jealousy and Love

Masculine Jealousy

IT has been supposed that exclusive personal claims over women originally arose in consequence of masculine jealousy. Dr Westermarck considers that the force of jealousy affords the strongest argument against ancient promiscuity. However, even a cursory inquiry shows clearly that, although instincts of sexual jealousy may be as strong in primitive as in civilized societies, or even stronger, the claims to which they refer differ completely from those which inspire the jealousy of a romantic lover—so completely as to make this argument irrelevant.

The almost universal assumption that the sentiment corresponding to jealousy exists in animals has already, I think, been shown to be a misconception. Male animals will battle with rivals for the opportunity of satisfying their sexual instincts in the same manner as they will battle with competitors for food, but when their hunger, nutritional or sexual, is satisfied they are indifferent. The word 'jealousy', as usually employed, denotes the choice of a particular individual; animal jealousy has no reference to individual mating, but is, on the contrary, conspicuous where such mating is absent. The natural outcome of such an attitude to sexual satisfaction would be, in human conditions, sexual communism and not individual association. The 'jealousy' manifested by men in the lower stages of society is identical with the 'jealousy' exhibited by male animals. Statements that the men of a given race of savages are 'extremely jealous' are very common, but are of little value and give rise to absurd contradictions. Thus Mr Curr asserts that among the Australian aborigines a husband is 'very jealous', yet on the next page tells us that he will often prostitute his wife. Morenhout reports that the men of Radak, in the Carolines, were 'extremely jealous'; pre-nuptial licence, exchange of wives and extreme licentiousness were, however, habitual amongst them. Dr Westermarck informs us that jealousy is a characteristic of the Tlinkit, the Aleuts, the Hawaiians and the Nukahivans, all these being peoples whose sexual customs are collective. He also instances the Eskimo. An Eskimo once told Captain Rasmussen that the only cause of unpleasantness between himself and his wife was that she was averse to receiving other men. 'She would,' he complained, 'have nothing to do with anyone but him—that was her only failing.' It is obvious that the use of the same term to denote these sentiments and the passion of an Othello arises from an unscientific confusion.

Dr Westermarck defines jealousy as 'an angry feeling aroused by the loss, or the fear of the loss, of the exclusive possession of an individual who is the object of one's sexual desire'. This is just what jealousy among primitive human races is not. What the savage fears is not loss of sexual possession but the actual loss of the woman in her sexual and, still more, her economic aspect. The offences commonly appearing in reports as adultery consist generally of abduction, and the anger of the husband is completely allayed by his being presented with another woman. Captain Tench tells us of a jovial Australian native who was fond of expatiating upon the merits of his wife, to whom he appeared deeply attached. Some time later, Captain Tench asked him how his wife was getting on. 'Oh!' replied the Australian, 'she has become the wife of Cotbee. But', he added with an air of triumph, 'I have got two big women to compensate for her loss!' He was obviously the gainer. In Northern New Guinea, if a woman runs away with a lover, her husband applies to her family, who either refund the bride-price or supply another woman. In New Britain, the men, who are stated to be 'fiercely jealous', never have any hesitation in parting with their wives to anyone who is prepared to refund the expenses incurred. In Samoa the abduction of a wife, we are told, was frequently the cause of tribal wars, but mere seduction was thought very little of. Gilyak husbands take little notice of their wives' infidelities, but if a woman leaves home with a lover it is quite a different matter. Similar attitudes are found among the Tartars, the Mishmis of Bengal and in many African tribes such as the Kuku, the Warega of the Congo and others. The general rule is that a woman is free to leave her husband for her lover if the bride-price is duly refunded. No additional compensation is claimed and no grudge borne. Among the Medge of the Congo, the seducer of the wife of a chief is liable to be mutilated and put to death; but if he supplies two new wives, he is neither blamed nor punished. These principles, universal in uncultured societies, obtained among our Anglo-Saxon forefathers within Christian times. A law of King Aethelbert (AD 560–616) provides: 'If a freeman lie with a freeman's wife, let him pay for it with his "wèr-geld" and provide another wife with his own money and bring her to the other.'

The abduction of women, even from tribal brothers, is extremely common in primitive societies, especially where patrilocal marriage obtains. One of the reasons which the Australian aborigines give for their polygamy is that an ample reserve of wives is an indispensable provision against the constant liability to the loss of one or two. In more matri-archal societies the woman is free to leave her husband. On the other hand, the sanction of the husband pledges a tribal brother or guest not to abuse the privilege by abducting the woman. Father Charlevoix asserts that the Iroquois were extremely jealous, although they them-selves 'utterly denied that they were given to such eccentricity'. What they claimed, as Hunter reports, was 'the sole disposal of their wives; and although in many instances they devote them to the sensual grati-fication of their friends without ascribing the least impropriety to the transaction, yet they regard a voluntary indulgence of passion on their part as an unpardonable offence'. Many North American Indians were wont to cut or bite off the nose of a woman convicted of actually running away, but freely lent their wives to fellow-clansmen or strangers. How-ever, if a stranger, after having knowledge of a woman by consent of the husband, were to repeat this without the husband making the offer a second time, he would be killed.

Many primitive tribes are described as extremely jealous because on the approach of strangers they hide their women. The reason is that they are afraid lest the women should be taken away, as would certainly be the case if the strangers were from a hostile tribe. Thus the natives of Easter Island, when visited by Captain Cook, hid most of their women; but, having learned that the white men had no desire to remove them, when visited a few years later, pressed their women upon the visitors with annoying persistence. The wild Veddahs of Ceylon guard their women so watchfully that it is difficult for a European, and much more for a Sinhalese, to catch a glimpse of them. But M. Moszkowski suc-ceeded in inducing them to let him see their women after he had pro-duced a photograph and assured them that he possessed a wife of his own. They are even more 'jealous' regarding their dogs.

Jealousy is also ascribed to Australian aborigines with as little reason. At night, when the old men are sitting round the fire, says Mr Oldfield, the whole neighbourhood of the camp resounds with the low whistles which are the recognized signals of invitation of the younger men to the women to come and join them. The older men, perfectly well aware of the meaning of these signals, do not interrupt their conversation, and take little notice of their wives' irregularities.

Indifference Concerning Connubial Fidelity

Widespread evidence that little notice is taken of adultery can be ad-duced. Throughout British Central Africa, says Sir Harry Johnston, infidelity is treated with indifference. Referring to Brazil, Father d'Anchieta says that, although adultery is habitual, he never heard of an adulterer being killed by an offended husband. They are, he says, absolutely indifferent to the conduct of their wives. Similar reports come of the Conebo tribes of the upper Amazon, the Tocantin tribes of the Maranhão region, the Guarani tribes and others.

The Aleuts, the Kamchadals, the Gilyak, the Samoyeds, as well as the Mongol tribes of Central Asia, follow the same pattern. Among the Kafirs of Hindu-Kush 'cases of infidelity are extremely common'. 'When a woman is discovered in an intrigue a great outcry is made, and the neighbours rush to the scene with much laughter. A goat is sent for on the spot for a peace-making feast between the gallant and the husband. Of course, the neighbours also partake of the feast; the husband and wife both look very happy and so does everyone else.' Among the Jats of Baluchistan it is a common saying that a tribesman who puts his camel to graze with a Jat becomes thereby the master of the Jat's wife. If a stranger casts his eye on the wife, the husband disappears discreetly. A similar attitude is found among the Aheriya of the North-western Province, the Chamars of Bengal, the Todas of the Nilgiri Hills, who can hardly 'conceal their scorn for European ideas on the subject', the Kunnuvans of the extreme south of India and many others. Similarly in the Pacific: jealousy is not displayed in the Marshall Islands, the Pelews or Tahiti. Among the Maori, who took a much more serious view of adultery than most Polynesians, 'in general the offence can easily be compounded for'.

Primitive Duels

In some primitive societies contests occur between the males, but they are institutionalised and do not go very far. Thus, among the Eskimo, if a husband and a lover quarrel they may only settle the trouble with their fists or by wrestling, the victor taking the woman. The Comanches, when fighting such duels, have their left arms tied together. The Slave Indians fight their duels by pulling one another's hair. The fight takes place in the presence of the assembled tribe, and the belligerents take care not to give a mortal blow. It is customary to request the opponent to strike first. All such duels are, in fact, staged under arranged rules, and are more in the nature of trials of strength than of mortal combat. These regulated contests bear no resemblance to the combats of animals for the possession of a female. (The abduction of women is a common cause of intertribal wars, but that is an entirely different thing.)

Primitive society is characterized by every form of communistic adjustment in regard to sexual relations, and the member of a group who is unable to procure a female companion is assisted in every way by other members, just as they provide him with food if he cannot obtain any himself.

Variable Manifestations of Jealousy

Where sharing of a woman is involved, reciprocity is the essence of the transaction. Among the Yao of Nyasaland the uneasiness caused to a husband by his wife's repeated misconduct is set at rest by the offender lending his own wife to the injured husband for an equal number of nights, or sometimes by an amicable understanding whereby they agree to share the wife, and possibly the household expenses. In New Zealand such a dispute is sometimes settled by both men becoming the woman's recognized co-husbands. Dr Hartland has shown by numerous examples that jealousy, as we use the word, does not exist in primitive society.

In the most highly developed societies, the lover's jealousy is aroused even by a thought or feeling in the beloved inconsistent with the exclusive attachment which he looks for. Indeed, even actual infidelity may lose its sting when it is clear there was no loss of sentimental attachment. Such sentiments are devoid of meaning in the lower phases of human culture. No such mental possession is either looked for or imagined. Of the Australian aborigines, Spencer and Gillen remark that 'for a man to have unlawful intercourse with any woman arouses a feeling which is due not so much to jealousy as to the fact that the delinquent has infringed a tribal custom'.

There are many instances of tribes with widely different attitudes regarding the seclusion of women. Thus, for example, the nomad Koryak are extreme puritans. 'Contrary to the custom of all neighbouring tribes, Koryak girls must have no sexual intercourse before marriage.' Sororal polygyny is forbidden. (Mythology and traditional tales show that these ideas are of comparatively late development.) They are so jealous that on a mere suspicion a man will kill his wife, and on any solid ground for suspecting her disembowels both her and the lover. After marriage the women are obliged to dress in rags and refrain from combing their hair or washing their faces. But the maritime branch of the same nation go to the opposite extreme. Their customs regarding the exchange of wives are similar to those among allied races and 'the caresses bestowed upon their wives are a source of gratification to the husbands'. They are said to be in the habit of positively pestering Russian officials, such as the postman, to lie with their wives.

In those relatively advanced societies where personal despotism has become established, infringement of sexual claims is often revenged with a severity which bears no relation to the sentiments with which a woman is personally regarded. In Africa, seduction of the wife of a king or chief, and even the mere fact of accidentally touching her person, is sometimes punished with death. A king of Angola had a man executed for giving a leaf of tobacco to one of the royal wives, although he had gone no farther than to place the leaf on a stone at a respectful distance.

The punishments inflicted by despots for the adultery, or suspected adultery, of their wives are often atrocious. The ancient Peruvians provided that a man guilty of adultery with the wives or concubines of the Inca, or even of attempting such a crime, should be burnt alive, together with the woman. In addition, 'his parents, sons, brothers and all other near relatives were to be killed, and even his flocks slaughtered; his native town or village was to be depopulated and sown with salt; the trees were to be cut down and all the houses destroyed'. African kings gouged out the eyes of the guilty parties and also of their relatives, and cut off the breasts of the women; the victims were sometimes compelled to eat their own amputated members. Such penalties are punishments for *lese-majesté* rather than for adultery. Among the Niam-Niam, seduction of the wife of a chief is punished with horrible mutilations, but among the ordinary people a present of cloth or of beads salves the feelings of the husband.

Conceptions of what will satisfy the honour of chiefs vary curiously. In New Caledonia a woman who has once been the bride of a chief is debarred from ever marrying any other man, but is at liberty to have as many lovers as she pleases, and in fact becomes what we should call a prostitute. The same rule for the protection of the honour of chiefs formerly obtained in the Caroline Islands and in Samoa.

The damage to the honour of a cuckold or husband constitutes an enormous part of barbaric jealousy: it is not infidelity as such, but the loss of reputation which is the grounds of complaint. As Father Dubois remarks of the Brahmans, so long as the adultery is kept secret it is regarded as a matter of small importance. 'It is the publicity which is the sin.' According to an old Chinese writer, if anybody reported to a Tungus the infidelity of his wife, the injured husband killed not only the wife's lover but also the informant, whom he regarded as the chief offender. As Burckhardt remarked of the Italians, not only the husband but the woman's brother and her father considered themselves bound to avenge their honour. 'Jealousy has therefore nothing to do with those acts; moral feeling little; and the wish to avoid ridicule is the chief factor.' The Statute of Tivoli excused the killing of a lover not only when found in unlawful intercourse with a man's wife, but also with the offended relative's daughter, his mother, his sister, or his daughter-in-law. The same conception obtains in several Eastern peoples, e.g. among the Druses of the Lebanon. But among the Moi of Indo-China, if a woman commits adultery, while she and her paramour incur no punishment, a heavy fine is imposed on the husband.

Penalties for Adultery

'The prevalence of jealousy in the human race', says Dr Westermarck, 'is best shown by the punishments inflicted for adultery.' Consideration of such punishments gives little support to the hypothesis that individual marriage is the oldest social institution of the human race, and that it arose from masculine claims to proprietory rights over females. If adultery were an offence against such a primary relation we should expect the offence to be universally regarded with more horror than any other social transgression. So far is this from being the case that, even in English law, adultery is not an indictable offence. If severity of reprobation is to be an indication of the antiquity of the institution, then the clan must be accounted more fundamental than the family, for breach of the law of clan exogamy—that is, the crime of incest—is regarded with infinitely greater horror and punished more severely than adultery.

Where adultery is not regarded with indifference, it may lead to brief outbursts of temper, followed by an amicable settlement. On the spur of the moment the angered husband may commit some impulsive act, such as disfiguring the woman, but such acts are subject to social restraints. Among the Afghan frontier tribes resort is made to European surgeons to remedy the disfigurement produced in the fit of temper. (An Afghan warrior, inquiring of an English surgeon the price of equipping his wife with a new nose, was informed that it would be thirty rupees. There was a silence, during which he was obviously weighing the situation. He pointed out that for fifty rupees he could obtain a brand-new wife.)

In such a fit of anger a man may kill his wife or her lover. Such an act is sometimes excused, but generally tribal law discourages leniency. In most societies in the lower stages of culture, the man who commits such a murder is exposed to the blood-revenge of the relatives of the victim, as for any other murder. In more developed societies, homicide in such a case is excused only when it can be clearly shown to have been unpremeditated. (Among the Pasema natives, the seducer of a married woman might be killed by the husband if found within the house, but not outside. Similarly, in Burmese law, if a man is found in the bedroom he may be struck, but not after he has left the bed.)

The statement that adultery is, or was at some former time, punished with death can only be accepted with the greatest caution. There is no well-authenticated instance in any lower culture of death being the ordinary legal penalty for adultery, except as an act of despotism on the part of an autocrat. In societies which have not advanced so far as to delegate judicial authority to a ruler or council, adultery and homicide are regarded as private torts concerning the individuals and families affected, and not punishable by collective action. The statement therefore can mean nothing more than that homicide under the circumstances is regarded as excusable; but since homicide itself is a private concern, it is difficult to see that the statement means anything. Speaking of the

East African Bantu, the Hon. C. Dundas says, 'I am convinced that the killing of an adulterer was not permitted under any circumstances.' As a matter of fact, the recognized penalty for adultery among them is a payment of ten goats. The Tuareg, when asked what they would do in the case of their wife's adultery, said that they would kill the culprits; but when pressed as to whether any such incident was known to have occurred they had nothing to say. Western ignorance has long supposed that the Turks, upon whom it has fastened a fantastic reputation for jealousy, punish with death the adultery of their wives. But 'the old story about the sacks filled with such degenerate beauties being sunk into the river where it is deepest are the illusions of the romanticist'. As a matter of fact, adultery among Turkish women, which is nearly as frequent as among Western women, is usually dealt with by the obvious prodecure of divorce. Although statements that the penalty for adultery is death abound, there are few instances. The statement is most frequently met with reference to Africa but, in point of fact, adultery throughout Africa is usually compensated for by a fine, and often a trifling one. Among the Ewe of Togo the penalty is two cowrie shells, value sixpence. In Abyssinia, it is slightly cheaper: fivepence sterling.

The claim for compensation for the breach of matrimonial rights may easily degenerate into a means of exploitation. Frequently husband and wife entice victims into adultery, or concoct false charges and share the proceeds. This is particularly common on the Guinea coast. The husbands 'make great gain of their wives and 'tis with this view that they marry many, who are so faithful that when they have admitted a spark, they immediately acquaint their husband, who directly fleeces him. Some pretend to be unmarried and so impose on the stranger, who, as soon as the affair is over, is undeceived by the appearance of the husband, in the same manner claiming his wife as the bullies in Europe do.' Among the Wataveta the husbands are 'affectionate and kindly in their family relations', and love their wives dearly. All they ask is that if the wife has lovers, the fine should be faithfully paid to them. Among the Bashamma of Nigeria it is customary to pay the fine in advance. The business details being thus disposed of, the co-respondent is free to commit misconduct. Other offences on the part of the wife are frequently regarded as more serious than adultery. A woman may be divorced for witchcraft, stealing, being a bad cook or a fool, but not if she commits adultery.

Tribal law is far from supporting claims to exclusive possession. Among the patriarchal Australians a man who has no wife has a right to challenge a man who has several and compel him, if he can, to surrender one of them. Among the Gilyak, if a woman absconds with a lover and the husband does not succeed in bringing her back within a year, his claim lapses. And among the Sakai of Sumatra the husband must achieve the return within seven days.

Far from lending countenance to seventeenth-century religious doctrines, as Westermarck supposes, primitive sentiments rule the theory of basic jealousy out of court. For if a desire for individual possession of females was really the chief factor in human society, how could indifference to such claims be so general in lower cultures?

Sexual Emotion

Since the eighteenth century opinions have differed much as to the emotional forms which sexual attraction may take in primitive humanity and as to whether savages are capable of romantic passion. Such controversies could hardly have arisen had more care been devoted to elucidating the psychological nature of those emotions.

The character of such sentiments varies enormously in different countries and periods. M. Kostyleff points out that the romantic emotions depicted by Stendhal are today extremely rare, if not impossible. Many people find it inconceivable that sentiments which play so fundamental a part in human life can be subject in any degree to cultural influences. But they overlook the fact that the form which they assume in cultured humanity is due to the fact that they are repressed. It is precisely because they are so fundamental that they are ready to avail themselves of any outlet offered and to assume any form which the culture may impart. The sexual instincts are the most malleable of any instincts. Let them be repressed, let their direct aim be denied them, and they will soon assume unrecognizable forms, from the depths of vice to the highest exaltations of art and religion. M. Kostyleff attributes the noticeable decay of romantic emotion today as compared with the mid-Victorian era to the greater physical activity of contemporary life, and in particular to the development of sport, which serves as an outlet for energy diverted from the sexual channel. But the chief cause of the change appears to be the greater freedom of intercourse between the sexes. Young men and women, brought up in seclusion from the opposite sex, who never met except under the primmest rules, were foredoomed to fall into the extremes of sentimental emotion.

In European societies the sexual instincts are repressed and denied their direct outlet at the very time when their operation is most insistent, namely puberty. This results in various forms of nervous disturbance, in romantic passion, in religious phenomena, in masturbation, in vice: manifestations which are, for the most part, unknown in primitive societies where no such repression exists. We are not concerned here with judging such effects. They include some of the most deplorable and some of the most exalted features of our culture. But the latter are no less artificial for being admirable. Psychiatrists describe love in pathological terms, such as 'obsession', '*idée fixe*', and 'rudimentary paranoia.' Even if one disagrees with psychologists in viewing romantic sentiments as pathological, one must regard the forms which those sentiments have assumed in European culture as, in a sense, artificial and abnormal. The overflowing of the sexual impulse is the outcome of the damming of those impulses. Their concentration upon one individual results from these restrictions. The diversity of an advanced culture extends the scope of sexual selection while restricting its operation. In short, the personal character of sexual attraction is not the cause of monogamy but, on the contrary, its product. These conditions are absent in primitive societies. The instincts are unrepressed; imagination has no power over the mind of the savage.

The profound differences which exist in the relations between the sexes in primitive societies and in our own is illustrated by the fact that throughout those societies, the kiss is unknown. Were the fact disputable, it would doubtless have been asserted that kissing is part of the nature of man, and that it is impossible to believe that there existed a time when such a spontaneous form of caress was unknown to human beings; for exactly the same forms of reasoning apply here as in regard to the sentiments of sexual love or of jealousy as we know them. The reason why the kiss is unknown to primitive humanity is that preliminaries to sexual relations are unknown. The development of emotional tenderness is rendered impossible by the fact that no pre-nuptial state corresponding to courtship exists in primitive societies.

It has been noted as remarkable that North American Indians, whose eloquence will bear comparison with the oratory of ancient and modern Europe, and who possess great gifts of poetic imagination, offer no specimen of erotic literature; they have no love-songs. The same is true of the Polynesians, who are far from being psychologically primitive, and who have a rich and flexible language and a store of imaginative myths and songs.[1] There are a couple of Samoan stories referring to sexual affection, but it is post-nuptial not pre-nuptial. The Ababua of the Congo also have no love-songs.

Suicide among Primitive Races
The fact that a man or woman who is thwarted sometimes commits suicide has been adduced as evidence of romantic love in primitive races, but suicide for all sorts of frivolous reasons is common among all

[1] A well-known Maori tale, the story of Hine-Moa, appears to be a solitary instance of a Polynesian love-story; it contains little that can be interpreted in terms of our notions of romantic love, and would seem to illustrate rather the 'swayamvara' usage, of which we find traces among the Maori, than romantic attachment.

primitive peoples. Perhaps this is because primitive man, like a child, lives almost entirely in the present. The impulse of the moment, however trifling in itself the object may be, determines action, uncounteracted by any far-reaching consideration. When Jesuit missionaries rebuked the North American Indians for not correcting their children, they replied that if they were to do so they would probably kill themselves. An old Dakota woman committed suicide because her granddaughter had received a thrashing from her father. American squaws kill themselves if spoken to crossly. In the Trobriands, a young man has been known to commit suicide because his wife had smoked all his tobacco. A native of the Gilbert Islands hanged himself because he had been scolded by his wife. Among the Banyoro a woman will hang herself if her husband finds fault with the dinner.

In every part of the uncultured world there is a curious disposition to commit suicide to cause annoyance to the survivors. Of the natives of Savage Island it is said that 'like angry children, they are tempted to avenge themselves by picturing the trouble that they will bring upon the friends who have offended them'. Married women often kill themselves to avenge themselves upon their husbands. Among the Goajiros, if a man quarrels with his wife, the latter often hangs herself from revenge, for the husband is obliged in such a case to pay for her a second time, and the woman exults in the trick which she is playing on her spouse. Among the negroes of the French Sudan, men commonly commit suicide 'to spite their wives', a practice also prevalent on the Gold Coast, where if a person commits suicide and, before doing so, attributes the act to the conduct of another person, the latter is required to undergo a like fate.

Often a Chuvash goes and hangs himself over his enemy's front door, a method of venting one's spite not uncommon in India also. Colonel Tod relates how four astute Brahmans committed suicide to evade the payment of their taxes. Thereafter the tax official was universally looked upon by the population as a murderer. Suicide is often connected with the belief that the ghost of the deceased person can plague survivors. Mr Manning reported of the Maori that no more marked change in habit has taken place than the decrease in suicide, which in the first years of his residence was an almost daily occurrence. He knew a man who cut his throat with a very blunt razor as a cure for toothache.

It would manifestly be difficult to infer from such frivolous acts of suicide an intensity of sexual attachment. Mr Gibbs mentions that among the western tribes of America many instances occur of young women destroying themselves at the death of their lovers, but he is nevertheless emphatic that there is little real affection. Herr Detzner observes of the Melanesians and Papuans, 'the momentary despair caused by the natural or violent death of wife or husband, the complete lack of energy to take up the battle of life singly, alone induce those resourceless people to take the step, and love for the deceased, which in our sense of the word is unknown to them, lends no higher hallowing significance to the wretched deed'.

In short, the anecdotes collected by several writers to demonstrate the existence of romantic sentiments among primitive peoples show just the opposite. Most of the instances put forward turn out to be suicides because the woman was compelled to marry an old and objectionable suitor and not because of unrequited love.

The existence of 'elopement' is sometimes cited as evidence of romantic attachment among uncultured people. Such elopements are in fact abductions; abductions are common among all Australian aboriginal tribes and are the customary mode of obtaining a wife among some of them. The procedure is hardly romantic; in describing it Dr Howitt has recourse to the decent disguise of Latin; before bringing home the bride it was the custom to perform a ceremony in which the companions of the Romeo were the chief actors: 'Postridie in loco quodam idoneo, a castris remoto, juvenes delecti a gente ejus abductam seriatim stupraverunt. Postea autem abductoris primi femina omnino habebatur.'

We shall return to the subject of elopement in considering the means of obtaining wives in patrilocal marriage. When not a mere form or a means of obtaining better terms from the relatives, such elopements are, like suicide, far more often the result of the young woman's dislike for an elderly or repugnant suitor than a personal attachment to a particular youth.

Primitive Love

Many testimonies to the lack of strong sexual attachment among primitive people can be cited.[1] That, in uncultured societies above the lowest levels, personal preference, and an emotional state analogous to 'falling in love', do occasionally exist appears probable. But such sentiments appear to have no depth or stability. Thwarting of individual desires may occasionally lead to impulsive acts of suicide, but appears in general to inflict little disappointment. Thus, speaking of the Sauteux Indians, Grant reports: 'They are not insensible to the charms of love, though indeed not so subject to its empire as Europeans are in general. Here the disappointed lover can bear the indifference of his mistress with the calmest fortitude.'

This does not imply that primitive man is incapable of affection or attachment. Quite the contrary. Other things being equal, there is probably a greater disposition to whole-hearted if perhaps less deep and

[1] See p. 40ff.

constant, affection in primitive than in civilized man. The whole structure of primitive society rests upon such sentiments. 'Affection with a savage', justly remarks Miss Kingsley, 'is not so deeply linked with sex; but the love between mother and child, man and man, brother and sister, woman and woman is deep, pure and true.' The savage can at once become devotedly attached to an individual in whom he feels he can confide. The admixture of such child-like affection with the sexual impulse in man is one of the elements in sexual love; it is the manifestation of transferred paternal instincts and the true basis of the mating instinct. But this affection is entirely distinct from erotic sentiment, and only related to it by artificial combination. Not being associated with the repression of sexual instincts, such affectionate attachment does not, as with us, have the opportunity of becoming blended with it, but remains distinct, as with those savages who are tenderly affectionate to their wives and yet share them with any lover. The post-nuptial affection which grows out of companionship is a different sentiment from sexual love, and not being linked with sex is compatible with the absence of jealousy. Such affection is a conspicuous feature of polyandrous families. Tibetan families are noted for the devotion which exists between brothers and wives, and the greatest harmony is apparent in Toda families. Primitive man is as prone as civilized man to sensual desire. He is equally capable of tender affection; what is unknown to him is the intimate combination of the two. Speaking of the Arabs, an observer as sympathetic as Burckhardt remarks: 'The passion of love is indeed much talked about by the inhabitants of towns, but I doubt whether anything is meant by them more than the grossest animal desire.' No Arabian love-poetry takes account of any other aspect. Throughout the East sexual attraction is looked upon as purely physical. Our fiction and our drama, the association of love with marriage, are unintelligible to the Japanese.

Late Marriage

Although sexual life begins extremely early with savages the resulting associations are transient. The decay of sexual life takes place correspondingly early, and a man of thirty may be regarded as past his prime. It is usually when the sexual instincts are thus on the wane that sexual associations acquire greater stability and that true attachment may manifest itself. In the lower stages of culture love in its most genuine form is an attribute, not of youth but of age. As the Eskimo say: 'Affection comes as a result of living together.'

The individual marriages of the Australian aborigines are an institution of advanced life. In some districts it is rare to find a married man under forty, and one is scarcely found anywhere under thirty. The same is true elsewhere. According to a missionary, the natives of Formosa seldom married before the age of fifty. The same is true among all the Dravidian races of Northern India. Among the northern barbarians of Europe 'the men did not as a rule marry until they had reached mature age and the restless period of youth had passed'. In America, among the Natchez, Iroquois, Hurons and Siouan tribes the usual marriage age was from twenty-five to thirty, but there were many who finally succumbed to importunity only at forty or fifty.

The Kaffirs of South Africa did not usually marry before the age of thirty or thirty-five, and frequently had to be pressed by the women. The Tuareg begin to think about marriage when they are about forty. Similar habits were general in South America.

Standards of Feminine Beauty

Primitive man's choice of a bride is scarcely ever determined by sexual attraction. He prefers to marry 'the weather-beaten and hardy women of the tribe, who are capable and hard workers'. An Indian chief, questioned as to his notions of female charm, 'seemed not to have made a study of them. Their faces', he said, 'might be more or less handsome, but in other respects women were all the same.' His further remarks are not reported, as they are said (though this is difficult to believe) to have caused a Canadian trader to blush. In the savage, discrimination as regards female charm is virtually confined to a preference for youth and plumpness over emaciation and age. Monteiro says of the African Bantu 'they are quite satisfied and content with any woman possessing even the greatest amount of the hideous ugliness with which nature has so bountifully supplied them'. Among the natives of Sunday Island, the young women are utterly neglected, the older women being much sought after, whether as wives or as concubines. In some parts of the Solomons, the men prefer an old to a young woman, as being more experienced. Among the Akikuyu, young boys are known to assault old and withered hags. Among the Fuegians, in about half the unions, the women are ten to twelve years older than the men. Among the Iroquois often a young warrior of twenty-five is married to a woman of forty, and Eskimos sometimes marry women old enough to be their mothers.

The primitive, indifferent to aesthetic standards, looks for purely utilitarian qualities which may seem to our taste coarse or repulsive. In Africa since the women are viewed as useful workers, the nearest approximation to the male type is regarded as desirable, instead of the accentuation of what we regard as femininity. 'All Negro races that I know', says Reichard, 'account a woman beautiful who is not constricted at the waist, and when her body from the armpits to the hips is about the same breadth—like a ladder.' Ears 'like an elephant' are also admired. A pendulous abdomen is accounted attractive, and an umbilical hernia is regarded as a specially charming trait.

The chief aesthetic character which the primitive values is adiposity. A female who is unable to rise from a sitting position without help is generally regarded as the ideal. In Nigeria, 'corpulence and beauty seem to be terms nearly synonymous. A woman of even modest pretensions must be one who cannot walk without a slave under each arm to support her, and a perfect beauty is a load for a camel.' Accordingly, girls in many parts of Africa and elsewhere (for instance, the Sahara and the Sudan) are subjected before marriage to a fattening process, and are severely punished if they do not co-operate. Among the Tuareg, girls of good family are entrusted at six or seven to energetic slaves who compel them to swallow large quantities of milk-foods and flour. The victims weep and implore to be allowed to remain ugly. In the evenings they are rolled and vigorously massaged in order to distribute the acquired fat uniformly and to suppress all angles and concavities. Thanks to this regimen and to complete idleness, they are towards the age of eighteen monstrously beautiful, being unable to rise or displace themselves without the aid of two vigorous slaves, and all the warriors vie for their favours.

Such ideals seem to be general among all uncultured races. The same fattening process is carried out for the bride of a Polynesian chief and by the Guanches of the Canary Islands. The Patagonians, the Eskimos and the Kirghis Tartars also appreciate corpulence. The Kaffirs justify their admiration for obesity on the grounds that a fat woman stands a much better chance of weathering a season of famine than a thin one. The countless figures of hugely obese women found in deposits throughout Mediterranean countries, which include the most ancient specimens of plastic art, show that the same idea of beauty obtained among the founders of European culture. It has been said that they indicate the former widespread existence in Europe of a race akin to the Hottentots. But this is unlikely since steatopygous women are an artificial product, and admiration for such forms is a universal primitive characteristic.

Most savages approve what we should regard as unsightly, namely long, hanging breasts, which permit the women to suckle the child which she carries on her back by throwing the breast over her shoulder. This feature is accordingly cultivated by means of manipulations from earliest puberty, and by use of bands to compress the base of the breast and elongate it. Firm, upright breasts are disliked as an indication of sterility.

Economic Grounds of Sexual Selection

The marriages of the most primitive peoples are governed by the same economic considerations which motivated the '*mariages de convenance*' of aristocratic families in feudal Europe. The Australian aborigine, asked why he wants a wife, replies: 'To fetch me wood and water and prepare my food.' Similar evidence can be adduced from many societies. In the Loyalty Islands, the choice of a wife is chiefly determined by her skill as a gardener. Among the Ainu of Japan, laziness on the part of the wife and failure to obtain good crops are recognized as grounds for divorce. A Singhalese, lectured on the sacredness of the marriage tie and the wickedness of divorce, asked what he should do if, having married a woman, it turned out that she was unskilled in cultivating rice. In the Ao tribe of the Naga Hills, if a marriage is arranged before concluding the alliance the couple start on a trading expedition. If the commercial venture turns out profitable, the marriage is proceeded with. If not, it is broken off. An Eskimo 'marries because he requires a woman's help to prepare his skins, make his clothes and so forth.' Among the North American Indians, 'industry and capacity for work are above all valued, and next, fertility'. In Brazil the chief qualities valued in a wife are that she should understand gardening and be able to brew good beer. Among the Banyoro, 'Marriages are . . . entered into for utilitarian and economic reasons.'

Today economic conditions in Uganda, as in many other parts of Africa, have entirely changed, and the men earn good wages in factories and on Government contracts. The result is that, although much wealthier, they tend to avoid marriage to an extent which is causing concern to the authorities. Marriage has fallen into disuse, not because the men cannot afford it, but because they can afford to do without it. The economic motive for individual marriage having disappeared, there is none other left.

To sum up: The origins of marriage cannot be found in a personal claim over particular women, arising from an innate masculine jealousy. We must therefore look elsewhere for such origins.

CHAPTER 14

Selecting a Husband and
Acquiring a Wife

Marriage Proposals by Women

IN primitive society, it is commoner for women to choose individual men than for men to choose individual women. Thus among the tribes of Queensland, 'it is never usual, it appears, for the young man to make the first advances to a young woman of his own tribe. The "gin" has the acknowledged right of showing her partiality for a particular person. We could not learn that the poor fellow had any right to refuse.' In the Torres Straits young men are lectured on the impropriety of proposing marriage to a girl. Even when the man has other wives, it is the woman who proposes. And even after the girl has declared her affection 'any forward conduct on the part of the young man would have been regarded as bad form'. Indeed, it was proper to ignore such proposals until they had been repeated several times, to avoid doubt as to the lady's intentions.

Female initiative in selection is reported from Papua to India, from northern Melanesia to South America. Similar usages appear to have existed among the Slavs and ancient Irish, while love-letters from ancient Egypt tell the same tale. Where, as among the North American Indians, it was customary for marriages to be negotiated among the respective mothers, it was normally from the girl's mother, not the man's, that the first move came. Among the Radeh, a primitive people of South Indo-China, the young lady who has taken a fancy to a youth, after inquiries as to whether her suit will be welcome, establishes herself in the youth's house and attempts to seduce him. Should she become pregnant within a year, she can remove her conquest to her own home without further formality—but if not, she must pay a bridegroom-price in cloth or cattle.

Such usages are far too widely distributed to be regarded as exceptions or aberrations. They are, as we might expect, observed in unmodifiedly matriarchal and matrilocal societies. Where male domination and a patriarchal social order have become fully established, the men naturally conduct the matrimonial negotiations, and often with little regard for the woman's wishes. For a woman to make any advances comes to be regarded as immodest. Thus in Australia, it is from Queensland, where the position of the women is distinctly less debased than is the rule with the aborigines, and where matrilocal marriage usages appear to have survived later, that feminine initiative in courting has been reported, as also from the Kurnai tribes, which have preserved an unusually primitive form of marriage organization.

Likewise in Melanesia courting by the woman is found in the New Britain and New Ireland groups, as also among the Melanesians of New Guinea, whereas it would be out of the question in the Solomons, in New Caledonia or in Fiji, where brutal male domination is established. Where the usage is found in a patriarchally organized community, it is probably a survival from times when women had a right of choice; while the deference which is often paid to the inclination of the young women, and the right of refusal which they often possess where marriage negotiations are conducted by parents or go-between, is probably also a legacy from such earlier times.

The reason for the woman's original right of choice is clear. In the conditions of primitive matriarchal societies the woman is far more interested in marrying than is the man. The economic value of a woman's labour is confined to the household in which she works; the man can take advantage of it only if he removes her to a household of his own. But if all marriage associations were originally matrilocal and a woman never left her group, she would be devoid of economic value to her mate. The product of a man's labour, on the other hand, especially when it consists chiefly of game, can be equally well distributed to his own household group or to that of his sexual mate. In such conditions, therefore, the economic inducement to association between sexual partners operates on the woman alone; it is she, and the group to which she belongs, who are gainers by the accession of a new provider of food and a new protector.

It is biologically irrelevant to adduce the 'passive' character of female germ-cells and the 'active' character of male germ-cells in support of a general social law that the male instincts must be the more active factor in bringing about a mating association. The relevant biological fact is that wherever *animal* mating takes place and there is a more-or-less prolonged association of the sexes, it invariably does so in relation to the requirements of the female and not to those of the male.

Love of Adornment greater in Primitive Males than in Females

Darwin's theory rested upon biological facts which everywhere show the selection of males by the females, not the reverse. In the animal kingdom it is the male which displays colours and ornaments; the female is invariably inconspicuous. Similarly in most primitive societies: the coquetry and love of adornment commonly assumed to be innate in all 'daughters of Eve' appear to be absent or rudimentary in primitive womankind. Thus in Australia, 'adornments are almost entirely monopolized by the men: females are content with their natural charms'. In the Gambier Islands the women not only 'have no ornaments of any kind', but they 'appeared quite indifferent to the beads and trinkets which we offered them'.

Throughout the American continent the same difference is conspicuous. With all the tribes of the South American continent 'the use of ornaments and trinkets is almost confined to the men'. Thus among the Muras the men display a wealth of ornaments, while the women are absolutely naked. Young Choroti men spend hours over their toilet before going to a dance, while the young women trust to their natural charms. Fuegian men have their hair dressed and brushed by the women; similarly among the Andamanese islanders.

In the Congo 'toilet and luxuries of dress are the attribute of the stronger sex, and the costume of the women is generally more simple'. The same is true in East Africa; the men affect the most elaborate fashions in hairdressing. The Mashukulumba have cone-shaped, tapering headdresses, sometimes a yard long; the women shave off their hair, and present their future husbands with their own locks to serve as padding for their extravagant coiffures. The Syrian traveller, Bardesanes, observed the same among the natives of Central Asia near Baktria. 'The Gelan women', he wrote, 'neither perfume themselves nor wear dyed garments, but are all barefooted, although the Gelan men adorn themselves with soft clothing and various colours, and wear gold ornaments and perfume themselves, and this not from any effeminacy in other respects, for they are brave and very warlike, and much given to hunting.'

Women's Choice determined by Economic Considerations

Primitive woman's choice of mate is determined by practical considerations. Thus, among the Sea Dayaks the women 'generally regard marriage as a means of obtaining a man to work for them' and a 'woman will often separate from her husband simply because he is lazy'. 'They cling to us', said an Eskimo, 'because we give them food and clothing.' When a hunter is sick, his wife goes to another man. Amongst all the North American tribes skill in hunting and prowess in war is the chief recommendation in a prospective husband. Similar reports come from all over the world. Among the tribes of Brazil, a warrior who has distinguished himself is overwhelmed with marriage offers. Among the Nilotic negroes 'a man with a reputation as a clever hunter can take his pick any day of all the girls in the district, whereas a youth who cannot shoot straight will find difficulty in getting a wife at all'. Of several communities it is expressly stated that a marriage lasts only so long as the man continues to provide adequately.

In the higher stages of culture, where economic pressure is less, other factors may operate. Tuareg ladies, who besides owning most of the property are superior in education and refinement to the majority of the men, are said to show a preference for somewhat effeminate men and *beaux raconteurs*. But such tastes are not to be found in primitive societies.

To demonstrate ability to support a wife is accordingly the indispensable preliminary to marriage. In the lower stages of culture, a man invariably pays court by presenting specimens of his efficiency as a hunter or proofs of his prowess as a warrior. Among the North American Indians, 'when a young man wishes to marry a squaw, he sends her a quarter of venison with the message: 'I can furnish you at all times with the game necessary for your food'. Similar usages appear to have been at one time customary in Scotland: the Caledonian hero Duchomar approaches the lady of his choice by sending her some venison. In hunting communities no youth may contemplate matrimony unless he has killed some animal. Among the Koyukuhotana of Alaska a youth who has not killed a deer is thought to be incapable of begetting children.

In warlike tribes it is usually a condition of marriage that a man should have proved his value by killing an enemy. Among the Yoruba 'whether the killing was done in fair fight or in the form of a murder did not matter.' The rules of hospitality were conscientiously observed, but a guest, after he had left the house, was often waylaid and his throat cut, thus enabling his host, as a fully qualified murderer, to enter the honourable state of matrimony. Among the wild tribes of Formosa a man was not allowed to marry until he had murdered a Chinaman. Of the Dayaks of the West Coast of Borneo Heer Francis writes: 'He who succeeded in bringing back a head, no matter how obtained, was immediately received as a distinguished member of the community and had a free choice of all the girls of his village.' With them, as also with the Alfurs of Ceram, of Minahassa, and of Sumatra, marriage was not possible unless such a trophy was forthcoming. So also among the Naga tribes of Assam, the Guaycurus and some tribes of the Amazon.

Tests of Endurance at Initiation and Marriage Ceremonies

In nearly all primitive communities, before a youth can contemplate marriage, he must take part in certain ceremonies, generally referred to as 'rites of initiation' or 'puberty' ceremonies. These rites vary in different parts of the world, and generally contain magical or quasi-religious elements. But they agree substantially in one respect: the candidates are subjected to ordeals in which their valour and powers of endurance are tested, affording an opportunity to judge their qualifications as hunters and warriors.

Such tests are commonly of the utmost severity. Thus in the Pueblo tribes the candidates were repeatedly flagellated with bundles of yucca, or 'Spanish bayonet'. Among the tribes of British Columbia the would-be warriors ran long distances over rough ground until their feet bled; dug large pits to test their arm strength; cut one another's chests, arms and legs with knives, and had the tips of their fingers slit open. Dry fir-needles were placed on their hands, arms, legs and chest, set alight and allowed to burn to ash. Anyone who could not endure the pain was ridiculed.

The refinements of torture endured by all candidates among the tribes of the Plains surpassed in ingenuity anything devised by Spanish Inquisitors. After a four days' fast and abstinence from drink, the young fellows had the muscles of their shoulders or breast transfixed with scalping knives jagged to a saw-edge in order to render the operation more painful; wooden skewers were then inserted through the wounds and ropes fastened to them, by which candidates were hoisted to the ceiling. Other skewers were similarly inserted in their arms and legs, with shields, buffalo skulls and other weights suspended from them. The victims were then twisted round and round so as to wind up the ropes and cause them to whirl rapidly as the ropes untwisted. This was but the first part of the ordeal. As soon as they had sufficiently recovered, they ran races before the assembled tribe, dragging after them heavy weights fastened by skewers to their bodies. All this had to be borne without showing any sign of pain; and the young fanatics frequently devised fresh refinements of torture of their own accord.

The famous 'huskanaw' ordeal to which boys were subjected at puberty among the tribes of Virginia was, like some other rites of initiation, calculated to promote the subjection of the youth to the authority and power of the old men; but it was declared that the test 'hardens them ever after to the fatigues of war, hunting and all manner of hardships to which their way of living exposes them.' Death sometimes resulted.

Among the Carib races of South America ferocious ants are often employed to test the powers of endurance of candidates. Thus among the Macusi of Guiana, the young men, besides thorough flagellation and the infliction of deep wounds on their persons, have receptacles containing ants applied to various parts of their body, or are sewn up in a hammock filled with them. If the candidate utters a cry, he is not permitted to marry. In addition, he must clear a space of forest, and bring as much game and fish as possible to show that he is able to support a family.

A peculiar trial to which the Mura lads were subjected was that they were compelled to drink an enormous quantity of fermented liquor; the women next administered voluminous enemas until their intestines were so distended that the abdomens were as tight as drums. They then had to perform violent exercises. Many succumbed to the test, and are said to have burst like a shell in the middle of the assembly.

In Africa, among the Kaffirs and Bechuanas, the candidates are prevented from sleeping and are compelled to take violent exercise, running and dancing till they drop from exhaustion. They are scourged mercilessly, and bear the marks all their lives. In the old days many of the boys died. If they want meat, they must steal it, and should a thief be discovered, he is beaten unmercifully for his clumsiness. The young Spartans, it will be remembered, were treated in exactly the same manner at the time of the manhood ordeals.

Circumcision is an indispensable preliminary to marriage, and is said by the Congo tribes to make the boys strong. The manner in which they bear the operation is a test of the boy's quality. Among the Orang Balik Papan of Eastern Borneo circumcision is performed immediately before marriage, as also among the Arabs of Djezan, where it is done in a particularly brutal manner, in the presence of the young man's intended bride 'If he betrays by any groan or gesture, or by the least contraction of the muscles of the face, the horrible pain which he feels, the bride declares that she does not wish to have a girl for a husband.'

The Australian initiation ceremonies consist of cutting with knives, hitting with the 'nullah-nullah', tearing the hair, burning the flesh, fighting with warriors and, wonderful to relate, delivering orations. If a candidate has the good fortune to kill or seriously wound an enemy, his claims are at once recognized and he is admitted as a warrior.

In some parts of Nyasaland and of East Africa dances are the only initiation ceremonials, and are at the same time the usual avenue to marriage. The same is true of Melanesian New Guinea, though it would appear that the obtaining of a human head was formerly requisite. The dances are, however, extremely strenuous. Speaking of the Gualola of California, Mr Powers remarks: 'The amount of dancing which they can endure for ten or fifteen days together, day and night, is astonishing, when we remember that the manner of dancing practised by the men is terribly hard work.'

In Polynesia, where exogamous clans and marriage-classes have disappeared, the conditions of life are exceptionally easy; elaborate manhood ceremonies no longer exist, but are represented by the operation of tattooing. The operation is extremely painful and protracted; the victim is held down by four or five young women, who sing to encourage him. When the tattoo is healed a great dance is held, 'when the admiration of the fair sex is unsparingly displayed'. In more primitive societies and among warrior tribes, the tattooing was but a certificate of prowess. Thus among the Natchez and other Mississippi tribes the youths are 'tattooed on the nose only until they have killed some enemy and have brought back his scalp when they have the right to have themselves tattooed elsewhere'.

Manifestly in their practical aspects the 'manhood ceremonies' of uncultured peoples are designed to afford a test of the strength, courage and endurance of young men, and of their efficiency as hunters and warriors. It might be supposed that these tests are imposed primarily in view of the community's interest in the quality of its hunters and its warriors, but this does not fit the facts. For, if so, one would expect that uncultured peoples would also seek to produce efficient hunters and warriors by a regular course of training, but there is usually very little such training, and what there is often follows, instead of preceding, the tests.

There is one institution only for which successful performance of initiation rites is indispensable—marriage is absolutely forbidden to a youth before he has been duly certified as having attained to the status of hunter or warrior. Indeed, the ceremony itself is sometimes spoken of as 'marriage'. Sometimes one and the same ceremony constitutes both the 'initiation' and the marriage.

Sometimes the initiation tests are applied individually as part of the marriage preliminaries or of the marriage ceremony itself. As we have seen, in many countries the bridegroom is soundly thrashed by the relatives of the bride. This is part of the rituals of violence which mark many marriage ceremonies; but it appears in many cases to constitute a test or ordeal in addition. Among the higher Hindu castes of the Punjab the bridegroom, in his progress towards the bride's home, passes between a double row of damsels and women armed with reeds. who strike him as he passes; the blows are quite harmless, but the ritual is doubtless a relic of a severer ordeal.

Frequently, such tests of endurance are applied in the presence of the proposed bride, or even by the women themselves. In Dongola it is the girl herself who tests the mettle of her suitors. She sits down between two of them, holding long knives in each hand, and slowly presses them into their thighs. The man who bears the torture best is chosen as her husband. In other instances, the women are excluded from such ceremonies, but there is reason to believe that this was not originally the case. Although women are, in general, quite willing to defer to the opinion of their male relatives in this matter, often they themselves are the judges. The procedure thus bears a close resemblance to the way in which, in ancient India, girls of noble birth selected a husband. Relics of these 'swayamvara' customs are still to be found among the Rajputs. Such marriage competitions were also much in vogue in archaic Greece, where, as in India, the bride was allotted to the victor in an archery competition, a foot-race or perhaps a bullfight. So also in mediaeval Europe. As late as the eighteenth century in County Derry, Ireland, it was the custom for the suitor of a marriageable maiden to compete for her hand in sports, which were generally arranged by the authorities as a Sunday entertainment.

Similar contests were widespread in South and Central America. Thus among the Chavantes 'he who can carry a heavy log over the longest distance, or excel in running, or cast a spear farthest, bears the bride home'.

Such organized contests are found among the rudest as among the most highly cultured tribes of the American continent. 'The most common gateway to sexual intercourse east of the Rockies', says Father Morice, 'was wrestling. Two young men would publicly wrestle for the possession of a maiden, and the same took place in connection with any married women as well.'

The Zulus, like most tribes of warriors, affect great contempt for women, but there are indications that things were once otherwise. Although women are now 'purchased', if there are a number of competing suitors, the right of choice lies with the women. In practice, the observance is now mostly formal. Each suitor, dressed in his best dancing attire, comes up for inspection, squatting in front of the lady's hut. If she is satisfied, he is instructed to come again the next morning and exhibit his paces in the cattle-fold before a large concourse of people.

Among the Chukchi at the present day, women sometimes choose as their husband the victor in an athletic contest or a foot-race in the same manner as did the daughters of Anætus and of Danaus. Among all the Turki and Mongol peoples of Central Asia the bride-race takes place on horseback. Among the tribes of the Malay Peninsula 'the bride-elect darts off, *au galop*, into the forest. . . .' A chase ensues, during which, should her inamorato return unsuccessful, he is met with jeers, and the match is declared off. Sometimes the bride-race takes place in canoes. The Aieta, a negrito race of the Philippines, have a similar custom. If the suitor finds the bride and returns with her before sunset, the couple is considered legally married.

Marriage by Service

The view that the primary function of such tests and ceremonies was originally to enable women to choose the ablest husband is confirmed by the fact that the same element of testing is present in 'marriage by service'.

In primitive matriarchal societies where no personal property exists, the sole economic contribution a man can make is to contribute his services. In comparatively advanced societies, the man may, in consideration of his devoting his labour for a period to the service of his wife's family, be permitted subsequently to remove her to a home of his own. But this period of service is far from being simply a contribution which may be commuted by some other form of payment. Thus, among the Tupi tribes of Brazil, whose marriages were in any case permanently matrilocal, the period of 'service', or probation, commonly took a competitive form. When a girl had a number of suitors, all would 'serve' for her for two or three years. They would work for her father, dig his garden, cut wood for him, fish, hunt and supply the household. The most effective provider was chosen as the husband.

That such service is not merely a form of payment is evidenced by the persistence of the usage even where the man is in a position to make, or actually makes, such a payment. Thus among the Awok of northern Nigeria a man pays a bride-price for his bride but, in addition, he must work for a time on the farm of his prospective father-in-law. Among the Koryak personal service cannot be commuted; even a wealthy suitor, the owner of large flocks, must serve many years as herdsman to his father-in-law. The way in which he is treated reveals the object of this. He is not treated as well as an ordinary servant, but is subjected to indignities, and unproductive labours are imposed on him. Mr Jochelson remarks: 'The principal thought is not his usefulness, but the hard and humilating trials to which he is subjected.' The Chukchi suitor likewise, no matter how wealthy, is compelled to serve for his first bride —but probations are not required in respect of her sisters, even if he has begotten children during his probation. He carries burdens, hauls heavy sledges, mends broken utensils. He must please the girl's father, her elder brother and other male members of the family.

If the Koryak or Chukchi suitor does not come up to the standard required, he may be dismissed without reward or explanation, even after serving five or ten years. Among the Yukaghir, according to their own account, 'the period of service is intended only to test the young man's ability to work. The bridegroom is required to be a good hunter and fisherman, and capable of doing everything necessary in the household.' In fact, an able suitor is permitted to take his bride after a reduced period, his qualifications having been sufficiently demonstrated. The tests imposed upon him have often no direct economic value. Thus the prospective father-in-law will go into the woods and fell a huge tree. The suitor must then drag it to his home, as in the 'log tests' of the

South American Indians. He usually ends by dropping the tree-trunk on the top of his father-in-law's 'yurta', and the delighted old gentleman exclaims, as his home comes tumbling down about his ears: 'This is a good man, he will be able to support us.'

All matrilocal marriage is 'marriage by service', and the evidence is, I believe, conclusive that this has everywhere been the most ancient form of individual marriage contract. For wherever the two usages exist conjointly, matrilocal marriage is either known to have formerly been the general practice, or is definitely preferred by the family of the woman, or is required in the form of a period of probation, whether or not a payment is made. Where the custom of acquiring a wife by the payment of a bride-price has come into general use, marriage by service may persist as an alternative to such payment, and it then appears to be a substitute for it. But it is, I think, clear in all such instances that the payment has come into use as a commutation of such service and not the reverse.

Marriage by Purchase

'Marriage by purchase' is by far the most widespread mode of acquiring a wife, and is found both in barbaric and advanced cultures. The ancient Semites called the bride 'she who has been paid for'. Hosea tells us that he paid fifty shekels for one of his wives. Wife-purchase was the universal rule in Vedic India, among the Tartars and Mongols and among the archaic Greeks. Among European peoples in Christian times the payment of a bride-price was normal. The essential features survive to the present day in southern Spain, where the bride-groom on betrothal deposits all his savings with the bride's family, who use the money to buy equipment for the new home—the bed and linen, however, being provided by the bride's parents.

Nevertheless, only in comparatively few barbaric societies does the transaction have the character which the phrase suggests to our ears. Such transactions obviously cannot be assimilated to a commercial traffic where commerce does not exist. There is no notion of barter in native Australia; materials and objects unprocurable locally are obtained by exchange of gifts, without any conception of exacting equivalent values or of getting the better of the bargain. Throughout North and South America the notion of traffic was equally rudimentary. (In European days shell-money, or 'wampun', and beaver skins became a standardized basis of exchange, but it is more than doubtful whether 'wampun' was so used in pre-Columbian times.) In New Zealand, as throughout Polynesia, 'buying and selling for a price as practised by us was unknown'.

Where the conception of private property is undeveloped, it is a universal rule that if a thing is desired it is asked for and accepted without any sense of obligation, and given, even if valued, without any expectation of adequate return. At their tribal meetings the Australian aborigines exchange gifts; they do so, as they say, in order, 'to make friends'. In the very lowest phases of culture it is customary for a man to present gifts to the relatives of the woman whom he wishes to marry; thus, for example, among the Hill Damaras the bride-gift consists of a bunch of onions and some striped mice. The Caroline Islanders give the girl's father some bananas or some fish.

In pre-Columbian days there was no 'marriage by purchase', in the proper sense of the term, in any part of the American continent. The Pacific tribes of California and British Columbia held that a substantial marriage-gift was essential; a system of aristocratic castes exists in those tribes, and the object of the bride-gift was to serve as a guarantee of the rank and wealth of the bridegroom, whose family must make a return present of at least equal value. Where the presenting of substantial gifts by the bridegroom has become customary among other American tribes, the same rule is observed; as for example among the tribes of the Oregon. The Fuegians have been described as 'buying' their wives, because they present otter skins to her relatives; but the wife, on the other hand, brings to her husband a canoe and a set of harpoons, a much more valuable contribution. Manifestly, these are not mercenary transactions. Far from constituting a sale of the woman, they are a guarantee of the social standing of her suitor and of his ability to provide for her. In later times, such guarantees may easily have excited the covetousness of the girl's family. Among the Navahos and the Apaches a considerable number of horses was required as a bride-price for a young woman; but traffic in horses was not an original habit of these Indians, for they had none.

Similarly, in Polynesia 'purchase' was unknown in regard to marriage or any other transaction. Yet very valuable presents were exchanged in Samoa between the respective families of persons of noble family. In Nakahive the bride's family was loaded with presents, but they were immediately given over to be looted by the people. In Raratonga the gifts were redistributed among the givers after the wedding.

In the most primitive cultural stages, the purchase of a wife is in any case impossible because the men possess no fundable property and therefore no purchasing power. The primitive hunter who joins the social group of his wife or 'serves' for her contributes the product of his labour, and this may be regarded as a form of payment. In more advanced cultural stages he owns possessions which may enable him to commute his obligation to serve his wife's group permanently. 'Marriage by purchase' is thus evolved from the 'mitigated form of slavery' of the serving husband.

Only when a man became an owner of domesticated cattle, his first form of real property, was he in a position to commute his service by a payment. Marriage by purchase in the proper sense is accordingly not found at all in Australia, Melanesia, Polynesia or in America, where no domesticated cattle, and consequently no man-owned wealth, existed. It is in pastoral societies, or in societies which have passed through pastoral stages, in Africa, Asia and Europe, that the purchasing power of the bride-gift has developed.

In the vast majority of instances such a payment is not regarded as commercial, nor is it so in fact. The 'purchased' wife may be a princess and the husband nothing. The princesses of the royal house of Ashanti, for example, took a succession of husbands, who 'purchased' them. They were dismissed after they had been completely depleted of their substance. What the complacency of Europeans has represented as the 'purchase of women' is thus not even an indication of female subjection. The Greeks were embarrassed by the fact that their ancestors 'bought' their wives, but the 'purchased' wives of the archaic age enjoyed a far higher status than the wretched dowried wives of later times.

Even where 'marriage by purchase' has assumed its crudest form, it is far from being regarded by the women as an indignity. The sum paid is a source of pride; the fact of payment is the criterion of the legitimacy of the union. In Australia a woman who has not been exchanged for another, or for whom nothing has been given, is socially degraded, and is regarded as we should regard a prostitute; in West Africa and many other places likewise. Yakut women do not think European women quite respectable, since they can be had for nothing, and even offer a dowry to a man as an inducement to marry them. Where, as in South Africa, the natives have been Christianized and have consequently been persuaded not to pay for their wives, this has brought about an enormous increase of immorality and loss of self-respect on the part of the women; conjugal unhappiness and desertion have greatly increased.

Even in Christian Europe the payment of the bride-price was once regarded as the main condition of the legality of the marriage. In the early Middle Ages marriages in which the husband had made no payment were regarded as illegitimate. We have, for example, a series of Merovingian legal documents in which a man goes to great trouble to obtain a court order establishing his children as legitimate, although he has not paid the proper purchase money for his wife. In Denmark when, owing to the influence of Christianity, men were becoming lax in this, King Frotho decreed that no one should be permitted to marry a woman unless he had paid for her.

To be sure, the acquisition of a wife by paying for her, although not originally an act of purchase, has, by an inevitable abuse, at times assumed that character. Thus in Sumatra, where marriage by purchase is a late innovation, a man in some parts of the country may, by paying double the usual bride-price, acquire complete rights over the woman, and may even resell her, hire her or pawn her. In East Africa, among the Mkamba, a wife 'is bought and sold, and may even be traded as a piece of goods'. Similarly, in Chinese Tibet a daughter may be sold over and over again; the speculation may thus be repeated as often as ten times. The Samoyeds also 'commerce with their wives'; and Georgi knew a Tartar who had disposed of eight successive wives at a profit, with their entire concurrence. (This remarkable business-man was at the time engaged in courting his ninth bride.)

Examples of wives being regarded as an article of traffic may be found nearer home. 'It is much to be lamented', stated Mr Grafton in a petition to Queen Elizabeth, 'that wards are bought and sold as commonly as beasts.' Numerous instances of wife-sale occurred in England in the nineteenth century.

Such mercenary instances are in reality exceptional, considering the wide distribution of the usage, and are found chiefly where the social organization has long been subverted by the development of slave traffic, and where the bride-price has consequently tended to become identified with the purchase money paid for a slave. That the people themselves are frequently aware that such a mercenary view is an abuse is indicated by the efforts which are often made to regulate the bride-price. In Uganda a universal rate was fixed as bride-price for all women, whether peasant girls or princesses, amounting to thirteen shillings and fourpence.

In Africa, above all, 'marriage by purchase' has developed into a mercenary bargain, but it is a corruption of comparatively recent origin, and the corruption is by no means complete. To take only one example, among the Zulus, 'marriage by purchase' is perhaps as crude a transaction as anywhere, but they 'never consider it as a sale'; the term 'to buy' does not apply to it, and the husband has no right to resell his wife. 'The practice of making an express bargain', says Mr Shooter, 'can hardly be said to have prevailed thirty years ago.'

The bride-price is sometimes sentimentally represented as the 'price of virginity'. Primitively it has no reference whatever to the right of sexual access to the woman and refers solely to the right to remove her and her children from her parental home to her husband's. In Indonesia, where the native custom of matrilocal marriage and the more recently introduced usage of 'marriage by purchase' commonly exist side by side, the latter confers on the husband the right to remove his wife and her children; but he is quite at liberty to marry the woman without any bride-price if he is content to take up his abode in her home. So also in

Tonkin, Cambodia, and many other places. Frequently, when the required bride-price is paid in instalments, the wife stays in her own home until payment is completed, and her children do not belong to her husband's, but to her parent's family—as among the Kafirs of Hindu-Kush, in Timorlaut, in the New Hebrides, among the Mishmis of Assam, and the Wakamba, the Makaranaga, the Kuku and other African peoples.

However, in firmly established matriarchal societies it is sometimes no easy matter for the men, even when they possess the power to offer a substantial bride-price, to break through the immemorial privilege of matrilocal marriage, and they resort to strange devices. Since in matri-archal law a man's property passes to his sister's children, not to his son, the men in several parts of Africa have adopted the plan of purchasing slave-girls, and of making over their property to their children by those concubines. Thus it comes about that those children whom we should call 'legitimate' do not inherit from their father, while those whom we should call 'illegitimate' are the only lawful heirs.

Marriage by Capture

One mode of obtaining wives which would apparently ensure female subjugation is the capture of women from neighbouring tribes or groups. McLennan and Lord Avebury held that this was the original mode of obtaining a wife; the former regarded it as the cause of the law of exogamy, and thus of the incest prohibition. If that were so, it would constitute the source of all marriage regulations.

Certainly, the forcible capture of women has occurred in every part of the world at all epochs in the course of warfare. It prevailed among the warlike tribes of central and northern Asia; and among the Germans, Scandinavians and Slavs. The archaic Greeks and Semites constantly captured women. Nevertheless, there is not, so far as I am aware. any clear instance of this being the habitual method of obtaining a wife, any more than it was among the Greeks or Hebrews. Such a practice would, indeed, involve the tribe concerned in perpetual warfare, for the capture of even one of its women is invariably regarded by primitive tribes as a *casus belli*. The resulting mutual extermination must usually check the practice; in fact, we are told that among the Bakyiga, the practice 'led to such fierce fighting that the clan gave up the practice . . . '; while in Australia the tribal elders discouraged such a dangerous practice.

In South America, the prevalence of the practice is doubtless due to the fragmentation of the native races into numerous tribelets which are constantly at war, a state brought about by the slave-hunting expeditions of the Dutch and Portuguese. In Africa, it was prevalent where the slave-trade reached its greatest development, as in Nyasaland and

British Central Africa—but the slave-trade is of relatively recent development in Africa. No North American tribe ever made a practice of obtaining wives by capture.

The term 'marriage by capture' also covers three other practices: the abduction of single women against their will; elopement with the woman's connivance, but not the parents'; and cases where the whole proceeding is more or less fictitious. Such fictitious abductions are very common, and much of the so-called evidence for wife-capture rests upon such simulated violence. Thus among the Kurnai, when, at the end of an inter-tribal festival, a young man elopes with a woman, her relatives make a great show of resentment; but it is understood that a suitable arrangement will be made, and their wrath is merely intended to ensure this. The man may have to meet the relatives in a formal combat, in which care is taken to inflict no serious injury, and which may reduce itself to tapping him on the head with a boomerang. Sometimes the abduction does not take place until all arrangements with the bride's parents have been completed, though the bride herself may not have been consulted.

Mock fights between the relatives of the bride and those of the bridegroom, the former pretending to prevent her removal from her parental home, are of almost universal prevalence. They are found in Australia, in Melanesia, in New Guinea, in Polynesia, in Indonesia, in India and other parts of Asia, and in Africa. Such fictitious combats at weddings are even more conspicuous in the higher phases of culture, and are a feature of customs among the country people in every part of Europe.

But there are serious difficulties in the way of interpreting these usages as reminiscences of real raids. In the first place, it is not easy to imagine why the memory of such supposed abductions and raids should have been so generally perpetuated by innumerable peoples as a ceremonial observance. The descendants of men who carried off brides in victorious raids might well celebrate their ancestors' deeds of valour, but there appears no reason why the defeated parties should be anxious to commemorate their humiliation. And in such instances the opposition of the bride's people is, in general, a far more conspicuous feature than the assaults of the bridegroom's friends. Some of the forms which those simulated captures assume are quite irreconcilable with the proposed interpretation. Thus, among several peoples the 'capture' of the bride is effected by women; this is the case in Greenland, among the Bedawi of the Sinai Peninsula and in the island of Nias. In Kashmir it is not the bride's house which is closed against the bridegroom's party, but his own; his sister barricades the door when the bride is brought home, and is only induced to admit her on payment of a compensation for receiving a strange woman into the household.

Perhaps the strongest ground for this view is the inadequacy of the alternative interpretations offered. Such usages are frequently interpreted as conventional displays of modesty or coyness on the part of the bride or of her friends. Thus, when among the Eskimo of Greenland a man removes his bride to his own home, it is etiquette for her to offer the most violent resistance, and for the man to drag her, screaming and struggling, to his dwelling. We are told that this is 'lest she should lose her reputation for modesty'. But since 'it would be difficult to find a people more cynical and more devoid of shame', it is hard to accept this. Again, among the Kamchadals, the bridegroom, to establish his right to the bride, is obliged to undress her and touch her vulva in spite of every obstacle. The woman is dressed for the occasion in many layers of leather gowns and pantaloons securely sewn on her and made fast by a multitude of straps, so that she looks 'like a stuffed figure'; moreover, the bridegroom's efforts are violently resisted by the elderly females of the family.

The suggestion that this procedure is inspired by a desire to make a display of the chastity and modesty of the bride can scarcely be reconciled with the fact that the Kamchadal bridegroom has a right to reproach the bride's mother for her negligence should he happen to find his bride still a virgin, nor with the circumstance that the ceremony is performed after the man and woman have cohabited for several years.

It has also been suggested that these displays of pretended violence are magic intended to avert the malice of evil spirits. To be sure, almost every act amongst uncultured peoples contains provisions to avert 'bad luck'; but that the desire to avert the malice of spirits should so often have taken the form of a simulated conflict between the families of the bride and the bridegroom is too much of a coincidence. Still less is it intelligible that the necessity for such magical safeguards should cease as soon as the due compensation has been paid.

Among the Banyoro there is no simulated violence in the customary wedding usages, but the traditional procedure includes precautions against such violence. If simulated violence be supposed to avert the wrath of evil spirits, it is difficult to see how precautions against the occurrence of such violence can effect the same purpose. Compared with such defective interpretations, the explanation that simulated opposition is an echo of real opposition is far more satisfactory. The only objection to the latter interpretation is that there is no evidence that forcible capture ever was the usual and normal mode of obtaining wives among any people.

The bride-price (as distinct from the customary presents out of which it developed) acquires its importance only where the woman is removed from her home; it is the price of that removal, not merely of access to her. Where marriage remains matrilocal there is no such development of the bride-price; there are also no ceremonies of resistance. Both are unknown in North America, where matrilocal marriage is the rule. In Indonesia, where matrilocal and patrilocal marriage are almost everywhere found side by side, no bride-price and no rituals of capture are found except where the bride is removed. The Biblical account of the marriage of Jacob offers a typical instance of 'marriage by capture'. Jacob runs away with his wives, and is hotly pursued by their incensed father and his kinsmen, who bitterly reproach him for the rape. But the capturing husband and the captured wives had been formally married for over fourteen years and had a family.

There is an even more potent reason for the display of resistance than the desire to obtain as high a bride-price as possible. The removal of the bride from her home to that of her husband constitutes a breach of the oldest usages of primitive marriage. Some peoples will not be induced by any consideration to allow their daughters to leave home and to follow their husbands. The Brazilian Indians, when one of their daughters was forcibly taken away by a European, followed her *en masse* and yielded themselves as slaves to the abductor rather than part with their women. Every breach of established usage, more especially of marriage usages, is humiliating if not actually wicked. Where patrilocal marriage customs are supplanting matrilocal marriage, proud aristocratic families refuse to adopt the change, and insist upon their sons-in-law joining their daughters in their own homes. The relatives who have been induced by economic considerations to yield to the man's desire to remove the woman, are bound to 'save their face' by the fiction that they are submitting to compulsion.

One of the most familiar usages which have suggested an attenuated survival of 'marriage by capture' is the widespread practice of lifting the bride over the threshold of her husband's house. It was observed by the Romans, and is still found in modern Greece; it obtains in India, in China, in Java, in Palestine, in Egypt, in Algeria and in various parts of Europe, including England and Scotland. The interpretation of the usage has given rise to a good deal of discussion. Plutarch though that it recalled a time when husbands, 'taking their wives by force, brought them to their house', a view which has been followed by many modern writers. Others (e.g. Frazer) have sought its explanation in superstitious ideas connected with the threshold as a place of particular danger and ill-luck, but it is not obvious why a bride should be the only person to be protected against such dangers.

It appears to me that the most natural underlying idea is that the entrance of the bride into her husband's home is the final act in her transfer from her own home to that of her husband. It is a common custom to carry the bride the whole way from the one to the other. Among the tribes of British Central Africa and Nyasaland the whole wedding ceremony is spoken of as 'entering the house'. Among the Baholoholo of the Congo the bride's entry into the man's hut is regarded as constituting the consummation of the marriage.

Where patrilocal marriage has supplanted the older matrilocal usage, the consummation of the transaction is in fact the crossing of the threshold of the husband's dwelling; it seems quite unnecessary to seek in magic or other ideas a more recondite explanation of the usage.

The view taken here coincides essentially with the most obvious and the most general interpretation of those widespread customs which are commonly included under the designation of 'marriage by capture'; but the conclusion to which we are led as regards their bearing upon social history is the exact opposite. Such usages are not evidence of the former prevalence of a custom of procuring wives by capture, but of the universal distribution of matrilocal marriage.

Patrilocal marriage is a violation of the time-honoured order, and must be excused by a show of yielding to force. But this change has not, in general, been brought about by mere force (save in the rudest stages of social evolution), but by economic conditions which women themselves have been the chief agents in creating.

CHAPTER 15

The Social Evolution of
Monogamic Marriage

LET us now consider the question: is it true, as Westermarck and others have claimed, that marriage was originally monogamous and that polygamy represents a decadent form of marriage?

The development of agriculture in its higher forms, and the consequent establishment of a regular food supply was the great turning-point in human history. It marks the boundary between civilization and uncultured 'primitive' states, and decisively affected the sexual constitution of human society. For, so long as men possessed no fundable wealth, marriage tended to remain matrilocal and the social order matriarchal, except where male dominance was established by brute force. It was the domestication of animals which first placed economic power in the hands of men, since animals appertain to the hunter. This power was commonly used to buy off the claims of women, and of their families, to the services of husbands; thus patriarchal society with patrilocal marriage became established among pastoral peoples. On the other hand, where agriculture, which was the province of women, developed on an important scale without any intervening pastoral stage, the matriarchal order has often persisted, and has even become accentuated as in North America. The matriarchal character of society has also been preserved among many African peoples who have remained chiefly agricultural, e.g. in Egypt where pastoral property was never very important.

Elsewhere agriculture has reached the highly developed stage only after passing through a long pastoral phase, as with the 'Aryans' of India and the Semites of Western Asia, who were driven by the desiccation of their pastoral lands towards the great alluvial plains, the granaries of the world. Among the Semitic nations of Western Asia women retained many relics of their primitive influence—the code of Hammurabi shows countless provisions protecting the status of women; women could own property, conduct business and plead in court. Yet Babylonian society contrasts sharply with that of Egypt in that 'the man is more important than the woman, the father than the mother, the husband than the wife'. Assyrian pictorial art, unlike that of Egypt, scarcely ever represents a woman. It seems that the development of agriculture in societies originally pastoral, instead of increasing the power of the earth-cultivating woman, accentuate the existing supremacy of the owners' flocks and gave rise to the most pronounced types of patriarchal society.

In the poorer, more broken lands of Europe there existed neither a fully-developed pastoral society nor large-scale agriculture. The men never became rich enough to purchase Oriental harems. The land, broken up into small holdings, long remained in the hands of the women who had formerly tilled it. Hence the man came as a suitor to the woman, through whom alone he could enter into possession of the land.

Where agricultural civilizations evolved *without* any preceding pastoral phase, the matriarchal position of women was enhanced by their traditional association with agricultural magic or religion, women retaining for a long time the character of priestesses. Nevertheless, this enhanced matriarchal influence was unstable and comparatively brief, especially in those regions where, as in Mediterranean Europe, the agricultural revolution took place amid highly developed cultural contacts and material industries. It was tradition rather than existing economic conditions which favoured it. Women had long ceased to be the cultivators of the soil; their traditional ownership of it had been reduced to a legal fiction. The assured food supply released the men from hunting. The male yoked his oxen to the plough, and gradually took over the bulk of agricultural labour. The household crafts which had hitherto been almost exclusively in women's hands, passed into those of men. The sexual division of labour found in primitive societies was abolished. Woman became economically unproductive and dependent. The contrast between the toiling primitive woman and the idle lady of civilization, which has been mistaken for an indication of the enslavement of the former and the freedom of the latter, indicates just the opposite. It is the primitive toiler who is independent, and the unemployed woman who has lost her freedom and is destitute.

One economic value alone was left to woman—her sex. In uncultured societies little sexual competition exists among women, hence the absence of 'love', i.e. individual preference; sexual selection is purely economic. Primitive woman is therefore little disposed to cultivate the arts of fascination—arts which have developed in proportion to the decrease of her value as a worker. The woman who was no longer economically self-supporting became competitive in terms of the only value which remained to her, as an instrument of luxury and pleasure. The Arabs forbid all manner of work to their daughters, lest their beauty should suffer. The appearance of the females in a civilized society presents to the biologist a unique anomaly. While the male is drab and inconspicuous, on the female's attire all the resources of art and wealth are lavished. To adorn her with the pigments and gloss of secondary male sexual characters, birds and mammals the world over are exterminated. The biological rule is reversed and so is the primitive relation between the sexes—in the substitution of the patriarchal for the matriarchal social order. Simultaneously the sexual instincts of the man became discriminating. Regard for personal attraction, imaginative desire, love, jealousy—all those sentiments which are often regarded as part of masculine sexual instincts—developed in consequence of the revolution wrought by the plough. Women became the symbol of the non-utilitarian values in which the fighter and the toiler sought refuge from the harshness of reality.

The loss of woman's economic value as a worker abolished the purpose for which individual marriage originally arose. In those societies which, after passing through a pastoral stage, reached a relatively high stage of material culture, the increasing purchasing power of the men enabled them to gather large harems of wives and female slaves; marriage assumed a purely sexual aspect, and became the chief form of sexual relation.

The position is different where, as in Europe, agriculture was not preceded by a pastoral stage. Throughout a considerable portion of European history the chief object of marriage, as in primitive societies, remains economic, but in a somewhat different sense. It is not as a worker that a wife is desired but as an heiress. The chief purpose of marriage is to gain access to the property, to the lands, which in a matriarchal social order were originally in the hands of women. Archaic European marriage was thus governed essentially by economic rather than sexual considerations. Hence, while polygyny was the Oriental ideal, European marriage was of necessity monogamic.

Monogamic marriage is thus rooted in the special conditions which led to European civilization. Religious and ethical conceptions became grafted upon the economic institutions, and imparted to the latter a religious and moral character.

In Europe the distinction between polygamy and monogamy has been invested with transcendent importance. In the writings of the older travellers scarcely any feature of non-European societies excites the same zealous denunciations as does polygamy; every vice is traced to polygamy, the head fount of all sexual immorality. This attitude is understandable, for the distinction goes to the root of the sexual code of Christian Europe.

It was a firm belief in the sixteenth and seventeenth centuries that polygamy had been invented by 'Mahomet', and its prevalence in Africa and in Asia was set down to the influence of Islam. The discovery that polygamy existed in the New World was most unpalatable. Efforts were made to suppress or minimise the fact; it was given out that representative North American peoples, such as the Iroquois and the Hurons, were monogamous, or had been so 'formerly'.

None of the European arguments against polygyny has any application in the conditions of uncultured society. Early Christian moralists who accounted marriage a necessary evil, favoured monogamy as a reduction of that evil to a minimum, but chastity and continence are not valued for their own sakes in uncultured societies. Monogamy accords with the sentiments of exclusive attachment which are assumed in European tradition to be the foundations of the union; but in primitive societies such a desire is not understood. Polygamy is thought to imply disregard for the feelings of women; but in uncultured societies women are the chief upholders of polygamy.

Absence of Jealousy amongst Women in Polygamous Families

Much evidence of the absence among primitives of the sexual jealousy which moralists assume to be an inherent human trait might be adduced, but a few examples will suffice. Among Kaffir wives 'jealousy', says Delegorgue, 'is unknown, and, far from dreaming of any sentiment of the kind, the first wife of a Kaffir will work doubly hard, and to the very limit of her strength, in order to acquire enough wealth to enable her husband to buy another wife. This second wife, once acquired, is bound to the first by bonds of affection for which we have no word in our language. Those women are far more intimate than sisters'. Similar denials of jealousy are made for the Ashanti and other African tribes, as well as for New Guinea, Australia and the Pacific region, as also the Eskimo and others.

In the accounts of travellers, we occasionally come upon references to discord among the women in a polygynous family. But bickerings between women who live and work together are liable to take place whatever their relation to one another; and the occurrence of such quarrels is as strong an argument against a multiplicity of servants or shop assistants as against a multiplicity of wives. The disputes seem mostly to do with economic matters. Women in West Africa, says Miss Kingsley, do not care 'a tinker's curse' about the relations of their husbands with other women, provided that he does not waste on them the cloth, etc., which they regard as their perquisite. If a man pays too assiduous attentions to another woman, his wives insist on his marrying her, so that she may share in the work of the household as well as in the profits. In Australia a wife will sometimes show indignation if her husband proposes to introduce into the household a woman older than herself, who might exercise the authority of age over her, but has no objection to a younger woman. An Akikuyu woman, speaking to a lady missionary, sent the following message to the women of Europe: 'Tell them two things', she said; 'one is that we never marry anyone we do not want to, and the other is that we like our husband to have as many wives as possible.'

Delager, writing of the Eskimo, mentions that he once asked a married woman why her husband had taken another wife. 'I asked him myself', she replied, 'for I am tired of bearing children.' The same thing has been noted among the Koryak, the Chuckchi, the Omahas, the Kirghis Tartars, the Ainu and among others. Hausa women encourage their husbands to buy more wives because it adds to the respectability of the family. Among the Ababua a wife 'to prove the great affection which she feels for her husband will, during his absence on a journey, buy him a young and pretty girl whom she presents to him on his return'.

Polygyny is condemned chiefly on the grounds that it implies an outrage on the feelings of women. Without doubt, were polygyny introduced in a European country it would offend feminine feelings. But feminine jealousy is a product of social conditions; it is not a cause, but an effect. It expresses the woman's desire not to lose the male whom she wants as an economic assistant and protector. It does not refer to the relations of the male with other females, so long as they do not constitute a menace to the economic association; and in a polygynous family, in primitive and uncultured societies, they do not. On the contrary, since primitive women are workers, it promotes the object of marriage.

No Condemnation of Polygamy outside European Countries

Biologically, polygyny provides the condition for efficient operation of the male sexual function, the object of which is to impregnate as many females as possible. Among bisexual plants one male serves for the impregnation of numerous females. The male palm-tree stands surrounded by an enormous harem of female plants. Among animals, monogamous pairing is, as we have seen, extremely rare and occurs only in special circumstances.

The European objection to polygamy is incomprehensible to uncultured peoples and is interpreted as a sign of mental degeneration. Indeed, polygyny is widely regarded as a moral virtue; to support as many fellow-creatures as possible is not only a mark of wealth but a form of philanthropy. The number of a man's wives is therefore the measure of his respectability, not only in savage society but also in the highest non-European cultures, as among Muslims and in China. The son of a Sherbro chief, being asked how many wives his father had, displayed considerable embarrassment, for his family was in somewhat decayed circumstances. He at last admitted that his father had 'only twelve wives'. Where economic conditions render polygamy difficult to achieve, it remains, however, the object of ambition.

Uncultured races vary considerably in the extent to which polygyny is practised, but no case is known, outside Christian nations, of a people among whom it is morally reprobated. Before the Christian era, the terms 'monogamy', 'bigamy', 'polygamy', in the sense in which we use them, were unknown. The 'prohibition' of polygyny, which was alleged to be 'natural' and 'to be met with among all nations in a state of refinement', was actually promulgated for the first time in any part of the world in the code of Justinian in the sixth century.

Limitations of Polygyny

Tribal custom is sometimes said to impose a limit on the number of wives a man may have. Such statements are often couched in terms similar to those in which the existence of polygamy is usually admitted it is said to be 'allowed', 'authorized' or 'tolerated', but it is unlikely that any uncivilized people ever thought to issue such an 'authorization'. To be sure, where women are difficult to obtain, a monopoly of wives by any individual is sometimes resented. In some Australian tribes the right of a man who is unable to procure a wife to challenge another who has several is recognized. Among the Wasania of British East Africa, for instance, men are not permitted to marry more than three wives, 'as it is considered that no man is able to provide food, etc., for more than this number'. Elsewhere the figure is four (the number prescribed in Islam), six or seven. Kings and chiefs, though privileged, are sometimes subject to a limit. The number of wives of the king of Ashanti is said to have been fixed at 3,333. Among the Jews, kings appear to have been limited to forty-eight wives, although the number was commonly exceeded. But neither economic necessity nor the natural objection of the majority to the monopolizing of available women, appear to have led anywhere to the enforcing of monogyny.

The term 'polygyny' is now employed in preference to 'polygamy' to denote plurality of wives. The usage draws a useful distinction between plurality of wives and plurality of husbands, or polyandry. But many writers do not make use of the distinction consistently, for they do not employ, in opposition to polygyny, the corresponding term 'monogyny', but speak of limitation of marriage to one wife as 'monogamy', thus conveying a misleading impression. The word 'monogamy' not only denotes a practice, but also connotes a moral or legal standard which precludes *anyone* having a multiplicity of wives. Statements that a given people are 'monogamous', or 'to a large extent monogamous', or even that (in a phrase of Westermarck's) they are 'generally rigorous monogamists' (whatever that may mean), are liable to suggest that a principle or law enforcing monogamy is recognized among those peoples. But monogamy in this sense is not known outside Christian nations. People among whom only one man in a hundred has more than one wife are no more 'monogamous' than those among whom every man has six wives.

Among primitives, to term a people polygynous or monogynous, polygamous or monogamous, conveys little concerning the actual extent and character of their sex relations. Even in Europe, it has been said, monogyny has never existed. The Romans and the Greeks were monogamous in their marriage institutions, but scarcely monogynous in their sex relations. In Abyssinia, among the Christian Shoa, 'monogamy, it is true, is established by the Church, but concubinage is the habitual and general custom, the king and his five hundred wives leading the way'. In polygamous countries, where a man cannot afford to keep more than one wife at a time, he makes up for the unfortunate circumstance by frequent changes. 'The Muslim of small means, who cannot afford to marry two or more wives or to purchase slave-girls,' observes Dr Rohlf with special reference to Morocco, 'compensates himself by marrying one woman after another.' In Egypt, partners were commonly changed as often as twenty or thirty times in a couple of years. A Bedawi will marry a young woman merely to enjoy her company for a few weeks. A Baghdad dyer, who lived in strict monogamy, when he died at eighty-five had had 900 wives! Frequent changes of partners, where polygamy is restricted, is equally conspicuous in the lower phases of culture. Thus, the Guaycurus and other tribes of the southern Chaco usually married only one woman at a time; but the connections were so transitory as to amount to general sexual promiscuity. As Dr Torres observes: '"successive polygyny" would be a more accurate designation than "monogamy".' Many peoples, theoretically classifiable as monogynous, because in old age they maintain monogynous marriage for economic reasons, are actually totally promiscuous—for instance, the Nagas, the Sakai forest tribes of Malaya, and the inhabitants of several parts of Indonesia and Micronesia. Such 'monogamy', of course, affords no sort of support to the view that sexual relations were originally monogamous.

The number of wives which a man is able to support is limited by economic conditions. 'The poor man is a monogamist all the world over', says Weule. Frequently the number of children in a family is likewise restricted by poverty. In several primitive societies a man is not considered justified in rearing more than two or three children; the rest are killed.

The limitation of polygyny to the point of virtual monogyny is found exclusively amongst forest dwellers, such as the Veddahs of Ceylon, the forest tribes of the Malay Peninsula, Borneo and South America, for life is extremely difficult to support in the interior of forests. Such tribes have no agriculture and few household industries; game is difficult to pursue. In such conditions a number of women cannot contribute more to a man's needs and comforts than can one woman, and each additional wife adds a burden to his resources. The position is radically different among the Australian aborigines or the Fuegians, for instance.

The distribution of polygyny among uncultured races appears to be governed by economic conditions exclusively. There is no reliable evidence to show that the numerical proportion of the sexes plays any important part in determining the extent of polygyny. (Estimates as to that proportion among uncultured populations are extremely unreliable.) Extensive polygyny is possible even where the number of females is considerably smaller than that of the men, since in uncultured societies females generally marry far earlier than males.

Estimates as to the extent of polygyny in a given community are equally misleading. In any polygamous society most of the men will probably be found at any one time to have only one wife, even though all of them will later have two or more. A man who begins by having one wife before acquiring three or four is no more a monogamist than an unmarried man is a celibate. Hence the statements, so commonly made, that 'many men have only one wife' or that 'the majority of the men are monogamists' are quite misleading.

The expansion of Western civilization has enormously reduced polygamy in every part of the world and in every phase of culture. Papuan savages now have 'an exaggerated idea of the wickedness of polygamy'; and African negroes 'call the ancestors of the tribe "polygamists" as if it were a swear-word'. In India, among wealthy Hindus, in northern China and Egypt, monogamy is becoming respectable, and in Turkey has been made the rule. This is by no means due solely to the influence of European opinion and of missionaries. The complete change in economic conditions brought about by European expansion has been an even more potent factor. The rise in the cost of living and of luxury has rendered impossible the harems of mediaeval pashas. The higher uncultured races are no longer dependent upon household industry, but on European products paid for with the wages of male labour; and in some parts of Africa those conditions have tended to abolish not only polygamy but marriage. The most remote tribes, in the lowest phases of culture, are no less affected. Their hunting-grounds have shrunk, their life has become one of squalor. Among the American tribes of Canada polygyny decreased within a few years of the first white settlements. Nowhere do the conditions in which native tribes are found by the traveller at the present day represent their natural state.

Alleged Instances of Primitive Monogamous Institutions

The extent to which monogynous marriage occurs as a general usage amongst uncultured peoples has been greatly exaggerated. Actually no uncivilized people is known with certainty to have monogamous institutions. In view of the prevalent misconceptions on the subject, we shall examine a few of the statements on this topic, particularly those of Dr Westermarck, which have been very frequently quoted without inquiry.[1]

Thus, among the Guarani tribes, according to Dr Westermarck, 'chiefs alone are allowed to have more than one wife'. The statement is given on the authority of Father Charlevoix, who actually is specifically referring to Christianized Indians. Westermarck adds a reference to Father Hernandez. What Father Hernandez actually has to say concerning the monogamy of the Guarani is as follows: 'The Guarani family, in their state of heathenism, suffered from a fundamental defect, for polygyny reigned amongst them, and they thus violated the natural law which is the basis of marriage.' Father Ruiz de Montoya loudly laments the unrestricted polygamy of the Guaranis; some of them had as many as thirty wives. D'Orbigny says: 'The customs of the Guaranis are almost identical in all sections of the race. . . . All of them practice polygamy.'

Among some of the forest tribes of the upper reaches of the Amazon basin, polygamy is reported to be rare or confined to the chiefs. Mr Whiffen, to whom Dr Westermarck refers, and who in turn refers to Dr Westermarck for theories of primitive monogamy, says that in some tribelets south of the Tikie, chiefs have no more than one wife, but adds the curious statement that 'it is extremely hard to distinguish at first between wives, concubines, and "attached wives".'

Dr Westermarck mentions by name eleven South American tribes as being, without qualification, 'monogamous'; to wit, the Guaycurus, Canellas, Shamboia, Paressi, Chavantes, Curetus, Purupurus, Mundrucus, Otomacos, Ackawoi and Macusi. But in eight of these cases travellers have reported polygamous practices. For instance, the polygamy of the Mundrucus was the chief obstacle met with by the Jesuit missionaries; their converts absolutely refused to give it up. Father Ignace says that 'the Mundrucus had for principle that it was licit to have as many wives as their husband was capable of maintaining'. Bates found the Mundrucus polygamous. We are therefore justified in regarding with some reserve Wallace's repetition of the same statement with

---

[1] In the revised edition of his work, Dr Westermarck has modified his former statements and eliminated several examples formerly adduced as evidence of 'primitive monogamy.' Thus, for example, the Iroquois were formerly represented as 'purely monogamous,' and were repeatedly appealed to as a conspicuous instance, statements now entirely withdrawn.

reference to the Curetus and the Purupurus, of whom he says that he never saw any and that 'little is known of their domestic customs'. No existing tribe is known by the name of Purupurus. According to Chandless, polygamy is practised by the chiefs among all the tribes of the Purus river; among the Ipurinas it is general. Von Spix and Martius did not form a high opinion of the sexual customs of the Curetus, who pressed their daughters on the travellers.

Father Gumilla is the source for the assertion that the Otomacs are wholly monogamous, but Baron Humboldt, who obtained full information from the missionaries living amongst them, speaks very disparagingly of Father Gumilla's account and says that 'all the Indians who will not be baptized live in a state of polygamy'. Father Gilii confirms this. Azara saw one of the last representatives of the Guaycurus: he was living with three wives.

In no instance is the alleged monogamy of any of those South American tribes established with anything like certainty. It is striking that an authenticated instance of a monogynous tribe should be so difficult to find where the aboriginal population has been broken up into innumerable warring tribelets and on the verge of starvation and extinction, conditions in which we might well expect to find monogyny. Many of the poorer tribelets consist of scarcely more than three families. When, in such tribelets polygyny is said to be confined to the headman, this represents a greater proportion of polygyny than is to be found in any Muhammedan country.

Again the Guanches of the Canary Islands are very generally described in modern accounts (including Westermarck's) as having been monogamous. The source of those statements is probably the work of Father Abreu de Galindo, who wrote towards the middle of the seventeenth century, when any surviving remnants of the Guanche race were Christians. His account is extremely edifying, but contradicts all the older accounts. Friar de Espinosa, who dwelt many years in the Guanche community of Candelaria, states that the Guanches 'had as many wives as they pleased and could support'. Gomara, Sir Edmund Scory, Galvano, Cadamosto and Bernaldez all confirm this.

The monogamy ascribed to some Berber tribes meagrely offsets the polygamy prevalent throughout Africa. Thus the Tuareg have several times been stated to be 'strictly monogamous'. But, if correct, the statement can apply to some of the north-western tribes only, for in the southern and eastern Sahara, the Tuareg 'usually have from two to four wives'. The monogamy of the northern Tuareg has been supposed to be a relic of their former Christianity. If so, it was certainly an innovation. 'Among the Numidians and the Moors,' Sallust tells us, 'each man marries according to his means as many wives as he can; some two, others more, and the kings many more.' The nomadic Tuareg commonly have establishments in the various villages which they visit; hence the appearance of monogamous households which has so often deceived travellers; in any case, they keep concubines in addition. Many do not marry at all, and are satisfied with a harem of purchased girls.

The western Sahara, or Moroccan region is, with the exception of a few patches, a land of extreme poverty. The men are haggard with hunger, and whole populations are decimated by famine. In such conditions it would be surprising if large households were common. Nevertheless, there is little definite evidence of general monogyny, except for a few communities, such as the Dads of the lower Atlas, and polygamy is found in every district. Dr Westermarck cites Chavanne, who refers to Vincent as stating that he 'did not meet a single man who had a plurality of wives'. Dr Rohlfs met one at Tafilet, in the heart of the same region, who had three hundred; and Mr W. B. Harris, who perhaps knows that region better than any other Englishman, speaks of the harems and of the large polygamous households and slave-girls of the Sharifian families.

From India, Dr. Westermarck has not succeeded in culling a dozen instances of tribes alleged to be monogynous. Among these are the Khasis. 'The practice of polygamy', says Mr Gait, 'is usually said to be uncommon amongst them'; but he adds: 'an educated Khasi whom I consulted assures me that polygamy is by no means unknown. It was formerly considered meritorious for a Khasi to beget offspring by different wives.' Among the Nagas, who are also alleged to be monogamous, 'polygamy is very common, and is limited only by the men's resources'. The Mikirs, who are cited by Dr Westermarck as monogamous, are expressly stated by Mr Stack to be polygamous. It is noteworthy that polygamy in India is characteristic of the more primitive rather than of the more advanced races. In southern India, the most ancient aboriginal inhabitants are supposed to be the Yenadie, Villee and Vede; they are polygamous.

'The early discoverers of the Philippines', says Dr Westermarck, 'found legal monogamy combined with concubinage.' What the early discoverers of the Philippines found, according to one of the oldest accounts, was that the natives 'marry as many wives as they can afford to keep'; what Magellan found was that 'they have as many wives as they wish'; what de Legazpi found was that 'the men are permitted to have two or three wives if they have money enough to buy and support them'. What the discoverers found in the Bisayan, or Middle Islands, was that 'all the men are accustomed to have as many wives as they can support. The women are extremely lewd, and they even encourage their own daughters to live a life of unchastity'. Father Chirino assures us that 'we are gradually uprooting that hindrance to conversion so common among those people and so difficult to remove, the practice of having several wives'. Dr Westermarck's remarks concerning the Subanu, the Italons, the Tinguianes, the Tagbanuas of Palawan and the Negritos of the Philippines are equally ill-supported.

The Igorots of Luzon have been specially instanced as an example of 'primitive monogamy', and also of a 'lofty ideal of chastity'. Various authorities contradict this, and the missionaries expressly denounced the polygynous habits of the Igorots. 'In case of adultery', says Dr Westermarck, 'the guilty party can be compelled to leave the hut and the family for ever.' Dr Jenks says that there is no tribal law against adultery, and that married men commonly frequent the 'olags' of the unmarried girls who solicit them.

We have seen that the 'primitive chastity' which has been ascribed to the forest tribes of the interior of the Malay Peninsula is as imaginary as that alleged of the Igorots. Among the Mantras (a tribe of the Jakuns) polygyny, Dr Westermarck tells us, 'is said to be forbidden'. 'It is nothing rare', says Father Bourien, 'to meet individuals who have been married fifty times'; and, in spite of the alleged prohibition, some nevertheless live in simultaneous polygamy. 'Most of the Binua, according to Logan', says Dr. Westermarck, 'have only one wife', but what Logan actually stated was: 'Most of the Binuas have only one wife, but some have two, and there does not appear to be any rule on the subject'; and he adds that separation is easy, that husbands commonly exchange wives, and that adultery is frequent and unresented.

'The Central African pygmies', says Dr Westermarck, 'seem to be mostly monogamous . . .'. Mgr Le Roy, who is perhaps one of the most competent authorities on the Central African Pygmies, says that 'polygamy is not condemned among them; on the contrary, if it is not universal, it is because it is not always possible'. Sir Harry Johnston says of the pygmies of the Tanganyika region: 'According to the evidence which I have myself collected, they seem to approach very near to promiscuity, and even incest, in their marital relations.' Similarly, the Bushmen have as many wives as they can afford, despite Dr Theal's assertion that they are monogamous.

Dr Westermarck has not been able to discover any suggestion of monogamy in Polynesia or in Melanesia. The Rev. W. Y. Turner received the impression that the natives of Motu were monogamous, but subsequently discovered that, in addition to the wives with whom they happened to be living, the men had other wives in the next village.

Nowhere among the Australian aborigines is there even a tendency towards monogyny. 'Polygamy to the fullest extent is an Australian institution'. Dr. Westermarck says that Mr Curr 'has discovered some truly monogamous tribes'. But nobody else has, and Dr Malinowski contradicts him, saying 'polygyny seems to be found in all the tribes'.

The customs of the now extinct Tasmanians appear to have been practically identical with those of the Australian aborigines. 'Plurality of wives was the universal law among them', says Mr Lloyd.

It would be difficult for any hypothesis to be so uniformly and directly in contradiction with the facts than the theological doctrine of primitive monogamy. 'The evidence', say Messrs Hobhouse, Wheeler and Ginsberg, summing up their collection of reports, 'does not make for the association of monogamy with the lowest culture, but only of monogyny with one particular form of that culture (the forest tribes), and that only partially'. Their extensive tables, though containing several disputable entries and open to certain criticisms, exhibit the general distribution of polygyny very well. The factors which are supposed to make for monogamy, the authors observe, 'in every grade, when considered as a whole, are seen to be overborne by the opposite forces making for polygamy'. The number of a man's wives reach as a maximum in pastoral societies, which are invariably polygamous.

While polygamy is everywhere disappearing with the advent of more complex economic conditions, there is no reliable instance of a people among whom monogamy was once the rule having adopted polygamy. Most allegations that a given people were 'formerly' monogamous, such as that of Father Charlevoix concerning the Hurons, or of Major Cremony's concerning the Apaches, are manifestly destitute of significance. Whenever it is stated on more solid grounds that a change from monogamous to polygynous marriage customs has taken place among a given people it will be found, I think invariably, that their earlier condition was one of unrestricted relations within the permissible degrees.

Thus, Westermarck mentions the Alfurs of the Minahassa peninsula of North Celebes as having formerly been monogamous; and he might have mentioned a much more authoritative statement of Professor Wilken to the same effect concerning the Alfurs of Buru. But the coastal tribes of the Alfurs are certainly not their primitive state. There are, however, several examples of tribes of the same race which have remained isolated from external influences. Their 'monogamy' bears little resemblance to what we understand by monogamous relations. Thus Heer Sachs admits with reluctance that he was unable to discover among the Alfurs of the interior district of Setie, in Ceram, anything that can be properly termed marriage. 'They live in a state of free love. The woman keeps company with the man of her choice for such length of time as it pleases both.'

Status of Different Wives in Polygynous Families

The women in a polygynous family are often spoken of in reports as 'concubines', with the exception of the one first married. Actually, the distinction between wives and concubines belongs in general to advanced stages of society, although some war-like tribes draw a distinction between captured female slaves and wives of their own nation. In some uncultured societies one wife (not invariably the one first married), is referred to as the 'chief wife'. It has been suggested that in such cases the 'chief wife' is in reality the only 'real' wife, and that the others are little better than 'concubines', thus implying that such marriages, although in appearance polygamous, are theoretically monogamous. But it can be shown that development has commonly taken place in the opposite direction. Where the wives are sisters, the eldest sister naturally exercises over the younger ones a certain authority and enjoys a certain precedence, which would be the same whether they were married or not; and an older woman usually has the privileges of seniority. But these distinctions are different from that between the 'chief wife' and other wives which is found in some societies, and which observers are prone to detect in uncultured peoples, among whom it is very rare.

Reliable reports from all over the world stress the complete equality of wives. The wife who is spoken of as the 'chief wife' is very frequently merely the favourite for the time being, and very often the last married. Thus among the Sioux, the oldest wife, being generally the eldest sister, enjoyed a certain precedence; but the one who was last married had an equal status. Among the Chukchi, and the Eleut Tartars an old wife is deposed and becomes the servant of the younger ones, or is driven from the home.

Distinctions between the various wives are found chiefly in Africa and Asia. Nevertheless, wives are on the same footing among the Central African pygmies, the Congo tribes, in Angola and Abyssinia, among the Banaka and Bafuku of the Cameroons, etc.

In Africa the term 'chief wife' commonly refers to the distribution of agricultural duties among the wives. A 'chief wife' is needed to direct the work of the others, like a foreman. In Senegambia, if the 'chief wife' proves incompetent, her position is given to another wife. Among the tribes of British Central Africa, a man may change his 'chief wife' whenever he thinks fit. Frequently, when a man possesses extensive fields, he has to appoint several 'chief wives'. Among the Medge, when a man's wives become too numerous to live in one hut, he divides his establishment, appointing a 'chief wife' for each group. Such practices are scarcely indicative of monogyny.

In certain advanced social conditions, however, the distinctions between a 'chief wife' and the other wives may have a real juridic significance; and one which has an important bearing upon the development of monogamic institutions. A woman of higher social rank naturally enjoys a superior status; such status is independent of whether she has been married before or after other wives and of the husband's predilections. Among the Binjhalsa of Bengal a man is bound to take a new wife when he succeeds to the rank of 'zemindar', or landowner, even though he is already married; the new wife is the 'pat rami', or 'principal wife'. The social rank of a man's first wife, who is usually selected for him by his relatives, is regarded as of the highest importance. It is obvious that the trouble and expense of securing a wife of suitable social qualifications can rarely be undertaken more than once. Hence it is a general rule that such social and mercenary considerations are taken into account in regard to a man's first wife only. These requirements once satisfied, a man must, as a rule, be content to select his subsequent wives by such less reputable considerations as love, youth, beauty and industry. The position of a man's first wife is thus often, quite apart from any relative status bestowed upon her by her marriage, socially superior to that of his subsequent acquisitions.

These considerations acquire an enormously enhanced importance, when, as in many advanced societies and in early patriarchal societies, the paramount consideration comes to be the breeding of legitimate heirs. A 'legitimate' wife is primarily a wife who can give birth to a 'legitimate' heir. It is the legitimacy of the heir which makes the wife 'legitimate'; a wife who is barren is not regarded as legitimate, and can in all lower cultures be divorced. Sometimes—as, for instance, among the Maori—when no distinction of social rank exists between the wives, the 'chief wife' is she who first gives birth to an heir. Where primitive tribal organization is still strong but is passing from a matriarchal to a patriarchal order, a 'legitimate' child means a child which belongs to his father's and not to his mother's clan; the breeding of illegitimate children in this sense defeats the main object of procreation, the increase of the tribe and its perpetuation. The breeding of such 'illegitimate' children is consequently as great an offence against patriarchal society as the transference of women to another tribe is against matriarchal society.

Islam condemned the once-common free contract between a man and woman, known as 'al-motah', because it gave the man no offspring that could be reckoned to his tribe and not to the tribe of the mother.

One of the merits of polygyny in the eyes of uncultured peoples is that it increases the number of a man's progeny. But where the transmission of private property becomes an important consideration, it is inconvenient to have numerous heirs, and the bulk of the property, or the whole, is sometimes transmitted to the children of the 'chief wife' only.

In such conditions—and they are the conditions of settled agricultural society—what is desirable is not a large progeny but an heir, and what is required is not a large number of legitimate wives but one legitimate wife. That other wives should be 'legitimate' is not only of no importance but is positively undesirable.

Obviously, the distinction in rank between the mother of the legitimate heir and other wives must become more sharply pronounced as private property grows more important. This differentiation will be accentuated by the reluctance of self-respecting families to allow their daughters to occupy an ever more disreputable and 'illegitimate' position.

In settled civilized society, the wife thus acquires an entirely new function. Whereas among primitive people she is primarily an economic associate, a provider of food, a labourer, and thus the chief source of wealth, in pastoral and higher agricultural civilization, only her sexual value is left. This sexual value consists in her attractiveness, in her function as an instrument of pleasure; the beauty of idle women is cultivated, and they are gathered together in large harems. Settled agricultural civilization bestows upon woman a new function and a new sexual value—that of legitimate wife, of mother of legitimate heirs to property.

The contrast which we have noted between pastoral and purely agricultural societies is thus accentuated. Pastoral property is readily subdivided and multiplies; the importance of transmitting undivided to one or a few heirs is not pressing. Essentially pastoral peoples, such as the Semites and the Arias of Asia, have in general retained their pastoral traditions with extreme conservatism. Yet, even here the acquisition of other forms of property has tended to reduce the extent of polygyny. In India, in like manner, polygamy has tended to become restricted. Modern economic conditions, together with the pressure of European opinion, are converting the polygamous institutions of the East into virtual monogamy.

Polygamy and its Decay amongst the Jews

An evolution similar to that now taking place in the Orient took place under the Roman Empire among the Jews. Like all other Semitic peoples, the Jews were polygamous; the harems of Jewish kings were vaunted for their exuberance (Genesis iv. 19; Judges, viii. 30; etc.). Nowhere in the fastidious Jewish law is there any condemnation of polygamy. Hebrew Law assumed polygamy. Among later Talmudist doctors opinion varies: some recommended that a man should not have more than four wives; others thought he might have as many as he could afford. Moses Maimonides said: 'It is lawful for a man to marry as many wives as he pleases, even to a hundred, either simultaneously or successively.' In Italy as late as the sixteenth century a Jew who had had no children by his wife married another, a formal dispensation for the bigamy being obtained from the Catholic Church. In Spain, Jews were polygamous as late as the fourteenth century, and still are so in some polygamous countries. The first pronouncement against polygamy among the Jews was made in the eleventh century at Worms, but was a merely local resolution. Since no law has ever existed against polygamy among the Jews, should a Jew in England at the present time contract a bigamous marriage, it could not be dissolved according to Jewish law without a formal divorce.

The object of Jewish marriage, as of all marriage in a settled order, was to obtain a male heir; hence, as in lower cultures, a barren wife might be divorced, or she might evade this by supplying another wife— for instance, one of her slave-girls. The offspring, of course, was accounted the son and heir of the husband. A male child was accounted the son of the chief wife, no matter who was the actual mother. Hence, respectable families became unwilling to sell their daughters except as 'legal' wives.

The Oriental Harem

The undignified status of secondary wives depends upon the accentuation of the distinction between them and the principal wife, and not on the fact of polygyny. In the most highly developed juridical polygamous families, such as those of the Muslim world, where the distinction of wives has no juridic significance, the position of women is very far from being one of degradation. Popular Western notions concerning the Oriental harem are, of course, little more than a tissue of myths.

Competent persons agree that the position of women in Turkey is, and was, actually higher, freer and juridically superior to that of women in Western Europe. 'I think I never saw a country', said Lady Craven over a hundred years ago, 'where women enjoy so much liberty and are freer from all reproach as in Turkey.' The Turkish woman is free to go and come as she pleases; she spends most of the day out of doors, usually absents herself for the night when visiting some friend, and is never called to account for the way she spends her time. From a juridic point of view, the position of Turkish women is certainly much higher than that of English women before the passing of the Married Women's Property Act.[1] A Turkish woman has equal rights of inheritance with her brothers. She has the uncontrolled disposal of her own wealth and property, and can inherit property without the intervention of trustees.

[1] Briffault is, of course, speaking of Turkey before the reforms of Ataturk.— G. R. T.

She can sue, or be sued, independently of her husband, and also sue, or be sued, by him. Although freedom of divorce is ostensibly greater on the part of the husband, yet the wife can obtain it without difficulty.

The Oriental woman enjoys, as a rule, more consideration and more deference from her husband than the average European wife. The great difference lies, of course, in the complete segregation of the sexes and consequent absence of intersexual social intercourse. This is not an Arab or an Islamic institution, but was introduced into Islam from Persia, where it had been customary from remotest antiquity. The Persian harem—the word means 'sanctuary'—derives not from any degraded status of women, but from the almost superstitious reverence with which they were regarded. All records bear witness to the high position of women in ancient Persia, a position which amounted to gynæcocratic domination. A man might not even sit down in the presence of his mother without her permission. The original harem was in all probability the matriarchal home of the mother, with whom her children remained, the father being excluded from even seeing them until they were five years old. 'The harem', says von Hammer, 'is prohibited to strangers not because women are considered unworthy of confidence, but on account of the sacredness with which customs and manners invest them.'

Much of that predominant position persists in Persia at the present day. As in Turkey, there is in fact very little real seclusion of women in Persia. Every woman goes as a matter of religious duty, each day to the 'hammam' or bath; and this is a sort of club where she meets her friends and usually spends seven or eight hours. The position of women in Persia is indicated by the form of the marriage ceremony: the woman places her right hand over that of her husband 'to show that she ought always to have the upper hand of her spouse'.

Inevitably, the harem has at times degenerated into an instrument of male domination; and seclusion has undoubtedly narrowed the mental outlook of the Arab women, formerly conspicuous for her achievements. But this atrophy has been greatly exaggerated. The frivolity and mental undevelopment of the harem woman is not in general greater than with many women of fashion in Europe. While the aristocratic lady cultivates such arts as embroidery, many of the Persian middle-class women are highly educated according to Oriental ideas. They read, and often write poetry; they sing, play and do plain and fancy needlework. The wife is consulted in all things to a much greater extent than is the case in Europe.

In the Oriental polygynous family, although there is a 'chief wife', there is no real social or legal distinction of rank between the several wives. Indeed, it is a current Islamic doctrine that the True Believer who displays any partiality for one wife above the others will incur a special punishment at the Day of Judgment. There is no juridic distinction whatever between the children; every woman who bears a child becomes thereby the legal wife of the father. There are consequently no illegitimate children in Turkey. If the man has already four wives, the woman becomes an odalisque, but her children have the same rank and rights as the children of the 'chief wife'. If the woman is a slave, motherhood makes her a free woman.

The evolution from polygamy to monogamy has been completed among the Osmanli Turks in our own day—not by reduction in the number of 'legal' wives, but by the gradual elimination of concubines.

Marriage and the Position of Women in China

In China, in contrast, the differentiation between the chief wife and other wives became so complete as to constitute juridic monogamy, while the Chinese woman gradually sank in status to perhaps the most depressed level found in any cultured society.

Chinese marriage institutions are virtually identical with those of the Mongols and Turkis of Central Asia. The same elaborate ceremonials involving 'go-betweens' are found in both; and the fact that these customs are regarded as immemorial institutions among the remotest tribes precludes the supposition that they were adopted from the Chinese. Among all Mongols, the same verbal distinction is made between the 'great' wife, or 'tsi', the 'little wives', or 'tsie', and 'concubines', and has practically the same significance as in China. The Mongols are frankly polygamous; yet such is the emphasis laid upon the position of the 'great wife' that they regard themselves as monogamous. The children of the 'little wives' have no legal right to a share in the inheritance, though they may be given one. Among the ruder Western Mongols we find the same situation; but, according to an early eighteenth-century account, the significance of the distinction between 'great wife' and 'little wives' and concubines was then very much looser. 'It is a constant rule among the Tartars, who look for nothing but youth in their wives, to give over lying with them when they draw near forty years, reckoning them no more than old housewives, to whom they give their victuals for taking care of the house and tending the young wives who may occupy their place in their master's bed.' Thus, the hierarchical distinction, so important in China, can scarcely be said to exist; the 'great wife' is merely, as in many African families, the favourite wife for the time being. Among the Kirghis the conditions are much the same. Among the Mongol Khans the legal distinctions up to the twelfth century were exactly similar to those noted among the Eleuts and the Kirghis. But no indignity whatever attached to the status of 'little wife'. Powerful khans gave their daughters in marriage to other khans irrespective of whether they went as 'great wives' or as 'little wives'. Jinghis Khan had over 500 wives and concubines, and all his wives were daughters of khans. His first wife was termed the 'mother of his sons'; his second wife was the daughter of the Emperor of the Manchus. Even children by concubines were regarded as perfectly legitimate, those of the legitimate wives merely taking precedence over them in the order of succession—though they could also inherit.

The usages of the ancient Chinese chieftains were identical with those of other Tartar khans, and it was common practice to marry two sisters or two cousins. Polygamy is the law of the land and is by no means confined to the well-to-do. Marriages of 'little wives' are performed with the same pomp and solemnity as with the 'great wife'; and they are officially presented to friends and relatives. The distinction between 'great' and 'little' wives is a purely juridic one, intended to preserve the unity of the inheritance. Hence 'little wives' cannot inherit, although their children, who bear their father's name, do so under the legal fiction that they are the children of the 'great wife', married with the assent of the 'great wife', and frequently at her request.

Marriage becomes indissoluble after the first three years. The union is contracted not only for this world but for the next. Formerly the wives of the emperor were killed at his funeral, as in Africa. Until lately a widow was expected to commit suicide on the death of her husband. It was, and is still, the correct thing for the announcement of her suicide to appear in the papers beside the death-notice. A widow may not marry again, nor may she return to her own family.

The position of women in China was, as we saw, formerly much higher and freer. Among Mongol tribes, both eastern and western, it is one of considerable independence and influence. 'In the household', says Prejevalsky, 'the rights of the wife are nearly equal to those of the husband'; and the latter is sometimes positively henpecked. Women have the right of divorce. Tartar ladies are viragoes, who may sometimes be seen pursuing a terrified husband with a whip. Throughout Tartar society the mother occupies a position hedged about with reverence and awe. Even the redoubtable Jinghis Khan, the 'scourge of Asia', 'the conqueror of the Universe', quailed before his mother and was compelled by her to alter his policy.

In historical and modern China, on the other hand, the status of women is abject; according to the Confucian dictum: 'The woman obeys the man: in her youth she obeys her father and her elder brother; when she marries she obeys her husband; when her husband is dead she obeys her son.' The education of a girl, according to the rules of the 'Lî Kî', consists in learning to spin and to be submissive, docile and obedient; a boy is taught to speak boldly and clearly, a girl submissively and low. A woman may be divorced because she is too talkative. 'Ignorance and retirement are proper to a woman.' Most Chinese women are illiterate. In the olden days, exceptions were common in mandarin families. The most famous is Pan-Hoi-Pan, who wrote a celebrated treatise on the duties of women. 'We occupy', she says, 'the last place in the human species, we are the weaker part of humanity; the basest functions are, and should be, our portion.' She proceeds in the same strain through seven learned chapters, citing authorities. From the age of seven the seclusion of Chinese women is absolute. Up to the seventh century women were veiled. Married women go out only in a sedan-chair with the blinds drawn—though women of the highest rank, when attended by a numerous train, have the blinds drawn up. At the present day [1927] if a woman or a girl should be seen in the open street, she is subjected to obscene remarks. In the house, it would be the grossest insult for a visitor to inquire after his host's wife. A woman may not eat with her husband or with her son, and she may not even remove the dishes from which they have eaten, for her touch would defile them. When a man entertains friends in his house and female company is desired, courtesans are called in.

It is not surprising that societies have frequently been formed of girls who are sworn to celibacy, and who vow to kill themselves rather than accept marriage except on purely matrilocal terms. 'It is not an uncommon thing', says Mr Dyer Ball, 'to read of girls in various parts of China committing suicide rather than be forced into marriage.'

Chinese marriage has nothing whatever to do with affections or sexual relations. It is regarded as a duty for the perpetuation of the family and the transmission of property. It is usually entered into as late as possible.

In Korea, marriage customs are identical with those of China. The marriage relationship is briefly summarized in the remark of a Korean gentleman: 'We marry our wives, but we love our concubines.'

As a consequence, the professional courtesan has attained the highest degree of development. There are various different classes of 'daughters of flowers' as they are called. 'One must not confound the accomplished and learned Chinese courtesans', says M. Bazin, 'with those who "publicly display their smiles", as the Chinese poets have it, and run after pleasure.' She must be proficient notably in music, dancing, history and philosophy, but must also be able to write the tao-te-king characters of the book which contains the doctrine of the philosopher Lao-tse. When thus qualified, she becomes a "free woman". She is emancipated from the duties of her sex, and may well account herself superior to the legal concubine and the legitimate wife. Many Chinamen of the better class marry such women, who become devoted wives.

Greek Marriage

The evolution of marriage in China is of interest because of its striking similarity to conditions in ancient Greece. The early Greeks were polygynous. In Homer and the tragic poets, the Trojans are represented as having legal wives, the Greeks as having 'concubines'. Polygamy was the rule in Troy. Priam had many honoured wives; the progeny of Antenor, wisest of the Trojans, was brought up by his chief wife, Theano, with her own children; Andromache even suckled the children of Hector's other wives.

The households of the Greek chieftains are described as abounding in 'concubines', but no great weight can be attached to the distinction: Thesaeus is expressly mentioned as having married his several wives 'in legal marriage'. Even in historical times Dionysius of Syracuse had two legal wives and Philip of Macedon had numerous legal wives, many of whom were princesses.

There was a very good reason why, in archaic Greece, secondary wives should have fallen to a subordinate status, and why one wife only should have come to be regarded as 'legitimate'. It was the princess whom a chieftain married who bestowed upon him rights to the throne and to her possessions; even Agamemnon only held his throne through his wife's rights. It would, obviously, have been impossible to have more than one such wife. The wife proper did not resent the presence of concubines provided that they were of lower rank.

In historical Greece, polygamy was never prohibited, and there is no reference in Greek literature to its being regarded as immoral; it was merely looked upon as a non-Hellenic custom. Indeed, during the Peloponnesian war, when Athens was depopulated by plague and casualties, bigamy was enjoined by law. The Greeks were not at all eager to marry. In his poem, 'Works and Days', Hesiod offers much Polonius-like advice to his younger brother, Perses, and counsels him to settle down to the quiet rustic life of a small farmer: he should procure a house and allotment, a ploughing-ox, and also 'a woman, purchased, not wedded'. Above all, he warns him against the enticements of a woman 'with waggling rump' that should 'seek after his home'. Marry some day he certainly should, but not until he has reached a mature age, at least thirty. It is also advisable that he should marry a virgin, 'so that you may teach her chaste morals'.

In Greece, as in China, marriage was a purely juridic procedure of which the object was that 'the heritage should not be left desolate and the name cut off'. In lieu of the right to the chieftainship and lands which heiresses bestowed in archaic times, the Athenians offered a dowry as an inducement. Medea, in Euripides, complains that 'We have to buy ourselves husbands at great cost.'

Between the dowry and the bride-price there is a developmental difference. When property accumulates in the hands of men, they will use it to 'purchase' wives; when it remains in the hands of women, they will 'purchase' husbands. The former, as we have seen, occurs in pastoral societies, such as the Arabs, the Jews, the Indian Aryans and the Tartars; the latter where arable land is the chief form of property, and the society is still matriarchal. This is precisely what we find in regard to the transmission of princely inheritance in archaic Greece. It was transmitted in the female line; and the sons of princes went forth from their home to marry princesses in order to obtain princely rights. Accordingly, the 'dowry' remained throughout the social history of Greece the pivot of legal marriage.

In historical times the position of the Greek wife was identical with that of the Chinese wife. She received no education beyond being taught by her mother to spin, to weave and to cook. She was 'not allowed to see, hear or ask anything more than was absolutely necessary'. She should not appear when her husband had invited guests, nor should she appear in public. Theban women were forbidden to walk in the street. No woman could inherit property; an 'heiress' did not herself inherit property, but had, on the contrary, to be inherited; the property lay fallow so long as the woman had no guardian or owner. When a man died his property might go to the most distant male relative but never to his wife, who had to return to her own people. In fact, a woman never really became part of her husband's family; Greek marriage remained juridically matrilocal; even after marriage, a woman remained under the guardianship of her father. On the other hand, a man might transfer his wife to a friend.

Greek marriage had no connection with love. Ottfried Müller knew of no instance of the marriage of a free-born Greek woman for love. Indeed, marriage and love were regarded as quite opposed. In a play of Terence (a translation from the Greek) the lovers lament that they are going to be married: 'Every lover feels it to be a sad grievance that a wife should be assigned to him.' Aristotle, endeavouring to put marriage in the most favourable light, speaks of friendship growing up between husband and wife; neither he nor any other author mentions love. The wife in Greece was a housekeeper and the bearer of lawful heirs; she was not the sexual companion of the man.

For his sexual life the Athenian Greek relied on 'hetairai'. The character and status of those women has been the subject of contradictory accounts, some representing them as being cultured Aspasias, others as common prostitutes. The truth is that there were all sorts. The word hetairai, which means 'companion', was, by a euphemism, applied to all.[1] Originally it was a perfectly honourable appellation. Doubtless its use dated from a time when the two orders of union, the patriarchal and propertied 'legal' marriage and the free matriarchal union by mutual consent, co-existed. This organization persisted in point of fact throughout the hey-day of Greek civilization. No social stigma attached in Greece to sexual freedom, because the standards of sexual morality had not yet developed. Matrons themselves had no scruple in associating with hetairai. They were honoured, as any other persons might have been, for distinction of talent, or of conduct, or of beauty. No obstacle lay in the way of their social advancement. Perikles sent away his 'legal' wife and installed Aspasia in his house; Myrrhina shared with Demetrios, king of Macedon, all but the crown; Thargelia married Antiochos, king of Thessaly; Pitho married Hieronymos and became queen of Syracuse. Thaïs was the companion of Alexander, and, after his death, married Ptolemy, the first Lagide king of Egypt.

The two opposite types into which woman, emancipated from economic production, had developed, are thus seen in Greece, clearly contrasted. Her two economic values, her two functions, as sexual companion and as mother in relation to the transmission of legal rights and property, remained separate. The attributes of each function were totally differentiated. The hetaira, elegantly adorned and highly educated, was a being of a different race from the cloistered housekeeper and breeder of heirs, to whom adornment was forbidden and whose mind was stunted. 'We have hetairai for our delight,' says Demosthenes, 'concubines for the daily needs of our bodies, wives in order that we may beget legitimate children and have faithful housekeepers.'

Roman Marriage

Roman marriage differed considerably from Greek marriage in origin and development. There are no traces of any phase of patriarchal polygamy or concubinage. The Italians were more exclusively agricultural than the archaic Greeks, and primitive Italian marriage relations point to loose matrilocal associations approaching clan promiscuity, in which the husband and father was of little account, such as appear to have survived until a later period among the Etruscans. No doubt where the

[1] Some of the hetairai, at least, were remarkably cultured. Leontion, the companion of Epicurus, could hold her own against Theophrastos in written philosophical disputation, and the purity of her Attic style is praised; Thaïs, Diotima, Thargelia were celebrated as philosophical disputants. The intellectual eminence of Aspasia is familiar. The famous 'funeral oration' of Perikles was said to have been composed by her; she opened a school for young women at which she herself taught. The relations of hetairai to their lovers could be sincere and unmercenary. The hetairai in the comedies of Plautus, though in Roman guise, are doubtless copied from Greek models; they spurn preferred wealth in their self-respect and fidelity to their lovers.

estates or titles of an heiress were at stake, the husband acquired them through a more formal matrilocal association, much as with archaic Greek princes. But, while Greek marriage appears to have evolved directly out of such a matrilocal association and remained to the last juridically matrilocal, in Roman usages everything points to a sudden revolution. The wife was transferred by a legal act from the jurisdiction of her father to that of her husband. This innovation was introduced in a society still essentially matriarchal; matriarchal influence, therefore, instead of gradually disappearing, as in Greece, was preserved by the very process which ostensibly abolished it, much as pagan temples have been preserved by being converted into Christian churches. Thus it is that in the emphatically patriarchal society of Rome women retained a much higher position than in the far less patriarchal society of Greece; and that the cleavage between the two contrasted functions of the woman, as wife and as 'hetaira', never became complete; thus arose the European conception in which marriage is identified with sexual mating, 'legality' with sentiment—in short, the fully-developed monogamic ideal.

Patriarchal Roman marriage was instituted by the patricians for their own purposes, much as the aristocratic class among the Yurok Indians remodelled the marriage institutions of their tribe to protect their interests. The patrician privilege consisted in having a legally recognized heir. The propertied patricians did not recognize the marriage arrangements of the propertyless plebians as being marriage at all, since the plebians 'did not know their own fathers'. Moreover, they refused to allow them to adopt legal marriage because they would thereby have become patricians, recognized owners of property with the right to transmit it, not to the clan, to which it went under the old law, but to their heir, to their 'family'.

Patrician marriage was deliberately evolved. Three forms of patriarchal marriage were current in Rome in earlier historical times: the most primitive was 'usus', by which, if a man and a woman had lived together connubially for a year, the marriage was recognized as 'legal'—that is, the children could inherit; this was orginally the only form of marriage. Second, 'coemptio', a 'legal' union, the contract of which had to be witnessed by five Roman citizens. The third form was in early times the specifically patrician marriage; the contract was witnessed by ten Roman citizens, and sealed by sacrificing a sheep. It was known as 'farreo', or 'confarreatio', because the ceremony included the sharing of a cake of 'far', the common Latin flour—our wedding-cake, in fact—consecrated by a flamen. The flamen, however, did not take any actual part in the ceremony.

It has been suggested that the difference between 'farreo' and other forms of Roman marriage lay in the former being a 'religious marriage'. We shall see later what a 'religious marriage', in the proper sense of the expression, a 'hieros gamos', really means; it means the marriage of a woman with a god, and in many stages of culture it was thought incumbent upon every woman to go through such a marriage.

But the Romans no more thought of marriage as a sacrament in the Christian sense than a modern bride thinks she is marrying a god. It is true that an attenuated relic of 'religious marriage' was celebrated at the same time as the Roman ceremonial, whichever of the three forms it took. The bride performed a most indelicate ceremony in connection with the statue of a god, the purpose of which was solely to make the marriage contract as binding as possible; it was a legal use of religion identical with the administration of an oath.

What was the contract which it was sought to make so binding? It was not the sanctification of the union, it was not an oath of fidelity. It was simply this—that the woman passed from the guardianship, or 'potestas', of her father to the guardianship of her husband. It was a deed of transfer. The Roman family rested on the notion of 'patria potestas', the absolute power of the father over the family. 'Family' comes from the Oscan 'famel', a servant, slave, a possession; and 'father', 'pater', means owner, possessor, master. The Roman 'pater familias' was thus literally an 'owner of slaves'. He had (theoretically) absolute power over his possessions, his chattels, his children. He could kill them or take them to the market and sell them. Accordingly, in Roman law the wife was technically her husband's 'daughter'. The contract was a consequence of the theory of 'patria potestas'. The transference of the woman from one 'familia' to another was called marriage with 'manus'. In later Roman legislation all three forms of marriage implied 'manus', but in their original forms neither 'usus' nor 'coemptio' did so.

'Coemptio' was a more archaic form of marriage; as the word indicates, it is a derivative of marriage by purchase. It was interpreted by Roman jurists as a 'mutual purchase'. Probably, as in all savage societies, the patrilocal family, the 'familia', first emerged when sufficient inducement was offered to the wife's parents to allow her to leave the home, i.e. by purchasing her. Subsequently, the patriarchal right was made more exclusive by the 'farreo', said to have been introduced by Numa, the Sabine king.

As soon as the legal distinctions between patrician and plebeian rights of property ceased to exist, all these forms of marriage fell into disuse. By the time of Cicero, and even as early as the second Punic war, 'farreo' and 'coemptio' were wholly obsolete. 'Farreo' became a mere opportunity for occasional ceremonial display. Throughout the later Republic and the Empire marriages were contracted, as of old, by 'usus' only. In Roman law the proof of marriage consisted in the deeds of dotal transfer; there was no ceremony.

In legal theory the woman who passed from the 'patria potestas' of her father into that of her husband was in a position of absolute subjection. 'If', said Cato, 'thou findest thy wife in adultery, thou art free to kill her without trial, and canst not be punished. If, on the other hand, thou committest adultery, she durst not, and she has no right to, so much as lay a finger on thee.' In the early days a law had to be passed making it illegal for a man to sell his wife. A woman was, in law, a perpetual minor. She could not own or transmit property or enter into any business transactions; even her children were not legally hers, she had no rights over them.

In practice, however, the position of women in Rome was from first to last more independent and dignified than among any other patriarchal people. Precisely because the law was so artificial and an innovation, the practice was very different from the theory. The matrimonial social constitution of Rome presented, in fact, a striking paradox. Compared with the Greek wife, the Roman woman was a free woman and a queen. Roman girls received the same education as boys, and in 'mixed schools'. There was no Oriental seclusion, although it was not thought becoming that she should resort too frequently to places of amusement. When her husband entertained, she acted as hostess. The Romans themselves noted the contrast. 'What Roman', exclaims Cornelius Nepos, 'would be ashamed to bring his wife in to dinner, and who amongst us does not regard the mother as occupying the first place in the house and in our regard? They do things very differently in Greece, for a woman is never present at a dinner, unless it be among her own relations, and she never sits down, except in the internal apartments.'

The explanation is that the matriarchal organization could not be swept away by a legal measure. The principle of 'manus' became absolute in the later times, simply because women would have none of it; and the law had to give way much as in our own day women object to promise obedience to their husbands.

Roman marriage was the last step but one in the evolution of our own institutions and conceptions. Roman marriage was converted by Christianity from a civil contract into a religious, a sentimental act, a sacrament. In Christian marriage the extraneous aspects of the relation between the sexes, economic and sexual, have for the first time become combined in one institution. Although Roman monogamic marriage is socially and juridically identical with the institution of marriage as it exists amongst us today, yet the sentiments with which it is viewed are the products of a momentous change, effected solely by the Christian religion. Later we shall sketch the development of these sentiments.

CHAPTER 16

Tabu

Primitive Ethics

MAN is a moral animal—the only moral animal. Among other animals there is no voluntary suppression of impulse and no self-reproach in yielding to it. In order that such a conflict of motives should exist, those motives must be consciously perceived. The natural instinct must be checked by the force of a conscious veto.

Curiously enough, these distinctively human prohibitions, instead of exhibiting a gradual development with the evolution of human society, are found in the greatest abundance in the most primitive phases of society. Every act of primitive man is burdened with prohibitions which would be accounted intolerable by civilized man. But remarkably enough, few of these countless prohibitions refer to what *we* should regard as moral values.

For example, we consider that nothing is more to be condemned than murder, especially the murder of a relative. Most primitive peoples, however, view murder with strange indifference. Speaking of savages generally, Steinmetz remarks that 'the only reproach which the slayer of a blood-relation incurs is that he has hurt himself by weakening his own family'. The injury inflicted by a murderer is held to be fully compensated if the loss which he has caused to a given family is made good by presenting the relatives of the murdered person with a substitute. Thus among the North American Indians the feelings of a mother, whose son had been brutally murdered, were assuaged by her adopting the murderer in his place. Similarly, a widow whose husband had been murdered might be consoled by marrying the murderer. Again, among the Habe hill-men of the French Sudan a murderer supplies the family of the victim with a woman from his own family; when she bears a son, the boy is given the name of the murdered man and all is well. (The principle that the shedding of blood constitutes a loss which must be compensated is carried to its logical conclusion by the Goajiros, among whom a man who hurts himself is required to compensate his relatives on the grounds that he has shed the blood of the family.)

Frequently little or no penalty attaches to murder. Among most primitive people the murderer of a fellow clansman is regarded as unclean, and is avoided or even expelled from the community; however, as Sir James Frazer has shown, this has nothing to do with moral condemnation, but arises from dread of the murdered man's angry ghost. In the island of Futuna 'in heathen days men-slayers were usually respected as well as feared'. Among the Fuegians a parricide is simply sent to Coventry. Among the Nandi, a man who has murdered a member of the clan is regarded as unclean—until he has murdered two members of another clan, when his moral purity is completely restored. In the Jewish code there is no definite penalty attached to homicide; homicide may be outlawed, but punishment, or rather vengeance, is entirely the concern of the victim's nearest relative.

There are two main reasons for this neglect of social principles. In the first place, social regulations are scarcely needed in primitive society. Human society arose as the outcome of the natural instinct of solidarity between members of the same brood. The individuality of each was merged in the solidary consciousness of the collective group-instinct. The individual did not defend himself as an individual; the group defended itself as a group. Being spontaneous, this sentiment did not need to be formulated as a law. All primitive societies are highly moral compared with ours in respect of just those rules which in our societies are enforced by laws and principles. Of the Marquesans, Mr Melville writes: 'During the time I lived among the Typees, no one was ever put upon his trial for any offence against the public. Everything went on in the valley with a harmony and smoothness unparalleled, I will venture to assert, in the most select, refined and pious associations of mortals in Christendom. There was not a padlock in the valley nor anything that answered the purpose of one. . . . I will frankly declare that after passing a few weeks in this valley of the Marquesas, I formed a higher estimate of human nature than I had before entertained.' Father Veniaminoff gives a similar account of the social morality of the Aleuts. He fancied himself among a community of primitive Christians. Their sexual morality, like that of the Marquesans, was of course scandalous. In fifty years the courts of law established by the Russian government could find no employment. In Hawaii, during the time that Lisiansky spent there, only one man was tried and executed, and that for eating a coconut on a tabu day. Of the Iroquois, a Dutch colonist, who gives a shocking account of their sexual morals, says of their civic morality, 'although they are so cruel, and have no laws and punishments, yet there are not half so many villainies and murders committed amongst them as among Christians'. Such illustrations might be multiplied. Only when the primitive constitution of society becomes sapped by the establishment of private property, and the instincts on which it is based are consequently supplanted by individualism, do social laws and formulations of moral principles become necessary.

Another reason why such laws are absent in primitive society is that such offences are regarded as a private concern. It is for the offended party or his relatives to take revenge, and the man who slays his father's murderer is congratulated by all. Primitive legislation deals only with group interests. It is in much more advanced stages that the right of personal revenge is delegated to the state, the king or the god.

Nature of Tabu and Sacredness

The moral character of ethical principles and their character as categorical imperatives have been imparted to them by their assimilation to primitive tabus.

When a savage is questioned as to the origin of a tabu, he is usually at a loss to explain it, and says that the thing has always been considered tabu. Tabus are, in fact, identical with what are among us spoken of as superstitions, such as the notions associated with spilling salt, stepping under a ladder and so forth; superstitions are, in fact, survivals of tabus. They still flourish in all secluded mountain, rural and fishing populations. The inhabitants of the Scottish Highlands, the hills of Switzerland, the Balkans, etc., are almost as rich in superstitions as are primitive tribes in tabus.

Tabus are observed from dread of the consequences of neglecting them. In more advanced stages of development the notion of tabu has given rise to two seemingly opposed sentiments: a thing may be tabu because it is too holy to be touched, or because it is unclean—a breach of the tabu would pollute the offender. Thus the tabu may be an expression of extreme reverence or extreme horror. But primitive tabu contains nothing of this distinction. Our word 'sacred', the Latin 'sacer', as also the Greek word '$ἄγριος$', originally corresponded exactly to the Polynesian word 'tabu'. Sacer meant equally holy and unclean, venerable and accursed. The bad meaning of polluting is by far the more prominent in the early use of the word. 'Sacer esto', let him be sacred, was the formula by which a man was outlawed, ex-communicated, e.g. for treason or homicide. Anyone had the right to slay a 'sacred' man—but I suspect that this was not the most primitive form of the rule, and that, originally, as among certain primitive tribes, no one would have dared kill him. Yahweh dealt with the first murderer, Cain, in this way, saying: 'Whosoever slayeth Cain, vengeance shall be taken on him sevenfold.'

In popular sentiment this idea persists. A lock of hair, a bone, or any part of a condemned criminal is a talisman possessing miraculous virtues. In Cornwall it was believed quite lately that a criminal who was going to be hanged could cure diseases by touching people. In Franconia a salve prepared from the fat of an executed criminal possessed such valuable properties that chemists had to put up a preparation to meet the demand. At public executions it was difficult to restrain the spectators from dipping their handkerchiefs in the blood of the victims; late in the last century in Berlin, men drank the blood of an executed malefactor, believing it a remedy for all ills. The reason undoubtedly is that a condemned criminal is a 'sacred' person. The execution of a criminal was, in ancient times, a solemn sacrifice to the gods. The Celts habitually sacrificed criminals, 'and if a man was cannibal enough to eat a bit of the victim's flesh, he by that act rose in the goodwill of heaven. He was supposed to have absorbed into his system much of the substance of what was consecrated to God.'

So completely did the good meaning of 'sacer' displace the bad that the Romans were puzzled by the hieratic use of the word. But primitive gods are not good; they are dreadful and dreaded, and worship of them consists chiefly in placating them. Thus they are sacred in the same sense as all tabu beings and things are sacred: the less one has to do with them the better. When Protestant missionaries tried to explain to the Dakotan Indians that the Bible and the Church were holy, they used the Dakotan word for tabu, 'wakan'. The Dakotas' natural reply was that, in the circumstances, they would rather have nothing to do with them. The ancient Jews themselves took much the same view of their holy books. A man had to purify himself and wash his hands after handling the Bible.

In short, no ethical value originally attaches to what is tabu. The differentiation which later takes place is not an unfolding of latent ideas but an addition. The notion of tabu, though it has come to be connected with gods, is not necessarily dependent upon the notion of God. Primitive gods are tabu and render anything pertaining to them tabu because they are dreadful, but a thing may be dreadful without being divine. The notion that a thing is tabu because it is the property of a god, or of the ghost of a deceased person, implies a clear idea of personal property, and it is therefore highly improbable that such a notion was the origin of tabu prohibitions. Tabus could not originally have been imposed by the authority of rulers and gods, for they are much older than such conceptions; in no primitive society is there a ruler invested with any degree of power, and in many primitive societies the authority of gods is hazy.

Different tabus have of course had various origins, but what calls for explanation is the whole notion of the origin of a prohibition from human instincts. Such prohibitions must have been imposed in the first instance in a very categoric form. The frequently-made assumption that they were imposed by the arbitary authority of chiefs is an untenable view, for there is nothing more foreign to the character of primitive man than respect for arbitrary authority, and truly primitive societies are nothing if not equalitarian. It is only at the human level, through the medium of language, that a prohibition can acquire the status of a principle. If I am right in considering that the authority of the female was paramount in the earliest human groups, a prohibition of this kind must have been the very first to come into operation.[1]

The Tabu on Menstrual Women

The most fundamental of all primitive tabus are those referring to women and sexual intercourse. Tabus on the approach of men to women during and after parturition, and during menstruation, are the most strictly observed of all primitive tabus. All the world over, and not only among savages, the tabus attaching to menstrual women are similar. And those which refer to women in childbed are practically identical with them. The latter have little reference to the child, but refer to the lochial discharge. Premature births and all issues of blood are treated in the same manner as full-time births as regards tabu.

It would weary the reader to recapitulate the vast array of evidence from societies in every part of the world which can be brought together to demonstrate the similarity of such tabus. The practices of the Eskimo may be taken as representative of all others. Four weeks before her confinement a woman retires to a separate hut, which no man is allowed to approach. She remains there for a month after she has been delivered, when the father is allowed to see his child for the first time. Should a woman be unexpectedly seized with labour pains, all the men stop work and build a snow-hut as quickly as possible. During her period of seclusion the woman cannot eat or drink in the open air; even the remains of her meals must be disposed of inside her hut. She has her own cups and dishes, which men must be careful not to use, and is subject to dietary regulations. If the few kinds of food which are permitted are unobtainable, she may have to go without eating. Among the Tlinkit, females are driven out of the house at the time of childbirth, and only some time after birth is a mother allowed to enter a rude shelter erected for the purpose.

In the same way, a menstruating woman is regarded as a being with whom all contact, however innocent, would entail dreadful consequences. In most societies a special hut is provided to which women must resort during their menstrual period. Special ceremonies regulate the first menstruation. Thus among the Déné a girl, at her first menstruation,

[1] There is one relation in which normal impulses are interdicted—the behaviour included under the term 'coyness'. However, the attribution of feminine diplomacy to lower animals is little short of absurd. The coyness of the female animal towards the courting male is the result simply of physiological conditions. The female is not prepared for impregnation except at stated periods of ovulation and rut. At other times the advances of the male are not desired. Among animals the male can only be repulsed or avoided by resistance or escape.

remains isolated for two lunar months. She must not touch even her own food with her hands, and is provided with a stick to scratch her head. In some cases the woman's head is wrapped up so that she can see nobody, and she is submitted to purges and fastings. In other cases a girl, at her first menstruation, is placed in a hammock near the smoke-vent of her hut so as to be thoroughly fumigated, and only at night may she rise to cook a little food for herself. The vessels which she has used are immediately broken and buried. Among the Guaranis and other tribes the girls are sewn up in their hammocks in the same way as corpses, only the smallest opening being left to allow them to breathe, and are suspended over the fire for several days. Not infrequently the unfortunate girls die under the process of disinfection. In some cases the women are beaten and all their hair is plucked out. Some observers have thought that this retiring of the women was due to an instinctive sentiment of modesty, but since, in some cases, the women are allowed to deliver their children upon their knees in the public street in the presence of everyone, this is hardly likely. In Russia, a woman after delivery is regarded as being in a state of impurity, and may not hold any communication with others until she has been purified by a priest. In the province of Smolensk she is confined in a barn or hut some distance from the house.

The Hebrews attached the greatest importance to the primitive tabu. 'If a woman have an issue and her issue in her flesh be blood, she shall be put apart seven days; and whosoever toucheth her shall be unclean until even.' Anyone who touched her bed or anything that she sat upon was required to 'wash his clothes, and bathe himself in water, and be unclean until the even'. On the eighth day after, she had to take two young pigeons to the tabernacle, one as a sin-offering and the other as a burnt-offering, and the priest had to make atonement for her.

In ancient Persia the very glance from the eye of a menstruous woman was so polluting that she must not look upon a fire or upon water, nor converse with any man. She was confined during menstruation to an isolated portion of the house, no fire was to be kindled and everyone was to remain at least fifteen paces from any fire or water. When the period was over, the clothes which she had been wearing must be destroyed, and she must be purified by being washed with bull's urine. The tabus attaching to child-birth were exactly similar. The rule mentioned by Herodotus that a man might not see his own child until it was five years old probably refers to a similar lengthy exclusion of a man from the house of his wife. The modern Parsees still observe most of the rules of their ancestors, and it is not long since there were in Parsee communities public menstrual houses to which women resorted at their periods.

The Hindus take as serious a view of the impurity of a menstrual woman as did the Persians, while the aboriginal races of India segregate menstruating women even more rigorously than the Arya Hindus. Thus among the Kamar, when a woman is menstruating, no man of the same household can enter a temple without previously having had a bath.

Much the same is true among wild races of the Malay Peninsula. In Africa, if an Akikuyu woman menstruates in a hut, it is at once destroyed as unfit for human habitation. Among the Menangkabau of Sumatra if a menstruating woman were to go near a rice-field the crop would fail. Among the Visayans of the Philippine Islands when a woman is overtaken by child-birth everything is removed from the house, else the weapons would no longer be efficient, the nets would catch no more fish, and fighting-cocks, their most valued possession, would no longer be able to fight. Among the Caroline Islanders, women are wrapped up in mats from head to foot during the whole duration of pregnancy, and seclusion continues for five or six months after delivery. They may not paint their faces nor anoint their hair, and are unfit to undertake any cooking. Were a man to touch so much as a drop of water from the pools in which they wash, it would be impossible for him to catch any fish. In Nauru, one of the Gilbert Islands, not only may no food be eaten that has been touched by a tabu woman, but it is considered that the nuts on any trees within a hundred feet of such a woman's dwelling are unfit for human consumption.

These ideas of the defiling and dangerous character of the menstruating or child-bearing woman appear in many forms. Thus in New Britain when a birth has taken place all the men must be disinfected. They subject themselves to fumigation and rinse out their mouths with ginger. Women, it would seem, can infect even themselves, for among the Pennefather and other Australian tribes a menstruating girl is buried up to her waist in the sand, a fence of brushwood is built round her, and she is provided with a stick to scratch herself. as she must not touch her own body with her hands. The Wakelbura tribe of south-eastern Australia believes that if a male should see a menstruating woman he would die. Sir George Grey observes that the more southerly tribes of Western Australia conform to the injunctions in Leviticus (xv. 19).

As these instances show, the tabus are not derived from any abstract principle, but from dread of the dire effects of contact with women in these conditions. The Déné believe that contact with menstrual blood will turn a man into a woman. The Tlinkit are persuaded that a single look from a menstruating woman would completely destroy the luck of a hunter, fisherman or gambler, and that it might even, like the Medusa's head, turn objects into stone; a view analogous to that of the Bushman, who believes that her glance can cause men to become fixed in whatever position they may happen to be, and to turn into trees. Similarly the Orang Belenda believe that contact with a menstruous woman will

deprive a man of his manhood; while some South African tribes believe
that if a man should touch a woman during the period his bones become
soft and he cannot in future take place in any manly exercise. Not only
men but their weapons and implements lose their virtues. An Indian
woman who inadvertently stepped over a man's gun while she was
menstruating had to flee for her life, and was only accepted back when it
was discovered, to the astonishment of all, that the gun could still
shoot.

Similar views obtained in primitive Greece; and sceptical as were the
Greeks of a later age, they still regarded the impurity of a lochial woman
and of a corpse as equal. Of the ideas of the Romans, Pliny has given us
a full account. 'Hardly can there be found', he says, in Philemon Holland's rendering, 'a thing more monstrous than is that fluxe and course
of theirs. For if during the time of their sicknesse, they happen to
approach or goe over a vessell of wine, bee it never so new, it will
presently soure; if they touch any standing corn in the field, it will
wither and come to no good. Also, let them in this estate handle any
grasses, they will die upon it; the hearbes and young buds in a garden,
if they doe but passe by, will catch a blast, and burne away to nothing.
Sit they upon or under trees whiles they are in this case, the fruit which
hangeth upon them will fall. Doe they but see themselves in a looking
glasse, the cleare brightnesse thereof turneth into dimnesse, upon their
very sight. Look they upon a sword, knife, or any edged toole, be it never
so bright, it waxeth duskish, so doth also the lively hue of yvorie. The
very bees in the hive die. Yron and steele presently take rust, yea, and
brasse likewise, with a filthie, strong, and poysoned stynke, if they lay
but hand thereupon. If dogs chance to tast women fleures, they runne
mad therewith: and if they bite anything afterwards, they leave behind
them such a venome, that the wounds are incurable.'

These beliefs are substantially current among most rural populations
of Europe. In the wine districts of Bordeaux and the Rhine, menstruating women are strictly forbidden to approach the vats lest the wine
should turn to vinegar, and I have seen the same rule observed in the
Chianti district. In northern France they are excluded from sugar-
refineries when sugar is cooking, and in Holstein no menstruating woman
attempts to make butter. No Frenchwoman would attempt to make a
mayonnaise sauce while in that state. In England bacon cannot be cured
by a menstruating woman. 'It is a very prevalent belief among females,
both rich and poor,' writes a medical man in 1878, 'that in curing hams,
women should not rub the legs of pork with the brine-pickle at the time
they are menstruating.' They even render bright mirrors dim.

The importance of a woman being properly 'churched' after her confinement is therefore manifest. Pennant records the practice in his *Tour*

in Scotland. One would scarcely expect to find in Europe the rule, so common among savages, that a puerperal woman must not touch her own head. Yet in Bavaria it is thought that if a woman in child-bed were to comb her hair it would turn grey.

Sexual Separation during Pregnancy and Suckling

Such tabus are not the only restrictions on sexual relations in primitive societies, for it is the general rule that all cohabitation must cease when a woman becomes pregnant, or at any rate during the later months of pregnancy, and this commonly continues during the whole time she is nursing a child, a period much longer among uncultured peoples than with Europeans. Children practically wean themselves after anything from four to seven years of suckling, though from two to three years is the most general duration.[1]

Restrictions of this kind are reported from all over the world. Thus among the Warega a wife will not allow her husband to approach her until the child can walk, though he may visit her if he sits quietly at the opposite side of the hut. Such restrictions are general among most African tribes. Among the Suk of Kenya Colony no marital relations take place until the child has cut two teeth.

It is reasonable to believe that such regulations were at one time even more general in primitive society than at the present day. The restrictions on the instincts of the male in the more primitive societies are evidently much more extensive than any observed by civilized Europeans. Even the tabus upon menstruating puerperal women are not regarded by Europeans with the same dread as attaches to them in uncultured societies. Although the Synod of Wurzburg reiterated in 1298 the prohibition that 'no one shall approach a woman who is near her confinement or in her menstrual fluxes', even theological opinion held such an act to be but a venial sin. Ecclesiastical exhortations during the Middle Ages show that abstinence at such times was by no means scrupulously observed. Among uncultured peoples today these customs are tending to become relaxed, and it is usually enough that a menstruating woman should give proper warning of her condition by such acts as painting her face yellow (as among the Mandingo), or wearing a brightly coloured scarf.

Origin of Periodical Sexual Prohibitions

This tendency of such tabus to fall into disuse appears inconsistent with the supposition that they first arose as a spontaneous inhibition of masculine sexual instincts by feelings of repulsion, since it implies a

[1] A bibliography of 31 titles is appended.

greater degree of squeamishness in savage than in civilized man. It has commonly been assumed that such tabus originated in some feeling of disgust. But primitive man is not disgusted by those things that Europeans regard as repulsive. In the matter of food, there is nothing too disgusting for savages to eat. Some use their cesspools as reserve stores. Primitive men exhibit no greater delicacy in regard to the satisfaction of their sexual instincts. Those savages who are most scrupulous in observing the menstrual tabus will also perform acts the very recital of which to us is nauseating. Australian aborigines who die of fright because a menstruating woman has touched their blanket habitually perform homosexual atrocities unknown to European vice.

When a savage manifests disgust, it is almost invariably at the breach of some tabu, such as eating some food, maybe quite appetising, which is prohibited by his customs. The tabu is the cause, not the effect, of his disgust.

The awful character of the menstruating woman has been set down to a supposed primitive 'horror of blood', notably by M. Durkheim, but there is no evidence of any such horror—blood is everywhere regarded as a delicacy.[1] Even peoples whose habitual diet is entirely vegetarian will miss no opportunity of indulging in a daught of warm blood. The Masai have a special method of shooting a blocked arrow into the jugular vein of an ox, so that they may drink the warm blood before they slaughter it. Sir Harry Johnston describes how, after filling their wooden vessels, they step apart from the crowd 'to drink the coagulating gore with utter satisfaction and a gourmet's joy'. The Australian natives, besides drinking one another's blood on every occasion, use it to bedaub themselves and to attach feathers and ornaments to their bodies. There is no instance known of blood in general being regarded with horror by any uncultured peoples.

It is frequently supposed that the menstruating woman is possessed of some dangerous spirit, and the fumigations and flagellations which we have noted are intended to expel this spirit.

That so many speculations should have been put forward is surprising, for these tabus are the only prohibitions which are not peculiar to mankind, but are common to all mammals. Among all animals the female admits the male only at such times as she is prepared for the exercise of his function; at others, her attitude to him is one of positive hostility. The description given by Pallas of the way the female camel rounds on the bull the moment she is impregnated, driving him away with snarling, is representative of the behaviour usual with mammalian

---

[1] There are special circumstances in which the blood of a particular person may, like any other substance, be the object of a tabu. It is not blood in general which is fraught with dread, but the blood of women.

females. Had the primitive human female admitted the male during menstruation, pregnancy and lactation, her behaviour would have constituted a biological abnormality.

As in all physiological functions, there is an adjustment between the inherited disposition of the male and that of the female. It has been too readily assumed by naturalists that all animals must have a special breeding season, but our information, fragmentary as it is, suggests that among most, if not all, carnivores the time of year at which the young are born varies, in the same species, within wide limits. In contrast to herbivores, there is no indication that at any time the sexual instincts of the male are completely quiescent. Where there is no definite yearly periodicity in the female, there can be no exact adjustment of the male instincts to that function. 'Among numerous higher species the males appear to be at all times disposed for sexual union, even though the females are not in rut.' In the primates the mutually-adjusted periodicity of sexual instincts has entirely disappeared. To regard these facts as imposing restrictions on sexual intercourse in primitive humanity is not a matter of hypothesis, it is inevitable. Those restrictions are imposed by biological necessities, and are in every respect the same as those obtaining among animals. As with every such traditional prescription, all manner of superstitious interpretations have become attached to the categorical prohibition. They are manifestly accretions on the original veto laid by women on the sexual instincts of the male. The formulated prohibition, like the biological restriction, must have been imposed by women upon men and not the reverse; nor are they restrictions imposed on themselves by the men.

It is often suggested that the restrictions upon sexual intercourse during pregnancy and lactation are dictated by concern for the welfare of the child. Sometimes the seclusion to which the woman is subjected is similarly explained, but these are manifestly attempts to account for the custom, and are of little importance as indicating its origin.

The terms in which many accounts are couched suggest that these observances are imposed upon the women by the tyranny and superstition of the men: the women are 'compelled' or 'driven out'. But there is little evidence that any compulsion is needed to force the women to segregate themselves at such times, and probably the wording merely expresses the assumption of the reporters that any ethical regulations must have been imposed by the men, except where such observances are set down to feelings of 'natural modesty' on the part of the women. Even where the men are most tyrannical, the women never carry out their arduous duties under compulsion, and similar tabus in their most rigorous form are observed in societies in which the women, far from being tyrannized, exercise an almost despotic power over the men. The women, in most accounts, segregate themselves of their own accord, without consulting the men.

It has sometimes been remarked that such customs are abused by the women as a pretext to get rid of their husbands. Speaking of the Beaver Indians, Mr Keith says, that a woman 'pretends to be ten days in this state and suffers not her husband except upon particularly good terms. Her paramours, however, are permitted to approach her sooner'.

Papuan tradition represents the men as quite enraged at their being repulsed by their menstruating wives. The women of the Tully River district in Queensland assert that they are anxious to menstruate regularly, for if they did not 'the men would be enabled to continually pay them sexual attentions, a course to which the women assured me they objected'. In the mythical Alcheringa days, when the tribesmen were celebrating the ceremonies of the bandicoot, their totem, a woman, through excessive repetition of the rites of fertility, began to bleed profusely. She said: 'I will no longer be a woman, but a bandicoot; and you cannot touch me.' And ever since then the women have had monthly periods, during which they are tabu.

The awful but undefined dangers which attend the breach of a tabu are identical with the dangers which result from a curse, than which nothing is more dreadful; and no curse is more dreaded than a woman's. Among the Damaras, if a woman curses her husband, he cannot, whatever may happen, cohabit with her again.

That curse has recoiled upon woman herself. The notions of her impurity which pervades the ideas not only of the savage but also of more advanced peoples, have their root in the primitive menstrual tabu. Woman is 'the cause of all evil'. All tabus fraught with vague dangers tend to become extended in their application. Thus the prohibited degrees of marriage have sometimes come to include the very persons who were originally prescribed as the natural sexual mates, such as cousins and wife's sisters. The tabu of modesty which originally applied only to the sexual organs has often come to include the whole body. In the same way the precautions taken with regard to the menstrual or parturient woman have frequently been extended to women at all times. In China the same care is used in handing anything to a woman as in Alaska in passing provisions to her when she is in quarantine. In Tahiti women were excluded from religious festivals, neither could they at any time eat in the company of a man, nor even sleep in the same house.

But it does not follow that because women were hedged about with such vexatious tabus that their position was one of degradation. Throughout Polynesia the position of women was the reverse of degraded; yet this is the country where the observance of tabus reached its most extravagant development. In Hawaii, since a woman could not eat in the company of her husband, and neither could he eat anything which she had cooked, there was no alternative for him but to do his own cooking, and he cooked for her as well. Thus the tabu results in the women being waited on by the men. Similarly, since it would be danger-ous for the woman to handle fruits and vegetables intended for food, the men felt impelled to take over the agricultural work, while the women had nothing better to do than to amuse themselves making gorgeous dresses. When, therefore, Mr Ellis and other travellers deduce the shamefully-degraded position of women from the fact that they may not eat with the men, they mistake the nature of tabu. An instance of the misapprehension to which observers who do not understand the nature of tabu is liable is afforded by a recent traveller in North Africa, who considered that no further proof of the degraded position of women among the polygamous Arabs is needed than that Arabs place women and pigs in the same class. But, of course, both women and pigs are tabu, which in primitive conceptions may mean either sacred or im-pure. In this sense, the ancient Jews placed both pigs and Yahweh 'in the same class'.

The tabus attaching to women were not originally identified with such ideas as impurity, though they have commonly become associated with them. Originally, they sometimes had the opposite meaning. In many primitive rites the sexual act is a sanctifying and purifying ritual. In this, as in all other instances, tabu means primarily 'dangerous'. According to Vedic conceptions, 'the blood of the woman is a form of Agni, and therefore no one should despise it', and the 'Institutes of Vishnu' lay down that to kill a menstruating woman is as great a crime as to murder a Brahman. In some instances menstrual and lochial blood has a sancti-fying and purifying influence. Among the Ainu menstrual blood is a talisman. When a man sees some on the floor of a hut, he rubs it over his breast believing he will thereby secure success. Although the Déné regard menstruating women with extravagant dread, if a child is not thriving his mother will fasten round his neck a piece of cloth soiled with menstrual blood. In such instances, the menstrual or lochial blood is, in all probability, regarded as scaring away the evil spirits and influences, rather than as communicating a positive blessing. By this principle the dreaded properties of the blood are often turned to a use-ful purpose. Among the North American Indians, when the corn began to ripen, a woman would leave her isolation-hut in the middle of the night and walk naked through the fields, thus destroying the caterpillars. The ancient Greeks had hit upon the same ingenious procedure, and Colu-mella recommends the same method, which was evidently used in Italy, where it is practised at the present day in the district of Belluno. In the sixteenth century the same device was used near Nuremburg to get rid of garden pests, and in Holland today it is usual for a girl at her menstrual period to go round the cabbage patch in order to dispose of the caterpillars. Northern Rhodesian natives, similarly, believe that this will drive away the tsetse fly.

It will be seen from these instances how easily the dreaded character of a sacred or tabu person may logically pass into the seemingly opposite notion of a wholly beneficent influence. In primitive conceptions things regarded as sacred are as often as not looked upon with horror and repulsion, and those which have come to be conceived as impure are as commonly regarded as divine.

The Menstrual Tabu as the Type of Prohibitions

The menstrual and puerperal tabus appear to be regarded by some as the very type of tabu. The Polynesian word 'tabu', or 'tapu', appears to be closely allied to 'tupua', signifying menstruation. The word 'atua', which is usually translated 'God' and applies to all supernatural phenomena, refers to menstruation in particular. The Dakotan word corresponding to tabu is 'wakan', which is defined as 'spiritual, consecrated; wonderful, incomprehensible; said also of women at the menstrual period'.

The assumption that the former meaning is derived from the latter is as probable as the reverse. Among the Arabs the expressions 'pure' and 'impure' originally referred exclusively to the condition of menstruating women. Among the Jews the medium of purification was known as 'the water of separation', a term used in reference to the menstrual seclusion of women. The tabu state is generally signified by marking a person or object with blood; red paint serves equally well, for the blood is not the cause of the tabu but the mark of it. The condition of a manslayer whose deed has rendered him 'sacred' is indicated by painting him red.

The practice of painting corpses and bones red, which is well-nigh universal in primitive society and has been so from earliest ages in Europe, may be regarded as connected with blood as one of the forms of the vital principle, or soul, but even this aspect is not unconnected with menstruation, for it is from the menstrual blood retained in the womb that human beings are believed by primitives to be formed. The Maori expressly state that blood is the substance of the human spirit. The condition of women in the tabu state is commonly indicated by their painting themselves red. Thus, several Australian tribes mark menstruating women with red paint, as do Kaffir women; while in India such a woman wears round her neck a handkerchief stained with menstrual blood.

The sign of blood is commonly used to make women tabu in marriage ceremonies. The theory of this is expressed by Brahmanic writers: 'The wife is pure to her husband and impure to every stranger.' Marking the bride is an essential of the marriage ceremony throughout modern India. The parting of her hair is commonly stained with vermilion. Among the Santals, if a young man succeeds in laying a dab of red paint on a girl's forehead, she is his wife. It is considered a serious offence to do so, but the marriage cannot be dissolved. The same practice obtains in China. The bride is smeared with blood among such peoples as the Chuckchi, the Koryak, the natives of Borneo, of the Congo, of the Solomon Islands and in Australia.

Men, on certain occasions, especially when embarking on some perilous undertaking, paint themselves red, a practice common in Africa. Pliny tells us that the Ethiopian nobles of his day did so, and Herodotus noted the custom among the Libyans and Arabs. It was common among the primitive Egyptians: cups of red ochre have been found in First Dynasty tombs. Among the early Romans, war-chiefs were painted red, and Camillus proceeded to the Capitol bedaubed with vermilion. The idea, no doubt, was to scare away evil and envious spirits; just as mothers among the Tlinkit Indians safeguard their children by painting their noses red. The door-posts of houses are marked with blood or red paint, especially in times of danger and epidemics. This is done in West Africa, among the Dayaks in Bengal, as it was in ancient Peru and among the Jews.

All sacred or tabu objects are commonly marked with blood or red paint. The sacred stones of various native tribes in India, in Burma, in Madagascar, are marked with blood; among the Estonians sacred trees. The Greeks painted the statues of Dionysos red, and the Romans applied red paint to the face of Jupiter before their festivals. The Banyoro, on the day of the new moon, waylay a man and cut his throat in order to smear with his blood the royal fetishes. The Australian Blacks, who pour blood over their sacred stones, and paint themselves red after their rites, volunteer the information that this red paint is really the menstrual blood of women. In a Hottentot song addressed to the spirit of rain she is addressed: 'Thou who hast painted thy body red like Goro; Thou who dost not drop the menses.' The deity referred to, there can be little doubt, is a form of the moon, and the red ochre with which they paint themselves is called 'gorod' after her.

Some other Tabus

All these facts point to the conclusion that the veto imposed by women upon masculine impulses during their periodical unfitness for sexual functions was the earliest formulated prohibition imposed upon instinct, and therefore the prototype of all such prohibitions. Actually all subsequent tabus tended to become assimilated to the pattern of the prototype. In some societies the arbitrary imposition of tabus became a form of tyranny in the hands of priests and chieftains, who imposed tabus to suit their purpose. The most highly-developed codes of moral prohibitions preserve the original type of such interdicts, for none are regarded as more important than those which refer to the restraint of the sexual instincts, and morality in the highest cultures is understood to be synonymous with sexual morality.

In primitive society sexual restrictions are connected with nearly every activity of primitive man—the hunter, the fisherman, the warrior, the agriculturist, the magician, regard abstention from intercourse and contact with women as essential to the success of their undertakings. Other tabus, less obviously connected with the primitive prototype, are nevertheless found on inquiry to be related to it. As illustration, we will consider two tabus still observed among us.

Few people would consider, I suppose, that any connection exists between the superstition that it is unlucky to step under a ladder and the tabu on menstruating women. The unsuperstitious regard it as a precaution against the possible presence of a paint-pot on the ladder, but the superstition is much older than the use of paint-pots or ladders. It is a survival of what appears to be a very widespread scruple against passing under anything at all, a superstition directly connected with the menstrual tabu. As Sir James Frazer says: 'The Australian Blacks have a dread of passing under a leaning tree, or even under the rails of a fence. The reason they give is that a woman may have been upon the tree or fence, and some blood from her may have fallen on it and may fall on them'; and he cites instances from the Solomon Islands, the Karens of Burma, the Siamese and others. A Maori will never lean his back against the wall of a native house, for Maori women have a habit of thrusting their soiled diapers through the houseboards. It is a common notion that a woman should not step over one's legs when one is sitting down, for if she does one will lose one's power of running. The Oraons of Chota-Nagpur are horrified if they see a woman climbing on to the roof of a hut.

The facts mentioned by Sir James Frazer are not adduced by him in elucidation of our superstition of walking under a ladder, but of the rule observed in Rome that the Flamen Dialis may not walk under a trellised vine, for the juice of the grape which was commonly regarded as the equivalent of blood might have fallen upon him. But there can, I think, be little doubt that our own superstition is connected with the same order of observances.

The Sabbath

A much more important example of a tabu still observed among our-selves, and one which is derived from the Hebrews, is the keeping holy, or tabu, of the Sabbath Day.

We have seen that it is an almost universal rule that a menstruating woman must not do any kind of work, a tabu which frequently extends to her husband. Among the Habe, a man whose wife is menstruating would not dare to go on a journey or hunt or sow; indeed, it would be pointless to do so, for the undertaking could not prosper. Among the Monumbo people of New Guinea the husband is subject to so many tabus during his wife's pregnancy that he is virtually a pariah. He must attend to all his wants himself and cannot borrow so much as a light for his pipe. An Eskimo husband is incapacitated for work for some weeks after his wife's confinement, and he should not enter into any commercial transaction. Sometimes the tabu on the woman affects the entire house-hold. Thus among the Naga tribes of Manipur even the fact that a bitch has laid a litter of puppies or that the cat has had kittens is sufficient to place the whole house under an interdict. These restrictions some-times extend to the whole community, all of whom remain at home the next day and do no work in the fields, for no good would come of it, owing to the influence of the lochial discharge.

General abstinence from all kinds of work is generally observed by almost every primitive community on inauspicious occasions, such as an eclipse, an epidemic or the death of an important personage. As Profes-sor Webster remarks, those general tabus 'are to be assimilated to those which rested upon individuals alone'.

Among many peoples there also exist regular tabu days recurring at fixed intervals. To the superstitious mind all days are distinguished into 'lucky' and 'unlucky'. An old resident of Ashanti calculated that there were only about one hundred and fifty or so days in the year in which any important business could safely be done. The ancient Greeks were almost as bad: Hesiod's poem on 'Works' lays down on what days it is safe to undertake farm work. The chief purpose of the ancient Egyptian and Babylonian calendars appears to have been to mark the lucky and unlucky days. The day of the new moon is generally looked on as especially inauspicious, and to this the day of the full moon is generally added. 'According to the rules of Astrology', observes Aubrey, 'it is not good to undertake any business of importance in the new moon, and not better just at the full moon.' To be on the safe side two more days should be added, the four days corresponding to the four phases of the moon. With many African peoples the day of the new moon is a day of general abstention from work. Thus among the Baziba it is 'a recognized day of rest'. Among the Baganda firewood must not be cut or food cooked on that day.

The two great monthly festivals of ancient Hindu religion, on which the sacrifice of the soma, or moon-plant, is celebrated, took place on the days of the new moon and full moon. On these days a Brahman might not trim his hair or beard or nails; he must not set out on a journey, nor sell any goods. The 'Vishnu Purana' lays down that anyone tending to secular affairs on these days will go to hell. These observances later became extended to the first days of the intermediate phases of the moon, making the tabu a weekly one. In contrast with observance of the sabbath in English and Scottish households, where it was a strict rule that secular literature should be put aside, the Brahmanical religious considered that the four monthly tabu days were the very days on which the sacred books should on no account be read, these days being in-auspicious. The Scriptures should not be exposed to the risk of pollu-tion. The four monthly sabbaths of Vedic and Brahmanical religion were adopted by Buddhism, and corresponding beliefs are found in Burma and Siam.

As we might expect, the observance of tabu days attained its most perfect form in Polynesia. The Hawaiian sabbath had quite an old-fashioned English aspect. 'Men were required to abstain from their common pursuits, and to attend to prayer morning and evening. A general gloom and silence pervaded the whole district or island. Not a fire or light was to be seen or canoe launched; none bathed; the mouths of dogs were tied up, and fowls were put under calabashes or their heads enveloped in cloth; for no noise of man or animal must be heard. No persons, except those who officiated at the temples, were allowed to leave the shelter of their roofs.' In Samoa the sabbath was similarly observed, but there was only one regular sabbath in the month, at the new moon. The Polynesians therefore took to the fourth commandment like fish to water when they were instructed in the truths of the Christian religion, but the Hawaiians complained that the missionaries were far too lax in enforcing the sabbath, and Sunday Leagues were formed amongst the most influential natives, who sent deputations to the clergy-men imploring them to be stricter. The missionaries, though shocked by the lasciviousness of the natives and by their cannibalism, felt that people so thoroughly imbued with the principles of Sabbath observance could not be wholly bad.

It has been argued that the fact that periodic observance is timed to take place at a given phase of the moon does not prove that it is associated with the moon, except in so far as the moon is a time-piece. But this view is untenable; no distinction is drawn in the primitive mind be-tween the relation of adventitious synchronism and that of cause and effect. You will not easily convince a savage that when two events habitually take place at the same time, the one is not the cause of the other. The moon, as will later be shown, is not regarded by primitives as merely the measure of time but as the *cause* of time.[1] It is abundantly clear from these examples that days of general tabu observance, whether arising from special eventualities or whether periodic, do not originate from belief in the benefit of rest from labour, but from the persuasion that no business undertaken on those days could possibly prosper. It is the moon which is regarded as exercising the dangerous, malign influence, which is at its peak at certain phases of the lunar cycle.

Though the conceptions attaching to the influence of the moon among primitives are complex, there can be little doubt that the original ground for the maleficent character universally ascribed to it is its association with the sexual functions of women. (As Darwin has suggested, the actual connection between the physiological and the lunar cycle is probably due to the fact that animal life developed originally in the sea, and hence was subject to the periodic environmental changes produced by the tide.) The correspondence between the cycle of sexual functions in women and the cycle of lunar changes has been noticed by even the rudest peoples. In every part of the world women reckon the periodicity of those functions by the moon. Menstruation—that is, 'moon-change'—is commonly spoken of by all peoples as 'the moon'. The peasants in Germany simply refer to women's periods as 'the moon'; and in France it is called 'le moment de la lune'. I have heard of a judge in a native court in India being puzzled by the statement that a female witness was unable to attend the court because of the moon. The idea that menstruation is *caused* by the new moon is universal. Papuans say that a girl's first menstruation is due to the moon having had connection with her during her sleep, and the Maoris speak of menstruation as 'moon sickness'. A Maori stated: 'The moon is the permanent husband, or true husband, of all women, because women menstruate when the moon appears. According to the knowledge of our ancestors and elders, the marriage of man and wife is a matter of no moment; the moon is the real husband.' We shall see that such conceptions are by no means peculiar to the Maori, but pervade primitive thought.

By all peoples in lower phases of culture the moon is regarded primarily as a male. This is doubtless due to the notion that menstruation is due to sexual intercourse between the moon-god and women. In later stages the sex of the lunar power is changed, and the moon becomes the chief goddess, the Great Mother. Every great female deity, every Great Mother—Isis, Ishtar, Demeter, Artemis, Aphrodite—has the attributes of the moon and is a moon-goddess.

[1] See pp. 295–6.

The cult of moon deities, whether male or female, is everywhere the cult of women. Thus among the Ibo of Nigeria the periodical sabbath on the day of the new moon is called 'The Women's Day'. In the Congo women observe special rites at the new moon. The Wemba women whiten their faces at this time, and the Aleutians dance in the moonlight. These feminine lunar observances are conspicuous in the more advanced religions of western Asia, Egypt and Europe. Relics of them were, until lately, found in our midst. Thus in Yorkshire and the northern counties, according to Aubrey, 'women doe worship the new moon on their bare knees, kneeling upon an earth-fast stone'. In Ireland, on first seeing the new moon, they fall on their knees, saying: 'O Moon! leave us as well as you found us.'

The Jewish Sabbath, as we know it, resembles that of the Babylonians, which was explained as a day of abstinence or propitiation. It is known as an 'evil day'. In the calendar of Elul II in the British Museum, the seventh days are marked out as days on which no work should be undertaken. All other days are set down as favourable. Probably in earlier times only two days a month, the new moon and the full moon, were observed as sabbaths. We know from cuneiform tablets of the fourth dynasty of Ur, dating from the third millennium B.C., that at that period these two days were the chief days for sacrificial observances in Sumer. With the early Semites, as with the ancient Hindus, the Dayaks and the Polynesians, the monthly or fortnightly observance of tabu days became extended to four monthly days.

It is not unlikely that on her 'evil day' the goddess was thought to be actually menstruating. The notion that goddesses are subject to the infirmities of mortal women is common in India today. Thus in Bengal it is believed that at the first burst of rain: 'Mother Earth prepared herself for being fertilized by menstruating. During that time there is an entire cessation from all ploughing, sowing and other farm work.' The menstruation of the Earth-goddess is thus observed by the Bengali as a sabbath. In Travancore there is an important ceremony known as 'trippukharattu', or purification ceremony, in connection with the menstruation of the goddess, which is believed to take place about eight or ten times a year, in which a cloth wrapped around the metal image of the goddess is found to be discoloured with red spots and is subsequently in demand as a holy relic. Another menstruating goddess is found at Chunganur. It is firmly believed even in some parts of Europe that the moon regularly menstruates. The peasants of Bavaria, for instance, when the moon is on the wane, say that she is 'sickening', using the same expression as they employ for a menstruating woman. Since the days of Homer, it has commonly been believed that drops of blood frequently fall from heaven, and this is commonly known among rural populations as 'moon-blood'. In Switzerland 'the peasants do not look upon the "moon-blood" as a figurative expression but as an actual physical fact, in the same way as they look upon the moon itself as a real living being. Hence the moon is spoken of as "sickening".' In Ashanti the day of the new moon is called 'the Day of Blood', and the Yoruba believe that if they were to work in the fields that day the corn would turn blood-red.

The Jewish Sabbath dates from before any contact of the Hebrews with the Babylonians. The Jews reckoned it among their oldest institutions. The explanation of it as a day of rest connected with the account of the creation was a late theory, according to most competent critics. The division of the divine labours into six days, followed by a day of rest, proceeds from the institution of the seventh-day sabbath, rather than the latter from the former. The Jewish Sabbath is primarily a new moon and full moon observance, extended later to each phase of the moon. In a subsequent chapter we shall see how intimately ancient Hebrew religion was associated, in its origins, with lunar cults, though traces of this association were carefully obliterated by editors of the sacred scriptures. Yet the connection of the Sabbath with the phases of the moon is constantly referred to in the Old Testament. Thus when the Shulamite woman wished to consult the prophet Elisha, her husband asked: 'Wherefore wilt thou go to him today? It is not new moon or Sabbath.' And Amos represents the Jewish profiteers as impatient at the restrictions placed on the business by the tabu days, and as exclaiming: 'When will the new moon be gone, that we may sell grain? and the Sabbath that we set forth wheat . . . ?' Isaiah, at a time when it was still uncertain what practices belonged to the religion of Yahweh and which were foreign corruptions, denounced in one breath both 'new moon and Sabbath'. The two are thus constantly associated. (See also Hosea ii. 11; Psalms lxxxi. 3.) This association has never been effaced. It is considered among Jews to be 'a very pious act to bless the moon at the close of the Sabbath'.

As with most primitive peoples, the observance of the Hebrew Sabbath is regarded as the particular concern of the women. Hosea, inveighing against the corrupt practices of Jewish women and speaking in the name of Yahweh, exclaims: 'I will cause all her mirth to cease, her feast days, her new moons, and her Sabbaths, and all her solemn feasts.' The character of the sabbath as a women's festival is several times referred to in Talmudic literature, and the sabbath itself is spoken of as 'the Queen', or 'the bride'. In the Kikur Sh'lh, it is set out that 'God has given the first day of the month as a festival more for women than for men'. To this day, among Jews, it is customary among women to abstain from work on the day of the new moon.

The Hebrew Sabbath did not differ in origin and character from the tabu days of the most primitive peoples. The Jewish institution, already popular in Roman society, where Oriental religious observances had become fashionable, was adopted by the Christian Church. But Greeks and Romans had been immemorially familiar with the observance of restrictions on certain tabu days, and especially the day of the new moon. When the trial of the bow of Odysseus was proposed to the suitors, they objected that it was the day of the new moon and therefore unbeseeming. The Greek lunar tabu days never extended to the four monthly phase days, but were mostly confined to the first. Although there was no general stoppage of business, most public activities except those of a religious character were intermitted, and it was considered unsuitable for farm-work. A less solemn monthly festival was held on the day of the full moon. The Romans observed the Kalends, or days of the new moon, in a similar manner, and in old-fashioned households it was customary for the paterfamilias to remain at home and offer prayers to the family gods. The introduction of the Hebrew usage did not, therefore, bring any startling change to the Romans.

Thus, although our inquiry into the connection between the Sabbath and the tabu on menstruating women may have taken us somewhat far afield, the connection is a close one; and the observance which in our own country bears most closely the character of a primitive tabu is immediately dependent upon what we have reason to regard as the first tabu, or moral prohibition, imposed upon the instincts of primitive mankind.

CHAPTER 17

The Totem

The Sacredness of Food

MOST tabus refer to food and to the manner of eating it. For instance, the strict rules regulating food preparation among Jews and Muhammedans are familiar. In the religion of civilized peoples the act of eating plays a prominent part; the chief Christian sacrament is a mystic meal, and meals are often begun and sometimes ended with a blessing. In Scotland neglect of these observances is considered dangerous, not only to the consumers but to anyone near. A man who suddenly felt faint in a Scottish village was told that he had passed a house where people had taken food without asking for a blessing; to counteract this, he must eat a piece of bread over which the name of the Trinity had been pronounced.

When a person is tabu, the tabu applies to everything which has been part of his body, such as his hair or spittle; also to *food* intended for him or left over by him. The strictest menstrual prohibitions refer to menstruating women handling or cooking food, which would thereby become poisonous. Since these rites conflict with the utilitarian value of food, they imply some underlying interest; the only such interest relevant to primitive psychology is the reproductive instinct. Just as food is the prototype of utilitarian and economic values, the reproductive impulse is the prototype of emotional non-utilitarian ones, and since the former are typically male interests and the latter female and non-individualistic, it is here that we must look for the explanation.[1]

Ignorance concerning the Physiology of Generation

The knowledge that the father contributes equally with the mother to the life of the offspring dates only from the seventeenth century, and Spallanzani's discovery in 1785 of the male germ-cells was greeted by fierce controversy. In Aristotle's view the child was formed entirely from menstrual blood; and, as Pliny said, 'The man's seed serveth in steed of runnet to gather it round into a curd which afterwards in process of time

---

[1] The comparative sterility of women in creative art appears to contradict this distinction, but it must be remembered that art represents an opposition between intellectual control and emotional motive. A woman, as Madame de Staël remarked, either has children or writes books.

quickeneth and groweth to the forme of a bodie.' This is a general view in the lower phases of culture.

Paternity was not regarded by the most primitive peoples as a physiological relation, but as a social and juridic claim. A father is 'responsible' for a woman's child in an economic and juridic sense; the Roman jurists declared that the relation between mother and child is a natural fact, whereas paternity belongs entirely to the sphere of civil law, and this is so not only because the actual paternity may be uncertain but because the physiological conception of paternity is absent. The peasant populations of Europe hold similar views. Physical or mental resemblance between father and child is accounted for in other ways, e.g. it is thought that the child is a reincarnation of some ancestor or that the mother's maternal impressions impart to the child the likeness to the father. When in the early days of Australia women gave birth to light-coloured children in tribes near to white settlements, this was accounted for by the changed diet, such as white bread obtained from the white man. Spencer and Gillen state that the Australian tribes they studied recognized no relation between sexual congress and reproduction, a report which, when first published, gave rise to much incredulity, but which has since been independently confirmed and is reported of almost all the wilder Australian tribes.

This is not surprising, for primitive ideas of reproduction are often extremely vague. Some tribes have been astonished to learn that menstruation could occur without sexual intercourse; others believe that pregnancy can only result from repeated connections. The Sinaugolo Papuans believe that conception takes place in the breast and have no knowledge of the female internal organs. Among savages pregnancy is usually diagnosed by comparatively late symptoms, often not before quickening takes place. The Baku Bahau of Central Borneo think that pregnancy lasts from four to five months; that is, they are ignorant of the date of conception. The Tuareg of the Ahir think it possible that pregnancy may last several years. Or again, in Europe, the southern Slavs believe that it may sometimes last only six weeks. The Baku Bahau expect to breed from castrated dogs. This is not too surprising, since Sicilian peasants do not suspect that the seminal fluid is secreted by the testicles, but believe it comes from the spinal marrow. In the Trobriand Islands girls who wish to avoid pregnancy are more carcful not to bathe at high tide than to abstain from sexual intercourse. The North American Indians, like the Australians, believe that women may be impregnated by the souls of the unborn.

In general, among uncultured peoples sexual congress is not looked upon as the cause of conception, even where it is regarded as related to it; a woman conceives because a spirit entered into her, and man can at most act as a medium for the transmission of that spirit. Thus the Nuer of the Upper Nile attribute pregnancy to their god, Kosz, 'with the assistance of the husband'. Analogously, the Roman Catholic Church teaches that the soul of the human being 'is created and united by God to the infant body yet unborn, which union is called passive conception, in which parents have no part'. The problem how children could be born from an adulterous union, since God is the real father of every child and yet condemns adultery, puzzled some of the early Fathers.

Immaculate Conception through Food, etc.

Belief in immaculate conception is universal. It is the usual manner in which gods and heroes are conceived even in non-savage societies, and legends of impregnation by non-human agencies are innumerable. The Subanu of Mindanao, for example, believe that conception may take place through the operation of the moon, the sun, by bathing in the sea or in other waters, by eating various foods. Pliny, Vergil, St Augustine believed that mares could be fertilized by the wind. In northern India, as in America, young women are careful not to linger in the sunlight while they are menstruating for fear of pregnancy. A Mongol princess conceived through the operation of a hailstorm, and another by an aurora borealis. We read similarly of the old inhabitants of Scotland that a young girl, walking on an old battlefield, became pregnant when a whirlwind threw some of the ashes in her private member.

In many stories of virgin births conception is caused by something eaten; the virgin goddesses and princesses of China usually conceived by eating a lotus flower; the Shang Dynasty was descended from a princess who became pregnant through eating swallows' eggs. The Divine Mother in Japanese tradition conceived through eating cherries. Hera conceived Hephaistos by eating a flower, and in the Finnish poem of Kalevala, Mariatta conceives through eating a bilberry. In several stories virgins conceive through eating bone-dust. Jacob, no doubt, was conceived by Rebecca from her eating the fruit of the mandrake, (*Genesis* xxx. 14–24). Throughout northern India coconuts are eaten to cause conception, and Hindu women, like those in Tuscany and Portugal, obtain consecrated food from priests with this object. The dew from a mistletoe bough or an infusion of the plant caused animals and women to become pregnant, according to the ancient Celts, from which derives our own attitude to the mistletoe. The Ainu of Japan and the natives of Mabuiag in the Torres Straits take a similar view.

Relation between Food and Offspring

Now, it is universally held that eating the flesh of an animal imparts its qualities to the consumer. Courage is acquired from lions and the like, swiftness from antelopes, ability to jump from kangaroos. Conversely, eating deer makes men timid and eating the flesh of cattle makes them slow. Eskimo children are given seals' eyes to eat so that their eyes may become bright and clear. The Greeks believed that to eat a nightingale would cause insomnia.

Sometimes it is thought that the person will become completely assimilated with the eaten. Thus in the Celebes a woman, after eating snake's flesh, turned into a snake.

The effect of food on pregnant women is particularly pronounced. Indian women of the Gran Chaco do not eat mutton after marriage lest their children be flat-nosed. The Ibibio of Southern Nigeria, like the natives of Anatolia, think that if a mother eats snails her baby will slaver. Similar prohibitions are found in every part of the world from South Italy to Penrhyn Island. So numerous are these dangers that primitive women are very restricted in diet. Gipsy women eat cocks or hens, according to the desired sex of the child, and in southern Hungary they eat slices of quince sprinkled with the blood of a strong man.

Most people believe that the fancies which pregnant women conceive for certain food must be satisfied at all costs, and men have been known to go fifty miles to obtain strange articles of diet, such as tadpoles or red ants' nests. The Hausa regard birth-marks as the result of leaving such fancies unsatisfied, and in Italy they are actually called 'voglie'—that is, 'fancies'.

The Importance of Food Animals

For primitive man the capture of animal prey must for long have been far from an everyday occurrence. Even today it is often a red-letter day. Savages are ravenously fond of meat, even where they are, from local circumstances, mainly agriculturists. Among the Baganda, women are said to have at times such craving for meat that they bite the ears of their own children. The Wachanga of the Kilimanjaro region will travel miles to have a drink of blood. The art of twenty thousand years ago deals almost exclusively with animals. *The animal on which his food supply depended was the centre of man's primitive interest; it was his totem.* (The notion of an intimate relationship between a man and a natural object, generally an animal, prevalent in many parts of the uncivilized world, is known among the Ojibwa as a totem, from which the word has been adopted.) Such traditions are also found in comparatively advanced cultures, but, since many changes in the food supply must have occurred in the course of migrations and altered conditions, we cannot expect to find totemism still in its original primitive form. To interpret totemic ideas is difficult. Though many totems consist of natural or even artificial objects, there is little doubt that they were originally animals or plants. The primitive identifies himself with his totem, believes himself to be of the same species and endeavours to assimilate himself to it. We find tribes whose totem is the wind or the sun, or even a tool or weapon, but it is clear that a man could not identify himself permanently with such things, and they must represent badges which are mere survivals of the original totemic idea.

The totem is frequently tabu. It may not be eaten, killed or injured; sometimes it may not even be looked at, but this is comparatively rare, and in Australia, as in North America, men kill the totem animals when opportunity serves, though the Western Australian tribes will not kill their totem 'if they find it asleep' and are said to 'kill it reluctantly'. In Chota Nagpur 'the general attitude of the Oraon to his clan-totem is that of a man to his equal, to his friend and ally'. Often the totem is killed only after the formality of offering it an apology.

It is therefore difficult to believe that the totem originally had a sacred character. As a rule, in primitive societies the awe with which a sacred being is regarded tends to grow rather than to diminish. It is therefore inconceivable that in societies which still possess a complete totemic organization, this character could have wholly disappeared. It is often suggested that where the totem is unceremoniously treated totemic ideas are in a state of decadence, yet the whole organization and many of the quasi-religious ideas of Australian tribes centre round the totem, although it is clearly not tabu.

It is in Africa, where totemic ideas are overlaid with others and where totemic organization is mostly in decay, that we commonly find rigorous prohibitions and sentiments of awe attached to it. Further, the tabu on eating the totem still has solemn force where every other trace of totemism has disappeared; while in the more primitive totemic societies the breach of food tabus is rarely regarded with horror. We must therefore regard the tabu character as secondary.

Among many totemic peoples a breach of the tabu is not only permissible but a duty, on certain occasions. Thus, the Edo of Nigeria must eat a mouthful of the totem animal on the occasion of the annual festival and at the funeral of any member of the totem clan. The food is merely tasted; sometimes it is only taken in the mouth and spat out. Similarly the King of the Banyoro, a pastoral people, lives normally on milk, but must eat a small portion of veal at the chief ceremonies, not as a meal but as a sacrifice to bring blessing on all the food of the land. Among the Central Australian tribes many of the rites refer distinctly to such a meal, although eating a totem does not today form part of the ceremony. They rub the sacred 'churingas' on their stomachs, for they are supposed to represent, or to contain, the essence of the totem. As they do so, each man says 'You have eaten much food'. These ceremonies take place at spots stated to be those where the ancestors of the clan cooked and ate the totem for food. Although the known instances of the ritual eating of a totem which is otherwise tabu are not numerous they are very widespread, and they so closely resemble the ritual meals of higher cultures that we must suspect that the latter had their roots in totemic ideas.

Long before the ritual usages of totemic peoples were known, Robertson Smith concluded that the ceremonial eating of the totem was a feature of totemic belief and he illustrated his view by the description left by St Nilus of the sacrificial eating of a consecrated camel among certain tribes of Arabs on the Sinai peninsula. One of the rules was that the whole beast must be consumed, hair, intestines and all, before the sun rose. This rule is almost universal in primitive ritual meals, and was observed by the ancient Hebrews when they partook of the Paschal Lamb. We have noted it among the Australian Narrinyeri; it was observed by the Algonkins. The Gallas of Abyssinia still practice rites similar to those described by St Nilus; they say that the eating of sacrificial flesh causes a spirit to enter their bodies. The Catholic missionary who reports this laughed when they told him; but when he saw how scandalized they were at his impiety he became more serious and he comments that 'the conviction that a supernatural being enters into them at the moment when they masticate the victim is akin to the fundamental idea of the Holy Communion'. When these same Gallas, in the seventeenth century, saw the Jesuits celebrating Mass, they were convinced that the consecrated hosts were portions of the spinal marrow of a hare.

The much-discussed question whether the eating of the totem is an essential part of totemic practices appears to be misleading. If the totem was originally the staple food of the tribe, to eat it would not be a ceremony but a necessity. Meal and ritual were originally one and the same. The Algonkins eat the meal with just the same ritual observances as the sacrificial communions just described, but this was simply the meal that they ate when they returned from the chase with a supply of food. As a Jesuit missionary comments: 'The heathen do not partake of any meal without making a sacrifice.'

Such meals are presided over by one of the older men of the tribe, who open the proceedings with a solemn invocation; and various rules were observed, such as that no cutting instrument might be used. The flesh of the animal had to be torn after the manner of primitive man. In the laws of Leviticus, none of the bones of the animal might be broken; the whole carcass must be consumed. These, in short, were ordinary meals; the special significance which attached to them was as much a question of the physiology of digestion as of the doctrine of transsubstantiation. In short, mystic and ritual meals were probably not originally religious ceremonies with symbolic meanings but ordinary meals. A ritual is a dramatic performance done in memory of the significance which the act once possessed. Primitive man never merely shoots an arrow, chops a piece of wood, lights a fire, but always accompanies such functional acts by words and actions of a magical character; thus there is primitively no distinction between ritual and utilitarian actions, between 'religious' and 'secular' acts. This is universally true; among the ancient Greeks cooks and butchers were regarded as quasi-priestly for, as Athenæus knew, the butcher was originally a sacrificer and the slaughtering of meat a priestly function.

In short, the totem was probably originally the food of the clan. In several instances, we find it continuing to be the staple or favourite food even when raised to a divine position. Thus the Huancas of Peru, who worshipped the dog as a deity, 'considered the flesh of a dog to be the the most savoury meat'. 'It may be supposed', remarks Garcilasso de la Vega, 'that they worshipped the dog because they were fond of its flesh.' Other Peruvians adored maize because it was their bread, and others the fish, which they caught in great abundance; while the Gollas worshipped the white sheep, for they were owners of innumerable flocks. The God of the Seri Indians is the great pelican, one of their chief sources of animal food, although there is the germ of a tabu in the prohibition on killing it during the breeding season. The Oraon clan regards its totemic fish as tabu today, but tradition states that they once lived by eating it. Some of the tribes of Western Australia were even more explicit.

Conception through eating the Totem

The transformation of the totem to a sacred food is logical enough for, if the totem was originally the food of the tribe, it is truly from its substance that every member of the tribe was formed. This is in harmony with the universal supposition that the child's characteristics are determined by the food which its mother eats. The Wogait of South Australia say that when a man kills game he must give some to his wife, believing that the food will cause her to conceive. Among the tribes of the Cairn district of North Queensland acceptance of food from a man by a woman is regarded, not merely as a marriage ceremony but as the actual cause of conception. Elsewhere the man who kills an animal tells its spirit, as it is dying, to go to a particular woman, from whom it is thereupon reborn as a child. A native told Mr A. R. Brown that his father had speared a small animal, now probably extinct, called a 'bandary', and he showed him a mark in his side where, as he said, he had been speared by his father before being eaten by his mother. The Eskimo and the Malays hold similar beliefs.

The presentation of food by a man to a woman is a customary wedding rite in every part of the world. It is essential among North American tribes, among the natives of Uganda and elsewhere. Even in the Upanishads we read: 'Animals spring from seed, and the seed is the food.'

With the passage of time, the food supply changes; some animals become extinct and their appearance is forgotten. When this has occurred, a woman's impregnation cannot be set down to an article of food which she has not in fact eaten, and the theory must be adapted.

Where the totem animal has vanished entirely, dreams and impressions must take its place as means of conception; thus among Western and Central Australian tribes conception is ascribed to the women having been near certain spots where the spirits of unborn members of a particular totem group are lying in wait, but we are told that these are the places where the ancestors of the tribe actually ate the totem. Since women who had actually eaten it would hardly ascribe the impregnation to the action of the totem spirit at a distance, we must assume that this represents an alternative way, developed when the practice of actually eating the totem had ceased.[1]

The Totem as Tribal Ancestor

The totem is also an expression of primitive social organization; the unity of the clan is conceived as founded on the bond which the totem constitutes. Most totemic people, asked to explain the significance of their totem, say that it is their father or the ancestor of the clan. With the most primitive totemic peoples the relation is not so much one of historical ancestry as of identity of substance. An Australian native said, pointing to a photograph which had been taken of him, 'that one is the same as me; so is a kangaroo'. The Bororo of Brazil, whose totem is a red macaw, believe that they are similar to it in appearance. They say: 'We are macaws.' Many North American tribes think likewise.

As man comes to think himself *descended* from a totem ancestor rather than identical with it, the totem tends to assume indefinitely human attributes. Thus among the Alcheringa of Australia a man of the Kangaroo totem may sometimes be spoken of as a man-kangaroo or as a kangaroo-man, while the ancestor, by natural evolution, tends to assume the character of a deity and a creator. Thus the Aborigines of Victoria say that the world was created by the eagle-totem and the crow-totem. The jay 'was at that time a man'. The iguana 'plays the part of an august divine being' at the initiation ceremonies of the Murring tribe.

[1] Sir James Frazer has set forth a theory of the origin of totemism which closely resembles the one here put forward, but he thinks that it may cause conception in a number of other ways besides being eaten, though, as he comments in many of these instances, 'this is totemism in decay'.

As in Australia, so in North America. Among the Wyandots the sun was created by the Little Turtle. The Manitu of the Delawares is an elk; elsewhere he is a beaver, a bison, a squirrel, an otter or a dog. This fusion between animals, men and gods is equally conspicuous among the peoples of northern Asia. Thus among almost all Siberian tribes the most important divinity is the Great Raven, and the Koryak declare that in his time 'there was no sharp distinction between men, animals and other objects'.

Obviously such a totem tends to become sacred, and, from being the ordinary article of food, it tends to become prohibited. By a common subterfuge only the least attractive parts of the animal are eaten, a device which was also found among the ancient Egyptians. Possibly some of the split totems may have resulted from the segmentation of clans originally having the same animal for their totem. However, no doubt many totems never had any connection with the food supply of the clan, for in every society new clans must of necessity come into being and they must then assume a totem which is little more than an arbitrary badge.

To recapitulate, then, we find a number of linked ideas:

(1) Many tabus refer to eating.
(2) A woman may be impregnated by eating.
(3) The child may be influenced sympathetically to resemble the animal eaten.
(4) Men identify themselves with their totem animal.
(5) The totem may become the tribal ancestor.
(6) The totem animal is eaten, sometimes with apologies or precautions.

This constellation of ideas seems explicable on the assumption that totems were originally the animals on which the clan depended for support but which have since become rare, and rituals in which the flesh of an ancestor-deity is eaten arise in this way.

Diffusion and Fundamental Conceptions of Totemism

Totemism, together with the exogamic totem-clan organization, exists in North America, among some tribes of Central and South America, in many parts of Africa, among several of the Dravidian races of India, and is prominent in almost all of the Australian tribes. Conclusive indications of its former existence are found in Melanesia, New Guinea, Micronesia and Indonesia. This makes it clear that we have to do with one of the most fundamental conceptions of the human mind, and its existence in Australia shows that such ideas date back to the Pleistocene age. The inference appears irresistible that this conception was once universal.[1] However, we are not justified in inferring, every time we find a people worshipping a god in the form of an animal, that such people once had an animal for their totem. It is improbable that bulls and serpents, which are constantly associated with gods, were formerly totems, for the symbolizm which has given rise to this association is clearly traceable, although the process of making such an association may derive from the traditional habit of associating animals with gods.

Furthermore, we come across conceptions identical with those of totemic peoples among peoples who show no other traces of totemism; for instance, the Eskimo, than whom no race shows a more complete absence of totemic organization.[2] Nevertheless, the conceptions we have been discussing are as prominent in the ideas of the Eskimo as in the most typical totemic society. The animals on which they live are not regarded as prey, but with sentiments of sympathy and almost veneration; the hunting of animals is subject to complex magical rites, designed to conciliate them, so that they will allow themselves to be killed, and this is done with apologies. After a seal, a walrus or a whale has been killed mourning rites are observed with the same ritual as for humans. The cooking and consumption of the meat are subject to ritual rules, and certain parts of the animal must not be injured. The soul of the slaughtered creature is supposed to reside in its bladder, and these bladders are the most sacred of Eskimo objects. The food animals are regarded as limbs of the Great Goddess Sedna, the moon, who is also represented as a walrus; at the same time, they are also represented as human beings. The Eskimo also have a notion of conception similar to that of the Australians; a pregnant woman may only eat game which her husband has killed, and should she eat any other animal food the husband would not regard her child as his. The extent to which the Eskimo retain or exhibit such ideas shows how fundamental they must be, and perhaps the failure of their conceptions to develop into a social tribal organization has helped to preserve their original character.

The primitive man's belief that his strength is derived from his food,

[1] The substitution of theriomorphic divinities as pseudo-totems for the original clan-totems is found in the lowest stages of culture. Thus the numerous snake, bird and stone 'totems' of the Melanesian races of eastern New Guinea are certainly not totems in the original sense. As Sir James Frazer says of the divine beings, represented as a shark and a crocodile in Yam, 'they seem to be on the point of sloughing off their animal skins and developing into purely anthropomorphic heroes or gods'.
Captain Cook directly observed the adoption of an animal as a totem on the Island of Atiu where he presented some people with a dog. The clan then adopted this animal as their totem and declared it was their ancestor.

[2] Though some authorities declare that the Inuit have no totemic system, Mr Nelson thought he noticed among the Eskimo of the Bering Straits some suggestions of totemic institutions.

and that his body and spirit were first formed from the food which his mother ate, leads to magical practices designed to promote the food supply, and when tribal groups are distinguished from each other, the organization is founded upon such conceptions, but this organization does not depend upon magical or religious ideas but is a corollary of totemic ideas which are probably more general in distribution.

Priestly Clans

We can see how, when totemism decays by the multiplication of totem clans, a priesthood could emerge. The members of a totem can exert a special influence over their totem animal: members of the Omaha bird clan can stop birds eating the corn, and members of the Kansas wind clan can create a breeze. When Mr Hollis's porters in East Africa were attacked by a swarm of ferocious bees and were compelled to abandon their loads, a Nandi, belonging to the bee totem, volunteered to quieten the bees, for, he said, 'they belonged to him'. Naked, he approached the spot and whistled the bees back into their hive without being stung. If a man is injured by his totem animal, this is often taken as a clear indication that he is not a true member of the totem. Analogously, ceremonies calculated to promote fertility are more effectual when carried out by members of a totem clan in regard to their own totem. Thus, such members enjoy a privilege belonging to them by birth. The specialization of a particular totem-group in such matters benefits the whole clan, and the clan whose totem has a general economic importance becomes a sort of magical society or, as it might be called, a college of priests. Such a group, therefore, comes to have magical powers with regard to the ancestors of the clan, and so over all forces vital to the clan's welfare, such as the control of rain or luck in war. Such clans will become sacred clans, royal clans; their power will be exercised on behalf of the people to propitiate the god who represents the transformed ancestral totem, and who can only be approached through their mediation. Their sacred character depends upon the fleshly kinship between the priest and the god, and this identity with the god is reproduced by rites of eating in many religions.

Primitive Tribal Solidarity

Such ideas have been the corner-stone of human social solidarity. The members of the clan regard themselves as members of one body through the community of food. In Arabic and in Hebrew the same word signifies 'flesh', 'kindred' or 'clan'. A similar nomenclature is used in Tibet and elsewhere. The word 'ebussia', for instance, is used by the Fanti of the Gold Coast to connote either the totemic animal or the maternal family. In the proto-human stage, the bond between members of a brood did not rest upon a concept but upon a spontaneous sentiment, the irradiation of the maternal instincts. A primitive man's solidarity is represented in his conceptions by the community of food. The Ojibwa Indians state that they have totems in order that 'they might never forget they were all related to each other, and that in time of distress or war they were bound to help each other'. It is a universal rule among totemic savages that when travelling in strange territory a man enquires for persons bearing his own totem, and is at once recognized by them as a brother. When there is any possibility of disloyalty, solidarity is confirmed not by rules and penalties but by exchanging blood and emphasizing the identity of substance. If the Arunta wish to prevent a stranger from revealing their war plans, they force open his mouth and pour down blood of the clansmen; after which it is inconceivable that he should give away their plan. From this derives the conception of the relationship created between host and guest by the partaking of common food, and Oriental history abounds with instances in which the animosities of mortal foes have been paralysed by their having taken food together. A robber who gained access to the palace of the prince of Sagistan, happening to touch some salt with his lips when he stumbled, had to withdraw empty-handed.

As totemic ideas decayed, concepts derived from them took their place—loyalties to divine kings, to a brotherhood, to the state, to the throne—but they have proved poor substitutes. Sometimes we can see among family groups in our own society the strange contrast of strong loyalty within the group and complete callousness to those outside it.

Where the interests of one member are the interests of all, an injury to one is an injury to all. There can be, as Mr Taplin says of South Australians, 'no personal property; all belong to the members collectively and are the possessions of the clan. Each man cares for his neighbour's property because it is part of the collective wealth'. A fisherman will call his friends to consult over the repairs to a canoe or to discuss the marriage of his son. He is surprised that one should expect him to act on his individual judgment; this would be dishonestly to ignore the rights of others. Similarly the individual has no personal rights over game or food which he may obtain, and the hunter may go short himself that others should receive the recognized share. 'Communism', says the Rev. W. Ridley, 'is another law of the aborigines. They hold the doctrine of M. Proudhon, "La propriété c'est le vol".' The same surprising ignorance of property has been noted among the Fuegians. 'The perfect equality among individuals composing Fuegian tribes is', Darwin thought, 'fatal to any hope of their becoming civilized.' A comparable communism is practised among the Eskimo, the Veddahs, in Tahiti and elsewhere. Of the North American Indians, Captain Carver says:

'The Indians in their common state are strangers to all distinction of property, except in articles of domestic use.' La Hontan notes that the Indians 'say that amongst us folks will rob, slander, betray, sell one another for money . . . they think it strange that some should have more goods than others . . . they never quarrel and fight among themselves, nor steal from one another or speak ill of one another'. 'What is extremely surprising', says Father Charlevoix, 'is to see them treat one another with a gentleness and consideration which one does not find among common people in the most civilized nations. This, doubtless, arises in part from the fact that the words "mine" and "thine", which St Chrysostom says extinguish in our hearts the fire of charity and kindle that of greed, are unknown to these savages.'

The steadfast fidelity of such men to their fellow-clansmen, found also among the Arabs, can be paralleled in Sparta.

Primitive human nature differed considerably from what we often assume to be human nature in general. Primitives do not think in terms of their ego and its interests, but in terms of the group-individual. Such ideas are not the result of totemistic beliefs; totemistic beliefs are the result of such ideas. The individualism which is the alpha and omega of the motives of modern man is not a primitive character but a product of social evolution, which has developed mainly, if not solely, in relation to social circumstances, and more especially to the growth of personal property. Where primitive man has had a few years of contact with Europeans a transformation occurs, and the chief cause is acquisition of private property and his taking part in individual transactions. The peasants of Europe closely resemble the savage in their traditions, but differ from him in one respect—they are proprietors, and instead of betraying sentiments of social solidarity they display narrow selfishness. It is not the operation of individualistic instincts which has given rise to the acquisition of personal property, but just the reverse.

CHAPTER 18

The Witch and the Priestess

Primitive Religion not Speculative

I T has been almost universally assumed that women have had little, if any, part in the development of religious systems, even though they have often been their chief votaries. Such an idea should not be accepted as self-evident. True, women are little disposed to construct speculative systems. But it would be profoundly wrong to suppose that religious ideas have grown out of intellectual systems; rather the reverse. Primitive man is strangely unconcerned about philosophical questions. The following questions were put to a very intelligent Zulu: 'Have you any knowledge of the power by whom the world was made? When you see the sun rising and setting, and the trees growing, do you know who made them and governs them?' The Zulu, after a thoughtful pause, replied: 'No, we see them, but cannot tell how they come; we suppose they come of themselves.'[1]

The Totem as Creator

The totem is by its very nature the tribe's progenitor and creator; this creative function is naturally extended to include the creation of the habitat of the tribe, i.e. the world. The animal nature of ancestral totems is, we have seen, but vaguely differentiated from their human nature. The iguana, the turtle, the emu in Australia, the Great Hare, the White Eagle in America, the Great Raven in Siberia, are all tribal Fathers, supreme magicians, creators. To the tribal ancestor are gradually ascribed all the the functions traceable to a superior agency controlling the destinies of the tribe. He instituted the tribal customs of which no one knows the origin, and is angry at any breach of them.

In more advanced stages the totem or mythic ancestor of the oldest and most influential clan occupies a position superior to that of all other

[1] Many similar statements have been cited to show that such savages have no gods. This does not follow; it only proves that the savage's conception of a god differs from the theologian's. Actually primitive man generally recognizes beings who may readily be viewed as divine though in many respects most undivine; when asked what beings he regards as possessing the divine attributes of the theologian's God, he has no hesitation in referring to them, and he recognizes his questioner's deity as being of the same order.

tribal totems. He is not merely a clan ancestor, but a tribal ancestor, a tribal god. He is not merely the source of a particular supply of food, but a dispenser of subsistence, the controller of the tribe's fortunes. The dominant clan is the mediator between the tribe and the controller of its destinies. The headman of the sacred clan is the representative of the god, his ancestor; he is his earthly avatar, his incarnation, indistinguishable from the god himself. In Madagascar the King is simply known as 'God on Earth', and the creation of the world is ascribed to one of his ancestors. The Queen of Angola, on being asked who made the world and who fecundated the ground and ripened the fruits thereof, replied without hesitation. 'My ancestors'. 'Then', rejoined the Capuchin who was catechising her, 'does your Majesty enjoy the whole power of your ancestors?' 'Yes', answered the Queen, 'and much more, for over and above what they had I am absolute mistress of the kingdom of Matamba.'

The divine king does not derive his status from any personal merit or attributes, but from the fact of his descent from the god. With the development, by ambitious conquerors, of royal power, the character of the divine ancestor is enormously enhanced. To us the identification of primitive kings with the supreme deity appears sacrilege or flattery. But, as a matter of fact, it is not so much the royal personage who is exalted by being assimilated to a god, as the primitive god who is exalted by the attributes of his earthly representative. The rude tribal god, who is in general treated with scanty reverence, first acquires majesty when impersonated by a powerful monarch.

The ancestral god has a special function, closely related to his original totemic character: rain-making. Whatever may be the source of a people's food supply, the most important factor determining its abundance is the weather, and especially the rainfall. It is difficult for us to realise fully the meaning of rain or drought to the primitive man. In Australia a drought means misery and death to the blacks. In South Africa, remarks Father Junod, 'drought is equivalent to famine, and famine to death'.

The rain from heaven has been the supreme determinant of the history of humanity. The great movements of pre-history, which have determined the present distribution of human races, took place mainly, if not solely, under the urge of the fatal drought. What is now the great African desert was one of the first regions from which peoples were driven northwards by the failure of the means of subsistence to people Mediterranean shores and Northern Europe.

Thus it is not by mere poetic fancy that heaven is the abode of the gods. The supreme gods of early religions not only dwell in heaven but *are* the heavens or the heavenly bodies, thought of as controllers of the seasons and of atmospheric conditions. Among the Tshi-speaking peoples the divine name 'Nyamkum' means 'sky' or 'rain'. Among the Makuas the same word means 'sky', 'clouds', or 'God'. With the Basetos of the Upper Nile the supreme god is simply 'the rain-maker'. The same nomenclature obtains in Asia. Among the Mongols the supreme god is Tengri, 'the sky'; in China, Ti, 'the sky'; in Vedic India, Dyaeus, 'the sky'; in Persia, Ahura, 'the azure sky'. In Greece he was Zeus, 'the sky', 'the cloud-compeller'. Yahweh, the god of the ancient Hebrews, was a rain-god; 'He shall come unto us as the rain', says the prophet Hosea, 'as the latter and former rain unto the earth.'

Thus it is that one of the chief, if not indeed the chief, functions of all primitive priest-kings was the control of the weather, and more particularly of the rainfall—as Frazer has pointed out. A king was primarily a maker of rain, and originally was probably the headman of the clan which was credited with the greatest power of wielding such control. All African kings were primarily rain-makers. For instance, the function of the King of Loango which most impressed the first missionaries was his obligation to make rain. In Somaliland a chief is known as 'Prince of Rain'. Throughout the continent, in fact, 'the chief was the great rain-maker of the tribe'. Even the kings of ancient Egypt were rain-makers, although Egypt, where it scarcely ever rains, would appear to be about the last place for a rain-maker to set up. Pharaoh's control of the waters was naturally applied more often to regulating the river; and he caused it to rise by casting into the Nile a written order to do so. Conversely, the most important ceremony at the court of the King of Siam was that at which the king, like Canute, issued through heralds a solemn order to the River Meinam to retire. The Emperor of China also had a similar office. Hindu doctrine teaches that Indra sends no rain upon a kingdom which has lost its king. Ulysses explains to Penelope that: 'Under a virtuous prince the earth brings forth barley and wheat in abundance, trees are loaded with fruit, ewes sit several times in succession, and the sea is filled with fish. Of so great worth is a good leader.'

The control thus exercised by sacred kings over heaven for the benefit of the people is thoroughly practical, and is exactly of the same kind as that exercised by members of a totem-clan over their totem. The purpose of primitive religion is eminently utilitarian. It is part and parcel of the means employed to supply and control the necessaries of life, to promote the prosperity of the tribe, and above all to provide its food.

'The really important question', as Robertson Smith remarked, 'is not what a god has power to do, but whether I can get him to do it for me.' This is why those divinities which, judged by a theological criterion, appear to correspond most closely to the conception of a god—the creators and controllers of the universe—are in most primitive religions not the objects of *worship*. Thus the Bahima, who worship a tribal ancestor, have also a god, Lugaba; but 'they know very little about him; he has no priests and so receives no sacrifices'. The supreme god of Dahomey is 'ignored rather than worshipped'. The same remarks apply to all African populations. In West Africa generally 'they regard the god as the creator of man, plants, animals and the earth, and they hold that, having made them, he takes no further interest in the affair'. 'The god, in the sense we use the word, is in essence the same thing in all Bantu tribes I have met with', says Miss Kingsley, 'a non-interfering and therefore negligible quantity.'

Similarly the American Indians 'nowhere adored the god they knew'. The tribes of Guiana, though they have the notion of a supreme being, 'concern themselves little about him'. In Australia, Baiame, in whom some enthusiasts thought they recognized a 'supreme being', is believed by the Queensland tribes, says Mr Thorne, 'to have gone away over the ocean so long ago that our informant could give no idea of the lapse of time, and never took further heed of the country or its inhabitants'. Of Daramulum, another Australian 'supreme being', 'there is no worship'.

The incongruity of divine beings who form no part of religion 'becomes intelligible when it is borne in mind that primitive religion refers to practical issues. The god in whom primitive man is interested is not the sky-god, but the tribal ancestor who is also the supreme magician, who can use his power to control the sky-god.

Since, then, primitive religion has little concern with philosophical speculations, the natural inaptitude of women for such speculations is irrelevant.

The Exclusion of Women from Religious Functions in the West

Nowadays, in Christian and other strongly patriarchal societies (e.g. Brahmanical India or China), the notion of women exercising priestly functions offends propriety. The suggestion that they should preach and administer sacraments is regarded as an extravagance of feminism. Such notions are comparatively recent.

The ancient world was full of priestesses. The Vestal priestesses were one of the most ancient and sacred institutions of Roman cult. When walking abroad, they were preceded by lictors bearing the insignia of supreme command; any insult was punishable with death. In earlier times they and other priestesses—the Regina Sacrorum, the Flaminicae —played an even more important part in Italian cult. Ancient Italy swarmed with priestly and prophetic women who often exercised greater influence than the official priestesses. The sibyls of classical tradition are the types of prophetic females, or shamanesses; the most sacred shrines of Greece, such as those of Delphi and of Dodona, were served by prophetic women. The priestess of Demeter, like the Vestals at Roman spectacles, occupied a throne of honour at the Olympic games. There can be little doubt that in these primitive cults, which later became connected with Dionysos, priestly functions were exercised exclusively by woman. In Aegean and Cretan religion, archaeological evidence shows us priestesses discharging all religious functions.

'As in Greece, so in Babylonia and Assyria', says Professor Sayce, 'women were inspired prophetesses of the god.' In Assyrian inscriptions, they are called 'The Mothers'.

None but women were allowed to enter the Holy of Holies of Bel-Marduk. In Carthage likewise women mediated between the Great Goddess and the people. In ancient Egypt the Queen was high-priestess of Rā. There were many orders of priestesses under the Old and the Middle Kingdom; and 'at the time of the New Empire there was scarcely a woman from the highest to the lowest who was not connected with the service of the temples'.

Priestesses in Uncultured Societies

In primitive cultures, the part played by women in religious cult is striking. In the state religion of Dahomey at least as many women as men exercise priestly functions; priestesses undergo a three years' course of initiation; they are called 'Mothers'. Their person is inviolable, and they enjoy great privileges. In most African kingdoms, such as Ashanti, Urua and Uganda, the temples of deceased kings are served by colleges of priestesses and vestals. The most dreaded deity of Matabeleland was served by a college of priestesses who were regarded as his daughters; even King Lobengula had at times to yield to it. The numerous female fetiches, or 'Mother fetiches', throughout Africa are served exclusively by women. Some of them rise to positions of enormous influence. In Loango, the priestess of Atida was called 'The Mother of God'. Throughout the Congo both sexes exercise magical and priestly functions.

Among the Eskimo the shamans, or 'angakut', may be either men or women. But Dr Rink maintained that formerly all magicians were women. Today, in East Greenland, there are two classes of sorcerers, the 'angakut' proper and the 'gilalik', an inferior order. The latter are nearly all women. Dr Rink believes that the male 'angakut' ousted them from their former positions.

Among the North American Indians 'medicine women' were as famous as medicine men, and on some occasions, such as the Corn Feast, they exercised almost unlimited authority. Their influence appears to have been greater among the prairie and western tribes than among the more advanced eastern nations. Among the tribes of California they are reported to have been particularly numerous. Among the Yurok tribes of the Klamath River district the shamans 'were almost all women'. So among the Zuñi, though today the rain-making ceremonies are in the hands of priests, and although the priestly college consists of men, at their head is a woman, the Priestess of Fertility. She can dismiss any of the priests at a moment's notice, without offering a reason. There are several 'secret societies', but 'there is only one person among the Zuñi who is a member of all the sacred societies and thus knows the secrets of all, and that person is a woman'.

Competition often develops between the sexes for the possession of the power derived from the exercise of magical and religious functions; accordingly they are frequently reserved to one or the other sex. But such a monopoly is not characteristic of societies which have reached a considerable degree of development under undisturbed matriarchal rule. Thus, among the Khasis of Assam the priestesses perform all the rites and sacrifices, but, as among the Pueblo Indians, the men are not excluded, although 'the male officiants are only the deputies' of the priestesses. The ultimate authority rests with the priestess, who is also invariably the keeper of the sacred magical objects.

From a cursory perusal of the most accessible accounts of Central America in the days of the European conquest, one would gather the impression that, although there was a considerable sprinkling of shaman-istic women, the wizard, or 'paje', was usually a man. Dr Brinton's close examination reveals a very different state of things. The 'pajes' were members of a closely organized and widely spread association which has been termed Nagualism.[1] 'A remarkable feature of this mysterious organization', says Dr Brinton, 'was the exalted position it assigned to women. Not only were they admitted to the most esoteric degrees, but in repeated instances they occupied the very highest posts in the organ-ization.' Pascual de Andagoya asserts from his own knowledge that some of the female adepts had attained the rare and peculiar power of being in two places at once. Spanish writings of the sixteenth and seventeenth centuries confirm the dread in which they were held. 'In the sacra-ments of Nagualism, woman was the primate and hierophant', Brinton declares.

In Guatemala the supreme ministrant of the gods was a priestess, and it was to her that the warriors applied to ensure victory. 'In many native American legends, as in others from the old world, some powerful enchantress is remembered as the founder of the state. Such among the Aztecs was the sorceress who built the city of Mallinalco, famed even

---

[1] The notion, common also in other parts of the world, that the shaman can transform himself into an animal, and that his power is somehow bound up with a spiritual double, or 'nagual', dwelling in the animal.

after the conquest for the skill of its magicians, who claimed descent from her. Such in Honduras was Coamizagual, Queen of Cerqui, versed in occult science, who died not, but at the close of her earthly career rose to heaven.'

The position of sorceresses in South America would appear to have been similar. Among all the tribes of the Amazon 'old women are the interpreters of the gods'. In Patagonia 'the old women, witches, prophetesses or divineresses are the chief ministers of their cult'.

Throughout the Indonesian archipelago the primitive aboriginal cults, where they have not been supplanted by Islam and other foreign religions, are predominantly and often exclusively served by women. Thus among the Bataks of Sumatra the shamans may be either men or women; but female shamans are far more common, and in several districts there are none but female shamans.

In numerous other Pacific islands, such as Timor and the southern Moluccas, the shamans are predominantly women.

Among the Dayak tribes of Borneo religious functions are almost exclusively exercised by women; the shamans 'are for the most part women, seldom men'. The same is true of the southern Celebes, where they are known as 'imitation women'. All the deities or spirits from whom sorcerers, whether male or female, derive their power are spoken of as their 'grandmother'. According to the tradition of the Land Dayaks, the magic art was first imparted by Tuppa, the women's deity, to a woman, and was taught by her to her successors. 'It seems to me more than likely', says Miss M. Morris, 'that manangism [shamanism] was originally a profession of women, and that men were gradually admitted into it, at first only by becoming as much like women as possible.'

We may here note that any attempt to draw a sharp line between the private magical practices of the shamaness and the more dignified office of the official priestess proves futile in practice. Thus in Indonesia, where the people themselves draw a distinction between the shamanesses and the priestesses, both Dr Wilken and Dr Kruijt, the highest authorities on the religious usages of the region, are compelled to admit that there is no psychological distinction between the two. Both priestesses and shamanesses are in exactly the same condition of spiritual possession, and the magical procedure ritually observed in the public cult is identical with the practice of the individual witch or shamaness. The distinction between the two is not religious or psychological, but social and official.

Among the Polynesian races, who originally came from the Indonesian region, power has become concentrated in the hands of chiefs and the aristocratic classes. To this is due both the decay of popular religious cult—the priestly offices being for the most part under the jurisdiction of the chiefs and ruling classes—and the masculine exclusiveness, if not the patriarchal character, of Polynesian institutions. Women were, as a rule, excluded in Polynesia from the sacred rites of men, so it is all the more remarkable that official priestesses, occupied a high position in many Polynesian islands. Thus there were priestesses in Rotuma, Tonga, Samoa, Paumotu, Uvea and Savage Island.

'Nearly all writers on Siberia agree that the position of the female shaman in modern days is sometimes even more important than that occupied by the male. . . . Among the Palæo-Siberians, women receive the gift of shamanising more often than men.' According to the traditions of the Yakuts, there were formerly no male shamans, or priests, but all magic functions were exercised by women. This was still the case until recent times among the Kamchadals and the neighbouring populations. The familiar spirit from whom every practitioner of the magic arts is supposed to derive his or her power is spoken of among the Yakuts as his 'Mother'. In the languages of the Yakuts, Altains, Torgut, Kidan, Mongols, Kirghis, Buryat, the term for shamaness is the same; while quite different words are used to denote male shamans. From this Troshchanski infers that, before the separation of these races, all practitioners of shamanism were women and that male shamans only appeared subsequently. Male shamans among the Yakuts wear long hair and dress as women, whether they are wearing their ordinary dress or their ceremonial costume, and two iron circles on their apparel represent a woman's breasts.

Male Priests dressed as and impersonating Women

The adoption of female dress by male shamans and priests is a worldwide phenomenon. It was prevalent among the North American Indians; invariable throughout Indonesia. In Tahiti and the Marquesas the priests of the Areois stained their skin a light or more feminine hue and affected the manners of women. When Zulu chiefs perform rain-making ceremonies they put on a woman's petticoat. Among the ancient Germans male priests dressed as women. In Babylon the priests of Ishtar and the Syrian goddess wore female attire. So likewise did the Korybantes, the Dactyloi, the Kouretes and the priests of Artemis at Ephesos. The priests of Herakles at Kos dressed as women when they offered sacrifice, as did male officiants in the festivals of Dionysos. The male assistants in cult scenes from Minoan Crete are represented wearing women's clothes. All priestly robes, skirts, aprons, sottanas are indeed everywhere of an essentially feminine character.

On the other hand, instances of a woman dressing as a man when exercising priestly functions are altogether exceptional, although women dress as men when exercising any prescriptively male occupation, such as soldiering or hunting.[1]

In primitive societies 'wearing the clothes that have been used by another transfers to another wearer the qualities of the former one'. Similarly it is a universal principle that the distinctive dress of each sex implies that the person wearing it is engaged in the occupations which are peculiar to that sex. Thus for instance, among the tribes of California every warrior, when too old to take part in active warfare, assumes female attire, and thenceforward helps the women with their duties.

It is frequently stated by those reporting that among a given people certain men dressed in woman's clothes and followed women's occupations, that such men served for the indulgence of unnatural vices. But it may be said positively, at least so far as regards the North American tribes, that no grounds exist for this inference.

In primitive societies the assimilating of men exercising priestly functions to women goes much farther than the assumption of feminine apparel. In the Pelew Islands, for instance, 'it often happens that a female deity chooses for her priest a young man, who is thenceforth regarded and treated in every respect as a woman. He assumes female dress, and wears a piece of gold round his neck, and he also frequently takes up the cultivation of a patch of taro.' In Cyprus, at the festival of Ariadne, the imitation was carried even farther—for one of the officiating priests lay in bed and imitated the groans of a woman in labour. Among the Yakut it was actually believed that male shamans were capable of bearing children. In California the male shamans assume female attire because this is regarded as bestowing greater power, and the same is true of the Chukchi. In short, this universal practice does not seem open to any other interpretation than that magic was orginally regarded as essentially a woman's function.

It is a curious fact that smiths are widely held to possess magic powers. Yakut traditions connect the appearance of male shamans amongst them with the introduction of iron. The first male shamans, they say, were smiths. The profession of smith is hereditary among Siberian tribes, and the Yakuts consider that at the ninth generation a smith becomes a wizard. Among the Buryat the spirits from whom men derive magical powers are called 'smiths', and are thought to have taught men the ironworkers' art also. A proverb of the Kolyma district affirms that 'the blacksmith and the shaman are of one nest'. Among the Mongols the same word denotes a male shaman and a smith. Among

---

[1] The women of the Mawungu secret society among the Pangwe dress as men at their festivals. The 'medium' of the god Mukasa in Uganda adjusts her clothes in male fashion when she is acting as the mouthpiece of one god; but at other times she remains purely feminine, and is, indeed, regarded as the wife of the god.

the Romans 'faber', smith, connoted 'magician'. In Russian popular tales smiths act as assistants to witches. The Kayan Dayaks believe smiths to be possessed by spirits, and that their skill is due to this. Similar estimates are general in Africa. Thus among the Fans the village blacksmith is the priest and sacred headman of the community. Tribes ignorant of the art of metallurgy regard smiths with such awe that if they obtain possession of a smith's bellows they place it in their fetich-house and address their prayers to it. The Arabs and Berbers ban all smiths from society. Dr Schneider is probably right in supposing that this 'indicates that the art of the smith is regarded as a branch of witchcraft, and those who practise it as the possessors of magical powers'. In ancient Egypt the priests of Horus were known as smiths. In Asia wizards were the particular disciples of Tubal-khan, the smith. In Ireland St Patrick pronounced against 'the spells of women, of smiths and magicians'. Such views accord with the belief (widespread in Europe) that smiths are the only men who share the magical powers peculiar to women.

Priestesses among the Peoples of Northern Europe

In the druids we appear to have a purely male priesthood. Their origin is disputed. Some authorities hold that they were always the priests of the Celtic races, others that they are of late origin. It is improbable that a highly organized religious corporation could have existed from the first in all Celtic countries. Cæsar, who enjoyed the friendship of the druid Divitiacus, tells us explicitly that 'the discipline [of druidism] is held to have had its origin in Britain, and to have been transported thence into Gaul . . .'. The facts appear to confirm this. The druids were certainly much more firmly established in Ireland and western Britain than in Gaul. They are said to have 'tamed the people as wild beasts are tamed'; this would hardly have been needed if they had been their spiritual rulers from the beginning.

That druidism was an importation at the cost of some earlier system is suggested by other facts. When Hannibal passed through Gaul it was agreed that all damages which might be caused by the transit of his huge armaments should be assessed by a council of women. It is scarcely conceivable that, had there been a powerful theocracy of druids at the time—and we hear nothing of them in this connection—they would have kept out of the whole business. Cæsar, it is true, does not mention any priestesses among the Gauls, though he states that the troops of Ariovistus were forbidden by their wise women to fight before the new moon; and Gallic women attached to the armies offered sacrifices and prophesied. (Some have spoken of 'druidesses', but there appears to be no evidence of any women being connected with the organization of the druids.)

Moreover, there is abundant evidence of the existence of priestesses, who appear to have been thrust aside by the druidical invasion in Gaul. Thus Pomponius Mela, in his brief reference to Gaul, observes: 'Sena in the British Sea is famous for its oracle of a Gaulish god, whose priestesses, living in the holiness of perpetual virginity, are said to be nine in number. They call them Gallizenae, and they believe them to be endowed with extraordinary powers, so that they are able to rouse the sea and the wind by their incantations, and to turn themselves into whatsoever animal form they choose; they can cure diseases which are incurable to anyone else; they know the future and vaticinate.'[1] Exceptional interest attaches to the account, for it enables us to detect tradition evolving. Sena is undoubtedly the island of Sein off the coast of Armorica, far-famed in Celtic legend as the site of the grave of Merlin. Now, in these (later) legends Merlin left the court of King Arthur accompanied by 'nine bards'. In other versions of the old druidical tales Merlin fell into the toils of the 'Lady of the Lake', who became so proficient under his instruction that one day, when he was asleep, she cast a spell over him, making him a perpetual prisoner in a castle or, according to other accounts, an oak-tree, whence he delivered oracles. Thus the oracular divinity of the priestesses of Sein appears to become a druid; but the priestesses of Sein do not appear to have had, in fact, any connection with druidical institutions.

This is not the only institution of the kind. A little farther south, on an island at the mouth of the Loire, near the present city of Nantes, there was, says Strabo, another great shrine served by a college of priestesses. They were said to celebrate 'the mysteries of Dionysos', and their cult is described as orgiastic. So little had the cult to do with druidism that no man was permitted to approach the shrine. Dionysius Periegetes tells us that in some of the Channel Islands the rites of Bacchus were performed by women crowned with leaves, who danced and made an even greater shouting than the Thracian bacchantes.

Similar evidence meets us in Ireland. In County Kildare is a monastery of nuns dedicated to the service of St Brigit. One of their chief duties was to tend, like the Roman Vestals, a perpetual fire. As Canon McCulloch remarks: 'The nuns who guarded the sacred fire of Kildare had evidently succeeded the virgin guardians of a sacred fire, the priestesses of a cult which was tabu to men.' This is likely enough, for Brigit was the chief Celtic goddess. It therefore appears improbable that her cult elsewhere, in Britain and in Gaul, was originally served by male druids. There are records of other shrines in Ireland where vestal fires were maintained. If cults existed in Ireland, the stronghold of druidism,

---

[1] 'Gallizenae' is obviously a MS. error for 'Gallae Senae', or some such expression.

in which druids took no part, it can cause little surprise that in other Celtic regions, such as western Britain, druids are scarcely heard of at all. The famous queen of the Iceni, Boadicea or Boudicca, was the high-priestess of the cult of the goddess Andaste. Pliny, again, refers to the rites of the British women who, probably in ceremonies of agricultural magic, dance naked, painted with woad.

It would thus appear that the exclusively masculine magical organiza-tion or 'secret society' of the druids was superimposed at a comparatively late date upon other cults in which the priestly functions were exercised chiefly, perhaps exclusively, by women. 'There is evidence', Canon McCulloch writes, 'that they [the druids] had ousted women as the earlier magic-wielding persons. . . . In Irish texts women as magicians performing all the magical rites ascribed to druids are much in evidence. But their magic was, so to speak, not official.'

Among the Teutonic and Nordic barbarians, on the other hand, no male priesthood ever became established. In nearly every instance where a priestly personage is mentioned it is a woman. The influence and power exercised by sacred women and prophetesses are frequently referred to, and several were actually worshipped as divine beings during their lifetime. Strabo reports: 'They say that the Cimbri had the follow-ing custom; their women, who travelled with them, were accompanied by sacred priestesses, grey-haired, white-robed, with a linen scarf buckled over their shoulder and a girdle of brass, and walking bare-footed. These priestesses, with a sword in their hand, met the prisoners of war when they were brought to the camp; and, having crowned them, they led them to a brass basin as large as thirty amphorae. They had a ladder, which the priestess mounted, and, standing over the basin she cut the throat of each prisoner as he was handed up to her. With the blood that gushed into the basin they made a prophecy.' One such cauldron has actually been discovered at Gendestrup in Jutland; the sacrifice is depicted on it; among the deities depicted on it is a moon-goddess.[1]

Among none of the Nordic races had the practice of the magic art been taken over by men at the time when Christianity was introduced. 'Our earliest antiquities', says Jacob Grimm, 'impute it pre-eminently

[1] Cauldrons similar to that of Jutland played, as we shall see, a very important part in Celtic religious ideas, and a number of epic myths relate the adventures of heroes who undertook to obtain the priceless gift of a sacred cauldron, or 'cauldron of regeneration', as they were sometimes called, from some divine woman. Those 'cauldrons of regeneration', which barbaric heroes coveted, were transformed in Christian times into the vessel of the Holy Grail; and thus the gruesome rites of the Cimbrian priestesses and the unholy mysteries of Celtic witches are intimately connected with the sublimest heights of mediæval Christian mysticism.

to women.' Thus among our own ancestors in Western and Northern Europe, as elsewhere, it would appear that formerly religious and priestly functions belonged originally to the women.

Traditions of Transfer of Religious Function from Women to Men

Further evidence of our thesis is afforded by the fact that in many parts of the world we find traditions which suggest that religious functions, now exercised by men, were formerly the women's prerogative.

In Australia, for instance, as we have seen, the women formerly played a much more important part in religious functions than now, and the traditions suggest that formerly women were not excluded, as they are now. They ascribe to women the magic powers today exercised exclusively by the men. There is definite evidence that the tooth-knocking ceremony, the mark of initiation, was performed on the women as well as the men, among some tribes, as recently as the first discovery of Australia by Europeans. Moreover, 'in tradition after tradition, we have accounts set out in great detail of how particular women of the Alcheringa carried sacred Nurtunja just as the men did, and how they performed sacred ceremonies exactly as the men did'. The Queensland natives explain that women have a natural aptitude for magic, which is precisely why they are debarred from practising it.

In several parts of the world traditions refer explicitly to the former exercise of magical and religious functions by the women. Thus the Fuegians still, like the Australians, use their religious ceremonies as a means of frightening the women and keeping them in subjection, but formerly it was the women who dressed up as ghosts and frightened the men. Tradition says the change was brought about by a revolution in which most of the women were massacred. The great religious yearly festival of the Fuegians is supposed to commemorate the event.

The South American tribes of the Upper Amazon and Rio Negro basin, particularly those dwelling near the Rio Uaupes, have similar ceremonies. The traditions of the Uaupes Indians, however, state that these ceremonies were formerly performed by women, and that their rites were instituted by a 'council of women'.

We come upon exactly similar traditions in Africa. In East Africa, among the Wanika, a terrorizing cult exists identical in social use with those just noted. In one district, however, at Rabbai Mpia, the situation is reversed; there is a society which is confined to the women, who simulate ghosts to terrify the men. Such women's religious associations, (or, as they are somewhat inappropriately called, 'secret societies') are common in West Africa. There is reason to believe that almost every woman belongs to such a society. What is known of their rules suggests that women were formerly leaders of society and of religious cult. One of the most famous and powerful is the 'Njembe', to which every Mpongwe woman is expected to belong. Initiation was formerly regarded as a sort of religious duty and as a sanctifying act. There are various degrees of initiation, and there is a supreme head, or Mother.

Europeans who have endeavoured to obtain a glimpse of the rites of the 'Njembe' have barely escaped with their lives. Hence little is known about them except that the meetings are held in secluded glades in the forest and involve a sacred fire. The women (who are normally modest) strip naked and dance until they are exhausted; phallic symbols and fescennine songs are part of the ritual, which is also associated with serpents, and each women must catch and carry one of the small snakes which live among the mangrove roots. In Liberia, 'If the tribe decides to go to war, the declaration of war is not complete until it has been referred to the women and they have approved of it.'

In the case of the Attonga sisterhood of Sierra Leone, 'If a man happens, through ignorance or inadvertency, to enter an Attonga house, he is made one of the society, though contrary to his inclination.' He is henceforth regarded as a woman, and when he dies he cannot be buried in the men's graveyard.

Special interests attaches to those societies admitting both men and women. In the southern Sudan, the Bir society is open to both sexes; but the women perform the essential ritual of maintaining the sacred fire. So is the secret society of the Butwa, a timid tribe of fisherfolk dwelling round Lake Bangwenlu, It is governed by five officials of each sex, but the women play the chief part. The female hierophants are called 'the mothers of the Butwa mysteries'. Butwa women compel their husbands to join the society. In the Purrah society of Sierra Leone, whenever a man is admitted, he must be introduced and accompanied by some female relative who is initiated at the same time. The head of the society is a woman. The neophyte swears allegiance to the high-priestess, saying, 'You are my mother; I cannot betray you.' Tradition relates that the society was formerly exclusively female.

What is more, some of the most influential religious societies of West Africa, from which women are at the present day excluded on pain of death, were, we are told, instituted by women and were once exclusively women's societies. One such is the Egbo, which flourished among the Efik and Ekoi people. On inquiring why their ceremonies sometimes involve an old woman, Mr Amaury Talbot was told that the Egbo was originally a women's society, and that the men had learned their rites and then forbidden the women to participate. At the New Year yam festival, the members of another man's society assemble and perform rites, which include songs by a member chosen for his sweet voice. He is dressed in women's clothes and is called 'The Mother of Ekong'. This society is also declared to have been formerly an exclusive women's society.

Associations similar to the 'secret societies' of Africa are found in most parts of Melanesia. In Duke of York Island the most important secret society is the Dukduk, from which the women are rigidly excluded. Yet we are told that 'the first "dukduk" was found by a woman at Birara, New Britain, floating on four coconuts. She dressed it, and soon exhibited it, and got lots of money. The men, however, got jealous, and said that women were not tall enough for it, and so they bought it and forbade women to go near it ever afterwards.' As in the West African societies, the head of the Dukduk societies, who is called 'the Old Woman', is a man dressed in female attire, and is often spoken of as 'she'. In British New Guinea, again, the initiation ceremonies of young men, which constitute the chief religious observances, are said by the Masuigam to have been instituted by a woman.

We thus find identical traditions in such widely different parts of the uncivilized world as Australia, Tierra del Fuego, the Amazon Valley, West Africa, Melanesia and New Guinea, to the effect that the rites from which women are at the present day excluded were once either instituted by the women, or that they took the leading part in them. These traditions reinforce the conclusion which has been reached independently in regard to Indonesia, America, Northern Asia and Northern Europe, that magical practices and primitive priestly functions formerly belonged to the exclusive sphere of women and that they were taken up by men at a comparatively late epoch.

Powers of Witchcraft ascribed to Women

In its primitive phases religion is indistinguishable from magic. All religion began as practical wonder-working. The distinction between magic and witchcraft refers not to the means employed nor the nature of the powers used, but to the purpose to which they are put.

It is therefore relevant to our thesis that the power of witchcraft is universally regarded as pertaining specifically to women. The witch is a woman; the wizard is a male imitation. In primitive thought every woman is credited with the possession of magic powers, wherever such powers are believed in. Thus the Chukchi declare that 'Woman is by nature a shaman'. In New Guinea 'the people will have it that all evil spirits are female. They are all women or enter women, giving them terrible power.'

In many different places tradition holds that women first taught the magic arts. In Sierra Leone, although (as in other parts of Africa) witches may be male or female, yet the power of witchcraft, which is considered to be inherited, can be derived only from the individual's mother. In India, according to Molwa, every woman was suspected of being a witch, and the same test as in Europe was applied of ducking her in a pond to see if she would float. In ancient Babylon the same notions were held.

Since it is a common notion that such power is counteracted by child-bearing, the power of witchcraft belongs particularly to *old* women or to young unmarried women. Young and beautiful women are often 'bewitching.' This notion is explained by Dalla Porta, who traces 'falling in love' to the magical properties of menstrual blood. 'If a person is ensnared with the desire of a fair and beautiful woman, although he be caught at a distance, yet he taketh the poyson in at his eyes, and the image of her beauty settleth in the heart of this lover, kindleth a flame there, which will never cease to torment him. For the soft blood of the beloved, being strayed thither, maketh continual representations of her: she is present there in her own blood. But it cannot settle or rest there, for it continually endeavoureth to flye homeward, as the blood of a wounded person spirts out on him that giveth the blow. But if it be a fascination of Envy or Malice, that hath infected any person, it is very dangerous, and is found most often in old women. And you will find more women than men witches.'

A seventeenth-century Italian bishop devotes a chapter to discussing 'Why witchcraft appertains to women and not to men'. 'For one wizard or necromancer that one may see [he notes] one finds ten thousand women.'

Modern anthropologists have generally sought to account for this predominance by reference to the nature of women. Women, it is said, suffer more from nervous instability than men; they are subject to hysteria and temporary delusions. Such nervous disturbances are similar to, or identical with, the state of 'possession' in which primitive priestesses and shamanesses become the medium of supernatural powers.

I regard this explanation as inadequate. Amongst primitive races nervous and hysterical phenomena are found almost as commonly in men as in women. 'Arctic hysteria', which in Northern Asia is regarded as closely connected with shamanistic powers, is reported to be common among both sexes. The analogous phenomena noted in Indonesia appear to relate almost exclusively to men. Again, men of Australian tribes commonly have attacks of hysteria, during which they yell, foam at the mouth and dance till exhausted; nothing is said about the women. In any case, it is not necessary to be in a hysterical fit to work witchcraft.

It seems unnecessary to call on such theories. Though women are commonly supposed to exercise power by virtue of their being witches it seems equally probable that they were originally regarded as witches because they exercised power. Where, as among the Seri Indians, the elder women were genealogically and socially heads of the groups, mediation between their children and supernatural powers would naturally fall to their lot. The primitive mother is, by virtue of natural position and function, the wielder of domestic magic. Among the Chukchi it is the mistress of the house who applies the sacred paint to all members of the family; she has charge of the sacred objects, and performs all the religious functions connected with the household. 'Consequently the women are more expert than the men in the details of the ceremonial', and 'the incantations and spells which are connected with household charms are better known by the women'. The same is true of the Eskimo. Among the Patagonians the magic or religious functions of the household are the exclusive concern of the mother of the family. Among the ancient Germans, Caesar tells us, 'it was the custom that the mothers of the families should declare unto them what they should do through divinations and vaticinations'. Thus, if our conclusions about the status of women in primitive society are correct the universality of the attribution to them of magic powers is self-explanatory.

The source from which magic powers are regarded as being primarily derived is, we shall see, closely connected with the physiological functions of women; the magic faculties which it imparts to them are, according to primitive conceptions, as much a part of their natural constitution as are their reproductive functions. This dread-inspiring power was primitive woman's natural means of enforcing her authority—her substitute for physical force. Her power was that of pronouncing curses, of casting spells. It was by that power, I believe, that sexual tabus were originally imposed upon mankind.

The diabolic nature ascribed to women, not only by the Christian Fathers but by all humanity, is rather the expression of the dread with which women were originally regarded than the cause of that dread. Inevitably, men revolted against that source of terror. On the other hand, it is quite inconceivable that female witchcraft should have arisen as an imitation of practices invented by male magicians, and then have come to be universally regarded as a faculty pertaining to the very nature of women.

Witchcraft and Religious Magic

It may seem paradoxical to say that the priest or priestess acts by virtue of the very powers upon which the witch or wizard depends. But, in fact, the distinction between good and bad magic depends on the use which is made of such powers in any given instance. The priest who bewitches and destroys the tribe's enemies appears maleficent to those same enemies.

Thus 'among the Matabele it is well understood that there were two kinds of witchcraft. One was practised by the witch doctors and the king, such as, for instance, the "making of medicine" to bring rain, of the ceremonies carried out by the witch-doctors to appease the spirits of ancestors. The other witchcraft was supposed to consist of evil practices pursued to cause sickness and death.' The only difference is that the user of white magic practises it openly, whereas the practiser of black magic does so secretly. But 'the same "medicines", the same dances, the same enchantments are used in both'.

Among the Eskimo, as among every other uncultured people. the practice of witchcraft is abominated; but the magic arts which constitute the ritual of actual religion are in every respect identical with the magic resorted to for private, maleficent purposes. The Samoyeds and Lapps make no distinction between 'white' and 'black' shamans, but every shaman may 'serve both for good and bad ends as occasion arises'.

Nor can we easily distinguish the witch from the priestess by referring to the deities from whom they derive their power, as our forefathers attempted to. Frequently the distinction between good and bad deities is not made. The same deity can bestow or withhold fertility, can send disease or withdraw it. Speaking of the divine beings of the Siouan tribes of North America, Mr Pond remarks that 'evidence is wanting to show that the people divide these "Take-Wakan" into classes of good and evil; they are simply "wakan".' Among all the people of Northern Asia, says Mr Staling, 'there is in the spiritual world of shamanism no absolute contrast between good and evil'.

However, even where beneficent and maleficent deities are recognized, it is more frequently the maleficent one who is the main, or sole, object of religious cult. The natives of Kadiak 'believe in a good and a bad spirit; they worship the latter because they are afraid of his ill-will, and do not sacrifice to the former because he will cause no harm to anyone'; similarly with the Patagonians. The Yezidis of Armenia, at Easter, sacrifice one sheep to Jesus Christ and thirty sheep to the Devil, 'because', they say, 'he is more difficult to propitiate'.

Primitive supernatural beings are essentially maleficent. In primitive society, power is synonymous with power to harm. The Santal of Bengal 'cannot understand how a being can be more powerful than himself without wishing to harm him'. The natives of South Africa represent their gods as 'mischievous, delighting to torment them in various ways'. The Hottentots 'have a vague notion of a benevolent spirit, but have a much clearer notion about an evil spirit whom they fear, believing him to be the occasion of sickness, death, thunder and every calamity that befalls them'. Sir Richard Burton spoke to some African Essas about God. They eagerly asked where he might be found, in order that they might kill him, for 'Who but he', they said, 'lays waste our homes, and kills our wives and cattle ?'

While maleficent magic is universally abhorred, beneficent witches are venerated. In Russia they 'stood high in popular estimation', and were thought in some respects more sacred than the Christian priests. Even in Scotland, where the persecution of witches was once so severe, witches have been held in high honour. In some districts fishermen would not put to sea until a witch had performed incantations to secure fair weather and a good haul. Conversely, priests are often called upon to perform deeds of 'black' magic. Thus, on the Gold Coast they are often asked to procure the death of persons who have offended the applicants. The god who is thus 'induced to gratify a personal enmity must be the god which the applicant generally worships; and it is imagined to be an extension of the protection granted by the god to his worshipper'; which notion does not differ fundamentally from the ancient Hebrew beseeching his god to destroy his enemies.

Witches are not thought of as possessing a power which is exclusively and necessarily evil in itself; but all magical power is dreaded, because it is susceptible of being used for harm. When such power is wielded by one sex alone, this must inevitably arouse alarm in the other. Little wonder, then, that men have sought to restrain women from using magic, and have sought to acquire the secrets of the art in self-protection. When magic comes to be exercised by organized male priesthoods, the illicit practice of the art by women is regarded as presumably malignant in intention. The magic woman who is no longer a priestess must necessarily be a witch.

The Christian tradition that women brought death and sin into the world is not peculiar to Christianity, but is universal. Father Lafitau compares the First Woman of the North American Indians, who did just this, to Eve, while Father Sahagun was struck by the same comparison in Mexico. Many African tribes regard the first woman as having brought death into the world, as do the Eskimo and the Melanesians. The Igorots of Luzon say that the first woman instigated men to fight.

We can obtain further clues concerning the significance of woman's mysteries by considering myths concerning the heavenly body with whom they have always and everywhere been especially associated— the moon, and to this topic we now turn.

CHAPTER 19

The Lord of the Women

Dangerous Character of the Moon

THE dangerous character ascribed to women is extended, in the mind of simple peoples, to that celestial body which is everywhere associated with women—the moon. The tabu on menstruating women attaches to the cause of menstruation also. In several of the myths which describe how the first woman introduced death and woe into the world, she and the moon are the same person—for instance, in the traditions of the North American Indians. The Iroquois warriors, before an expedition, consecrated themselves to the moon as to the spirit of relentless vengeance—a practice also observed by ancient Greek warriors. A Wyandot tradition relates how Aataentsic, the first woman, planted fever-breeding plants in order to destroy men. The myth calls up a picture of the witch gathering magic herbs by moonlight.

> *In such a night*
> *Medea gathered the enchanted herbs*
> *That did renew old Aeson.*

The natives of New Granada tell how a woman of surpassing beauty, called Chia (i.e. the moon), appeared and taught doctrines contrary to those received from their tribal god, and eventually caused a flood which almost destroyed the human race. This myth has parallels in most parts of the world: sometimes we are specifically told that the woman is the moon, at others it can be inferred. Thus, in ancient Egypt mankind was supposed to have been almost destroyed by fire and flood produced by the moon-goddess Hathor or Isis. The prominence of the flood in most mythologies is probably due not so much to dread of the damage which floods cause as to their association with the moon, which is universally held to control all waters.

In general, the moon is regarded as the mother of mankind. It has even been suspected that Eve herself, whose name 'Chawwa' means the 'round one', was originally the moon; a Rabbinical tradition represents her as having at first consisted, like other lunar deities, only of a face. A missionary once explained to a Syrian woman's children that Adam and

Eve were our first parents, but she protested against such new-fangled notions, saying that our first parents were the sun and the moon.

The dangerousness of the moon is universally conceded. The Solomon Islanders believe that she is always on the lookout to kill men, and the Eskimo regard her as the cause of all plagues. The Tartars of Central Asia regard the moon as inhabited by a giant who used to eat men, and the peasants of modern Greece still regard the moon as anthropophagous. Among the Maori the moon was called 'the man-eater', and was the source of death; similarly elsewhere. The Bushmen throw sand in the air and shout loudly when they see the new moon—their usual procedure when they wish to drive away evil spirits. Other African tribes have similar customs. One of the most familiar lunar superstitions is that it is unlucky to see the new moon through glass. Obviously, in its primitive form this myth could not have referred to so recent a luxury as glass windows; the myth was that it was dangerous for the new moon to enter a house, or what was the same thing, to be seen from within the house. Hence all savages come out of their dwellings to see the new moon. The Bushmen are careful to build their huts in such a way that the moon cannot shine in at the door, and in Louisiana the window shutters were bolted at the new moon.

As we have seen, many uncultured peoples believe that in certain phases of the moon it is inauspicious to undertake any work or enterprise; the new moon or the full moon being regarded as the most dangerous phase. The malignant character popularly ascribed to the moon reflects the predominance of lunar power in primitive religious ideas.

Precedence of the Moon in Primitive Cosmology

'Moon-worship naturally ranking below sun-worship in importance', wrote Tylor, 'ranges through the same districts of culture.' Tylor was surprised to find that there were tribes who regarded the moon as a deity, and ignored the sun, for he assumed that sun-worship took precedence of moon-worship; and that they normally co-existed. This idea derives from the fact that people with whom we are most familiar have reached the agricultural stage of development. Actually, moon-worship long preceded any form of sun-worship and ranges through different cultural areas.

Many students have reported this. 'It is not the sun that first attracted the savage', remarks one writer; 'we find moon-worship among most utterly savage tribes in Africa and America; and it is noteworthy that with them the moon is always regarded as a male, the sun as a woman; not until later are those relations inverted. From this we may infer that lunar worship is older than solar worship.' Similar comments are made by Professor Hutton Webster, Dr Schultze, Dr Welcker and many others. Usener says: 'Originally the moon was the only deity that was worshipped.' 'As far as can be known, the veneration of the moon has everywhere preceded the veneration of the sun', observes Reclus. We shall find similar conclusions with reference to particular regions and peoples later. It is significant that innumerable popular superstitions (which are relics of primitive conceptions) refer to the moon, while scarcely any refer to the sun. The moon-cult survives to this day in our countryside in the form of bowing and courtesies made to it.

The greater impressiveness of the sun (as it appears to us) is easily explained away, if need be. The Nagas of Upper Burma, for instance, believe that the sun shines by day because, being a woman, it is afraid to venture out at night, whereas the bolder male moon is alone powerful enough to face the darkness. It is pointed out that the moon is obviously more powerful than the sun, for he commands the host of stars which are his children, whereas the sun, if a monarch at all, is without subjects. According to the Guaranis the light of the stars is derived from the moon. Again, although the sun is more brilliant, we are assured in almost every primitive cosmological myth that this has not always been so. The Metheis say that there were once two suns but they quarrelled, and the wounded one became pale; while the Huitotos of Columbia hold that the moon was once the sun and vice versa. These traditions persist even in advanced religions. Thus in Brahmanical literature it is stated that the sun 'took to himself the moon's shine'. Though in the Old Testament the moon is 'the lesser light', in Talmudic literature, where many ancient ideas are preserved, it is stated that originally the sun and moon were equally brilliant. The Arabs also believe this, holding that the angel Gabriel rubbed his wings against the moon and thus deprived it of part of its brightness.

The suppositions which have been put forward to account for this precedence of the moon are extremely inadequate. Thus Professor Arrhenius suggests that, the difference between the seasons not being so marked in the tropics as in temperate climes, the effects produced by the sun have not been so noticeable to populations near the equator. But in America, for instance, it is precisely among the inhabitants of the arctic and antarctic areas that lunar worship is more pronounced, while it is replaced by sun-worship in the equatorial region. Tylor, because he was misled by the current theory that the religious ideas of primitive man were moulded by impressions of natural phenomena, thought that the sun must 'naturally' be regarded as more powerful.

In point of fact, primitive man is no more impressed with the spectacles of nature than the boor who gapes at the enthusiasm of the traveller for picturesque scenery. 'Children and savages', observes

Hoffding, 'have as a rule no sense for the beauties of nature.' 'The negroes of Congoland, as elsewhere in Africa, take surprisingly little notice of the heavenly bodies or the phenomena of the sky.'

If the sun and moon were deified, it was because they were credited with more or less power of influencing the welfare of men. The moon is more important to the savage than the sun, because it is the marker of, and therefore the cause of, time and change, and, in particular, of the changes in women's reproductive life. And it is everywhere dreaded because of its association with the sexual functions of women, and it is regarded as the source of the awful powers ascribed to the witch.

The Moon as the Cause of Conception

As we have already noted, the moon is the regulator and cause of menstruation, which is frequently regarded as being the result of actual intercourse between the moon and women. Thus, for instance, among the Murray Islanders, 'the moon was supposed to be a young man who at certain periods defiled women and girls, causing a bloody discharge'. Menstruation is, according to many uncultured peoples, a form of pregnancy; the fœtus is supposed to be formed from the menstrual blood. Pregnancy, as well as menstruation, is primitively considered to be dependent upon or due to the moon. The Papuan natives, who ascribe menstruation to the moon-god's embraces, go on to explain that such attentions aroused the jealousies of the husbands. He then appointed that 'in revenge all girls and young women should bleed when he appeared, but the older and pregnant should be excepted, since in the latter case he was responsible for their condition'. The Maori expressly affirm that 'the moon is the real husband of all women', and that their mortal husband is only, as it were, a subsidiary. The Gilbert Islanders held that the first man and woman were forbidden to have sexual relations, the woman being exclusively reserved for the moon, who begat children by her. The Hindus held a similar view. The Australian aborigines represent the moon as claiming that all women belong to him by right. In Greenland, the Eskimo believe that the moon has intercourse with their women, and 'young maids are afraid to stare at the moon imagining they may get a child by the bargain'.

The belief that the moon is essential to pregnancy is found among a wide range of peoples, from the Indian tribes of Texas, where directly after their marriage the women stand naked over a bucket of water which has been exposed to the rays of the moon, to the Saorias of the Rajmaha Hills, who believe that when the moon is absent from the sky, copulation cannot result in pregnancy. 'Among all negro races the moon and generation are closely connected.'

In Central Europe it is believed that if a girl were to drink from water in which the moon is reflected and thus 'swallow the moon', she would certainly become pregnant. In Brittany the women are careful not to expose the lower part of their bodies to the rays of the moon, especially in the first and last quarters when the moon is horned, for should they do so they would at once conceive, or as they say, be 'mooned'. In Germany a pregnant woman must not linger in the moonlight lest she bear a lunatic, as also in Iceland. In Africa the waxing moon is supposed to produce male children, the waning moon female. In Cornwall there is a saying, 'No moon, no man'. In the Highlands of Scotland, girls were wont to refuse to be married except at the full moon; and in the Orkneys brides invariably visited megalithic circles, known as 'the temple of the moon', and there prayed to the lunar power.

Moles, which are commonly known as 'moon-calves', are stated by Pliny to be produced by women without sexual intercourse. The Romans held a similar notion of the regulation of pregnancy by the moon, and thought that satisfactory delivery depended upon its phases. In ancient Egypt the fertility of women was thought to depend upon the moon, and an inscription at Thebes states that 'through his agency women conceived'. The sacred bull Apis was held to be the outcome of the impregnation of a cow by the moon. In Babylon pregnancy was controlled by the moon, and the sex of the child was determined by whether the moon had a halo or not at the time of conception. The belief that a child born during the moon's eclipse would be born incomplete was held in Mexico and by Hindus and Malays.

The notion that the moon reveals to young girls their future husbands is general in Europe. It is found in England, Ireland, Brittany, Germany, France, Belgium, Portugal, Greece and among the southern Slavs. In France, girls sing to the moon: 'Lune, lune, belle lune, faites me voir en mon dormant le mari que j'aurai de mon vivant.' Girls among the Indians of the Paraguayan Chaco address an identical request to the moon. Among the southern Slavs the bridegroom at a wedding is sometimes called 'Mr Moonshine'.

The Vedic view that the moon is the real husband of all women passed over into Buddhism, and in a Buddhist legend Buddha himself was begotten by the moon. In Persia the title of the moon was 'the keeper of the seed of the bull', for, according to a very ancient myth, the primeval bull or male principle of generation deposited his seed in the moon. In ancient Babylon the moon-god, Sinn, is also a bull. The Greeks and Romans retained the memory of similar views.

It is a world-wide custom for mothers to hold their new-born children up to the moon, which is beneficial to the child. Sir James Frazer regards this as an act of sympathetic magic, the growth of the child being assimilated to that of the waxing moon. But actually among the Kashubs the waxing of the moon is regarded as causing weakness in the child; it is the waning which imparts strength. The true explanation is indicated by the Isubu of the Cameroons; when the mother shows the child to the moon she says, 'This is your grandfather'. And among the Kaffirs of South Africa, when a mother presents a child to the moon, she says, 'See, your child is growing'. So also among the Pelew Islanders.

It is true that conception is also ascribed to many other causes, e.g. to eating the totem animal. But the totem or tribal spirit is frequently confounded in primitive thought with the cosmic deity or moon-god, and usually identified with him. In Western Australia impregnation is ascribed both to the totem animal and to the moon. Numerous other agencies are credited with producing pregnancy, but many of these are also emanations of the moon. Supernatural impregnation is often by water—but everywhere waters are regarded as being under the control of and derived from the moon; or it takes place through the medium of flowers, especially the lotus and its analogue, the lily. But these are moon-emblems. In India the moon is called 'the Lord of the Lotus', and in Egypt and Babylon the lotus was the emblem both of water and of the moon deity.

Again, the sun frequently appears as the cause of impregnation—a world-wide notion among agricultural peoples, but at this phase of cultural evolution all the attributes, and especially the fertilizing attributes, of the moon have, as we shall see, been transferred to the sun.

The Moon Primitively a Male

In primitive thought the moon is generally regarded a male. In primitive mythology all spirits or gods are male or female as suits the occasion, and primitive thought finds no incongruity in this. This does not mean that the personified power is thought of as bisexual or asexual; on the contrary. Primitive mythical conceptions are not a system of theology; everyone is at liberty to regard a power as male or female, as circumstances demand. This is particularly the case with lunar deities, who commonly have a male and female form. The female lunar deities do not become prominent until relatively advanced phases of culture, and, in particular, until the development of agriculture. In every instance it would seem that the conception of the moon as male is the more ancient. Thus among the Australian aborigines the moon is exclusively regarded as a male; the sun, on the other hand, is female. The moon is preeminently male in New Guinea and in Melanesia. In Polynesia the moon is currently feminine, but in old myths it is represented as male. Among the agricultural populations of Indonesia it is feminine but among the more primitive populations it is masculine. It is male among the Eskimo and the races of North-west America, and often remains male even after the development of considerable agricultural activities. It is still male in Mexico and among the Caribbean races of Central America, and among most, if not all, of the tribes of South America. It is male among Mongolian tribes and Tartar populations, and among the Japanese. With the Chinese the moon is a goddess, but in popular tradition it is represented as a man. It is male in Indian mythology and among the Nagas, the Todas, the Khasis, the Shans, the Siamese; as also among the ancient Persians and the Armenians. In all Semitic languages the moon is masculine and the sun feminine. The same is true among all the more primitive tribes of Africa, among the Slavs, the Finns, in Scandinavia and in Iceland, as well as among all Teutonic races. The moon was male among our own Anglo-Saxon ancestors, and the word remained masculine in English up to the time when arbitrary genders disappeared from the language. It still remains male in English folklore, which knows only the man in the moon. Our habit of regarding the moon as female is due only to our training in classical mythology—but even in Greece and Rome the moon was originally masculine. It was universally masculine among the Celts. In France, where classical tradition has been prolonged, the moon is feminine, but among the Bretons and the Basques the original sex reappears.

The Moon as a Source of Magical Power

But while the moon, as 'the real husband of all women', is thought of as a male, it is at the same time associated with the functions, not of men but of women, It is the source, not only of their reproductive powers but of all their other powers, and especially of their magical powers.

The moon is everywhere regarded as the source of magic; the 'Lord of the Women' is also the Lord of witches and magicians. Thus among the North American Indians the moon was 'the chief of manitus', or wizards. Among the Eskimo the power of the 'angakut' derives from the moon, and when he is in a trance his spirit is transferred to it. A Chukchi shaman 'when he desires to make especially powerful incantations, must strip himself naked, and go out of his house when the moon is shining' to invoke the moon. The Tartars of Central Asia consider that women can practise witchcraft only once a month, at the new moon; and in India witchcraft must be performed by moonlight.

Many other instances can be given. On the Gold Coast the same word means both moon and witchcraft. In ancient Greece all witchcraft was held to derive from the moon, and the moon-goddess, Hekate, was the special patroness of witches. It is still held by Greek peasants that no witch can work without the aid of the moon. In the Shetlands a witch, to strengthen her powers, lay for hours in the moonlight to become thoroughly saturated with its influence. Among the survivals of pagan-

ism especially condemned in the Carolingian capitularies is the belief
that women can exercise witchcraft by means of the moon. In Germany
deeds of witchcraft are particularly looked for on Mondays. Cornelius
Agrippa, to reconcile this view with astrological doctrine, said that,
though magical power came from all heavenly bodies, it could only be
transmitted to the earth and its inhabitants by the intermediary of the
moon.

The fascination which woman exercises, her beauty (which many
uncultured peoples regard as a form of witchcraft) is also bestowed by
the moon. The Vedas state that woman's beauty is derived from the
moon, and is promoted by eating the flesh of the moon-hare, or by
applying preparations obtained from it. The beauty of women is expressed in all Oriental languages, as well as in Southern Europe and in
Polynesia, by assimilating it to the moon. The moon-goddesses are the
goddesses of beauty and love.

The faculty of prophecy is likewise derived from the moon. 'The
ancients', says Lydus, 'regarded the moon as the leader in all divination.' In primitive Greece and among the Semites all oracles originally
derived their inspiration from lunar deities.

The Moon as Cause of Time and as Destiny

The association of the moon with prophecy derives from the fact that
throughout primitive culture the moon is the only measure of time. The
solar year is a relatively late discovery, made possible only by ingenious
astronomical observations. The cycle of seasonal changes is, of course,
visible to all peoples living in temperate climes, but this affords no fixed
point which can serve to measure duration. Throughout the greater part
of human development the moon, whose name in our language is from
the root 'mas', measure, 'mensura', has been the sole marker of time.
Even in cultures so advanced as Islam the sun is never thought of as
affording a measure of time. That function belongs to the moon. 'God
created the moon and appointed its 'houses',' says the Koran, 'in order
that men might know the number of the years and the measure of time.'

But in the primitive mind the function of the moon is not simply to
measure time but to create it. The word moon is not derived from
'measure'—the word 'measure' is derived from the name of the moon.
It is the cause of time, just as it is the cause of menstruation. Hence the
moon stands for the conception of fate or destiny which pervades the
thought of uncultured humanity.

Further, the moon, as we shall see in greater detail, stands in primitive
thought for perpetual renewal, immortality, eternity. The Siouan tribes
of America, for example, called her 'the Old Woman who never dies'.
Her name, Aataentsic, among the Iroquois tribes means 'the Eternal

One'. In Polynesia, the moon was regarded as possessing the secret of immortality; she was perpetually renewed. Among the Chams, the moon has the gift of eternal youth; she is never more than thirty. Similarly among the Chinese. Among the ancient Egyptians the moon was 'the maker of eternity and creator of everlastingness'. In Latin inscriptions her epithet is 'the eternal'. In Russia she is 'the deathless one'.

In primitive thought the eternal time-creating nature of the moon imparts to it an inexorable character, setting it above all other powers. The Iroquois recognized that there was a power above that of all 'manitus', whose decrees were unalterable. This conception, which has its parallel in all primitive mythologies, corresponds to that of the Greek Moira, who stood above the gods. But the Moira, or the three Moirai, or Fates, were originally the moon. 'The Moirai', says Porphyry, 'are referred to the power of the moon', and in Orphic writing they are spoken of as parts of the moon. Destiny is assimilated by Sophocles to the moon. The Arabian goddess, Manat, was the moon and was also Fate. The Teutonic Norns, like the Greek Moirai, were moon-goddesses and were 'older than the gods'.

Mr Cornford has shown the attributes of the Greek Moirai to be the prototype of the scientific conception of natural law; he points out that the Greek conception of Moira, or Fate, is essentially that of a dividing divinity and measurer of lots, who apportioned his special sphere of activity and functions, not only to every human being but also to every god. These are likewise the functions of the primitive mother, who allots to each his portion of food, and who, in early agricultural phases of culture, is also the apportioner of cultivable land.

Lunar Divinities commonly Triune

Like the Moirai, lunar deities are usually threefold. Among many uncultured peoples the waxing, the full and waning moons had three different names and were conceived as three different persons. Thus in New Britain the moon consists of the 'White Woman' and her two sons, the waxing and the waning moon. Among the natives of Northern Ashanti 'it is well-known that the satellite is inhabited by three beings, similar to men in appearance but provided with enormous ears which completely cover their faces. One of these is white and the other two black'. In Dahomey the badge of moon-priestesses consists of a white shell and two black beads. The Indians of New Granada represent their lunar deity by three crosses, one large one flanked by two smaller ones. The month was divided into three parts among the Germans and the Celts, as likewise among the Greeks, the Romans and the Semites.

Countless triads of Greek goddesses, such as the three Charities, the three Horai, the three Syrens, the three Hesperides, the three Gorgons, the three Erinyes, are primitively scarcely distinguishable from one another or from the Moirai. The Muses were originally also three in number, and were deities of the night heavens, governing the stars. The Mothers, Nurses or Nymphs, who bring up infant gods, are also forms of the Moirai, who preside over the destiny of every child, and were, like them, threefold. These triads of Hellenic goddesses were regarded at will as one or three. They were triune, or three in one. Like them, the great goddess of the Semites was worshipped at Mecca in threefold form as three sacred trees, and was spoken of as the Three Virgins. In Phœnicia and Carthage, as in Krete and ancient Greece, the great goddess was represented by three pillars. The Jewish god, Yahweh, appeared in the form of three men whom Abraham addressed as one. Threefold deities are prominent among the races of Northern Europe and among the Celts. Thus Brigit, the Norns, the Walkyries had the threefold character. They were impersonated by three priestesses who officiated over the birth of every child. They became the three weird sisters. The three Fatal Sisters survive in popular tradition as the three fairies, or fays. In many of the stories in which they figure two of them are deformed and one of them is rounded and beautiful like the full moon. Just as the moon-god of the Ashanti is black in two persons and white in the third, so the Erinyes were similarly two parts black and one white.

The principle by which the threefold division of the month was applied to lunar deities has sometimes been extended to solar and other deities. Thus Zeus has been described as having three hundred heads, corresponding to the three hundred days of the year. More frequently, however, the threefold character of lunar deities having once set the pattern, other deities are represented as triune. Thus Zeus was represented at Corinth with three eyes. Similarly the ancient Mexicans worshipped their gods as a trinity denoted by three crosses. The heathen Slavs similarly represented their deity with three heads. The Nordic gods were worshipped at Upsala as a trinity.

The profane mimicry of the mysteries of the Christian religion by heathens has naturally been a cause of annoyance to missionaries. 'It is strange', says Father d'Acosta, 'that the Divell, after his manner, hath brought a trinitie into idolatry, for the three images of the Sunne called Apomti, Churunti, and Intiquaoqui, which signifieth father and lord Sunne, the sonne Sunne, and the brother Sunne. . . . I remember that being in Chuquisaca, an honourable priest showed me an information, which I had long in my handes, where it was prooved that there was a certaine "huaca", or oratory, whereas the Indians did worship an idoll called Tangatanga, which they saide was one in three, and three in one.

And as the priest stood amazed thereat, I saide that the Divell by his infernall and obstinate pride (whereby he alwayes pretendes to make himself God) did steale all that he could from the trueth to imploy it in his lyings and deceits.'

Pagan symbolizm has been extensively adopted in Christian myth. Thus the three Moirai, or Mothers, have survived as the three Maries, the three daughters of Holy Sophia, who is stated to be the moon, or as Faith, Hope and Charity. In a shrine at Vallepietra, near Anagni, a threefold Christ is held in high repute (Fig. 1). Even cruder ikons were common until lately, representing God with three heads, or with three faces (Fig. 2). The Church did its best to put down this disguised

FIG. 2
A Triune Christ from a Mission Chapel in Bolivia (F. Keller, *The Amazon and Madeira Rivers,* p. 158).

FIG. 1
The Christ of Vallepietra

heathenism; Pope Urban VIII had a number of three-headed gods removed from the churches of Italy, and in 1628, caused these Holy Trinities to be publicly burned.

The Moon as the Source of Lunacy

Lunacy, 'demoniac phrenzy, moping melancholy and moon-struck madness', are universally regarded as caused by the moon. Mental derangement is also a qualification for the prophetic, magic or saintly character. The powers of the prophet, magician or priest are thought to depend upon inspiration or possession, and are manifested by various nervous phenomena—convulsions, trances, hypnosis, somnambulism. The word 'shaman', like the Greek word 'mainad', means 'the raging one'. Aspirants to prophetic and magic powers seek to cultivate nervous hyperaesthesia and instability. In Egypt, 'they look upon all madmen, imbeciles, lunatics, and such as are afflicted with the falling sickness, as saints'. Lunacy is regarded with reverence throughout the East. The ancient Hebrews held that 'the prophet is a fool, the man that hath the spirit is mad'. The Baralonga honour demented persons, 'believing them to be under the direct influence of their tutelary deities'. 'Regard for lunatics is a universal trait among the American tribes.' 'The association of poetry, prophecy and idiocy', observes Sir John Rhys, 'is so thoroughly Celtic as to need no remark.'

Not insanity alone, but every disease involving convulsions, is ascribed to the moon. Epilepsy, 'the sacred disease', was formerly spoken of as lunacy. Jesus, for instance, cured 'lunatics', σεληνιαζομένοι, which word is translated in the R.V. as 'epileptics'.

Lunar Animals: the Dog, the Hare, the Cat

Hekate's attendant animal was the dog, which worshipped her by barking at the moon, and announced her coming by howling. The Peruvians, during eclipses of the moon, used to beat their dogs to make them howl, 'thinking her affectioned to dogges'; so did the Hurons and Iroquois, while the Apache honoured the moon by yelping. Sometimes an Indian, having shot a dog, found the corpse of a woman.

The association in primitive thought between witches and the moon is illustrated by the connection of both with certain animals. It is a widespread notion that witches may assume the form of a hare. 'The hare', says Mr Henderson, 'is the commonest disguise of the witch in all the northern countries of Europe.' He has 'personally heard of and known many women who were regarded as having the power of shifting themselves into hare-shape'. In Wales, 'only the women can become hares'. In the Isle of Man witches regularly become hares; there is one instance of a man doing so, but he was a smith and thus a warlock. In Scotland a witch-hare cannot be hit with ordinary shot, but can be wounded with a crooked sixpence. In many stories found all over the world the wounded animal enters a cottage, and the hunter, following, finds there a bleeding, wounded woman.

The transformation is sometimes effected in a manner reminiscent of totemic rituals; namely, by the witch anointing herself with hare's fat. Indeed, hare's fat is believed to bring out the witch-nature of any woman, as was believed in medieval Europe. Dalla Porta describes how modest women 'set a lamp with characters graved upon it, and filled it with hare's fat; then they mumble forth some words and light it. When it burns in the middle of women's company, it constrains them all to cast off their clothes, and voluntarily to show themselves naked unto men; they behold all their privities which otherwise would be covered, and the women will never leave dancing so long as the lamp burns'.

For a hare to cross one's path is regarded as most unlucky. In Scotland, Ireland and Brittany the very word must never be mentioned. Sailors believe that the presence of a dead hare on board ship will cause bad weather. In France to eat hare's flesh is regarded as making women more attractive; that is, imparting to them powers of bewitching men. Hare's flesh was eaten for this purpose in ancient Rome. Eating hare's flesh is also believed to render women fertile. According to a widespread belief among the Jews, Greeks and Chinese, all hares are female and are impregnated by the moon. The antiquity of their association with witchcraft among the Celts is testified by the fact that Queen Boadicea, when opposing the Roman armies, drew a hare from her bosom and followed its guidance in directing her attacks.

The hare is also widely associated with the moon throughout India, where the moon is called the 'bearer of the hare'. In Tibet and among the Mongols of Central Asia, as in China and Japan, the spots in the moon are interpreted as a hare, put there by a great magician, a myth which is found as far south as Ceylon. The hare plays a prominent part in folklore throughout South Africa. 'He is a small creature, but with one exception all the animals are as clay in his hands'; and is often regarded as the messenger of the moon, who pronounced upon mankind the doom of mortality.

Such myths are equally popular among the Indians of North America, but the hare is often substituted by the rabbit, never clearly distinguished from the hare. There can be little doubt that the Great Hare, the most familiar form of the Great Manitu among the Iroquois nations, was originally the moon. Hekate was a hare, and in Karia was worshipped as the hare-goddess, and her chief shrine was at Lagina, the hare-city. Artemis was a hare and hares were sacred to her. Even in the present day, in some parts of Albania they 'consider it a sin to kill a hare'. Dionysos, who was a moon-god, changed himself into a hare.

The close association of the hare with witches and with the moon is found in Northern Europe equally. The part which the hare played in the agricultural cult of the ancient Germans is indicated by the importance attached to it in connection with Easter. It is the Easter-hare which lays the Easter eggs, and it figures in association with them in Easter cards. Much circumstantial evidence indicates that it occupied an equally important place in the Celtic cults of Great Britain and Ireland. The custom of hunting the Easter-hare was kept up until lately with much pomp by the mayor and aldermen of Leicester. We know that the hare was tabu as food to the ancient Britons, and that it was eaten as a sacred food by the kings of Ireland. The hare upon which Boadicea relied was probably the sacred animal of her goddess.

Why is the hare so universally associated with the moon? There can be little doubt that its original relation to the lunar deity was sacrificial. In the cults which belong especially to women, the animals sacrificed are almost invariably small animals, such as birds, dogs, rabbits, hares and pigs, for women are seldom able to obtain the large animals used in sacrifice by hunters and herdsmen. Furthermore, the moon's fructifying powers are paralleled by the fertility of the rabbit or hare, which in Aztec hieroglyphics had the same ideogram as does the earth.

In West Africa the cat is the commonest animal into which a witch may change, and was the usual disguise of the familiar spirit of witches in Western Europe. The cat is accordingly credited with having nine lives, with being able to see in the dark and with being able to cause storms. It is a widespread superstition in Europe that a cat washing herself behind the ears forebodes rain, while in Asia Minor rain is expected if a cat licks her paws. In Indonesia to compel a cat to wash herself is considered a good way to bring about a good downpour; while the natives of southern Celebes, when there is a drought, carry a cat round the fields in a sedan-chair, squirting water over it. In the Middle Ages heretics were commonly accused of worshipping cats. The Cathari were said, erroneously, to have derived their name from the practice, and the charge was brought against the Knights Templar. The Stadinghi, a heretical sect of the thirteenth century, were accused in a Papal Bull of the crime of keeping black cats.

The important part played by cats in the ritual of witches 'is clearly derived from an early form of sacrifice'. Shakespeare appears to refer to the practice, and the sacrifice of cats to produce rain is widespread. In Bohemia and in Russia a black cat is buried alive in a field to promote the fertility of the land; and in some parts of Lancashire it is still thought that to shut the cat up in the oven promotes good luck. Cats are supposed to become fat or lean with the waxing or waning of the moon, and Cornelius Agrippa says their eyes grow wider or narrower according to its phases. They are 'lunar animals, and are of the same nature as menstrual blood, with which many wonderful, miraculous things are wrought by magicians'. The Australian aborigines and Tasmanians identify the moon with a wild cat, and the North American Indians believe that there is a cat in the moon. The cat was sacred to the goddess Freija, who rode on a chariot drawn by cats; and in Egypt cats were sacrosanct. So abundant are cat-mummies in Egypt that shiploads of them have been brought to Europe to use as manure. According to Plutarch, the cat in Egypt denoted the moon. 'Though this may look like a fiction, yet there can be no doubt that the eyes of cats seem to grow larger at the full moon, and to decrease again and diminish in brightness upon the waning.'

The Moon as Spinstress

All feminine attributes, not only fertility and magic, are dependent upon the moon. One of the activities most commonly ascribed to it is spinning and weaving. The moon is a spinster in innumerable folk-tales in Germany and Italy, and the same idea is found among the North American Indians, in Central Brazil, in the Banks Islands and elsewhere. In Borneo the moon assumes the form of a spider. In ancient Egypt, the moon-goddess, Neith, invented weaving. Artemis, Athene, Aphrodite and the Nymphs were spinstresses, as was the Nordic goddess, Freija, and the Teutonic goddesses, Holda and Bertha. The hare is also found in folk-tale as a weaver. Jewish women did their spinning and weaving by moonlight, while German women held that spinning must on no account be done by moonlight. The Dayaks believed a woman could not weave beautiful patterns without the inspiration of her divine protectress.

It is natural enough to connect the moon as a measurer of duration with the spinning of the thread, or the weaving of the web of time and destiny. Nevertheless, the primary connection between such pursuits and the moon was probably not poetical, but more direct, for the moon is engaged in almost every other occupation belonging to primitive women. It is known as a maker of bark-cloth, as a basket-maker, pot-maker, grinder of seeds, maker of fires and as a cook. Among the Eskimo the fires of the sun are stoked up by the lunar deity.

In Europe the man in the moon is most commonly shown as carrying a load of firewood, which is interpreted as a punishment for Sabbath-breaking, and in some popular myths he is Cain or Judas Iscariot. The representation, however, is much older than Christianity. The Yoruba of the Gold Coast see a Sabbath-breaker in the moon who carries a load of firewood, and the same idea is found among all the southern Bantu. The firewood of the man in the moon has baffled many. But the gathering of firewood is simply one of the occupations of primitive women. Among the Banyoro the first act of a bride, after marriage, is to draw a small pitcher of water from a well and to gather a small bundle of sticks. 'The drawing of water and the carrying of fuel typified', says the Rev. J. Roscoe, 'the duties of the wife.'

The Moon regarded as the Producer of Vegetation

In tradition, there are trees and shrubs in the moon. In some representations the moon-man is surrounded by thorn bushes. Thorn bushes were sacred among the Celts and Teutons, and were used for cremating the dead. Trees are observed in the moon in various Molucca Islands, in Melanesia, in the Malay Peninsula, in China and in Sweden. In modern Greece the man in the moon, who is Cain, is engaged in cutting down a tree which grows again every month. The same notion is current in China.

One of the most prominent attributes of the moon is, in fact, that of producer of all vegetable life: it is known among the Brazilians as the 'Mother of Vegetables'; among the agricultural tribes of North America as the 'Mother' of corn, and is assimilated by the Cherokee to the maize itself. This notion is also found in many other parts of the world. Thus in India, the moon is known as 'the bearer of seed, the bearer of plants', and is identified with some, 'the Lord of Plants'. The Caribs picture the world as having arisen from a gigantic tree, resembling the world-tree of Nordic mythology, Yggdrasil, which in the Völuspa is called 'the tree that metes out the fate of men'. It is also the Tree of Mimir, who appears to have been an ancient Nordic moon-god. All Semitic moon deities were similarly associated with trees and sacred bushes, while in the Admiralty Islands the moon is identified with the coconut-palm. On some Babylonian cylinders, the moon-god is represented as the trunk of a tree with branches growing from every part of his person. In Krete and archaic Greece also lunar deities were worshipped as trees.

The moon is particularly identified with the juices of vegetables and the sap of trees, which is supposed to rise and fall with the phases of the moon; hence the rule that timber must be felled at the waning of the moon. The juices of vegetables are regarded as their life-blood or soul, and so as the life-blood or soul of the moon. Accordingly the highest forms of divine inspiration are attained by drinking the juice of the soma, or, in South America, the concoction known as chicha, or the juice of the grape, which was regarded in Western Asia as the blood of the deity. To chew the leaves or fibres of the lunar plant is a necessary preliminary to divine and prophetic inspiration. Among the Semites, those trees which exude thick saps of aromatic gum were regarded with special reverence, and the fluid was employed as incense. 'The value of the gum acacia as an amulet', says W. Robertson Smith, 'is connected with the idea that it is a clot of menstruous blood, i.e. that the tree is a woman.' The moon was thus the divine counterpart of the primitive cultivator of the soil. Hence the presence of trees and shrubs in the moon.

The Moon as Controller of Moisture

The moon has, by universal consent, control of all water and moisture, as part of her office of bringing forth vegetation. Primitive women secure the fertility of the earth by watering it and by performing rain-making incantations, in which they are assisted by the moon. According to the Eskimo, snow comes directly from the moon. In British Columbia the moon is represented as bearing water-pitchers. The Indians looked upon the moon as being the actual cause of rains and gods, and among the Algonkin tribes the terms for moon and water were the same. Similarly the serpent goddess of Mexico, who was the moon, was also the goddess of water and the ocean. The moon is represented in Maya manuscripts by a pitcher of water. The idea that the moon is ruler over waters is found in China and Japan, in Central Australia and Central Asia, in Brazil and in many other parts of the world.

Frogs who croak to the moon never fail to obtain rain from him. In the Ganges valley, the women, when there is a drought, slowly crush a frog to death, and its croaking is believed to be an infallible rain-charm. The frog, often interchangeable in myth with the toad and with the dragon, is a universal emblem of water and the moon. Among the Pueblos, the frog-clans are the rain-making clans, and the great goddess of Mexico, who is the moon and the ruler of waters, was represented by a huge emerald frog. The North American Indians see in the moon the 'Primeval Toad', which contained all the waters of the world and caused the flood by discharging them. Many races, e.g. the Chinese, see a frog in the moon. The toad is also regarded as an emblem of the womb; and in Germany women suffering from uterine troubles present images of toads to the Virgin Mary. In Semitic mythology the moon deity is invariably the controller of water and the primal ocean out of which all things arose. So, also among the Greeks and the Romans, the moon was regarded as the source of all moisture. This list could be lengthened almost indefinitely: medieval writers supported the idea. 'Water', says Cornelius Agrippa, 'is the lunar element, the water of the sea as well as that of rivers, and all things humid, the humours of trees and of animals, and more especially those humours that are white, such as the white of eggs, fat sweat, pituitary discharge and superfluities of the body.'

The notion that the moon is 'the governess of floods' persists among ourselves in the notion that the phases of the moon are related to changes in the weather, an idea which persists in spite of repeated demonstrations of its falsity. It is anything but obvious why on grounds of mere nature symbolism the moon should be universally associated with moisture. The connection between the moon and the tides appears to be unknown to most uncultured peoples. Those daring seafarers, the Polynesians, had no such notion and thought them due to the presence of a huge monster which breathed twice a day. If any connection between the tides and the moon is recognized by some uncultured peoples, probably it is deduced by them from the moon's character as ruler of the waters, and not the other way about.

On the other hand, nothing would be more logical than that the source of magical power should be the controller of the waters upon which fertility depends. Woman is the primitive water-carrier and also the primitive rain-maker. The two functions, practical and magical, are scarcely distinguished from one another. The drawing of water and the watering of the fields are regarded as magical operations, and are carried out with the solemnity of a ritual.

In short, the attributes of the moon in primitive thought are not the products of poetic symbolism, but are the transferred characters and activities of primitive women, which are regarded as being derived from and controlled by the magic power of the moon. Everywhere—from China to Peru, from Tierra del Fuego to the Arctic—the moon is regarded as the counterpart of women, their special deity, the controller of their beings and the source of their powers. 'The nature of women', as Rabelais says, 'is figured by the moon.'

Now, just as the functions of the moon-deity reflect woman's share in the sexual division of labour, so also the moon's supremacy as the primitive cosmic power is the counterpart of the magical powers of primitive woman. Hence wherever we find the moon pre-eminent, we are entitled to conclude that women are, or were, pre-eminent too. This is perhaps why Spartian says: 'All the learned, especially in Harran, believe that those who honour the moon as a female deity and give it a feminine name remain for ever enslaved to their women, but those who worship it as a male deity and give it a corresponding name, rule over their women.' Likewise, according to Palgrave, our Anglo-Saxon ancestors 'had an odd notion that if they addressed that power as a goddess, their wives would be their masters'.

CHAPTER 20

The Resurrection and the Life

The Serpent and Eternal Life

WITH the fall of man and the origin of death, with woman and the moon, who are held responsible for these disasters, is associated the serpent, an animal which plays a larger part in religious myth than any other. In all symbolism it is the emblem of immortality because, instead of dying, it changes its skin. Uncultured peoples hold the serpent to be the only animal (together with lizards and other reptiles, and also crabs, which are regarded as equivalent) which possesses the gift of immortality. Savages, it should be remembered, do not regard death as a natural event, but ascribe it to witchcraft—woman's witchcraft, or, what is the same thing, the moon's. True, the effects of old age are recognized in the wrinkling of the skin; the natives of British Columbia consider that men die because their skin is too soft. If men could change their skins as serpents do, they would also be immortal.

The belief that the first human beings preserved their immortal nature by this faculty, and that serpents were involved in its loss, is very widespread. Thus the Tsimshian of British Columbia relate that their tribal hero, or first man, applied to the moon-god for the gift of renewed youth. The divine physician purified him by bathing him, and his skin fell from him in the form of scales, leaving him as white as snow. The tribes of central California say that death was introduced among men by the machinations of the lizards, who obtained from men the power of changing their skin; before this men did not die, but merely moulted— a view also held by the Caribs. The ancient Mexicans also had a god, Xipe Totec—originally a moon-god, but regarded later as a god of vegetation—who regularly renewed his youth by putting on a new skin. Again, the Arawak of the Orinoco tell how a boy was swallowed by a serpent and re-emerged, to the admiration of his friends, with a new skin, which was mottled like a serpent's. We come upon an almost identical story in Australia.

Some Australian tribes believe that the dead put on incorruptibility by an opposite process; instead of being swallowed, they themselves eat a serpent. In New Caledonia the serpent is replaced by a sea-monster, but fishes and serpents are often interchanged in popular conceptions.

In Tonga the god Tangaroa, who is a lizard, is said to have sent his two sons with their wives to people the island. One of those sons was all that a son should be, but the other turned out badly. So Tangaroa appointed that the good son and his descendants should have white skins and should go to the land of the immortals; but the bad son and his people were condemned to have black skins and to remain in Tonga. The same story is told in Samoa, but the personages are lizards.

In the languages of Melanesia the term for 'to slough one's skin' is equivalent to 'living for ever'. In the New Hebrides the origin of death is accounted for in the following story: an old woman went down to the sea and, casting off her old wrinkled skin, as lobsters cast their shells, she became a young and beautiful woman. But her grandchild failed to recognize her in her disguise, and would not let her take her in her arms. So she returned to the sea and put on the old skin. The same story is told with unimportant variations throughout most parts of Melanesia; we find it again in Papua.

The myth takes another form in the New Hebrides, in the island of Ambryn. The two gods, Barkolkol and Buglian, who respectively represent the bright aspect and the dark aspect of the moon, created man. When man began to age and his skin grew wrinkled; Buglian said to Barkolkol: 'Our man is getting wrinkled, what shall we do?' Barkolkol replied: 'We will skin him like an eel; he will grow a new skin like the serpent, and thus he will be made young.' But Buglian said: 'No. When he is old and ugly, we will dig a hole in the earth, and put him in it.' In a similar story from the Gazelle Peninsula of New Britain the good god Kambinana said to his wicked and foolish brother Korvouva: 'Go down to the men and tell them to cast their skins, so shall they avoid death. But tell the serpents that they must henceforth die.' But Korvouva, the fool, reversed the message. The Annamites also regard mankind as having been defrauded of immortality by the serpents, who so terrified the god's messenger that he reversed the god's message.

The same notions are widely current throughout Africa. In the forests of the upper basin of the Congo, an account of the origin of death is current similar to that which is so widespread in Melanesia. The first man, it is said, had two wives. In course of time their skins began to get wrinkled. The elder wife then went to a hut, and proceeded to take off her old skin, and laid it down on the winnowing fan. Unfortunately the second wife happened to need that implement and went to the hut to fetch it; there she saw her co-wife radiant with renewed beauty. But the process of renewal had not been quite completed, and her entry broke the spell, causing both women to fall dead; death was thus introduced into the world. The serpent, on the other hand, never dies, and cannot be killed unless it is completely crushed.

This myth of a disastrous error or fraud is common. Among the Gallas, tradition asserts that the order to slough their skin was by mistake delivered to the serpents instead of to the human race. Similarly the Wafipa and Wabende of the shores of Lake Tanganyika relate that God once asked the creatures of the earth, 'Who wishes not to die?' Unfortunately all were asleep except the serpent, which answered, 'I do.' The Sea Dayaks have the same story.

In the more common African form of the tradition the lizard is the chief means of defrauding mankind of the gift of immortality. Thus, for example, among some Basuto tribes it is related how the good king Leobu, grieved at the sufferings of his people, decided to send his own beloved son to announce the good news that they should not die but have life everlasting. The king's instructions were, however, overheard by a professional runner, whose name was Khatoane—that is, the Lizard —and he ran to the people and gave them the opposite message. In a Zulu version, the chameleon is sent with the message 'Let not men die', and the lizard with the message 'Let men die'. The lizard naturally arrives first. This story, in slightly varying forms, is current throughout the greater part of Africa, from the Cape to the Sahara.

Identical conceptions were familiar to the ancient Greeks. The term by which they spoke of the cast skin of a serpent was $\gamma \tilde{\eta} \rho \alpha \varsigma$, that is to say 'old age'. Aelian tells how Zeus, taking pity on man, decided to bestow immortality on him, sending the gift on the back of the donkey. The donkey, however, was defrauded of his burden by a serpent in exchange for a drink. In another story, the wise Polyidos brings about the resurrection of Glaucus, the infant son of King Minos, who died from falling into a cask of honey, by rubbing the child with certain herbs, with which he had seen a snake resurrect a dead companion. In another version, Glaucus obtains possession of the herb of immortality—from the moon-hare. (The idea that the moon-hare possesses this herb is also found in China.)

The ancient Egyptians likewise associated immortality with the serpent. In a passage of the 'Book of the Dead', the deceased prays that he may become like a serpent. 'I am the serpent Sata, whose years are many', he says; 'I die and I am born again. I am the serpent Sata which dwelleth in the uttermost parts of the earth. I die and I am born again, and I renew myself, and I grow young each time.'

In the Gilgamesh epic, one of the most ancient literary monuments of the world, a story exactly similar to that of Glaucus is told. In Genesis, which appears to have been largely inspired by Babylonian myths, the serpent, as in the traditions of the whole uncultured world, defrauds the human race of immortality. But the Biblical narrative has been adapted to later conceptions of Jewish theology. A Rabbinical commentary on Genesis iii. 14 explains that Adam, after the Fall, did not possess the same skin as before, his first skin having presumably been immortal; it is in consequence of thus having changed the skin of the first man that the serpent is compelled to moult his. An early Muslim doctor, drawing, no doubt, from the same traditional sources, gives further particulars. 'When the fruit had descended down Adam's throat and reached his stomach, the skin which Adam had in Paradise fell from his body. That of Eve fell off likewise, and the soft flesh of their bodies remained exposed as it is with us at the present day; for the skin which Adam had in Paradise was similar to the substance of nails. When it became detached, only a small portion of it remained on the tips of the fingers; and thereafter whenever Adam or Eve beheld the nails of their fingers, they were reminded of Paradise and its delights.'

The Redeemer Himself was likened by the apostle to the serpent: 'As Moses lifted up the serpent in the wilderness, even so must the Son of Man be lifted up: that whosoever believeth in him should not perish, but have eternal life' (John iii. 14–15).

Later, the notion that the serpent possesses the gift of immortality was a definite tenet in Europe among the alchemists and practitioners of occult arts. Serpents, being undying, are accordingly widely regarded as the spirits or souls of the departed.

Immortality Dependent on the Moon

The serpent thus shares the moon's gift of immortality. The moon itself is thought by some peoples to owe its faculty of rejuvenation to the power of casting off its old skin. The 'old women' and other personages who, in the Melanesian and Papuan myths, renew their lives by sloughing their skin are, in fact, personifications of the moon. In the languages of Melanesia the only way of expressing the notion of eternity is the phrase 'ul ta marama'; that is to say, 'casting off one's skin like the moon'. So when the missionaries desire to explain that God is eternal, they are obliged to say that he sloughs his skin like the moon. In Australia, the natives of Queensland believe that the moon sheds its skin every month. In Togoland, the Ewe believe that the moon has scales like a serpent and casts them off each month; while an ancient Babylonian inscription describes the body of the moon-goddess Ishtar as 'covered with scales like a snake's'. Moon-gods and moon-goddesses are usually represented as serpents.

In a more general way the moon is conceived as dying every month and as being born again after three days, and the power of men to survive every month, or the hope that they will survive after death, is regarded as being derived from the moon. Thus the eternal moon is not only the cause of death, but also the source of renewed life and resurrection. The natives of the Caroline Islands, for instance, think that men formerly went to sleep as the moon waned, slept during the three days of the interlunary period, and rose again with the new moon. Accordingly they rejoice at the appearance of the new moon, and say that they are born again. The Sakai of the Malay Peninsula relate that the moon, which falls to the earth during the three days of the interlunary period, has to be assisted back into heaven by the use of magic rites. Unless this is done, all men must die. In India it has been recognized since Vedic times that 'the moon makes life long'. At the full moon, in the month of Kuar, the Hindus place food on the house-tops; when it has thoroughly absorbed the rays of the moon the food is distributed among the family. 'This is supposed to lengthen life.' In the Upanishads the moon is represented as the cause and controller of metempsychosis. The Indians of California, as they dance before the moon sing: 'As the moon dieth and cometh to life again, so we also, having to die, will live again.' The same belief obtains among other American Indians, as it did in ancient Mexico and Peru. The ancient Babylonians prayed in much the same manner. 'May the gods', they said, 'give me a life which, like the moon, is renewed every month.' In Loango the women prayed to the new moon: 'So may I renew my life as thou art renewed.' The Christian Abyssinians address long prayers to the new moon. 'He is risen!' the women exclaim.

In the African stories in which two messengers bring respectively the message of death and the message of eternal life to mankind, the sender of the message, in what appear to be the more primitive versions of the tale, is the moon. The story is current in this form among the Bushmen. Among the Tati Bushmen the moon is said to have given the message to the tortoise. The tortoise being incredibly slow in delivering the message, the moon repeated it to the hare, which perverted it so as to make it mean the opposite of what the moon intended. The moon is the sender of the message among the Hottentots and among the Nandi and Masai of East Africa. In other versions of this widespread African myth the sender of the message is simply the personage who is most prominent in the mythology of the particular tribe or people; but it is probable that these personages were originally the moon.

In Madagascar a current myth relates that the first men were given the choice of dying like the moon or like the banana-tree; that is to say, of dying periodically and being born again, or of dying altogether, but propagating the species as does the banana-tree, by its root. The first parents foolishly chose to propagate and die like the banana-tree, and thus lost the chance of being immortal. This last version of the myth of the origin of death differs somewhat from African versions, where, as far as I know, no reference is made to the alternative of propagating like the banana. It may have been brought to Madagascar from the Indonesian region by the Hovas, for the allusion to the banana in similar myths is frequently found there among the Mantras of the Malay Peninsula, the Alfurs of Poso and on the island of Nias.

The reason the banana is chosen as an emblem of sexual propagation is probably its phallic form. It is implied in the foregoing myths, as in the narrative of Genesis, that men lost, or gave up, their hope of immortality through their fatal subjection to women and to their sexual passions. In a creation myth from the Gilbert Islands the creator, after bringing the first man and the first woman into existence, expressly forbade them to have sexual intercourse with one another, although he himself had intercourse with the woman. Propagation by sexual intercourse thus appears to be regarded in primitive thought as an alternative to eternal life. Mankind cannot have both; men must choose between the moon and the banana.

In Polynesia also stress is laid on the contrast between the immortal nature of the moon and human mortality. In various parts it is related that Maui endeavoured to obtain the gift of immortality from the relentless goddess by force. The means by which he proposed to accomplish this were identical with those by which young men in Australia, on the Gold Coast of Africa, and in Guiana, are fabled to have changed their skins, and thus, presumably, acquired a new life from serpents, namely by passing through the bodies of the monsters. Maui similarly endeavoured to jump into the mouth of Hina or, according to another version, to enter her womb. This attempt to be born again is said, however, to have ended in failure. In the Melanesian stories of the origin of death which we have noted, the bestower of life and death is the moon. The old woman who changed her skin and wished to bestow the gift of immortality on her grandchild was the goddess 'Round Head'—that is to say, the moon. The good Kambinana, who wished men to live for ever, and the wicked and foolish Korvouva, who bestowed the gift on the serpents instead, are the Melanesian gods of the full moon and of the new moon.

Similar beliefs are general among the Australian aborigines. Thus the tribes of Central Australia believe that formerly men did not die permanently, but rose again after the third day. The belief that blackfellows rise up again as 'white men' is universal in Australia. When the body of an Australian black begins to decay the loosened epidermis assumes a whitish appearance; friends assist the dead man to cast off his skin by scraping it off with shells. The ghosts of Australian blackfellows are, in fact, white; and in the corroborees the dancers, who are supposed to impersonate them, paint themselves white with a preparation of pipe-clay, which they call 'the moon'. Thus in the most intimate beliefs of peoples in the five parts of the world, the gift of renewed life, the hope of resurrection and life everlasting, are connected with the moon and the serpent.

The Serpent as Representative of the Moon

Among the founders of European civilization also, immortality is derived at times from the moon, at times from the serpent. In one of the Greek myths of Glaucus, the secret of resurrection is acquired from a serpent; in another version from the moon-hare. Endymion derived his eternally renewed youth directly from the moon. The serpent and the moon are similarly interchangeable in the beliefs and myths of the peoples of Melansia, Australia, Indonesia and Asia, Africa and America. The association between the moon and the serpent is thus clearly founded upon the possession by both of the gift of immortality through perpetual renewal, and the serpent is accordingly regarded as a form of personification of the moon. Amongst the Greeks it was a popular belief—Aristotle gravely reported it as a fact—that serpents have as many ribs as there are days in the lunar month. The Pawnee Indians believe serpents to be subject to the moon. The Iroquois thought that the moon fed on serpents. Among the Algonkin tribes the serpent 'crowned with the lunar crescent was a constant symbol of life in their picture-writing.' Their mythical 'grandmother', the moon-goddess Aataentsic, was represented either as an old woman or as a serpent. In Mexico the serpent-woman was the moon-goddess. In Australia, serpents are the 'dogs' of the moon. In Uganda the sacred serpents' festival took place on the day of the new moon. Among the ancient Hindus the Naga kings, or Serpent-people, who were supposed to be descended from a serpent, were known as the Lunar dynasty.

So intimate is this association that it may safely be laid down that, wherever we find the serpent in symbolism or worship, we may confidently expect to find a lunar cult. In the religions of civilized societies, as well as in those of uncultured peoples, serpent deities are lunar deities. In India the great serpent 'that had been worshipped there since the world began' is specially associated with the moon-worship of the ancient Aryas. Among all Semitic peoples the serpent is the avatar of the moon deity. The moon goddesses of Hellenic cults were associated with serpents. The Arcadian Artemis, Hekate, Persephone, hold serpents in their hands. The Erinys, Gorgons, Graia are serpent-goddesses whose hairs are serpents. There is a popular superstition in Central Europe that a hair plucked from a woman who is under the influence of the moon—i.e. who is menstruating—will, if buried, turn into a serpent. The hairs of a witch, according to Breton tales, turn into serpents. The notion is current in Japan. 'The myth of Medusa has many counterparts in Japanese folklore, the subject of such tales being always some wonderfully beautiful girl whose hair turns to snakes only at night, and who is discovered at last to be a dragon's daughter. But in ancient times it was believed that the hair of any young woman might change to serpents—for instance, under the influence of repressed jealousy,' All women, being more or less witches, are thus thought to have something of the serpent in them. It is said in the Congo that at the time of the great flood all human beings, through fright or otherwise, resumed their original shape; the men turned into monkeys and the women into lizards. A mediaeval legend asserts that women were made out of the legs of the serpent, which lost its limbs as it entered Paradise. It is supposed to be not uncommon for women to give birth to serpents and other reptiles. 'Neither is it hard', says Dalla Porta, 'to generate toads of women's putrefied flowers; for women do breed this kind of cattel, together with their children . . . as frogs, toads, lyzards, and such like; and the women of Salerium, in times past, were wont to use the juice of parsley and leeks, at the beginning of their conception, and especially at the time of their quickening, thereby to destroy this kind of vermin with them. A certain woman lately married, being in all men's judgment great with child, brought forth instead of a child, four creatures like frogs, and after had perfect health. But this was a kind of Moon-calf.'

In a Tartar poem the hero finds it impossible to kill a witch, even though her bowels be torn out of her body, for she keeps her soul in a snake. In China serpents are regarded as the source of all magical powers. In Hebrew and in Arabic the terms for magic are derived from the words meaning serpent. According to Philostratus, the Arabs held that a man acquired magical powers by eating the heart or the liver of a serpent. In Brittany supernatural powers may be acquired by drinking a broth prepared from serpents. The Iroquois regarded serpents as the usual disguise of witches, and believed that all magical powers were derived from serpents, although their source was at the same time the moon. Among the Algonkin tribes a 'manitu' was defined as 'he who walketh with a serpent'; and among the Siouan tribes the words 'manitu,' 'wakan' denoted both wizards and serpents. Among the Missouri Indians, Captain Bossu saw 'an old woman who passed for a magician; she wore round her naked body a living rattlesnake', to whom she spoke. Many other examples might be cited. We have seen that in some West African religious associations the women who take part in the magic rites must be provided with serpents. It is not improbable that the countless images of goddesses in Western Asia, in Krete and in Greece who hold serpents in their hands reproduce the attitude of their priestesses, who were wont to handle sacred serpents, from which they derived their magic power. There can be little doubt that the 'wisdom of the serpent', the wisest of all beasts of the field, refers to the proficiency of the reptile in the arts of magic.

Women and Serpents

As some of the foregoing beliefs indicate, women are as closely associated with serpents as they are with the moon. In southern Italy it is a current saying that serpents make love to all women—a belief familiar from the most ancient times, for the 'fauns' of primitive Italy were worshipped in the form of serpents; and, as is well known, women were in constant danger of being assaulted by them. Even the Good Goddess was ravished by the god Faunus in the form of a serpent. The notion was well known to the ancient Greeks. Euripides describes the women of Thebes as washing at sacred springs, whence issue serpents that girdle round them, fondling them and licking their cheeks. The predilection of serpents for women was associated with the sacred functions of women in the agricultural rites which came to be associated with Dionysos and Orpheus. Plutarch tells us that Olympias, the mother of Alexander the Great, who was an enthusiastic devotee of the women's religion, 'was wont in the dances proper to these ceremonies to have great tame serpents about her, which sometimes creeping out of the ivy in the mystic fans, sometimes winding themselves about the sacred spears and the women's chaplets, made a spectacle which men could not look upon without terror'. The ancient Celts also believed that serpents are attracted by women. In several stories serpents are described as fastening upon women in such a manner that it was impossible to separate them. Tenau 'of the golden breast' was so called because a serpent had clung to her nipple so tenaciously that the breast had to be cut off and replaced by one made of gold. In Germany women are said to become pregnant by a serpent entering their mouth while they are asleep. In northern France and Portugal at the present day women are believed to be in constant danger of being assaulted by lizards.

In Japan and India, as in Europe, Abyssinia and Algeria, girls are warned to be careful in approaching serpents lest they should be ravished. A love-sick serpent will, it is said, constantly follow a woman. Woman are supposed to conceive a passion for serpents, and to take pleasure in allowing the reptiles to bite them, for they are thought to be immune to their poison. The condition is known as 'nar-ashakh' or 'serpent-love'. It is to serpents that women turn when desirous of offspring. The Brahmans 'think that children can be obtained by worshipping a cobra'. (Children who have been thus obtained are usually named after the serpent.) It is a very ancient notion in India and in neighbouring countries of the East that women at the time of menstruation, or at least of puberty, before thay have menstruated or had intercourse with a man, are possessed by a malignant spirit in the form of a serpent.

Among the Jews it was a common Rabbinical opinion that menstruation owes its origin to the serpent having had sexual intercourse with Eve in the Garden of Eden. The ancient Persians likewise believed that menstruation was originally caused by the serpent-god Ahriman's relations with the first woman. The ancient Eygptians had fables about women being pursued by serpents. Among the Hottentots snakes are supposed to have connection with women while they are asleep.

In several of the notions just noted serpents are regarded as being the cause of menstruation; they thus play the same part in regard to the functions of women as the moon. In New Guinea the idea also appears to be familiar. Although, as we have seen, the Papuans commonly ascribe menstruation to the moon having intercourse with girls and women, in their elaborate wood-carvings women are often represented as being bitten in their genital organs by lizard-shaped animals. Throughout Polynesia women are supposed to be in danger of being violated by lizards and by eels.

This notion has been thought to derive from the phallic shape of the animal, and that idea is undoubtedly present in those world-wide beliefs. It was thought by the ancients, and is still believed by the European peasantry, that during sexual conjunction the male serpent introduces its head into the mouth of the female, and that the latter gnaws and bites it off, thus becoming fecundated. The same idea appears to obtain in Polynesia, and is, no doubt, general among uncultured peoples. In parts of the world where there are no serpents, lizards and other animals which are understood to change their skins, appear in the same role. In most of these myths, the animals in question are regarded as impersonations of a moon-god.

A variant of the same ideas represents serpents as stealing women's milk, e.g. among the Namaquas of South Africa. The same belief is current in Madagascar and New Guinea, and has also been popular in Wales from time immemorial. In Italy the restlessness of babies is frequently attributed to a serpent sucking the mother's breast, to the exclusion of the child.

The Eskimo have stories of reptiles falling in love with women and of serpents caressing women clinging to their breasts. The North American Indians likewise have numerous stories of serpents having connection with women and falling in love with them. Among the Déné, as among the Jews and the Persians, tradition relates that the first woman mated with a serpent.

In South America serpents are generally regarded as the cause of menstruation. Pregnancy as well as menstruation may, of course, result from the assaults of serpents. The Arawaks believe that such accidents are quite common. In the Upper Amazon region the god Jurupari, who is a serpent, is said to pursue women and to ravish them; they thereafter give birth to serpents. He himself was conceived by a virgin, who had no sexual parts at all, but was bitten by a reptile while she was bathing in a pool. The superstitions of the Tupis of northern Brazil bear a strong likeness to the rites of the Theban women described by Euripides. 'The Devil', says Father Yves d'Evreux, 'has persuaded those Gentiles of various delusions concerning waters, fountains and streams. Some are inhabited by nymphs, others by goddesses; some produce one effect, some another; some are injurious and dangerous, others agreeable and safe; some are sacred, others profane. Those savages have likewise a superstitious opinion that when they see a certain kind of lizard, which resemble those we call "mourons", or venomous snakes, running in the waters, they esteem that the fountain is dangerous to women, and that Giropari (their chief spirit) drinks of that water. This superstition goes so far that they believe that those lizards cast themselves upon women, that they send them to sleep and have company with them, so that they become big with child in consequence, and give birth to lizards instead of children.'

Serpents the Guardians of the Waters of Life

The association of serpents with sacred springs, just noted, is common in many other parts of the world. In an Indian tale a beautiful girl is taken by the King of the Serpents as his wife while she is admiring her reflection in a spring. The Zulus of Natal have a similar story. In Brazil every spring and lake is regarded as being under the control of a serpent-deity. So also among the North American Indians.

In innumerable myths, of which that of Perseus and Andromeda is the type, the sun-hero liberates a woman who has been given as wife to the serpent of the sea, or of a river, or spring. There can be little doubt that the opponent of the sun-god in these myths was originally the moon-god. In numerous tales the latter is credited with assaulting or kidnapping women while they are drawing water at a spring or well, just as the serpent-guardians of the springs. Wells and springs are, in fact, particularly dangerous to women. In several Irish tales the water of a spring or well overflows and pursues women. Wells also, especially very sacred ones, are credited with the property of causing women to fall pregnant. We have come upon the belief in South America and in Polynesia. Kaffir women, when their children ask them where babies come from, tell them that they are found by waters and springs, and that 'women bring them back with them when they return from fetching the day's water'. Banyoro women refuse to cross rivers unprotected, for fear of assault by the serpents dwelling in them. Recently a well near Oxford was regarded as being almost as potent as the sacred wells of the Tupis. 'Child's Well,' we are told, 'by the holiness of the chapleynes successively serving there, had vertue to make women who were barren to bring forth children.''

Whether it be the serpents which dwell in the wells and springs, or the waters themselves, which get women with child, the original cause of the mischief is the moon. It may appear strange that serpents should be so generally and intimately associated with water. Serpents are not usually aquatic animals. But primitive zoology does not look closely into classificatory affinities: the serpent is interchangeable in fable with almost any reptile, and with the eel and the crocodile, and is generally supposed to have once possessed legs; it is likewise regarded as identical with the worm, and is often so spoken of. Fishes are commonly regarded as closely allied to serpents. The Bechuana, for instance, 'have a prejudice against eating fish, and allege a disgust to eating anything like a serpent. This,' remarks Livingstone, 'may arise from the remnants of serpent-worship floating in their minds.' The Caribs of the West Indies appear to have had the same notion. The Tasmanians did not eat any fish that has scales, nor did the ancient Egyptians.

Babylonian gods were conceived in the form of serpents or of fishes, interchangeably. Ea, or Oannes, who was the serpent Tiamat, identified with the primal waters of life, was also the great Fish. The Syrian form of the Semitic goddess, Derketo, was a fish, and her dying and resurrecting son, Tammuz or Adonis, was also a fish-god, and was spoken of as Dagon, the Fish. Similarly the Hebrews regarded Leviathan,—that is, the primal serpent—as a huge fish covered with scales. Joshua, the first saviour of Israel, was called 'the son of Nun', that is to say, 'the son of the Fish'. Nun, or Ji-nun, the Fish, was, according to learned Rabbis, the true name of the Messiah, which he bore before the sun was created. He was currently regarded as identical with Leviathan, who having died, rose again after three days. The symbolism passed over into early Christian ideas, and a fish, an image of which Clement of Alexandria recommends all Christians to wear, was as common an emblem of the faith as the cross.

The serpent's constant association with waters is not, however, due to its fancied resemblance to a fish, but to its being a surrogate of the moon, the ruler of waters. Throughout Indonesia the ocean is regarded as a serpent, the Great Serpent of the primordial waters, from which all things have arisen. The great serpent or dragon, so prominent in Chinese mythical representations, is the representative of the waters above the earth. The association of the serpent with rain has led many to suppose that this is the primary significance of the serpent in universal mythology. But rain is only one of the forms of the waters over which the moon exercises her control. The moon's faculty of eternal renewal is frequently ascribed to her bathing periodically in the waters of pools, lakes or of the sea. In Polynesia the moon preserves her youth by bathing in the waters of Tane. The Jukon of northern Nigeria say that the moon goes to renew its youth in its home in the waters. So do the Huitotos of the Upper Amazon. The water which by that baptism imparts renewed youth to her is thus the Water of Life. It seems not unlikely that the virtue of those waters is thought to be due to the presence in them of their guardian serpents, and that the moon is regarded as deriving her powers of rejuvenescence from the serpent, which renews its skin.

CHAPTER 21

Primitive Cosmic Religion

As we have seen, primitive religious ideas are hopelessly parochial. They are not general theories of the universe, but are connected with primitive man's immediate needs and purposes. Superstitions concerning the moon, however, are of especial interest since they constitute the germ of a cosmic religion. Like the totem, the moon is regarded as the progenitor of the tribe, and the tribe is equated with 'mankind'. But the moon naturally tends to broaden out into a universal deity, whose sphere of influence is the whole world; such a conception may be called cosmic, in distinction from purely tribal and local ones. In this chapter, therefore, we shall survey the religious conceptions of the less advanced peoples, and shall see how far the moon occupies the chief place in them.

There is little evidence to support the idea, once popular, that one of the earliest forms of religious belief was 'nature worship'. Primitives, it is true, readily regard natural objects as the abode of spirits, but cosmological views do not seem to have developed out of such haphazard 'animism'. Nor are the gods of winds and storms true deities; they are usually simply aspects of more generalized powers. The facts suggest that religious ideas arose from the desire to acquire magical powers and not from an intellectual desire to interpret nature. The interpretations subsumed under the term 'nature worship' appear to be late phenomena.

All religious conceptions tend to detach themselves from the ideas from which they arise. Once a deity emerges with a name and personality, these constitute a sufficient account of him, and the ideas from which the deity arose are usually repudiated or regarded as a mere allegory. The deity is, perhaps, remembered as the Light of the World, and the sun is 'naturally' likened to the god. Clans which have become pre-eminent frequently assimilate themselves to the sun, and favour the substitution of the more brilliant luminary. The respective sexes of sun and moon become changed. In solar theologies, the moon is belittled and discredited; a regular controversy develops between the solar and lunar conception of a heavenly ruler. But the attributes of the solar god are, in point of fact, just those which have been handed down to him from the older lunar deity. In primitive thought the sun is destitute of significance. Equinoctial time, and the relation between the seasonal changes and the course of the sun, are unknown to primitive humanity. The most uncultured races do not realize that daylight is due to the sun; it is believed to be an independent phenomenon. The sun's brilliancy and heat—the attributes which constitute the manifest grounds for its importance—count for nothing in primitive ideas of the supernatural which are not a result of the impressiveness of natural phenomena but an endeavour to secure benefits by obtaining or controlling magical powers. It is the moon, the regulator and transformer, and not the sun, which is everywhere regarded as the source of magical powers; no primitive magician turns to the sun to obtain that power. In a Lettish myth the moon is represented as saying to the sun: 'What have you to be proud about? Is it that you give heat to the world? I do more, I cause all growth and all existence, I bring to life and I bring to death.' The solar gods of later stages of development are but transformed moon-deities, whose functions they inherit. They are life-giving and fertilizing, they renew their youth in cycles. But such functions are the attributes of the primitive lunar deity. Hence it is that we repeatedly come upon incongruities which disclose the substitution: we encounter sun-gods who die a monthly death and rise again after three days, or sun-cults which are celebrated by night.

Nor are solar cults alone derived from older lunar cults. The more highly developed religious systems of advanced cultures, which have the universal bearing and philosophic scope which we associate with a religious conception, also betray their development from lunar cults.[1]

Cosmic Religion in Melanesia and New Guinea

The Melanesian islands provide an unequalled opportunity of approaching the root of primitive cosmic religious conceptions—although to be sure Melanesian religious ideas certainly are not primitive in the absolute sense. The Melanesians have a copious oral literature of myths, all of which, from the northernmost groups of New Britain and the Admiralty Islands to New Caledonia and Fiji, repeat essentially the same themes. These themes are exclusively lunar; the sun only appears in a quite subordinate character.

[1] 'Observers', remarks Sir James Frazer, 'ignorant of savage superstition, have commonly misinterpreted such customs as worship or adoration paid to the moon. In point of fact, the ceremonies of new moon are probably in many cases rather magical than religious.' True, the rituals by which primitive humanity endeavours to utilize and acquire the virtues which it believes to reside in the moon may be regarded as operations of magic. Yet if procedures which are intended to secure the continuance of life, the redemption of human nature by a new birth, and which are addressed to a power which is regarded as the controller of human destiny, and as the resurrection and the life, are not religion, it is difficult to say what is.

The lunar deities of Melanesia are characteristically represented as a pair of gods, corresponding respectively to the lucky waxing moon and to the unlucky waning moon. The one is beneficent and wise, the other maleficent and foolish. Thus, at Aurora, in the New Hebrides, 'Tagaro wanted everything to be good, and would have no pain or suffering; Suqe-matua would have all things bad. Whatever Tagaro did was made right, Suqe was always wrong; he would have men die only for five days.' Whatever Tagaro ate increased as he ate it, but Suqe could not plant things aright. Suqe is the ruler of the dead. His head is forked. In New Britain the two brothers are called Kabibabam, 'the Wise,' and Karvuvu, the 'Left-hand god'. (In the southern hemisphere the new moon crescent appears on the left-hand side of the moon to an observer facing north, the dark shadow being on the right-hand side.)

The lunar character of these deities is shown in many small ways; sometimes they are known as skin-changers, sometimes they are globular in shape and sometimes the deity has eleven brothers. They create men and constantly resurrect them after three days. Often the bad deity seduces the wife of the good deity.

The bright moon-god is commonly regarded in Melanesian myths as corresponding to the full moon. In the island of Erub in the Torres Straits, the moon is represented by two sacred stones, one circular, the other crescent-shaped. The same symbols recur in almost every religion. In ancient Egypt, almost every high god and goddess bore the emblems of the full orb and the crescent; these two symbols have often been supposed to represent the sun and the moon—but we find the emblems surmounting the figure of the moon-god. Similarly, the various attributes of the waxing, or full-moon god, as we find them in Melanesia, may easily be adapted to a solar mythology; all that is needed is to interpret the brilliant and beneficent full-moon deity as the sun, and to leave unchanged the contrast between him and the deformed, dark, maleficent, crescentic moon-god. Thus, according to Mrs Hadfield, the natives of the Loyalty Islands worshipped the sun and the moon. 'They say the sun reached old age in one month, but owing to some secret and special attribute was enabled to renew his youth.' On the notion of a solar deity who passes through a monthly cycle of ageing and rejuvenation, comment is superfluous. Reporting from Pentecost Island the myth of Tortali, who absents himself from the heavens for several days at intervals while with his wife, Father Suas refers to Tortali as the sun, but it is difficult to see on what principles of nature symbolism the sun is represented as being absent from the heavens during the interlunar days, which the moon is usually supposed to spend in the company of his wife, the sun.

The two contrasted moon-gods of Melanesia are often associated with a moon-goddess, their mother, who is sometimes represented as giving birth to them by splitting into two. In New Ireland she is spoken of simply as 'the Mother', or 'our grandmother'. In New Britain she is the mother of Kaninana and Karvuvu, whom she moulded out of her blood, and is known as 'the Old Woman', or 'the Shining Woman'. In the Banks Islands she is the mother of Qat and the Tangaros, and is called 'Round Head,' or 'the Skin-changing Woman.' In San Cristoval she is the Snake-woman and the mother of mankind. But the serpent deity of San Cristoval, though regarded in its local forms as a female, is in its generic form a male, and has a brother; it is thus a form of the double moon-god. It is regarded as the supreme deity, the creater of the world and of all creatures, and is the object of deep reverence. The Great Serpent, the creator of mankind and of all good things, occupies the same position in the Admiralty Islands, and in Pine Island, at the opposite extremity of Melanesia. The same triad of the two moon-gods with their mother is also found in New Guinea.

A misconception which has had a paralysing influence on the interpretation of primitive belief is the assumption that a given personage cannot be a god because he is not treated with reverence, or because ludicrous stories are told about him. Such beings, it is supposed, must at best be classed as 'demi-gods', or 'heroes'. But these distinctions, so important to the Christian theologian, do not exist for the savage. He makes no clear distinction between gods and men. The magical attributes of supernatural beings are but a superlative form of the powers daily exercised by medicine-men; the function of creator does not establish a gulf between the god and the man; all magicians are more or less creators, and the circumstance that he has created the world is often an incidental detail, hardly worth stressing. As often as not, the drudgery of creating beings and things is delegated by the god to a subordinate demiurge. The god is commonly supposed to have dwelt at one time amongst men, living much the same life as his savage companions, and changing his residence to heaven by a mere accident in the course of his adventures. The character of awful majesty, which we associate with a veritable god, the attitude of reverence which we regard as characteristic of a religious view of him, are foreign to primitive man's conception of supernatural beings. These may be dreaded as dangerous and evilly disposed, but dread does not prevent a sly delight in their misadventures; they may be looked upon as well-disposed and willing to be helpful, and are then treated all the more freely with friendly good-nature, but not with reverence (cf. 'the man in the moon.') Thus it is that the gods of Melanesia and of Polynesia have commonly been described as 'tribal heroes' or 'spirits'.

Melanesian secret societies, when they first came under the notice of

Europeans, were already in an advanced state of decay, but enough of their primitive character survives to show that their central object was admission to the company of deceased ancestors by obtaining resurrection and eternal life from the moon. 'It is possible', observed Dr Rivers, 'that further knowledge will show the presence of features derived from the cult of the moon in the ritual of Melanesian "ghost" societies.' And, in fact it does. At Vanikoro, in the Santa Cruz group, where, as everywhere else in Melanesia, the creation of the world and of the human race is ascribed to the moon; its cult in the stone circles constitutes, in fact, a regular religious worship.

Thus the Qat, Qatu or Qetu societies of the Banks Islands and northern New Hebrides are associations of the moon-god Qat.

In Rook Island, between New Britain and New Guinea, the boys were supposed to be swallowed by a monstrous spirit, and were delivered shrieking and trembling to the masked personages representing it, and compelled to crawl between their legs. In the Koko Islands the candidates for initiation are seized, blindfolded and thrust between the jaws of a vast crocodile effigy, while their parents shout: 'Do not kill my child!' Bull-roarers swung inside the building represent the roaring of the monster. At last, yielding to the entreaties of the agonized parents, the master of ceremonies consents to beg the crocodile to disgorge his prey, on consideration of a payment of some pigs as a substitute for the boy, who is accordingly vomited forth a fully-initiated man. Almost identically similar proceedings constitute the initiating rites of the Yabim, the Bukua and the Kai tribes of northern Papua.

It would be a misconception to imagine that these proceedings are mere pantomines designed to instil terror into the uninitiated. The monster is the most sacred and venerated object in the religious ideas of those tribes. Offerings and sacrifices are presented on solemn occasions to the beasts; and they are consulted as oracles. After a war expedition, prisoners are immolated and their bodies are placed in the stomachs of the wicker-work crocodiles; they are subsequently removed and eaten communally by the men. The holy crocodiles are called 'kopiravi', and are spoken of as 'kai ai imunu'. that is to say, 'imunu from the sky'. The term 'imunu' is explained as meaning 'the principle of life'.

The crocodile monster which devours and regurgitates the candidates for initiation is thus no other than the 'kopiravi', or 'principle of life from the sky'. In the Kiwai tribe, the initiators representing the 'spirit' are masked as crocodiles. This conception, 'which would appear to correspond to the "mana" of the Melanesian Islands,' says Professor Haddon, 'runs through all their religions.' The crocodile occupies, in fact, a conspicuous place in Melanesian New Guinea. In the Solomon Islands, says Dr Codrington, the sacred animals 'are chiefly sharks, alligators, snakes, bonitos and frigate-birds'. The shark, and the 'bonito' fish which resembles it, are in all likelihood regarded as marine equivalents of the crocodile. In Polynesian languages the shark and the lizard, the nearest Polynesian equivalent to the crocodile, are both denoted by almost the same word, 'mako' and moko', respectively. (We have seen that women are represented as being bitten in their genital organs by the crocodile.)

In New Guinea initiation ceremonies the candidates are often said to be restored by the monster which has swallowed them—on consideration of some pigs being supplied by the parents as a ransom. This is not exploitation on the part of the hierophants—though, of course, it may degenerate into such. In some tribes, in which the ceremonies have become reduced to a simplified form, the final investiture of the candidate takes place while he stands on the carcass of the dead pig which he has provided, and, before this, he is steamed as if he, and not the pig, were about to be eaten. The slaughtered animal is thus regarded not merely as a payment, but as a *substitute*, whose life is given in ransom for that of the candidate. The Namau offer their prisoners of war to the 'kopiravi' crocodiles in the same manner as the ancient Celts. In the sacred stone circles at Wagawaga and Wani a man was solemnly decorated, tied to a stone, sacrificed, roasted and ritually eaten. In these forms of the ritual the substituted victim is frequently assimilated to the deity itself; the Papuans doubtless considered that they acquired the virtues of the deity by eating the sacrificial victim. In the Solomon Islands it is said that formerly men cut up the moon and each ate a piece of it. The substitution of a redeemer who gives his life for the people is not infrequently enacted symbolically in the same manner as the symbolic death of the candidate for initiation is represented by a mimic death.

In Melanesia the lunar power is associated with sacred stones. 'Sacred places have almost always sacred stones in them,' and deities are associated with them. As already noted, in the island of Erub, the moon is represented by two sacred stones. In the Solomon Islands, the creator, Tantanu, is regarded as a stone. In Fiji the chief god, Ndeugei, is a serpent in the upper part of his body and a stone in the lower. The goddess 'Round Head', the mother of Qat, is represented in the Banks Islands by a stone. On Lepers' Island 'all the stones that are sacred are connected with Tagaro'. On San Cristoval a magic stone spoke and announced the coming of the Great Serpent, and was in fact his daughter. In the Massim area of eastern New Guinea, the circles of standing stones, which were of old the scenes of human sacrifice and cannibalism, are marked with the remains of ancient pictographs; one bears a cross; another is called 'the Serpent'. Dr Seligman was unable to imagine why, as it is wholly unlike a serpent. In New Caledonia all magic and religious practices are associated with sacred stones, and these bestow fertility. In the Belep tribe the sacred stone is regarded as 'the principle of life'. The god Doibet, who is ruler of the dead and of the underworld and is manifestly the representative of the dark moon, is represented as being, in the lower part of his body, a stone. These sacred stones play the same conspicuous part in every district of Melanesia, from the Admiralty Islands to Fiji. Moreover, individual fetiches are adopted by selecting a stone from which the owner believes he derives magic power, or 'mana'.

Sacred stones are a world-wide feature of archaic religious cult, from Japan to Brazil and from Madagascar to Scandinavia. Every Semitic deity was embodied in a sacred stone, and could be called down by the worshipper by setting up a stone; aniconic stones played a conspicuous part in primitive Greece. Sacred stones represented the gods in all Celtic countries; and they are found throughout Africa.

It might seem that stones afford such an obvious means of setting up a durable symbol that the practice of 'worshipping' stones scarcely calls for any explanation. Yet it appears that the identification of stones with the moon comprises something more. The sacred stones of Melanesia are not the aniconic idols of a people unable to produce more like-life representations of their gods, for few savages excel the Melanesians in wood-carving. In the island of Yam, as already noted, two deities, doubtless forms of the double moon-god, are represented by elaborate images of a shark and a crocodile adorned with tortoise-shell and bird-of-paradise plumage and painted in brilliant colours. But the richly carved figures are merely presentments; the actual souls or spirits of the divinities are situated in two rough stones which lie beneath the images. In the myth of the Alfurs of Celebes the symbol of immortality, instead of being the moon or the serpent, is a stone; and we are told, in the name of the moon-god, that the stone is the symbol of immortality because, like the moon, it is not subject to decay. In New British myths, mankind was defrauded of the gifts of immortality, not only by the serpents but also by stones. The Melanesians do not merely represent their gods by stones, but as being stones. In short, it appears probable that they are deliberately identifying the 'principle of life' with stones because, like the serpent, stones partake of the moon's gift of immortality.

Australia and Tasmania

Australian religious conceptions do not centre exclusively round the totem. The control of life and death and the resurrection of the dead are, throughout Australia, regarded as depending upon the moon. The Queensland tribes and the Dieri regard the moon as the creator of

mankind. The sun has no place in Australian conceptions of the supernatural; when personified it is regarded as a female, presumably the
wife of the moon.

The initiation rites of the Australians have both practical and
magical purposes. I have suggested that the practical purpose may be to
aid in sexual selection. Be this as it may, these ceremonies, like all rites
of initiation, whether into 'secret societies' or into bridal manhood, are
regarded as conferring certain magical powers, and admission to the
ranks not only of living tribesmen but of their departed ancestors, after
the initiate's death. The latter object is achieved, as usual, by ceremonies
in which the initiate is supposed to die and be resurrected.

The method of resurrection often resembles the Australian story already noted, in which a youth is supposed to acquire a new skin through
being swallowed by a serpent, and those initiation rites of Indonesia and
New Guinea in which the neophyte is imbued with new life by passing
through the body of a monster. The supernatural being is supposed to
swallow the candidate or to bite his head off. The performance is sometimes represented in a fairly realistic manner. 'I have seen one of the
old men', says Dr Howitt, 'rush furiously at one of the novices, seize
him by the head and apparently bite part of it.' Mathews says that 'before cannibalism ceased to be practised by the tribes he studied, 'it was
the custom to kill and eat a man during the "burbung" ceremonies'.

The Australian 'bora' divinities, in whom some authorities have
thought to detect moral and august deities[1] and who thus initiate the
youth are, in fact, not remarkable for either their moral or august character. In these myths, they break almost every one of the ten command-
ments. Their connection with the moon is evident. Baiame 'appears
occasionally during the day, but mostly by night'; and is described as
painted white with the pipe-clay which is known as 'moon'. On the
bora ground he is pictured by a huge figure moulded in mud and sand;
at its head stands a tree on which is represented the lunar crescent.
Moreover, the magical powers of Australian medicine-men are intimately associated with the possession of pieces of rock-crystal, which are
supposed to be obtained directly from the heavenly magicians. They are
symbols of the Great Spirit. Daramulum is represented with quartz
crystals on his head, and Baiame with similar crystals growing from his
shoulders.

[1] Westermarck cites, as the *piéce de resistance* of his account of Australian gods,
a paper by J. Manning from the *Journal and Proc. of the Royal Society of N.S.
Wales* (1882, p. 157 sqq.). Actually 'Cockatoo' Manning was a farmer who
obtained entry to a meeting of the society and read a paper which was a farrago
of nonsense. Under the rules of the society, the paper had to be printed despite
the protests of members of the society, who had heard it with mixed amusement
and disgust. Its worst puerilities were deleted before publication.

Seeing that various Australian tribes are stated to regard the moon as their creator and father, and that the origin of death and the faculty of resurrection are even more generally ascribed to the moon, it seems no very daring conjecture that their 'Great Spirits', the source of all magical powers, who are seen at night adorned with moon-paint and crystals, who are represented with crescents over their heads, and who kill the young men in order to resurrect them, are none other than lunar deities. They appear to be, in fact, essentially identical with the moon gods of Melanesia and Papua. The two best-known Australian bora deities, Baiame and Daramulum, are an associated pair. Baiame occupies the superior position, Daramulum acting under his orders as his deputy or demiurge in the initiation ceremonies. Baiame is represented as white, Daramulum as 'one-legged' and deformed; Baiame is on the whole benevolent or at least innocuous, Daramulum is evil and maleficent. They stand in fact in the same relation to each other as the bright full moon and waxing moon-god and the dark waning moon-god of Melanesia. Indeed, there is substantial evidence that the Australian initiation deities and their rites are culturally connected with the corresponding cults of Papua and the Torres Straits. The bull-roarer and the supposed 'swallowing' of the candidates are prominent features of both. The bull-roarer which in Papua as in Australia is the voice of the initiating 'spirit', is in the Borli tribe of Papua called 'bora'. It is difficult to avoid recognizing in Bomai and Malu the Australian Baiame and Daramulum. Malu, the 'bad' god, is stated to be like Daramulum in the habit of biting off men's heads. Malu is a crocodile; Daramulum is an iguana—there are no crocodiles in Australia. Bomai is a shark; in Queensland Baiame is a tortoise.

The death and resurrection which the rites are supposed to effect are sometimes dramatically represented. One of the older men is buried in a deep grave, which is then lightly covered with branches and earth; at the conclusion of the ceremony he rises again, bearing in his mouth the magic crystal which he is supposed to have received from Daramulum. By a converse argument the candidates, instead of being swallowed, may be made to swallow a piece of the magic rock-crystal, 'the symbol of the Great Spirit'.

Here a short digression on the meaning of these sacred crystals may not be out of place. The Nutka of British Columbia also achieve rebirth and initiation by ingesting pieces of rock-crystal; the Butwa of the Congo acquire immortality in the same way. The rite has analogues in the eating of the bark of the moon-palm by South American 'pajes', or the drinking of a moon-draught by the Thonga medicine-men. All stones partake of the lunar nature since they are everlasting and indestructible, and hard, crystalline gems which seem to emit light especially so. In fact, gems are regarded by the wise men of the East as owing their virtues to the moon; thus pearls are the products of the moon, emeralds of the waxing moon, cat's-eye stones of the waning moon. Other gems are associated in astrological lore with various planets and stars; but, as we have seen, the magic virtues of these heavenly bodies are supposed to have their source in the moon. Furthermore, it is widely believed,—e.g. in China—that serpents carry in their head a magical gem. The notion was familiar to the ancient Germans, and the 'snake-stone' is mentioned in some of the most ancient German poems. In Salzburg and the Jura Mountains it is believed that one of the eyes of the undying serpent is a diamond. The ancient Greeks believed likewise. Diamonds are popularly supposed in France to be produced by snakes, while the Danubian peasants believe that all gems have their origin from serpents; a serpent's nest is supposed to contain a wealth of precious stones. Among the ancient Celts those 'snake-stones' or 'serpents' eggs' played an important part in religious belief, and bestowed magic powers on the possessor. The veneration for such 'snake-stones,' 'adder-stones' or 'clach-nathrach' is still prevalent in all Celtic countries.

The Melanesians of eastern New Guinea hold similar views; the indispensable means of acquiring magical power is, they believe, to obtain a snake-stone. Among the American Indians it was believed that certain mythical serpents have horns on their heads, and possession of one of them bestowed magical powers. The Armenians tell of a queen serpent who paralyses her enemies by means of a magic stone which shines brightly when, on certain nights, she takes it in the air. Another Armenian tradition tells of a man who unknowingly married a serpent-woman. An astrologer revealed to him the true nature of his consort, and advised him to shut her up in the oven and roast her. This he did, and her ashes were found to possess the property of transmuting metals into gold. The magic 'snake-stone', or 'moon-stone', is in fact no other than the philosopher's stone, and naturally derives its power of transmuting baser metals into incorruptible gold from the moon. The true formula for transmuting metals into gold is to treat them with a preparation obtained by burning a serpent to ashes; alchemists were commonly spoken of in the Middle Ages as 'serpent-burners'.

The Nutka of Vancouver, the Congo natives, and the Australian aborigines, when they endeavour to renew their life by swallowing rock-crystals, are thus guided by the same ideas as the mediaeval alchemists.

The ceremony which constitutes the central rite of Australian boras, and which takes the place of the immolation and resurrection of the candidates, is the knocking out of one or two of their front teeth. This is represented as a commutation of more severe proceedings. It is said that Daramulum always pretended to kill the boys and resurrect them, but that, in reality, he contented himself with extracting a tooth. The evulsion of teeth thus appears to be regarded as equivalent to being swallowed and restored to life by the initiating spirit. The evulsion or filing of teeth at initiation is a widely distributed custom.

The teeth are, according to many uncultured races, the part of the body in which the immortal soul resides. This is in accordance with savage logic. The most enduring or immortal part of man is regarded as being his bones. The Choctas say that 'the real seat of the human soul is in the bones'. The Hurons likewise called the bones 'the soul'. The ancient Hebrews appear to have had similar notions; the word for 'bone,' 'etzem,' meant with them a man's self, his person. Among the Central Australian tribes, the word 'kutchi', means both 'bones' and 'ghost'. The bones of the dead are accordingly the object of elaborate attention the world over. The bones which are regarded as possessing in the highest degree the quality of immortality are the lower jaw and teeth. In Uganda the jawbones of the kings are alone preserved; they are spoken of simply as 'the King', and are consulted in all important affairs. The Ewe of Togo state that babies are formed out of the jaw-bones of the dead, thus reincarnating them. Warriors adorn their trumpets and drums with the jaw-bones of their slain foes, thus effectively conciliating their ghosts. For the same reason, in Porto Novo, the executioner keeps the jawbones of his victims securely in his house.

This conception parallels the view that stones possess the virtue of immortality; and that the teeth should be accounted as possessing that virtue in the highest degree follows by the same logic which sees in crystals the most immortal order of stones. The bones of the dead are referred to in Mayan codices as 'precious stone bones'. In Samoa the spirit of a shark-god was supposed to be immanent in a shark's teeth which were consulted as oracles. The holy tooth of Buddha is similarly worshipped in Ceylon. The dragon's teeth which Kadmos sowed, from which armed warriors arose, probably contained the spirit of the divine animal. Teeth are also associated with the moon in primitive thought, because they possess to a certain extent the property of being renewed. Among the natives of the Loyalty Islands 'it seems to have been the general opinion that the moon possessed an unlimited supply of teeth to dispose of; so that whenever a man pulled out a decayed tooth he was mindful to throw it over his house on a moonlight night, calling out at the same time to the moon: 'Here is my old tooth, take it away and send me another in its place'. This faculty of renewal is shared by the hair, the growth of which is commonly believed to depend upon the moon. Accordingly, the cropping of the hair or complete depilation is an essential part of the Australian rites of initiation. When, therefore, Daramulum bites off the teeth of the initiates as a compromise for biting off their heads or swallowing them bodily, he is selecting the most appropriate substitute for the whole man, and the portion best suited to receive the gift of immortality.

In short, among the Australian aborigines, who exhibit one of the most primitive surviving examples of religious conceptions, rites and conceptions of lunar origin are no less important than those associated with totemic animals. The same appears to have been the case with the now extinct natives of Tasmania.

Traces of Lunar Cults in Indonesia

Where agriculture has become the chief means of subsistence, the sun naturally assumes a special importance. Since the races of the Malay Archipelago are mostly dependent upon primitive agriculture, the most general cosmic conception amongst them is that of Father Su, the husband and fertilizer of Mother Earth. Their religious theories have, however, been influenced by Hinduism and Islam, as shown by the fact that the Bataks, the most primitive race of Sumatra, have a trinity which in some respects conforms in nomenclature to the Hindu triad, while even the wild tribes of Borneo Dayaks call their supreme being Hatalla or Magatalla, which is simply the Arabic Allah ta'ala.

Nevertheless, more ancient ideas everywhere gleam through such advanced concepts. Thus, the triad of gods of the Toba-Bataks, although adapted to Hindu ideas, is known as the 'Lords of the Moon.' With them is associated a moon-goddess, who, having bestowed upon her children the power of controlling demons, retired to the moon to watch over them. 'When we are in need, in trouble, or in anxiety,' say the Bataks, 'when a child, a woman, or an oppressed person amongst us is in need of help, we look to the moon, and take courage.'

This strange combination of primitive with later cosmic conceptions is manifested in the Kei Islands and in Aru even more incongruously; the chief god is spoken of as the 'Sun-Moon'. In Ceram-laut, and in the island of Gorom the moon is feminine; but the women address her as 'Our Grandfather'.

In the sixteenth century Barthema noted that the moon was worshipped in Java. In the Kei Islands and in Timor the moon is the chief object of worship. In Timor she is served by aged vestals, who tend an undying fire. In the island of Babar the supreme god dwells in the moon. In Nias the cosmogony is purely lunar. In the Middle Celebes, among the Bataks of the Tomori region, sacrifices are offered to the moon at harvest-time, with songs in which it is addressed as 'Mother'. Among the Dayaks of Borneo, we are told, the 'veneration for the moon, formed the chief basis of their worship and myths'. When the Spaniards first visited Borneo, the only worship which they noticed amongst the natives was that 'they pray to the moon, and ask her for children, abundance of cattle and of the fruits of the earth, and other similar things'.

The moon is regarded by the Dayaks as the cause of time and of every event. 'It is certain that solar mythology was originally foreign to all purely Indonesian peoples.'

Survivals of Primitive Cosmic Religion in Polynesia

The decay of the original conceptions upon which Polynesian myths were founded has proceeded much further than in Melanesia. Though the Polynesians preserved their myths with wonderful unity, their interpretation was not an object of religious or of magical interest. Hence, so far as they are 'interpreted' at all, they are interpreted 'naturally': that is, in accordance with the more obvious aspects of natural phenomena rather than with their primitive religious and magical significance. Solar interpretations, if not insisted on, are at least accepted. This has given European inquirers the impression that Polynesian myth presents a typical example of the primitive 'solar religion' imagined in the theory of 'nature worship', and the Polynesians have even been sometimes termed 'The People of the Sun'.

Actually there is no trace of sun-worship or solar mythology anywhere in Polynesia. The sun plays no part in Polynesian myth, except as the wife of the moon. The most prominent mythical figure is Maui, the 'creator of land,' the 'creator of man'. He has been identified with the sun; he is, however, the son of the moon, Hina; and the most famous of his myths relates how he conquered the sun. Maui is demonstrably identical with the moon-gods of Melanesia. His name means 'left-handed'; and he is thus, like the 'left-handed Karvuvu' of New Britain, the new moon-god that grows from the left (west) in opposition to the 'right-handed Kabinana'. His name is also used as a synonym of 'witchcraft'.

As in all traditional mythologies, the same deities are known in Polynesia and in Melanesia by various names, and the traditional names become transferred from one deity to another. An instance of the confusion which may thus arise is presented by the myth of Rona, who in her best-known form is the woman in the moon, abducted there by the moon-god, while she was drawing water. In other versions, however, Rona is a male and an ogre. 'Rona is lord of the sun and moon. Rona eats the moon and the moon eats Rona; but as each becomes exhausted and devoured in the monthly battle, they go to the Life-waters of Tane to bathe and be restored to life and strength, by which they become able to renew the struggle.'

The two moon-gods, the favourable and the unfavourable, not infrequently change places. Maui-tiki, who figures in western Polynesia as a good-natured hero anxious to confer benefits upon mankind, is in Tahiti a fiend who desires to slay men.

The wife of Maui is Rohe or Rau. 'She was beautiful as he was ugly, and on his wishing to exchange faces with her, she refused his request. He, however, by means of an incantation, managed to gain his point. In anger she left him, or refused to live any longer in the world of light, but proceeded to the under-world.' As in the parallel Melanesian myth, the wife of the moon-god is the sun. In the Solomon Islands, in the Loyalty Islands and in New Guinea, the sun and the moon formerly travelled in company, but quarrelled and separated; in New Zealand the moon said to the sun, 'Let us travel together at night'; but they disagreed and separated. Rohe, the wife of Maui, is in fact said in New Zealand and in the Chatham Islands to be 'the sister of the sun'; but it appears manifest that, like Ro Lei, she was in reality the sun itself. In Polynesian myth, the supposed sun-god is thus, under the thinnest of disguises, a female and the wife of the moon.

In western Polynesia, Tangaroa occupies the place which Maui occupies in eastern Polynesia. A Tongan version describes four Tangaroas, and associates them unambiguously with the four phases of the moon. Tangaroa has, of course, been claimed as a sun-god. In Samoa he dwells in the moon. In Hawaii and in eastern Polynesia, Tangaroa is an evil and maleficent god; he is the ruler of Hades; in the Marquesas, he is a god of darkness and is defeated by the god of light, Atea. He is identical with the Tangaroas and Tagaros known throughout Melanesia. 'It would be quite erroneous', remarks Professor Schimdt, 'to regard him [Tagaro] as a loan from the Polynesian Tangaroa. He is, of course, identical with him—not, however, as an imitation, but as an earlier form of him, which has more distinctly retained its lunar character.'

Maui, Tangaroa and other corresponding Polynesian gods are, like those of Melanesia, incarnate in serpents, lizards and eels, and in stones. The deities of Polynesia and their mythology are in fact identical with those of Melanesia.

Polynesian kings were primarily 'sacred' kings,—that is, representatives of the gods—from whom their power was derived. The Tuitonga, the sacred king of Tonga, was regarded as the direct descendant of Maui, Tangaroa and the goddess Hikuleo. Thus they were associated with the moon. In Samoa, where the name of a chief might not be pronounced, least of all when he was dead, the phrase by which his demise was announced was: 'The moon has fallen.'

Few particulars are available concerning Maori initiation rites but, there can be little doubt that they included a symbolic representation of death and resurrection. In the sacred enclosures human sacrifices were offered; the officiating hierophant was attired in a shroud. After initiation the candidate, painted red, received a new name. The death and resurrection of the god himself formed an important part of the rites of the Areoi, although the ritual was of a solar and not a lunar cycle. But the god whose death and resurrection were thus celebrated—mostly, it appears, by night—was the moon-god of Polynesia and Melanesia.

The dualism represented by the two moon-gods, the bright and the dark, which is so conspicuous in Melanesian and Polynesian myth, and of which we find clear traces in Australia, is met with everywhere in primitive lunar cosmological conceptions. This is not the expression of a sense of the opposition between good and evil forces, but derives in every instance from the contrast between the two beings who, in primitive belief, are supposed to contend for mastery in the course of the lunar cycle, the one loving darkness rather than light, and seeking to destroy the other who would bestow light and the power of regeneration upon the world.

Primitive Cosmic Religion in North America

This contrast is expressed by the Greenland Eskimo as clearly as by the Pacific Islanders. They relate that in the beginning there were two brothers, one of whom said: 'There shall be night, and there shall be day, and men shall die one after another.' But the other said: 'There shall be no day, but only night all the time, and men shall live for ever.' Here, as often elsewhere, the good and evil attributes are intermixed, for it is from the power of darkness that eternal life is obtained.

For the Eskimo, the moon, Aningahk, is the supreme deity. With him is associated a female form of the lunar power, the goddess Sedna, who presides over the food supply and to whom propitiating rites are directed. The sun, who is the sister of the moon, plays no part in their theology; its heat and light are supposed to be derived from the moon.

The conceptions of the tribes of north-western America appear to be similar. Among the Tlinkit and the Nutka, the sun is likewise the wife of the moon, and is regarded as a poor creature, while the moon is wealthy and powerful.

Initiation ceremonies depicting rebirth in essentially the same pattern are found from Alaska to Vancouver. In the rites of the Tsimshian the tribal chief impersonates the divinity. An agent of the Hudson Bay Company declares: 'He imitates the rising sun, which they believe to be a shining man, wearing a radiated crown, and continually walking round the earth, which is stationary. He wears on this occasion a curiously constructed mask, set round with seals' whiskers and feathers, which gradually expand like a fan; and from the top of the mask swan-down is shaken out in great quantities according as he moves his head. The expanding bristles and feathers represent the sun's rays, and the showers of down, rain and snow'. As the Tsimshian hold that the sun is the wife of the moon, from which all rain and snow are believed to come, it is difficult to understand how the sun-goddess should be represented by them as a snow-producing man; and it appears probable that, seeing a representation of a radiating heavenly body which controlled the weather, the European assumed it as a matter of course to be the sun. Moreover, the Tsimshian believe that their rites were instituted by the moon-god Haiatlila'qs, the founder of all the tribe's institutions, It is the moon which is supposed to renew the life of the Tsimshian by causing them to change their skin. And, accordingly, 'everyone who wants to go to heaven must pass through the House of the Moon'.

Our information concerning the fundamental cosmic religious conceptions of the native races is deficient and contradictory. Modern investigations have unfortunately been carried out at least two hundred years too late. The reports of the earlier travellers are marred by anthropological naïveté and distorted by preconceived theories. The Indians have been described as polytheists and as monotheists. Their religion has been characterized as pure 'shamanism', a mere jumble of disconnected superstitions, and as forming a deeply philosophical system; it has been defined in turn as a worship of ghosts, a worship of the elements and as pure sun-worship.[1] The religious conceptions of the North American Indians now generally held by anthropologists to be essentially a form of 'shamanism'; that is to say, they had reference to the acquisition and exercise of magical power. Such powers were thought of as derived from supernatural sources. Medicine-men were believed to be inspired or possessed by 'manitus', and were themselves spoken of as 'manitus'. Every Indian sought to place himself under the special protection of some manitu. The Indians told by missionaries of the Christian Creator sometimes identified him with the Supreme Manitu; but the Supreme Manitu had no transcendental character. In the numerous tales about him every trace of an august nature is lacking; he is treated with good-humoured familiarity, and is indistinguishable, except by his superior magical powers, from an ordinary mortal. Nor does he possess moral attributes; he is called 'the liar' and 'the clown'. The Supreme Manitu was, in fact, not conceived by the North American Indians as a solution to speculations concerning the origin and government of the universe, but as the most powerful source of magical power.

But the Great Manitu often assumed a specific nature. The Algonkin and Iroquois tribes regarded all magical power as derived from the moon. It was the moon-goddess Aataentsic who imparted the arts of sorcery and who determined the destinies of men. She was to the Iroquois 'the

[1] Dr Daniel Brinton ridicules the last idea, at one time very prevalent, saying that in North America the Natchez alone were avowed sun-worshippers.

head of their nation'. The Siouan tribes, whose expression, the 'Kitchi Manitu'. literally translated, gave rise to the term 'Great Spirit', had the same conception. 'In the moon, they say, lives the Old Woman who never dies.' The great magic ceremonies which the Mandans carried out in order to obtain a plentiful supply of maize and buffaloes were intended to propitiate the 'Old Woman who never dies'.

'At the appearance of the new moon,' says another traveller, referring more particularly to the Creeks, 'I have observed them with open extended arms, then folded, with inclined bodies, to make adorations with ardour and passion. At the time of harvest and at the full moon, they observe certain feasts and ceremonies which it would seem were derived from some religious origin.'

The Navahos likewise addressed themselves chiefly to the Old Woman, Etsanatlehi. The name signifies the woman who changes and rejuvenates.[1]

The supreme divinities or sources of magical power were represented under identical mythological forms among all Algonkin, Iroquois, Siouan and Athapascan tribes. The moon appears in the mythological conceptions just mentioned under female form, as the Old Woman, the Changing Woman, Aataentsic, the Eternal Woman. In the myths of all these tribes, the moon-goddess has, however, two sons, whom some of the early missionaries compared to Abel and Cain or to the Dioscuri. They are known by a variety of names, though their myths are identical; —such as the 'White One' and the 'Black One'; the beautiful and the ugly Manitu; 'the Slayer' and the 'Controller of Water'. The Dark Manitu is commonly represented as a toad or bull-frog, which contains all the moon-waters. The White Manitu, who is horned, bursts the toad and thereby causes the waters to flood the earth. The Dark Manitu was the 'Lord of Death', while his brother ruled over the living, and was therefore the 'Lord of Life'.

It is a characteristic of lunar gods, that although they are engaged in mortal combat, they are never killed, or their death is only temporary. In his contest with his brother, the Algonkin Manitu is killed but comes to life again after a while. The god Iosheka, 'when he is old, becomes young again in a moment, and is transformed into a young man of twenty-five or thirty, and thus he never dies and remains immortal, although he is somewhat subject to corporal infirmities like ourselves'. Among the Mandan, he is at times a young child and at others an old man. The Great Manitu was, furthermore, a serpent-god. The Chippewa

---

[1] Mr W. Matthews comments that 'in the light of this narrative we see her as none other than our own Mother Nature, the goddess of the changing year, with its youth of spring, its middle of summer, its senility of autumn, growing old to become young again'. The reader may form his own conclusion.

represented him as brandishing a rattlesnake, and the Algonkin as clothed in a garment of serpents. The mythic great serpent, Chepitch-calm, was supposed to have horns on his head; these appear to be the same as the magic horns of the Great Manitu with which he transfixed the toad.

Of the Great Manitu, under his various appellations, a multitude of stories are related in which he appears as a good-natured Indian, playing tricks and practical jokes. He teaches men all the arts, above all the arts of magic and sorcery. But he is at the same time the creator of the world and the ruler of human destinies. He is also a 'vegetation god', the giver of fertility.

One of his most familiar forms is that of the Great Hare or Rabbit. The Hare plays the same conspicuous part in North American folklore as in Africa, and presents the same character as the 'culture heroes' with whom he is interchangeable. The Great Hare 'seems half wizard, half a simpleton; nevertheless, he is 'the Chief God'. In one form of the myth the Great Hare, instead of avenging his mother's death, eats her. 'However, he did not touch the child which she still bore in her womb.' The child, in turn, kills the hare who ate his mother.

One of the most familiar exploits of the Great Manitu resembles Melanesian and Polynesian myths: he snares the sun. The Ojibwa tell the adventure in reference to Hiawatha, one of their names for the Great Manitu. The enmity between the Great Hare and the sun is the theme of various tales. The Great Hare, or Rabbit, having got his back scorched by the sun, vowed vengeance. After a long struggle, the sun fell on the earth and set everything on fire. The Hare himself was so burnt that he was reduced, like some Melanesian gods, to nothing but a head which rolled over the world. His eyes struck against a rock, and such a flood of tears gushed out that a universal deluge resulted which extinguished the conflagration. The Great Hare dwells with his 'grand-mother', the Moon; he is the provider of all waters, the master of the winds, the brother of the snow.

He has frequently been stated to be the sun; but one of the Jesuit missionaries, who did not trouble about theories, says that the Indians worshipped nothing except the Moon and the Wolf. The men, at their religious festivals, danced the 'dance of the moon'; When a distinguished person was sick they danced to the moon to obtain his recovery. The Déné tribes knew no other supernatural power than the moon, of which they stood in great fear and which they invoked for success in their hunting. Their only religious festival was their 'Feast for the Renewal of the Moon', at which they sacrificed a reindeer, setting up a cross over its bones.

Such cosmic notions are found throughout North America. Among the tribes of California the two moon-gods were called Wiyot and Chinegchinick or Waklaut; that is, the Frog. They had once lived on the earth and had ascended into heaven in consequence of dissensions as to whether men should change their skins and live for ever or should die. On the advice of the lizards it was decided that men should die. 'While Wiyot was alive they called him Wiyot; now he has two names, Maita, the Moon, and Wiyot.' The opponent of Wiyot is also represented as the Cojote, who eats Wiyot when the latter is sick. The Cojote, who is equivalent to the Wolf of the eastern tribes, plays a prominent part in the stories of the Californian Indians. He was the fertilizing moon-god who made women pregnant. He could make people young again and, like the Menomini Wolf, he was drowned and revived. The god of generation and resurrection is thus the dark god. It was the bright god who said: 'I want people to live so that an old man may be a boy again, over and over again.'

With the Pueblo Indians, myths are so burdened with detail that it is difficult to discern the leading ideas. But from the multitude of tribal divinities, the Goddess of Fertility, or 'Mother of Germs', and her son the Serpent God, emerge as supreme. 'Muyenwuth, Goddess of Germs', says Mr Fewkes, 'is prëeminently the divinity of the underworld, and has many remarkable similarities to the Nahuatl Micthantecudi of his female companion, Mictlancihuatl. The name is very similar to that of the Moon. This was the ruler of the world of shades visited by Tiyo, the snake hero.'

It is probable that among some of the argicultural tribes the chief Manitu came to be loosely assimilated to the sun. No doubt, many of our reports are coloured by the European assumption that the heavenly body 'worshipped' by the Indians must be the sun, and by the ready assent almost invariably given by uncultured peoples to such suggestions. 'When it is borne in mind', observes Leyland, 'that the most ancient and mythic of these legends have been taken down from the trembling memories of old squaws who never understood their inner meaning, or from ordinary "senaps" who had not thought of them since boyhood, it will be seen that the preservation of a mass of prose poems equal in bulk to the Kalevala or Heldebuch is indeed almost miraculous.'[1]

Cosmic Religion in Central and South America

The solar character of the various ancient Mexicans deities also re-

---

[1] The only instance of a regular cult of the sun in North America is the sun-cult of the Natchez of the Lower Mississippi; but this was of a definitely political character, and directly connected with the claims to supremacy of a clan, the Sun-clan, which constituted the nearest approach to monarchical institutions found in North America, and was, it appears, imported from Central America.

sulted from the claims of aristocratic ruling and priestly classes. It was the thinnest of veneers, laid over traditions and beliefs referring to the moon. All the gods of the Mexican tribes have been recognized by scholars as being originally moon-gods. Thus the great god Tezcatlipoca, whom the missionaries identified with Jesus Christ, 'was a sorcerer who roamed in the night, and certainly developed from the conception of the new, waxing moon.' Quetzalcoatl, the 'Bird-Serpent', conspicuous in Toltec and Aztec myth, has also been recognized as a moon-god. He was the inventor of the calendar. He was a white god who was overcome by the god of darkness, Tezcatlipoca. A magic draught caused him, when old, to become a child again. 'The moon', says Dr Seler, 'held a paramount position in the beliefs and conceptions as also in the cult of the ancient Mexican and Central American races.'

Again, the names of the sun show that, as usual, it was originally regarded as feminine and the wife of the moon-god. The assimilation of the primitive gods to the sun was not generally accepted; the Xaltoca continued to worship the moon as the supreme deity.

The only other instance of a sun-cult on the American continent is that established by the Incas of Peru, who were compelled to build temples to the sun. This forcible reform met in general with obstinate resistance. The ancient gods of the people, whose worship appears to have continued as the popular religion, were Cons and Pachacama. Cons was probably the same as the deity, worshipped at Tauca in Conchucos, who was called Cati-quilla or Lord of the Moon. Conchucos was a Mecca for people from all parts of the country.

The Incas, however, established an association with the ancient deities by claiming the moon, Mama-quilla, as their mother, and by associating her cult with that of the sun-god at Cuzco. The Indians of Peru still pray 'to the great moon that it may give them strength.' In the southern Chilean provinces 'there is not a trace of sun-worship'; and 'the strange circumstance has attracted attention that they bestowed more honour on the moon than on the sun'.

The Caribbean races of the Antilles, observes an old traveller, 'esteem the moon more than the sun'. Their supreme deity is a dual one, consisting of two gods, one well-disposed and one malevolent, and who is in the habit of eating the moon.

The moon was the chief cosmic object of religious conceptions throughout South America. Jurupari, the serpent-god who caused menstruation, is mentioned as the supreme being from Maranhão to the Andes. Jurupari was in the habit of swallowing the moon. His counterpart, the bright and beneficent moon-god, Tupan or Tupanan, was represented as horned. As is usual with non-agricultural peoples, the dreaded dark god occupied a more prominent place than the bright and beneficent god. With the tradition of the former prominence of women in the cult of Jurupari, which is probably the foundation of the legend of the South American Amazons, is associated a sacred lake called the 'Mirror of the Moon', by which they were said to perform their rites on full-moon nights. There the Mother of Frogs gave them certain amulets of green jade, called 'frog-stones'.

Our fullest account of the myths of the South American forest tribes is Dr Preuss's report on the Huitoto of the Upper Amazon; they are of the same type as we have noted in North America. Their lunar deity is sometimes represented as a child, sometimes as a corpse. Sometimes it consists of a face only, which is liable to lose one of its eyes. All fertility is held to be derived from the moon, which may be represented by a tree or a stone. The Tupi and Guarani hold similar beliefs, while the moon festivals of the Tocantin Indians have been vividly described; in them naked women and splendidly-clad men dance from moonrise to moonset. The Uaupes hold similar ceremonies.

The cosmic religion of the Patagonians is distinguished 'by an absence of any trace of sun-worship, although the new moon is saluted, the respectful gestures being accompanied by low muttered words'. And we come again upon myths essentially identical with those of the tribes of Canada.

Although few details are available concerning the religious conceptions of the Fuegians, there can be little doubt that they are similar to those of other South American peoples. We are told that the Fuegians worship the moon and dance all night in his light, and tradition says that their rites were formerly celebrated by women.

Cosmic Religious Conceptions in Africa

The cosmic religious conceptions of the primitive races of South Africa, the Bushmen and Hottentots, are strikingly similar to those of Oceania and America. They refer to two contrasted beings, one on the whole well-disposed, the other not. The former is known as the Lord, or the moon, the words for the two being practically identical. His opponent is called 'the Destroyer,' or Kaggan, which is the name of the Mantis insect. (The latter is also credited with devouring everything, and each is spoken of as 'the all-devourer'.) Kaggan's messenger is the hare and has the power of bringing people back to life. Many of Kaggan's attributes recall those of moon deities; for instance, he is sometimes large and handsome, sometimes small and deformed; he often dies and rises again.

All accounts describe the moon-dances held by the Hottentot and Bushmen as their chief form of cult. 'On the dying or disappearing of the moon, great anxiety prevails.' When a male dancer fell exhausted to

the ground, as often happened, the women danced backwards and forwards over his body, and placed upon it a cross. The collapse was perhaps regarded as a state of temporary death, and the measures taken by
the women may have been intended to promote resurrection.

What are spoken of as 'dances' are generally not so much festive
entertainments as religious ceremonies or 'mysteries'; in fact, with all
African peoples the terms for 'dance' and for religious worship or prayer
are the same. On the Gold Coast the general appellation for a priest is
'dancer'. Dancing is, of course, prominent in all primitive religious
rituals, but the connection of dancing with primitive moon-rites is
particularly close. The Iroquois state that the moon-goddess, Aataentsic
compelled the ghosts of the departed to dance before her. In fact such
dancing was absolutely essential to her health; the dancers 'dance for
the sake of her health, when she is sick'; that is to say, when she is on
the wane or not fully grown. The Indians of California state that their
religious dances were 'to please the moon and prevent her waning'.
Strenuous persistence is commonly regarded as necessary; thus the
Caribs, during an eclipse, considered it imperative to go on dancing
until the recovery of the luminary.

Dancing is probably regarded as an act of sympathetic magic promoting the revival of the moon. The Sakai consider that it is necessary to
aid the moon by magical measures, in the inter-lunary days, in order to
restore it to health. In Melanesia the restorative effects of dancing are
evidently regarded as universally applicable, for the moon-gods themselves are represented as reversing the process, and as bringing human
beings to life, after having fashioned them in wood, by dancing to them.
In the cults of primitive Greece dancing in the moonlight was also
continued to the point of exhaustion. The main function of the priests
who had charge of a young god, the Kouretes, Korybantes (or, as they
were generally called in Rome, the Salic, or 'Jumping', priests), was to
dance and jump; no doubt to assist the growth of the divine infant. It
appears that the Olympic games were not instituted to promote physical
culture but to assist the course of the heavenly bodies. The Diegueños
of southern California were in the habit, when the new moon appeared, of
running foot-races, hoping thus to speed up its progress. The Hurons
did the same and when a chief was sick they held 'games in honour of
the moon'. (In Rome the circus was under the patronage of the goddess
Luna.) The Pawnees say that the games of ball which were popular with
the North American Indians were first instituted by Manibush, the
Rabbit or Great Hare, 'in memory of' his brother the Wolf, that is to say,
the dying moon. The tossing about of balls was apparently thought
to be an even more realistic and effective means of promoting its recovery than dancing; and it is thus possible that our own games of ball,

such as cricket and football, derive from attempts to assist the recovery of the moon.

We have noted how Bushmen women placed a cross on the prostrate bodies of unconscious votaries. The cross played an important part in their religious practices and those of the Hottentots. Women made a point of keeping a wooden cross over their bed, especially prior to confinement. Since the moon and its representatives were their only deities, it seems probable that the cross was an emblem of that deity which is everywhere regarded as helping women in labour.

The sign of the cross is one of universal distribution, and it is almost invariably regarded as possessing a deep magical significance. The cross seems to be uniformly regarded as symbolic of infinite extension in all directions and, by analogy, of eternal life. Thus in Polynesia the moon is said to have formerly occupied all space, and to have ruled over the day as well as the night, by extending her four limbs in all directions. The Luiseño Indians of California represent the Great Mother with her limbs extended in the form of a cross. The cross is stated by North American Indians to indicate the four points of the compass or the four winds. In Egyptian pictures, extension in space is usually indicated by the extended arms of the personage, and the same convention is observed in archaic Greek icons. This symbolism was familiar to the ancients. Plato, in a passage which appears to be a paraphrase of Pythagorean doctrines, describes the Creator as forming the soul of the world in the shape of a cross. 'What is the aspect of the cross', says St Jerome, 'but the form of the world in its four directions.'

The cross, symbolizing the outstretched limbs of the moon-goddess Hina, was worn as an amulet by the Maori (Fig. 3). The statues of Easter Island are marked with the cross, as also the sacred stones of eastern New Guinea. The Algonkins marked the trees near their camps with the cross, to protect themselves against evil spirits; and the cross, pointing to the four winds appointed by the Great Hare, is prominent among the Algonkin and the Siouan tribes. The Athapascan tribes erected a cross

FIG. 3

Greenstone Maori amulet (J. White, *The Ancient History of the Maori*, vol. iii, facing p. 96)

when offering a sacrifice to the new moon. In Central America also the cross, which occupied almost as conspicuous a place as in any Catholic country, was associated with the four winds and with the rain. It was also identified with the 'Tree of Life', prominent in Central American myth, and regarded, as amongst the Algonkins and in Western Asia, as identical with the deity of fertility and vegetation. A cross was usually worn as a pendant by Assyrian monarchs and noblemen (Fig. 6). The cross was specially connected with the cult served by the Araucanian moon-priestesses, and was employed in their rain-making ceremonies; figured prominently in the shrines of the Great Goddess in China; and

FIG. 4
From the pyramid of
Men-kau-ra

was a cult-symbol in Tibet. It was widespread as a religious symbol and magic talisman among the Semites and throughout Western Asia.

The Egyptian looped cross, or 'ankh,' which, as the symbol of life and resurrection, was held by deities to the nostrils of their votaries, imparting to them renewed life, has received varied interpretations—as a key, a nilometer, a knot, a uterus and appendages. It appears to be in accordance with the conventions of Egyptian, as also of Western Asiatic pictography, that the 'loop' which forms its upper limb is simply the schematic representation of the head of the deity with outstretched arms, or the disc or egg of the moon as a surrogate. Innumerable such figures appear on Semitic monuments, and one at least on the pyramid of Men-kau-ra (Fig. 4). The sign of the moon-goddess Ishtar, or Aphrodite, is a cross surmounted by a disc, ♀. The plain four-limbed cross was likewise an alternative of the 'ankh' among the Egyptians, and is found both as an amulet (Fig. 5) and in association with the god Moon, hanging as a pendant from his neck (Fig. 7).

FIG. 5
Pendant amulet from Tell-al-Amarna. (P. E. Newberry and J. Garstang, *A Short History of Ancient Egypt*, facing p. 88)

A monumental cross is the central object in the shrine of the Kretan goddess, and it takes the place of the crescent on the brow of the

FIG. 6
From a monolith stele of Samsi-Adad IV (A. Jeremias, *Handbuck der altorientatischen Geisteskultur*, p. 99

FIG. 7
Aah, the god Moon, after R. V. Lanzone and E. A. Wallis Budge

FIG. 8
Vase fragment from the acropolis of Susa. (*Délégation en Perse*, vol. xiii, p. 214, fig. 428)

Ephesian Artemis. In Western Asia, the cross was usually associated with the lunar crescent and was an alternative symbol of the moon (Figs. 8-12.) Surmounted by the crescent, it was placed on the sacred

FIG. 9

The Crescent-Cross. (W. Ward, *Seal Cylinders of Western Asia*, p. 395) Cf. p. 248

FIG. 10

Babylonian Sacred Stone (J. Menant, *Pierres gravées de la Haute-Asie*, vol. i, p. 136)

FIG. 11

Intaglio from Sardinia (G. d'Alviella, art. "Cross" in Hastings's *Encyclopædia of Religion and Ethics*, vol. iv, p. 326 after J. Menant).

stones of the moon-deity in Babylonia (Fig. 10). The cross and crescent appear again on Iberian coins (Fig. 13).

Demonstrations similar to those made at the various phases of the moon by the Bushmen and Hottentots are general in most parts of Africa. 'All Africa dances at night,' says an old writer. Thus among the

FIG. 12

Fragment of pottery from the acropolis of Susa. (*Délégation en Perse*, vol. xiii, p. 40, fig. 135)

FIG. 13

(*a*) Coin from Asido. (*b*) Coin from Turiregina. (J. Zobel de Zangronitz, "Spanische Münzen und bisher unerklärten Aufschriften," *Zeitschrift der deutschen morgenländishce Gesellschaft*, xvii, plates iii and viii)

Ekoi, 'though dancing is carried on during every hour of the day and all seasons of the year, it is by the light of the full moon that the Ekoi most love to indulge in the pastime'. It is exceedingly doubtful whether it was originally regarded as a pastime. At Oban, in the country of Ekoi, there is a circle of unhewn stones where women and girls dance at the new moon, men and boys being excluded. It is believed that unless they do so no woman can have a child.

Such rites take place most frequently at the new moon. 'To the African generally', says the Rev. John Roscoe, 'the new moon is always a time of rejoicing; it is watched for and hailed with songs and festivities.' Among the Bambara, as among the Ekoi, the women and girls meet every month at the new moon, and perform dances presided over by a high-priestess. No man may be present. The negroes of Ashango say that the moon calls them her insects and devours them. 'The moon, with them, is the emblem of time and death.' In Loango, 'at the appearance of the new moon the people fall on their knees, or cry out, standing and clapping their hands, "So may I renew my life as thou are renewed" '.

In the religious associations or secret societies, the same ideas are central to the process of initiation. It would, of course, be unlikely that such notions should be connected with the power of resurrection ascribed to the moon in one case but not the other. And in fact in some of those stories the power of resurrection and the origin of death are expressly associated with such rituals. Thus, in a varient of the story in which a man's second wife spies on the first just as she is restored to youth and beauty, with the result that both fall dead, the incident takes place in the 'vela', or special building in which the secret society's resurrection rites take place, on which no one may spy. We are told that the man and his two wives, who figure in these stories, are the moon and his two wives, the morning and the evening stars.

The Bantu have strikingly little mythology, and do not distinctly individualize their personalities. The Bantu turns for supernatural assistance to individual workers of magic, whose powers derive from a spirit or fetich, and his superstitious fears are associated with the powers of these innumerable fetiches to work evil. The magical powers that are near at hand have obliterated in his mind the remoter cosmic powers. If the point be pressed, the native African will, however, generally recognize that the power of the fetich is ultimately derived from some higher and more general source of power, much as the magic virtues of the sacred stones of the Melanesians are derived from the moon. In fact, among the Baluba tribes of the Congo, at the new moon, all fetiches are taken out of their niches or sacred huts, and are presented to the moon. It is apparently thought that their magic power will be invigorated by saturating them with moonlight.[1]

---

[1] A partial exception to the general disintegration of religious belief and cult by the practice of fetichism was presented by the religion of Dahomey, which was identical with that of other Bantu peoples, and was characterized by the same substitution of fetich deities as for the supreme deity. But the connection between the two was less completely obliterated; the supreme being, Mau, we are

Some of the stories concerning the origin of death are directly associated with the supreme deity as an alternative designation of the moon. Among the Herero, he is the giver of immortality; he is also the personification of fate. The tribes of northern Rhodesia relate that Leza (as they call him) gave the first men the choice between mortality and immortality, but that they made the wrong choice. Death from old age is spoken of by them as 'Leza's death.'

The name Leza, and its variations, such as Kabezya, Wezia, etc., are, according to Father Colle, connected with the root 'wez' or 'Kwez.' In the Luba region of the Congo, 'Kwezi' is the ordinary term for the moon. Among the Ashanti the generic term for all gods is 'Boshun'; it is the same for the moon. There is no indication in any part of Africa at the present day of any solar cult or cosmology.[1]

Cosmic Religion of Ancient Egypt

In one notable instance, however, a regular solar cult arose in Africa, viz. in ancient Egypt. Though far from primitive, it derived directly from the conceptions which survive in savage Africa, and forty centuries of theological development have not completely obliterated its primitive outlines. A glance at some of its aspects may be instructive.

The sun-god Rā heads the national pantheon. All other gods are represented as emanations of the supreme solar divinity, the creator and governor of the universe. All Egyptian religious conceptions, such as those relating to the judgement and resurrection of the dead, were associated with Rā. The divine kings of Egypt were styled 'sons of Rā', and were regarded as his representatives; the princesses and queen were called 'the wives of Rā'.

We know how the sun-god became established in Egypt. From the Westcar Papyrus, it appears that it was not until about 3500 B.C. that Rā became supreme. At this point 'the sun-god Rā advances to the first place, which, in conjunction later with the Theban deity Amen, he holds ever afterwards, Horus becoming in some respects identified with him.' Sir A. E. Wallis Budge says: 'The astute theologians, either by force or persuasion, succeeded in making the official classes and priest-

---

told, is the moon fetich, and his priestesses bear as their emblem two black beads and a white shell. At the new moon they run shouting like mænads through the streets and are then said to be 'seeking the moon'. Other fetiches were the sacred serpent and that for evoking rain.

[1] The solar name used by the Shagga tribes, Raum believes, is 'probably the effect of foreign influence. To perceive God in the sun or in the vault of heaven does not appear to be a genuine Bantu belief.' But the statement of Frobenius, that 'the greater part of Africa is in the stage of moon-worship', is only partially true, for the primitive cosmic cult has broken down for the most part into fetichism.

hood believe that all the indigenous great gods were forms of Rā, and so secured his supremacy.' Nowhere is Rā worshipped in his own name alone, but always in combination with the name of some other god.

At Thebes, when it became the capital of the New Empire, Rā was worshipped as Amen-Rā. But Amen does not appear originally to have had the slightest connection with solar cult. His name, 'the Hidden,' or 'Obscure', seems highly inappropriate for a sun-god. His representation as a frog, an animal held sacred at Thebes, hardly suggests solar attributes. Amen was the horned god, familiar to the Greeks as the horned Ammon. Much more ancient than his association with Rā was his identification with Min, probably a variation of the same name. Amen-Min is 'the Fiery Bull, Lord of the New Moon, who becomes the Full Moon; who shines in the night at the beginning of each month'. Hence Amen had various forms corresponding to his different ages—Amen the Child and Amen the Old.

At Heliopolis, Rā was similarly associated with the local gods, notably Tum (Atum, Temu) who was described as a personification of the setting sun. 'I am Khepera in the morning, Rā at noonday, Tum in the evening,' states an oft-cited formula. But Tum is represented in his infant form as a child with the moon on his head. At Pi-Tum, Tum was worshipped in the form of a python; he is also represented as a lizard.

Ptah, the great god of Memphis, was in Heliopolitan theology regarded as identical with Rā, or as his father. Ptah is referred to as the 'Lord of thirty years'; like the moon-deity of Cochin-China, he was never more than thirty. He was a two-headed god, 'of multitudinous forms'. Sometimes he was 'Ptah of the Beautiful Face'; sometimes 'Ptah the embryo', and was represented as a lame dwarf, resembling the Melanesian and Polynesian embryo gods Qat and Maui-Tiki. It is significant that the dwarf form of Ptah, common under the Old Empire, disappears almost completely under the New Empire. Ptah is described as the creator of the egg of the moon, to which is sometimes added the egg of the sun. The former is a common symbol of the moon, the latter a most uncommon symbol of the sun. Probably Ptah was originally the moon-egg itself.

Horus, as the royal god of the early Egyptian dynasties, was assigned an honourable place as the god of the rising sun in the solar mythology of Heliopolis. Like some of the moon-gods we have noted, he was sometimes regarded as consisting of a head or face only; his name, 'Her' means 'Face'. Horus was called 'the Lord of Transformations'. He was also spoken of as the old man who becomes young again', or 'who becomes a child.'

He was 'He of the Lotus', and the phrase was regarded as equivalent to 'He who renews himself and becomes young again'. The feast of He of the Lotus was celebrated on the last day of the month, i.e. at the new moon. The Pharaohs, who impersonated Horus, were crowned on the day of the new moon when gods granted them 'to commence happily the year, and to become young again'. On this occasion the Pharaoh also ceremonially put on a new skin.

Horus was engaged in a continual fight with his brother Set, the dark god; Eusebius, who saw the traditional representations of the fight, says this was an allegory of the double light of the moon. Horus and Set were regarded as heavenly twins; they sailed the heavens in the same boat. The double deity was sometimes pictured as having two heads—that of Horus and that of Set—on the same body. They periodically lost their human form, becoming indiscernible; 'they spent three nights and three days in this state', until released again by Isis. Set not only fought Horus but also threw filth in his face, thus producing the spots that may be seen thereon.

The two eyes of Horus play a conspicuous part in all the symbolism referring to him. Like those of the moon-god of the Huitoto they were subject to vicissitudes. In the fight with Set, the latter swallowed the right eye of Horus. The left eye of Horus was one of the commonest emblems of the god and of the moon. The waxing moon appears in Egypt on the right side of the lunar disc, so that it constitutes the left side of the Face-god, the right side or his right eye, being eaten by Set, who, as Plutarch says 'is the name given to the shadow of the earth cast upon the waning moon'. Ultimately the Face-god has no eyes left at all; he is then called the 'Blind', or 'Dark Horus'. Set, however, is ultimately compelled to regurgitate the right eye of Horus.

At Panoplis, Horus was worshipped as the moon without ambiguities, and was regarded as identical with Min, which appears to have been an alternative name for the moon; the temple of Horus was called 'the House of the Moon'. Her-Min was one of the oldest and most widely worshipped of Egyptian deities, and the great agricultural festivals were celebrated all over Egypt under his auspices.

'Those mythological subtleties which may seem surprising', writes an eminent Egyptologist (Pierret), 'have their explanation in the fact that the perpetual succession of the phases of the sun are personified in those divine forms which reciprocally engender one another.' But the sun does not die, nor does it come to life again, and no uncultured people, ancient or modern, is known ever to have supposed that it does. The sun, on the contrary, is contrasted by them with the moon on account of its unchanging and undying character; it is only during an eclipse that the sun is ever thought to die. The moon dies, not because it sets but because it dwindles and disappears entirely for three or four days; and the Zulus have grown sceptical concerning their ancient doctrines because they have discovered by careful observation that the dark moon may be perceived even during the inter-lunary days. Primitive conceptions may be puerile but they have never engendered such a monstrosity as a waxing and waning sun. It was reserved for the learned to give birth to such an astronomical curiosity.

'Among certain Oriental nations', Sir E. A. Wallis Budge remarks, 'the worship of the moon always preceded that of the sun, and there is reason for thinking that several of the oldest gods of Egypt were forms of the moon in her various phases.'

From the multitude of figures of the moon-god (says Lorisato) 'it appears that his cult was extremely widespread throughout Egypt.' Indeed, while everywhere in Egypt we come upon numerous moon-emblems and figures of acknowledged moon-gods, scarcely a trace is to be found of the sun, or emblems of the sun-god.

The interpretation of ancient Egyptian cult in solar terms by the priestly theologians of the Middle and New Kingdoms has been referred to by learned Egyptologists as sublime, but, as Sir E. A. W. Budge says: 'The confusion and contradictions which appear in the religious texts written under the XXth and following dynasties, prove beyond all doubt that the knowledge of the early dynastic religion of Egypt possessed by the priests in general after, let us say 1200 B.C., was extremely vague and uncertain. It seems to me that the existence of the cult of Rā does not affect the inquiry into the indigenous religion of Egypt in any way.' Professor Wiedemann, although accepting the existence of sun-worship uncritically, observes: 'The bulk of the people clung to their ancient cult of the Moon, and to their sacred beasts and birds, and worshipped the spirits that dwelt in them, wholly undisturbed by the spread of the foreign and official cult of the Sun-god.'

Horus, who occupied a high place in Egyptian religion from earliest times, was represented as a hawk; and some Egyptologists—e.g. Wiedemann—have supposed that the hawk must be an emblem of the sun. But elsewhere Wiedemann himself says: 'Khunsu is in the first place a lunar deity . . . He was figured as a hawk-headed god.' In point of fact, the hawk was the totem animal of the royal dynasties who first unified the Egyptian people and cults, and as such was naturally identified with the chief cosmic god just as the eagle-hawk is identified with the cosmic deity by some Australian tribes. Manifestly the priests of Rā would seek to impart a solar character to the royal totem-bird.

It has been suggested that the reason for the sharp opposition between the popular and the official theology of Egypt was that the priests of Rā at Heliopolis were Asiatics and the cult of Rā an imported cult. But Western Asia, where cosmological conceptions preserved their lunar character to the last and were never supplanted by a solar religion, seems about the last place from which to import a solar cult.[1]

We come upon this phenomenon everywhere; and foreign solar worshippers would have to be postulated in Persia, in Polynesia, in Peru, in Mexico, no less than in Egypt. But nowhere can a primitive solar religion be found unpreceded by lunar cult. All solar mythologies exhibit the inconsistencies which reveal the clumsy adaptation of lunar attributes by which they have been produced. They are invariably the products of priesthoods and sacred monarchies; they are never the spontaneous outcome of popular religious ideas.

The vital religious conceptions of the ancient Egyptians centred not around Rā but around Osiris. There is nothing to indicate that Osiris differed in his original character from any other Egyptian high god. He was regarded as the special god of the resurrection; but almost every other Egyptian god was periodically a waxing and waning god, a dying and resurrecting god, and a bestower of eternal life.

The sacred beetle, or scarab, which rolls its ball of eggs and dung, whence a new generation is born, is regarded as a symbol of the resurrection in many parts of Africa. In the Congo the beetle symbolizes the moon and eternal renewal. The Egyptian priest Horapollo describes how the scarab propagates itself by depositing its ball of ox-dung in the earth for twenty-eight days, after which the scarab emerges, and he adds: 'The second species is that which is horned and bull-formed and is

FIG. 14

Khepera, from C. R. Lepsius, *Das Todten-buch*, plate ix.

consecrated to the moon.' Khepera is represented as a beetle with wings outstretched in the form of a lunar crescent (Fig. 14). In fact, there is not a single high god in the Egyptian pantheon, with the exception of Rā, who is not a god of the dead and fitted by his characteristics to play the part of god of the Resurrection. Like so many other peoples, the Egyptians believed that the power which made resurrection possible was associated with the moon.

Osiris was, like every other Egyptian god, identified in Heliopolitan theology with Rā. But that association was even more flimsy than similar identifications with Rā of the moon-gods Sud or Khons. His very name appears to mean 'the Lord of the Moon'. Countless inscribed figures

---

[1] The ground upon which Sir E. A. Wallis Budge thinks it necessary to have recourse to this desperate hypothesis is that 'it could not have been sun-worship which they disliked, for they had been sun-worshippers from time immemorial'. But for this statement there appears to exist no sufficient evidence.

represent and name 'Osiris, the Moon'; on the other hand, there does not exist a single figure representing Osiris as the sun. The moon was termed the 'abode of Osiris'. As a form of the adult Horus, he had been the special resurrecting god of the great earlier dynasties. Osiris was represented as having reigned or lived twenty-eight years—obviously a translation of the moon-god's life of a month into years. The body of Osiris was supposed to have been cut up by Set into fourteen pieces, one for each day of the waning moon. A conventional representation of Osiris pictures him enthroned at the top of a flight of steps; the same convention is observed in representations of the moon; we commonly see the lunar crescent, surmounted by the left moon-eye, resting on the top of a flight of fourteen steps (Fig. 15 to 19).

In his mysteries at Denderah, the funeral rites of Osiris lasted nine days, ending on the last day of the month, when he was buried; the ceremonies were thus celebrated during the nine days of the waning moon. (Similarly, the Nandi in East Africa celebrate mourning rites during the duration of the last phase of the moon). The figure of the god, which was moulded afresh for each performance, was a lunar crescent, as Plutarch tells us.

One of the most popular alternative names of Osiris was Un-nefer, the Great Hare.

The bull Apis, which was 'the life of Osiris, the Lord of Heaven, with his horns on his head', 'symbolized the moon'. Its mark was the lunar crescent on its flank; it was begotten 'by a ray of generative light which appeared from the moon, and rested upon the cow his mother'.

It is wholly improbable that the lunar attributes of Osiris were super-added to his original character. In the oldest texts the lunar attributes constitute the whole of his character and ritual. Moreover, to suppose such attributes to have been assigned as an afterthought implies an evolution of ideas from more abstract to more concrete. Universal

FIG. 15

From a tablet of Semti (1st Dynasty), British Museum, Third Egyptian Room, Table-case L, No. 124

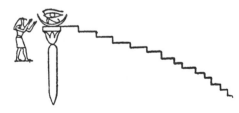

FIG. 16

The Moon on fourteen steps (R. V. Lanzone, Dizionario di mitologia egizia, plate 39).

FIG. 17

The Moon and the gods of the fourteen steps (E. A. Wallis Budge, The Gods of
the Egyptians, vol. ii, p. 321)

FIG. 18

From the mace-head of Nārmer, (J. E. Quibell, *Hierakonpolis*, Part i, plate
xxvi B)

FIG. 19

"The Ennead" from the "Book of Gates," British Museum

ethnological experience teaches that the development of human thought takes place in the reverse direction.[1]

Since solar cosmogonies are merely reinterpretations of those primitively connected with the moon, they have but a slender connection with cosmological ideas at all. Hence they are particularly apt to assume vaguer, more generalized, more abstract forms. In the theological system of the priests of Rā, the sun, was in itself of very little direct account. It was not the object of the superstitious awe with which primitive man regards the moon; it was a mere symbol—the sun was not the god but the visible emblem of the god. Being of no vital significance, that similitude assumes an even more abstract form, as the contest between Good and Evil. The dark god who endeavours to eat the bright god becomes blacker and blacker in the spiritual sense, and comes to be looked upon as the embodiment of evil. Set is, in the priestly recension of the Book of the Dead, 'an abomination unto Horus.' Rā, taking the place of Horus, was represented as bruising the head of the enemy, in the form of the serpent, under his heel, and, like St George, transfixing the Evil One with his spear. Primitive lunar deities, in contrast, have no absolute moral attributes; the dark god is not wholly evil, nor is the bright god wholly good. The more 'unfavourable' and more dangerous a god is, as we have frequently had occasion to note, the more important to conciliate him.

The god Set appears in the Pyramid Texts and in the Book of the Dead as one of the Great Gods to whom all honour and worship are directed. Being, like his brothers Horus and Osiris, a moon-god and a god of resurrection, he could bestow eternal life; he was pronounced the 'supreme god', the 'Lord of Heaven and Earth'. It was not until the relatively late times of the XXIInd, or XXVth Dynasty that Set was definitely recognized as the spirit of evil and his temples abolished.

The local deities of Egyptian nomes, who were assigned various position and functions in the 'pantheon' of solar theology, were, in fact, one and all, but local names or forms of the primitive moon-god, either in his bright or in his dark aspect. Like all primitive deities, they were usually associated with some local totem animal or with some pseudo-

---

[1] It has been suggested that Osiris was originally a river-god and symbolized the annual rising and falling of the Nile. But, as Plutarch noted, the Egyptians 'regard the rise of the Nile as being regulated in accordance with the light of the moon'; and with their predilection for expressing their conceptions in numerical symbolisms they supposed that 'the maximum rise measured at Elephantine [was] twenty-eight cubits in accordance with the monthly cycle of the moon'. Sir James Frazer thinks that Osiris was originally a personification of vegetation. But the growth of vegetation and the fertility of fields, as well as that of animals and human beings, are universally attributed to the moon, and all moon-deities are 'vegetation-gods'.

totem of significance in their cult or in lunar symbolism. Thoth, whose name is usually understood to mean 'the ibis', is most commonly represented as ibis-headed, the ibis being the local totem of the ibis-nome in the delta. He was also an ape or baboon.

Ancient Egyptian notions concerning the baboon are mentioned by Horapollo: 'The beast cynocephalus rejoiceth at the coming of the moon, for then he stands up, lifting his fore-feet towards heaven, and with a royal ensign upon his head. And he hath such sympathy with the moon, that when she meets the sun, as betwixt the old and new moon, so that she gives no light, the male, or he-cynocephalus, never looks up, nor eats anything, as bewailing the losse of the moon. And the female, as malcontent as he, all that while pisseth blood. For which causes these beasts are nourished and kept in hallowed places, that by them the times of the moones meeting with the sun may certainly be known.' Among the Bechuana, the baboon is likewise associated with the moon.

In short, in Egypt the evolution of religious ideas may be followed from primitive lunar and magical conceptions intermingled with totemism, identical with those of the Bushmen and Hottentots, to the most transcendental and abstruse metaphysical abstractions.

The latter are the term of the process of religious evolution; the common error of interpreters has been to mistake them for its germ, and to set the pyramid of religious development upon its apex. 'The Egyptian was never a profound theologian and in primitive times his religion was largely a mixture of magic and materialism. Modern investigators of the Egyptian religion read into the texts ideas and meanings which were, and are, wholly foreign to the African mind.'

CHAPTER 22

The Magical Origin of Queens

THE transformation of primitive lunar deities into solar ones is often associated with the transfer of magical and priestly functions from women to men. Thus in Peru the ancient official cult of the lunar deity at Cuzco was served by priestesses, while the service of the sun-god was performed by priests. This change is often associated with the establishment of powerful rulers or priest-kings, who are disposed to claim the protection of a deity distinct from the gods of the people.

Plutarch observes: 'The effects of the moon are similar to the effects of reason and wisdom'—that is to say, of magic knowledge and art—'whereas those of the sun appear to be brought about by the power of physical force and violence.' Accordingly, monarchical rulers almost invariably tend to regard the sun as their special deity; nowhere are regular solar cults found in societies that have retained their primitive democratic character. Of course, the development of agriculture also tends to impart the solar character to primitive cosmic conceptions. In such cases male priests may become concerned with the magical practices promoting fertility, which were originally the speciality of the women. In the primitive division of labour, the preparation and cultivation of food are the special occupation of the women, as hunting is that of the men. In many savage myths, agriculture is held to have been invented by women. All uncivilized peoples regard agriculture as depending, even more than other operations, upon magical power rather than on skill and labour. Nothing so astonished the Pueblo Indians, when Europeans first settled amongst them, as to see them plant corn without performing any religious ceremonies, and it was the profoundest shock to see that the corn grew, nevertheless. The fact did more to shatter their faith than all the crusades of the missionaries.

Naturally, the magical or religious rites to secure the fertility of the fields were within the competence of the women who cultivated them and whose fertility was likened to the earth's. The immediate object of most of these ceremonies is the production of rain, and in most parts of the world rain-making ceremonies are performed by the women. In Europe, such practices survive in a few places into modern times— in Germany and elsewhere. (Thus in Worms, when a severe drought was experienced, a naked girl was led to the nearest stream to bathe.)

This explains why in Europe the raising of storms has always been regarded as one of the powers of witches. 'No one imbued with mean sense', says Reginald Scot, 'but would deny that the elements are obedient to witches and at their commandment, or that they may at their pleasure send rain, hail, tempests, thunder, lightning, when she, being but an old doting woman, casteth a flint over her left shoulder towards the west, or hurleth a little sea-sand up into the element, or wetteth a broom sprig in water, and sprinkleth the same in the air . . .!' A common story, of which many variants are found, is that of a hunter who, annoyed at a prolonged spell of rain, fired a shot at the clouds, from which a naked women fell mortally wounded, and the clouds at once dispersed. Hence the expression, 'It is raining cats and dogs and old women.' The cats and dogs are, of course, but disguises of the old women.

In Africa, where rain-making is so prominent a function of the sacred king, the association of that function with the special powers and activities of women is nevertheless apparent. Thus, among the Baronga, the women perform elaborate ceremonies at which no man may be present; these strongly recall those of the Greek Bacchantes.

Indeed, the magical powers of a wizard are often thought to be largely dependent upon the character of his wife, and in many tribes a man cannot become a doctor by himself. Among the Zulus, a rain-maker loses his power if his wife becomes pregnant, for pregnancy is believed to impair the magical powers of women.

Vestal Fires

Incidentally, agricultural magic is often associated with the practice of lighting fires or with carrying lighted torches around newly sown seeds —a practice observed in most parts of Europe and among the Basuto, the Koreans, the North American Indians, the Zuñis, etc. In France it was repeatedly condemned by ecclesiastical councils as a relic of paganism, and it has been noted quite recently in Lancashire. The fires might either produce rain or check excessive rain.

Fire is everywhere accounted sacred, and must be protected against inauspicious influences. For example, all fires are put out on the death of a king in Uganda, and this is still the custom in some parts of the Highlands of Scotland when a person dies. Fires must also be extinguished on inauspicious or Sabbath days—hence the Jewish law against kindling fire upon the Sabbath. The rekindling of the fire was a solemn ceremony. The Andamanese islanders extinguish or cover up all fires whenever the moon rises after sundown, as it is thought that the moon will be jealous. When St Patrick first came among the heathen Irish and lit candles in a chapel on the day of Beltane, to whom sacred fires were consecrated, the horror caused by this sacrilegious act was such that he was obliged to extinguish them. The extinction of lights is observed in most countries by the Christian Church on the Saturday before Easter, and at the Church of the Holy Sepulchre in Jerusalem constitutes one of the great festivals. Indeed, with many Eastern Christians it is regarded as the chief ceremony of their religion. The new fire is believed to be supplied by the Holy Ghost.

It is commonly supposed that such rituals are an index of the sun-cult, but they are, in fact, much older. The Sabbath observance of the Babylonians and of the Jews were monthly, not yearly, and in primitive religion the renewal of life is associated not with the sun but with the moon. In Greece, sacred fires were kept burning in the shrines of countless deities who had no connection with solar cults, such as Demeter and Kore, Aphrodite and Pan. In Rome a fire was maintained in the temple of 'Luna noctiluca'.

Magical Functions of Queens

In many societies, the magical powers reside particularly in the wife or wives of the king. Thus the wives of the king of Dahomey are the priestesses of the rain-making god and are spoken of as 'the Mothers'. The vestal priestesses of Peru were also called 'the Mothers', and were regarded as the wives of the great Inca, who had the right to take any of them as his actual wives. The institution of the Peruvian Mothers, which was adopted by the Incas, belonged to the most ancient religious usages of the people. The vestals of Cuzco were specially devoted to the cult of the moon-deity Mama-Quilla, and tended a perpetual fire, baked the bread and prepared the beer. The native priestesses of Peru and of Chile served, in particular, the 'Mother of Maize' and performed the rain-making ceremonies.

The similarity between these and the Vestals of Rome is manifest. Our conception of the cult of the Vestals is derived from later Roman times, when the Vestals were held up as models of domestic virtue. But originally the cult was very different. Vesta was associated with a male god, Pales, and they were jointly the god of food. Pales appears to have been identical with Priapus, and was represented in the temple of the Vestals by a phallic image, also by a sacred serpent. One of the chief festivals of the cult was the Feast of Bakers, and the Vestals themselves prepared loaves of bread according to an elaborate ritual. They also cared for the water supply and, at the Ides of May, threw into the river twenty-four dummies, bound hand and foot and representing men.

Sir James Fraser has sought to show that, like their American and African sisters, they were originally the wives of the Roman kings. Several Vestals were, we know, the mothers of kings of Rome; and each received, on her consecration, the name Amata, 'beloved', which was the title of the wife of a Latin king. The Flamen Dialis who, as representative of the sacred king, occupied the position of head of the College of Priestesses, was hedged by many tabus designed to maintain him in a condition of ritual purity. But, strangely enough, he was not vowed to chastity. On the contrary, it was compulsory that he should be a married man. The most remarkable of the rules was that, if his wife should happen to die before her husband, the latter automatically ceased to hold office and at once lost his sacred character. Thus the status of the Flamen Dialis did not differ essentially from that of the headmen of the Seri Indians. It would be impossible to account for these strange rules if we were content to accept the old conception that Roman society had from the first been strenuously patriarchal, and that the priestly functions had, accordingly, been exercised chiefly by males. In primitive times, priestesses were even more important than priests in Roman religion and the cult of the Good Goddess (from which, even in later times, men were entirely excluded) was one of the oldest and most sacred in Roman religion, and was served by the Vestal priestesses.

Archaic Queenships

It seems, then, that in the primitive monarchies of America, Africa and Archaic Italy, it was considered appropriate that the wives of the god, or of his representative the sacred king, should take an important part in the fertility ceremonies, especially those connected with water. It is difficult to suppose that women were introduced into religious rituals originally in the hands of male officiants.

Sir James Fraser has shown that the office of royalty and its semi-divine character originated not in political organization but in the magical functions which the monarch was expected to discharge. Indeed, in ancient kingships the king has no despotic power and is frequently treated with scant reverence. In many societies the spiritual and temporal leaders are quite distinct, but in others the successful war-leader legitimizes his claim to supreme power by assuming the magical role, and it would seem that this is how the monarchial office has developed.

Sometimes we find a society developing into an actual gynæcocracy, in which supreme power is vested in the queen and the war-leader remains merely a delegate. For instance in the matriarchal communities of Assam the religious and sacerdotal functions have remained in the hands of women, while Chinese annals (A.D. 581–905), describe the bellicose kingdom of Su-pi—that is, the Kingdom of Women—comprising the whole of northern Tibet, where the women had men to serve them and held their husbands in light esteem.

The matriarchal constitution of royalty, far from being exceptional, is the general rule in barbaric kingdoms. In North America, where the democratic character of primitive society has, in general, been fully maintained, nevertheless among the tribes of the lower Mississippi, particularly the Natchez, the system of royal (female) power developed. In the Sun-clan the female genealogy alone counted. The women might take what sexual partners they pleased, and their husbands were treated as servants. They might not even sit down in the presence of their royal mistresses, who spoke of them as 'curs', and could have them executed.

Where royal power is transmitted through the female line, we may suspect the existence of an earlier mother-cult, as among the Incas. This often leads to the practice of dynastic incest, for this is the only way to avoid the king's own son being excluded from the succession. Such a system is found in Bogota, in Hawaii and elsewhere. In Tahiti royalty was hereditary through the women. Although Polynesian society was not in a matriarchal phase, the magical character of royalty was regarded as transmitted through the women. One observer remarks on the extraordinary veneration shown by Samoan chiefs for their sisters, and explains it by the belief that it was into their descendants and not those of the brother that the family god would enter. A similar pattern is found in many places in Africa. The organization of royal power among the Ashanti is almost identical with that among the Natchez. The paternal descent of the king is unimportant and, if the princess who is heir to the throne dies before her father, he is obliged to commit suicide on her grave. The chief among the princesses is called the Queen-Mother and she administers the state when the king is absent. She also has the power to depose the king. The commander of the British expedition which established a protectorate in 1895–6 considered that 'the real ruler of Ashanti was the Queen-Mother'. The conception of a royal family consisting of women only seems to have been deeply rooted among African peoples. 'In the oldest times', says Dr Rehse, 'there were no reigning princes in Africa, but the negroes had large kingdoms which were ruled by goddesses. The goddesses and priests and priestesses, who transacted the affairs of government in the name of their divine mistresses.' Very similar circumstances ruled among the Loango, in the kingdom of Dahomey and among the Lunda. Even among the war-like kings of the Uganda, two women, the queen-mother and the queen, the latter being the king's sister, reign by their side and each of these women bears the title, 'Kabaka'; that is, king. If the Queen-Mother died, fear seized the people. These principles and usages are not peculiar to the Bantu races, but are observed in kingdoms where the ruling classes are predominantly Hamitic—for instance, among the Shilluk of Fashoda. Here the sacred kingship illustrates Sir James Fraser's well-known theory that the sacred king was ritually put to death before he became senile. Such treatment is intelligible if the monarch was originally little more than the slave-husband of imperious royal women. Among the Shilluk the term of the king's office and of his life was determined by the queens who decreed his demise as soon as his generative powers began to fail.

The same principles are found in Egypt, where, says Sir Flinders Petrie: 'It is very doubtful if a king could reign except as the husband of the heiress of the kingdom, the right to which descended in the female line.' Every princess of the royal house was known as 'Royal Mother', while the chief title of the king, 'Suten Net', originally meant high-priest, not 'king'. The queen and princesses were entitled to the royal totem from birth, whereas the king wore only the crown of high-priest and did not receive his Horus-name until his coronation. Queens were born but kings were made.

When Egypt reverted to semi-barbarism, the matriarchal features became accentuated. The kings of Egypt adopted the device of dynastic incest but, failing this artificial combination of the male and female line, the succession reverted to the female line. The royal office could not be transmitted by a king to his descendants.

It is needless to go to Africa for examples of kings legalizing their titles by marrying the widows of their predecessors. Almost every conqueror and usurper shows the same anxiety: Absalom, Alexander, Canute. Alboin, the Lombard king, married Rosamund. Hamlet's uncle, Feng, married Hamlet's mother; and the latter's successor, Wiglet, did similarly.

In Egypt, according to Manetho, Sethosis, setting out on a journey, appointed his brother regent, on condition that he did not touch the queen or the royal wives. However, the brother made himself master of the kingdom by marrying his brother's wife. The famous intrigue of Antony and Cleopatra was, no doubt, much more political than romantic, and the Roman adventurer endeavoured to follow the immemorial precedent of all aspirants to the double crown of Egypt.

The reason so much importance was attached to legitimacy in the royal succession was the transmission of magic power through women. This is shown, for instance, by the fact that, among the Kuku of the Upper Congo, no man can become a rain-maker unless he is born of a rain-making woman. Such facts as these offer strong confirmation of the conclusion, to which we were previously led, that magic and priestly functions were originally exercised by women. The power of sacred monarchs and priesthoods is founded upon magical attributes which originally belonged prescriptively to women. Agricultural religions have developed out of rites that were the domain of the women. And the deities which priestesses serve derive their significance from their association with the functions of women.

These conclusions take us a long way away from the assumption that women have had little or nothing to do with the development of religious ideas, even though in its advanced phases and intellectualised forms religious development has indeed been the work of men. Just as primitive emotions and sentiments have been transmuted into creative art by the intellectual operation of the masculine mind, so primitive magic and superstition have been transformed by the male intellect into theological religions.

CHAPTER 23

The Great Mothers

PRIMITIVE lunar deities are predominantly masculine: the moon is a man and the sun is commonly his wife. But when solar gods or more generalized deities take over the fertilizing function, the sexes of the heavenly bodies commonly become reversed, the moon becoming the wife of the sun. This reversal is facilitated by the fact that the moon-deity is intimately associated with the functions and activities of women. (This reversal explains why we sometimes find a female moon kidnapping a male lover, as Artemis Endymion.) Because of its feminine associations, the primitive moon-deity is sometimes found playing a female role; this is so among the Eskimo, the Ainu and the Nagas, for whom the moon is normally male. Among the Akamba, it is treated indifferently, as male or female.

The incongruity of a male deity traditionally engaged in spinning, weaving, making pots, carrying firewood and cooking sometimes perplexes inquirers, and it has been suggested that the deity is bi-sexual. Such a conception is foreign to primitive thought. The sexual character of primitive deities is, on the contrary, emphatic, and the primitive moon-god is the very principle of masculine generative power. Primitive thought is often inconsistent, and the change of sex does not disturb established ideas. As soon as the moon has lost its functionally male character it readily assumes the form of a female divinity and becomes the prototype of womanhood—the Mother.

The Primitive Goddess as Mother of God and Primal Ancestress

However, in primitive myths the moon is in any case associated with a female deity, the mother of the moon. In matriarchal societies it would be inconceivable that a masculine person should have no mother, while the notion of a self-begotten god does not enter into primitive theology. (A male god may have no father, however, for women can procreate by immaculate conception.)

The mother-deity has a more generalized character than the moon-god. She is essentially the Mother of God, the goddess of fate. She is also generally the mother of all mankind; the mother of American or Melanesian myth is indistinguishable from the Eve of Semitic myth.

Often each tribe or clan has its primal mother. All good and bad luck comes from the mothers; it is they who, when angry, send diseases and death. Among the aboriginal populations of India, especially in the south where Aryan influence has been weakest, the native cults are represented by local deities who, with few exceptions, are female and are frequently spoken of as, simply, the Mother. While overtly recognized as tribal ancestresses, they may be anything from a totem to a moon-deity, but their character as controllers of life and disease, as arbiters of destiny, suggests that they may have been originally derived from the magic-wielding lunar deities who exercised those functions in primitive thought. At the same time, it is plain that they contained at least the germ of Earth Mothers and, but for the influence of Hindu religion. which is non-agricultural, might easily have developed into Great Mothers, similar to those of America and Europe.

The Primitive Goddess as Mother of Animals

The mother-deity, in her capacity as generating goddess, is also the mother of animals as well as men; and as mother of the tribe she is the dispenser of food. Artemis, the hunting goddess of the Greeks, was specially thought of as the protectress of wild animals, not excluding fish. Similar deities are found in India and elsewhere. Among the Eskimo, Sedna, 'the Woman', is the chief deity; her principle function is control of the animals which provide the Eskimo with food, and she is identified with the cosmic power which the Eskimo regard as controlling their destinies, namely the moon. The Chukchi have a goddess who appears to be identical: she is called 'the Mother of the Walruses'.

The Primitive Goddess as Mother of Corn

When food comes to be mainly cereal, as the mother of vegetable and animal food she comes to be the mother of corn. The great goddess of the Siouan tribes of North America, the First Woman, has assumed the character of Corn-Mother so completely that she manifestly parallels the Hellenic Demeter and the Asiatic corn-goddesses. Nevertheless, she is expressly said to be the moon. Similarly, among the Tupis of Brazil, Mother-Moon is chiefly regarded as the mother of all vegetables. They have the following myth concerning the origin of the manioc plant. A young woman became pregnant without intercourse, after a young man, white and shining, had appeared to her. She presently gave birth to a child as white as snow, which, however, died after a year. From its grave arose a plant which bore fruit, on tasting which men felt as if the spirit of a god had entered into them. This was the first manioc plant. Mother-Moon is here a corn-mother, and her offspring, or divine son, a dying vegetation god, who dies after a year, instead of after a month, as with the children of the moon.

Mother Earth

The Great Goddesses of Western Asia are Earth Mothers who bring forth the corn. In primitive thought, the fecundity of the earth and the fecundity of women are viewed as one and the same quality. Women should plant maize because women know how to produce children. The sterile wife, according to the Baganda, is injurious to a garden. Many customs connect a new bride with corn: corn is thrown over her or she is crowned with it. In New Zealand, the same ritual precautions apply to a pregnant woman as apply to one who is cultivating a patch of sweet potatoes. Many peoples believe that seed grows best when planted by a pregnant woman.

The same means which fertilized the earth are also thought to fertilize women and vice versa. Thus the fertilizing rains can also fecundate women. Virgil, in the Georgics, echoes the conceptions of Australian aborigines. 'The mother and the soil are alike,' is a principle of Roman jurisprudence. In ancient India, at the wedding ceremony, the woman was called a 'seed-field', and the priest exhorted the bridegroom, saying 'Sow her with your seed'.

Thus it is that in many religions man is stated to have been created out of the earth. In Vedic hymns the earth is the mother of man; in Persia also. The word 'homo' is a derivative of humus, and Adam was fashioned from the earth. Lucretius declares that 'animals cannot have fallen from the sky, nor the inhabitants of earth have issued out of lagoons of salt water; rightly has the earth been called 'mother', for out of the earth all things have been created'. This explains the widespread custom of depositing a child on the ground directly after its birth, a custom honoured by the Romans and by the rudest savages such as the Veddahs of Ceylon, and one of which the English abbott Aelfric complained.

Nevertheless, Mother-Earth has scarcely any place in the cosmological conceptions and rites of people in pre-agricultural stages, a fact all the more remarkable since the conception of Mother-Earth is far more obvious than that of Mother-Moon. Even far above the level of primitive culture, Mother-Earth plays no part. Both in Vedic literature and Hindu religion we find no great Earth-Mother, which may be explained by the fact that the Hindu Aryans developed their high civilization without ever becoming agriculturists. They established themselves in Northern India as warriors, leaving agriculture to the native inhabitants, and despising it.

In the archaic stages of agriculture, the bringing forth of the fruits of the earth is ascribed not to the earth but to the moon. In Brazil, the moon, not the earth, is the mother of all vegetation. It must be remembered that nowhere did religious conceptions originally develop as a symbolic interpretation of nature; they arose from functional magic. No clear instance is to be found in any culture, either primitive or advanced, of a female divinity who originally arose, solely or chiefly, as a personification of the earth.

At the same time it is true that the moon and the earth are curiously identified in primitive thought as aspects of the same thing. Many mythologies claim that the moon was formed out of the earth. The Chinese, whose primitive notions have been systematized, represent both the moon and the earth as belonging to the same cosmic principle, the feminine principle. The Greeks expressly called the moon a 'heavenly earth'. Such an identification seems unintelligible in peoples ignorant of modern astronomical conceptions, let alone in uncultured nations such as the Caribs and the Polynesians. It becomes intelligible only when the ideas connecting both the moon and the earth with women and their functions are apprehended.

In fact every earth-goddess is at the same time a moon-goddess. (The converse is often but not universally true.) Primitive agricultural goddesses retain the character of the primitive universal mother, the mother of God.

The Great Mother in Mexico

The point may be illustrated from Mexico, where the Great Mother fulfils the many functions commonly assigned to lunar deities—she was the goddess of all waters, the source of diseases and of healing, and the protectress of women and of child-bearing. She was represented as a frog or a serpent. The statue of her which was displaced by the Christian missionaries in Mexico City was white above the mouth and black below, thus resembling the Greek Erinyes. But, although the Mexican Great Mother is Mother-Moon, she commonly appears at the time of the Spanish Conquest as 'She of the Maize Plant', and presides over every agricultural occupation.

Nordic Goddesses

Many learned authorities have identified the goddesses of Europe and the Near East as Earth-Mothers. Nevertheless, closer examination shows this to be implausible. As Grimm says: 'They are mothers who travel round and visit houses, from whom the human race learns the occupation and arts of housekeeping and husbandry, spinning, weaving, tending the hearth, sowing, reaping'. One does not think of a personification of the earth as spinning and tending the hearth, nor as careering around the country in a wagon. In some of her forms the goddess does not travel in a wagon but a ship, a startling mode of locomotion for Mother-Earth. Sometimes she rushes through the air, often riding in a cart. Celestial bodies are habitually provided with chariots for this purpose, and the sun and moon are everywhere thought of, like the planets, as wanderers. Tacitus tells us that the great goddess of the Germans, after her journeys in a cart, was given a bath. It is usually the heavenly bodies which undergo periodic immersions and ablutions. Jacob Grimm, although in his earlier writing following established tradition, in a later work concluded that Freija resembled most closely the Thracian moon goddess, whom Herodotus calls Artemis. There are indications that Freija, who is the possessor of a golden necklace, was originally a sun-goddess, but the radicle of her name is the same as in 'fru' or 'frau', and means the 'woman'. She was but vaguely differentiated from Frigga, the horned goddess, who is avowedly the moon. Cæsar, who was perhaps in a better position than Tacitus to know, says, 'the only gods of the Germans are the Sun, Vulcan and the Moon'.

Wotan, of whom it was related that one of his eyes was swallowed by a watery god, also seems to have been a moon-deity, as is also suggested by his name 'the Wanderer', and the fact that he was sometimes triune.

The Great Goddesses of the Celts

The Great Goddess was general among the Celts. The Irish Gaels claimed to have been descended from the goddess Danu—probably a contraction of Dea-Anu. She was also called Bu Anu, 'the Good Mother', and was the mother of the gods. She was also known as Brigit; and Brigit was the great goddess of all the Celts, both in Britain and in Gaul. Brigit has been called in modern times not only the Mary of the Gaels but even the Mother of Jesus. Like most religions, Celtic heathenism was both monotheistic and trinitarian. There were three Brigits, represented either as sisters or as daughters of the goddess, and Brigit had three sons who had three wives and three concubines, but only one son between them. 'The Mothers' are usually represented as bearing babes or carrying baskets of fruit, and are thus regarded as goddesses of fertility.

The Celtic goddesses also displayed characteristics which we have noted elsewhere. Anu was supposed to make men mad; she ruled the sea and presided over rivers, springs and wells—Bridewell is named after her. Black Anu was represented as a savage woman who ate men; the priestesses of Nantes offered her a human victim. By the Sequani she was worshipped as Mona, 'moon', and in the south of France was called 'The Shining One'. She was a wonderful reaper and carried 'the moon's sickle'. In Ireland she was 'the old woman with the horns'. The great midsummer festival is called in the Limousin 'La Lunade'.

Solstice festivals are not, as is sometimes assumed, necessarily solar festivals but frequently refer to the moon. Primitive peoples are familiar with the changes in the seasons, and where the solar year is unknown, the mid-summer and mid-winter ceremonies are not at fixed dates. The Lunade did not begin at sunrise but at moon-rise, as did the Irish festivals. On the three days following Lammas Day all work ceased and the Irish were careful to avoid bathing or fishing. A legendary king erected a magnificent temple, sacred to the priests of the moon—such temples were doubtless originally megalithic circles. Strabo mentions that the priestesses of Nantes unroofed their temple once a year at the chief festival, which implies that originally it had no roof. In the Orkneys stone circles are still known as 'The Temple of the Moon'.

Associated with Anu was Crom Cruaich, 'the bloody crescent'. He represented Dagda, the supreme god of the Irish who was the racial ancestor and the triune deity common to all the Celts. Dagda was a god of fertility. The divine son of Dagda was Lug, who frequently changes place with him. He is the British Ludd whose name appears in Ludgate, where he was worshipped in association with the moon-goddess. The original name of Paris was Lug Tetia—so named for him.

Celtic mythology, like Hebrew mythology, has reached us in a form much edited by Christian redactors. This is why Sir John Rhys's lectures on Celtic heathendom, composed in the eighties, assume that Celtic myths are solar myths; but it is astonishing, after 600 pages of warlike sun-gods, including Lug, to find that in all Celtic languages the sun is feminine. Rhys points this out, and is at a loss to account for such an extraordinary disregard on the part of his ancestors for the views of Professor Max Mueller. The Celtic year was lunar, Pliny tells us; and Caesar says: 'They reckon all time not by days but by nights' (hence the word fortnight). It is doubtful whether there were ever any native sun-gods among the Celts. In Scotland, Ireland, France and elsewhere people fall on their knees when they see the new moon, and as late as the seventeenth century the French were speaking of the moon as 'Our Lord' or, as they did at Noyon, as 'The Lord of Lords'. The moon was the supreme deity of the Basques; and the Celtiberians—that is, the Celts who crossed the Pyrenees to Spain—worshipped it after the orthodox manner of primitive savages, dancing all night at the full moon.

Primitive Semitic Religion

The moon was from earliest times the foundation of all theological development among the whole Semitic race, even after the Semites had become agriculturists. Moses Maimonides expressed this by saying that moon-worship was the religion of Adam; and the crescent is still the badge of Islam, as it was once the emblem of Israel—for when Mohammed overthrew the old religion of Arabia, he was not strong enough to defy immemorial sentiment. Arab women even now insist that the moon is the parent of mankind. A curious Talmudic tradition represents Yahweh as making a sin-offering because he has caused the moon to lose its pristine importance.

Numerous ancient Arabian inscriptions show the moon-deity as the most prominent object of cult everywhere, whether in the Hadramaut, Kataban or Minaean kingdoms. In early Babylonia the moon-cult was the national religion: the name Chaldeans means 'moon-worshippers'. Herodotus says that the Arabs 'have no other divinities than Dionysos and Urania'. Both were definitely lunar deities. The moon was the 'protector of women', and was associated with a feminine counterpart.

The great goddess of Arabia was most generally known as Al-Uzza; Al-Kindy says that Al-Uzza was the moon, her chief shrine being the Ka'aba at Mecca, where she was worshipped in the form of a sacred stone, doubtless the very stone which the pilgrims to this day visit Mecca to kiss. This Arabian goddess was triune, being also known as the three Holy Virgins, and was the bringer of good and bad luck, just like the Greek Moirai and the Nordic Norns. The Arabian goddess was regarded by the Babylonians as identical with Ishtar but although Ishtar is definitely a moon-goddess, her name is not that of the moon but that of the planet we still call Venus, whereas Al-Uzza is never identified with Venus. This identification of Ishtar with the moon and the evening star throws an interesting light on the origin of goddesses. It has nothing to do with the comparatively late adoption of lucky stars by the Arabian tribes, due to the influence of Babylonian astrology, but derives from the common idea, found in the Congo and many parts of West Africa, Australia and elsewhere, that the morning and evening stars are the two wives of the moon. In Egypt Isis was identified with the star Sirius; but probably Isis and Nephthis, the two wives of Osiris, were originally the evening and the morning star. Similarly, the Hebrew god Yahweh was worshipped at Elephantine with two wives, and the god Abraham also had two wives, Sarah and Hagar. When the female aspect of the lunar deity came to displace the male, the wife of the moon-god became identified with the moon itself, while the goddess Ishtar maintained her association with the planet Venus. This identification is symbolically represented by the lunar crescent, enclosing the star within its horns, which is still the crest of Islam.[1]

The oldest and most fundamental Babylonian deities known are a triad of male gods—Anu, En-Lil and Ea—who constitute a triune god.

[1] The relationship between the male and female counterpart of the moon was, however, variable. Ishtar is sometimes the daughter of the moon; sometimes the moon is the son of her male avatar.

Anu is the deity of the waters above the earth; En-Lil is the father of the moon and also a god of storms; Ea is the primal ocean; Tiamat, the deep out of which all things rose, and also the ancient serpent, the fish-god or Leviathan mentioned by Berosus. Ishtar is mentioned as the daughter or female counterpart of each of the three members. It is true that there were sun-gods in Semitic religion, but they were, originally, inferior deities, regarded as female and as the daughter or wife of the moon. They had no cult until relatively late. Curiously enough, though the moon was viewed as the giver of life and promoter of growth, the sun was associated with death, darkness and the underworld. Thus the notion of the Caribbean savages who 'esteem the moon more than the sun', and which Tylor found so singular, was shared by a particularly enlightened people.

The cult of the moon-god Sinn is found in every Semitic land, and he was 'the father of the great gods, the Lord of Heaven'—the sun-god being merely an attendant deity. His supreme character passed in later times to his female counterpart, who finally replaced him. She was the creatrix, the mother of all men. Ishtar was Queen of Heaven astronomically as well as theologically. She was horned, and was brought up out of the foam by water-gods, like Aphrodite. She was triune, and St Augustine, with scathing irony, taunts his pagan countrymen with the absurdity of the notion that the goddess could be one person and at the same time three persons.

Nevertheless, she also had a fertility aspect: she was 'Queen of the earth and mistress of the fields'. Her character of earth-deity is emphasized in the Syrian form of the cult by its association with the god Tammuz or, as the Greeks called him, Adonis. Tammuz appears as the lover and son of the goddess. He is a vegetation god whose yearly death, corresponding to the decay of the vegetation after the harvest, and whose resurrection in spring are generally known from the pages of *The Golden Bough*. But until recently his cult was regarded as a late one. Nothing could be further from the truth. Tammuz, the divine son, is one of the oldest elements in Babylonian religion, figuring as far back as the records reach. As Professor Langdon observes: 'We do not know, among historical peoples possessing written records, a more ancient god.' He was represented as born from a tree, his material image being a rough wooden figure or a mere log of wood, over which the women mourned at his death. We have already come across such a god elsewhere, e.g. among the North American Indians. In India also goddesses are frequently sacrificed by drowning, and in some early Egyptian rituals Osiris was drowned.

Tammuz is 'the Healer', 'the Saviour' and often 'the Shepherd'—but not an earthly so much as a heavenly shepherd, and the flocks which he originally tended were the stars. He is also known as 'the Wanderer', a common epithet of the moon, and as a lord of moisture, which suggests that he was originally a lunar god. In one liturgy, he is expressly addressed as the moon-god.

There is not a single Babylonian trinity in which the 'Son' does not appear as the 'Saviour', though he has many alternative local names. Thus Bel-Marduk was a Divine Son and was called the Lord of Lamentations. The Hebrew god Yahweh was identified with Tammuz. The concept of a Divine Son, who dies and rises again, seems to be older than any formal myth. The cult was general throughout Mesopotamia and Syria, one of the chief shrines in Palestine being in Bethlehem. St Jerome says:' The very grotto where the infant Christ uttered his first cries, resounded formerly with the lamentations over the lover of Aphrodite.' The cult continued in many parts of Asia long after the Christian era, and was more particularly observed by the Sabæans, until at least the tenth century.

There is evidence that, in primitive Semitic states, the king, or a prince chosen from amongst his sons, was sometimes actually sacrificed for the good of the people, as was done until recently by the Shilluks of the upper Nile and other uncultured peoples.

Ideas and cults similar to those connected with Tammuz appear to have been widespread in Asia, far beyond the limits of Mesopotamia. A second-century Chinese writer reports them from Samarkand. The mourning rites persisted even into Christian times, as St Augustine complains; while the old Roundhead, Northbrooke (fl. 1570), reports: 'It is better that women should pick wool or spin upon the Sabbath day, than they should dance impudently and filthily all day long upon the day of the new moon.'

European nations also practised virtually identical rites, which the Christian Church repeatedly denounced. In the South of France the yule log, or as it is often called the Christ log, was solemnly anointed with olive-oil before being ceremoniously invoked and placed on the fire. In southern Italy, it was the custom to place on the log a portion of all the food eaten, and this was said to be the share of Jesus Christ. In many districts the ashes of the log were regarded as ensuring fertility. When the yule log was lit, all other fires were extinguished, and it was not permissible to spin or wash clothes until the twelfth day. These observances were substantially equivalent to the cult of Tammuz, for it was a common practice among the Semites to sacrifice Tammuz by burning him. The story of Phœnix, the father of Europa, who was represented as being periodically burned and as arising from the ashes, is a version of the myth of the Tyrian Tammuz. Talmudic tradition ascribes the same fate to Abraham. Similar rituals are also found among the North American Indians. In Thrace, Dionysos suffered yearly sacrifice with fire in the same way, and an almost identical ceremony may be witnessed at the present day in Florence at Easter.

'There are abundant indications', observes Prince Teano, 'that the Jehovah of the Hebrews and the Allah of Islam are merely transformations of the primitive lunar deity of Arabia.' The Hebrews (the term is a political not an ethnic one) were migrants from a land which they referred to as Sinim, the Land of the Moon, where the cult of the god was associated with a sacred mountain, Sinai, that is, the Mountain of the Moon, where the cult was in the hands of a special tribe of priests and priestesses known as law'iu, or Levites. To this clan belonged the traditional leaders Musa (Moses), Jethro, Aaron, Joshua and others. The name Levi means 'serpent', and the deity was commonly worshipped under that form. The Levite priests wore as their head-dress a lunar crescent, and the high-priest sometimes wore a representation of the full moon. The moon is regarded as the emblem of Israel in Talmudic literature and Hebrew tradition. The mythical ancestor of the Hebrews was Abraham of Ur, who is no other than the god of Ur, the mooncity, and he migrates to Harran, the other great centre of Semitic mooncult.

When the Hebrew tribes, under the leadership of the votaries of the Moon-God, came into the land flowing with the milk and honey of the Queen of Heaven, they found their own race there and their own religion, but modified by the effects of agricultural civilization. The Baal of Sinai had his female form or counterpart. The temple of Jerusalem was simultaneously dedicated to Yahweh and to the Queen of Heaven, and before it stood the asherah, the symbolic trees, which are associated with the female aspect of the deity. In the excavations at Gezer, in Palestine, a number of figures of bulls have been found, the usual representation of Yahweh, and with them the corresponding figures of cows. Abraham, a close double of Yahweh, was worshipped with his female counterpart Sarah. But in this agricultural society the Queen of Heaven eclipsed the male god, and Adon, the Lord, instead of being her spouse, or father, was her son and a subordinate deity. The bulk of the Jewish people, especially the women, transferred their devotion from Baal to the Holy Mother, but, to the more conservative elements, these agricultural forms of the cult were an abomination. They repudiated the local homologues of Yahweh as false Baals, and claimed that Yahweh was a better rain-maker than the Baal of the Phoenicians. Just as the Babylonian gods had decomposed into a good and a bad aspect, so the god of Sinai dissociated himself from his serpent form, Leviathan, whose sacred image was destroyed by Hezekiah. Yahweh became so completely assimilated to Adon that the two cults were confounded and the names blended—

Yahweh being frequently spoken of as 'the Lord Adon'. (It was the vocalizing of the tetragrammaton *jhvh* with the vowels from Adonai which, in the hands of ignorant translators at the time of the Reformation, gave rise to the barbarism 'Jehovah'.)

The Yahwistic reformers met with opposition in their attempts to press on the people the claims of the male form of the deity. They were met with the answer: 'We will certainly burn incense under the Queen of Heaven, and pour drink offerings unto her, as we have done, we and our fathers, our kings and our princes, in the cities of Judah and in the streets of Jerusalem.' The struggle was one of patriarchal principles against matriarchal ones. It was the women who resisted giving up their allegiance to the Queen of Heaven.

The character of the new Yahweh most persistently emphasized was that he was unchanging. Now, it is possible for a god to be eternal without being unchanging. The reason this point was made was that it was a way of affirming that he was not a moon-god; he did not wax or wane; above all, he did not die and rise again after the third day. In other words, he was not Tammuz. The ancient histories and scriptures were heavily edited to expunge all astral myths and illusions; the early deities were reduced to the status of men, and cosmological myths translated into history. Nevertheless, Jewish women still recite a prayer when they see the new moon; 'May God cause thee to increase and mayst thou be enabled to bestow upon us a blessed month'.

It was the great development of agriculture that gave rise to the preeminent position which the great goddesses occupied at the dawn of our culture. Men, however, took up the labours which formerly appertained exclusively to women, and were anxious to obtain control of the magical powers thought to be essential to cultivation. The male gods, reinterpreted as solar or more generalized deities, ultimately ousted the Great Mothers, not only amongst the pastoral Semites but throughout the Western world. Religious evolution was thus an aspect of the social evolution which led to the obliteration of the matriarchal character.

Greek Religion

The most striking feature of the earliest Ægean civilization, centred on Krete, is the predominance of female deities. No male idol has been found, and there are not above two representations of a male god on seals of a late date. The female divinity appears under varying forms, associated more often with serpents than the Babylonian, but also with doves, a conventionalized mountain, and other symbols common to Western Asia. It is difficult to escape the conclusion that Kretan religion was derived from, or profoundly influenced by, the religion of Syria and Babylon. The Kretan Great Mother was triune, and commonly represented under the attributes of the tree, the pillar and the cross. Thus we may regard her as a moon-goddess and, in fact, the lunar crescent is a ubiquitous symbol in Krete. Like Ishtar, she had some chthonic attributes, but this does not justify the conclusion of some scholars that she was an earth-goddess.

In Anatolia and the northern portion of the Ægean, the son of the Great Mother bears the name which in all languages of the Aryan family means the moon, Men. Men, in fact, and not Selene is the proper Greek term for the moon, and, as in all other languages, it is masculine. The term 'Men' is always used by Homer; and those who preferred primitive conceptions regarded the moon as masculine. To this day Greek peasants persist in regarding the moon as male. Men was, of course, a dying god, and appeared in infant and adult form. In classical theology the male lunar deity occupied a prominent position from earliest times, the name by which he is best-known being Dionysos. Dionysos has always presented a problem of peculiar interest. He stands apart from the circle of Olympian gods, but not, as has been said, because he is a late importation. The deity appears in every region of Greece in the most primitive strata of religious ideas. It would be nearer the truth to say that Olympian religion was a late importation into Dionysian cults. He was represented both as teaching a religion and as inventing agriculture, and such culture-gods always come down as strangers and dwell amongst men. This explains why Greek legend does represent him as a new god, coming from abroad. The Mænads were the priestesses of the Dionysiac cult and were assimilated to the mythical nurses or Mothers. They were three in number, and each had charge of a troupe of women. The agricultural rites of primitive Greece remained, even in historic times, conspicuously a special and often an exclusive woman's cult. In latter times men were admitted to the trieterica, but originally were in danger of being torn to pieces if they so much as spied upon the woman's mysteries. They were similarly rigorously excluded from the thesmophoria, which took place in October, at the time of sowing. When men took part in the cult of the woman's god, they frequently donned feminine attire. In Attica, Dionysian priests were arrayed in women's attire and Dioynsos himself has a feminine character. He wears women's clothes and, according to one myth, was brought up as a girl.

These are clearly archaic rites. Among the conceptions which were super-added, the most conspicuous was the association of the god with the vine. The vine appears to have been first brought to Greece by the Phœnicians. One of the first miracles ascribed to Dionysos was the turning of water into wine, and similar miracles of transubstantiation took place in his chapels. In this character, he closely resembles the Indian moon-god, Soma. Soma is the name of a climbing plant closely resembling the ivy, from which an intoxicating drink is brewed. This drink was used in sacrificial offerings in ancient Persian and Vedic ritual. Soma was completely identified with the moon-god, so that at the present day Soma actually means moon-god. The moon occupied the central place in Vedic belief and cult. Soma is the healer and the owner of all women. This notion of an association between intoxicating beverages and the moon is widely diffused. The mistletoe of the Celts derived its significance from being regarded as the sap of the oak. In Greece prophetic women prepared themselves by chewing ivy or laurel leaves. In Northern Europe and among the Celts beer was regarded in a similar manner, and Dionysos himself, in his Thracian form, appears to have been connected with beer before wine. In Egypt, Osiris was regarded as the discoverer of the vine, and Tammuz, in his earliest form, was identified with it.

But there could be no greater error than to suppose that Dionysos was the manifestation of the vine. The vine was, on the contrary, a manifestation of Dionysos. The vine was by no means the only plant with which he was connected. His association with the ivy was even more ancient; the Dionysiac women chewed ivy leaves. His thyrsus was encircled with ivy, his votaries were crowned with it. At Acharnae he was worshipped as 'the Ivy.' Almost equally closely he is associated with the evergreen pine, and like, Tammuz, was often represented by a mere pine log. Elsewhere he is associated with the fig tree, the plane tree, the maple, the oak and with barley, beans, apples and all fruit. He is, in short, a vegetation god, and is the inventor of ploughing and sowing. Modern writers recognize him as identical with Osiris, Attis, Adonis and other vegetation gods. But the Greeks had not read Sir James Frazer and knew of no vegetation gods, and it is unlikely that they assimilated them on this principle. Dionysos, says Plutarch, is the generative principle which gives life to all. Dionysos was identified with many gods, such as the Sinn of the Arabs, which were not typical vegetation gods.

The primitive deities of Greece, essentially older than the Olympians, became unified under the name of Dionysos. They belonged to lunar not to solar cults. The Arcadians, where primitive cults survived, were moon-worshippers. The Spartans were so observant of lunar influences that they missed taking part in the battle of Marathon because the moon was not in the proper quarter for a journey. There is evidence that, in Arcadia, the moon had earlier been regarded as a male deity. Athene herself bore the moon on her shield and lunar serpents all over her. Her priestesses wore moon halos.

Like all the gods with whom he was identified, Dionysos was certainly in nature and origin a moon-god. Like all primitive moon-gods, he is the Lord of generation and of moisture. One of his most common epithets is 'nocturnal'. Nonnus calls him 'night-shining Dionysos'. His ritual vestment is a dark, star-spangled robe and a crescent-shaped mitre. Though alien to the Olympian deities, the worship of Dionysos is everywhere associated in Greek cult with that of the moon-goddess, Artemis. He was likewise intimately associated with the moon-goddess Ariadne and she was his wife.

Jane Harrison has made familiar the dual character of Greek religion. On the one hand, the Olympian gods grouped around the sky-god Zeus, and typically represented by the sun-god Apollo; on the other, the non-Olympian deities such as Demeter, the Great Mother. This group is concerned with the very forces of life and death, and has a mystic character which is lacking among the sky-gods. But these deities which are often called chthonic, or earthly, were not, in any sense, deities of the earth. They are deities of the underworld simply because, as heavenly bodies, in the course of their cycle they pass under the earth, and they appertain to the primitive lunar religion. In Greek religion, the sun-deity never became supreme. Apollo, in Greek religion, is in the incongruous position of possessing none of the attributes of a heavenly fertilizer. He is associated instead with perscriptively lunar functions, such as prophecy, divination and the control of diseases. He is the god of Parnassus, but ivy-crowned Parnassus is the sacred mountain of Dionysos. Though established at Delphi, the holiest spot of Greek cult, it must be remembered that Delphi was originally the seat of an older cult of the great goddess, under the names of Gaia, Themis and Phoibe. The Delphian priestesses bore the name Melissai, the name reserved to the priestesses of Demeter and the favourite epithet of the moon. Among the deities displaced there is Dionysos, and, when Apollo set up to be a doctor, he pretended to be the same as the Serpent-God, Asklepios; but here again he found Dionysos in the field before him. In Phrygia, he had to be satisfied with the third share of the medical practice. In fact, the sun-god Apollo had no functions other than those which belong, in far higher degree, to Dionysos.

The Olympian and chthonic deities were always at feud, It was a gross insult to introduce so much as an ivy leaf into the temple of Hera. This battle between patriarchal and matriarchal outlook is demonstrated in that strange play of Aeschylus, *The Eumenides*. In it, Apollo introduces the strange new physiological theory that the son is not produced by the mother but by the male, the woman being no more than the nurse of the newly-conceived foetus. It is quite possible, he says, to become a father without the assistance of a woman.

The ancients everywhere worshipped Demeter and Dionysos together, although they were historically strangers, for they were indissolubly associated by virtue of their character. Greek goddesses are conspicuously triune, though more rarely they are double. Lunar phases are often simplified into two, as we see in the old Latin god, Janus. Demeter has long been regarded as the personification of the earth-mother, and her name was once analysed as Ge-Meter, a derivation which is inadmissible. Probably the name was a derivation of Dea Meter, the Goddess-Mother, and she has many lunar attributes. (The extreme confusion of Greek divine names and attributes is due to the fact that the basic deities were worshipped under many specialized aspects. Demeter is as much an Erinis, a Moira and a ruler of the dead, as she is a corn-goddess.)

The great goddesses owed their existence not to the earth but to their motherhood; and the Great Mother, whether we find her in the ice-fields of the Arctic or the corn-fields of Krete, existed before ever an ear of corn had been ground in the mill. Her origin was heavenly not earthly, and she had fertilized the dark earth and been the mother of all her fruits long before she was crowned with corn. Hence, however closely Demeter and analogous goddesses may have become assimilated to the Earth-Mother, they could never entirely lose their heavenly character.

The goddess's primitive character was preserved, above all, by her relation to the male god with whom she was associated. These gods are not her husbands, nor merely male counterparts of her. Divine pairs are merely male and female aspects of the same divinity; indeed, their relationship is usually that of husband and wife. Such pairs were the general rule in primitive Semitic religion, and are found in native Italian cults. Sometimes these pairs are sharply contrasted as masculine and feminine principles—as heaven and earth. But the relation of the Great Mothers to their male deities is entirely different. Thus Demeter, who as Mother-Earth should be the legal wife of the sky-god Zeus, is a total stranger to him, and scarcely ever meets him in the course of mythological story. The Great Mothers have no husbands. They are 'virgins'. This word meant, originally, not a woman who had no sexual experience, but one who was independent. (The correct Latin expression for an untouched virgin is not *virgo* but *virgo intacta*.) Aphrodite herself was a virgin, and the term was applied to all the goddesses of the early Aegean cults. Thus it was that the Virgin Ishtar was frequently addressed as 'the Prostitute.' Children born out of wedlock were called parthenioi; the Greek word 'parthenos' has the same meaning as the Semitic 'bathur', or 'unwed'. It was only in later patriarchal society, when the term had acquired a new meaning, that such goddesses were transformed into types of maidenly purity. Artemis, for example, though she was the mother of Telephos and the fifty daughters of Endymion, came to be regarded as the patroness of chastity. The motherhood of Athene, the mother of Erechthonios, was explained away by a somewhat coarse story, and Erechthonios was made the son of Earth, Athene acting merely as his foster-mother. In the same manner, the Roman Vesta was deliberately set up as the patroness of virginity, though she retained her title of 'Mother' and was even the mother of the gods, while phallic emblems continued to figure in her cult. Her relation to Priapus was obliterated by a similar expedient. Her virginity was saved by the timely interference of an ass—incongruously enough, as the ass is an emblem of lubricity. The ancient British Moon-Goddess, Arianrhod, was called 'The Virgin', although she had several children. The Chinese Holy Virgin, though the pattern of purity, is still like Ishtar, the patroness of prostitutes. This explains why Demeter 'execrated marriage', and presided not over marriage but over divorce. The same character pertains to all the goddesses of the Eastern Mediterranean world in just the same way as the great goddess of the Eskimo is known as 'she who will not have a husband'.[1]

The Moon-god was originally mutable. As the lunar deity became eternal and unchanging, the son retained the mutable attributes and was pre-eminently a dying god, and the culture god who assumed human form and as a Man-god instructed men. He is a generative force, a master of magic; he causes death and he heals. He is a chthonic god who periodically descends into the dark underworld, rises again and ascends into heaven.

In agricultural religion, he is identified with the fruits which the divine mother bears forth. The bread is his body; the juice of the grape, his blood. The wails of his worshippers at his death and their rejoicings at his resurrection are the wails of the savage at the death of the new moon and their rejoicings at its reappearance.

Throughout primitive society, lamentations and mourning are performed by the women. All wailing, however ritualistic, devolves everywhere upon the women, and the care of the dead is usually their function. Women alone took part in the mourning rites among the ancient Karians and Lokrians, as among the Arabs, the Romans and others. Among the Lyknians, when a man mourned for a beloved dead, it was the custom for him to dress in female clothes. Thus it was that the Valkyries had the function of collecting the souls of fallen warriors on the battlefields.

The lamentations of the women of Syria, Egypt, Babylon and Greece

---

[1] Isis presents an apparent exception, but her relationship to the moon-god is complex. She is his sister and wife, but conceives from him after his death; she is at the same time his mother and becomes the wife of her perpetually-dying son. This composite relationship is inevitable in the primitive lunar myths of uncultured peoples. Tammuz is at the same time the son and lover of the goddess; Attis is the son and lover of Kybele.

over the Divine Son were also lamentations for the Saviour who had paid for them the price of death. For the Divine Son was ever the 'Saviour', whose death is the pledge of the moon's gift of eternal life. Initiation into the mysteries of Dionysos was believed to secure eternal salvation. He who had received the sacraments of initiation lived in joy and hope; for him death was robbed of its sting and the grave of its victory.

In both Christian and pre-Christian times, pictorial art seldom depicts the son in the company of his father but always in that of his mother, and as a young god who is never more than thirty at the most. In China, 'the most common of female deities is the Holy Mother. . . . This lady is the exact counterpart of the Indian Ganga, . . . the Isis of the Egyptians and the Ceres of the Greeks. Nothing shocked the missionaries on their first arrival in China so much as to find the image of this lady, in whom they thought they discovered a striking resemblance to the Virgin Mary'. They were told that she had conceived and bore her son while yet a 'virgin'. The priests informed Mendez Pinto that, after the flood, the moon sent her representative to earth to re-people the world.

The divine son is man and god in one. He came down among men, was his own prophet, established his own religion. Men doubt whether he is god or man. Thus Egyptologists still seriously entertain the possibility of Osiris-Horus having been an actual king. Every Semitic martyr-hero or prophet has been identified as Tammuz, the anointed One. The Dionysos of Euripides has been regarded as a human prophet. Miss Harrison is persuaded that his double, Orpheus, was a historical personage.

The Great Mother and the divine child were the first divinities to whom women, at any rate, turned with feeling other than those of dread. Tenderness, love, maternal instinct entered the sphere of religion for the first time. Hitherto, all spirits, tribal gods, sky gods had been feared and placated. If anywhere a distinction is to be drawn between religion, properly considered, and that from which it sprang, it is here.

Women, therefore, influenced importantly the evolution of religion and religious ideas, if indeed it was not mainly their creation, for it is highly improbable that the mother and child were fashioned by the hands of men. The fierce tribal gods of hunters became transformed under the influence of the women's religion, their attributes changing in harmony with the character of the universal Mother. The All-Mother is older than the All-Father. Ishtar and Isis were the universal Mother long before any sky-god or tribal male deity had evolved into universal fatherhood. She was not tribal, not national, not the jealous deity of a chosen people. Apuleius makes her say: 'There is no other power but I. I am worshipped under as many aspects . . . as there are peoples on the earth.' When the heavenly fathers who had almost faded out of existence reasserted themselves, they were no longer the same. The Queen of Heaven was put away by the solitary God. Christian and agnostic theology restored, however, his original three-fold nature. The son was the off-spring of the father and of divine Sophia, for the Queen of Heaven had ever been the goddess of Wisdom. The Holy Ghost which is identical with her, and is in Hebrew feminine, was regarded by the Nazarenes and early Christians as the Mother of Christ. It was by a grammatical accident, $\pi\nu\varepsilon\tilde{v}\mu\alpha$ in Greek being neuter, that the third person of the Holy Trinity came to be dissociated from the Mother of God. Nevertheless, it was represented by the dove, the immemorial bird of the Great Goddess, and Philo regarded the bird as identical with Sophia, i.e. wisdom. Jesuit theologians have asserted that the Holy Virgin was omniscient. In Eastern Europe the dove is still associated with the Holy Virgin, rather than the Holy Ghost, and to this day Russian peasants will not eat pigeons for fear of sacrilege. The practice of offering cakes, etc., to the Queen of Heaven survived until very recently. Demeter was worshipped at Eleusis until the year 1801. In Sicily as at Eleusis, the goddess Ceres did duty for the Madonna in Christian churches, and at Castrogiovanni there is still a statue of the Virgin whose divine child is not a boy but a girl, the figure having earlier served as Ceres.

It was after the doctrine of the Incarnation had become the central dogma of the Catholic Church that the substitution of Mary for Sophia or the Holy Ghost acquired importance, In the fifth century, the Marianites were condemned for regarding the Holy Virgin as a goddess; but a few centuries later, the ascription to her of divine titles was commonplace, and she came to be pronounced identical in nature with the first person of the Trinity. It was even asserted that she created the world. 'At the command of Mary', says St Alphonse, 'all obey, even God.' Traces even remain of her role as mother of corn. St Ambrose remarks: 'In the most pure womb of Mary there was sown one sole grain of wheat, yet it is called a garden of wheat . . . .' Like Persephone, she is Queen of the Underworld, and therefore 'Mistress of the Devils'. To retain her ancient association with the planet Venus, she is 'the star of Ishtar', 'the star of the sea', 'the ruler of the ocean'. She is universally identified with the moon and is said to control it. In most parts of Europe the peasantry fail to distinguish the Virgin Mary and the moon. Thus in France the peasants of the Perche district call the moon 'Notre Dame'. In Portugal they call the moon 'the Mother of God'. Not only St Bonaventure but even Pope Innocent III compare her to the moon.

Let us now turn back again to the question of marriage and explore how, from being simply an economic association, it came to be considered a sacrament and a 'mystery'.

CHAPTER 24

Holy Matrimony

In European society, marriage is not merely a union for economic and reproductive purposes but has a religious character: the Church holds it to be a sacrament. But if we go back into pre-history we find that the focus of religious feeling lies not in marriage, which is primarily an economic union, but in the union bètween gods and women. This is the so-called Hieros Gamos or Holy Matrimony.

In this chapter, therefore, let us explore the stages through which the notion of a divine union has passed.

In many primitive myths, the tribe is said to be derived from the union of women with animals—the totem animals of the tribe. Thus the Iroquois regard themselves as springing from the intercourse of women with bears, deer or wolves. Many peoples—e.g. the Ainus, the Déné and some Eskimos—believe themselves descended from a woman and a dog. The Kirghis Tartars reckon their descent from forty girls (=kirg kiss) who had intercourse with a red-haired god. (Our own reigning house was probably descended from a wolf, for Guelph or Welf is the same word as whelp or wolf.) The Tlinkit of Alaska say that some tribes sprang from a woman and shark. The house of Cleves traces its descent from a woman and a swan. The union of a woman and a serpent is a genealogy found the world over.

Many rituals contain allusions to such a union; thus in the major religious ceremony of the ancient Hindus, involving the sacrifice of a horse, the queen actually had congress with the slaughtered animal. These animal cults were common in Egypt, and Theban princesses in the early Middle Kingdom period were buried in the company of sacred bulls which were presumably their divine husbands. The women at Mendes had connection with a divine he-goat, a rite still practised in the time of Plutarch; perhaps the early Semites observed a similar rite, for Jewish women were forbidden to offer sacrifices to goats with which they had fornicated. A reminiscence of this sacred zoogamy survived in England until Tudor times at Haberden, where women desirous of off-spring touched a white bull, kept for the purpose, in an elaborate ceremony. This also explains why European witches were believed to copulate with the devil in the form of a goat. 'It pleaseth their new maister oftentimes', says an old writer, 'to offer himself familiarly unto them, to dally and lie with them, in token of their more near conjunction and, as it were, marriage unto him.'

Such ceremonies were often associated with dances in which the persons concerned disguised themselves as animals; and such dances ended in orgies which were believed to ensure the fertility of the totem animal, and thus of the tribe itself.

The Divine Bull

By far the commonest of these animal forms of deity are the serpent and the bull. We have already seen how the serpent was the emblem of the lunar deity in its generative aspect. In ancient Persian religion the 'primal bull' was regarded as representing the soul of the world and as residing in the moon. 'I invoke and glorify the supreme bull who causes the grass to grow in abundance, the pure bull who has given being to the pure man,' says one hymn; while another enjoins 'address your prayers to the pure, heavenly bull, holy and uncreated'. In India the bull Agni and the moon-god Soma were often treated as one god; the bull was also an impersonation of Indra and Siva. All the Semitic gods have been assimilated to bulls: Yahweh was worshipped in the form of a bull throughout earlier times, and in Krete the generative power was conceived as a bull, as the myths of the Minotaur and of Europa show. Many of the Greeks represented Dionysos in the form of a bull. It was in the form of a bull that the god led Pentheos to his mysteries.

Celtic gods are commonly horned. The sacred bull of Cooley forms the theme of the most important Irish epic. Now in the great religions in which bull-gods were prominent, the divine bull is either expressly identified with the moon or is especially associated with moon-gods. The horns of cattle and the lunar crescent are equivalent symbols, and the lunar disc is placed between the horns of the bull Apis. The North American Indians assimilated the horns of buffaloes to the crescent of the moon, and described the moon circle as 'horned'. Throughout the lake dwellings of the bronze and early iron ages lunar crescents are found modelled in clay which vary in form from the regular crescents to bulls' horns.

In many places women are thought to have an injurious effect upon cattle. This is probably a special instance of the emasculating influence which women are thought to exercise on men's weapons and appliances. As the drawers of the plough, bulls are also specially connected with the transfer of agricultural work from the women to the men.

Rites of Sexual Licence

When food came to be derived chiefly from the cultivation of the soil, instead of from hunting, ritual magic to increase the earth's fertility became important; and rites involving sexual licence, intended to achieve this aim by sympathetic magic, are so widely diffused and have been so frequently reported that there is no need to reproduce all the evidence here. The Roman Saturnalia were feasts of sowing. One need only add that this licence is not necessarily orgiastic in nature. For instance, among the Dayaks, the licence lasts exactly a quarter of an hour, after which perfect order is restored. These festivals of promiscuity have survived in European countries in such forms as the May Day carnival and the May Day celebrations. In Russia, promiscuity took place as late as the sixteenth century at the festivals of Midsummer Day and at Christmas. Church festivals involving scenes of indecency abounded in Europe up to late times, notably the Feast of Fools, and became associated in some country districts with the Festivals of the Holy Virgin. In South Holland the peasants regard such ceremonies as necessary even today.

The increase of fertility was not, however, the only motive of such festivals, which often served to avert illness or other misfortune, which was seen as bestowed by an angry God. For it was felt that promiscuity would pacify and conciliate the gods. Such ideas were also familiar to the Greeks of the luxurious colony of Lokria in Magna Graecia, who, when hard pressed by the Rhegians, vowed to expose their women for sacred prostitution if they were saved. Having secured the victory, however, they avoided fulfilling the vow. (This would appear to be a temporary reversion to a belief already obsolete.) Ribald jokes and gestures and the use of phallic images were also thought helpful. These were not the depravities of barbarians nor of sensual Orientals; noble Athenian women exchanged such jests and carried such images at the Thesmophoria, and so did Roman matrons at the Feast of Bona Dea. Traces of this belief survive to this day in Christian countries, for instance among the Portuguese population of Brazil.

The fact that all religion, whether crude or highly developed, in the great civilizations is pervaded with such sensual licentious conceptions is commonly expressed by saying that the generative powers of nature are the object of worship, but the term is unsatisfactory, for the object of these primitive cults was not to bestow praise on a God, but the purely practical one of avoiding danger or achieving fertility. The notion of worship is unknown to the primitive mind. The explanation of these rites lies in the notion that it is the function of every woman to have union with God who bestows generative powers, and this union is a necessity to women, though not to men. The sexual character of the rituals also pertains to all magical operations carried out by women; thus it is a universal rule that witches must strip themselves of clothing when performing a magical act, and nudity is essential in all rain-making ceremonies.

Holy Matrimony of Priestesses and Queens

This union with the divine bridegroom formed the central ritual in many religious ceremonies, and was celebrated by the high priestess or the queen as the representative of all womankind. Such ceremonies were found in India, in Europe and in North America, as also in Babylon and elsewhere. This union was usually consummated with God's representative—but among the Arapahos of Colorado, at the last moment the woman, with a quick movement, threw her blanket on the ground and fell, exposing her body to the moon.

The priestess of a god is the wife of the god, and her magical powers are derived from her union with him. As a rule, such priestesses cannot marry men, for they are property of the god, but they are not debarred from sexual commerce; often quite the contrary. The priestesses of Bel-Marduk commonly had numerous children. We know of virgin priestesses only where the power of the sacred king is already highly developed.

But while gods have priestess-wives, the true Great Goddesses have no priest-husbands, and when men serve them it is not as husbands or lovers, but by renouncing their sex and assimilating themselves to women. They dress as women; they emasculate themselves, as did the priests of Ishtar, of Pessinos, of the Ephesian Artemis and others. They are probably secondary introductions into the cults of goddesses who were originally served exclusively by women. Where women serve goddesses, considerations of chastity have no application, and they serve as sacred prostitutes. Herodotus says that nearly all people except the Egyptians and the Greeks have intercourse with women in sacred places, but even these two exceptions are not substantiated. It is sometimes said that sacred prostitution among the Hellenic peoples is due to Asiatic influence; but this is not so, and the famous courtesans of Corinth, who were in later times regarded as *filles de joie*, originally served a religious function. A sacred brothel was attached to the temple of Dionysos at Sparta, hardly the place to find imported Asiatic customs. In mediaeval Europe, brothels were frequently attached to churches and religious houses. Queen Joanna instituted a brothel called 'the abbey' in the Papal city of Avignon; it was regulated after the model of religious houses, none but good Christians being admitted; it was closed on Good Friday and Easter Day. Pope Julius II, by a Papal Bull, instituted a similar brothel in Rome, the proceeds being devoted for the comfort of the Sisters of the Order of St Mary Magdalene. From such sources perhaps derives the more modern jocular practice of referring to a brothel as an abbey.

Obligatory Sacred Marriage

Sacred prostitutes are often members of a religious association and frequently married well. As sacred prostitution fell into disuse and the concept of virginity acquired a new significance, the principle of ritual chastity was extended, and even the priestesses of a goddess sometimes came to be vowed to chastity. Yet such ideas have persisted to our own day. Until recently, the Egyptian government used to pitch special tents for the sacred prostitutes, numbering six hundred, during the great annual feast of Ahmed al-Bedawi at Mecca. Women still offer themselves to the holy pilgrims.

In many cultures it is regarded as essential that all women should have connection with the deity at least once in their lives to ensure fertility and, in particular, before their human marriage. Such connection may take place by marriage to an image of the god, often with defloration by a sacred lingam. In India they spend the night in the temple of the god who, in the person of one of his priests, visits them in the darkness. Such visits would be repeated by married women who had proved infertile. The demand, exhibited in many cultures, for the ritual defloration of young girls, if possible by strangers, may be seen as a development of this theme. Strangers performing the office among the Portuguese were lavishly entertained, but it would have meant death to have attempted to repeat the act. Such practices are found throughout the East; for instance, in Burma, the Celebes and Malabar, in North and South America, in Central Africa and elsewhere.

The Nasamonian Custom

In some respects analogous is the 'Nasamonian custom', namely that the bride, before her husband exercises his rights, should yield herself to all the wedding guests, and in some districts specifically to the husband's relatives, before having connection with her husband. Herodotus reported it of the Nasamonians of Cyrenaica, and Diodorus found it practiced in the Balearic Isles; but similar usages are observed at the present day in many parts of the world. The widespread custom of male guests at the wedding kissing the bride or dancing with her may derive from such usages.

The Divine Bridegroom Impersonated by a Priest or Sacred Personage

These practices also reflect, in some instances, the recognition of tribal and communal rites above the husband's individual claims, but certainly in many cases the main object is to placate the deities. The ritual defloration also embodies the dread which attaches to the haemorrhage resulting from rupture of the hymen, which is regarded as analogous to menstrual blood.

A further extension of the idea of connection with the deity is found in the widespread belief in the desirability of union with a holy man. In India, Yogis sometimes, instead of performing penances, make a vow to deflower two or three thousand girls and go about performing this charity. In Egypt, saints, or 'Maslub', go about stark naked and may seize upon women and have connection with them, there and then, in the street, which is regarded as a great honour, and a similar practice is even found among the Yezidis, a semi-Christian sect of Armenia.

From these practices derives the *jus primae noctis*, which, though it may sometimes have assumed the form of a tyrannous claim, was originally greatly desired. Indeed, unless the act was performed, the husband's children would be regarded as bastards and the marriage annulled. In some accounts, the first child of a woman was alone regarded as legitimate and all others bastards, when according to our ideas it should have been the other way about.

Nuptial Continence

Such facts explain why, in most parts of the world, it is customary for newly-married people to observe continence for one or more nights. Such practices have nothing to do with the merits of chastity, and are often observed by people whose moralities are the reverse of puritanical. Several of the people observing this custom are polyandrous. In some cases, though the husband must be continent, the wife is obliged to yield herself to any of his clan-brothers. In others she yields herself to the priest.

The Christian Church recommended deferring consummation for three nights, known as the Tobias nights. The observance was first recommended by St Augustine, and is laid down in the Carolingian capitularies. Arnoldus makes a holy man explain to his bride that these three nights should be spent praying to God that he may procreate children—an idea which echoes the divine marriage. Sanction was found in a reference in the apocryphal book of Tobit in which Tobit, or Tobias, observes such abstinence. But the narrative makes it clear that Sarah had already had seven husbands, each of whom had been slain by a jealous devil, and that Tobias was merely anxious to avoid any clash with his rival. In the Vulgate and Aramaic versions, Tobias not only refrains from challenging the demon but actually performs a well-known fertility charm.

The Divine Bridegroom impersonated by the Husband

In the final phase of development, the husband himself comes to be seen as the vehicle of the divinity, or as the accessory who opens the road for the divine impregnation. Often this is proclaimed by the fact that the husband is regarded as a usurper. Thus in India, the bridegroom repeatedly declares that not he but the moon-god is the rightful husband of the bride, and he formally surrenders her to the god before advancing any claim himself. Among the Romans, that the husband is the representative of the deity is shown by the formula, pronounced by the bride: 'Ubi tu Gaius ego Gaia.' The name Gaius means bull—the bull being the commonest form of the deity in his fertilizing aspect. In just the same way, among the ancient Celts the woman would signify her choice by saying to the man :'You are the bull, and I am the young cow.' Plutarch tells us that the senator Manilius never had intercourse with his wife except during a thunderstorm, feeling himself then to be more thoroughly assimilated to Jupiter.

It is by this ultimate identification of the husband with the deity that ordinary marriage ends by taking on a religious character. In the early Christian church the suggestion that marriage should be regarded as a sacrament would have been blasphemy. As Conybeare says, nothing is further from the truth than the contention of modern divines that the Church from the first patronized and sanctified an institution which in reality was only imposed upon her. For many centuries the consent of both parties was sufficient to constitute a marriage. In A.D. 537 it was laid down that nobles should marry in church, but it was not until the Council of Trent in 1563, in the case of Catholic countries, and until Lord Hardwicke's Act in 1753 in the case of England, that a religious ceremony was made the condition of the legality of a marriage.

St Paul referred to marriage as a 'mystery', thus indicating its connection with the Hieros Gamos. The word translated in the Vulgate by *sacramentum* was elsewhere applied by the translators to 'the sacrament of the Woman and the Beast'.

It was in this way that the sacrament of Holy Matrimony came to be regarded as a sacrament of the Christian Church, and that a religious conception which normally had reference to a divine marriage separate from and even opposed to the human one, came to be blended with the economic and sexual relation—while the primitive tabus attaching to the Holy Marriage were extended to earthly marriages also.

Let us now turn to the question of how an ideal of chastity emerged in western thought, and how this came to influence the conception of marriage.

CHAPTER 25

Modesty

As we have seen, the ethical ideas of primitive society present a strange paradox. Those rules which seem to us indispensible to social welfare are not insisted on nor invested with solemnity, while to those which have no apparent utility the greatest importance and awe attaches. Murder, theft and fraud may or may not be condemned; they are, in any case, viewed as civil offences. On the other hand, the breach of traditional tabus, such as holding converse with one's mother-in-law or exposing one's open mouth while eating, are fraught with vague but dreadful consequences—not only to the guilty party but to the whole community, and this even when the breach is accidental.

However, we have little right to laugh at the savage, for such tabus are also to be found in the field of sexual morality in our own society, although their very sanctity prevents us from seeing their incongruity.

Our existing morality is composed of two elements, both of which have originated from certain primitive tabus. The first is the curse pronounced by women in refusing sexual intercourse at the menstrual period; the other is the tabu against incest, which was also probably imposed by women actuated by maternal jealousy. But though women laid the foundation of sexual tabus, they seem to have had little part in their subsequent development. There is no original disposition in women to chastity. Though sexual indifference may be commoner in women than in men and sensuality rarer, even frigidity is very different from a bias towards chastity.

Generalizations as to the physiological dispositions of the sexes are unreliable, however, and we are on firmer ground when we turn to ethnology, which affords no evidence that women have ever used their influence to extend sexual restrictions and to impose chastity on men. Women are constitutionally orthodox, and their morality consists in ascent to established usages. It is noticeable that in areas where missionaries have imposed puritanical ideas on a previously amoral society, the women soon begin to speak of the new rules with as much conviction as they formerly observed the old, and this can be shown by reports from places as far apart as Polynesia, Turkestan and Paraguay.

Far from women having been instrumental in establishing puritan standards, it is precisely those societies where the power is wielded by women which are characterized by greater sexual freedom. Bachofen—although he thought that matriarchal society had become established by a feminine revolt against promiscuity—nevertheless recognized (with strange inconsistency) that 'hetærism' is characteristic of matriarchal societies. The fact can be illustrated by many North and Central American tribes, such as the Hopi, the Iroquois and the Pueblo, by Malayans and Nayars, by Tibetans and Tongans. History also confirms: Bardesanes in Eusebius says that the women of Central Asia, who 'receive more attention than the men, are not chaste and consort promiscuously with their slaves and with strangers, and are not blamed by their husbands over whom they, in a manner, domineer.'

It might be supposed that feminine jealousy might have tended to foster the development of monogamous marriage. Certainly matrilocal marriage, where it persisted until advanced stages of culture as in Egypt or early Greece favoured monogamy, for it was generally impracticable in such stages of culture for a man adequately to maintain several households, as appears to have been sometimes done in Egypt; but this factor is economic not psychological. In the northern Targi tribes, where marriage is matrilocal and monogamous, the presence of concubines in the household is not in the least resented by the wife, and the same appears to have been the case in early Greece. In countries where marriage customs are, or until recently were, polyandrous, women emphatically favour this. Usually it is the most influential who have the largest number of husbands. Wherever individual women enjoy, in a cultured society, a position of power, far from imposing or observing chastity, they avail themselves of their independence to exercise sexual liberty. The princesses of Uganda used their position so freely that 'all Uganda was said to be their husbands'. In Sierra Leone it is reckoned 'extremely impolite and ill-bred for a married woman to reject the offers of a lover'. Similar stories come from Madagascar and the Marshalls, from Hawaii, Tahiti, Paraguay and Arabia.

To sum up: while we everywhere find chastity imposed by men upon women, it would be difficult to find any instances of a corresponding imposition of chastity by women upon men, apart from the primitive tabus which have reference to menstruation, pregnancy and suckling.

Concealment During Sexual Intercourse

It is often claimed that women have an innate or natural sense of modesty. Old writers used such stereotyped phrases as the sentiments which 'nature has implanted in the human mind', and allude to the sexual organs as 'those parts which nature has taught human beings to conceal'. Since there is no evidence whatever of a sense of modesty in animals, such statements are strictly meaningless. True, some animals return to secluded places for intercourse, but it would be natural to do so for safety. Some authors have argued that primitive man may have sought concealment for the same reason.

Such a view is not in accordance with the sociological and psychological facts, for it is not around the sexual act that modesty centres but about exposure of the sexual organs. In the lower cultures there is no sense of embarrassment in satisfying sexual urges before witnesses. Among the Australian aborigines any native man will, on request, call a woman from the camp and copulate with her before the visitors, without the slightest manifestation of embarrassment on the part of either. Cook reports the same from Tahiti, and it may be observed today among the Maori, as also the Negritos of the Andaman Islands, the Indians of Paraguay and others.

A woman commonly displays modesty at the very time that she willingly yields herself, and she manifests it by a desire for darkness and the avoidance of exposure in the actual act of giving herself to her lover. (The contrary view, that modesty refers basically to the sexual act and only by extension to the sexual organs, has been maintained by several writers, notably Westermarck.)

Clothing for Purposes other than Modesty

Christian writers maintain that the original purpose of clothes was to cover the sexual organs, but in fact this concealment is far from being primitive, although personal apparel, often of an elaborate character, is used by many peoples. For instance, among the majority of South American tribes the women are usually completely naked, the men elaborately decorated with crowns, armlets, garters and collars, but leaving the sexual organs exposed. Some Melanesians who go naked, so far as regards sexual modesty, are yet so sophisticated in the arts of the toilet that they actually wear wigs.

Arctic peoples wear ample garments for warmth and protection, but their lack of bodily modesty is conspicuous. Dr Middendorff relates how, when entertained by a well-to-do Samoyed, he mistook his host's daughter for his son. His host removed his daughter's pantaloons in the most natural manner in order to prove to the traveller his error, although half the village was present. Eskimo men and women, when inside their huts, remove their clothing and place it outside to get rid of vermin, remaining completely naked without self-consciousness no matter what strangers may be present. The Eskimo, says Father Petitot, 'is completely ignorant of morality and cannot imagine that what is natural and necessary should not be done openly'.

However, the use of clothing for warmth and protection is limited to very few primitive peoples. The bulk of primitive clothing consists of what is commonly called 'ornaments'. The term is naturally employed by travellers to describe any object which does not serve the purposes of protection or decency, and the use of which is not known. In point of fact these objects usually have a magical function, and travellers have noted how natives will rarely dispose of them even where the beads and ribbons offered in exchange are of the same kind but more showy. As a matter of fact, it is odd how slow primitive peoples have been to think of employing even easily-available materials, such as furs, to protect themselves from cold. In Central Australia, where the nights are extremely cold, the natives have not thought of using the fur of the bandicoots as a protection. In Tierra del Fuego, where the climate is one of the most inclement in the world, the natives prefer to crowd round the fire with chattering teeth until they sustain serious burns.

Magical Purpose of Attire

In undisorganized primitive societies there is overwhelming evidence that the motives for tattooing and other supposed decorations were magical. Even decorations employed for the express purpose of aiding sexual attraction act not by virtue of their aesthetic value but by their power as magic charms. As M. van Gennep remarks: 'It seems superfluous at the present day to insist on the fact that the origin of tattooing lies not in any single "aesthetic instinct", or "in desire for means of sexual attraction", but in medico-magical mutilations.'

Some savage ornaments and attire seem to have originated from a desire to increase the wearer's resemblance to his totem animal or to a supernatural being. The Fuegians, who go naked most of the year, during their religious ceremonies wear hideous masks, one of the objects of which is not to attract but to repel and terrify the opposite sex. Again, in many parts of the world admission to the company of one's deceased ancestors depends upon having the requisite recognition mark. In several parts of New Guinea, for instance, it is necessary to have the septum of one's nose perforated, and should a child die before having undergone the operation, it is performed post-mortem so that he may not be excluded from the abode of his fathers. In Fiji, Bechuanaland and Brazil similar practices obtain.

Such ornaments may also be amulets designed to secure safety or ensure fertility. Among the Eskimo an effective charm for the latter purpose is a piece of an old European shoe, for they take our nation to be more fertile than their own. A woman is careful to place her amulets for three days in the bladder of a female bear, so that the magic virtues of the animal may be communicated to her. There is no article which cannot form a magic amulet. When the Jesuits first settled in Canada many natives were influenced towards conversion to Christianity by their desire to possess one of their magic talismans; that is, one of their rosaries; an old woman who had succeeded in obtaining one immediately set up in businesss as sorceress. The feather garters worn by the Lenguas of the Gran Chaco are a protection against snake-bite, while those of the Negritos of the Philippines give the wearer greater powers of endurance. A young Shan woman, having obtained some European dress-material, was anxious to know the meaning of the 'charm' printed on it. This read: 'Made in Germany.' Cowrie shells are often worn, usually as charms against sterility. Like all fertility charms the cowrie and other shells have come to acquire magic protective virtues against all evils. The Japanese, if a cowrie shell happens to be unavailable, use a pornographic picture representing the female genitals as a substitute. Coral ranks almost as high, but its virtue is removed if it is polished or treated artistically. Coral is regarded in Italy as regulating the menstrual flow. It is believed that it becomes pale during the menstrual period, and regains its bright red colour when it is finished. In Algeria, as in most parts of Asia and Africa, it is an indispensable part of woman's attire.

Gems are also of profound importance, and are usually regarded as the quintessence of powers derived from the moon. In ancient Peru emeralds were called 'daughters of the Moon' and assisted women in child-birth. They are called the 'sons of the Moon' in India. Glass beads, on which savages set so high a value, are believed by them to possess virtues scarcely less potent than gems.

The discovery of metals was accounted a revelation of magic power, and all metals are regarded as possessing talismanic properties. Such is the reverence with which gold is regarded in India that it is not considered proper to wear any below the waist, as this would be an indignity to the holy material. There can be little doubt that the adoption of a gold standard of currency was, as with cowrie-shell money, due, in the first instance, to magical and superstitious notions. When nickel annas were introduced into India, the natives entertained great doubt as to their worth, and did not consider that they could be used for solemn purposes, such as offerings in the temples.

Amulets are worn, particularly in the neighbourhood of the various openings of the body, through which, according to universal belief, evil spirits and influences may enter, or the soul may escape or be drawn out. Hence the nostrils are guarded by nose-rings, the ears by earrings, the mouth by skewers or the knocking out of teeth and so on. On the coast of Guinea, women wore rings over every opening of their body and a gold ring in the labia. When an opening of the body is thus protected, it is thought not only foolhardy but grossly indelicate to remove it or to be seen without it. American Indians, when the over-stretched lobes of their ears became torn, so that they were unable to wear their usual huge ear ornaments, were so overcome with shame that only with difficulty were they prevented from committing suicide. When, after persistent requests and bribes, Alaskan women were induced to remove their mouth discs, they hid their mouths with their hands in the same confusion as a European woman would display if discovered semi-naked.

Magical Protection of the Sexual Organs

The sexual organs naturally call for special protection. It must be remembered that they are exposed to constant dangers. Impregnation at a distance may take place through countless magical agencies. Sinhalese women believe that if the sexual organs are carelessly exposed, 'the devil, imagined as a white and hairy being, might have intercourse with them.' In ancient Greece and Italy the women stood in the same danger from fauns and satyrs. Eskimo women rub saliva on their abdomen in order to protect themselves from the embraces of the moon-god.

In primitive thought the principle that 'he that looketh after a woman to lust after her, has already committed adultery with her in her heart', has a literal significance. Hence among many peoples, who are otherwise naked, the sexual organs are concealed, and sometimes the concealing object is an exact copy of the member it is meant to conceal. The belt, the primal rudiment of all apparel, is universally regarded not as a utilitarian contrivance but as a magic instrument. Japanese women, noted for their ingenuous lack of prudery and accustomed to bathing publicly, never lay aside their girdles except at the bath, and not always then. Among the Ainu the most effective remedy for barrenness is to drink some water in which the leather girdle of a woman who has borne children has been boiled. In Brazil, in the province of Magalhan, the costume of the women in pre-European times consisted of a minute triangle of carthenware, which fitted closely over the mons veneris, but did not cover the vulva; made from fine china, the surface bears elaborate geometrical designs which differ in each specimen. There can be little doubt that they have magical significance. The 'ururi' worn by the women of the Bakairi tribe does not conceal the labia but occludes the opening of the vagina. Similarly the men in many Brazilian tribes, as also in some parts of Polynesia and Melanesia, tie a piece of tape or string around the prepuce, thus occluding the urethra. Disturbance of this string causes the greatest embarrassment. The Zulus wear a minute cap over the prepuce.

In numerous parts of the world similar tabus refer to the mouth. In Tahiti, when men and boys wished to eat a snack, they would sit two or three yards away from each other, and turn their faces away from the company. It was thought particularly obscene for a woman to be seen eating. The ladies with whom the officers of Captain Cook's ships had such a good time sometimes forgot themselves so far as to take some light refreshment in the cabins, but they begged their lovers not to let it be known that they had been guilty of such a gross breach of modesty. In Polynesia and Melanesia, when a man is surprised he clasps his hand over his mouth to prevent himself from gaping. In Brazil the traveller von den Steinen once shocked his companions by eating a fish in their presence; though they had not a stitch of clothing on their persons, they did not know which way to look.

From this derives our habit of covering our mouths when yawning. Among the peasants of Germany and the Tyrol, it is the custom that if one yawns one should cross oneself in the name of the Trinity, in order that no evil thing may enter. In Norway, when a child yawns, the mother makes the sign of the cross; as also in Italy and in Spain. All Arabs believe that the devil would jump into their mouths, if they were to yawn without covering it.

The Hebrew tradition that clothing originated from using leaves—as the most easily available material—in order to cover the sexual organs is scarcely borne out by the ethnological facts. The use of leaves and branches as sexual coverings is by no means the most general form of primitive clothing; but leaves and boughs are regarded as having the magic properties associated with trees and are widely used as protective charms.[1]

Leaves are almost invariably worn to promote fertility. The women of the Koragars caste in South Canara, who until lately wore the classical costume of Eve, today are fully clothed in Manchester goods, but still wear their leaf-apron over their clothes. In Ross-shire girls sew ivy leaves to their petticoats to bring luck. The Jesuit fathers in the Orinoco were distressed because the women tore up the clothes with which they supplied them, saying that they would be ashamed to wear them. Father Salvado had the same trouble in Australia. In the Congo, some of the natives are now supplied with trousers, but for the sake of convenience leave them completely unbuttoned, thus defeating the missionaries' purpose.

[1] The Hebrew myth is no doubt, a comparatively late one, perhaps owing its origin to an agricultural ritual, of which the object was to promote the fertility of fig-trees. These, according to primitive ideas, were regarded as male and female, and their fertility was promoted by a sacred marriage in which the trees were presented by a man and woman, or a man impersonating a woman, clad in fig-leaves. The fig-leaf was one of the most common emblems of fertility and reproduction, the wood being the usual material for phallic emblems, such as the statue of Priapus, and the fruit being regarded as a surrogate of the female genital organs. The hideous use of fig-leaves on statues is a practice introduced by the Jesuits in the seventeenth century.

Among the peoples who are altogether nude, the desire to protect the sexual organs has given rise to the notion of a natural sentiment of modesty, for if strangers are suddenly introduced there is a certain commotion, and they alter their position so as to conceal the vulva by means of their foot. This is done with a certain amount of ostentation and, after the strangers have been present some time, the precaution is dropped. This is because the stranger may have the evil eye, and until reasonable assurance has been given, it is common sense to take some precaution. All savages have a strong objection to being stared at, and in particular staring at their genitals arouses alarm. Drs Ploss and Bartels, when discussing modesty, attribute it to 'a natural sentiment', chiefly on the basis of some photographs of Fuegian girls who are covering their genitals. As ethnologists, they should have known something of the universal terror with which most savages look on the camera.

Similarly, although amongst most peoples up to an advanced stage of civilization a woman's breasts are not a subject of modesty, yet there are certain circumstances even among the most uncultured peoples when to expose them is regarded as highly undesirable, for fear of the evil eye. The Germans thought that the milk could be dried up in the feeding mother's breast by an envious look, and witches were burned in Burgundy for that crime. Hence nursing mothers who at other times would wear very little attire may conceal themselves in a mantle.

The sexual organs are not only liable to be influenced by magic influences, but may themselves be the source of such influences, as the primary menstrual and lochial tabus indicate. Thus it is that in the Madras province women expose themselves in order to quell a storm. Pliny says that ghosts can be laid by a woman exposing herself, and the women of ancient Egypt used this method to drive evil spirits from the harvest field.

Magic influences may affect men almost as much as women, and may come equally from women or from men. Hence male 'modesty' is often more conspicuous in primitive societies than in higher cultures, and refers to exposure before other men as much as before women. Among a considerable number of peoples the men alone wear protective charms or coverings. In the Admiralty Islands, a man is filled with confusion when the shell which he wears over his sexual organs is removed, and in the New Hebrides the sight of another man's penis is regarded as fraught with the gravest magic dangers; the organ is accordingly wrapped in yards of cloth, forming a preposterous bundle sometimes two feet in length. The pygmies of Dutch New Guinea wear as their sole article of clothing a prodigious case made of a gourd, in which they enclose the penis; its length commonly equals a quarter of the man's height. The Siamese were shocked at the shamelessness of the French soldiers when they saw them bathe naked, and the Fijians were equally scandalized at seeing sailors naked. On the other hand, among many peoples the men utterly scorn the idea that such a covering is called for. The Masai, for instance, consider it wicked to cover their sexual organs, and in some parts of British New Guinea, the natives consider clothing to be fit only for women. It is therefore clear that the extreme modesty of Papuan men is not the outcome of a natural sentiment but of special notions and traditions. Such a tradition is readily instilled. Father Gilii had the joy of bringing the nude Orinoco women to such a sense of modesty that they would on no account remove any part of their clothing, even when going to bed. 'This', exclaims the good Father, 'is a matter of great consolation.'

Extension of Sentiments of Modesty

Ultimately such sentiments become transformed by confluent ideas. Often the covering of female sexual organs becomes associated with the proprietary rights established over a woman by her husband through individual marriage. Thus it is a very general rule in primitive societies that the clothing of women is lengthened and extended after marriage. In some, if the husband dies, the widow removes her skirt and returns to her pre-nuptial state of nudity. Queens in their own right, however, often show their independence by dispensing with such proprieties. One such replied to Livingstone, when he urged her to clothe herself: 'It is not proper for a chief to appear effeminate.'

The concealment of married women has gone to many extremes: in some parts of Sumatra it is indecent to expose the knee, among the Baganda to reveal the calf; among the Chinese the neck, the bare hand and even the foot constitute obscenities. When the Jesuit fathers displayed some beautifully-coloured pictures of saints in classical drapery, they were horrified to discover that these were regarded as pornographic.

To sum up, primitive modesty has no reference to any notion of impurity attaching to the sexual organs or to their functions. As Mr Cross remarks, with regard to Africa, as a rule 'modesty is in inverse proportion to clothing'. In modern society, the fact that an exposure which is customary on the beach would give rise to confusion in the drawing-room, reminds us that the sentiment of modesty derives from a tabu. No doubt, if complete nudity were once more to become general it would cease after a while to produce either sentiments of offended pudicity of or stimulated lubricity. No feminine attire is less stimulating sexually than complete nudity. The youthful Goethe described the feeling produced by his first contemplation of the naked female body as one akin to fear. Flaubert says, 'The first time I saw the two breasts of a woman, I nearly fainted.' Such an avowal reveals the nature of the abyss which has been

created between the natural sexual instincts and the artificially stimulated instincts of the civilized male. Pruriency and obscenity depend,
like modesty, upon the breach of tabus and not upon natural sexual
values. Where no tabu exists, lubricity cannot exist. Modesty, in short,
far from being 'natural', is an artificial product of irrationality.

CHAPTER 26

Purity

THOUGH the primitive sexual tabus were established by women, men transmuted them to produce the moral character of sexual modesty and chastity. While the primary tabus are universal, this male sexual morality is comparatively rare and appears only in advanced stages of culture—a fact which significantly indicates the original matriarchal character of human society and the late growth of patriarchal influence. True, there are some less-advanced peoples—those among whom the theory of marriage-by-purchase has been fully developed—where virginity is claimed, but such people are in a far from primitive state, and the view that they take of the matter differs profoundly from European conceptions.

Indeed, even in European society, among the lower orders and peasant populations, where patriarchal influence is weaker, little importance is attached to the virginity of a bride. In a village near Lisbon, one writer says: 'Young girls who reach the age of sixteen and are still virgins are the object of so much ridicule that, in order to avoid the shame, they yield themselves with the greatest readiness to the first man who courts their favours.' In many parts of Italy, says a sixteenth-century writer, the men would not think of marrying a woman who had not given proof of her popularity by the multitude of her amours. Pre-nuptial unchastity is not regarded as a bar to marriage in Holland, nor in the rural parts of Austria, Bavaria, Switzerland, Norway and elsewhere.

In the earlier phases of society, there is an actual preference for women who are not virgins, for one of the chief objects of marriage is to obtain children; hence, to enter into a binding contract with a virgin would be 'to buy a pig in a poke'. Indeed, in these phases marriage is not regarded as being fully contracted until a child is born. In stages slightly above the primitive, sterility either annuls the contract and the bride-price is returned or another woman is supplied by the bride's parents. It is fertility, not virginity, which is the dominant consideration. Among some peoples, a pregnant girl is the most eligible spouse, exactly as if she were a cow with calf. Among the Kaje of Nigeria and other tribes, the price of a girl who has borne a child is far higher than that of a virgin. Among the Makeo of British Papua, when a young man courts a girl who has already had a child, he advertises the fact by wearing a yellow feather in his head.

Apart from the question of fertility, the desirability of a woman is often thought to be enhanced by her being sought by many lovers. Marco Polo says that in Tibet, the more tokens from her lovers a girl carried around her neck the sooner she got married. Plautus records the same of the ancient Etruscans.

To say that no importance is attached to virginity in primitive society would be scarcely accurate; virginity is, on the contrary, the object of superstitious dread. It is obvious why this should be so. The hæmorrhage from hymeneal rupture is regarded as similar to the menstrual flow, most dreaded and fundamental of all tabu objects of fear. Menstruation is thought to be the effect of sexual intercourse, and the latter is therefore accounted necessary for the establishment of the physiological function. Hence precocious intercourse is not merely permissible but indispensable. In some instances, sexual relations cease at the appearance of puberty. Hindu law enjoins as a most important rule that a girl should be married before the age of puberty, and among the Nayars and other peoples defloration had to take place before puberty.

Moreover, as we have seen, human marriage cannot achieve its object unless it is preceded by divine marriage—and this union is effected by various means, such as unrestricted promiscuity, prostitution with strangers, ritual defloration by a priest or mechanical defloration by the image of the god. These measures not only secure the fertility of the women, not to mention fields and cattle, but also protect the husband against the perils of defloration.

A remarkable feature of the promiscuity which precedes marriage among many peoples is that the first men selected to have intercourse with the bride belongs to the same division of the tribe as herself. Diodorus reports similar usage from the Balearic Islands, and the practice is found in Fiji, New Granada, Assam and elsewhere. When the dread of incest is borne in mind, it is clear that there is a purpose in this: only a person of the same blood is immune from the perils attaching to menstrual or hymeneal blood. Since there is no breach of a tabu when an act is performed with a religious purpose, the incest tabu can be overridden—just as it is also permissible to eat tabu food ritually.

Mechanical Defloration

The fear attaching to intercourse with a virgin has very generally led to the use of artificial means of defloration. The material instrument sometimes represents the god, as in India and primitive Rome. In Morea, in the last century, the bride 'avant de se mettre au lit est admise à l'épreuve de sa virginité qu'elle doit prouver en enfonçant un crible en peau sur lequel elle monte'. Chinese 'ammas' think it their duty to wash their charges so thoroughly that the hymeneal membrane is destroyed, and European parents not acquainted with the customs of the country are sometimes horrified to discover that their daughters have lost all physical signs of virginity.

While ritual defloration by priests or parents is widespread in a great many cases, it is achieved by an extensive cutting of the vulva with a razor, so that the procedure constitutes a very thorough form of female circumcision. This practice was observed until recently by all classes throughout Egypt and by the ancient Egyptians. It is an immemorial practice among the Arabs, and was said to have been first practised by Sarah on Hagar. Afterwards both Sarah and Abraham, by order of Allah, circumcised themselves. We have no evidence that female circumcision was practised among the Jews, though Strabo states that it was, and the Virgin Mary was said to have been circumcised.[1] Many instances can be quoted from India, and it is very widespread in many parts of Africa.

Circumcision of Males

There are grounds for thinking that circumcision in the male originally arose as an imitation of these mutilations of the female genitals. Like all puberty rites, these mutilations are an essential part of the ceremonies of initiation into the tribal organization or religious association, and are, therefore, passports to the ancestral paradise and means of salvation. If, as we have argued, the religious ceremonies of re-birth originated with the women and were taken over by the men, it would naturally follow that the mutilations which constituted a part of these rites would also be adopted by the men. The most widespread form of circumcision is not the amputation of the prepuce but a slitting of the penis along the whole length of the urethra. And the name by which the slit penis is known in the Boulia district of Australia is derived from the word 'vulva'. The conclusion is obvious. The operation is an imitation of the puberty operation of the female. The sub-incised men are known as 'the possessors of a vulva'. Indeed, there are recognized marriages between men who have undergone the operation and youths who have not yet done so. The tribes which practise sub-incision are also those which practise sub-incision of the perineum of the female.

Throughout Polynesia and the greater part of Melanesia, the operation of circumcision does not consist in the excision of the prepuce, but in making a longitudinal slit over the foreskin or the dorsum of the penis. Among the Papuans of a small island off New Guinea, the penis is bored through, as also in the Celebes, among the Dayaks of Borneo, etc.

---

[1] This was probably on the principle that every incident in the biography of Christ had to have its exact counterpart in that of the Virgin.

This is described by some travellers as a voluptuary device, and women are said to appreciate the additional stimulation caused by inserting foreign bodies in the aperture. To anyone familiar with the psychology of savages who, however licentious, are ignorant of the refinements of vice, such a view is quite untenable. It is found among the primitive and most unsophisticated and not among the more advanced and corrupt races, which shows that it is traditional and ritualistic in origin.[1] A perforation would be a natural alternative to slitting as an imitation of female defloration.

On the American continent, where cultural influence cannot be held responsible, artificial defloration and complete circumcision of the female are far more prevalent than circumcision of the male. The existence of simple incision in many African tribes shows that the practice of circumcision is not due, as has been sometimes supposed, to Arab influence, nor is that of female circumcision. Indeed, circumcision by amputation of the prepuce appears, with few exceptions, to be confined to the Semitic races and those who come under their influence. The Jewish rite, we know, did not assume its present form until so late a period as that of the Maccabees. At that date it was still performed in such a manner that the jibes of Gentile women could be evaded, little trace of the operation being perceptible. The nationalistic priesthood enacted that the prepuce should be completely removed. Originally it was understood among the Jews that it was in some way necessary or beneficial for procreation; but it assumed a religious significance, and the notion of a sacrificial offering, or the casting off of an impurity, represented amputation as the essential feature. In the male it imitated not only the defloration of the female but also the tabu resulting from the hymeneal blood.

In the Biblical account of the origin of circumcision, Zibborah rescues her husband, Moses, whom Yahweh is attempting to kill, by pretending to circumcise him. He thus becomes 'a bloody husband', and Yahweh dare not touch him. The blood from the operation is in Kikuyu regarded as tabu—the boys after circumcision are tabu until the wound is healed, and are secluded like girls at their first menstruation, and are sometimes dressed as girls. Among Egyptian Muslims boys undergoing circumcision are attired in a woman's skirt and cap. Intercourse as soon as possible after circumcision is imperative. This is intelligible in the case of girls, where unless steps are taken adhesions would be formed. In Peru, for instance, an artificial penis is inserted after the operation to prevent this.

---

[1] The theories of voluptuary ingenuity appear to be more felicitously illustrated by the practice reported by old travellers of the Burmese, who 'weare a bell upon their yard, and sometimes as big as an acorne, which is made fast between the flesh and the skin'. But even in this instance, it turns out that the object inserted is an amulet intended to ward off evil spirits.

However, among the Arabs and other Muslim peoples the practice of circumcision among females has tended to fall into disuse, and even to be looked on as objectionable, while as regards males it has acquired a nationalistic significance, and today the male rite is more prevalent than the female rite. Nevertheless, artificial defloration, which is still practised by all Mongol peoples and most Muslims, is still the rule with the majority of the human race.

The Concept of Virginity

In primitive societies the concept of virginity is almost unknown, and when asked for some term to describe it, the Congolese savage can think of none more appropriate than one meaning 'mental defective'. Among the Basoga-Batamba of Uganda virginity in women of marriageable age is considered almost a crime.

The value set upon virginity in a bride owes its origin to the practice of infant betrothal—one which prevails among all uncivilized peoples without exception. It is particularly common where a high bride-price is demanded. Men in the prime and vigour of life are betrothed to babies two and three weeks old; in West Africa 'no man except the husband dares come near a betrothed or married woman, even to shake hands'. Nevertheless, in more primitive society no such claims are made. Thus among the Todas betrothal among girls in infancy is the universal rule, but not the slightest importance is attached to virginity, and intercourse is unrestricted from childhood. In somewhat higher cultural stages a clear distinction is sometimes drawn between a girl who is betrothed and one who is not, and a betrothed girl may even be put to death if guilty of unchastity. It is probable that in some societies, such as those of Polynesia, the claim to the virginity of the bride was first put forward in regard to chiefs who, apart from any despotic privileges, are in their sacred character more or less immune from the dangers attaching to virginity. On the same principle, the sacred King of Tonga was the only person in the community who dispensed with circumcision.

The claim to the virginity of the bride among uncultured races is especially developed where the theory of marriage by purchase attains its crudest form—namely, in some parts of Africa, Siberia and Indonesia. Among the Ibo of Nigeria the daughter is not in any way guarded—on the contrary, the father arranges liaisons for her. In a number of African tribes the seducer of a girl, if he does not marry her, is required to pay the bride-price. But 'her market value having been received, any excesses she may commit are regarded as of no importance'. Where missionaries have abolished the bride-price, pre-nuptial chastity has often fallen considerably.

Of many uncultured peoples it has often been stated that the seducer of a girl is obliged to marry her. Such statements may easily give the impression that standards of pre-nuptial chastity are identical with our own, but this is misleading. Unacknowledged children are objectionable for several reasons, which have little to do with chastity; for instance, their maintenance falls upon the girl's parents. In many areas, although the bearing of a child before marriage is forbidden, intercourse itself is not. Among the Masai, the bride is guarded for some time before the marriage—apparently to ensure that the first child born is that of the husband. Again, the Bahima of Ankole are perhaps the strictest of all puritans as regards pre-nuptial chastity, transgression being punishable by death; but after marriage the utmost looseness prevails, and for a man to place his wife at the disposal of a guest is a recognized rule of hospitality. The claim to the virginity of the bride thus represents sentiments entirely different from those which we attach to such a claim. In Southern Russia, if the bridegroom was unable to consummate the marriage on the wedding night while the guests were still assembled, the most vigorous-looking among them was requested to take the bridegroom's place so that the all-important proofs of virginity might be forthcoming. Manifestly, in such instances the value attached to the virginity of the bride does not spring from a feeling akin to jealousy towards women who have had previous intercourse with other men.

Great importance was attached to the demonstration of virginity among many peoples. In the Southern Celebes the proofs of virginity were demonstrated to the guests on a silver salver, and the public exhibition of proofs is widespread all over the world. Among the Turks it was customary for the marriage to be consummated in the presence of the mothers of the parties. Many devices for ensuring that the proofs shall be forthcoming, as by the judicious use of chicken's blood, are adopted and, commonly, the bridegroom takes care to connive in any fraud, for the sentiments involved have no reference to his feelings towards the bride but to the public upholding of the established standards as regards his honour. Throughout barbaric cultures the chastity of a bride is not regarded as a virtue of the young woman but ascribed to her parents and particularly her mother, as acknowledgment of her watchfulness. The marketable value of virginity is not preserved by moral principles but by guarding the girls. Among the Yakut, virginity was protected by an intricate arrangement of leather trousers secured with straps, which girls were not allowed to remove even at night. In Egypt and neighbouring areas, an operation is performed which causes adhesions which close the vaginal aperture, only a small opening being contrived by inserting a quill and the parts being immobilized by stitches. The operation is frequently repeated after each confinement. In Burma, 'they sew up the privy members of the female children as soon as they are born, leaving but a little hole to void the water'. In Sind, the procedure has been modified by the use of a detachable metal ring in the labia. Thus an operation originally intended to facilitate intercourse has been adapted to precisely the opposite purpose.

In China, where marriage does not take place until maturity and is therefore preceded by strictest guarding and seclusion, a standard of female virtue has been created which cannot be matched in any other country, and even surpasses the highest ideals of primitive Christianity. The first Jesuit missionaries were put to shame by the ingenious prudery of the Chinese. Chinese girls have been known to commit suicide because they felt themselves dishonoured by having been in the company of a man, albeit for the inadequate reason, as it seemed to them, of saving him from imminent death. In desperate cases of illness, Chinese ladies may call for the advice of a physician, and in order that he may feel their pulse a silk thread is tied to their wrist and passed through a hole in a partition. The Jesuit fathers were perplexed how to administer baptism or extreme unction to a female convert. Nevertheless, in the vast and minute Chinese literature of moral precepts, not a single reference to chastity or purity, as virtues applicable to the male sex, can be found.

Greek Sexual Morality

In Greece, we have a very different position. Chastity and fidelity were regarded as essential in wives and prospective wives, but it cannot be said that they constituted an ideal. Women were consistently regarded in Greek thought as inferior beings. Adultery appears to have been common. It was the concern of husbands or guardians not to afford women the chance. Plato advocated sexual communism. So did the Cynics. The Epicureans are said to have practised it; and in, a somewhat later age, the Stoics, despite their ascetic tendencies, attached no special merit to chastity. Jones says, 'There does not appear to have been any respect for moral purity in the modern sense.' This attitude is in perfect accordance with the Greek spirit, which considered no natural impulse as evil. It was not until a later stage of Western culture that the current values, which have been regarded in European sentiment as of absolute validity, as grounded in the constitution of human nature, have been developed. The Roman conception came nearer to those of our own society than any other. The Roman woman was placed upon her honour.

Ritual Purity

Continence is regarded as one of the conditions required for the successful carrying out of magical operations and for securing the satisfactory result of certain enterprises. Among the Motu of New Guinea, when a good crop is looked for, a tabu is imposed upon the chief, who must remain chaste. Similarly in Assam just before the harvest continence is exercised by the whole community, for any licentiousness would obviously stimulate the rain-god and ruin the crop. Among the Romans, who celebrated the feast of sowing with Saturnalia, harvesters were careful to remain chaste until the corn was safely gathered. In the same way, chastity had to be observed before the Roman Bacchanalian feasts, and a similar circumstance attached to the Greek Thesmophoriae.

Continence is generally observed by hunters, fishermen and warriors in the course of preparation for an expedition, and this is not simply to raise their efficiency. Dakotan warriors prepare themselves by most elaborate measures, including rigorous chastity and starvation; they stay awake all night, gash their limbs and even cut off one or two fingers, working themselves up to such a pitch of delirium that they see visions. Among the Masai chastity is a necessary condition for the brewing of poison, and among the Kwakiutl it is needful in order to be able to digest a cannibalistic meal. Purity is often required of cooks.

Ritual purity is often thought of as akin to cleanliness, but, in fact, saints and ascetics are as a rule very dirty. St Jerome declared that for an adult to wash was a practice to be wholly condemned, and he expresses his admiration for women who abstain altogether from ablution. The monk of St Gall refers to a certain deacon who 'resisted the course of nature; for he took baths and had himself closely shaved . . . '. Such cleanliness is the reverse of ritual purity.

Sexual continence is a necessary part of ritual efficiency, on the same principle as all forms of self-mortification. The primary rationale of such practices is that the envy of maleficent powers must be warded off by voluntary suffering. Continence is identical in theory with rites of mourning. The Greeks expressly identified ritual purity with rites of mourning, and used the same word to denote the mourning ceremonies in honour of dying gods. In India craftsmen never produce a work of particular beauty without some intentional flaw so as not to tempt Providence, and the most beautiful Oriental manuscripts are generally defaced in some part by an intentional blot. It is significant that in Oriental cultures ritual chastity is observed by priests and holy men solely as a magical qualification, without reference to its intrinsic virtue—just as it is in the most primitive societies. According to Hindu theory, says Sir M. Monier-Williams: 'The performance of penances was like making deposits in the bank of heaven. By degrees an enormous credit was accumulated which enabled the depositor to draw to the amount of his savings without fear of his draft being refused payment . . . .' Even gods are described as engaging in austerities—presumably not to be outdone by human beings.

In India ritual purity is as intimately associated with ritual licentiousness as anywhere. Thus the priests of Siva, while ministering to the god in the form of a gigantic phallus, are under the strictest obligation to be chaste, both in thought and in deed. Asceticism is an alternative to licentiousness: an aspirant to sanctity may tie a heavy stone to his penis and thus effectually mortify the flesh, or he may make a vow to deflower a thousand virgins. Chastity is always a means and not an end, and 'undue craving for chastity is, like all other forms of clinging to conditions of earthly existence, essentially evil'.

Had chastity arisen from a deep-rooted instinct, we should have expected it to have assumed the character of a merit and moral virtue, but nothing of the sort happened in India. The same is true of all the other cultures and civilizations out of which our own has developed. In Western Asia, in Egypt, in Greece chastity was recognized as a condition of magical power but not as a virtue. Indeed, so far were the Greeks from inferring a moral quality from magic ritual that to require young women appointed to the service of the gods to remain chaste was thought unreasonable. The Delphic prophetess was usually an old married woman who complied with ritual requirements by dressing as a virgin.

Christian Morality

The usual practice of tracing the tendencies of Christianity to Eastern influence is thus unjustified. The Jews were distinguished among all other peoples for the importance they attached to ritual purity, which was not a condition of the priestly office but a condition of citizenship of Jewishdom. The word 'Law' came to mean religion itself, so that the 'Jewish Law,' the 'Christian Law', refer to these religions. The Jews thought moral excellence synonymous with accurate observance of the rules of purity.

The moral character of the Jews was not due to their raising morality to the level of religion, but to their elevating religious observance to constitute the whole of morality. No ethical principle was formulated by the Jews that was not recognized equally by the Egyptians or the Romans. It was not their principles but their observance which was superior, and the religious sanction which they attached to it. The whoredoms of Babylon, the customs of the Gentiles, were not denounced as immoral but as opposed to Jewish Law—or rather no distinction was drawn between the two viewpoints. We never find Jewish doctors discussing, as did the Romans and Greeks, whether an act is just or unjust, beneficial or harmful.

The Jews did not invest chastity with any merit, while adultery, fornication, nudity, breaches of the primitive tabus were regarded with horror; virginity was not exalted. Indeed, celibacy was looked upon as a

religious crime equivalent to murder, and men over twenty were compelled to marry. Celibacy was not even tolerable in priests.

The Jews were divided into three types when Christianity first began
to differentiate itself. the Pharisees, the Sadducees and the Essæans.
This last sect did sometimes practise celibacy. Philo says: 'No Essene
marries but all practise continence. . . .' Josephus says that although
they did not absolutely condemn marriage they condemned sexual
desires as sinful, and some Essæan sects practised trial marriage,
marrying a woman only if after three years she had proved her fertility.

Other Eastern ascetics practised continence as a form of self-mortification, but with the Jews the concept of ritual purity had supplanted
this. The preparation of the purifying holy water with which a man
might be purified of the various sources of infection entailed more precautions than surgery. The priest who carried out the final stages was
insulated in mid-air on a specially-constructed bridge. The Essæans
went even farther, and on joining the communion each was supplied
with a spade so that he could dig a pit whenever he wanted to relieve
himself, after which he must wash. They were also vegetarian. The
Essæans, though ritually pure, were not as strongly opposed to marriage
as were the Roman Christians of A.D. 300, who carried such views to an
extreme previously unknown in history. In the Gospels no special stress
is laid on chastity, and there is no denunciation of unchastity.[1]

The Clementine Homilies speak of chastity in the sense of connubial
fidelity, and dwell in a charming tone on the joys of married life.
Marriage of priests is strongly insisted on. It was only when Christianity spread to populous Roman cities that the conception of sexual
purity assumed such significance. Saturninus at the beginning of the
second century drew large crowds by declaring that 'Marriage and procreation are of Satan'. He is thought to have been the first to have introduced such doctrine 'among those who call themselves Christians'.
The sexual aspect of holiness came to eclipse all others, and morality to
mean what it has connoted ever since in Europe—sexual purity.
Athanasius declared that the appreciation of virginity and chastity was
the one supreme revelation and blessing brought by Jesus Christ.
Tertullian said: 'The Kingdom of Heaven is thrown open to Eunuchs.'
Numerous Christians followed Origen, castrating themselves, and surgeons were besieged with requests. In the literature issued by the
Churches of Asia Minor in the second century, 'the married life is
treated as absolutely unlawful'. It is denied that married persons who
have been guilty of sexual intercourse can share in the resurrection.

St Jerome pours scorn upon motherhood—'the tumefaction of the

---

[1] Matthew xix. 12 is manifestly figurative. Matthew v. 28 refers to adultery,
not to ritual purity.

uterus, the care of yelling infants, all those fond feelings which death at last cuts short'. Tertullian insisted in lengthy arguments that marriage was nothing but fornication, and that captious distinctions drawn between it and adultery were mere legal fictions. St Ambrose declared 'that married people should blush at the state in which they are living'. Gregory of Nyssa held that Adam and Eve had at first been created sexless, and, but for Adam's fall, the human race would have been propagated by some harmless mode of vegetation, a view endorsed by John of Damascus. Ambrose and Tertullian declared that the extinction of the human race was preferable to its propagation by sexual intercourse.

These views were not, as has sometimes been represented, exceptional and extreme opinions. It would be hard to find many Christian writers in the first four centuries who have not composed a tractate in praise of virginity; and none of them speaks of marriage and family affection in the human tone of the Clementine Homilies. John Chrysostom was one of the most moderate of the Christian fathers; he concludes his discussion by saying: 'Marriage is good, but virginity is better.' The Council of Trent embodied the principles of the Fathers in its canon: 'Whosoever saith that the marriage state is to be placed above the state of virginity, let him be anathema. . . .'

CHAPTER 27

Romance (1)

Sex Morality Among the European Barbarians

NOTHING is more incongruous than the effects which Christian morality had upon the ideas of the western barbarians. These societies were little removed from matriarchy. Their sagas show us a picture of free, masterful women, often holding the position of queens, commonly exercising the functions of priestesses, almost invariably endowed with magic powers. Their husbands or lovers come to them at their invitation and are dismissed at pleasure. In the case of chieftains marriage was almost always an economic transaction into which no other motives entered, and it mattered not at all whether the lady in question was a maid, a widow or was married. For instance, when Kilydd, a British king, thought of getting married, one of his counsellors advised him: 'I know a wife that will suit thee well and she is the wife of King Doged.' And they resolved to go and seek her, and they slew the king and brought away his wife. When a marriage was founded not upon economic considerations but on love, it was frankly regarded as a temporary arrangement. Thus Fionn, being the guest of Eanna, falls in love with his daughter Sgathach, and offers two hundred head of cattle and a hundred ounces of gold if the chieftain will bestow her upon him as his wife 'for one year'. Her father is honoured by the request and the nuptials are solemnized. The famous queen, Medb, had at least three living husbands who were constantly quarrelling over her. Frequent changes of partners were common until late in mediæval history.

Although polygamy was rare, there was no recognized principle of monogamy, and chieftains were often polygamous. Diarmaid had two legitimate wives, apart from concubines. Conchobar married Derdri, although already married. When Cuchulainn wooed Emer, she inquired, after a number of other questions, as an afterthought: 'Hast thou wife already?' Irish literature of about the first century mentions fraternal polyandry. Clothru, Queen of Connaught, had three brothers for her husbands. Brothers shared the same mistress. The traditions of clanbrotherhood made it a point of honour to supply a guest with a temporary partner. When King Conchobar travelled, his host placed his wife at his disposal. The son of King Aed Mac Ainmerech, when travelling through Ireland, was provided each night with the wife of a different chieftain. When the King and Queen of Connaught sent ambassadors to a certain chieftain to negotiate for the purchase of a sacred bull, they mentioned, among other terms of payment, that the queen 'would receive him in her bed'. Ordinary travellers enjoyed the same hospitality. These customs survived in Ireland as late as the seventeenth century, as we know from Fynes Moryson, who tells us that a nobleman, coming to the house of an Ulster chief, was met at the door by sixteen women, naked but for their loose mantles.

There was no notion of pre-nuptial chastity; princesses of the noblest families, besides being freely offered to guests, bestowed their favours on whomsoever they pleased. Medb, Queen of Connaught, boasted to her husband, 'Before I was married, I was never without a secret lover, in addition to my official lover.'

Nor was there any sense of bodily modesty. Celtic warriors, in full fighting costume, were entirely naked but for their weapons and ornaments. Young unmarried girls attended them.

Our knowledge of Irish pagan society is comparatively detailed owing to the early development of literary activity there. But there is ample evidence that the customs of other barbaric nations were not appreciably different. Celtic-speaking peoples in Britain and Gaul had identical usages. As a modern historian says, the chronicles of the Nordic peoples make constant reference to their ceaseless desire 'to overcome the chastity of matrons and make concubines even of the daughters of the nobility.'

For a long time, these ideas were little modified by Christian influence, for although in savage societies conversion to a new religion will take place rapidly under the prestige of missionaries whose magic is felt to be superior, the magical powers which the Roman missionaries could manifest was scarcely of a nature to impress the barbarians.

The Age of Chivalry

The tradition of an 'age of chivalry' has contributed to draw a veil of misconception over the origins of European societies. In the later Middle Ages, it was firmly believed that the romances of chivalry composed in the twelfth and thirteenth centuries, which referred to the times of Charlemagne and his predecessors, and especially to those of a chieftain called Arthur, represented accurately at least the manners and customs and ideas of European societies during those periods, if not actual historical events.[1] In this romantic literature, we are in the midst of a

---

[1] In the Middle Ages it was a matter of Christian faith to accept the truth of these romances, and especially those referring to Charlemagne. Never has imagination dealt more freely with recent historical events; for instance, the ignominious raid of Charles into Northern Spain, in which he never crossed swords with a Moor, furnished the theme of countless recitals of epic glory.

fantastic world of knights-errant roaming in search of 'adventure', rescuing distressed damsels, joining in the pageantry of jousts, holding exalted ideals, and scarcely more real than the giants and dragons which they overcome, the enchanters and magic castles which surround them. If, from these pictures, we turn to the historical data, we find a society very different from this and surpassing in grossness any savage or barbaric community known to ethnology.

Gildas, the British monk, who spent his life in the midst of this society, describes the knights as 'sanguinary, boastful, murderous, addicted to vice, adulterous and enemies of God'. He adds: 'They are generally engaged in plunder and rapine, and they prey by preference upon the innocent; if they fight to avenge anyone, it is sure to be in favour of robbers and criminals. . . . They lose no opportunity of exalting and celebrating the most bloody-minded amongst themselves. . . . Although they keep a large number of wives, they are fornicators and adulterers.'

Gildas does not refer to King Arthur, but contemporary manuscripts reveal that his character was similar. An old gloss in some of the manuscripts of Nennius informs us that Arthur was 'from his boyhood renowned for his cruelty'. Layamon confirms this. His own warriors held him in such dread that they were afraid to speak in his presence. He informed them that anyone incurring his displeasure would be drawn by wild horses or would have a limb lopped off. At one of his banquets, which are described as wild orgies, his knights attacked each other with carving-knives. After several had been killed, Arthur entered the hall and ordered the warrior who started the disturbance to be buried alive in a bog. He then ordered his knights to strike off the heads of all the male relatives of the culprit and cut off the noses of all the females.

Gregory of Tours' history of the Franks, although written in a spirit of astounding flattery, presents a picture a thousand times more lurid than that of Gildas. There is no parallel in human annals to the interminable recital of murders, massacres, perfidies and cruelties which fill the record.[1] The mass of the people do not differ from them—'the entire population is sunk in vice; each man loves evil and indulges his criminal inclinations without restraint'. The sexual morals of Chilperic are thus described: 'It is not possible to picture in thought any form of licen-

[1] One of the favourites of Gregory is 'the good king Gontran'. Sismondi sums up his good qualities: 'He is only known to have had two wives and one mistress; his temper is, moreover, reputed to be a kindly one, for with the exception of his wife's physician, who was hewn to pieces because he was unable to cure her; of his two brothers-in-law whom he caused to be assassinated; and of his bastard brother Gondobald who was slain by treachery, no other act of cruelty is recorded of him than that he raised the town of Cominges to the ground, and massacred all the inhabitants, men, women and children.'

tiousness or vice which he did not perpetrate in deed.' The race became exhausted through the excesses of debauchery.

The most famous hero in the cycle of Carolingian romances, Roland, is probably mythical, but Charlemagne's warriors do not seem to have differed from their predecessors. Charles himself behaved like his fore-runners. Having accepted the submission of the Saxons, who delivered to him their arms and their leaders, he summoned their chief men to Verden and, after extracting what information he could, had them beheaded, to the number of 4,500. After this massacre, continues the annalist, the king 'proceeded to his winter quarters at Thionville to celebrate the Nativity of our Blessed Lord. . . . As soon as the grass began to sprout again . . . he spread massacre, arson and pillage in every direction.'

The revolting 'Capitularies concerning the Saxons' have preserved a record of the reign of terror by which Germanic Europe was won for Christianity. Charles Martel is represented as informing an ambassador that he will hang every knight he takes prisoner, cut off his nose or put out his eyes, and that all common soldiers and even merchants will have their hands or feet lopped off. One of the most distinguished paladins of Charlemagne, Vivian, cuts off the noses, ears, hands and feet of the ambassadors sent to treat with him. Another Carolingian hero tears out the eyes and cuts off the noses and lower lips of his prisoners.

The chivalry of the heroes towards women is notable. When a lady contradicted a Carolingian knight 'he raised his fist, which was large and square, and hit her full on the nose, so that the bright blood streamed down'. In one of the earliest *chansons de geste* that have reached us, the hero, Raoul de Cambrai, while engaged in dispossessing some neighbours of their domains, roasts one hundred nuns alive.

This is the society in which the 'age of chivalry' was retrospectively located. The twelfth- and thirteenth-century writers depicted the heroes and heroines of this period in contemporary terms. Thus Roland and King Arthur are represented as clad in complete suits of armour and as dwelling in feudal, moated castles. The age of chivalry is that of the readers, not of that of the heroes of the romances; that is, it was not the age of Charlemagne but of the Crusades.

But the manners of the knights of feudal Europe of the period of the Crusades were scarcely less rude and barbarous. For example, Richard Cœur de Lion, later romanticized as the soul of magnanimity, to revenge the defeat of his Welsh auxiliaries, had some prisoners thrown from a cliff into the Seine; he put out the eyes of fifteen French knights. Philip Augustus, the pattern of French chivalry, retaliated by treating fifteen English knights in the same way 'in order that it should not be thought that he was inferior to Richard in prowess and valour'. As proof of the valour of English knights, Richard mentions Guy de la Marque, instancing as proof of his prowess that he killed his father's butler with a blow of his fist. The brother of Henry III, being dissatisfied with his dinner, had his cook tortured to death. The pages of Ordericus Vitalis, of Giraldus Cambrensis, of Guibert de Nogent are scarcely less full of atrocities than those of Gregory of Tours. Bernard de Cahuzac married a sister of the Count of Turenne. Both spent their lives robbing churches, stripping travellers and mutilating innocent persons. 'In one monastery alone... we found 150 men and women with their hands and feet amputated, their eyes torn out, or otherwise injured. The wife of this tyrant, oblivious of pity, used to cut off the breasts of poor women or lop off their thumbs', says a chronicler.

Raping and robbery were as much knightly attributes in the age of professed chivalry as in that of mythical chivalry. 'Knights', says a troubadour of the thirteenth century, 'distinguish themselves by stealing cattle, and robbing travellers and villeins'. They sallied from their castles to strip travellers of their belongings. When Joanna, the daughter of Henry II, went to Naples to get married, she had the misfortune to pass near the domain of Hugh, Duke of Burgundy. She and her escort were stripped of everything, and the Duke's knights, to amuse themselves, 'caressoient les damoiselles'.

Burglary did not detract from the character of a knight. One of the highest nobles of Roussillon, having blackened his face, climbed into the castle where the king was staying, by means of a ladder, and stole the silver. The knights did not disdain to stoop to petty thefts, to steal a few sous, the cheese from a farm or the boots from a house. The Archdeacon of Bath, Peter of Blois, said: 'The order of chivalry consists of living in the midst of every disorder, the art of indulging in every excess and of leading a life of folly.'

However, the knights of the twelfth and thirteenth centuries differed from the heroes of the primitive sagas in one respect. Whereas the latter society was equalitarian, and warlike prowess was the sole criterion of merit, in the feudal system rank and power depended upon territorial possessions. The subjects of a feudal lord held their lives at his pleasure. The aristocracy constituted a close corporation, and the people were regarded as being scarcely human. 'To the warrior knight the labouring man was but an instrument of service to whom no courtesy was due.' The rite of investiture of a knight was only a variant of the rite by which he was invested with a territorial domain. A knight had not only to be valiant but also 'gentle'; that is, well-born. Hence showy display was essential in feudal chivalry. St Bernard taunts them with their ostentation. 'You deck your horses with silk and gewgaws, and cover yourselves with I know not what tawdry draperies; you have your lances, shields and saddles painted, your horses' bits and your spurs of silver and gold adorned with gems.' Frequently the knights were very poor. We read of a lady assisting her chosen knight with a sum of five shillings. One scarcely hears of a knight presenting his ladylove with a gift of any value: many a knight lived exclusively on the bounties she supplied.

The great worth of chivalry lay in the conception of honour. It has been alleged that the conception was a new one but, in fact, it was immemorially established among the northern barbarians, and was developed in a far higher degree among the Arabs, where it included conceptions of generosity unknown to European chivalry. The word 'honour' primarily means 'renown' or 'fame', and the word 'praise' is commonly used as a synonym. A man was dishonoured by a charge of cowardice, and battles consisted of a succession of duels. Gaulish warriors frequently came out of the ranks and challenged an astonished Roman to single combat. Such combats had to be fought under equal conditions. Similar rules are observed among the Australian aborigines, the Indians of Brazil and other savages. The rules of fair play were known among the ancient Irish as 'fir fer'. In an Irish lay, a warrior, coming upon his enemy asleep, first wakes him and tells him to take up his weapons and defend himself. Such a contest usually took place in connexion with banquets, and these banquets were served at round tables or among people sitting in a circle. Hence the name 'Round Table' was also applied to the armed contests. Probably the word 'tournament' referred to the whole practice of indicating the merit of a warrior by his place, from right to left, as the company sat at the round table.

Secondly, after bravery the concept of honour was attached to the faithful observance of promises. A large proportion of Celtic stories turns upon the obligation to fulfil a promise. The obligation imposed by a promise was in reality a conditional curse, called by the Irish a 'geis', a word which also had the meaning of tabu. Thus Cuchulainn, whose name means the Hound of Culan, was under a geis not to eat dog's flesh, which would have been a breach of the totemic tabu. Similarly, Conaire, who was descended from a bird, might not kill birds. The hero, Diarmaid, was under a geis, whenever the cry of hounds was heard, to follow the hunt. Thus the geis was equivalent to a vow, such as those which play so important a part in chivalry. The honouring of a vow was thus much more in the nature of a superstitious fear than an ethical principle. It was in no way inconsistent with perfidy and lying. Celtic heroes, when they have to redeem their geis, commonly attack or endeavour to outwit the person by whom they have been deprived of the promised gift, and clever deceit enhanced a knight's reputation.

The attitude of knights to women is explained by Chrestien de Troyes: 'The usage and rule at that time were that if a knight found a damsel or wench alone, he would, if he wished to preserve his good name, sooner think of cutting his own throat than of offering her dishonour. . . . But, on the other hand, if the damsel were accompanied by another knight, and if it pleased him to give combat to that knight, and win the lady by arms, then he might do his will with her just as he pleased.' However, the first part of the rule does not seem to have been strictly regarded. Gawain, the pattern of knighthood, when Gran de Lis refused to grant him her favours, ravished her in spite of her tears and screams. In Marie de Frances' 'Lai de Graelent' when the hero meets a lady in the forest and who rejects his advances, he knocks her down and ravishes her. The lady, however, forgives him his ardour, for she recognizes that 'he is courteous and well-behaved, a good, generous and honourable knight'. To neglect to acquire a woman when the occasion offered was accounted dishonourable. Among the instructions given to Percival by his mother, was: 'If thou see a fair woman, pay thy court to her, whether she will or no, for thus thou wilt render thyself a better and more esteemed man. . . .'

The lady usually repaid the service of the knight by her favours. Nutt says that the relationship must not for one moment be looked upon as platonic. The tenderness of women for knights in mediaeval times had utilitarian rather than romantic motives. When Iseult first beheld Tristan naked in his bath, she was struck by his fighting qualities. 'If he is valiant as he is handsome,' she says to herself, 'he must be sufficiently strong to sustain a hard fight.' No woman ever had anything to do with a man who had not the reputation of being a good warrior and whose 'praise' was not in people's mouths.

To win the woman was generally to win the land of which she was the owner, for the woman and the fief were inseparable.

In the oldest sagas, the marriage of the hero was not by capture but by service. The woman who was bestowed upon a warrior as a reward for his services was not expected to become his wife. The prize consisted in the enjoyment of the lady's favours, and the warrior might please himself about retaining her. For example, the lord of the Chateaux du Port promised his daughter to Gawain if he should rid him of his enemy. This being achieved, the girl was brought to the hero, undressed, after supper. There was no word of marriage, and she made it clear that she did not expect him to marry her. When Charlemagne visited the Emperor of Constantinople, the latter gave his daughter to Oliver, merely to prove a boast made by the hero as to his phenomenal virility.

Such usages are identical with those of the ancient Britons, to say nothing of those of the North American Indians and the Araucanians of Chile. It was an honour for a girl to offer herself to a warrior of repute. Gawain praises the good taste of his own lady-love, Orgueilleuse, for giving her favours to so valiant a warrior as the Red Knight. A girl who has bestowed her favours on a knight laments, when she hears that he has been killed, that he did not leave her pregnant. The women make the running, and a celebrated hero like Gawain is pestered with women's solicitations.

There was, in fact, in pagan society no such definite distinction as we make between marriage and a more or less temporary liaison. The same terms were used for both relationships. The 'guerdon' which a knight expects as payment for his services is referred to in the most direct terms. 'Jesus!' exclaims a love-sick knight, 'that I might hold her naked in my arms!'

As already indicated, a host customarily offered his daughter to a guest to keep him company. Similar customs were usual in ordinary intercourse. The practice known as 'bundling', which has lingered in some districts until modern times, is manifestly a survival of these mediæval customs.

For centuries after Europe had become Christian, marriage retained this character. The matrimonial history of Henry VIII would not have attracted attention in the eleventh or twelfth centuries. Doubtless that there were many chaste and faithful wives: William of Malmesbury assures us that he was personally acquainted with several men, both lay and clerical, who led sober and chaste lives, but he represents them as exceptions. The Norman nobility were in general, he says, 'given over to gluttony and lechery'. It was usual with them, 'when their concubines became pregnant, or they tired of them, to establish them as public prostitutes, or to traffic their favours amongst their acquaintances'. Shortly after the battle of Hastings, a large number of William's knights asked leave of absence, and hurried back to their Norman castles on receiving news that their wives were entertaining lovers. When Richard I arrived at Marseilles to embark for the Holy Land, he found that his barons, who had preceded him by a few weeks, were penniless, having spent all the money they had collected to redeem the Sepulchre of Christ on women. John of Salisbury said: 'After a young woman has come out of the bridal chamber, her husband is regarded more as a procurer than as a spouse.' These manners are set down by ancient and modern writers to 'the corruption of the times'. But, in fact, if we go back to an earlier period we find a worse 'corruption'. The condition of things differs little from that represented by Cæsar's statement that 'the Britons possessed their wives in common'. St Boniface laments that the English 'utterly despise legitimate matrimony'. They 'refuse to have legitimate wives, and continue to live in lechery and adultery after the manner of neighing horses and braying asses, confounding all things in their wickedness and corruption'.

Things were no better in Gaul and Spain. The fact is that the character of marriage and of sex relations had remained to a large extent
unchanged since the days of paganism. M. Gautier appears to be justified when he claims that 'the ideas and customs in regard to marriage
were established by the Church; it was the Church which created
marriage'.

St Boniface complains that nunneries were no better than brothels,
but it must be remembered that throughout the Middle Ages people
did not enter monasteries or nunneries from motives of religion; the
monasteries were a godsend; they offered homes which were luxurious
compared with those of the majority of the population.

The immorality of the monasteries it too well-known to need detailing.
In the early Irish monastic foundations, monks had women to wait on
them. As Professor Zimmer shows, the lives of early Irish saints are
marked by conceptions of morality which differ little from those of
pagan times. St Brigit is described as blessing the womb of a pregnant
nun. King Ethelbald and other potentates, in regarding the nunneries
as their harems, continued the immemorial usage by which priestesses
are looked on as the wives of the king. The Christian priests, codifying
the laws, abolished polygamy, but for a considerable time the prohibition was not taken seriously. It was common among the kings and chieftains of the Merovingian and Carolingian era, and Charlemagne himself, the Defender of the Faith, was said to have at least two legal wives
and a seraglio of concubines. A beginning was made by insisting that
priests should have not more than one legal wife. In the later Middle
Ages and thereafter the word 'bastard' is one of abuse, but in the early
heroic sagas it appears to have been almost obligatory for every personage to be a bastard. All the heroes of Irish epical myth—Conchobar,
Cuchulainn, Mongan, Fionn, Conaire—were bastards. King Arthur was
a bastard, so was Gawain. Clothwig, Charles Martel, Charlemagne,
Roland and other genuine and mythical characters were declared to be
bastards, as was William the Conqueror. It was Christianity which
turned 'bastard' from a word of credit to one of dishonour. The
Anglo-Saxon synod of 786 decreed: 'We command then, in order to
avoid fornication, that every layman should have one legitimate wife
and every woman one legitimate husband in order that they may have
and beget legitimate heirs according to God's law.'

The Literature of Pagan Europe

The change in feelings about sexual morality is far more clearly exhibited in the literature of early Christian Europe than in the manners
of its people. In fact, the change of view was first manifested in literary
productions and only subsequently in life. Among the barbarians, the

lays reciting the adventures of heroes and goddesses and the abduction of princesses and queens formed a part of every entertainment. The Germans had no other literature. The bard was a privileged person, a magical individual to whom nothing could be denied. The Germans considered that to sing deeds of valour was as meritorious as to perform them. According to a minstrel, 'the fables of Arthur of Britain and the songs of Charlemagne are more dearly cherished and more esteemed than the Gospels. The minstrel is listened to more keenly than St Paul or St Peter.'

This whole literary heritage was of pagan origin, and it was to these compositions in the current speech that the term 'romance' was applied by the people of France who had, since the days of Roman domination, been proud to call themselves Romans. The word originally was an adverb, meaning 'in the Roman tongue', as opposed to the Latin or the German. Romantic literature therefore means the popular French literature of the early Middle Ages, as opposed to the learned literature of Clerks written in Latin. Today, of course, 'romance' and 'romantic' are understood to refer to a form of amatory sentiment distinctive of European feeling. The identification of the two meanings is perfectly justified, for it is out of the romantic literature of the Middle Ages that the type of European amatory sentiment developed.

As Andreas the Chaplain explains in his book on romantic love, the heart of the true lover palpitates at the unexpected sight of his lady-love. He is always a prey to anxiety, eats little and sleeps little. The image of his love never departs from his mind. Here, if the Hibernicism may be allowed, we have the classical picture of romantic love. It is explicitly an extra-conjugal love. The Countess of Narbonne declared: 'Conjugal affection and the true love between lovers are two absolutely different things which have nothing in common. . . . We say definitely and considerately that love cannot exist between married people.' Such explicit statements are scarcely necessary. The poetry of romantic love dealt exclusively with extra-conjugal relations. 'Married women alone were idealized by chivalry, and it is to them that is addressed the homage of poets and of knights.' Husbands had no right to jealousy, and when Count Raimond killed the troubadour who loved his wife and his wife committed suicide, the whole country rose. Knights moved a punitive expedition against him and seized his castle. King Alfonso publicly degraded him, distributed his lands to the relatives of the lovers, who were given a sumptuous burial, while the count was imprisoned for life. The love stories which for ages thrilled the imagination of European populations, in England, Italy and Spain from Tristan and Lancelot to Eric and Paolo, are presentments of illicit relations. In Chrestien de Troyes' *Cliges*, unlawful love is put before the duty of a wife to her husband. In Tristan it is put before the duty of a husband to a wife. In *Le Conte de la Charette* it is even put before the duty of chivalric honour.[1]

The process of idealization of the conception of love began with the re-editing of the mythical and epic material of pagan tradition by Christian redactors. No specimen of that literature which has reached us has not been thus edited. Strangely distorted scraps of classical annals and literature were commingled with Biblical and pagan myths, producing the most amazing medley. The Irish mythical king, Conchobar, was assimilated to Jesus Christ. His birth and death were made to coincide with the Nativity and Crucifixion, and he fell endeavouring to avenge the death of Christ, which had been predicted to him by a Druid. Oberon, that is, the Nibelung king, Albericht, performed his feats of magic in the name of Christ and professed to derive his powers from Him. The redactors refer to the wars between David and the kings of Rome. Brutus is described as the grandson of Æneas and, after the siege of Troy, becomes the first king of Britain. Julius Caesar, king of Austria and Hungary and prince of Constantinople, was the son of Brinhylde, the daughter of Judas Maccabaeus, and married Morgana, the fairy, by whom he became the father of Oberon and of St George. Cæsar, despite his putting Hanygos to death by torture, was 'the flower of chivalry'. He had unhorsed countless knights, and often lifted his opponents bodily in the midst of a fray and carried them off.

The traditional stories of the adventures of Celtic gods and goddesses and tribal heroes became transformed into the romantic narratives centring on King Arthur and his knights. The name Arthur, which is to say 'the Black One' (arsu = black), is almost certainly the same as 'Bran', 'the Raven', and has no historical foundation.[2]

Morgana, the 'Lady of the Lake', is a form of the Celtic moon-goddess who rules over lakes and springs, another of whose appellations is 'The White Lady'. In Celtic literature, the theme of the fairy-wife is common. In it the hero abducts her from her divine husband, who later

---

[1] The learned M. Gaston Paris is utterly perplexed that the legend of Tristan glorifies a love which 'so absolutely contravenes the laws which stand for the family and which are often more sacred in primitive cultures than in more advanced societies'. I do not know whence M. Paris derives his impressions of primitive cultures—possibly from Dr Westermarck.

[2] The view that a nucleus of historical fact underlies the legend of Arthur is untenable. The passage of Nennius which constitutes practically the only support for such a hypothesis is in reality strong evidence against it. Arthur has none but mythological relatives—his father is the dragon Uther, his sister the goddess Anu. As William of Newburgh long since remarked, Geoffrey of Monmouth 'disguised under the honourable name of history the fables of Arthur which he took from the fictions of the Britons, and increased out of his own head'. Arthur who disappeared from the world for three nights, who fought twelve battles per year, and at whose death the moon was chief mourner, is a mythical figure.

recovers her and finally the hero gets her back again. Each of these three
stages occurs in the myth of Arthur and Gwenn-Wyfar, that is, 'the
White Lady'.

Such stories of the abduction of women abound in Celtic literature,
and constitute a class of stories known as Atheida. Many of them breathe
a spirit of deep passion; the love of the women is often obsessing,
haunting, persistent. They sacrifice everything to it. They face dangers
and death in defence of their husband and assist them to their utmost
power. At the loss of the man they love they will not be comforted. They
are tales, as an Irish bard puts it, 'that make women sorrowful'. It is that
element of primitive passion that has supplied what ever true art there
is in 'romantic literature'. Yet, conjoined with that passion there is a
crudity which appears to us incompatible with it, and which runs
counter to the whole concept of romantic love. Thus the wooing of Emer
by Cuchulainn has been cited for its modern tone and the constancy
which pervades it, yet even during the first period of his wooing the
hero has half a dozen other love adventures. Sentimental editors have
gushed over the character of Emer and cited her as an instance of
fidelity, but actually Emer offers herself to any man that she pleases with
an effrontery and obscenity which defy description. She takes a fancy to
a Scandinavian visitor and induces him to elope with her: they spend a
long 'villegiatura' in the Isle of Man, in the Hebrides, and in Scotland.
Similarly, when Iseult is forced to betray herself and give herself to
King Marc before her lover's very eyes, there is not the slightest hint of
horror in the situation. On the contrary, we are actually told that she
took pleasure in the caresses of Marc, for he was young and agreeable
company. Women do their wooing with a directness which ignores re-
buff. The terms with which they make their advances will scarcely bear
repeating. It is indeed a feature of primitive Celtic tales that the men are
represented as reluctant lovers, doubtless a sign of the marked matriarchal
feature of the society. In all the stories of women passing backwards and
forwards from one associate to another, being exchanged, won as the stake
in a game of chance, or demanded as a companion of a night, there is no
inkling of any appreciation of chastity as a virtue, still less of virginity.

In the later courtly redactions traces of the same manners persist.
When the ladies of King Arthur's court were subjected to a proof of
chastity by trying on a magic mantle that would only fit a virtuous woman,
not one was found to answer the test. When a similar test was applied
to the men, King Arthur was the only one who passed successfully.

The Christianization of Pagan Literature

Nevertheless, the translation of this literature into terms of Christian
morality was finally achieved with great thoroughness. In Ireland a good

deal of sympathy with pagan conceptions lingered under superficial Christianity, but it was far otherwise on the continent. The Christian clergy pursued the bards with fierce denunciations, and regarded their total suppression as essential to the triumph of Christianity. Alcuin, that dark obscurantist whom modern historians still represent as a promoter of culture, was untiring in his activity and wrung from Charlemagne a decree abolishing the poets. Many later bishops and archbishops made similar rulings. The duties of kings were defined by the Sixth Council of Paris as being 'to prevent thefts, punish adultery, and to abstain from feeding "jongleurs" '. Minstrels were denied communion; it was declared that they had no hope of salvation, 'for they are ministers of Satan'.

However, all these efforts proved in vain. The bards survived by incorporating into their romances the triumphs of Christian knights, the lives of saints and other Christian topics. This disarmed the ecclesiastical authorities to the point at which some Churches even maintained their own troops of 'jongleurs', as for example at Amiens and Fécamp. The valuable assistance which they rendered in making Church festivals and pageants attractive made them indispensable. Mystery plays were probably their creation—they certainly took a prominent part in their production.

This process of modification never achieved a more important change than when it adapted the myth of the Magic Cauldrons into the sacramental vessel of the Last Supper, in which the blood of Christ was collected by angels as He lay on the Cross. This San Graal, containing the true blood of the redemption (*Sanguis realis*) was said to have been brought to England by Joseph of Arimathea. Just as the Celtic magic cauldron was credited with resuscitating dead warriors, so wounded knights requested to be taken to the Graal to be healed of their wounds. Magic cauldrons were also the source of prophetic inspiration, and they sometimes supplied unlimited banquets, such as the cauldron of the King of Alba, which never became empty. The Holy Grail had in like manner fed Joseph of Arimathea during his imprisonment, and in the Grail Castle 'it proceeded to every place in the hall . . . and filled them with every kind of meat a man could desire'.

In its original pagan form the adventure of the magic cauldron was in no wise a mystic quest, but a conquest like any other. As was natural among war-like tribes, the conquest of the magic lance and sword was originally more important than that of the magic cauldron, but in later versions they became three accessories, the former being explained as the lance which pierced the side of Christ, the latter as the sword which beheaded John the Baptist.

The most serious difficulty was, however, presented by the character of the heroes. The chosen guardian of the eucharistic vessel must naturally be ritually pure. It was scarcely sufficient that he should merely be reputably chaste. His function seemed to require that he should be a virgin. How could this office be filled by Gawain, who of all the heroes of the Arthurian cycle had the most firmly established amatory reputation ? In the later stages of the Romance period Lancelot almost supplanted Gawain in popularity, and there was a disposition to transfer to him, as Gawain's understudy, the High Adventure; but the lover of Guinevere was scarcely better qualified from the moral point of view than the original Gawain. The best solution that could be found in these difficult circumstances was to assign the part to Perceval. This attribution presents one of the most curious incidents in literary history. In Celtic folk-lore the character of Perceval is well-defined. He is not a mythological hero, but a pure product of folk-lore humour. He was in fact the clown or comic personage of the traditional cycle, and was spoken of as 'Perceval the Fool'. He leaves his rustic home on a bony piebald with imitated trappings and armed with a pitch-fork, and rides into the hall of Arthur's court amidst jeers and laughter; while clumsily manœuvring his farm-horse he knocks off King Arthur's cap. He attempts all the exploits of the prototypes, accomplishes them with the proverbial fool's luck, and then, owing to his phenomenal stupidity, fails to reap the fruits of his success. His feeble-mindedness is exhibited by his scrupulous observance, at the most inopportune moments, of any advice given to him. When he attains the magic talisman, he observes the advice given him not to show curiosity and thus remains ignorant of its properties.

The incident which commended him to the Christian editors was this: Perceval had been instructed by his mother to make love to every fair woman he met, whether she was willing or no, but of course bungled his amatory successes. The first woman he comes upon he finds asleep in a tent; he kisses her, steals her jewellery and eats up all her provisions—his appetite is gargantuan. Having thus faithfully carried out his mother's instructions, he departs, taking no notice of the lady's hints and advances. When Blancheflor implores Perceval to rescue her realm, which is being ravaged, he does so. When she comes to her guest's bed, coquettishly excusing herself 'por ce que je sui presque nue', he receives her literally with open arms, but in accordance with his character, after covering her with kisses, falls asleep in her arms and thus spends the night.

This incident was assimilated to the trials of chastity of earlier Christian saints and, in the later adaptations of the myth, Perceval comes to be represented as a maiden-knight and a worthy protagonist of the quest of the Grail. Actually, the original Perceval was in no way more austere, though less courteous, than his prototypes. There is certainly nothing austere in his behaviour with the lady and the chess-board. He draws her to his arms, kisses her, 'and would have done more if he could and she had consented'. Not only is Perceval a married man, but his matrimonial arrangements appear to be multiple. One of his traditional amours is with a certain heathen princess. In one manuscript, she is expressly said to be given in marriage to Perceval by King Arthur after a tournament. In two other versions which give the incident in the same way, the writers show a remarkable embarrassment, stating that she was given by King Arthur to a most distinguished knight, but positively declining to mention his name. From the Mabinogion version, we learn that the lady was the Empress of Cristinobyl the Great. She entertained Perceval for fourteen years, and he had a son by her, named Morien. In the Dutch 'Lancelot', the perplexed editor states that some books declare that Morien was the son of Perceval,' but that cannot be true, because, as is well known, both Perceval and Galahad remained virgins'.

In the German 'Parsifal', the difficulty of explaining Blancheflor's visit to her guest's bed, though adorned with rhyme, is certainly destitute of reason. The reason given is that she feels inclined to confide her troubles to her guest, although she has had the whole afternoon and evening to do so. In Gerbert's addition to Chrestien's poem the story evolves further, and is even more devoid of reason. Blancheflor's visit to Perceval takes place on the very eve of their marriage. The betrothed couple, whose indecent haste is quite unaccountable, sleep with the bed-cover between them, though we are not told which of the two runs the risk of catching a death of cold by sleeping outside it. Their wedding is celebrated next day, but no sooner are they married than Blancheflor, in a discourse paraphrased from Origen, proposes to her husband that they should remain chaste for the rest of their lives, and this they decide to do. As a reward, a heavenly voice announces to them that from their seed shall spring the Knight of the Swan and the deliverer of the Holy Sepulchre. Since Perceval's only living relatives are a holy hermit and a nun, it is difficult to imagine how the prophecy can be realized.

Even this is not the last word in the evolution of the story, for the author of *La Queste del Saint Graal* goes even farther. Perceval meets Blancheflor in a desert and she seduces him by her blandishments. but as he is about to step into bed, his eyes fall on the cross-shaped hilt of the sword; he is reminded of his vows and instantly tent and damsel vanish. A hermit tells him that the damsel was no other than Satan.

Despite these resourceful modifications, Perceval was still not a wholly successful protagonist, and a brand-new hero was created in Galahad, a character unknown except for a casual mention of the name in Celtic tradition. The author of *Le Saint Graal* makes him the sole hero of the quest of the mystic talisman, eliminating the name of Perceval from his account.

By such methods, the belief was made current that the relations between knights and their 'amie' had always been platonic. Thus literature, enshrining the doctrines of Ambrose and Origen, became an instrument of edification not, only to the mediæval but to the modern world. The Victorian editor of *La Queste* sees in the example of Galahad and Perceval a feeling 'founded on a deep reverence for women, which is the most refining and one of the noblest sentiments of man's nature'. Actually, for the mediaeval, woman was the means whereby sin came into the world, the arch-stumbling-block. As Mr Nutt says: 'It would be hard to find a more striking instance of how the editorial ideal may override perception and judgement.'

Thus the Christian Church transmuted the secular literature which had sprung from pagan traditions into a glorification of the patristic doctrines of the value of chastity and the vileness of sex. No more amazing transformation could be imagined.

CHAPTER 28

Romance (11)

THE conception of chivalry and courtly love was not elaborated in the romances of chivalry of Northern France, with which it is so closely associated, but in the lyrical poetry which attained its greatest development in Provence. This poetry is the source from which the lyrical poetry of the whole of Europe, including Germany and England, has been derived.[1]

While the taste for the romantic narrative vanished almost completely, the love-poetry of the Provençal poets handed down a way of looking at amatory relations which has grown into the blood and bone of every subsequent European literature. Whereas in the Romances love was dealt with without subtlety, in troubadour poetry the treatment was elaborate.

In pagan Europe, love poetry had not occupied an important place. Love-songs had been regarded as magic spells, and to address a love-song to a girl was a form of assault, often severely punished, like other forms of witchcraft. Thus the Scandinavian poet, Ottar the Black, was convicted of having dedicated a poem to the daughter of King Olaf of Sweden, and was condemned to death. In one version of the Tristan story, the hero-poet is killed by King Marc for singing a song to Iseult. These pagan barbarian love-poems were extremely crude.

In the twelfth century Provence enjoyed exceptional peace and prosperity; in the absence of any calls for martial valour, the aspect of chivalry which assumed the chief importance was that of amatory adventure. Troubadour poetry inherited the twin traditions of chivalry—the knightly interest in arms and in love. As Andraud says: 'All the people of that society lived manifestly for the chief purpose of enjoying themselves. The nobles . . . are the friends of poets but are, above all, engaged in their attentions to the ladies and always in quest of some new amorous adventure.'

Like the bards of pagan times, the early troubadours belonged to the

---

[1] It may seem strange that early German lyrical poetry should be derived from Provence, but the German emperors held claim over the kingdom of Arles and the relations between the two countries were close. Frederick I paid a lengthy visit to the south of France, bringing many minstrels with him.

ruling class, and the love-service which the minstrel-knight offered his lady, in the form of poetical homage, was identical with the service by which he could win her with lance and sword. The poet owed allegiance to his mistress, and she to him when she formally accepted him as her bard. This literary chivalry was a knightly privilege, conferring upon men and women of gentle birth a freedom in extra-connubial amatory relations, as the word 'gallantry' in modern French continues to suggest. Prudery and jealousy were ungallant, uncourtly, and betrayed ignorance of polite usage.

Just like the knightly journeys, this literary service was regulated by convention. Poetic inspiration was confined within fixed literary canons, and the merit of a composition was praised by its conformity to precedent. Originality in troubadour poetry is confined almost entirely to the skill displayed in varying set forms and themes. It was a rule, for example, that an amatory song should begin with some reference to the season of the year.

The same conventionalism regulated the relationship between the lover and his mistress. The canons of romantic love-making were worked out with amazing exactitude: every sigh, every blush, the cruelty of the lady and the despair of the lover, the graduated scale of favours, were measured and timed according to established rules. The situations to which a love-relation may give rise were formally debated in dialectical discussions, modelled on scholastic disputations, and judgment was pronounced at conferences of experts on erotic problems.[1]

This strange theoretical interest in amatory sentiment is a singular phenomenon. Such a pedantic dealing with erotics is without parallel either in pagan barbarian or classical literature. The reason this refinement of analysis appeared in a society which had scarcely emerged from the rudest barbarism is that these conventions expressed the desire to give the sanction of cultivated taste to customary sex-relations. Thus the application of Christian standards was eluded and the charge of immorality parried.

This idealized sex-relationship was, as we have seen, exclusively extra-conjugal. The homage of the troubadour poets was, without exception addressed to married women. This was emphasized as an essential part of the distinction between refined and 'courtly' love and gross, vulgar relations or 'villeiny', as the poets called it. A woman who pleaded the duty of fidelity to her husband was stigmatized as bourgeoise and the

---

[1] Much controversy has centred on the question whether 'courts of love' existed. It seems clear that the assembled company often debated theoretical issues, and, no doubt, real instances were often raised, but the rule of secrecy excludes the possibility that a formal demand for judgment was made, and it was the whole company which gave its opinion.

jealous husband as dishonourable. This tradition persisted until a late date. Thus Petrarch, a canon of the Church and a person of the greatest respectability, celebrated in a lengthy series of songs his love, real or fictitious, for a married woman.

Romantic love was thus 'immoral'. However, that Petrarch could write such poetry was due to the fact that, in the intervening centuries, a profound change had occurred. Petrarch's long-drawn literary passion is, from a moral point of view, well-nigh unobjectionable, for while it is adulterous it is also so highly sublimated and so dissociated from gross sex relation that one may wonder whether it was not purely fictitious. It is interesting to trace how this purification and spiritualization took place in the development of troubadour poetry.

There is no vestige of such delicacy in the earlier Provençal poetry. The first troubadour whose name has come down to us is William of Poitou, Duke of Aquitaine. His apotheosis of love as the supreme fact in life indicates no thought of sublimation. His grossness cannot be reproduced in printed English, and he furnished Boccaccio with the prototype of one of his more salacious stories. Other early troubadours, such as Marcabru and Cercamon, are equally direct and unsophisticated. Raimon Jordan prefers a night in the arms of his beloved to his chance of Paradise; and Gauçelm Faidit is even more lascivious. Arnaut de Maroill defines his passion as 'the desire which I have of your sweet body'. Raimond de Miraval expressly declares that it is 'bodily and not spiritual possession which he desires'. Arnaud Daniel, the 'master of love', asks that it may be the merciful God's pleasure that 'my Lady and I shall lie in that chamber where precious assignation convenes us . . . and that I may, amidst smiles and kisses, uncover her fair body and feed my eyes upon it by the light of the lamp'.

Daniel sets aside the rule that every lover must be despairing and every lady pitiless. He sings: 'Beautiful is life when orbed in joy; let those to whom the Fates are harsh decry it; no cause of plaint my lot affords. She is not cruel whose friend I am; nor is a fairer this side of the Alps. Fondly I love her, nor ever greater joy did Paris have of Helen of Troy.' Not until the period of decadence is there any ambiguity as to the troubadours' conception of love or any suggestion of platonic sentiments. Frankly sensual as Daniel is, he expresses only contempt for 'Shameful pleasures, unredeemed by honour and refinement'. Similarly, Andreas the Chaplain, the most detailed exponent of courtly ideas, repudiates 'mere' sensuality and lovers who confound everything by their behaviour, which is no better than that of dogs'. Marcabru inveighs against mercenary women, whom he calls in plain Provençal, 'putanas'—'harlots'. Mercenary motives were, in fact, the chief sin against courtly love. 'A woman must yield her favours to her lover as to a friend, not as to a master,' a poetess declares. One of the rules of gallantry was that no woman should have a lover of more exalted social status than herself. With the later troubadours of the thirteenth century these distinctions became even more pronounced. The frank language almost vanishes, and they explicitly disclaim the reward of their services.

The humble lover declares himself sufficiently recompensed by a kiss or a smile, or by the gift of the hair from his lady's cloak or a thread from her glove. The affectation becomes more pronounced, the poems more prolix; the humility and resignation of the lover is unendingly dwelt upon and becomes abject; his tears flow in a perpetual stream; we hear a great deal more of the cruelty and heartlessness of his fair enemy.

What were the causes of this evolution? Simple causes may be found in the social conditions of the period. As Christian legislation became more fully established and feudal society more firmly organized, extra-conjugal relations became illicit. Love became platonic because changed social conditions required that it should. The conduct of courtly society in France, Italy and Norman England never became puritanical, but the opposition between things permissible and things illicit became, in theory at least, more definite. In a later age the dictates of the code of honour became, in effect, reversed. Sordello implored his lady-love not to be moved by pity to grant him favours which might compromise her honour.

Whereas the early troubadours had belonged to the ruling classes and knighthood had been a necessary qualification, literary talent came to be independent of class distinctions. Bernard de Ventador was the son of a scullion and a kitchen wench. Folquet de Marseille was a burgher in business. His editor comments upon the absurdity of supposing that he would create a scandal by making love to the Viscountess of the Manor who, with her husband, was good enough to patronize him. Sometimes the love-poetry of the professional troubadour was composed in order to forward the intrigues of his noble patron or patroness, and the 'drue' whom he celebrated became a gracious patroness of literature, upon whom the poet was dependent for his bread and butter.

These altered social circumstances were not, however, the only cause of the change. The time had come when the voice of the Church, which the elegant culture of Provence had been in a position to defy, became effective. The hosts of Simon de Montfort pounced upon the abodes of profane culture and heresy, reducing whole districts to deserts. Nevertheless by 1218, when de Montfort was killed, the southerners had almost reconquered their devastated country. But what the swords of the Crusaders failed to achieve was achieved by the Holy Inquisition. 'In the twelfth Century', says Lea, 'the South of France had been the most civilized land in (Christian) Europe. There commerce, industry, art, science had been far in advance of the age. The cities had won virtual self-government . . . the nobles, for the most part, were cultivated men . . . who had learned that their prosperity depended upon the prosperity of their subjects, and that municipal liberties were a safeguard rather than a menace. The Crusaders came and their unfinished work was taken up and executed to the bitter end by the Inquisition. It left a ruined and impoverished country with shattered industries and failing commerce. The native nobles were broken by confiscation and replaced by strangers . . . a people of rare gifts had been tortured, decimated, humiliated, despoiled. The precocious civilization which had promised to lead Europe in the path of culture was gone, and to Italy was transmitted the honour of the Renaissance.'

Now, bishops and Dominicans illustrated their own view of 'reverence for women'. Even though sick, women were dragged from their beds and burned at the stake. When troops, led by the Archbishop of Narbonne, had besieged a castle and reduced its inhabitants to surrender from lack of food, they made a huge fire and, as over 200 men and women came out of the castle, they were seized and tossed into the flames. As the Dominican prior of Villemier said, in a theological poem: 'If you do not believe this, look at that raging fire which is consuming your comrades. Reply in one word or two, for you will either roast in that fire or join us.'

Such methods affected a transformation in the conception of love. 'Provençal poetry became penetrated with the theory of the sinfulness of love, invented by the Church.' The leading spirit in bringing about this reform was Guilhem Montanhagol. 'Lovers must continue to serve love,' he said, attempting to reassure those who, terrified by the prohibitions of the clergy, were turning away from the cult, 'for love is not a sin but a virtue which makes the wicked good and the good better . . . chastity itself comes from love, for whosoever truly understands love cannot be evil-minded.' That is the first mention of the word 'chastity' in Provençal literature.

Montanhagol claimed that the noble knights of old sought nothing in love except honour, in accordance with the usual apologetic method of claiming that the moral notions which one preconises have always been the rule. The principles of this poetical reformation were set forth by Malfre Ermengaud, in a prodigious versified treatise of 27,445 lines, the *Breviari d'Amor*, where the argument is prosily set forth in true scholastic fashion, supported by citations from the old troubadours. Satan, he says, makes men love women more than God, but those who do so certainly adore Satan. This new interpretation was voiced by the last bards of Provence as they scattered to foreign lands. Chief among them was Guiraut Riquier, the last of the troubadours. He said: 'I account myself well-repaid by the inspiration which has been derived from the love I have bestowed upon my lady, without being requited by any love on her part.'

The Italian troubadours, such as Lanfranc Cigala, Zorzi, Sordello, outdid their masters, but when Sordello proclaimed that he wanted no favours from his beloved, his fellow bards were amazed; Bertran d'Alaman thought that he had taken leave of his senses. At first these Italian poets wrote in Provençal but later in their native tongue, thus creating the first Italian poetry, immediately preceding Dante and now generally known as the 'dolce stil nuovo'. It developed a flexibility and variety of expression, surpassing in charm the Provençal product, but the conventions remained unaltered.

It has been erroneously associated exclusively with the Sicilian court, but in fact the imitations which were produced in Sicily show no trace of the later doctrines. The Provençal poets who took refuge at the semi-pagan court of Frederick II were not likely to belong to the set of Montanhagol and his friends. In the poems of Guido delle Colonne, Jacopo Lentini, Pier delle Vigne and the other poets of the Sicilian school, not a word is to be found about the merits of chastity. Various poems of the north Italian school, on the other hand, seem almost to be translations of the *Breviari d'Amor*. The 'sweet new style' assumed its full development with Guido Guinicelli of Bologna, who stresses the sublimated purity of his love. His lady 'is crowned in heaven and in his hope of Paradise'. Indeed, if she is not expressly identified with the Holy Virgin. she is assimilated to the moon: 'The lady who in my heart awakened love seems like unto the orb that measures time and sheds her splendour in the sky of love.'

Dante's Beatrice, leading him through the seven spheres while she lectures him on theology, is here clearly pre-figured. Cavalcanti gave out a new version of Andreas' law of love from which all objectionable principles were eliminated. One of the troubadours of the earlier period, Garin le Brun, wrote a poem, in which, after the fashion of the time, the opposing promptings of 'Mezura' (moderation) and 'Leujairia' (sensuality) are contrasted. 'Moderation whispers sweet and low, telling me to proceed with my affairs step by step. "Leujairia" says, "Wherefore wait ? If thou dost not hasten, the opportunity of reaching the goal may pass." ... And thus am I equally divided between "Mezura" and "Leujairia".' It is easy to see how this choice would be represented as the opposition between pure and impure love, between chastity and lechery.

However, it was necessary to do much more than reinterpret the terms of this poetry. Nothing short of its conversion into purely religious poetry could satisfy the requirements of the times. 'Love,' abstracted and personified, was freely identified with God, with Christ, with the Holy

Ghost. Likewise the 'Lady' towards whom poetical sentiment was directed was identified with the Holy Virgin.

A recent Catholic writer states that 'respect for women rises and falls with veneration for the Virgin Mother of God', and there is some truth in the claim. In pagan Europe, where women were independent and influential, the Virgin Mother was fervently worshipped, but she was not as yet Christian, and her worship was, as we have seen at first, put down by the Church. But by the time of the revival of culture in the twelfth and thirteenth centuries it had become completely re-established. The Holy Virgin, called by Albertus Magnus the Great Goddess, had, in Southern Europe at least, well-nigh replaced the male Trinity in the current devotion of the people. God the Father was regarded as terrible and unapproachable; Christ, in spite of his compassion, held the office of a judge; the Queen of Heaven alone could show untrammelled mercy. She wrought more miracles than all male divine and saintly beings put together, and had, in fact, entirely regained her position as divine prototype of magic-wielding women. She was the chief Source of healing. Thus she cured a monk who was on the point of death from an ulcerous disease of a very suspicious nature, by applying the milk from her own breasts to his sores. When the reverend abbess of a convent was pregnant, the Blessed Virgin came to her assistance and acted as midwife. A nun who, becoming bored with convent life, went off and became a prostitute, then, repenting, returned, found that her place had been taken during her absence by the Virgin so that no one knew anything of her escapade.

In the best period of Provençal poetry, some of the troubadours composed religious pieces, but the Holy Virgin was never referred to. Peire Cardinal was the first to compose a hymn to the Virgin. These early troubadour poems to the Virgin are merely paraphrases of church hymns. It was the troubadours of the decadence who transferred the formulas of Provençal love-poetry to the celebration of the Virgin, merely substituting the name of the latter for that of the object of their effusions. Riquier even reversed the procedure, calling the Virgin by the name he had used in celebrating the Countess of Narbonne. The pattern was taken up by the Italian troubadours, and became an established tradition. Even the 'divine' Aretino supplemented his pornographic sonnets and his directory to the prostitutes of Venice with hymns to the Madonna.

The changes in the attitude towards amatory themes were not psychological changes or even (as is commonly said) in the conception of love, so much as changes in literary convention. With the later court poets, the rules of composition were so strict that their poems could never be spontaneous effusions of feeling. Some troubadours continued to produce poetic laments until they were well over fifty. In such circumstances, it is easy enough to sublimate the conception of love. As a rule, they keep one conception for their literary activities and another for their relations with actual women. Sordello himself, whose extravagance in idealization surprised his contempories, was distinguished for his exploits as a libertine and eloped with at least two married women. Yet, ultimately, it is not possible to separate literature from life. The culture of every civilized people is built around its Bibles. The transformation in the conception of romantic love and the idealization of the relationship between the sexes were not dictated by changes in public sentiment but by the influence of the Christian Church, and were imposed upon popular literature by those patristic conceptions which pronounced the extinction of the human race to be preferable to its reproduction by sexual intercourse.

These conceptions, the extravagances of a disordered asceticism, would be accounted by most people morbid aberrations, for today sexual morality has nothing to do with the insane vilification of sex and the condemnation of marriage as a necessary evil. Yet it is to this ascetic ideal that current European standards owe their existence. It was not moderate and considered views which transformed barbaric usages, but patristic ideals in their most uncompromising forms. The moral standards now applied to sex relations are the product of that exaltation of ritual purity which pronounced a curse upon sex and stigmatized women as the instrument of Satan.

But this is not all. As the freedom of paganism became abolished, the idealization which had been used to excuse it was transferred to legitimate relations, and came to be regarded as the foundation of monogamic marriage, with which it had formally been regarded as incompatible. The idealization of a relation, long essentially economic, has continued in the European tradition. Sexual instincts, confined within one prescribed channel, have become directed, as in no other phase of culture, towards a single personal object, and have availed themselves of an emotional sublimation of which the romantic and lyrical literature of the Middle Ages supplied the elements. Monogamic relations have created monogamic love. The sentimental idealization of the sex-relation has thus assumed a character which is without equivalent in any other culture, and was unknown in the cradle of European civilization, the Hellenic world.

CHAPTER 29

The Mothers

CIVILIZATION has been created chiefly, if not exclusively, by man's rational faculty, and its achievements have taken place in societies organized on patriarchal principles; they are, for the most part, the work of men. Women are innately conservative and, if it is true that a man learns nothing after forty, it may be said that a woman learns nothing after twenty-five. Her intelligence differs in kind from masculine intelligence. But the rich world of civilization has sprung from more ancient types of society, in the development of which the human mind has played a much smaller part and instinct a much larger one. In these societies, the notion of magic took the place which creative thought takes in higher societies. Abstract conceptions could have no place where every relation of life was concrete. In these societies, it was from the woman's sphere of interests and activities that the chief stimulus was derived, and social organization itself was the expression of feminine functions.

The source of social cohesion lies in the maternal instinct. The non-rational sentiments which united the primitive maternal groups have given rise to more varied and generalized loyalties; it is in this sense only that the family should be regarded as the foundation of society. The patriarchal 'family' of academic social science is but a euphemism for for the individualistic male with his subordinate dependents. Human society could not have arisen out of conflicting individualistic interests. The primordial family was not the unit but was the whole society. The expansion of primitive social groups into larger aggregates was rendered possible only by the bonds which made the primitive group a social entity, and the evolution of other forms of loyalty from them. The maternal instinct is the only true altruism. No people, probably no individual, has ever been actuated by love of the human race. The leaders of men, who founded kingdoms or expanded the primitive matriarchal into an extensive society, inherited from the primitive mother and priestess her sacred magical character.

If today the cohesion of Western societies appears precarious, it is because these sentimental bonds have been enfeebled. They derive from the reproductive function, the primary purpose of the group. Important as are cultural influences, biological facts are antecedent to them.

In the foregoing pages it has frequently been contended that a given institution or sentiment owed its origin, not to the higher motives and conceptions now associated with it, but to more trivial and, in our eyes, less worthy causes. But it must not be supposed that to trace it it a humbler origin is to detract from the intrinsic worth of the product. In studying human phenomena, one should adhere to the principle 'judge not'. There is no element in our social heritage which is wholly good or wholly bad in its effects. The restrictions imposed upon the sexual instincts by primitive tabus, superstitions and selfishness have so transformed the manifestations of those instincts that they cannot operate in civilized man as they did in primitive humanity. They have created sentiments unknown to the savage, who knows not love as the banking up of primitive passions into one channel. Even though the confined flood may beat against its banks, and its course be full of storm and pain, few would readily forgo the baptism of its living waters.

But the factors which have sublimated primal instincts have also given rise to mephitic products as a result of their simultaneous stimulation and thwarting. Restrictive sexual morality, aimed at purity and chastity, has been the source of vice and lubricity. European morality places a tabu upon the sexual instincts at a time when these first develop, and thus indelibly impresses a certain form upon the whole sexual life of the individual, which is poisoned at its source. Thus it is that civilized man imparts to uncultured races morals and vice at the same time.

At the present time the relations between the sexes are in an exceptional and perhaps unprecedented situation. We live in a patriarchal society in which patriarchal principles have ceased to be valid. Nevertheless, woman cannot return to being the chief producer and controller, as she was in the housekeeping stage of material culture. Many aim at a compromise, at economic independence, and take up the avocations of men, thus abolishing to some extent the economic lever upon which patriarchal dominance is founded. But this is very different from the primitive division of labour, and the economic independence cannot be part of sex-relations as at present established. Either the woman worker eventually marries, thus returning to patriarchal conditions, or she adopts forms of sex-relations other than patriarchal marriage.

The Christian form of patriarchal marriage combines the economic with the sexual aspect of the association between men and women, but both these aspects have undergone transformation. The primitive division of labour has vanished, and the economic relation consists in the maintenance of the woman by the man. Whereas formerly the economic aspect provided the moral basis for marriage, today it is the sentimental aspect which does so; and, whereas in former times the economic aspect provided the overt motive for the association, today the woman who sells herself for her maintenance acts immorally.

But marriage cannot be reformed merely by legislative action. Legislative action, which prescribes a form of marriage and overrides the personal agreement of the parties involved, stands upon the same footing as the Australian tribal council which allots sexual partners or the negro who sells his daughter. The function of the law is to protect individuals; it is not concerned with sexual morals; but the law of civilized countries has not yet adapted itself consistently to that principle. The state's only function in the matter is to register the agreement; it is not the concern of the state to institute a particular form of marriage or to lay down any form of sex-relation. People are either united by love and agreement or united by an institution, and if the latter is the only bond, it comes near to being synonymous with prostitution.

Since individual men and women differ profoundly in their fitness for one or another form of sexual association, marriage may have to take varying new forms. Some women are by nature patriarchal wives, others are courtesans. Lifelong monogamy constitutes the ideal sex-relation, the most precious that life can offer, but it calls for special qualifications and special effort. The belief that it is a 'natural' relation, founded on biological functions, and that it can be left to the spontaneous operation of those functions, is one of the commonest causes of its failure. It is, on the contrary, a social product and a compromise.

Social evolution has emphasized the fundamental opposition between the aims and interests of the two sexes. This antagonism is rooted in the profound biological reproductive differences—periodic bearing of offspring in one sex, maximum dissemination of the breed in the other. While in the primitive division of labour, a mutual collective loyalty was developed in existing society, there is scarcely a collective social interest common to both sexes. For women the spheres of masculine activity are little more than means to the ends of their primal interest—independence. The relation between the sexes thus acquires an intensified individualism, Whether she aims at freedom or a home a woman is thrown back on the defence of her own interests; she must defend herself against man's attempt to bind her, or sell herself to advantage. Women is to man a sexual prey; man is to woman an economic prey.

The hope of amelioration lies in a clearer understanding of the facts. Men have much of the 'patriarchal theory' to unlearn; women have to learn that all racial ideals that are worthwhile are ultimately identical with their own elemental instincts, and no advantage can accrue to either sex by the accentuation of sex-antagonism, or from the endeavour of one sex to impose the aims of its own instincts on the opposite sex. Men and women must view one another's standpoint with sympathy, not with antagonism, that they may co-operate in the eternal effort to face realities.

As of old, it is the part of the Vestal mothers to tend the sacred fires. Upon women falls the task not only of throwing off their own economic dependence, but of rescuing from the like thraldom the deepest realities of which they were the first mothers. Women are the repositories of those values, and it is upon the rude foundations which they laid that the restless energy of man has reared a mighty structure of achievement.

In the second part of *Faust*, Goethe—recalling those threefold divinities who appear in the most ancient beliefs of European peoples, ruling human destinies, dispensing life and death, bringing forth and nursing the gods—referred in mystic terms to the mothers that dwell beyond space and time, and from whom the manifestations of life proceed. This conception applies equally to the racial spirit of Motherhood, of which the higher avatars human life are manifestations. And with this symbolic thought of the great poet our long journey may fittingly conclude:

> In your name, ye MOTHERS! who upon the throne
> Of the Illimitable dwell eternally alone—
> Yet not uncompanied. Life's Idols swarm
> About you, lifeless, yet in lifelike form;
> What has been is, and shall be; for with you
> Abide what things are ageless, unfading, ever new.

INDEX

GORDON RATTRAY TAYLOR

Gordon Rattray Taylor, writer and lecturer, was born 1911 in Eastbourne, England, and was educated at Trinity College, Cambridge. He served with the British Psychological Warfare Division during World War II, news monitoring service. As a journalist and editor he has contributed to numerous journals and newspapers, written and directed science programming for BBC television, and lectured in England and the United States within the area of his special interest, which is to broaden understanding of social change. His books, *Sex in History*, 1953, and *The Angel-Makers: A Study in the Psychological Origins of Historical Change, 1750-1850*, 1958, offered a theory of the influence of mother and father figures upon the development of society.

His long list of books include: *Economics for the Exasperated*, 1947; *Conditions of Happiness*, 1949; *Are Workers Human?*, 1950; *Eye on Research*, 1960; *The Science of Life: A Picture History of Biology*, 1963; *Growth*, written with Dr. James Tanner, 1965; *The Biological Time Bomb*, 1968; *The Doomsday Book: Can the World Survive?*, 1970; *Rethink: A Paraprimitive Solution*, 1972; and *How to Avoid the Future*, 1975.